THE KING'S COUNCIL DURING THE MIDDLE AGES

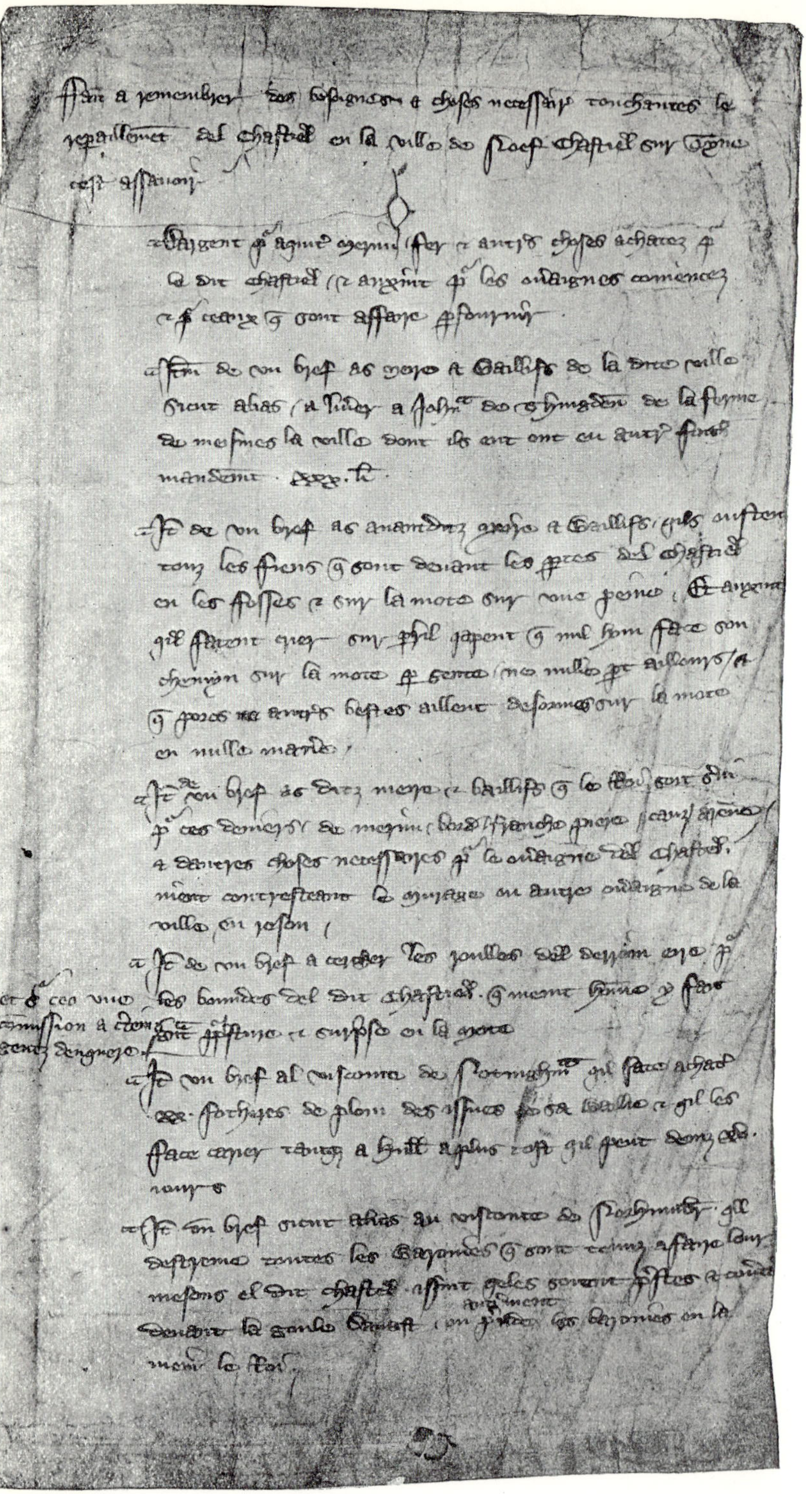

ORDERS FOR THE REPAIR OF THE CASTLE AT NEWCASTLE-ON-TYNE, 10 EDW. III.

Frontispiece

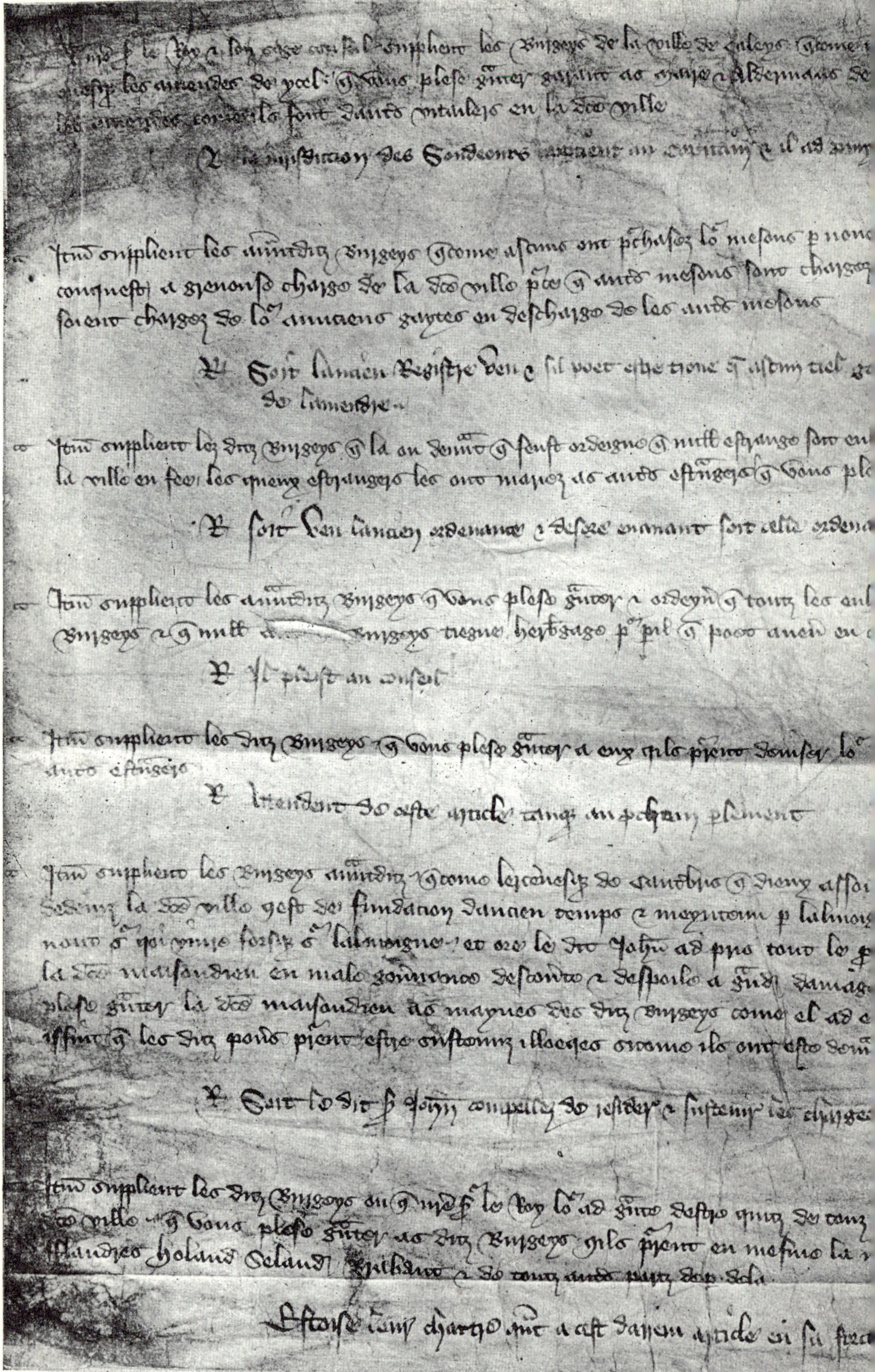

Petitions of the Burgesses of Calais

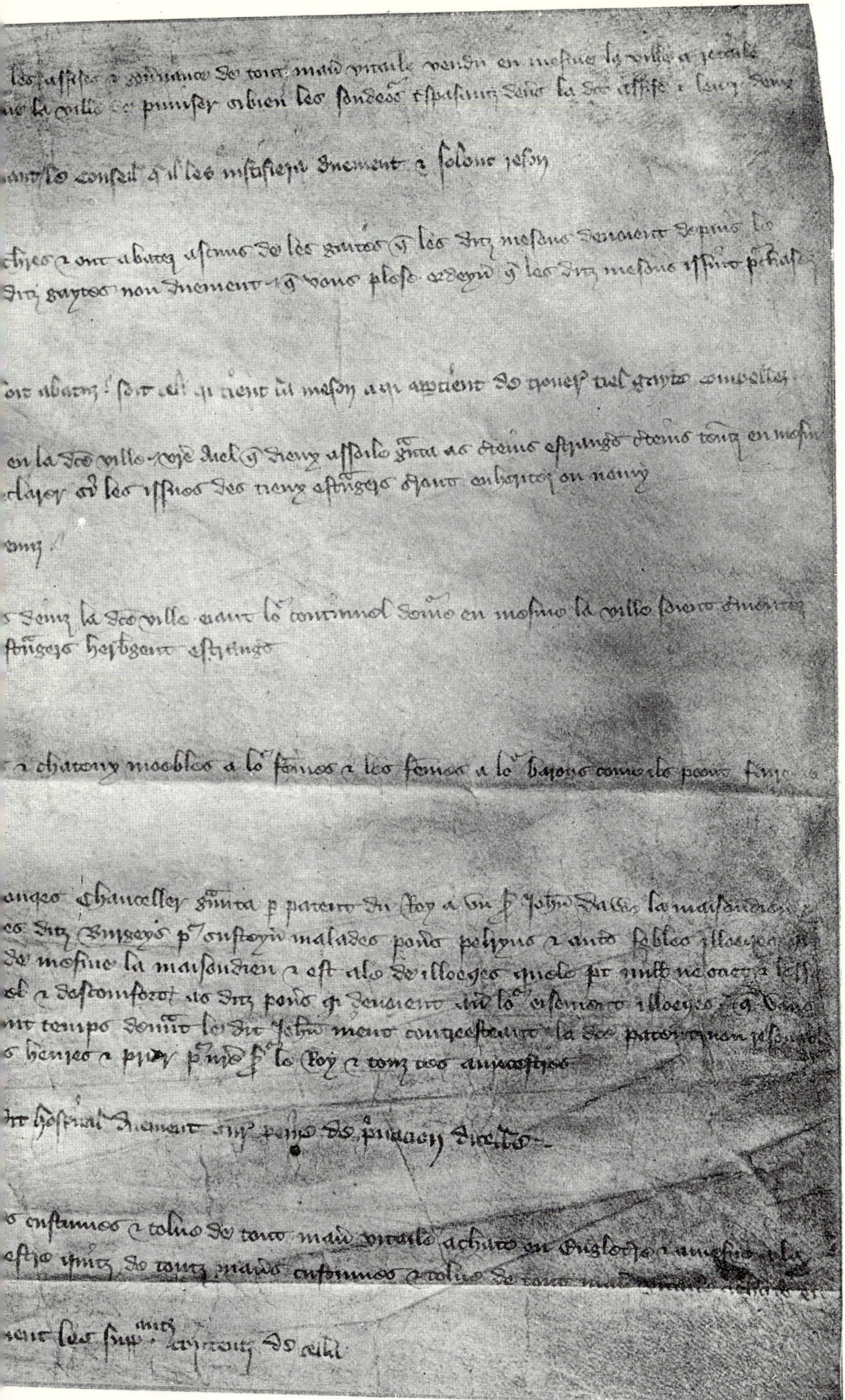

ANSWERS OF THE COUNCIL, TEM. RIC. II.

Frontispiece

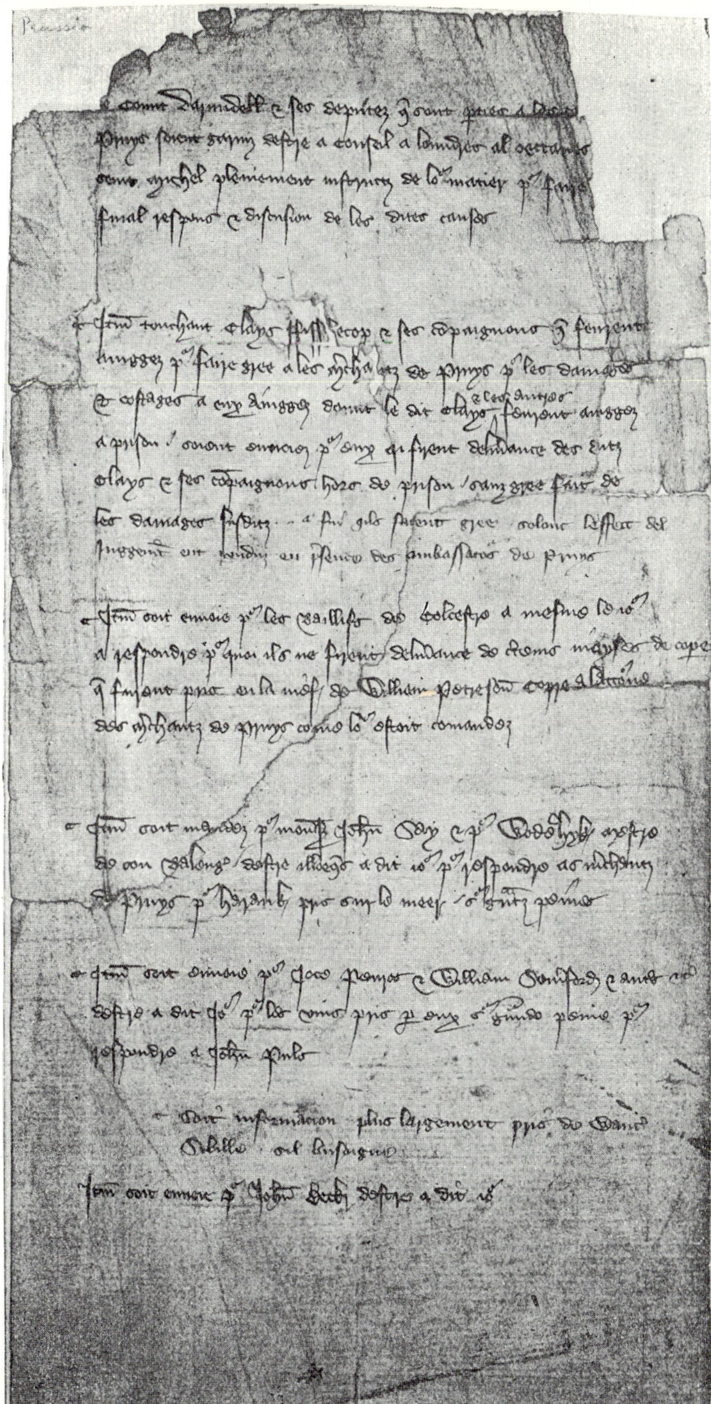

ORDERS OF THE COUNCIL WRITTEN UPON PAPER, TEM. RIC. II, 1388.

Frontispiece

THE KING'S COUNCIL IN ENGLAND DURING THE MIDDLE AGES

BY

JAMES FOSDICK BALDWIN

OXFORD

AT THE CLARENDON PRESS

Oxford University Press, Ely House, London W. 1

GLASGOW NEW YORK TORONTO MELBOURNE WELLINGTON
CAPE TOWN SALISBURY IBADAN NAIROBI LUSAKA ADDIS ABABA
BOMBAY CALCUTTA MADRAS KARACHI LAHORE DACCA
KUALA LUMPUR SINGAPORE HONG KONG TOKYO

FIRST PUBLISHED 1913
REPRINTED LITHOGRAPHICALLY IN GREAT BRITAIN
FROM CORRECTED SHEETS OF THE FIRST EDITION
AT THE UNIVERSITY PRESS, OXFORD
BY VIVIAN RIDLER
PRINTER TO THE UNIVERSITY
1969

PREFACE

ABOUT ten years ago the subject of this work was first suggested to me as a topic for investigation by the late Professor Charles Gross, whose learning was ever devoted to the inspiration and guidance of students in his chosen field. The material aid and encouragement which was generously given by my former friend, especially during the earlier stages of the study, I have sought to recognize in the dedication of this book.

My first intention was a monograph of much more limited scope and modest dimensions, which should be confined perhaps to the thirteenth century, or at the most should deal with the period prior to the reign of Richard II. Out of the material that was most readily discovered I published several articles, which appeared in the *Transactions of the Royal Historical Society*, the *English Historical Review*, and the *American Historical Review*, treating different phases of the subject during the early period. But like many another investigator I was drawn irresistibly from one question to another, and as every question proved to be worthy of study I did not rest until substantially the whole ground had been covered. That such a task had never been undertaken before lent a zest to the effort. Moreover, it was impossible even to understand any single phase of the history until it was considered in connexion with every other part. After the method of Seebohm and Maitland also it was necessary to read the order of events backwards as well as forwards. The council of Henry III, for example, was not intelligible until the clearer lines drawn by Edward I made tendencies visible, and the councils of Edward II and Edward III were an enigma before the events of Richard II brought certain hidden forces to the surface. Ultimately, for reasons that will be made apparent, it seemed to me that there was no satisfactory settlement of the chief problems connected with the mediaeval council until the reign of Henry VIII was reached. Not only in extent of time, but also in respect of its breadth the problem of the king's council was not so simple as first appeared, for it was in the beginning not a clearly defined institution, but a body very vaguely outlined and by no means clearly separated from other branches of the original organ of government. So that if the subject was to be fully understood it must be considered in every practical bearing, particularly in its relations with several closely affiliated bodies such as the house of lords, the exchequer, the king's bench, and the court of chancery.

'For obvious reasons', one writer has said, 'the history of the king's council cannot be written.' This statement is true in the sense that a continuous narrative of a body that was in its very nature more or less secretive, the actions of which were never strictly a matter of record, can hardly be constructed. Probably no such history has been written of the house of lords, although its principal features are well understood and are clearly presented; certainly nothing of the kind has been offered concerning the exchequer, the king's bench or the chancery. That the council is in no wise an insoluble problem at any stage of its history has become my own very firm belief, although it is for others to say how far the present attempt has been a successful one. To a certain degree the feasibility of the effort has been proved by the well-known contributions of Sir Matthew Hale, Sir N. Harris Nicolas, Sir Francis Palgrave, and Professor Dicey, who have treated the subject, each according to his purpose, in various limited aspects. It was the avowed intention in fact of

Harris Nicolas to follow his great collection of the sources with a more specific history of the council, but for some reason not explained this promise was never fulfilled. To a great extent the lines of my own work, its points of emphasis and explanation, have been determined by its predecessors. Besides availing myself of all the learning of others, I was led to investigate particularly the questions which they had neglected or left in doubt, and my chapters are mainly the treatment of these specific topics. More than any one else I have inclined toward the administrative side of the history, and in tracing the effect of this or that administrative method have found the essential factor of an institutional development. It was not so much a definite body of men, I believe, as it was certain methods of procedure that gave the council its distinctive character.

The material assistance that has been received from others at every stage of the work it is difficult justly to recognize. First of all it is customary to mention the unfailing courtesy and efficiency of the officials of the Public Record Office in the discharge of their duties. My own sense of obligation goes far beyond any perfunctory statement of the kind, for the assistance that a student most needs and appreciates can never be a matter of official routine, but is afforded only by men who are scholars themselves and have a genuine interest in all such work. Particularly have I been in contact with Mr. Edward Salisbury, who has assisted me in reading the most difficult manuscripts, and Mr. Charles Johnson, who has placed in my way many sources of information and also has read most of the chapters in detail. I have been fortunate too in the services of my transcribers, Miss Mary Martin and Miss E. Salisbury, who have done practically all the work contained in the appendices. With reference to particular questions and lines of study valuable counsel has been given by the late Professor Maitland, Professor Tout,

Professor Cheyney, and Professor Adams. Finally, I take the opportunity to express my gratitude to President James M. Taylor and the Trustees of Vassar College, who have allowed me the extended vacations that were necessary for the completion of the work.

JAMES F. BALDWIN.

POUGHKEEPSIE, N.Y.

CONTENTS

CHAPTER I

PAGE

THE INITIAL PROBLEM 1

Acknowledgement of the difficulty—feudal theory of the constitution—the Anglo-Norman *curia regis* as a starting-point—a twofold development of the *curia*—the exchequer specialized for certain purposes—expansion of conciliar functions—great councils and small councils—counsellors of John—different aspects of *consilium* and *curia*.

CHAPTER II

THE COUNCIL UNDER HENRY III 16

The king's minority—was there a selected council ?—existence of an active small council—but still undefined—no new institution conceived—the same usages after 1223—strife concerning the king's council—changes of counsellors—plan of the barons in 1244—more definite proposals in 1257 and 1258—scheme followed in 1264—reaction after 1265—a sworn council in 1271.

CHAPTER III

THE COUNCIL AND THE 'CURIA REGIS' . . . 38

Continuance of a single governing institution—formation of distinct courts a gradual process—how the steps are best followed : (1) its relation to the exchequer ; (2) its relation to the court of common pleas ; (3) its relation to the king's bench—distinctive character of the council.

CHAPTER IV

THE COUNCIL FROM EDWARD I TO EDWARD III . 69

The institution how far defined—a group of councillors sworn, ordained, and retained—a body of official character—the great officers—the justices—retired officers—clerks—foreigners—knights—magnates retained in few instances—the 'council in parliament'—aims of the barons under Edward II—the ordinances of 1311—the councils of 1316, &c.—similar efforts under Edward III in 1327, 1341, &c.—general inability to maintain a council of lords—the council a heterogeneous body.

CHAPTER V

PAGE

THE 'PRIVY' COUNCIL, THE 'GREAT' COUNCIL, AND THE 'ORDINARY' COUNCIL 103

Various expressions of current usage—a deficiency of the Latin language—the 'secret' council—the great councils—a sworn great council ?—the 'whole' council—the 'ordinary' council not existent during the middle ages.

CHAPTER VI

THE COUNCIL IN THE TIME OF RICHARD II . . 115

Notice of a change of organization—a well-marked period, 1376–1437—the Good Parliament in 1376—a new council—failure of the plan—the minority of Richard—the council of 1377—a change in 1378—attack in the parliament of 1380—failure of the parliamentary plan—impeachment of Suffolk in 1386—attempt to form a council—another attempt in 1388—the council after 1389—the ordinances of 1390—prominent councillors—proceedings 1392–3—the council at Eltham 1395—Richard's absolutism 1397–9—individual councillors—their fall in 1399.

CHAPTER VII

THE COUNCIL UNDER HENRY IV AND HENRY V . 147

Special problem of the Lancastrians—the first years of Henry IV—lords of the council and lesser men—councillors attending the king—weakness of the council—plan of reform in 1404—the parliament of 1406 and the council then appointed—supreme power of the council 1406–7—failure to sustain itself longer—the plan in the parliament of 1410—the council under the Prince of Wales—last years of Henry IV—policy of Henry V—his councillors—an active period in administration and judicature.

CHAPTER VIII

THE COUNCIL UNDER HENRY VI 169

Renewed problem of a royal minority—appointment of officers and councillors in parliament, 1422—powers of the council—stability of the arrangement—salaries—conduct of the government—dissensions among the lords—passing of the king's minority in 1437—changed relations of the council—its continued

PAGE

power and stability—rise of the earl of Suffolk—quarrels of Lord Cromwell—impeachment of Suffolk in 1450—Cade's rebellion—efforts to reform the council, 1450–1—strifes and failures in 1453—the duke of York, protector, 1453–4—alternations during 1455—failure of the protectorate and decline of the council in 1456—utter disintegration and powerlessness during the last years of Henry VI—reflections of Sir John Fortescue.

CHAPTER IX

THE COUNCIL AND THE EXCHEQUER . . . 209

Return to the subject of the courts—the exchequer as a general secretariat—and court of general assemblage—how assembled—why assembled in this manner—wide range of functions—foreign affairs—judicial authority—restrictions upon this authority—illustrative cases—amounting to an equitable jurisdiction—methods of procedure—a check to this development in the time of Edward II—ascendancy of the chancery and contraction of the powers of the exchequer—survivals of an equitable system here—contest over appeals—the court of exchequer chamber.

CHAPTER X

THE COUNCIL AND THE CHANCERY . . . 236

Unique development of the chancellor's office—the chancery considered as a branch of the *curia regis*—its function as *officina brevium*—as a court—as a court of extraordinary jurisdiction—impetus given by statutes—its efficiency and popularity—the court was the council—steps toward an independent position—petitions to the chancellor and council—petitions to the chancellor alone—stage of advancement under Richard II—later form of the court—a distinction between council and chancery—methods of the privy seal—advancement of the keeper—the council (privy seal) distinguished from the council in chancery.

CHAPTER XI

JURISDICTION OF THE COUNCIL 262

Distinction of ordinary from extraordinary jurisdiction—records both of the chancery and the privy seal—origin of council cases—its treatment of violence—fraud—cases affecting the rights of the crown—maritime and mercantile cases—the admiralty—heresy—poverty of suitors—trusts and uses cases—restrictions

PAGE

made by parliament—development of a special procedure—petitions—suggestions and delations—summary writs—arrests and detentions—parties before the council—suits—inquisitorial examinations—a star chamber case—the use of committees—assistance of the judges—expedition *v.* delay—leniency and weakness.

CHAPTER XII

THE COUNCIL AND PARLIAMENT 307

The problem stated—the 'council in parliament'—comprehensiveness of the early parliaments—the groups in parliament—the council in legislation—conflict of the magnates and the councillors—altered status of the judges in parliament—the council in parliament is the house of lords—two bodies distinguished—peculiar powers of the council—peculiar methods of the council—difference in respect of jurisdiction—as seen in form of petitions—in subjects of litigation—ultimate failure of petitions in parliament.

CHAPTER XIII

ANTIQUITIES OF THE COUNCIL 345

(1) The oath form of 1257—of 1307—of Edward II—in Ireland—in Gascony—derivatives from the original oath—later forms; (2) The council chamber—various houses used—the star chamber—its equipment—continued use of the Black Friars and other houses; (3) Expenses—refreshments—breakfasts and dinners—itemized accounts; (4) The clerk of the council—dispute upon the question—clerks first noticed—clerks of the privy seal—John Prophet—duties of the clerks; (5) The 'head' of the council—mention of a chief councillor—the chancellor regularly the presiding officer—the presidency a later creation.

CHAPTER XIV

RECORDS OF THE COUNCIL 372

An important question—proceedings and ordinances collected by Sir H. Nicolas—the council never a court of record—the endorsements of petitions—extensive use of the petitionary form—concrete examples—responses sometimes on separate parchments—bills framed by the council—instruments of all kinds inspected and passed—responses and notes made by the king—articles of 1339—utility of the notes—advances made under Richard II—the clerk's journal—the Book of the Council—was it continued ?—a new view offered.

CHAPTER XV

PAGE

The Councillors in Relation to the King and to One Another 395

Relations of the king and the council not usually defined—the king frequently on journeys—correspondence—messengers and 'reporters'—a royal audience—duties of a councillor—difficulties of free expression—requirement of secrecy—of honesty—maintenance and bribery—privileges—letters of councillors—the 'term'—quorum—attendance of non-members—unpractical ideals of the age.

CHAPTER XVI

The Council from Edward IV to Henry VIII . 419

Apparent loss of records 1460–1540—was there a loss? or a period of reduced activity?—councillors of Edward IV, lords, knights, doctors, clerks—reversion to an official body—no *consilium ordinarium*—activities in the government—judicial cases—changes noticed—the same tendencies under Richard III—vigorous policy of Henry VII—aim at riots—the statute *de camera stellata*—explanation—the court of requests—branch of the council remaining with the king—two co-ordinate boards—their relative importance—the 'ordinary' council at last defined—great success of the Tudors in solving the old problems.

Conclusion 459

APPENDICES

Appendix I. Acts and Articles from Edward I to Edward III 465

An ordinance by king and council, 26 Edw. I.

Memorandum of a letter from the king in Scotland to the council at York, 31 Edw. I.

Articles from Gascony with recommendations of the council, 5 Edw. II.

Advice of the council concerning the government of Gascony, 7 Edw. II.

Ordinances of the council with responses of the king, 9 Edw. II.

Preamble of articles brought by Elias Jonestone, 11 Edw. II.

PLATES

FACSIMILES OF TYPICAL DOCUMENTS

CHAPTER I

THE INITIAL PROBLEM

THAT there is a problem in the early history of the king's council has been admitted by all writers upon the subject. As Sir Francis Palgrave has explained, 'partly from the absence of records, and partly from their ambiguity, the history of the council, a tribunal which occupied the most prominent station in the government of the country, is involved in great obscurity and perplexity.'[1] In the face of the difficulties which have been confessed also by such men as Sir Harris Nicolas, Bishop Stubbs, and Professor Dicey to be insurmountable, probably no one would be so bold as to offer a work upon the council unless he were able to point to the evidence of much new material. With this in hand, he may well feel justified in offering a reconsideration of the body of material already known. To say nothing of the vast amount of unpublished documents which the opening of the Public Record Office has made available, there has been during the present generation an accumulation of published sources that are yet to be utilized. Every year new volumes are added to the calendars of state papers, which alone present a great amount of evidence that was practically unknown to earlier writers.

On the whole, however, it is the belief of the present writer that the difficulty in the past has lain not so much in the scarcity or ambiguity of the records, as in a failure properly to understand them. In the minds of the men of a former generation there was a prevailing rigidity of thought which failed to comprehend the extreme flexibility of institutions in a formative stage. Such words as *council*, *curia regis*, *exchequer*, *parliament*, and others were given a precision

[1] Palgrave, *Original Authority of the King's Council* (London, 1834), p. 19.

of meaning that is true of modern times but not of the middle ages. An excessively insular mode of study also tended to treat the governing institutions of England apart from their real connexions in Europe. Above all, a false theory regarding all these bodies was given, in the tendency to look for their origins in the earliest history of the nation, so far as possible in the Saxon period, and thus from the very start their fundamental character was perverted. The work of the last twenty-five years has done much not only to bring forth many needed matters of detail, but also to clear the air of certain false conceptions. As a general basis for the study of the English constitution, the nationalist theory of its origin no longer stands. By the successive studies of Stubbs, Maitland, Round, and Adams, it has been broken down at one point after another, and in its stead the theory of the feudal origin and character of practically all the institutions of the central government is at present strongly established. This view in itself is by no means a new discovery. It is surprising how near to the truth in this regard Sir Matthew Hale, in the seventeenth century, was able to come.[1] Professor Dicey also began his admirable treatise on this line.[2] But the argument was either overpowered or unheeded by the more influential contemporaries of Professor Freeman, so that it has remained for the scholars of the present day to present the thought with adequate proofs, to give it due emphasis, and to carry it to its ultimate conclusions. This has been done step by step, until at last, during the past year, it has been declared that England at the time of Magna Carta was 'the most perfectly logical feudal kingdom to be found in Christendom'.[3] The arguments sustaining this view need not be repeated here. They are germane to the present work only as they give a new colour to the study of any part of the constitution, and

[1] He speaks of the jurisdiction of the king in council as 'the origin of all the courts of justice in the realm', and again as the 'common mother' of the chancery, the king's bench, the exchequer, and the common pleas. *Jurisdiction of the Lords' House* (London, 1796), chap. iv.

[2] *The Privy Council*, Arnold Essay, 1860 (reprinted, London, 1887).

[3] G. B. Adams, *The Origin of the English Constitution* (New Haven, 1912) p. 149.

particularly as they give a certain starting-point or key to the early history of the king's council.

In accordance with the theories and methods of the past, attempts have been made to find a fixed time for the beginning of the king's council as a constitutional body. From different points of view it has been traced to the time of Henry II, of Henry III, Edward I, and Richard II. Now there is truth in any one of these statements, according as one feature or another of the council's history is considered, but the larger truth lies in the discovery that the council never had a point of beginning or initial organization. Its origin is found in the prevailing theory and practice of the feudal world, according to which the king, like any other lord, was accustomed to receive the 'aid and counsel' of his vassals. It was vaguely the right and duty of the lord to demand this, as it was also the right and duty of a vassal to give it. This mutual dependence of lord and vassal was in keeping with the feelings of the age in its lack of confidence in individual initiative and its distrust of individual authority. So there was a council, whether of a king, a duke, or even a minor lord, in practically every feudal state. In Normandy there was the *curia ducis*,[1] in England the Witenagemot of Saxon times, which was superseded by the *concilium* or *curia regis* of the Norman Conquest. This council or *curia* had then reached a high stage of development in certain respects, while in others it was still in a primitive stage. It still maintained the simple organization of an assembly court, a gathering essentially of the king's vassals, among whom were counted the officers of the royal household. Besides the clergy there were no 'discreet', learned, or professional men, although some persons were more constant in their attendance than others. From the first the court appears in two aspects, that of a large body which could have met only on fixed occasions and general summons, and a small body which could meet at frequent intervals for a continued term. Between the large *curia* and the small *curia*, it must

[1] See L. Valin, *Le Duc de Normandie et sa cour* (Paris, 1909); C. H. Haskins, *Eng. Hist. Review*, xxiii. 502–8; xxiv. 209–31; *Am. Hist. Review*, xiv. 453–76.

be understood, there was no positive difference of organization; much less was there any fixed division of labour. As Professor Adams has recently written, 'These, then, are the two essential things to have clearly in mind in beginning to study the constitutional history of England: that all the functions of the state were exercised by a single institution, and that the institution existed under two forms which were distinguished from each other only by size and manner of meeting.'[1] Another essential characteristic of the king's court during the feudal age is found in its lack of differentiation or specialization. This was not incompatible with a high degree of centralization and an effective control of all the agencies of the government. It means that the same body, whether large or small, was a royal council, a court of justice, or a general assembly, according to the needs of the moment; it exercised executive, judicial, or legislative functions alternately without clear discrimination. A certain classification of business like that of finance there certainly was, but even this was slow to create a distinct branch of the court.

This ill-defined but very practical organ of the Norman kings, it is understood, was the common mother of all the later central courts, including the exchequer, the common pleas, the king's bench, the council, and the parliament. The emphasis of its original feudal character explains many anomalies in the later history of these bodies, which have never before been properly understood.[2] It is made clear, for instance, that in spite of many divisions and subdivisions the idea of the single institution still lived on; the various individual courts were slow to separate, and long maintained a practical connexion with the parent stem; the newer courts were not for an indefinite time widely separated,

[1] Op. cit., p. 345.

[2] The conception of the common origin and consequent interrelations of the various courts is, of course, not entirely new. Madox has said, 'After the division of the courts, there still remained such a communication between the Court *coram ipso Rege*, and the Exchequer, and the Bank, as might be naturally expected between three courts springing out of one common stock.' *History of the Exchequer* (London, first ed. 1711; enlarged 1769), i. p. 796. But there is even more than this to be said of the courts in their common relations.

and they were easily reunited in a single body. With this mobility of the units themselves there went a certain interchangeability of the names, *curia*, *consilium*, *parliamentum*, and others. This does not seem strange when it is remembered how much these bodies, with all their points of divergence, continued to hold in common. Yet the apparent ambiguity of the word *consilium* in particular has proved a stumbling-block to every one seeking an accurate terminology. Stubbs turns in despair from a subject that confuses several differently organized bodies, as well as the occasions of their meeting.[1] It is likely that the various councils and parliaments to which the historian refers did not seem in the eyes of contemporary observers so differently organized as we have tried to make out.[2] In the subsequent differentiation of the *curia regis*, therefore, one will only be confused by attaching great weight to the use of names. The features of the institution can be discerned only in its actions and means of organization.

The history of the *curia*, in all its wide and general bearings, it would be quite impossible to follow in any single work. For the sake, then, of showing a definite purpose it must be avowed as the intention of this book to follow the steps which lead to a council of permanent character, such as is ultimately known as the privy council. This would be an outgrowth naturally of the original *curia regis* in its smaller rather than its larger form, although this line was by no means fixed. To create such a body was bound to be a long and laborious process in the face of certain real difficulties. It was quite practicable to hold occasional councils, great and small, and to require the more or less casual attendance of the king's

[1] 'The fact that the word council implies both an organised body of advisers, and the assembly in which that organisation meets; that it means several differently organised bodies, and the several occasions of their meeting; that those several bodies have themselves different organisations in different reigns, although retaining a corporate identity; and that they have frequently been discussed by writers who have been unable to agree on a common vocabulary or proper definitions, has loaded the subject with difficulty.' *Constitutional History* (Oxford, 1880), ii. 283.

[2] Says Mr. Round, ' Once admit that in the feudal *curia*, an institution of which the existence is undisputed, we have the common origin, at once of the *consilium* and of the *curia regis*, and all these difficulties vanish.' *Peerage and Pedigree* (London, 1910), i. 349.

vassals. But to train a body of regular attendants, especially among the nobles, was another matter. There were in the king's employ the officers of the household, and shortly the barons of the exchequer and justices, but would these be sufficient to form a council of influence and authority? In view of the invariable feudal tradition that the king's vassals, particularly the barons, were the king's advisers, how could a considerable number of bishops and barons be induced to give their regular attendance? To suggest another question of a practical bearing, how would the general body of the king's vassals and subjects regard a council composed of a small and select number? All of these tendencies indeed were so far contrary to the prevailing feelings of the age, that they could be worked out only with the utmost effort. In fact, like many other reforms which were destined to transform the feudal *curia*, they were brought forth not by any inherent tendency in the court itself, but by the strong and persistent assertion of the royal prerogative.

Because the *curia* of England was of the general feudal type that existed everywhere in Europe, one might expect that a comparative study of the king's council in England and the councils of other monarchies would prove fruitful. There is no doubt that the example of one government was readily followed by another, especially at a formative time. Some interesting parallels certainly can be drawn between the conciliar systems of England, France,[1] Scotland, Burgundy,[2] and the Spanish states. The councillor's oath, for instance, appears in France at about the same time as it does in England. But the comparison breaks down or proves unprofitable as soon as one passes over the elementary stages and finds how much more highly organized was the English

[1] On 'the great and secret council', as it was usually called, of the king of France, see especially Noël Valois, *Inventaire des arrêts du conseil d'État* (*Henri IV*), 2 vols., wherein the Introduction gives a review of the history of the council; also by the same author, *Le Conseil du Roi aux* XIVe, XVe *et* XVIe *siècles* (Paris, 1888); also Edgard Boutaric, *La France sous Philippe le Bel* (Paris, 1861); and Boutaric, *Actes du Parlement de Paris*.

[2] See Arthur Gaillard, *Le Conseil de Brabant* (Brussels, 1898), and Eugène Lameere, *Le Grand Conseil des Ducs de Bourgogne* (Brussels, 1900).

government than any other of the time. Nowhere else surely was there in equal strength the threefold development of the council, the subordinate courts of law, and the estates general or parliament. Outside the English sphere of influence, which includes Ireland and Gascony, the councils of European states in a large measure filled the place of the parliament of England. On the other hand, their separation from the courts equivalent to the exchequer and the king's bench was by no means so distinct. Sometimes, as in the Burgundian territories, the council of the prince was subdivided along provincial lines. Moreover, the most distinctive feature of the English council, as well as of English law, was the peculiar growth of an equitable jurisdiction apart from the common law. For this essential part of our history, there is no parallel to be found upon the Continent. And finally, in view of the fact that the records of England at this point are far more extensive than any discovered elsewhere, one is bound to admit that beyond a few general suggestions there is not a great deal to be gained for the present purpose from the observation of councils abroad.[1]

If these premises be taken as a starting-point, there is immediately to be observed a twofold development in the Norman council or *curia*. In the first place there begins a process of differentiation in the branches of the original body, so that the exchequer, and later the court of common pleas and the king's bench appear as bodies of distinct character. The relationship they bore to the king's council, how far they were separated, and to what extent they remained united, will be the special question for consideration. In the second place there was a marked expansion of the political power of the council, in its capacity as an advisory body, until in this sphere also it was given special recognition.

[1] In comparing the scanty records of the king's council in France with those of England, M. Valois observes, ‘ Quelle pauvreté est la nôtre, si l'on se reporte au temps où le Conseil intervenait dans les affaires politiques et dressait journellement des actes du plus haut intérêt pour l'histoire ! Qu'avons-nous à mettre en pendant des *Proceedings and Ordinances of the Privy Council* que l'Angleterre a su conserver ? ’ *Inventaire des Arrêts*, I, p. cxli.

In the inevitable process of differentiation which took place in the original *curia*, the first court of special functions to be formed was the exchequer. This appears with a certain degree of distinctness during the reign of Henry I, when its peculiar name *scaccarium* first emerges, and likewise a special staff known as the 'barons of the exchequer'. In a way, no portion of our history is better understood than this, for the sessions of the exchequer and its methods of business, even the table, the accounts, the assays, and the tallies, have been described by a contemporary observer in utmost detail and with wonderful clearness.[1] But as regards the origin and fundamental character of the court, one speaks with less certainty. Was it conceived as an organ distinct from the *curia regis*? or was it merely the *curia regis* in financial session? Although its financial procedure was closely defined, in the time of Henry II certainly the exchequer was not as yet a fully differentiated body. In the first place it was still maintained as a court of general assemblage, which included not only the king's officers, but also a varying number of barons, as is sometimes expressed in the words, *et aliis baronibus domini regis tunc praesentibus*.[2] For this reason great councils were likely to be called in October, when they would coincide with the Michaelmas sessions of the exchequer. The appointment of the several officers known as barons of the exchequer, who were especially responsible for the conduct of the business here, did not alter the general character of the court, which in point of *personnel* did not differ from the small *curia regis* as usually known. Moreover, the same body acted as a royal council and a court of general jurisdiction. But whenever the court is named one speaks not of the court of exchequer, but always of the '*curia regis ad scaccarium*'. Some say this means that the *curia* occupied the place of the exchequer after the sessions of the latter were over,[3] but this is to make a distinction

[1] Among many works dealing with the subject the most recent is R. L. Poole, *Exchequer in the Twelfth Century* (Oxford, 1912).

[2] 'Concordia facta in curia Domini Regis ad scaccarium coram R. Wintoniensi episcopo (etc.), et aliis Baronibus Domini Regis tunc praesentibus.' Madox, *History of the Exchequer*, i. 213.

[3] Bigelow, M. M., *History of Procedure* (London, 1880), 127.

without a difference. According to the thought of the time there was but one king's court, which was essentially the same whether it was held before the justices at Westminster, before the justices itinerant, or at the exchequer.[1] As regards its conciliar side the Dialogue tells us that the exchequer was attended by the great men of the kingdom, ' who share familiarly the royal secrets,' and for the purpose of taking counsel there was near by a ' chamber of secrets ' to which the members were wont to withdraw. ' Hither the barons repair when a doubtful point is laid before them, concerning which they prefer to treat apart rather than in the ears of all, but especially that they may not hinder the accounts which are being rendered.' [2] From various allusions we are not to understand that the deliberations thus taken were confined to subjects of finance. In the reign of Richard it is stated that when Walter of Coutances was raised by the barons of the kingdom to the justiciarship, he promised to do nothing in the government except by the will and consent of his associates and ' by the counsel of the barons of the exchequer '.[3] In the way of judicial proceedings a case is described in 1185, when the prior of Abingdon went to the justiciar, Ranulf Glanvil, who took counsel ' with the bishops and other justices who sat with him at the exchequer ', and finally pronounced the decree of the entire *curia*.[4] At this point, therefore, it does not appear that the exchequer was a specialized body except for certain purposes, namely, its care of the king's revenue. In other

[1] Madox has pointed out that the records make a distinction between the pleas in the king's court held ' before the justices ', the pleas ' before the justices itinerant ', and the ' pleas at the exchequer '. ' But in what manner the Chief Justiciar, who presided in the Curia Regis and in the Exchequer, ordered or distributed between those two Courts the several Pleas that were brought into a superior Judicature, I cannot determine.' *Hist. of Exch.*, chap. vi, § iii. At this time there was no distinction as regards either the kind of pleas or the procedure that was followed. It was purely a matter of convenience whether they should be held in one place or another.

[2] The *Dialogus*, ed. Crump, Hughes, and Johnson (Oxford, 1902), chap. iv, § vii.

[3] ' Qui nihil operari voluit in regimine regni, nisi per voluntatem et consensum sociorum suorum assignatorum, et per consilium baronum scaccarii.' Hoveden, iii. 141.

[4] *Chronicon de Abingdon*, ii. 297 ; Bigelow, *Placita Anglo-Normannica*, p. 235.

respects it still maintained the general character of the *curia regis*, in its uncertain composition and unrestricted activities. It was not as yet separated from the council, nor was the council distinct from it, so that a further discussion of this problem must be deferred to a later date.

At the same time that such branches of the *curia regis* were beginning to take form, there was also the other development of the council in its function of giving *advice* in matters of policy. This was perfectly in accord with the simplest feudal principles, but it had not yet been carried beyond a rudimentary stage. On various occasions, it is true, the Norman kings laid their plans before a council of their barons, to ask for their assent and co-operation.[1] This was not always gained without difficulty, and there are instances when it is known to have been refused. Yet so little was the actual influence of the council at that time upon the conduct of the government, that some have considered the monarchy then to have been a practical absolutism. 'By the counsel and consent of all my archbishops, bishops, earls, barons,' &c., was a current but usually a very perfunctory phrase. It was soon vitalized, however, into a real constitutional right. Under Henry II, especially during the strife with Becket, the great councils became truly a debating ground between the rival interests of church and state. Under Richard the barons collectively effected the deposition of one justiciar and the appointment of another, and again in the great Oxford debate of 1197 the clear voice of an opposition to the king's proposals was heard.[2] Still further, in the reign of John, the barons were able so to formulate and enforce their demands as to bring about the enactment of the Great Charter. But it was not only in the general or great councils that the function of giving the king advice can be seen to develop. There were also small councils held with considerable frequency, while at all times the king is found consulting with men who enjoyed his special confidence. Such

[1] The incidents of Duke William before his vassals at Berkhamstead, of Henry I receiving advice on his negotiations with Rome, and also on the choice of his second wife, will readily be recalled. Stubbs, *Constitutional History*, § 125.

[2] Ibid., i. 572; Round, *Feudal England* (London, 1895), 528 ff.

counsellors are known in the chronicles as *consiliarii*,[1] *consultores*, *familiares*, *domestici*, or *aulici*, and included barons in uncertain numbers, as well as officers, knights, and clerks of the royal household. Except as they are casually mentioned from time to time, it is not possible to describe them closely. They form no definite group, and in this capacity have no legal standing; their relation to the king was a purely personal one, but their influence nevertheless is unmistakable. They may be regarded as an exception to the feudal rule in that they were not necessarily the king's vassals; even if they held by serjeanty they appear rather in the light of officers and attendants of the royal household.[2] In the great councils which they commonly attended they formed a special element of stability, possessing acquaintance with the usages of the government and showing devotion to the king's interests.[3] In the smaller councils they easily became the principal element, and sometimes the king is represented as holding conferences with them exclusively. Counsellors of this type are mentioned under William II, Henry I, and Stephen, but it does not appear that there was yet any regular custom in this regard.[4] Under Henry II, especially during the stress of the clerical conflict, the king's counsellors or partisans were a calculable political influence. At every point in the contest the king is found advising with his counsellors, sometimes in secret. At the great council of Northampton, in 1164, the king is said to have deliberated with them apart from the general assembly, and to have been dissuaded by them from attacking the clergy.[5] On

[1] The word *consiliarius* for the present I translate 'counsellor'; a little later it will bear the meaning of 'councillor'. See p. 24 *n*.

[2] Stubbs, *Const. Hist.* § 122.

[3] In the great Easter council of 1136, according to the names of witnesses upon a charter then given, there were present the chancellor, two constables, two chamberlains, a dapifer, and a butler. A similar classification of the officers is made upon other charters. Once we notice four constables, four dapifers, and two butlers; and at another time four clerks of the chapel. Round, *Geoffrey de Mandeville* (London, 1892), pp. 19, 263, 427.

[4] 'Rege et suis secretius in Anselmum consilia sua studiose texentibus,' Eadmer, *Hist. Nova* (Rolls Series), 53; also Malmesbury, *De Gestis Regum*, ii. 314; Florence of Worcester (Eng. Hist. Soc.), ii. 57, &c.

[5] 'Rex cum familiaribus suis secretius agebat,' *Materials for the History of Becket*, i. 35; also, 'Porro rex cum familiaribus suis in remotiori camera consistebat,' ibid., iv. 46.

another day letters were read before the counsellors and such others as could be brought together.[1] Many of the counsellors were known as opponents of Becket, and as such became known to the friends of the archbishop as 'evil counsellors'. Not all were such, however, for we are told of certain friends of Becket, who were 'of the king's council', informing him of the danger to his life.[2] In 1166 the clergy of the province of Canterbury, in a letter to the pope, speak of the *fideles et familiares, regiis specialiter assistentes secretis in quorum manu consilia regis et regni negotia diriguntur.*[3] During the later years of Henry II, as well as under his sons, without giving further illustrations, it may be sufficient to say that the prominence of the counsellors was by no means diminished. As to small councils, we learn that under Richard, in 1190, at a meeting attended by ten of the bishops and barons, besides the queen and the sister of Philip Augustus, the king appointed William de Longchamp chief justiciar.[4] Again, in 1191, during the absence of the king, action was taken, we are told, according to the counsel and consideration of the archbishop of Rouen, of other *familiares* of the king, and of his *curia.*[5] But in all the various ways that counsel might be given, whether it were by a great council, by a small council, or by individual counsellors, it is necessary still to insist that there was, legally speaking, but one *consilium.* That is to say, there was as yet no standard of size or definition of the composition of the king's council. Naturally usages of this kind could not fail to have political effect, so that as they came to be understood there would be sure to arise occasion for definition.

There is a current belief that John was too much of a

[1] 'Postera die, lectis litteris in conspectu aulicorum et aliorum qui pro loco et tempore cogi poterant.' *Materials for the History of Becket*, i. 123.

[2] 'Interim nuntiatur archiepiscopo a quibusdam amicis et fidelibus suis qui erant de consilio regis quia rex iam de morte illus tractaret.' Ibid., iv. 48.

[3] Ibid., v. 407; also, 'saltem autem in regni maiores et regis familiariores manum (archiepiscopus) extendit, quorum scilicet consiliis rex agebatur et ministeriis ad concussiones utebatur.' Ibid., iv. 114.

[4] 'Habito cum illis consilio, dominus rex statuit Willelmum Eliensem episcopum, cancellarium, iustitiarium Angliae,' Hoveden, iii. 32; Benedict of Peterborough, ii. 105.

[5] Hoveden, iii. 136; also, 'communi familiarium et fidelium nostrorum consilio,' Gervase, i. 509.

tyrant to be willing to take counsel. According to the standards of the age, a tyrant he certainly was, for he acted in defiance of the general opinion of his barons. For this very reason he was all the more disposed to take counsel with men of his own choice. Stimulated by the incessant strifes of the reign, small councils and special groups of counsellors were more in evidence than ever before. The chronicles are filled with references to the 'evil counsellors', especially the foreigners and favourites, who are named as the king's supporters.[1] The celebrated song of William Marshall contains many vivid passages describing the relations of the king and his counsellors. A few lines of the poem are worth quoting in this connexion:

> Un jor, après mengier, avint — Years 1207–8.
> Que li reis en sa chambre vint
> E Girard d'Atées o lui,
> & Melier i ert autresi,
> E tuit si mestre conseiller
> Qui l'amoent a conseillier.
>
> (Lines 13589–94.)

and

> Lors mena li legaz aval — Year 1216.
> A une part le Mar; (i.e. the earl marshal)
> S'apela le conte de Cestre
> E puis l'evesque de Wincestre,
> E une partie apelérent
> Des hauz homes qui laienz érent
> En une chambre a conseiller,
> Mes tant ne sourent travailler
> Que nul conseil certain eüssent.
>
> (Lines 15537–45.)[2]

Of far more consequence in the long run was the participation of the king's counsellors in the practical work of the

[1] The St. Albans chronicler undertakes to give a list of the evil counsellors of John in 1211. 'Habuit autem rex hac interdicti tempestate consiliarios iniquissimos, quorum nomina pro parte hic ponere non omittam.' He mentions over thirty men by name, besides 'many others' who were accustomed to give the king counsel. The great length of the list, and the changes which the same chronicler makes in a later attempt to name the king's counsellors, fail to suggest anything like a fixed or limited council at this time. Roger of Wendover, *Flores Historiarum* (Rolls Series), ii. 59, 118.

[2] *Histoire de Guillaume le Maréchal*, ed. Paul Meyer (Paris, 1891–4).

government, as is shown in many official documents. Among the letters of the great seal, which first appear in the reign of John, it is manifest that the concurrence of the council was desired and given in countless ordinary acts of the government. According to the usages now woven into the letters close and patent, orders were issued 'by the advice of the council', 'by the counsel of Geoffrey fitz Peter and other faithful,' 'by the counsel of the archbishop of Canterbury and others.'[1] These were not empty phrases, for sometimes the names of the counsellors were given in a list of greater length. In 1209 is the statement that letters from Llewelyn were read before the bishop of Winchester, the bishop of Bath, Walter Gray chancellor, Geoffrey fitz Peter justiciar, William Briwer, Hugh archdeacon of Wells, Roger Thorn, Gerard de Atyes, and others who were then present.[2] Again, in 1214, the king, who was then on the Continent, sent a letter to his barons urging them to hasten to his service across the sea, 'except those who by the counsel of the bishop of Winchester, the justiciar, the bishop of Norwich, the chancellor, William Briwer, and others were to remain in England.'[3] In the last instrument drawn by John, namely, his will disposing of his personal property, he appointed thirteen executors, 'without whose counsel', said he, 'I should ordain nothing even though I were in good health.'[4] The practice of employing small councils and groups of counsellors to such an extent undoubtedly helped to incite the barons to insert the fourteenth article in the Great Charter, which defined the great council as it should be summoned for the purpose of granting aids. For other purposes, however, no requirement of the kind as yet was made. Still it is to be understood that there was nothing permanent or stable in the shifting groups of counsellors that took part in the government of John. The utmost importance which can be assigned to them is the frequent, perhaps constant, exercise of the function of *counsel* in the govern-

[1] *Rotuli Litterarum Clausarum*, and *Rotuli Litterarum Patentium, passim.*

[2] *Rot. Lit. Pat.* i. 88. See similar passages in *Rotuli Chartarum*, i. 13, 125, &c.

[3] *Rot. Lit. Pat.* i. 118.

[4] *Foedera* (Record Ed.), i. 144.

ment. This proves to be of great value as the basis for the settlement of a permanent council in the future.

The process of institutional development just outlined resulted finally in a change of usage in respect of the very words *consilium* and *curia*. Upon this point Mr. Round has tentatively offered a most helpful suggestion,[1] which is well supported by the evidence in hand. For some time after the Norman Conquest, it is admitted by all, these terms were used synonymously and interchangeably. They afterwards became differentiated in meaning, the *consilium* denoting the *curia* in its consultative aspect, and pointing toward the parliament, the house of lords, and the privy council of the future; the *curia regis*, on the other hand, represented the same institution in its judicial aspect, and so the name was applied to the exchequer as well as to each and all of the special courts of law. Already by the beginning of the thirteenth century we have such expressions as *consilium curiae*, *consilium in curia*, and *consilium et curia*, which suggest that the two words were not identical. The particular problem as to how the *curia regis* came to be differentiated and in a measure separated from the council will form a study to be treated in one of the succeeding chapters. From the evidence brought forward in these preliminary pages, the only inference to be drawn is that the king's council had no particular time of initial organization; its origin lay in the general and unspecialized court of a feudal monarchy; it was associated very closely with the officers and attendants of the royal household; its subsequent development lay in the branching forth of a number of special courts; but whatever the number of specialized courts, the need of a council of general and undefined powers continued to exist.

[1] *Peerage and Pedigree* (London, 1910), i. 348.

CHAPTER II

THE COUNCIL UNDER HENRY III

The minority of Henry III as a starting point.

THE reign of Henry III has generally been understood as a time when, out of the uncertain usages of the past, a council of permanent character began to be formed. It has been said that for the control of the government during the king's minority the positive organization of such a body was then effected. This view in its extreme form has been stated by Gneist in these words: 'Under Henry III a government council was first formed as an administrative body for the discharge of the whole business of the state, which formed a basis for the administrative nature of the permanent councils of later times.' [1] Stubbs also has said, 'The king's personal advisers begin to have a recognized position as a distinct and organised body, of which the administrative body, the judges, and other officers of state and household, form only a part.' [2] With more caution Professor Tout says, 'We also discern, almost for the first time, the action of an inner ministerial Council which was ultimately to develop into the *consilium ordinarium* of a later age.' [3] M. Bémont holds the singular view that during the minority of Henry III there was a special council of regency, which is to be distinguished from the king's council of other times.[4] In view of the uncertainty of the ground, as shown by the

[1] *History of the English Constitution* (trans. Ashworth, London, 1889), chap. xxiii.

[2] *Const. Hist.* ii, § 171.

[3] *Political History of England* (London, 1905), iii. 29.

[4] 'C'est seulement à partir de Henri III que l'on constate l'existence d'un conseil privé, nettement distinct, à la fois, du Parlement dont il vient d'être question, et de la cour du roi dont il sera parlé plus loin. On ne peut pas cependant considérer comme tel le *supremum* ou *supernum consilium* qui dirigea les affaires générales du royaume pendant la minorité de ce roi. Ce n'est pas là un conseil privé, c'est un conseil de régence ; il n'assiste pas le roi, il le dirige ; ce n'est pas le roi, c'est le Parlement qui le nomme.' *Simon de Montfort* (Paris, 1884), p. 111.]

hesitancy of these opinions, the question of the actual beginning of an appointive council is worthy of careful investigation. Whether any of the foregoing statements can be accepted without modification remains to be tested.

In the first place, it must be admitted that upon every page of the history of the time there is evidence of the constant presence and activity of a king's council, and there are not lacking signs that a new view of it was taken. Writers of the period designate it by such expressions as *regale consilium*, *familiare consilium*, *supremum* or *supernum consilium*, *nobile et prudens consilium*, *secretum consilium*, *secretiora consilia*, and the like.[1] It is to be noted, however, that these expressions are to be found only in chronicles and literary sources, and therefore must be looked upon with caution in defining a legal institution. Official language was much more conservative, and was usually confined to the general term of established usage, *consilium regis*. But even in the rolls there were sometimes departures from the set phrase, as when mention is made of *magnates qui sunt de consilio nostro*, and *quidam magnates de consilio nostro*.[2]

Was there a selected council?

It has been suggested that for the purpose of a regency a standing council was in some way appointed or sanctioned by the first great meeting of the barons, which was held at Bristol, November 11, 1216. It was then that William Marshall was accorded his special title of 'guardian of the king and of the realm', and that two of his associates, the pope's legate and the bishop of Winchester, were named to have 'the care of the king and the realm'.[3] As to Hubert de Burgh the justiciar and other officers, there is no evidence that any new appointments then were made. In 1218 it was decided by the council itself that commissions of John's reign still were valid.[4] As to the king's council there is even

[1] *Dunstable* (Rolls Series), pp. 68, 87, 89; *Royal Letters of Henry III* (ibid.), i. 5, 94, 123, 148; Matthew Paris, iv. 87, &c.; Hemingburgh, ii. 20.

[2] *Cal. Patent Rolls*, 2 Hen. III, pp. 167, 181, &c.

[3] 'Commissa est ex communi consilio cura regis et regni legato, episcopo Wintoniensi, et Willelmo Marescallo.' *Walter of Coventry* (Rolls Series), ii. 233; Matthew Paris, *Chronica Maiora*, iii. 2.

[4] *Cal. Patent Rolls*, pp. 135, 181.

less reason to suppose that any special body of men was at that time either named, appointed, or sanctioned. It would be strange, indeed, if any such novel proceedings could have taken place, with no one to mention the fact! Whatever council there was, therefore, must have been either so far in accordance with established usage as to excite no comment, or else it was of gradual formation too slow to be realized as anything new.

An active council there was.

And yet the presence and participation of a council is found in nearly all the actions of the government. It is 'by William Marshall and the magnates of the council', 'by the counsel and consent of the legate and the magnates who are of the council', 'before the justiciar and council', that grants, appointments, and treaties were constantly made.[1] For certain periods acts of this kind can be shown to have been made during every month of the year.[2] In 1217, to give sanction to the peace which was then made with Louis of France, the magnates of the council placed their own seals upon the treaty,[3] and in 1218 they gave their personal security for a loan of 6,000 marks.[4] Under the conditions then prevailing it is safe to say that no minister would act in any matter of importance unless in some way he had obtained the sanction of the council. Even so, no grants of the crown were made in perpetuity, but only provisionally until the king became of age. In 1220 an exceptional incident is given, when the legate Pandulf wrote to Hubert de Burgh, that in order to effect a truce with France, the justiciar should proceed without delay, and not await further counsel, it being sufficient that 'we wish and advise it'.[5] This is not to be understood as an intentional usurpation of authority on the part of Pandulf, for in another matter of the same year he expressed himself as unwilling to proceed without the

[1] *Rot. Lit. Claus., passim.*

[2] See for instance the attestations during the year 1223 in the *Close Rolls*, wherein actions of the council appear on January 30, February 1, 4, 11, 23, March 12, May 30, June 3, 4, 26, July 6, 13, 14, 30, August 3, 24, September 23, October 9, &c.

[3] *Foedera* (Rec. Ed.), i. 148.

[4] *Cal. Patent Rolls*, 2 Hen. III, p. 181.

[5] *Royal Letters* (Rolls Series), i. 76.

counsel of the justiciar.[1] There can be no doubt that on the whole the government of the early years of Henry III was a government by council as fully as it well could be. But before we fall into the conception of a distinct and newly organized body, we must explain the idea which then prevailed concerning the council.

But still an indefinite body.

Not only is there lack of evidence of any appointed or limited council at this time, but there were in fact strong reasons against anything of the kind. The period in view was one of civil war and feudal reaction, when amid the dangers of further rebellion and foreign invasion the government was thrown back upon the most elementary principles.[2] It needed, indeed, all the support it could get. Now to gain the counsel and consent of a baron was in a measure to gain his co-operation. Such 'aid and counsel', therefore, the ministers were bound to have in every possible way, whether it were by means of a large council, a small council, or only the individuals who happened to be present. Large councils could be assembled only on occasions, but small councils and consultations could be held perpetually. This fact the regents emphasized and proclaimed at every opportunity. In their acts they gave lists of names, and, as in the signing of a charter, the longer the list and the more prominent the persons mentioned the better the act was considered to be attested and sanctioned. When it was not practicable to give names, they proclaimed their acts with general attestations in some such form as, *coram S. Cantuariensi archiepiscopo et H. de Burgo iusticiario et omni consilio domini Regis.*[3] At other times the names of two or three ministers sufficed, as most likely these were all that could be obtained.

In making and comparing the lists of names which are given on numerous occasions, one finds indeed the greatest irregularity in the attendance of the magnates. After the Earl Marshal, the legate, the bishop of Winchester, the

[1] *Foedera* (Original Edition), i. 236.

[2] For a special treatise upon the period see J. G. Turner, *Minority of Henry III*, Royal Historical Society Trans., New Series, xviii. 245–295; Third Series, 205–262; also, Kate Norgate, *Minority of Henry III* (London, 1912).

[3] *Rot. Lit. Claus.*, i. 403, 404, &c.; *Cal. Patent Rolls*, 9 Hen. III, p. 544, &c.

justiciar, the archbishop of Canterbury, and one or two others are mentioned, there is no certainty whatever as to the personnel of the king's council.[1] Even two lists, drawn up on the same day, will show variations. It was in fact anything but an organized or even a stable body which is thus revealed, and consisted rather of a shifting group of bishops, barons, and officers, as many as happened to be present or as could be induced at the time to come. An element of stability, it is true, may be found in the fact that the supporters of the present government were largely the same as those who had been the counsellors of John. Often the barons without doubt, both individually and collectively, had reasons in their own interests to attend the court, for they were constantly concerned with the issue of charters and the conduct of law cases. At other times plainly it was difficult to induce them to come, so that it was necessary to remind them constantly of their duty to attend the king's councils—the plural form being frequently used—as many an urgent letter shows. Referring to the archbishop of Dublin, in 1217 the king wrote, *ipsius consilio vix carere valeamus*.[2] In 1222 the king commanded the earl of Derby to come to the council, but, he writes, ' you went away without holding colloquy, which we bore hardly '.[3] Again, in 1224 he says of the bishop of Winchester and the earl of Chester, *familiares habere debemus in consiliis nostris*.[4] Likewise the ministers and barons urged one another, as when Henry de Trubleville wrote to the bishop of Chichester, *sitis in auxilium et consilium ad loquendum coram domino Rege et domino Iusticiario*.[5] Under these conditions it is hardly correct to speak of ' members of the council ', and at the time certainly no such definite expression was used. With much less precision men were said to be *consiliarii* or simply *de consilio nostro*. Moreover, the king's council is not to be understood in any

[1] In the *Transactions of the Royal Historical Society*, New Series, xix. 57–9, I undertook to give a list of the bishops, barons, and officers who appeared prominently in the king's council. There is no reason, however, to say that there was anything like a fixed membership. With equal correctness the list might be made longer or shorter according to the immediate circumstances.

[2] *Cal. Patent Rolls*, p. 57.

[3] *Rot. Lit. Claus.*, i. 502 ; also p. 387.

[4] *Royal Letters*, i. 224.

[5] Ibid., i. 328 ; also p. 80.

exclusive sense. It is not likely that any baron who was willing to come and give counsel would be excluded except for grave political reasons. In 1219 the queen mother Isabella was said to have been removed from the council of the king, and of this she bitterly complained.[1] Again, for special reasons in 1224 the bishop of Winchester and the earl of Chester saw themselves superseded by Hubert de Burgh, and excluded *a secretioribus consiliis*.[2]

No new institution conceived.

With all the facts at our disposal—and these are many—it seems impossible to suppose that any new institution, equivalent to a privy council or a council of regency, at this time was created. There was, indeed, nothing more than the quickening and adaptation of the *consilium*, as already understood, to the needs of new conditions. The modifications which were required because of the regency had very important effects upon the council, in the rapidity of its development and in bringing certain features soon to the point of definition. But these technical features must not be assumed until they are made clear in the course of events.

Did the council, in the sense which was then understood, include others besides the bishops and barons, such as the justices, the barons of the exchequer, and the officers of the household ? It may be too soon to say that there was a professional class apart from the barons, but there was a strong inclination expressly to mention the justices and other officers in this relation. For example, actions were taken, as it is said, 'before the council *and* the barons of the exchequer', 'before the king and his council *and* the justices', although more often it is expressed 'before the justices *and others* of the council'.[3] Again, mention is made of 'the archbishops, bishops, earls, barons, *and* our council'.[4] The first men of whom we may speak with confidence as professional lawyers, namely Martin Pateshull and Stephen Segrave, certainly were associated constantly in the council with the

[1] 'Multum et enim grave nobis fuerit, si nos a consilio filii nostri oporteat removeri.' *Royal Letters*, i. 34.

[2] *Dunstable*, p. 87.

[3] *Rot. Lit. Claus.*, pp. 361, 438, &c.; also 'coram dilectis et fidelibus nostris, Henrico de Bathon', Henrico de Bracton, Henrico de la Mare, et Nicholao de Turri, et aliis de consilio nostro in curia nostra venire facimus'. *Foedera* (Rec.), i. 320.

[4] *Foedera* (Orig.), i. 232.

magnates. So that the council continued to include all the elements of the old *curia regis*. It expanded or contracted according to the occasion, while the number present, so far as it was not a matter of accident, depended on the character of the business in hand. Occasionally the magnates appeared in force; more often a few bishops and barons were combined with the officers;[1] and again the officers remained alone. A special recognition of the men of the household in this regard was made in the pope's bull of 1223, which declared the king to be of age and acknowledged his right to govern *cum suorum domesticorum consilio*.[2] The barons, seeing their influence threatened, took exception to this pronouncement. Their right to counsel the king at all times they considered to be incontrovertible.

The same usages continue after 1223.

The king's minority in one sense was considered to end in 1223, although he remained under tutelage until 1227. In either event there was no positive change in the form or functions of the king's council. What has been said as to the need of counsel during the minority, remained almost equally true because of the king's weakness whether in youth or in old age. Probably a more substantial ground for the permanent power of the council is found in the well-established usages of the chancery, wherein letters were commonly attested in some such form as *per ipsum regem coram Wintoniensi episcopo, iusticiario, et aliis de consilio regis*.[3] Moreover, like any mediaeval king, Henry III did not regard it as a sign of weakness, but a source of strength, to have competent 'aid and counsel'. This he proudly announced not only in his acts at home, where there might have been some constraint, but in his foreign correspondence, where his liberty was greater. In 1228 he declared to Llewellyn, *nunquam ita fuimus consilio destituti, quin consilium nostrum ad maiora et difficiliora sufficit* (*oper*)*anda et*

[1] The attendance at a trial held in 1227 is described as including the king himself, the justiciar, the chancellor, four other bishops, nine barons and knights, of whom at least four were members of the royal household, four justices, and five clerks. *Red Book of the Exchequer* (Rolls Series), iii. 1010.

[2] Matthew Paris, *Chronica Maiora*, iii. 79.

[3] *Rot. Lit. Claus.*, ii, *passim*.

emendanda.[1] Whatever usages, then, as regards the council had been established during the minority, these were not now reversed, but so far as possible were maintained and extended. It only remained to be seen who should be the king's counsellors, and what new usages concerning them should be established. It is true that immediately after 1224 Hubert de Burgh's influence was dominant, and that there are then fewer instances of conciliar action than during the previous years. Throughout the eleventh, twelfth, and thirteenth years, the number of administrative orders in the name of the council are exceedingly few, while in the close roll of the thirteenth year there is not one to be found. It has been suggested that Hubert de Burgh more than any other man was instrumental in giving the council its initial organization.[2] But the few facts which can be gathered do not point to this inference. His position of supremacy was a dangerous one for any minister then to hold. The barons made complaint against him on the ground that he had made himself 'the only counsellor', that 'he held his fellow counsellors for naught',[3] and with the addition of other charges they were successful in 1232 in bringing about his downfall. The continued vitality of the council at this time is shown further by a letter from Gregory IX to Henry III, in which he granted the bishops permission to assist in the king's councils.[4] Certainly it was no new thing for the bishops to attend councils and to hold offices, as the pope readily acknowledged,[5] but prior to the present reign, as a rule, they had not been required to give so much of their time to these duties.

Strife over the king's council.

Henceforth, it is generally known, the history of the reign consisted largely of a struggle over the king's council and his

[1] *Royal Letters*, i. 335.

[2] Bémont, *Simon de Montfort*, p. 112.

[3] 'Conquestus est in primis de rege Anglorum, quod solummodo omnia regni negotia per consilium Huberti iustitiarii, aliis spretis magnatibus, disponebat.' Matthew Paris, *Chronica Maiora*, iii. 165, 205, 222; ibid., *Hist.*, ii. 294.

[4] *Royal Letters*, i. 549.

[5] 'Asseris introductum, quod reges Angliae semper consueverunt habere consiliarios aliquos episcopos regni sui, de cuius statu cum consilio disponerent eorundem.' Matthew Paris, *Chronica Maiora*, iii. 549.

counsellors.[1] As soon as the king was able to adopt a policy of his own, he showed a marked preference for foreigners, whom he chose as his personal attendants and rewarded richly with grants of every kind. This was the policy that had formerly been followed by John, and now it was suggested anew by Peter des Roches, the Poictevin bishop of Winchester, whose influence was dominant after the fall of Hubert de Burgh. In his relations with his advisers it is common to speak of Henry's capriciousness and lack of trustfulness, so that his more steadfast purpose is obscured. The intention plainly was to secure a class of office-holders and counsellors who should be detached from the interests of the barons, and therefore the more subservient tools of the royal authority. Among the Poictevin and Savoyard courtiers who then flocked to England, it is fair to observe there were found many able men who greatly strengthened the government on its administrative side. But the men whom the king chose to honour were not entirely foreigners. At times allied with them there were certain Englishmen who had gained experience in the *curia regis*, whose only hope of further advancement lay in the royal favour. On the other hand, some of the foreigners, most notably Simon de Montfort, became identified with the English baronage. It was not then a contest purely of the native English against the foreigners, but rather that of an official class, strengthened, it is true, by an influx of foreigners, who were grasping the powers of the government against the claims of a militant feudal baronage. Here was a cause of irritation that cut much deeper than any national feeling at the time. The barons threw the blame especially on the foreigners, but they were equally incensed at the promotion of clerks and judges whose only claim to distinction was their service in

[1] The word *consiliarius* means either 'counsellor' or 'councillor', just as *consilium* or *concilium* may be understood either as 'counsel' or 'council'. At this time the abstract and the concrete ideas were completely blended, or rather had failed yet to be distinguished. The transition to the conception of 'council' and 'councillor' is seen to grow very gradually. For the present period, I think, the word of less definite meaning is usually the better translation, although there are times when the other undoubtedly would be correct. At a later stage I have swerved to the term 'councillor' as the preferable one to express the meaning.

the *curia regis*. They proclaimed themselves to be the king's ' natural counsellors ', while they stigmatized their opponents as ' evil counsellors '. In the long contest which now ensues there could not fail to be taken many steps toward a clearer definition of the king's council, not only as regards its larger and more formal sessions soon to be known as parliaments, but also in its aspect as a smaller and more permanent body.

After the fall of the great justiciar, it was now one group of counsellors and now another which alternated at court. First it was the Poictevin party under the bishop of Winchester that gained the ascendancy. But the changes that were now made in the administration were of far greater consequence than a transfer of political power ordinarily implies. The chief justiciarship was never again given to a great baron. It was filled at the time by Stephen Segrave, the son of a small landowner, who was known solely as a lawyer who had held many judicial and administrative positions.[1] Hereafter the great Norman office became a chief justiceship, the head of a staff of judges, instead of the viceregal position it formerly was. The steadfast intention of lowering the dignity of the principal offices is seen also in the suspension of the chancellorship a few years later. At the same time, Peter de Rivaux, who is described as a nephew of the bishop of Winchester, was appointed treasurer, and Robert Passelewe, who was formerly a clerk in the employ of Falkes de Breauté, was made deputy-treasurer. Two-thirds of the counties of England likewise were placed in the custody of the bishop and his dependants. The intention to exclude the English barons from their accustomed political strongholds was unmistakable. As the chronicler who voices their

[1] In 1203 Segrave was constable of the Tower of London, and was known to hold the favour of John. Under Henry III, especially after 1217, he was frequently employed as a justice itinerant. He was sheriff of Essex and Hertford during the years 1221–3, sheriff of Lincoln 1222–4, and of Buckingham, Bedford, Warwick, Leicester, and Northumberland between 1228 and 1234. He was violently hostile to Hubert de Burgh, and worked with the bishop of Winchester for the justiciar's downfall. Professor Maitland regarded Martin Pateshull and Segrave as the earliest examples of the type of a purely professional lawyer. Segrave's abilities as a jurist are acknowledged to be very high, but his character is marred by his avidity for rewards and his alliance with the Poictevins to secure them.

sentiments declares, 'the king cast out all his counsellors, that is bishops, earls, barons, and nobles of the realm.'[1] The bishops in retaliation threatened to excommunicate the aforesaid ministers for giving evil counsel, and Richard Marshall uttered threats in the name of the barons, while in particular he accused the counsellors of perjury to the oath which they had sworn 'to furnish the king faithful counsel'.[2] This passage is of special significance, as it is the first reference which is made to a counsellor's oath. The counsellors, also, assert their position in a positive manner, when they argue with the barons saying, '*nos, quorum consilio rex et regnum regitur.*'[3] In a parliament, as we may now call the assembly of 1234, a concerted attack upon the king's counsellors was made. The bishops declared, '*consilium quod nunc habetis non est sanum.*'[4] Under the threats of the archbishop and the menacing attitude of the barons, it is said, the king 'dismissed his iniquitous counsellors, and recalled to his following the natural men of his realm, submitting to the counsel of his prelates'. Peter des Roches, Peter de Rivaux, Stephen Segrave, and other Poictevins were removed, while nine new counsellors, including Hubert de Burgh, Gilbert Basset, and Richard Siward were received, it is asserted, '*inter domesticos et familiares consiliarios.*'[5]

Changes among the counsellors, 1234–7.

The changes which were made in the king's council from time to time are described as being effected with the utmost facility and least formality. Except as one was appointed to office, it was commonly sufficient to say that he was 'admitted', 'dismissed', or 'removed'. This was in keeping with the unfixed and informal character of the institution as it was still conceived. The restoration of Stephen Segrave and other unpopular counsellors provoked another eruption in the parliament of 1237.[6] In answer to the murmurs of the barons, the king was forced to make the usual kind of

[1] Wendover, iii. 47; Matthew Paris, *Chronica Maiora*, iii. 240, 252.

[2] 'Periuri sunt de fideli consilio quod iuraverunt domino regi praestituros.' Of Stephen Segrave the justiciar, it was said, 'qui iuravit iustas leges observare.' Wendover, iii. 67; Matthew Paris, *Chronica Maiora*, iii. 260.

[3] Ibid. 266.

[4] Ibid. 269.

[5] Ibid. 271; *Dunstable*, 136; Matthew Paris, *Hist.*, ii. 367–71.

[6] Segrave was not again appointed justiciar, but in 1236 he was appointed justice of Chester. *Dic. Nat. Biog.*

concessions, and to return to his 'natural counsellors' again. On this occasion with more caution and precision than before, there was named a council of twelve, at the head of whom was placed William bishop-elect of Valence, a militant prelate who had come from Savoy to England in the company of the queen. Although he was a foreigner he was not unpopular with the native barons. He was designated as *consiliarius regis principalis*, and with him were associated such sturdy representatives of the baronial party as the earl Warenne, the earl Ferrers, and John fitz Geoffrey. These men, we are told, were then sworn upon the gospels to furnish the king faithful counsel, and likewise the king gave his oath to follow their counsels. This is the first instance in which a group of counsellors is described as appointed and sworn.[1]

But the weakness of constitutional devices that did not have the sincere support of the king was soon made apparent. In the absence of parliament there was nothing to prevent the king choosing and removing his counsellors at will. Neither was it, on the other hand, at all sure that the barons named in parliament would stand at their posts. In the same year, at all events, mention is made again of such unpopular counsellors as John of Lincoln, Simon de Montfort, and Geoffrey the Templar.[2] In 1239 Stephen Segrave again was recalled, who is described as *praecipuus consiliarius*, and as taking in his hand 'the reins of the royal council'.[3] He was now influential solely as a counsellor, for since his removal he had not been made justiciar again. Among the others whose names were made prominent in the same relationship were Otto the pope's legate, Peter of Savoy the queen's uncle, Peter of Aigueblanche bishop of Hereford,[4]

[1] Matthew Paris, *Chronica Maiora*, iii. 382 ff.; *Hist.*, ii. 394; *Dunstable*, 145. Unfortunately the names of the twelve are not all given.

[2] Matthew Paris, *Chronica Maiora*, iii. 412. On inheriting the earldom of Leicester, Simon de Montfort became steward of England.

[3] Ibid. 524, 545.

[4] Peter of Aigueblanche was a Savoyard of high rank who came to England in 1236 as a clerk of the aforesaid bishop of Valence. In 1239 he became keeper of the king's wardrobe, and in 1240 was made bishop of Hereford. He was known as the king's 'special councillor', and was sent on more than one diplomatic commission to the Continent. He remained a royalist during the barons' war.

and John Mansel.[1] Among all the men who gained prominence at this time in the king's council, no one was more capable, diligent, and assertive than John Mansel. He was not a foreigner, but the son of an English country priest, who had practically been brought up in the king's court. In 1234 he is found filling an office which Madox believed to be that of the chancellor of the exchequer. Several times during the period when there was no official chancellor of England he was given the custody of the great seal.[2] Concerning his relations with the king, M. Bémont has said, 'the simple title counsellor gave him greater influence than the right of the proudest baron.'[3] His influence was exerted to obtain for himself and others many grants of the crown, and it was said finally that he held as many as three hundred benefices, and it was believed 'there was no wealthier clerk in the world'. For all these reasons he became especially an object of the barons' wrath, until they brought about his ruin during the war. At one time Mansel is mentioned as 'moderator of the royal counsels'. But the phrase must not be taken too literally, for the chronicles are repeatedly pointing out one or another of these men as 'principal counsellor' or 'special and familiar counsellor'. It has even been suggested that something like a presidency of the council here is indicated. The expressions, however, are used too freely and with too little consistency to be admitted to have more than a momentary significance. Certainly no presidential office was in course of evolution.

A plan of reform, 1244.

On the renewal of the parliamentary strife in 1244 the barons became more insistent and positive in their demands. According to Matthew Paris, a particular scheme was drawn up for the reform of the king's council.[4] This plan is given to us in the form of a draft, which may never have been

[1] Matthew Paris, *Chronica Maiora*, iv. 87, 190, 237.

[2] In 1238 the seal was taken away from Bishop Neville. After this time the seal was entrusted to one keeper after another, who was preferably a skilled officer rather than a magnate. The chancellorship was restored by the 'Provisions of Oxford', but its character henceforth was changed in favour of a salaried officer. See the article of Miss Dibben, 'The Chancellor and the Keeper of the Seal under Henry III.' *Eng. Hist. Rev.*, xxvii. 39–51.

[3] *Simon de Montfort*, p. 112.

[4] Matthew Paris, *Chronica Maiora*, iv. 366–8.

acted upon. It was proposed, at all events, that by common consent there should be chosen four of the most capable and noble men of the realm to be of the king's council, and sworn to manage faithfully the business of the king and the realm. Among the four might be included the justiciar and the chancellor. These men should personally attend the king, and if all could not be present, at least two should be in attendance at all times. As they were to be chosen by the assent of all the barons, so without common consent no one of them should be removed. It does not appear that this plan was ever presented to the king, or even that it was formally passed by the barons, although there is reason to think that it was known and had some effect. At all events the king was moved to present to the barons the names of four new counsellors of his own choice. This action seems to have forestalled any further consideration of the aforesaid scheme, for by this announcement the barons were said to have been in no small degree conciliated.[1]

From this time there are a great many references to a council of limited personnel. In 1250 Matthew Paris speaks of the magnates of the land, *praecipue eorum qui de consilio domini Regis sunt.*[2] In 1253 the king went abroad, leaving the queen and his brother Richard as regents during his absence. It appears that he then appointed a council also, for during this time he wrote, 'we are unwilling to have other counsellors than those whom we have ordained.'[3] This is an expression of a more exclusive idea of the council than has appeared heretofore. That Henry was disposed to determine his policies in small councils without the assent of his barons, is seen in the curious scheme which was devised to place the king's younger son Edmund over the kingdom of Sicily. In 1256 there was framed a memorandum of the liberties to be granted to Apulia, and in the list of the king's

[1] Ibid. 294, and *Hist.*, ii. 48. This is the reverse of the order of events given by the chronicle, but as Mr. Prothero (*Simon de Montfort*, pp. 71–2) has pointed out, the chronology of this year has been badly mixed. The place which I have given for the scheme concerning the council seems the only possible one. It would hardly be sensible for the barons to propose the plan after the king's appointments had been accepted.

[2] *Chronica Maiora*, v. 118.

[3] Prynne, *Register*, i. 390.

council which is given therein not more than two were great barons.[1] According to the prevailing ideas as to the right of the barons to participate in the king's councils, certainly no national policy could safely be determined in this manner.

More definite proposals, 1257–8.

It was particularly the Sicilian scheme of the king and his counsellors that brought to a head the great crisis of the reign. In 1257 the clergy, in their own assembly under archbishop Boniface, refused to grant money until they had drawn up for the reform of the government a series of articles, which they forced the king to accept. More than half of these articles were concerned with the statement of a counsellor's oath, which was said to have been taken by the bishop of London, the bishop of Worcester, and others then elected to the king's council.[2] The same oath, we are told, was taken by the barons of the exchequer, the justices, and all of the king's bailiffs except the sheriffs. This is the first time that we are given the form of an official oath, and as it proves to be the basis for all future oath-forms of the kind, there will be reason to refer to it again. In the following year the barons followed up the work thus begun by the famous 'Provisions of Oxford', which have been described as an elaboration and extension of the principles previously enacted in Magna Carta.[3] But the advance that had been made during the past forty years is shown nowhere more clearly than in the prominence that was now given the king's council. In the attempts to provide for the enforcement of the charter (Article 61), the best that the barons could then do was to name a committee of emergency. The safeguard of the 'Provisions of Oxford', however, was to rest with a permanent standing council, although the council was not permitted to stand clearly apart from a series of special committees. In the very complicated constitution which then was drawn up the barons show a certain confusion

[1] The names were Peter bishop of Hereford, Aymar bishop-elect of Winchester, William of Valence, Geoffrey of Lusignan, Richard earl of Gloucester, John earl Warenne, John Mansel, Philip Louvel, treasurer; and to these another list was added, including Ralph fitz Nicolas, Roger of Turkelby, Henry of Bath, Henry de la Mare, Henry of Bretton (Bracton ?), and Nicholas de la Tour. *Foedera* (Rec.), i. 332.

[2] *Ann. Burton* (Rolls Series), p. 395; Matthew Paris, *Chronica Maiora*, v. 638.

[3] Adams, op. cit., pp. 298 ff.

of mind between the two methods of action, naming first a special commission of twenty-four, who should ' reform the state of the realm ', and then by a devious process of indirect election a council of fifteen for the general control of the government. With a view to reconciling the interests of the two parties, twelve of the twenty-four were named by the king and twelve by the barons, and they were given an extensive commission to reform the realm. They were also delegated to select the king's council, and this was done in the following manner: the twenty-four selected four, two from each side, and the four electors proceeded to name the ultimate fifteen. The members of the council were duly announced and sworn—*ceo sunt ceus ke sunt jurez del cunseil le rei.*[1] Whatever may be thought of these electoral methods, the results were entirely favourable to the barons, for nine of their own committee of twelve were given places in the council against three of the king's twelve.[2] 'The which council', the king was required to concede, 'we have promised and do promise to create for the redressing and amending of all the affairs which belong to us and our realm. And we will that the aforesaid council, or the greater part of it, may elect a wise man or wise men to be members of it in place of him or of them who may fail. And we will hold firm and stable whatever the aforesaid council or the greater part of it shall do.'[3] Even this council, though decidedly anti-royalist in its personnel, was not allowed to remain without being guarded by another committee of twelve appointed by the ' community '. In the events which follow, it would be difficult to distinguish between the actions of one junto and another. In practical work certainly the lines which were laid down with so much artifice were not

[1] Stubbs, *Select Charters* (Oxford, 1895), p. 389; *Cal. Patent Rolls*, 42 Hen. III, p. 645. Prothero, *Simon de Montfort*, App. III, gives the lists of each of these committees. See also Tout, *Political History of England*, iii. 100 ff.

[2] Of the latter group there were Archbishop Boniface, John Mansel, and the earl of Warwick; while of the barons' group there were the bishop of Worcester, the earls of Leicester, Norfolk, Hereford, Gloucester; John fitz Geoffrey, Peter Montfort, Richard Grey, and Roger Mortimer. The remaining three were Peter of Savoy, James of Audley, and the earl of Albemarle.

[3] *Royal Letters*, ii. 362.

observed with any degree of consistency. In 1259 the enactments known as the ' Provisions of the Barons ' were made, it is said, *par le rei et sun conseil et les xii par le commun conseil esluz.*[1] Again the same year Richard Grey, one of the barons' twelve and also of the fifteen, was appointed keeper of Dover Castle, *par nostre conseil,* ' that is, by the good men of the land elected to the king's council '.[2] But on another occasion a writ was issued by the assent of eight men, of whom two had been named among the twenty-four, five were of the fifteen, and one belonged to neither body.[3] In 1260 a letter of the king to ten barons asking for counsel contains the new name of Philip Basset.[4] From all that we know of the habits of the barons, their attendance at the council in the manner intended could not have been held for any considerable length of time. In the same year the defection of the earl of Gloucester helped to cause the confederacy of the barons to break down, so that in 1261 the king, with the sanction of a bull from the pope, definitely repudiated the 'Provisions of Oxford' with all of his promises thereto.[5] There were still efforts, however, in his behalf to maintain a council, for in 1262 Peter de Montfort wrote to several of his fellow barons, ' wherefore I pray and request you, fair lords, since you are of the council of our lord the king, that you will tender the king counsel.' [6]

Scheme of 1264.

Not discouraged by their failures in this direction, the barons, after their victory under Simon de Montfort in 1263, made one more signal attempt to organize and control the king's council. In this way, they had learned, the government could be taken completely out of the king's hands without the necessity of deposing him. According to a plan devised at the parliament of Lewes in 1264, three electors were chosen by the barons, and the three in turn were to select nine counsellors.[7] This scheme in its simplicity was

[1] Burton, pp. 471 ff. [2] *Cal. Patent Rolls,* 43 Hen. III, p. 19, &c.
[3] *Lords' Report on the Dignity of a Peer,* p. 132.
[4] *Royal Letters,* ii. 153. [5] *Chron. Wykes* (Rolls Series), p. 128.
[6] The letter is directed to the earl of Norfolk marshal, Philip Basset justiciar, John Mansel, and Robert Walerand. *Royal Letters,* ii. 368.
[7] Stubbs, *Select Charters,* p. 413 ; *Cal. Patent Rolls,* 48 Hen. III, p. 370 ; *Foedera* (Rec.), i. 443.

a marked improvement over the former one, especially as the council was not confused with interlocking committees. By letters patent in the name of the king, Simon de Montfort, Gilbert earl of Gloucester and the bishop of Chichester were given the right to nominate the nine, *de quorum consilio negocia regni nostri, secundum leges et consuetudines eiusdem regni, regere volumus.*[1] It was further enacted with considerable care for details, that the king should receive their counsel and give credence to them in the administration of justice, in the creation and appointment of offices, and in the observance of charters. The counsellors were also to provide that the king should not make immoderate expenses. In the creation and appointment of all offices Englishmen and denizens of England only should be recognized. Another clause, which reveals an inherent difficulty in every council of barons, was the requirement that of the nine counsellors three at least should always be present in the *curia.* Finally the counsellors and all other officers were required to be sworn in a manner which recalls the oath form of 1257.[2]

As to the actual operation of the council of nine we are not given any definite information. But we are sure that the government of Simon de Montfort, as it is commonly called, was not in a position to do anything without the sanction of a council of some kind. There is hardly an act that does not bear witness to this fact in one form or another, as may be illustrated by the following phrases: *per comitem Leicestriae et totum consilium; de consilio praelatorum et baronum nostrorum de consilio nostro existentium; cum baronibus et consilio nostro; de consilio magnatum nostrorum qui sunt de consilio nostro.*[3] In the same year the king writes to Simon de Montfort and the earl of Gloucester, '*mittatis etiam ad nos aliquos ad eundum nobiscum usque Doveriam, et*

[1] *Foedera*, i. 444.

[2] The names of the new counsellors do not appear. Besides the electors, Simon de Montfort, the earl of Gloucester, and Stephen Berksted, bishop of Chichester, there were probably Peter de Montfort, Roger St. John, and Giles of Argentine. Hugh Despenser was justiciar at the time, and Thomas of Cantilupe, a doctor of canon law, was made chancellor.

[3] *Foedera*, i. 454; *Royal Letters*, ii. 258, 276; *Patent Rolls*, 49 Hen. III, n. 32, &c.

ad consilium impendendum et responsum nuntiis euntibus et redeuntibus nobiscum de consilio vestro faciendum quousque personaliter veniatis'.[1]

But what the council was from time to time in its personnel and method of work is not revealed, and this concealment was probably for good reasons. From every circumstance in the politics and warfare of the time, we cannot fail to infer that as a working body it was irregular and uncertain to an extreme degree. Before the downfall of this régime in 1265, an effort was made to support its failing strength by a charter in the name of the king, which confirmed all the ordinances and articles previously made *per nos et consilium nostrum,* and declared further that any one acting contrary to these enactments or against the tranquillity of the realm should be punished, *per consideracionem concilii nostri et magnatum terrae nostrae.*[2] In this passage the king's council is mentioned as distinct from the general body of the barons, although they are indicated as acting together. But what is of greater importance than any of the particular acts of this unsettled and short-lived government, is to observe the well-sustained growth of a definite conception of the king's council in its political sphere as an indispensable organ in the state.

Reaction after 1265.

The defeat of Simon de Montfort in 1265 and the fall of his party meant the failure of this particular experiment of government. But the ideas of an age were not so readily destroyed. Neither the parliament nor the council in its other aspects were long retarded in their normal development because of another revolution. Under the government of the restoration, therefore, one can continue to follow the working of forces which had long been striving for expression. During the few remaining years of Henry III's reign there continues to be evidence of a king's council in constant operation. The king himself makes mention of *quidam nobis assistentes, quorum consilio regni nostri negotia disponuntur.*[3] There is no doubt, moreover, that out of the experience of previous years the council which now emerged was emphatically a barons' council. The foreigners and

[1] *Royal Letters,* ii. 262. [2] *Foedera,* i. 453. [3] *Royal Letters,* ii. 303.

favourites had been effectively removed and do not appear again as a political factor. The council of barons is frequently referred to by the phrase, *de consilio magnatum qui sunt de consilio nostro*, and among the barons the name of the king's son Edward is given prominence together with *alii fideles de consilio nostro*.[1] It remains, however, to be asked whether the council thus indicated was in any way selected or appointed, or did it revert to the unorganized and uncertain condition which existed at the beginning of the reign? Now there are various reasons for inferring that for the time being the latter alternative was true. The royalist reaction was naturally opposed to all that the appointed councils had previously meant, while the party of barons now dominant had no reason to insist upon anything of the kind. Moreover, the loose way in which the word *consiliarii* is used points very positively to the same conclusion. In particular the edict of Kenilworth in 1266 contains an award which was determined by twelve lords, who were declared to have been given power *a domino Rege et aliis baronibus, consiliariis Regni et proceribus Anglie*.[2] The twelve were a committee such as might be selected at any time for a particular purpose, but the real counsellors were the barons of the realm.

A sworn council again, 1271.

But just as had happened before, a loose principle gave way before the need of a more fixed and responsible body. Before the long reign drew to a close, the aged king grew sick and feeble, while his son and heir left the country on a pilgrimage to the Holy Land. Very likely the events of former years were remembered, when again the government was entrusted to a body of sworn counsellors. Evidence of this is given in a letter which Henry wrote in 1271, *a nostre cher frere le noble Roy de Allemagne, nostre honurable pere Wauter Arceveske de Everwyk primat Dangleterre e as autres de notre conseil iurez*.[3] In this letter the king explains how, in gratitude for what he believed was a recovery from his illness, he had made a vow to go to the Holy Land. This task his son Edward had undertaken for him. He needed money greatly, and he gave the council power to use the resources

Letter of April 16, 1271, from the king to Richard of Cornwall.

[1] *Foedera*, i. 458, 469, &c. [2] *Statutes of the Realm*, i. 12.
[3] *Patent Roll*, 55 Hen. III, m. 16.

of the royal domains to the utmost for this purpose. This passage is of great significance, for it contains the first proof that we have of a council which was appointed and sworn under ordinary conditions. On previous occasions, so far as we can be sure, the council had been sworn under pressure of the barons, but now the oath appears as a normal part of the king's government. Possibly we should still say that the sworn council was but a temporary expedient. The letter declares that the authority then given was to endure for a year, in order that at the king's pleasure it might afterwards be renewed. The question is immaterial, because Henry lived only a little more than a year from this date. When the king died in 1272, John de Kirkby gave up the great seal in the presence of the archbishop of York and other counsellors, and at this point the close roll ends.[1]

It required the entire reign of Henry III to bring the king's council, in its aspect as a permanent body, to this point of definition. The period of the minority shows the existence of a council in constant attendance and active service, but it was still of a shifting and indeterminate character. The presence of the foreigners and royal favourites had the effect of bringing the council into antagonism with the barons, and in this way caused the demand for appointments, removals, and a formal oath. The later strife with the barons and the revolutionary crises forced the appointment on several occasions of a select number of councillors who should be responsible for the government. Even these councils were lacking in elementary stability. The restoration shows a tendency to revert to the original conditions of a general body, with the reappearance of committees for special purposes, but soon a reason was found for the employment again of a sworn responsible council. This brings the subject to a slightly advanced stage of its development, which will be treated in succeeding chapters. It is not to be understood, however, that the counsellor's oath materially altered the character of the council; it only brought the duties of a counsellor into a clearer light and caused these to be better understood. There is still to be

[1] *Excerpta e Rotulis* (Record Com.), p. 590.

considered the question how the council in any feature is to be distinguished from the exchequer or any other branch of the *curia regis*. While we turn now to deal with such specific and technical problems, let not the early and primitive ideas of an undefined *consilium* be forgotten. Most historic institutions, in fact, retain something of their original character, and this tendency to a marked degree was true of the council, which was never so closely bound by legal forms as other constitutional bodies, and therefore enjoyed a remarkable freedom of action.

CHAPTER III

THE COUNCIL AND THE CURIA REGIS

Continuance of a single institution

In the last chapter the council was considered in its relations with the king and barons so far as it was a subject of political discussion. During the conflicts of the time, particularly in 1258 and in 1264, there was a near approach to the recognition of a group of councillors distinct from the *curia regis* and the exchequer.[1] But the events of those revolutionary years were exceptional, and the view of the council then expressed was by no means the usual one. The normal conception was clearly set forth in the oath form of 1257, in which the king's council was defined as including the barons of the exchequer and the justices, as well as the bishops and barons then especially chosen. Not for an indefinite time to come, in fact, can we speak of the council as an organization apart from other bodies in the state. In the thirteenth century, undoubtedly, it was an active organ of political influence, but it did not cease for this reason to exercise the functions of a court. Likewise we find the exchequer and the other branches of the *curia regis* taking their positions as distinct courts, but according to the conceptions of the time these did not cease to be an integral part of the council. Moreover, whenever the case required, any of these courts might be reinforced or expanded, and made to assume the complete form of the king's council. The transition from the system of a single institution to that of many was bound to be a slow and laborious process. For our present consideration, then, there is the problem of the relations of the council and its offshoots. How were the different courts separated and distinguished from the

[1] It would be difficult to prove the point, but it is not my belief that even at these times there was any intention of separating the council, as a political body, from the *curia* in its usual operations.

council? and at the same time to what extent was their fundamental unity maintained? Furthermore, after the formation of the new courts may be said to have been accomplished, what functions were still retained by the king's council?

Its differentiation gradual and obscure.

Now the differentiation of the branches of the *curia regis* is a process which can be followed only with great difficulty, because contemporary writers have given us no description of the steps that were taken. Even the lines of cleavage upon which the divisions occurred are nowhere clearly drawn. The uncertainty of thought that prevailed concerning the exchequer, whether it was in anywise a court separate from the *curia regis* has already been mentioned. Likewise men spoke of the common bench and the *coram rege* in a tentative way, showing that they were only beginning to make distinctions, which again they readily lose sight of. Usually they referred to the *curia regis* or the *consilium* in the same manner as before. In this apparent confusion of mind it is easy to say that the people did not realize the changes that were going on about them. This is true, but their lack of forethought shows also that the changes were made under actual necessities. With a certain reluctance to accept the new conditions, they preferred to think of the council or *curia regis* as a single organ of authority, which comprehended indeed a wide diversity of operations. Possibly a trace of the original thought is found to the present day, when as a mode of expression one speaks of 'the court' irrespective of any particular tribunal. A reason for this conservatism becomes manifest as soon as the nature of the changes in view is considered.

The lines of differentiation.

It has been suggested in this connexion that a division of powers executive, legislative, and judicial, must inevitably occur. The development of the council, the parliament, and the law courts, it is said, followed on these lines. With proper qualifications this may be a correct statement of the principles of government as they are tending to-day, but it will not bear scrutiny for a moment when the thirteenth century is considered. No step was then taken in fact with any such aim in mind or with any such practical results. The more usual view concerning the basis of the division of the courts is that it occurred in response to the necessities of certain *kinds* of business, such as finance, common pleas, and pleas of the crown. This also fails to be a satisfactory explanation, because the exchequer without any irregularity received common pleas, and the court of common pleas also freely heard pleas of the crown. A truer explanation, it is believed, finds a basis for the multiplication of the courts not in the *kinds* of business, but in the diverse *modes of procedure* which came to be followed. The great change that was eventually to transform the feudal *curia regis* into the courts of common law was not primarily a division of the original body, or a classification of its functions, but an introduction of certain new methods of business. These were not a product of the court itself, but were imposed by royal authority and in many respects were opposed to the older feudal ideas and interests. In this light the new processes may well be denoted as prerogative actions. The assertion of the principle is first visible in the exchequer, where questions concerning the king's revenue at an early date were treated according to rule and routine. It next appears in the judicial reforms that are connected with the name of Henry II, as seen particularly in the *itinera*, the assizes, the jury, and the judicial writs. It is carried further in the elaboration of a great system of formulary actions that are associated with the development of the common law. By the operation of the methods of the common law, courts of defined authority necessarily follow. These differed from the older stem, and from each other, not so clearly in respect of the subjects of their jurisdiction as by the modes of procedure which they were bound to observe. To this extent, and only to this extent, were they differentiated from the council; in other respects they were still an integral part of the single dominating court that for certain purposes still survived. To carry out this thought in all its practical bearings it will be necessary to trace some of the steps in detail. We shall therefore observe the relations of the council in turn: (1) to the exchequer under Henry III, (2) to the court of common pleas, and (3) to the king's bench.

1. *Its Relation to the Exchequer.*

It has already been shown that in the time of Henry II the exchequer was hardly more than a phase of the *curia regis*. It was then a differentiated body only in the respect of certain well-defined methods of dealing with the king's revenue, but in other respects it was not different from the original court of general assemblage and general authority. While the meetings of the council or *curia* were by no means confined to the semi-annual sessions of the exchequer, it was no doubt a convenience to bring together and transact as much of the king's business as possible at these stated times. At the beginning of the reign of Henry III, it is clear that early usages in this regard were still actively maintained. Whether to say that this is made evident by the more explicit statements of the records, or that during the prevailing feudal reaction there was a positive reversion to primitive conditions, we cannot be certain. At all events, there is no doubt that the government of this period, not merely in its strictly financial affairs, was largely carried on by the council meeting at the same time and place as the exchequer.

The exchequer a general court

In the first place, the attendance of a more or less general body of consultation is constantly noticed. This is now usually known as 'the council at the exchequer', in preference to the older expression '*curia* in the exchequer'. In the second year, for example, a judgement is recorded upon the pipe roll as having been rendered 'by William Marshall, the bishop of Winchester, Hubert de Burgh, and the king's council'.[1] Again in the same year a clerical appointment was made with the words, *provisum est per concilium domini regis ad scaccarium*.[2] Likewise a certain convention is made *coram consilio nostro et baronibus de scaccario*.[3] The close relations of the king's council with the barons of the exchequer are noticed further under various forms of expression. One speaks of 'the justiciar, the magnates of the council and the barons (of the exchequer)'; 'the council, the treasurer, and barons'; 'the barons of the exchequer and

attended by the council.

[1] *Pipe Roll*, 2 Hen. III, m. 4 b.; cited in Madox, ii. 26.
[2] Ibid. 27.
[3] *Rot. Lit. Claus.*, i. 361.

others of the council'; 'the treasurer, the chancellor, and others of the council'; sometimes also 'the council of the exchequer'.[1] From these and other passages it is evident that according to the traditional usages of the *curia regis*, the attendance at the court varied indefinitely according to the convenience or necessities of the occasion. Whenever it is possible there is an emphasis of the presence of the ministers and other great men of the kingdom, while at other times the council at the exchequer appears to be only a conference of the barons thereof with one or more of the justices.[2] But at all times the records seem to be striving to show that the exchequer was not mainly a segregated department, but a general organ of government wherein the council was seated.

Consultations at the exchequer.

That this was the view taken by a minister of the time is made evident by a letter of the legate Pandulf to Hubert de Burgh in 1220. The legate is deeply concerned, he writes, over the misdeeds and excesses committed by Philip of Ulecot, and thinks that some form of punishment for his offences should be devised. It would be rash, he admits, for himself alone to proceed without the counsel of the justiciar and other men, and for this purpose he hopes to confer with them shortly at Worcester. If only the question had been discussed lately at the exchequer, he would have taken action immediately.

'Si enim super hiis vestrum et aliorum qui sunt in scaccario expressissetis consilium, processissemus forsitan adhibeto consilio vestro.'[3]

Necessities of Henry III's minority.

There were certainly very strong reasons for bringing the council, including as many of the magnates as possible, to the exchequer during the early years of Henry III. As a result of the civil wars the finances had broken down more completely than at any time since the reign of Stephen. From Michaelmas, 1216, for the following year the ferms of

[1] *Rot. Lit. Claus.*, i. 361, 410; *Excerpta e Rotulis Finium*, i. 67, 88; *Memoranda Rolls*, 45 Hen. III, m. 2 d.; 55 Hen. III, m. 6 d.; 55 Hen. III, m. 1.

[2] One attestation is *per consilium scaccarii et M. de Pateshull* (*Rot. Lit. Claus.*, i. 406).

[3] *Foedera* (Rec. Ed.), i. 158.

the sheriffs were not accounted for at all, while the rolls at one time were captured by Louis of France.[1] Military services had been rendered by royalist barons and expenses incurred without royal warrants and without official record of the facts. Wardships and escheats also, which rightfully belonged to the crown, were somehow withheld. At such a time men could not be held to account, after the strict legal methods for which the exchequer is noted, but had to be dealt with in a spirit of fairness and conciliation. To do this successfully required all the wisdom and counsel which could be brought together.

Expenditures.

In the first place there were numberless claims for services rendered under John, of which the exchequer evidently had scanty record. Such claims lasting during the whole period of the minority, the council sought to adjust, either by judicial process or otherwise. The close rolls in fact are filled with orders in the name of the council that acquittances should be made of scutages charged for the expedition to Poitou, the council receiving testimony and deciding that parties so charged had actually served. Services in the civil war had to receive compensations and rewards, as did Falkes de Breauté for his services to 'our father and ourselves'.[2] These rewards were given generally in the form of remittances of ferms or other dues. In 1220 William Briwer 'for his good and faithful service' was acquitted of various obligations amounting to £452. The order was attested, *per eundem* (i.e. the justiciar) *et consilium domini regis*.[3] In 1222 the citizens of York were acquitted by the council of the sum of £1,000 which they owed King John, as it was testified that they had given the money for work upon the king's castles.[4] A letter close of the fifth year, addressed to the barons of the exchequer, shows very clearly how the council took such questions in hand. 'Know that we have learned by our council and by the rolls of the exchequer that Robert de Vallibus once made fine with King John of 2,000 marks for quittance of all that he then owed the exchequer.'

[1] G. J. Turner, *Trans. Royal Hist. Society*, New Series, xviii. 282 ff.
[2] *Rot. Lit. Claus.*, i. 481.
[3] Ibid. 413.
[4] Ibid. 496.

It was found on the rolls that of the debt he had rendered 1,000 marks, in that he had given the service of two knights and twenty serjeants with horses and arms for one year, and of one knight and twenty serjeants in the following year. Protestation having been made before the council that Robert had rendered King John this service, it was commanded that he be acquitted at the exchequer of all the aforesaid debts.[1] Altogether the financial obligations left over from John's reign were a serious load for the government of the minority. In 1218, in order to raise a loan of 6,000 marks, to be used by an embassy sent to Rome, for the better security of the creditors, the bishop of London, the bishop of Winchester, and the Earl Marshal gave pledges 'with the assent of the legate and the magnates who are of our council'.[2]

Increase of the revenues.

That more of the revenues due to the crown might be brought in, the council in many cases scrutinized the work of the sheriffs. In the third year the justices itinerant in the county of Nottingham were directed to make an inquisition as to the revenues of certain manors since the fifteenth year of John, and to direct the sheriff of Nottingham to come before the council at Westminster to answer concerning all the issues of those manors.[3] In 1220 the sheriff of Canterbury was ordered to inquire by the oaths of legal men as to the services due from a certain piece of land, whether they were one-sixth of a barony or more, and to report without delay to the justiciar and council.[4] In the same year the sheriff of Lancaster was ordered to pay damages of chattels he had wrongly seized to the extent of 40 marks. If he did not, he was to appear before the council and the barons of the exchequer to show cause.[5] In the second year Robert Courtenay was required to make a convention before the council and barons of the exchequer that he would answer for the revenues of the county of Devon, for which he had already had a summons that he had not obeyed.[6]

[1] *Rot. Lit. Claus.*, i. 472; a similar case, p. 521.
[2] *Cal. Patent Rolls*, 181, 304.
[3] *Rot. Lit. Claus.*, i. 406.
[4] *Excerpta e Rotulis Finium*, i. 46.
[5] *Rot. Lit. Claus.*, i. 438; also p. 436.
[6] Ibid. 361.

The council a body of reinforcement.

After the minority of Henry III was passed, the general conferences at the exchequer were not sustained with the same regularity. Under the more normal conditions that were now resumed there was less reason for any exceptional body of consultation. The attendance of the council, however, was by no means given up; it reappears whenever anything out of the usual routine occurred. In the twenty-ninth year, for instance, Alexander Swerford, a clerk of the exchequer, for an answer to a question of procedure, repaired *ad loquendum cum consilio Regis*.[1] In the thirty-fourth year it is described how the king in person, attended by his council, came to the exchequer and there gave commands to the sheriffs, which were then enrolled in a series of ordinances.[2] In 1264 the issues of a certain manor were to be answered for, 'in the form to be provided by the king's council and the barons of the exchequer.'[3] In 1270 the methods of keeping the records in the exchequer were reformed, we are told, by the magnates of the king's council.[4] On another occasion the king commanded the treasurer and barons to make a postponement to a time when the matter could be considered also by others of the council. All these instances suggest the very narrow scope of authority that was allowed the treasurer and his associates in their separate capacity.

Separation of the chancery.

At the same time another step was taken which served to define the exchequer more closely in its administrative procedure. It is well understood that a vital part of all its methods in fiscal affairs lay in the writs, which were the king's orders to the treasurer and barons, or the treasurer and chamberlains, as warrants for every kind of expenditure. During the present period such warrants were issued often by the authority of the justiciar or other great officer, as well as by authority of the council. To a considerable extent,

[1] Hall, *Red Book of the Exchequer* (Rolls Series), i. p. xliv.

[2] *Memoranda Roll*, 35 Hen. III, m. 2; Madox, ii. 102.

[3] *Cal. Patent Rolls*, 49 Hen. III, 392.

[4] 'Coram nobis, Ricardo Rege Romanorum fratre nostro, venerabilibus patribus Waltero Eboracensi Archiepiscopo, Godefrido Wigorniensi Episcopo, Edwardo primogenito nostro, Willelmo de Valencia fratre nostro, Rogero de Mortuo Mari, Philippo Basset, Henrico de Alemannia, Roberto Aguylun, Roberto Waleraund, et aliis magnatibus qui sunt de consilio nostro.' *Red Book of the Exchequer*, iii. 843.

we know, these orders were determined by the advice of the council sitting in the exchequer itself.[1] The close connexion with the king that was maintained by the exchequer, and the council at the exchequer, was made the easier by the fact that from the beginning the chancellor was one of the regular attendants of this body. But an important change in this regard took place when, for reasons that are not entirely clear, another branch of the *curia regis*, namely the chancery, was formed and became a separate department. Possibly it was due to the initiative of Hubert Walter that a new series of rolls begins to appear in 1199. The next step, which was believed by Madox to have been taken about the eighteenth year of Henry III and by the editors of the *Dialogus* near the twenty-second year, was the withdrawal of the chancellor from attendance at the exchequer, while his place in the older organization was taken by his clerk, henceforth known as the chancellor of the exchequer.[2] Whichever date be taken, the event was an important one in causing a 'shifting of the centre of gravity' in the political power of the exchequer, and also in setting a line of demarcation between the council and the exchequer. For the chancellor attended the king, and continued to act for the king and council as a general secretary,[3] while the proceedings of the exchequer were controlled by the writs that passed through this channel. The actions of the council then, so far as they appear in the records of the chancery,[3] are clearly distinct from any of the methods of the exchequer. Ultimately we shall be required to speak of the 'council in chancery', but the practical value of this point can best be appreciated at a later stage.

Dual functions of the exchequer.

Henceforth it is necessary to make a sharp distinction between the financial operations and the judicial operations

[1] The formula of the writs closed with the words, *testibus hiis ibi ad scaccarium* (*Dialogus*, lib. i, c. vi).

[2] Madox, ii. 51; *Dialogus*, p. 17.

[3] To cite a few examples: in 1224 Walter Lacy asks the chancellor to assemble the council in order to expedite his business (*Deputy Keeper's Report*, v, App. II, No. 830). In 1225 the king consents to come and make a truce with the Welsh *cum domino cancellario et consilio nostro* (*Foedera*, Orig. Ed., i. 277). Again in 1265 certain letters under the great seal were said to have been made before the whole council, approved, and immediately signed and delivered (*Cal. Doc. Scotland*, i. 473).

which were carried on simultaneously in the exchequer. 'In our view', says Maitland, 'it may be a compound institution, in part a judicial tribunal, in part a financial bureau.'[1] The anomaly has not always been perceived that in its aspect as a financial bureau the exchequer was a body of closely restricted powers, while outside this field, in its judicial activities, it was not placed under any similar limitations. At the time that the courts of common pleas and the king's bench were being defined in their respective spheres, for a considerable period the exchequer held its position outside the system of the common law. In this field then it was still in character the older *curia regis*, and identified with the king's council. Its proceedings in this capacity were not permitted to be held without an assemblage of consultation to which at least the justices were called. For this very reason the exchequer was more and more sought for its adjustment of cases, so that it was inevitably brought into rivalry with the courts of fixed procedure.[2] But before this phase of the subject is considered, it will be necessary to determine the position of the other courts of law, regarded especially as branches of the king's council.

2. *Its Relation to the Court of Common Pleas.*[3]

The *itinera* a special departure.

Apart from the exchequer the beginning of an important departure in the *curia regis* is found in the itinerant justices as first employed by Henry I. Henry II extended the system by dividing the country into regular circuits, while to the existing *itinera* he added the visiting justices of assize. It was not the original intention to divide the *curia*, but to bring its facilities to all parts of the country. Never-

[1] Pollock and Maitland, *Hist. of Eng. Law*, i. 191.

[2] Says Maitland, 'We are at a loss to account on the one hand for the offence that they (the barons of the exchequer) thus gave to the community of the realm, and on the other for the persistent recourse to their tribunal, unless it be that a creditor might thus obtain the advantage of some of those expeditious and stringent processes which had been devised for the collection of crown debts' (Pollock and Maitland, i. 193). There was also the reason that here the court was not subject to the writs and other requirements of the common law.

[3] For the ideas contained in this section I am especially indebted to Professor Adams, who has given me suggestions beyond those presented in his recent book. See *The Origin of the Court of Common Pleas*, op. cit., 136–43.

theless a special feature was introduced which was ultimately to affect the entire system of justice most profoundly. The new point of departure is found in the fact that the visiting justices were royal commissioners, who were appointed for certain purposes, not exclusively judicial, and for these purposes only. In 1170 we are told that such justices were appointed and were given a 'form' according to which they were to act.[1] It was afterwards customary to give them articles of instruction.[2] The well-known reforms of Henry II, elaborating the possessory assizes, the use of the jury and the writs, were intended primarily for the royal commissioners, that is, the itinerant and other visiting justices, who were bound to act according to the rules of procedure thus laid down. The degree of authority given to the royal commissioners on different occasions varied greatly; sometimes they were charged to undertake only the new possessory assizes, and again they were to receive not only the assizes but all pleas in a county.[3] But in every case the restricted powers of the commissioners and their obligations to follow a more or less definite form of procedure is made manifest. When the justices were uncertain of their ground they could only refer the question to the *curia* of general authority. To give a single illustration, in a Cornish eyre of 1201 an assize of *mort d'ancestor* was held, in which the court was uncertain of the existence of an elder brother, there being no proof either that he was living or dead. To determine the point whether a jury ought to be employed or not, a day was given at Westminster, where the matter was to be discussed by the council.[4] The same idea is expressed more forcibly in the following order which Henry III made in 1218 to his itinerant justices in Kent, directing them to reserve all questions of difficulty for the consideration of the council.

Their limited authority.

'Si quae et loquelae arduae coram vobis emerserint quae coram vobis sine difficultate terminari non possint nec *sine*

[1] 'Rex autem convocatis optimatibus suis instituit abbates et clericos, comites et milites qui circuirent terram, dans formam inscriptam quo modo eis esset agendum.' *Gervase of Canterbury*, i. 216.

[2] A form of 1194 is in Hoveden, ii. 334, and Adams and Stephens, no. 21.

[3] Maitland, *Select Pleas of the Crown* (Selden Society, vol. i, p. xx).

[4] Baildon, *Select Civil Pleas* (Selden Society, vol. x, no. 170).

consilio consilii nostri, eas similiter in respectum poni faciatis (usque . . . coram consilio nostro apud Westmonasterium).'[1]

In this way began the development of that peculiar feature of English law which Maitland has called 'the formulary system'. After the middle of the twelfth century, he says, 'the old oral and traditional formalism is in part supplanted and in part reinforced by a new, written, and authoritative formalism'.[2] From a few simple formulae such as are given by Glanvil, there developed by the time of Bracton a complex and rigidly binding system. The pivotal point of this system lay in the writs, especially the original writs, which were the commands of the king through the chancery for the justices to take this or that action. Three of these original writs are traced to the reign of John, but from that time they multiply rapidly until toward the latter part of Henry III's reign they easily numbered over a hundred.[3] According to Bracton, there should be a writ for every possible form of action in the king's courts—*tot erunt formulae brevium quot genera actionum*.[4] It was against many of the new writs in particular that the opposition of the barons was strenuously directed. In describing this transformation in legal methods most writers give the impression that the new prerogative procedure, as we may call it, extended *pari passu* through all branches of the *curia regis*. Certainly no one has shown that the truth lies quite to the contrary, and that the adoption of these forms by the courts in unequal measure proved to be the great factor in bringing about their separate organizations. In order now to follow this line of argument, it must be understood that the so-called formulaic and restrictive procedure began, and could begin, only in the courts held by the royal commissioners—that is, first the itinerant justices and then the central court established on similar lines.

The bench also a restricted court

Such a central court, or central branch of the *curia*, was formed by Henry II in 1178, when he appointed five justices, who should remain permanently at the *curia regis* to hear all

[1] *Rot. Lit. Claus.*, i. 383.
[2] Pollock and Maitland, ii. 558 ff.
[3] Maitland, *Harvard Law Quarterly*, iii. 97, 167, 212.
[4] *De Legibus Angliae* (Rolls Series), vi. 262.

complaints of the people; with the proviso that if any question should arise which they could not decide by themselves, it should be brought to the king to be determined by him and his *sapientiores*.[1] This was the court soon to be known as the 'bench residing at Westminster'; it was the beginning not of the king's bench but of the court which is afterwards called the common bench or court of common pleas. It is to be noted that in its very inception it was like the itinerant justices, a court by royal commission, and was given only a restricted authority. The very words of the restrictive clause are similar to the instructions already quoted as being given to the itinerant justices in 1218.[2] So close was the connexion at first between the bench and the itinerant justices, that in a year when an eyre was proclaimed in all of the counties there was no business before the bench at Westminster.[3] Moreover, as early as the pleas in this court can be studied—that is, from about the year 1200—it is found that the royal formulary procedure has full sway here. While there was naturally a strong survival of the older *curia regis* procedure, fully one-half of the litigation consisted of the new possessory assizes, and actions by original writs were followed apparently as rapidly as these were invented. For example, a case is quashed because a plaintiff demands by word of mouth another thing than she demands by her writ of dower, and she is instructed to seek another writ if she will.[4] Again, a case cannot proceed because the writ is in the wrong name.[5] The court was not devoted solely to common pleas, for pleas of the crown also were freely dealt with. But its character as a tribunal of formulary procedure is made perfectly clear from the start.

of inferior jurisdiction.

The bench at Westminster is also marked as a court inferior to another branch of the *curia regis* which begins to appear in the reign of John. The latter was known as the court *coram rege*, which consisted of the justices and other members

[1] Benedict of Peterborough, *Gesta Henrici Secundi*, i. 207.

[2] Lest this statement seem to be a hysteron-proteron, I only mean to say that the usages were parallel, without reference to which was first.

[3] Maitland, *Bracton's Note Book* (Cambridge, 1887), i. 141–2.

[4] Baildon, *Civil Pleas*, no. 16.

[5] Ibid. 31.

of the *curia* who followed the king on his journeys. For some time it was not maintained so regularly as the common bench, but it was recognized nevertheless to hold a higher degree of authority.[1] Thus the king commands the justices of the bench that a certain assize of *mort d'ancestor* by preference be held not before them but *coram eo*—that is, in the court attending the king himself.[1] The necessity of holding the sessions of the common bench with regularity was in a measure secured by Magna Carta, article 17, providing that 'common pleas shall not follow our court but shall be held in some certain place'. The identity of either court as a distinct branch is easily lost to sight, as the two readily coalesce and form again an undivided *curia*, which in the time of Henry III is more often called the council. The individual justices also might alternate in attending the bench at Westminster and in holding pleas before the king. As an illustration of the continuance of the old form of the *curia*, which must be acknowledged still to be the normal form, there is an interesting record of the attendance of the court in 1227, when the bishop of Hereford, in a dispute with the citizens of his town, came before the king, who was personally present with certain magnates in the chapel of St. John's, Westminster. Besides the king, there were also in attendance the chief justiciar, five bishops, four justices of the bench, nine knights and barons, of whom four were officers of the household, and five clerks, among whom was Alexander Swerford.[2] But for the most part the bench at Westminster is clearly marked as a court which differs from the older *curia* and from the bench known as *coram rege* by its formulary procedure and inferior authority. The same question with regard to the specialization of the *coram rege* branch will be more difficult to answer.

3. *Its Relation to the King's Bench.*

Continuation of the old *curia*.

The origin of the court ultimately to be known as the king's bench was very different from that of the common bench. It was, in fact, never at any particular time created, but came into its peculiar sphere by a very slow process. While the

[1] Baildon, no. 11.

[2] *Red Book of the Exchequer*, iii. 1010.

common bench was an offshoot from the original *curia regis*, the court following the king was more truly a continuation of the life of the older tribunal in its organization and methods. In the reign of John, as has been said before, the king at times had justices in his train, and with their aid held court *coram ipso rege*.[1] There was no permanence to this body as yet, however. When the king was in France it disappears for the time. During the minority of Henry III there were no sessions or pleas held *coram rege*, nor was any roll of such a court kept, but instead there were pleas which are indicated as held *coram consilio nostro, coram H. de Burgo iusticiario*, and *coram nobis et consilio nostro*.[2] After Henry came of age, in 1224, the pleas *coram rege* reappear, and henceforth there are to be found two sets of rolls, which at first were maintained with imperfect regularity, namely the *coram rege* and the *de banco* rolls. Still comparatively late in the reign, as in 1242 and again in 1253, when the king was absent from the kingdom, instead of *coram rege* there were pleas held *coram consilio, coram W. Eboraci episcopo et consilio domini Regis*, and *coram domina Regina et consilio domini Regis apud Westmonasterium*.[3]

Coram rege distinct from the bench.

Now the distinction of the court *coram rege* from the bench located at Westminster is from the start fairly clear. It was a valid defence for a party to declare in words to the effect: 'this plea should not follow the king, since it is a common plea and (according to the charter) common pleas ought to be held in a fixed place.'[4] On the other hand, in order to have their claims settled in a higher court parties would pay substantial fees that they might be heard *coram rege*. Moreover, the definite superiority of the court *coram rege* over all other courts is shown in its power to review and correct decisions in a manner shortly to be described. These facts are well known in every legal history, but an

[1] Maitland, *Pleas of the Crown*, pp. xii ff.

[2] *Rot. Lit. Claus.*, i, *passim*. Specific instances will be cited in the succeeding pages.

[3] *Abbreviatio Placitorum* (Record Com.), 118, 129.

[4] Ibid. 105, &c.; Madox, i. 102. In the first of these cases it was answered that the plea was not a common plea, since it specially touched the person of the king, and so it should be determined *coram rege*.

unsolved problem appears as soon as the council is mentioned in connexion with the court *coram rege*. Were the units thus designated the same or equivalent ? is there any difference, in fact, which can be shown to exist between them? and if there is no difference at the start, at what point can divergence be shown ? Now it must be remembered that the original *curia regis* was a body of no particular size, membership, or limitations. Thc number present, so far as it was not a matter of accident, depended upon the character of the business in hand. It varied in personnel from a handful of household officers to a large and general assembly. The appointment of special justices in the thirteenth century 'to hold pleas before the king' did not alter this fundamental principle and practice of the court.[1] Whether it was held before a single justice, or in the presence of the king in person and attended by an indefinite number of magnates, it was in any case the *curia regis* as held *coram ipso rege*.[2] In its expanded form it was also called the *consilium regis*, but at the beginning of the reign of Henry III there is nothing which can be said positively to draw a line between the two.[3] Whether it was designated by one name or the other, there was as yet no difference in point of organization, functions, or procedure. That is to say, the prevailing idea of the *curia* or council was sufficiently elastic to include every

[1] A certain commission of the year 1258 has incorrectly been cited as relating to the formation of the king's bench. By letters patent Roger de Thorkilby and others were appointed *ad tenendum bancum regis* at Westminster, to attend the office of the said bench 'according to law and custom' (*Patent Roll*, 42 Hen. III, m. 2). Plainly this was not the court *coram rege*, the king's bench, as we are accustomed to call it, but the court at Westminster, the common bench, or court of common pleas.

[2] A case in which Richard Scroty offered to fight his opponent was postponed because neither the king nor a sufficient number of his council were present. 'Et quia Dominus Rex absens fuit, nec fuerunt ibi nisi pauci de Consilio Domini Regis, noluerunt illi qui praesentes fuerunt adiudicare duellum nec aliud, in absentia ipsius Domini Regis vel maioris Consilii sui, et ideo datus est dies.' *Coram Rege*, Mich., 25 Hen. III, m. 6 ; Madox, i. 120.

[3] 'In modern terms', says Maitland, 'we might say that the court held before the king in parliament and the court held before the king in council are the court of king's bench raised to a higher power' (Pollock and Maitland, i. 199). It was not a higher power in the sense of a superior power ; much less was it a different power. In its enlarged and conciliar form it was still the same court, however much it gained in collective wisdom, dignity, and moral weight.

activity of this body, whether it was giving counsel, administering justice, or framing laws. Before the end of this reign there will appear a line of divergence, but first we must give a view of the varied and undifferentiated functions which were exercised by the council or *curia*.

Not distinct from the council.

The substantial identity of the court known as *coram rege* and the council is abundantly shown in the plea rolls themselves. Conciliar cases alternate with *coram rege* cases without any material distinction. A *coram rege* case becomes a case before the council without change of venue or break in its continuity. The only change which is noticeable from time to time lies in the augmentation of the court by the attendance of a larger number of members. For example, in 1238–9 an important case was being heard, in which the question arose whether the county palatine of Chester was partible or not. Since the few magnates who were present in the *curia* did not dare to give judgement, 'for the reinforcement of the court' a postponement was made. The case was afterwards continued and the decision rendered *coram Domino Rege . . . et pluribus magnatibus Anglie tunc praesentibus.*[1] More often without any such explanation, after the preliminary stages of the case had been passed, the final judgement is rendered with the words, *postea consideratum est per consilium.*[2]

Cases in first instance.

In the first place, there were of necessity a number of cases that were heard before the court in first instance. The number was never large compared with those coming before the bench, but there was a constant stream of 'great causes' affecting great men and the political interests of the day. In the instructions to the itinerant justices of 1218–19, as previously quoted, the amercements of earls and barons were expressly reserved for the consideration of the king's council. To give a few examples of these conspicuous cases,

[1] *Bracton's Note Book,* no. 1273; *Abb. Plac.*, 107, &c.

[2] In a case, 51 Hen. III, a defendant pleaded that he ought not to be heard *coram rege*, since the matter was a common plea. On the other hand it was claimed to touch the king's person. The record says, *postea recitata fuit ista loquela coram domino Rege et Consilio suo, ipso domino Rege sedente pro tribunali apud Westmonasterium*; and judgement was given against the defence. *Coram Rege*, 51 Hen. III, m. 13 a.

there was that of Falkes de Breauté in 1217, who appealed to the justiciar to be heard by the council in his contest with the men of the Earl Marshal.[1] In 1218 a contention between Engelard de Cigony and the earl Warenne over the custody of the county of Surrey was made a plea before the legate, the archbishop, and other magnates.[2] In 1221 a contest over the stewardship of the royal household was settled before the king and council by a convention between the earl of Chester and Hugh Bigod.[3] At this time of feudal reaction there were cases for the attention of the council in the adulterine castles. The council proceeded judicially in deciding whether castles were lawful or adulterine, and sought to compel the destruction of unlawful ones. Thus in 1220 an order from the justiciar and council to the sheriff of Northumberland asked him to make inquiry with twelve men concerning the castle of Richard of Umfraville which he had strengthened since the war. If he should not stop fortifying the castle, the sheriff was to find out how much he had strengthened it since the war.[4] In dealing with such cases the council did not always itself hold the trial, but remanded the parties to other courts, exacting from them bail and surety for their appearance. It was sometimes expedient not to hold a trial, but to seek a settlement by means of conciliation. The council was equally adapted for either method, whether it were political or judicial. The extraordinarily large number of pardons granted by the discretion of the council give evidence of this spirit. In 1222 permission was given to hold the sentence against the earl of March in suspense.[5] Many titles to lands and castles in England and Ireland were in confusion, owing to confiscations and conflicting grants. A number of claims which had been held over from John's reign were settled by the council, not always by judicial decision, but also by direct orders of restitution. Prior to the formulation of the rules of common law there was nothing extraordinary

[1] *Royal Letters of the Reign of Henry III*, i. 5.

[2] *Cal. Patent Rolls*, 135, 181. Incidentally, in this case it was decided that commissions issued under John were still valid.

[3] *Rot. Lit. Claus.*, i. 455.

[4] Ibid. 436.

[5] *Foedera* (Rec. Ed.), i. 168.

in the great freedom of procedure which was assumed in the king's court. Thus far, it is only in certain branches of the court, as previously described, that these rules were of binding force. As regards the rights of earls and barons, there were several cases of this time which served to strengthen the claim, already broadly recognized in Magna Carta, that they should be tried only by their peers. Besides the examples already cited there was the conspicuous trial of Hubert de Burgh in 1234,[1] and also that of Stephen Segrave, who was not a baron but an officer and councillor.[2] The claim was even tentatively extended to civil suits.[3] It is to be noted, however, that in none of these cases was there any need to form a special tribunal or to alter the organization of the *curia* as it was commonly known. Bracton restates the rule that earls and barons are to be amerced only by their peers, but this, he explains, does not require a separate court, since the peers of the accused are only to be associated with the regular justices.[4]

Cases for consultation and correction.

More frequently the council (or court *coram rege*) acted as a court of consultation and correction. The instructions to the itinerant justices and the justices of the bench, as previously cited, required them to refer questions of law to the council. This the justices were by no means reluctant to do, for a professional trait which they display from the beginning is a marked dislike of assuming responsibility of this kind. In a Worcestershire eyre, in 1221, the jurors declared that the assize of cloth was not observed as it should be. Amercements were respited until what was to be done should be provided by the king's council.[5] It behoved the justices to move cautiously, for they were liable themselves to be put on trial for any faulty decision. A county court which had adjudged the *lex defensionis* as a means of settlement was uncertain whether the defendant could offer a substitute or not. The court was all the more in doubt

[1] *Bracton's Note Book*, no. 1108. [2] *Royal Letters*, i. 444.

[3] This was done by the earl of Chester in 1236–7. *Bracton's Note Book*, no. 1213.

[4] *De Legibus*, ii. 242, 266; also L. W. V. Harcourt, 'Amercement of Barons,' *Eng. Hist. Review*, xxii. 732–40.

[5] Maitland, *Pleas of the Crown*, no. 148.

because the defendant was a great man and a baron of the king. The case was postponed until another meeting of the county, so as to obtain in the meantime the opinion of the king's council.[1] Under the system which was now growing up it was possible also for litigants to appeal to the council against the decision of a court, which might have exceeded its authority or have made a faulty construction of the law. A jurisdiction over the errors of inferior courts, therefore, was an immediate corollary to the system of specialized courts. An early instance of this kind is found in 1223, when the record of a case in the king's court in Ireland was reviewed by a council of magnates and judges. In this plea the defendant had been called to warrant for a piece of land which he held by a charter of the king, and because he did not come he was considered to have lost by default. He claimed that under the charter of John he should have had peace until the king was of age. The council considered that the court was in error in two respects. In the first place, according to the charter, the defendant should have been left until the king's minority was passed. In the second place, it was not in the power of the plaintiff, or even of the court, in a proceeding of this kind, to call one to warrant, and to declare a default if one failed to appear. This would amount to calling the king himself to warrant; 'our court is not above ourselves,' declared the council.[2] The right to review and correct the errors of all inferior courts was freely exercised by the council from this time forth. So far were the proceedings regularized, that in 1256 we find mention made of a writ of error.[3]

Appeals on error.

Often an appeal took the form of a complaint by an aggrieved party against the judges who had wronged him by a decision. In one such case certain justices in eyre were summoned before the king's council and justices of the bench, by whom they were convicted of hanging a man unlawfully. In another case several justices of the bench, answering

[1] *Royal Letters*, i. 103.

[2] *Rot. Lit. Claus.*, i. 549.

[3] *Cal. Doc. Ireland*, ii, nos. 427, 497; *Abb. Plac.*, 138, &c. A question for the future inevitably is whether these cases according to the precedents belonged to the council or the king's bench.

for their mistakes in law, pleaded that they knew no better.[1] At another time a justice was acquitted of the charges made against him and commended for his conduct.[2] It was a well-understood rule with the justices that in matters touching the rights of the crown they should not proceed without consulting the king or his council. On this ground defendants frequently set up claims that their own rights in some way affected the royal prerogative, and therefore they should not be required to answer in the usual way. The council was always zealous in defending the rights of the crown, but at the same time it made short work of many flimsy claims of this kind by ordering that the actions proceed.

A complicated case.

In 1223 a case occurred in Ireland involving complications which were resolved by the council in the following manner. In an assize of *mort d'ancestor* a question of legitimacy was raised, and this point was referred for settlement to an ecclesiastical court. Here long altercations and delays took place, during which appeal was made to the pope. A new issue arose when two girls under age appeared, and made appeal that the assize should not proceed lest they should be prejudiced and precluded from afterwards seeking their inheritance. The king's letter simplified matters by pointing out the following facts: that in the original assize no mention was made of the girls; there were only two parties to the assize; 'you are not called upon to pronounce upon them' (the girls); an assize is a question of possession, not of property. By the council of magnates then the justiciar of Ireland was directed to delay no longer, and to cause the assize to proceed.[3] In most of these instances, it may be noticed that only the point in question was determined by the council, and then the hearing was resumed in the same court as before.

Consultations or discussions.

The practice of holding consultations in the council or court thus constituted is frequently indicated in phrases like the following: *discussum est per eos mediante consilio nostro; tractatu habito intra magnates et iurisperitos,*

[1] *Bracton's Note Book*, no. 67; also nos. 73, 1166.
[2] *Cal. Doc. Scotland*, i. 275.
[3] *Rot. Lit. Claus.*, i. 629.

and the like.[1] But the expressions which occur with most repetition, receiving the recognition both of Glanvil and Bracton, are, *de consilio curie, de consilio et beneficio curie, per consilium magnatum de curia.*[2] As Maitland has explained, such phrases always point to an exercise of that original power of the court to depart from the strict rules of law and to do whatever a sense of justice demands. 'Our king's court is, according to very ancient tradition, a court that can do whatever equity may require.'[3] In a case of horse-stealing, for example, on one occasion it was judged that the thief must lose his foot, with the warning that 'by action of the council he is dealt with mercifully, since by law he deserved a worse penalty'.[4] This is to say, that while every other court was being moulded in accordance with the forms of the common law, the council was not bound by these rules, but could create its own rules as cases arose.

Instructions to the justices.

Another mode in which the general powers of the council were exercised is found in the directions or mandates which were given to the justices in their work. In 1219 an act of some importance appears in certain letters patent which were given to the various itinerant justices in words to the following effect:

> Inasmuch as it is uncertain and undetermined at the outset of your itinerary what judgement should be imposed on those detained for robbery, murder, arson, and similar crimes, since it has been prohibited by the Roman Church to use judgement by fire and water; it is provided by the council for the present that those detained for greater offences should be held in prison; those detained for moderate crimes should abjure the realm; and those detained for minor offences should find sure pledges.[5]

Beyond the definite instructions given by the council, the judges were to use their discretion. Another provision of the council, made in 1220, was that no subject of the king of France might plead in an English court until Englishmen

[1] *Bracton's Note Book*, no. 1110; *Rot. Lit. Claus.*, i. 549; *Cal. Patent Rolls*, 11 Hen. III, 90.

[2] *Bracton's Note Book*, no. 1106; Glanvil, lib. iii, c. 2; lib. xiii, c. 2.

[3] Pollock and Maitland, i. 189.

[4] Maitland, *Pleas of the Crown*, no. 192.

[5] *Cal. Patent Rolls*, 186.

were permitted to plead in the French courts.[1] More often the mandates of the council dealt with individual cases. It decided in which of the courts pleas belonged, where itinerant sessions should be held, and ordered the necessary writs. In 1219 a letter to the itinerant justices of Sussex and Kent required that pleas of the crown in the Cinque Ports and elsewhere should be held in suspense, until it might be provided by the king's council where and before whom those pleas should be held.[2] In 1228 a letter of the king to Pateshull and Segrave said that it was a long time since pleas of the crown had been held in Shipway, wherefore the place had become a refuge for law-breakers. It seemed best then to the king and council that pleas should be held there without delay. In this matter the king asked especially for the advice of the above-named justices before he would decide.[3]

Acts of legislation.

Orders of the council easily broaden into veritable acts of legislation, although there was no recognition of this as a distinct function. What we may call examples of legislation were hardly more than the instructions which were framed for the guidance of judges, sheriffs, and other officers. Of the many ordinances of this nature that were certainly framed by the council no separate record was kept. In 1234 upon the *coram rege* roll in the midst of the usual array of law cases, there appears a series of enactments of a legislative character. Among these is found the well-known answer of the barons concerning the proposed change in the law of bastardy, *quod nolunt leges Anglie mutare que usitate sunt et approbate*.[4] In 1237 a new writ of cosinage, framed by William Raleigh, was sanctioned by the magnates in council.[5] In 1238 certain orders of the council on the management of the royal forest were likewise of legislative character.[6] To what extent this power might be carried was afterwards shown by the Provisions of Oxford, which undertook to effect a general reform in the government.

[1] *Bracton's Note Book*, nos. 110, 1396.
[2] *Rot. Lit. Claus.*, i. 406.
[3] *Cal. Close Rolls*, 108; *Royal Letters*, i. 328; also *Abb. Plac.*, 142.
[4] *Bracton's Note Book*, no. 1117.
[5] Ibid. 1215.
[6] *Cal. Patent Rolls*, 216.

It is commonly said that the existence of a legislative power in the state was hardly realized during the middle ages. As all of these cases show, there was no assertion of a distinction between a legislative act and a judicial act. But this is only to say that there was a failure to discriminate between general rules and individual cases. We must concede, how ever, that there was at this time a fairly clear perception of the fact that the law was undergoing a change, and might be changed still further, especially when it was claimed that this should not be done without the counsel of the magnates.[1] What is legislation in its essence but an intentional change of the law ?

The courts according to Bracton.

As to the precise status of the courts in the middle of the thirteenth century there is a very illuminating description given by Bracton. In regard to the question of the council and the court *coram rege*, the passage is equally suggestive both for what it says and for what it fails to say. Of the council as a distinct court Bracton makes no mention. As a legist he prefers the older term *curia*, where other writers would more likely say *consilium*. To him it seemed that there were but two central courts of permanent standing: the first he describes as a group of justices residing by the side of the king, *item iustitiariorum quidam sunt capitales, generales, perpetui et maiores a latere regis residentes*.[2] The likelihood of the justices being aided by the added presence of the magnates is not mentioned in this connexion, although there is reference to the practice elsewhere. The authority of these justices is stated to be of a general and superior kind, which was not for the purpose of hearing cases in first instance or of receiving pleas of any particular sort, but it is said they were 'bound to correct the injuries and errors of all the others'. The second group of justices is defined more specifically as *alii perpetui, certo loco residentes, sicut in banco*. Their authority is indicated as of more limited scope than that of the former, since it is said they are to

[1] Thus Bishop Grosseteste writes to Justice Raleigh: 'nec tam idiota sum quod credam ad alicuius suggestionem te vel alium sine principis et magnatum consilio posse leges *condere* vel *commutare*' (*Epistolae*, p. 96).

[2] *De Legibus*, ii. 180 ff.

determine those arguments respecting which they have a *warrant*, and they are to commence their jurisdiction by taking an oath. The itinerant justices are described with some emphasis as holding still narrower and more limited powers according to their commissions: 'They cannot extend their jurisdiction, nor take cognizance of other things than of those which are contained in their commissions, since the limits of their mandate are to be diligently attended to.'

Separation of the king's bench from the council.

But it is not long after Bracton's day that a line of cleavage begins to appear, which in the end serves to set off the king's bench as a court distinct from the council. This is found in the tendency of the court to hear cases in accordance with the formulaic procedure already observed in connexion with the common bench. Early in the thirteenth century, certainly in the reign of John, the *curia regis* in its *coram rege* capacity began to try cases under these forms. It heard possessory actions, it made use of the jury of inquest, and decided upon the validity of writs. Probably most of these cases, some of them certainly, had been begun in some other court, and were in this wise only transferred and continued *coram rege*. At all events the court was by no means bound to follow these forms, and for the most part it continued the comparatively free and unrestricted procedure of the old *curia regis*. That is to say, in practice it was not bound like other courts to proceed upon a writ from the chancery; it was not required to follow one or another of the formulaic 'actions'; it received the parties who came without writs to make their complaints, appeals, or demands; it permitted the parties freely to plead, first one side and then the other; if proof were necessary this could be secured either by the old or by the new legal methods; and judgements could be given in the spirit of equity. A technicality also might be waived aside, as was done on one occasion when certain writs of assize, whereby jurors had been elected and the survey of land made, were lost, causing the business of the trial to stop. The council directed the justices, if they found the jurors actually were elected and the survey made, to proceed without the writs.[1]

[1] *Cal. Patent Rolls*, 3 Hen. III, 210.

But the tendency to permit actions by writ of the chancery to be heard *coram rege* clearly appears after the barons' war, when there were strong reasons for employing the power of this court to restore the tranquillity of the country. Naturally this is not the only time that new legal departures can be traced to the stress of a revolutionary period. There was then the problem of a number of cases of violent entry and forcible dispossession of property, which by the newly devised writ of trespass were freely brought to be heard in the court before the king.[1] This is the first time also that criminal cases were systematically received here. Simultaneously there appears in the same court a special possessory action, which, according to an ordinance of the king and the magnates, was to give seizin of their lands to all those who had adhered loyally to the king during the war. The tendency to employ the court for actions of this kind was carried further in the reign of Edward I, until Britton (*c.* 1291) practically defines the king's bench as a court of common law.[2] Concerning justices assigned to this court, he declares 'that they have cognizance of amending false judgements, and of determining appeals and other pleas of trespass committed against our peace, and that their jurisdiction extend so far as we shall authorize by our writs'. In another passage, concerning the power to amend false judgements, the same legal writer assigns this jurisdiction to 'the Justices who follow us in our Court (i.e. *coram rege*) who are authorized by us for the purpose, *or* ourselves, with our Council'.[3] Thus in thirty years from the time of Bracton a very positive advance has been made, since a lawyer is now able to distinguish between the council and the king's bench.

The civil war a turning-point.

But even at this time the separation of the king's bench from the council was only at a certain stage of advancement. The common law procedure was thus far adopted in the court,

The king's bench not entirely separated.

[1] One of the first entries of this kind reads as follows: 'Nicholaus de Haversham optulit se versus Reginaldum de Molendino et multos alios de placito quare vi et armis occasione turbacionis nuper habite in regno bona et catalla sua in manerio suo de Haversham ad valenciam centum marcarum ceperunt et asportaverunt.' *Abb. Plac.*, 160 ff.

[2] (Ed. Nichols, Oxford, 1865) vol. i, chap. i, § 4.

[3] Ibid. § 11.

so far as we may feel sure, only for certain actions, especially criminal,[1] while other cases were treated very much in the same manner as before. Throughout the reign of Edward I and beyond, the older usages continued, and to this extent the two courts did not cease to coincide. There was still upon the rolls a mingling of conciliar cases and cases *coram rege* without any apparent distinction as to character or procedure. A case *coram rege* at one stage or another of the proceedings might be considered before the council or the parliament without any breach of continuity. At any moment by the attendance of magnates and ' others of the council ' the court might be brought again to its most expanded form. The recurrence of pleas *coram rege et consilio suo* in this manner can hardly be said to be discontinued until the reign of Edward III.[2] But long before this time the usual proceedings of the king's bench were manifestly of common law character in that they were begun on original writ and were treated according to the rules of action.

Distinctive character of the council.

In distinction from the branch of the *curia regis*, which became the king's bench, the council was not swept into the current of the common law. True to the traditions of the older court *coram rege* and the original *curia*, it remained a body of indefinite powers and of unrestricted procedure. It is this fact which explains the vitality of that ' fertile parent stem ' which, having put forth such mighty branches as the common law courts, was not drained of judicial power or exhausted in its ability to create. While the common law courts in this way were being assigned to their respective spheres, there were certain very necessary functions left

[1] So far as the records have been printed, the actions of trespass were the most frequent. At the same time there were actions for conspiracy (*pro brevi de conspiracione*), for damages (*ad dampnum*), for assault, insult, and debt (*per breve de debito*). Juries were commonly employed, and a frequent source of difficulty was the default of jurors (*pro defectu iuratorum quia nullus venit*), especially when they were required to come from the counties to London. See Phillimore, *Placita Coram Rege*, 1297 (British Rec. Soc., 1898).

[2] The attendance of magnates in the capacity of ' auditors ', taking little active part but giving the proceedings an added dignity, was a custom that continued indefinitely.

to the council. Some of these have already been pointed out. There was the duty of giving counsel, not in the political sense only, but in advising and directing the actions of all the lower courts. This power also took positive legislative form. Already there were ordinances upon the *coram rege* roll; some too can be found upon the close rolls and elsewhere without definite arrangement. Most of these enactments do not appear in their original form, so that there was real danger that important ordinances might be lost in the confusion.[1] In the reign of Edward I a new roll appears, which had the purpose of such enrolments particularly in view. It was the recognized right of the council also to assent to new forms of procedure, especially in the creation of new writs. But as legislative processes still were slow to meet new legal demands, probably on the whole the most important function reserved to the council was that of providing special remedies for special cases. In earlier times a person with a grievance might come directly to the *curia* and make complaint, as the records commonly say, *A. venit et queritur.* The court was not then so restricted in its powers as to be prevented from hearing and treating any case upon its merits. There were dangers, of course, of a judicial tyranny in any such untrammelled legal system. But with the development of the well-known features of the common law, the justices were permitted to receive cases only as they had general warrants or were given specific writs. In the face of the fact that suitors could not always find in the chancery an appropriate writ, while at the same time the creation of new writs was being checked by a jealous baronage, the right of petition to the king and council became of utmost importance. It was, in fact, one of the prescribed duties of the king's councillors 'to hear the complaints of individuals and quickly to provide remedy for those suffering injury'.[2] In other words, the remedy which was not provided according to any general rule might yet

[1] One is presented by G. J. Turner as 'a newly discovered ordinance'. *Law Quarterly Review*, xii. 299–301.

[2] This is mentioned in the schedule of 1244 as well as in the oath of 1257. Matthew Paris, *Chronica Maiora*, iv. 367; Burton, 395.

be secured by action in an individual case. Now the use of petitions in legal proceedings is found at a very early time. In the reign of John, for instance, on *petition* of the parties a great assize is postponed without a day.[1] Again *A. venit coram Domino Rege . . . et petit iustitiam sibi fieri.*[2] Bracton uses the word *petitio* apparently as equivalent to 'complaint'.[3] Few written petitions of the time of Henry III are extant,[4] because such complaints were then generally made orally. Because of the prominence that this feature is soon to assume, the few examples that can be cited for the reign of Henry III are worthy of attention. In 1237 there is the record of a petition on behalf of the king of Scotland claiming seizin of the county of Huntingdon, in the following form: (the attorneys) *uenerunt ad Dominum Regem et petierunt a Domino Rege quod ipse redderet Regi Scocie domino suo comitatum Huntingdone cum pertinentiis, &c.*[5] The petition was considered judicially, and answered by the king and council—*quibus ita responsum est a Domino Rege et consilio suo.* In 1268 the sheriff of York in a letter to one of the justices complains that the ferm of his county had been reduced, and asks, *quare si placet Domino Regi et eius consilio predicta constare velitis.*[6] Probably no settled form in this procedure was yet attained, but there can be no doubt that the method of petition to the king and council was well established before the close of the reign of Henry III. Under Edward I this function of the council, particularly of 'the council in parliament', is recognized by Fleta (*c.* 1290), who describes it as the court 'where judicial doubts are determined and new remedies for new wrongs, and justice is done to every one according to his deserts'.[7] One may observe the emphasis which is placed upon the remedies which are provided not by general rule but for individual instances.

[1] Baildon, *Civil Pleas*, no. 151.

[2] *Bracton's Note Book*, no. 1106.

[3] 'In adventu iustitiariorum ad omnia placita . . . pertinent ad eos audire querelas singulorum et petitiones, ut unicuique iustitia fiat.' *De Legibus*, ii. 206.

[4] There is a small petition of Philip de Ulecot addressed to the king in 1220. *Dip. Doc. Chancery*, no. 673.

[5] *Bracton's Note Book*, no. 1221.

[6] *Royal Letters*, ii, 325.

[7] *Commentarius Iuris Anglicani* (London, 1685), lib. ii, cap. 2.

The council is the original court.

Thus out of the two imperfectly outlined tribunals which existed at the beginning of the thirteenth century, three are now recognized to exist. The question has been propounded whether we shall regard the council or the king's bench as the new formation. It is customary to speak of the council as 'rising above the king's bench'. Naturally the council was now upon a higher plane than had been held before. But in the light of what has been given, it seems more nearly the truth to say that the council is the strictly lineal representative of the original court, from which the exchequer, the common pleas, and ultimately the king's bench, have branched off. The court *coram rege*, as it continued to be called, changed character fundamentally, while the council remained *curia regis* in function and prerogative throughout the thirteenth century. During this time, in response to new conditions, its activities were greatly quickened and expanded, but there was no necessity for it to acquire any new functions whatever. Even the petitionary system was not new, but a latent and undeveloped feature of the twelfth century *curia*. Much less were its legislative activities under Edward I a new departure. In time there will arise certain distinctive features of the council's procedure which will call for attention.

No line of distinction between the large and the small council.

In this discussion no distinction has been made between the council in its form as a large assembly and its alternative aspect as a small body. Beyond the fact that the council was an assemblage of constantly varying dimensions, there is no line of legal distinction as yet to be drawn. A general council, it is true, required the special formality of summons, but this did not in anywise prescribe the scope of its authority or its methods of work. There were many occasions, too, when a large assembly was deemed to be necessary, and business was deferred for the sake of holding a general consultation. The presence at these times not only of large numbers, but of important individuals, was particularly emphasized. But so long as there was no settled usage or understanding as to what was appropriate for one body or the other, we cannot speak of two institutions. In any case, it was the king's council with the same rights, powers, and functions. As has been said, the small *curia* 'was not a committee of the larger, it was not responsible to the larger; it was the larger'. And yet the two lines of development, one in the direction of the greater assembly known as parliament, the other towards a narrower and more permanent body, were every day more apparent. With the sanction of official usage the former was known as the *magnum consilium*, the *commune consilium*, the *parliamentum*, and the *consilium in parliamento*, while the chroniclers extend these terms with such expressions as *magnum parliamentum generale* and *generalissimum parliamentum*. On the other hand, except for the informal references of chroniclers to the 'secret' or the 'familiar' council, there is no such positive recognition of the smaller body. In all the official language of the day it was known simply as the *consilium regis*, without further qualifying adjective. A difference certainly was perceived, but why should the fact be so persistently obscured? A reason is found in the conceptions which still prevailed concerning the constitutional position of the council. It was still in theory the court of all the king's vassals. That it was frequently, even most of the time, of necessity reduced to the attendance of a few officials and appointed members, did not immediately alter this fundamental thought. The idea of a small or secret council lacked dignity and moral value, so that a legislative or a judicial act would never be put forward by such a sanction as *per secretum consilium*. In the obscurity that attends the formation of the small council, the important fact to be noted is that it was not as yet set off from the great council either by the kind of business that was undertaken or by the manner of its performance. The situation caused no special difficulty until parliament afterwards assumed a form that was distinguished from the council, and consequently questions arose as to their respective spheres of authority. At the present stage, however, the precedents belong alike to either.

CHAPTER IV

THE COUNCIL FROM EDWARD I TO EDWARD III

The statesmanship of Edward I is considered to have consisted largely in bringing to definite form many of the features of the law and the constitution which were hitherto in an incomplete or formative stage. Out of the experiments of the former reign came then the further organization of the law courts, the parliament, and also, to a degree, of the permanent council. This was recognized by Stubbs, who says of Edward I, that 'he seems to have accepted the institution of a council as part of the general system of government, and whatever had been the stages of its growth, to have given it definiteness and consistency'.[1] The only mistake in this statement is the implication that the council was a new feature of the government, which the king was in a position to accept or refuse. At all events, so far as it was given definiteness and consistency, there is now the practicable task to consider what the council was, with regard to its form, composition, and character.

The council a settled institution,

The problem is by no means a simple one, for contemporaries have given us no adequate description of it, its membership in ordinary times was never openly stated, and its proceedings were not generally a matter of record. Strange to say, we are never given such explicit information concerning the king's council in England as is afforded on one occasion of the council in Gascony, when, in 1310, certain royal commissioners went forth and caused all of the councillors there to be sworn.[2] The councils which were appointed under stress of revolution, as had been done according to the 'Provisions of Oxford' in 1258, and as was attempted again

but difficult to define

[1] *Constitutional History*, vol. ii, § 230.

[2] 'Eodem die (November 12, 1310) ibidem fecerunt subscriptum iuramentum in presentia dictorum dominorum (the king's commissioners, namely, the bishop of Norwich, the earl of Richmond, Guy Ferre, William Inge, and Amanieu d'Albret), hii qui de consilio Vasconie sunt.' *Dip. Doc. Chancery*, no. 228.

under Edward II, are of exceptional character, and do not reflect normal conditions. A certain amount of information in this regard one might expect to gain from the writs of summons to parliaments. In the great collection known as 'Parliamentary Writs', after the lists of prelates and barons who were summoned to parliament, there are found certain groups of judges and other officers who are called to consult together 'with others of the council'. But even these lists, it will be shown, cannot be relied upon to show fully or precisely those who were attached in any permanent way to the king's council. In spite of the lack of any direct account, however, there is a great deal of evidence which can be gathered from various incidental and indirect sources. Especially are we informed in many instances of the men who belonged to the council, of the manner of their appointments, and of their duties as councillors. In this study it will be necessary to have in view a considerable period of time, that of the reigns of the three Edwards, because the data afforded for any single reign alone are not sufficient. Moreover, in this stage of its history the council did not change character rapidly, so that the period will be found for the present purpose to be a fairly homogeneous one.

A writer of the period, who is responsible for the unauthentic work known as the *Modus tenendi Parliamentum*, describes the king's council as consisting of 'the chancellor of England, the treasurer, the chamberlain, the barons of the exchequer, the justices, all the king's clerks and knights, together with the serjeants-at-law'.[1] Sir Francis Palgrave has further elaborated this definition, saying that 'the council was composed of the chancellor, the treasurer, the justices of either bench, the escheators, the serjeants, some of the principal clerks of the chancery, and such others, usually, but not exclusively, bishops, earls, and barons, as

[1] *Modus tenendi Parliamentum* (Record Com.), p. 27. The date of this anomalous work has been a matter of conjecture. By some writers it has been ascribed to the beginning of the fourteenth century, by others to the very close of the same period. Without making any study of the treatise as a whole, I wish merely to point out that the aforesaid passage bears the stamp of the earlier part of the century, as suggested by Hardy and Stubbs, rather than of the later time. No one would be likely to refer to the council in this manner during the reign of Richard II.

the king thought fit to name.' [1] Likewise Maitland speaks of it as consisting particularly 'of men who in one capacity or another are doing the king's work, and receiving the king's pay'. [2] Now these statements are each of them true and satisfactory, so far as they go. But is it meant that *all* of the men in the king's employ were regularly sworn of the council? or that they belonged to the council only in a more general and indefinite way? Did the king's clerks and knights belong to the council in the same manner as bishops, earls, and barons, or were there differences in this relation which were felt and understood? Undoubtedly there still survived the use of the word *consilium* in a loose and indefinite sense, meaning any body of men or assemblage in the king's interest, but there was also the idea which was gaining ground of a council in a more limited sense. [3] Already in the reign of Edward II the terms *secretum* and *privatum consilium* begin to appear in the official records. In the face of these uncertainties, and at times ambiguities, there are many explanations and modifications which must be made in all of the foregoing definitions. Moreover, what was true at one time and under one set of circumstances was not true at another. Within the period in view there were certain important changes and transformations which must be accounted for.

The oath a distinctive feature.

As has previously been suggested, the oath was the earliest and most distinctive feature of the council's organization. Such an oath was already, under Henry III, being formulated and at least tentatively applied. It is not to be understood that the oath as yet fully defined the council, in the sense that every one who served therein was necessarily sworn; this was far from being the case. But it is true that the oath was the means of suggesting a permanent membership and of making clear the duties of a councillor. The swearing of councillors became a regular practice from the beginning of the reign of Edward I. In the very first year

[1] *Original Authority*, p. 20.

[2] Maitland, *Memoranda de Parliamento* (Rolls Series), p. xlvii.

[3] This is clearly expressed in the following passage of Fleta: 'Quod nullus cancellarius, thesaurarius, iusticiarius, vel alius de consilio regis, vel de cancellaria, de hospitio, scaccario, nec aliquis minister, clericus regis, vel alius laicus recipiat praesentationes,' &c. (i.e. gifts in the nature of bribes). *Commentarius*, lib. ii, c. 36.

this fact may be discerned in a list of witnesses to a process in the exchequer, who are named in the following manner :

> . . . Hiis testibus, venerabilibus patribus W. Eboracensi Archiepiscopo Anglie primato, G. Wigorniensi et R. Cestrensi episcopis, dominis Rogero de Mortuo Mari, Ricardo de Middelton cancellario Domini Regis, Roberto Burnel cancellario domini Edwardi predicti domini Regis primogeniti, cum *juratis de consilio* ipsius domini Regis, magistro Rogero de Peyton tunc Justitiario de Banco, magistro Ricardo de Clifford tunc Eschaetore domini Regis, magistro Williamo de Clifford, Johanne de Kirkeby clericis ipsius domini Regis, dominis Hamone Hauteyn, Rogero de Shirland, Nicholo le Peyson, Galfrido de Brodeleyr et aliis.[1]

In this passage it may be seen very clearly that it was not the bishops and barons who are mentioned as sworn of the council, but the minor officials at the end of the list.

Members 'ordained' and 'retained'.

The form of this oath and the obligations which it imposed, so far as they are of a technical nature, it will be convenient to reserve for a subsequent chapter. For the present it will be sufficient to ask and, if possible, to answer the more fundamental question, what was the council in its general form and composition ? In the reign of Edward II and afterwards, with a similar meaning, men were said to be ' ordained ' or ' retained ' of the king's council. In some cases they were given fees or wages for their services, and these were announced in letters patent. For the purposes in view, the surest ground will be to make a study of the men who are known to have been sworn or retained in the council, taking them conveniently first by classes and then as individuals, noting particularly the formalities of their appointments, the reasons for appointing them, and also their services as councillors. After this has been done, it will be possible to make some observations of the council in other aspects.

Distinctly official character of the council.

In the first place, it is evident that the council of Edward I, in its growth apart from the parliament, proceeded from the general usages of Henry III, and not from the suggestions that had been made by the barons in 1258. There was indeed no change of principle, but the natural development

[1] *Exchequer Plea Roll*, 1 Edw. I, m. 6.

of a more orderly plan of government. Considered as a permanent body, the nucleus of the council then consisted not of a particular group of nobles, who were rarely to be relied upon for any regular service of the kind, but upon a body of officers employed in the king's court and household. Chief among these without doubt were the chancellor and the treasurer, who were recognized as bearing a kind of *ex officio* relation to the council. 'The chancellor, the treasurer, and others of the council,' was the phrase by which this body was most frequently designated. The order of precedence, however, was quite as often in favour of the treasurer, and not until a later time did the chancellor become the acknowledged head of the council. To one or both of these officers it was customary for the king to send letters of the privy seal with the command to summon others of the council, to decide the matter in question, and to do what should be done. This procedure, to which there will be reason to refer again, may be illustrated by the following writ of the time of Edward II:

'Edward, &c. A noz chers et foialx l'onorable piere en Dieu l'evesque d'Excestre, nostre Tresorier, et Mestre Robert de Baldoke nostre Chauncellier, Saluz. Nous vous enveoms ci dedeinz enclose une bille que nous feust baille par nostre chere cousine la countesse de Pembroke ; et vous maundons que, regardee la dite bille, et eu sur ce pener et bon avisement od ceux de nostre conseil, nous conseillez et avisez selonc ce que vous verrez que mielz fait a faire a nostre profite.' [1]

Officers of the household.

No other ministers of the time certainly were given similar prominence. But there were several officers of the royal household, particularly the chamberlain, the steward of the household, the keeper of the wardrobe, and possibly the controller of the wardrobe, who were brought into the same political circle. The keeper of the wardrobe, says Fleta, was sworn of the council, and for this reason he was exempted from taking any other oath when he rendered his accounts.[2]

[1] H. Hall, *Formula Book of Official Documents* (Cambridge, 1908), p. 100.

[2] 'Officium autem thesaurarii garderobe (i.e. the keeper) est pecuniam, iocalia, et exenia Regi facta recipere, receptaque Regis secreta custodire, et de receptis expensas facere rationabiles, expensarumque particulas

It was not the invariable rule, however, especially when great men were concerned, that all members of the council should be sworn. More closely than the chancellor or the treasurer were these officers of the household in personal contact with the king, and so they were in a position to act as his confidential advisers.[1] Many of the grants of the crown, in fact, are stated to have been made 'upon information of John Drokensford', 'of John Benstead', or some other one of these intimate councillors. As the departments of the government increased, the king's secretary emerges as a distinct functionary, and likewise the keeper of the privy seal. In accordance with the importance of the latter office, by the time of Edward III the keeper of the privy seal is regularly given a rank in the council next to the chancellor and the treasurer,[2] and for certain purposes was permitted to act as its presiding officer. There was an inclination then to include also the escheators and the admirals, and so the list might have been extended indefinitely. Counting the justices, the barons of the exchequer, and the clerks of the chancery, there were as many as thirty or thirty-five professional men, who, in accordance with the writ just quoted, might be called upon at any moment to form the requisite council. Much of the time they were practically the only councillors in attendance, while many of the acts of the government, including grants of the crown, judicial decrees, and sometimes even the statutes, were passed by their exclusive sanction. Had the plans of Edward I been carried out to their logical conclusion, there is reason to believe that the council, in all its usual functions,

inbreviare, et de particulis compotum reddere ad scaccarium singulis annis in festo Sanctae Margaretae absque sacramento praestando, *eo quod de concilio Regis est iuratus*, et unde post debent distincte et aperte compotum reddere de omnibus receptis separatim per se in uno rotulo.' *Commentarius*, lib. ii, c. 14.

[1] In the parliament of 1305 Maitland indicates an inner circle of 'discreet men' who had not been formally summoned, because they were too 'discreet' or intimately associated with the king to require any writ. These were John of Drokensford keeper of the wardrobe, John of Benstead controller of the wardrobe, and John of Berwick clerk, possibly holding the privy seal (*Mem. de Parl.*, xliii). For several of the facts which I have given concerning the wardrobe I am indebted to Professor T. F. Tout.

[2] This occurs in the fourteenth year of Edward III. *Statutes of the Realm*, i. 283.

would have become entirely, or at least mainly, a professional body, while the parliament would have remained an organ of the three estates, wherein the lords naturally dominated. But the barons powerfully resisted the tendency of the court to supersede them in the exercise of their historic rights. In their great rebellion under Edward II, it was their particular aim not only to dictate the appointment of the king's ministers, but to reduce the number of officers retained in the council. In respect of the second point they were more successful than in regard to the first. As a result of the pressure which continued to be exerted during the reign of Edward III, the official element within the council was materially lessened. In 1376 only the chancellor, the treasurer, and the keeper of the privy seal were recognized as belonging there. In the first year of Richard II the chamberlain and the steward of the household were also given places, and henceforth the number of ministers was rarely increased beyond the aforesaid five, while more often it was reduced to the first three. Because of the interests involved, there was an almost ceaseless conflict upon this question. But before we speak of the nobles and their actions in this regard, there is more to be said concerning the councillors of minor official rank.

The judges

Next to be mentioned in Palgrave's definition were the justices and other professional men of the *curia regis*. With the justices one should not fail to class also the barons of the exchequer, who held an analogous position in this respect. There is no doubt of the fact in a general way, but the precise position of these men in the council, and likewise in parliament, has been a question of some difficulty. Originally, it is clear, the justices and other officers formed the main body of sworn councillors, while at this time very few of the magnates in fact were retained in this manner. The oath of 1257 was constructed especially for the officers in its statement of judicial and financial duties, and the same thing was obviously true of the oath which was administered under Edward I. Probably most of the justices and other officials, such as are found in the lists of men summoned to parliament, were then sworn of the council. But this cannot be true of all of them.[1] As is shown in the case of Hugh Louther, a justice who had served on the bench since 1303 was not required to take the oath till 1306;[2] while William Inge, another justice who was sworn in the same year, had been summoned to parliaments 'with others of the council' since 1295.[3] It would seem, therefore, that at the time of Edward I some selection was made among the officers in determining the permanent members of the council. Moreover, there was no need of these men taking the councillor's oath, as oaths of their own respective offices were soon separately devised. In the twenty-sixth year of Edward I an oath of the justices is mentioned, which proves to have been in large part a germination from the earlier one.[4] Moreover, the councillor's oath which appears in the reign of Edward III does not contain the articles which pertained especially to the duties of these officers. That the justices were regarded as having a different status from the prelates and barons of the council, even in the reign of Edward I, is suggested by such phrases as *consilium domini regis et iusticiarios* and *coram consilio vocatis thesaurario et baronibus et iusticiariis de utroque banco*.[5] A little later the same idea is emphatically stated in the words, *tam iusticiariis per quos iusticia fit et redditur . . . quam aliis magnis et peritis de consilio nostro iuratis*.[6] From the reign of Edward III, and so nearly as we can state, from his fifteenth year, it is clear that the justices and other officers of similar rank ceased as a class to be sworn of the council, although they were still constantly summoned to attend its proceedings.[7] In the reign of Richard II they are spoken of

[1] Stubbs believes all of the judges and officers of the household were included. *Const. Hist.*, ii. 281.

[2] *Rot. Parl.*, i. 219; and *Parl. Writs*, Index.

[3] Ibid.

[4] A justice is declared in that year to have been sworn according to a form provided by the council (*Memoranda Roll*, Exch. K. R., 26 Edw. I). The clause of the justice's oath, as afterwards given, proved to be derived in part from the original councillor's oath (*First Report on the Public Records*, p. 236).

[5] *Rot. Parl.*, i. 39, 67; *Parliamentary Proceedings*, file 1, no. 14.

[6] *Patent Roll*, 20 Edw. III, part ii, m. 22; *Calendar*, p. 135.

[7] A summons of this kind to the chief baron of the exchequer runs *de veniendo ad consilium regis pro avisamento habendo coram dicto consilio super quibusdam secretis negotiis domini regis*. *Issue Roll* (*Pell's*), 46 Edw. III, m. 29.

as advisers or assessors who were called on occasion by the authority of the council. It was furthermore enjoined repeatedly by ordinances of parliament that the council should summon these advisers in all legal questions, and that the justices should not fail to attend and to render their services.[1] In at least one instance it is shown to be a ground for an allegation of error, that a writ was granted by the council when no one of the justices was recorded as present.[2]

Still, it is not sufficient to say that the justices and their fellow officers stood merely in the relation of assessors. In the council their position beside the lords was not lowered so much as in parliament. In certain ways older traditions continued, and the justices were designated and treated as members of the council. Often indeed the justices and law officers were the only persons in attendance. This was true particularly in judicial proceedings, which were clearly understood to be separated from political interests. The inchoate court of chancery consisted of 'the chancellor, the justices of either bench, the serjeants-at-law and other *periti* of the council'.[3] Under these circumstances there is no reason to believe that these members of the court acted in any secondary capacity, but had full power to decide questions of law and to render advice to the crown. On one occasion a case was determined 'because it seems good to those of the council learned in the law'.[4] It is possible, indeed, to think of the council as differently constituted for one purpose from what it was for another. This is shown in the appointment of one Lawrence Drew, a baron of the exchequer under Richard II, who was declared to be 'of the council for law cases, not otherwise'.[5] In the following

[1] In 1377 the commons petitioned that Magna Carta be confirmed, and that if any point be obscure it should be declared 'by those who shall be ordained to be of the continual council, with the advice of all the justices and serjeants and other such men whom they shall see fit to summon'. *Rot. Parl.* iii. 15; also Nicolas, *Proceedings of the Privy Council*, i. 80, 191, &c.

[2] *Year Book*, Mich., 13 Hen. IV, no. 10; cited in L. W. V. Harcourt, *His Grace the Steward* (London, 1907), p. 365.

[3] *Close Rolls, passim*; W. P. Baildon, *Select Cases in Chancery* (Seldon Society), pp. 89, 140, 150.

[4] *Cal. Patent Rolls*, 28 Edw. III, 153.

[5] 'Que Laurence Dru soit de conseil en cas coursable de la ley et non pas autrement.' Nicolas, i. 76.

century the justices themselves maintained this position, declaring that, while they were 'the king's councillors in law', they were not to be considered such 'between party and party', that is, in politics.[1] The same idea also was expressed by Sir John Fortescue, a judge under Henry VI, who said that the justices, the barons of the exchequer, the clerk of the rolls and others 'may be off this counsell when thai be so desyred and ellis not'.

Retired officers

It was customary also to retain in the council a number of justices and other officers who had retired from their regular positions after long terms of service. They were still called to parliaments and councils as a special mark of honour. Thus in 1316 Roger Brabazon, the aged chief justice of the king's bench, was relieved of his office with the permission 'to remain one of the secret council all his life, to be admitted to all the king's courts and councils, to attend parliaments at the king's summons, and to share the king's secrets'.[2] In the ninth year of Edward III William Herle, because of his infirmities and in consideration of his great services as a justice of the common pleas, was allowed to retire from office on condition that he remained one of the king's secret council and attended his parliaments and councils on summons.[3] Again, John Stonore, chief justice of the common pleas, after a long career on the bench, was permitted to retire, and as a mark of special confidence was retained as one of the privy council.[4] In the tenth year of Edward II Walter of Norwich, on his own request, was relieved of the office of treasurer, but the king, wishing to retain him in service, made him chief baron of the exchequer, willing that when able he should be present at the king's council, both secret and others.[5] At other times may be found a baron of the exchequer[6] and a king's clerk,[7] who on retirement from office were similarly retained of the council as a mark of distinction. Of a certain William of Leicester it was said

[1] *Rot. Parl.*, v. 376.
[2] *Cal. Patent Rolls*, 9 Edw. II, 437; *Parl. Writs*, ii. 162.
[3] *Cal. Patent Rolls*, 9 Edw. III, 153.
[4] *Cal. Close Rolls*, 28 Edw. III, 4.
[5] *Cal. Patent Rolls*, 10 Edw. II, 655.
[6] Ibid., 16 Edw. II, 247.
[7] Ibid., 11 Edw. III, 434.

that 'on account of his ripe counsel, whenever he be summoned to parliaments or councils, he is to be one of the council to whom the secrets of the king are opened '.[1]

The clerks. The clerks of the chancery, whom Palgrave next mentions, before the close of the thirteenth century had attained an official rank only one degree lower than the justices and the barons of the exchequer.[2] Together with these should be considered also the clerks of the wardrobe, a closely allied department, wherein at the time of Edward I the privy seal was kept and used. The clerks of higher grade were necessarily men of learning, 'having full knowledge of English law,'[3] while some of them were doctors of canon or civil law. Among them especially were those 'more discreet' and 'more secret' than the others, who were entrusted with confidential correspondence or were employed as messengers or as proctors or agents in dealing with foreign courts. Moreover, there was always one, possibly there were two, in the position of 'king's clerk', who particularly attended the royal person. In the reign of Henry III several clerks of this stamp are recognized as the king's confidants and counsellors,[4] while under Edward I it is clear that a considerable number of them were formally retained as members of the council. In 1295 there were writs of summons to parliament addressed to 'the deans sworn of the council, and other clerks of the council',[5] the expression 'clerks of the council' frequently recurring.[6] As was true of other officials, it is possible that at first all of the clerks, at least

[1] Ibid.

[2] There were two grades of chancery clerks, 'principal' and 'secondary'. Of the former the number was traditionally six, although it was sometimes not more than three or four.

[3] Fleta mentions 'the honest and circumspect clerks sworn to be obedient to the king and having full knowledge of English laws and customs.' *Commentarius*, p. 75.

[4] See article of L. B. Dibben, 'Secretaries in the Thirteenth and Fourteenth Centuries,' *Eng. Hist. Review*, xxv. 430 ff. Matthew Paris speaks of Lawrence of Saint Martin as *domini regis clericus et consiliarius noster* (*Chronica Maiora*, v. 185), and of John Mansel as *clericus et specialis regis consiliarius* (ibid. iv. 213; v. 261, 355).

[5] *Parl. Writs*, i. 29; *Cal. Close Rolls*, 23 Edw. I, 446.

[6] The king is asked to *assigner clercs de son conseil a survoer ses busoignes* (*Parliamentary Proceedings*, file 5, no. 14; also *Diplomatic Documents, Chancery*, no. 266).

those of the higher grade, were considered to be included in the king's council, but it soon appears that there were only a few who were formally retained, and these for special reasons. In 1305 we learn that a clerk, Master Robert Pickering, was especially excused from remaining with the council held at that time.[1] Together with the clerks of the council, it will be convenient to consider certain other servants of the king of similar rank. Under Edward I there were two friars, William of Gainsborough, a Minorite, and Hugh of Manchester, of the Order of Preachers, who were declared to have been sworn of the king's council.[2] In 1294 they were sent on an embassy to France ;[3] in 1295 they were entrusted with messages of the king each to the chapter of his order, the one at Assisi, the other at Argentan.[4] A reason for Edward I's special favour to the Minorite is seen in the fact that the order supported him in Gascony during his controversy with the king of France.[5] In 1300 the same William was sent on an embassy to the pope as one of the king's special envoys and proctors, and again in 1302 he went to expedite negotiations of peace with the king of France.[6] In time of war there was an obvious advantage in employing 'religious' men as envoys. The two friars were among those summoned to a great council in 1297.[7]

The policy of Edward I in this regard was followed to greater lengths by his son. In the face of the opposition of the barons, who were seeking to control the higher offices, the king was driven to place greater confidence in such functionaries as the keeper of the wardrobe and the clerks who were the more obedient tools of royal authority. Again and again were his acts determined 'upon information of Master Thomas Charleton', or 'of Gilbert Roubery, a clerk of the council'.[8] In spite of the antagonism of the barons

[1] *Parl. Writs*, i. 158.

[2] *Cal. Close Rolls*, 23 Edw. I, 440.

[3] *Cal. Patent Rolls*, 22 Edw. I, 85.

[4] *Cal. Close Rolls*, 23 Edw. I, 440.

[5] Ibid., 27 Edw. I, 302.

[6] *Cal. Patent Rolls*, 28 Edw. I, 511, 543 ; *Cal. Close Rolls*, 30 Edw. I, 584, 600.

[7] *Parl. Writs*, i. 55.

[8] The Patent Rolls of Edward II are very specific in indicating the king's advisers ; also *Statutes of the Realm*, i. 216.

to all councillors of this type, as was expressed in their successive revolts, the king's policy was not then effectively checked. In the fifteenth year of Edward II occurs a memorandum that three clerks, Master William Weston, Master John of Shoreditch, and Master Richard Binteworth, were sworn of the king's council in the Tower of London.[1] Weston, a doctor of laws, was in the seventeenth year appointed one of the king's proctors for all cases affecting the king which were pending in the *parlement* of Paris by reason of the duchy of Aquitaine.[2] In the following year he was sent with others upon an embassy to the guardian of the king of Castile, 'whom they were to inform secretly concerning the king's wishes and upon divers other things';[3] at another time he was sent as an envoy to the pope, when he was captured and held a prisoner by the duke of Brabant.[4] On two different occasions he was summoned 'with others of the council' to parliament.[5] John of Shoreditch, likewise a doctor of civil law, was sent several times on the king's service beyond the seas.[6] As a reward for his labour, in the seventeenth year he was appointed to the custody of the rolls and writs of the court of common pleas.[7] He was named with Weston as one of the proctors to make excuses and defence before the king of France, because Edward II did not come to Amiens to do homage for the duchy.[8]

In spite of the objections that were expressed against the practice, clerks continued to be engaged and promoted in the same way under Edward III. To give a few examples, in 1336 Master John Walwayn, a canon of Lichfield, by letters dated December 14, was retained as one of the king's council with an allowance of twenty pounds a year.[9] Upon the very next day he was said to have been sent on an errand to the archbishop of Cologne 'upon certain things near to the

[1] *Cal. Close Rolls*, 15 Edw. II, 503.
[2] *Cal. Patent Rolls*, 17 Edw. II, 390.
[3] *Cal. Close Rolls*, 18 Edw. II, 350.
[4] Ibid., 20 Edw. II, 647.
[5] *Parl. Writs*, vol. ii, part i, pp. 289, 335.
[6] *Cal. Patent Rolls*, 16 Edw. II, 271; 17 Edw. II, 347, 426.
[7] Ibid., 17 Edw. II, 340.
[8] Ibid., 426. In 1336 we learn that he was made second baron of the exchequer. Ibid., 10 Edw. III, 341.
[9] Ibid., 10 Edw. III, 341.

king's heart', and in a patent of December 16 he received his commission for this service.[1] Master Simon Islip was another king's clerk who, in the nineteenth year of the same reign, was engaged as one of the king's council, with a grant of 50 marks a year.[2] He had already in 1342 served on an embassy to treat for a truce with the king of France,[3] and in 1345 was one of the council appointed to assist the king's son Lionel, who was acting as guardian during the king's absence.[4] In 1346 he was one of a commission named to receive with courtesy the envoys coming from Spain and Hungary, and to open and answer the letters which were then brought.[5] Islip was a rising man at court; he was in turn king's secretary,[6] clerk and keeper of the privy seal,[7] and in this capacity was attendant at certain judicial proceedings of the council. A doctor of canon and civil law, he received also various church preferments until in 1349, as the king's candidate, he was elected archbishop of Canterbury.[8] Master Andrew Ufford, a brother of John Ufford, chancellor and archbishop-elect of Canterbury, was a doctor of civil law and a king's clerk, who had already served on several royal commissions,[9] when in 1346 he was retained as one of the king's council with a fee at the rate of 100 marks a year when beyond the seas, and 50 marks a year when in England, besides two robes each year.[10] He was immediately appointed one of the proctors in behalf of the king to treat with Philip of Valois, 'styled king of France.'[11] The accounts of Master Andrew for his fees at the exchequer in accordance with this patent are preserved, and are of interest as the earliest record of a councillor's wages.[12]

[1] *Cal. Patent Rolls*, 347; *Cal. Close Rolls*, 731. Walwayn afterwards was appointed receiver of customs beyond the seas, and also escheator south of the Trent. *Cal. Patent Rolls*, 11 Edw. III, 542.

[2] *Cal. Patent Rolls*, 19 Edw. III, 536.

[3] *Foedera* (Rec. Ed.), vol. ii, part ii, 1185.

[4] Ibid., iii. 50.

[5] Ibid., 85; *Cal. Patent Rolls*, 20 Edw. III, 138.

[6] *Cal. Patent Rolls*, 22 Edw. III, 131.

[7] *Cal. Close Rolls*, 23 Edw. III, 99.

[8] *Dictionary of National Biography.*

[9] In 1343 he was one of a commission sent to Avignon, whence he returned to explain the negotiations before the council. Murimuth, p. 147; also *Foedera* (Rec. Ed.), iii. 19, 50, 58.

[10] *Cal. Patent Rolls*, 20 Edw. III, 91.

[11] Ibid. 478.

[12] These accounts state his days of service and wages as councillor from

The services of these professional men in the judicial and administrative work of the council will be brought into a clearer light when these functions shall be separately considered. The need of their assistance in all tasks of a technical character was never denied by the barons. The point of friction came from their being raised to the position of councillors with all the political influence which that implied. In the words of a complaint that was made in 1341, 'these same men now make themselves governors and counsellors more than their estate doth warrant '.[1] Although the barons failed at first, by a continued pressure in this direction they ultimately succeeded in displacing the clerks even more positively than the justices and barons of the exchequer. In the councils of Richard II, which were appointed under parliamentary influence, this class was practically eliminated. Even the clerk of the council of that time was not considered to be a member. The clerk or master of the rolls was then an important official, and his presence in the council can hardly be considered as an exception to the rule.[2] Likewise there were at times doctors of law who were of sufficient dignity and importance still to be found in the council.[3]

Foreigners. Another element in the composition of the council, overlooked in Palgrave's definition, consisted of a few foreigners who were even formally sworn and retained. More clearly than any other class, they reflect the personal policy of the king, who thus honoured them and in some instances gave them large rewards, either out of favour or for the special

May 11 of the twentieth year until October 24 of the twenty-first year. They are given as follows:

	£	*s.*	*d.*
May 11 to July 12, 1346, in England, 62 days	5	13	$4\frac{1}{2}$
July 12 to December 24, abroad, 166 days	30	6	$4\frac{1}{2}$
December 25 to July 17, 1347, in England, 204 days . .	18	12	$6\frac{1}{2}$
July 17 to September 4, abroad, 49 days	8	18	$11\frac{3}{4}$
September 4 to October 24, in England, 50 days	4	11	$5\frac{1}{2}$
Robes, one of 20th year, and two for 21st year at 4 marks each	8	0	0
Total	£76	2	$8\frac{3}{4}$

His accounts continue in this way until February 24 of the twenty-third year. *Accounts, Exchequer K. R.*, bundle 96, nos. 2 and 3.

[1] Avesbury, 326.

[2] Nicolas, i. 64.

[3] Henry V speaks of 'our faithful councillor', Master Philip Morgan, Doctor of Laws (*Foedera*, ix. 221).

services which they might render. To further his schemes with the Frescobaldi, the great Italian bankers, Edward II formally appointed Berto, the head of the house, to be 'of his secret council', at the same time that Antonio, bishop of Florence, was likewise retained for similar reasons.[1] The Frescobaldi were bitterly assailed in the Ordinances of 1311, but the general policy of retaining foreigners in the king's council was not then seriously affected. Most of them were dignitaries of the church, cardinals of the church of Rome, or nuncios of the pope, upon whom this honour was conferred to improve the king's relations with the papacy. For example, in 1314, Edward II appointed three nephews and two other adherents of Clement V,[2] and in like manner three years later named Peter d'Euse, a brother of John XXII, and two nephews of the same pope to be of his council for life.[3] A letter of the king to d'Euse and his two nephews, granting their annual pensions and requesting their influence at the papal court,[4] explains the reason for these appointments. At various times under Edward II and Edward III in the same relation may be noticed as many as four cardinals, a pope's notary, and a papal nuncio.[5] A special reason for cultivating the pope's friendship at this time is found in a letter of Edward II, wherein the king beseeches the pope to intercede

[1] As an example of these letters patent the one issued in favour of the bishop of Florence reads as follows: 'Rex venerabili in Christo patri et nobis predilecto domino Antonio de Ursis Dei gratia Episcopo Florencie salutem. De fidelitatis vestre constantia et maturitate consilii quibus laudabiliter noscimini insigniri specialem fiduciam optinentes ac sperantes per vestre provide circumspectionis industriam nostra negocia posse pro patria dirigi et maturius procurari, vos de nostro consilio secreto duximus retinendos mandantes universis et singulis de consilio nostro quod ad tractatus et consilia nos et nostra negocia tangentia vos admittant et inter ipsos collocent ac vobiscum communicent de eisdem. In cuius etc. quam diu nostre placuerit voluntati durature. Teste Rege apud Berewick super Twedam Scocie xv die Ianuarii. Per breve de privato sigillo.' *Patent Roll*, 4 Edw. II, part i, m. 2; Cal. 305. See also *The Italian Bankers in England*, Owens College Essays (Manchester, 1902); Davidsohn, *Geschichte von Florenz* (Berlin, 1908), vol. ii, part ii, pp. 462, 540.

[2] *Cal. Patent Rolls*, 7 Edw. II, 82.

[3] Ibid., 11 Edw. II, 50.

[4] This letter of 1322 requests that they procure the cessation of the annoyances to which the king has been subjected in the court of Rome: 'Velitis sic viriliter et efficaciter interponere partes vestras.' *Foedera* (Rec. Ed.), vol. ii, part i, 495.

[5] *Cal. Patent Rolls*, 7 Edw. II, 82; 11 Edw. II, 25, 59; 8 Edw. III, 29; 10 Edw. III, 247; 17 Edw. III, 111.

with a view to making peace between himself and Robert Bruce.[1]

There was evidently a policy of strengthening the king's friendly relations with Genoa, when in 1315 Carlo de' Fiesci, a captain of the city whom Edward II calls his kinsman, was retained as one of the king's council, household, and following.[2] In 1317 the Marquis of Careto was similarly honoured.[3] After the fall of the Frescobaldi, Antonio Pessagno, a merchant of Genoa, became the king's most favoured money-lender and buyer for the royal household.[4] Under Edward III he is designated as *dilectus et fidelis miles et consiliarius*, and as such he was repeatedly sent upon the king's business to Rome, to France, and to Aquitaine.[5] In 1336 Niccolo de' Fieschi, also a citizen of Genoa, was engaged as one of the king's council with a yearly fee of twenty pounds, and forthwith was sent from Genoa to hire galleys and ships for the transport of horses in the king's service, mention being made of the long friendship existing between the kings of England and the city of Genoa.[6]

During the period when the struggle with France was imminent and all possible alliances were promoted, the friendship of England and Aragon was expressed in a similar way. In 1329 Raymundo Cornelio, a subject of the king of Aragon, who came to England with messages from the government of that kingdom, was engaged as one of the king's council for life, with an annuity of 200 pounds out of the revenue of Aquitaine, saving his fealty due to the king of Aragon.[7] It was declared that Raymundo had always been a well-wisher

[1] This letter of 1320 concludes with the words: 'humiliter supplicantes quatinus tam gratam benivolentiam erga nos . . . dignemini continuare.' *Foedera* (Rec. Ed.), vol. ii, part i, 438.

[2] *Cal. Patent Rolls*, 9 Edw. II, 340.

[3] Ibid., 11 Edw. II, 59.

[4] In the sixth year Pessagno is commissioned to raise a loan of £20,000, and in the eleventh year one of 20,000 marks. *Foedera* (Orig. Ed.), 214, 346. In 1317–18 he appears as seneschal of Aquitaine taking part in the administration of the duchy. *Archives municipales de Bordeaux*, v, 489 ff.

[5] *Cal. Close Rolls*, 6 Edw. III, 581, 582; *Cal. Patent Rolls*, 6 Edw. III 269; *Foedera* (Rec. Ed.), ii. 403, 420.

[6] *Cal. Patent Rolls*, 10 Edw. III, 247, 321, 328; *Cal. Close Rolls*, 10 Edw. III, 686, 733.

[7] *Cal. Patent Rolls*, 3 Edw. III, 416; in 1332 there was an order for the payment of the arrears of his pension. *Cal. Close Rolls*, 6 Edw. III, 532.

to the royal house of England, and the king opened to him the secrets of his heart concerning certain things to be explained to the ruler of Aragon.[1] It was also with reference to the war with France that an alliance, which already had some foundation, was contracted with Odin, lord of Cuijk in Brabant.[2] In 1329 two knights were sent to persuade him to be of the king's council and retinue all his life, the envoys being given discretion as to the lands, revenue, and money to be offered him. In accordance with the agreement then made, Odin received an annuity of 250 pounds besides an indemnity for his losses in the war. In addition to serving in the war he was especially empowered by the king to treat for alliances with the emperor and other princes.[3] In like manner, in 1345, while certain negotiations with Flanders were pending, two citizens of Ypres and one of Ghent, who were then acting as envoys, are mentioned as being sworn of the council with a grant of robes each year.[4] In 1352 John de Crespy, a Frenchman, did liege homage to the king and was engaged as one of the council with a grant of three shillings a day, until some other provision should be made for him. The purpose of this retainer does not appear, because in the following year Crespy was released from his fealty and permitted to return to France.[5] In most of these cases probably the oath of fealty was similar to that given by Arnold Garnier, a collector of papal dues in 1372, 'to give faithful counsel when required, to keep secret the king's counsel, not revealing it to any man living '.[6] The practice of retaining councillors abroad, particularly lawyers who conducted suits in the *parlement* of Paris, caused the king sometimes to speak of his *consilium in partibus transmarinis*.[7]

[1] *Cal. Close Rolls*, 3 Edw. III, 565, 566.

[2] In 1295 John, lord of Cuijk, had done homage to Edward I. *Foedera* (Orig. Ed.), ii. 677.

[3] *Cal. Patent Rolls*, 3 Edw. III, 445; *Foedera* (Rec. Ed.), vol. ii, part ii, 773, 895, 914, 1076, 1102, 1178; vol. iii, part i, 32, 65, 66.

[4] *Cal. Close Rolls*, 17 Edw. III, 185.

[5] *Cal. Patent Rolls*, 26 Edw. III, 253; *Foedera* (Rec. Ed.), vol. iii, part i, p. 268.

[6] *Cal. Patent Rolls*, 46 Edw. III, 424.

[7] Ibid., 11 Edw. II, 53, 59; *Foedera* (Orig. Ed.), iii. 677.

Dislike of the foreigners.

Edward III's preference for foreigners, which was carried to the extent of raising one of them to the peerage,[1] was naturally disliked and was opposed in parliament, as is shown in the following example. Master Raymond Pelegrin, a Gascon and special nuncio of the pope, in view, it is said, of his approved fidelity to the king, was sworn of the council and numbered among the king's clerks and councillors.[2] In the twentieth year the commons in parliament petitioned that his pension should be annulled, but they were answered that Master Raymond was a liege man of the king, born in Gascony, and sworn of the council.[3] It was further declared on the part of the king that for his good service and faithfulness Master Raymond was to be considered not an alien but a denizen of England, and therefore not affected by any ordinance touching the property of aliens.[4] Although the lords and commons then failed, they succeeded ultimately in excluding the foreigners from the council and other political positions. In the time of the ascendancy of parliament under Richard II and under the Lancastrians, no members outside the native estates were appointed,[5] so that like the clerks already mentioned the aliens were a transient element which came to be practically eliminated from the council.

Knights of the council.

Another group of considerable importance, not noticed by Palgrave, consisted of a select number of knights and bannerets, who came to be known as the 'bachelors' in distinction from the lords of the council. As one of the newer estates, unlike the lords, the knights had no historic claims to be regarded as the king's councillors. Under Edward I and Edward II scarcely any of them in fact are noticed in this connexion. But the war with France gave a new value to military titles, and these were widely conferred sometimes for deeds of valour and sometimes for

[1] Guiscard d'Angle, lord of Angle in Poitou, was made earl of Huntingdon in 1377. Courthope, *Historic Peerage*, p. 262.

[2] *Cal. Patent Rolls*, 17 Edw. III, 111.

[3] *Rot. Parl.*, ii. 163.

[4] *Cal. Patent Rolls*, 23 Edw. III, 346.

[5] The presence of Master Peregrino de Fano, an Italian, is noted in the council of Richard II at the time of his reactionary policy. *Issue Roll* (*Pells*), 16 Ric. II, Easter, July 15, August 28 ; 17 Ric. II, December 3.

political reasons. Just as Edward II had shown a special preference for clerks, so Edward III found a body of knights peculiarly useful in the government. Some of his judges and clerks in fact were given the distinction of knighthood,[1] while a number of his knights were made officers and councillors. The first time the chancellorship was given to a layman, in 1341, it was held by Sir Robert Bourchier, and the treasurership at the same time was given to Sir Robert Parning. Others who were retained as councillors were allowed wages or annuities, and formed a material addition to the permanent staff of officers, judges, and clerks, by whom the work of the council was ordinarily performed.

An expression of this tendency is given in 1344, when the bishop-elect of Norwich, before going on a mission to Rome, was sent to consult with the archbishop of Canterbury, accompanied by certain of the 'more secret knights and clerks of the council'.[2] One of the knights mentioned particularly for his faithful service was Robin Forest, who in 1338 was engaged as a king's councillor with an annual fee of 100 marks for life.[3] Another was Guy Brian, first known as an esquire in the royal household, was knighted by the king himself during the campaign of 1346, and afterwards bore the king's banner at Calais. He is called a 'knight of the king's chamber', and was prominently connected with the council before he was made a baron in 1350. Of all the knights of the council at this time, the most assiduous in the work of the government certainly was Bartholomew Burghersh. He had gained a reputation in the war, and in 1347 was in attendance upon the king as his chamberlain. At about this time he first appears in the council, where he is given wages at the rate of twenty shillings a day. From his

[1] The aforesaid John of Shoreditch, before his death in 1345, is mentioned as *doctor legum advocatus et miles de concilio regis existens.* Murimuth, *Contin.*, 149.

[2] 'Et idem dominus rex misit eum (i.e. bishop Bateman) ad archiepiscopum Cantuariensem apud Ortefordiam cum quibusdam militibus et clericis secretioribus sui concilii, cum quibus etiam misit custodem sui privati sigilli, ut ibidem fierent literae regiae de archiepiscopi et eorum consilio per dictum electum sedi apostolicae remittendae.' Murimuth, *Contin.*, 157.

[3] *Cal. Patent Rolls*, 12 Edw. III, 189, 465, 523; *Cal. Close Rolls*, 15 Edw. III, 88; *Foedera* (Orig. Ed.), v. 529.

accounts at the exchequer, which run from the twenty-fifth through the twenty-ninth year, some idea of the labours of a councillor may be formed. In the first of these years his services, extending through different terms, amounted to 82 days, and in the succeeding years to 109 days, 249 days, 240 days, and 207 days respectively. The 249 days are reported to have been spent entirely at London.[1] From various parallel records Burghersh may be observed as one of the council hearing cases in the star chamber, assisting the justices by sitting in the king's bench, examining petitions, and drawing up a compact between the king and certain merchants, while in the many ordinary tasks of administration no name occurs more frequently than his.[2] He was afterwards rewarded with the profitable post of Warden of the Cinque Ports and Constable of Dover Castle. In 1360 Sir William Burton was retained in the king's council with an annuity of 40 pounds, and was employed in several diplomatic missions.[3] Walter de Mauney was a banneret, a foreigner, whom the king retained 'of his most secret council', and gave him more land in England, it is said, than had ever been held by a banneret before.[4] Two other knights of the royal household gained an unenviable prominence during the later years of the reign. These were Sir Richard Stury, who is described

[1] 'Particulae computi Bartholomei de Burgherssh de reditibus et vadiis suis existentis super consilium regis per diversas vices.' *Accounts Exchequer K. R.*, 96, 4–7. During the twenty-sixth year, 1352–3, Burghersh's days of service as a councillor with wages at 20*s.* a day were as follows:

	Days	£
October 5–9 and 16–31	19 . . .	19
November 2–15 and November 27–December 4	20 . . .	20
December 8–19	11 . . .	11
March 8–April 7, 1353	29 . . .	29
May 15–29	15 . . .	15
June 1–7 and 15–22	15 . . .	15
Total	109 days .	£109

Accounts Exchequer K. R., 96/5.

[2] *Coram Rege Roll, Trinity*, 24 Edw. III, m. 32; upon one petition is the note *Tradatur ista petitio B. de Burghesse ad inquirendum*, &c. *Anct. Petitions*, E. 876; *Cal. Patent Rolls*, 20 Edw. III. 136; *Cal. Close Rolls*, 23 Edw. III, 98; 27 Edw. III, 618, &c.

[3] *Cal. Patent Rolls*, 34 Edw. III, 329, &c.; *Foedera* (Orig. Ed.), v. 665, 689.

[4] *Chronique de Jehan le Bel* (Brussels, 1863), i. 154.

as *regi familiarissimus*, and Sir Richard Stafford, brother of the earl, who has been called *dux regis et ejus consiliarius principalis*.[1] They were especially attacked in the Good Parliament of 1376 as 'evil councillors' and were for the time removed from the council. As distinguished from the justices, clerks, and other minor officers, the knights, since they were of parliamentary estate, were considered legitimately qualified to hold places in the council together with prelates and barons. In each of the councils of Richard II named in parliament it will be found that two or more of them were appointed, and again in the latter part of the reign they were to a still greater extent employed and favoured by the king in carrying out his personal policy.

Finally, as to the great men, specified as the 'bishops, earls, and barons whom the king thought fit to name', some of the most difficult questions arise.

The magnates

As to the number of magnates, who were in any way designated or retained as special councillors, in normal times we are never given any definite information, nor has any method of dealing with this question led to satisfactory results. They cannot be ascertained from the parliamentary writs, because the bishops and barons were summoned not as members of the council, but in all cases as lords spiritual and temporal. For this purpose it has been suggested that the names of witnesses upon the charter rolls may be taken as a guide.[2] No doubt there is much to be learned in this way of the men who week by week and day by day were in the king's presence, but there is no indication here who were sworn of the king's council. Indeed the strongest impression made by the charter rolls is the ever-varying and shifting character of the group of nobles attending the

[1] *Chron. Angl.*, ed. E. M. Thompson, p. 87. There is a letter of the king to Sir Richard Stafford in Avesbury, 446.

[2] Maitland once tabulated the names of the witnesses found upon the charter roll of the year 37 Hen. III (*Eng. Hist. Review*, viii. 726–33). This is a point which requires further investigation, since we cannot be sure that witnesses of a charter were all present at the date of sealing. Especially after the chancellor ceased regularly to attend the king, were the witnesses supposed to attest the grant of the charter in the presence of the king, or the execution of the charter by the chancellor ?

court.[1] Even when several charters were dated on the same day the lists of the witnesses would fail to coincide. For our present purposes, therefore, the charters only serve to emphasize the difficulty which was met in maintaining steadily a body of nobles in the council.

It has been conjectured that the barons were members of the council only as they were specially summoned or as they chose to attend. Nevertheless, it can be shown that at all times there were great lords who were regularly sworn and retained of the king's council. But it is believed that the number was not large, and that this was done only for special reasons which are generally apparent. For instance, in 1296 the archbishop of Dublin and Hugh Despenser, who were said to have been sworn of the king's council, are found assisting the treasurer and barons of the exchequer in trying a case.[2] In 1305, at the close of a parliament, Edward I issued a proclamation dismissing the archbishops, bishops, and other prelates, earls, barons, knights, citizens, and burgesses who were present, but requiring the bishops, earls, barons, justices, and others who were of his council to remain.[3] This passage suggests that at least a selection was made among the bishops and barons. In 1306 we are told that John Salmon, bishop of Norwich, a man who had been summoned to parliaments for four years previously, was sworn of the council.[4] To this step it seemed necessary to urge him, for the king sent the following letter to the treasurer and the chancellor concerning him.

Retained in few cases.

'Edward, par le grace de Dieu, roi d'Engleterre, seigneur d'Irlaunde et duc d'Aquitaine, as honurables peres en Dieu par la mesme grace W. evesqe de Cestre, nostre tresorer, et R. evesqe de Londres, nostre chancellier, saluz. Por ce que nous tenoms l'evesqe de Norwys a bon homme, et l'avoms amez depieces, vous mandoms qe vous le facez queire

[1] I have found this to be true even in the years 1316 and 1318, when the nobles especially undertook to control the king's council.

[2] The passage declares *Et per Thesaurarium et Barones, fratrem W. de Hotham et H. le Despenser de consilio Regis iuratos eis assidentes concordatum,* &c. *Memoranda Roll, Exch. K. R.*, 25 Edw. I, m. 54 d. Hugh Despenser will be remembered as the son of a judge, who had recently been made a baron.

[3] *Rot. Parl.*, i. 159.

[4] Ibid. 219.

hastivement et au plus tot quil serra venuz a vous : et le priez de par nous quil vueille estre de nostre Conseil deci en avant et *le facez faire serment* si comme affiert. Donne souz nostre prive seal a Cardoill, le secund jour de juyn, lan de nostre regne xxxv.' [1]

A reason for retaining the bishop in this manner is found in his appointment a short time before on an embassy to the court of Rome.[2]

But the more usual relation of the lords to the council is expressed in the following letter which Edward II sends to the bishop of Hereford, commanding him to come upon a certain occasion and give counsel. The writ was similar to those used for summoning parliament, except that it was issued under the privy seal and does not suggest any general assemblage.

'Edward par la grace de Dieu Roy Dengleterre, etc., al honorable piere en Dieu, Adam par la meisme grace Evesqe de Hereford, saluz. Por acunes grosses et chargeauntes busoignes tochauntes nous de lestat de notre Roiaume dunt nous voloms avoir conseil et avisement de vous, nous vous maundoms et chargeoms en la foi et en la ligaunce que vous nous devez, que veues cestes lettres totes choses lessees, giegnez a nous a Loundres, a tote la haste que vous unques porrez. Et ceo en nule manere ne lessez. Et par vos lettres et par le portur de cestes nous remandez a queu jour vous y serrez. Done sous notre prive seal a Waltham, le xvi jour Doctober, le an de notre Regne xi.' [3]

The council in parliament not to be identified with the sworn councillors.

In a brilliant editorial preface to the Memoranda of the parliament of 1305, Maitland has given us an essay on the king's council, with special reference to its proceedings in the formal sessions of parliament.[4] He shows that the term was still used, as it was under Henry III, in a wide and general sense, and included probably all of the lords and officers present. He then offers, admittedly with diffidence, a list of the 'councillors whose presence in this parliament there is evidence', among whom are included as many as thirty bishops and barons. There is no ground for criticism

[1] *Warrants* (*Chancery*), file 57, no. 5696.
[2] *Cal. Patent Rolls*, 34 Edw. I, 410.
[3] *Registrum Ade de Orleton* (Canterbury and York Society, vol. v), p. 50.
[4] *Mem. de Parl.* (Rolls Series), especially pp. cvi–cviii.

here, but it should be explained that this was the 'council in parliament', that is, the expanded sessions of the council which only met on special summons. Any lord who was summoned was considered to be 'of the council' for the time being, but this was not the same as though he were appointed, sworn, or retained with the extra obligations thus implied. Within the period in view, we may be sure, there were never at any time so many lords who were sworn councillors, although it was by no means infrequent for that number to be present on occasion. As to the line of distinction which was drawn between the 'council in parliament' and the council in its ordinary aspects, we shall have more to say in a subsequent chapter.

Aims of the barons under Edward II.

Concerning the attitude of the barons and their relations to the council, there is much to be learned from the revolutionary years of Edward II. Already, before the reign of Edward I was completed, they were deeply disaffected by the tendencies at court. The promotion of clerks, the prominence of household officers, the filling of the great ministries with men of the *curia*, and above all the patronage that was enjoyed by the king's personal confidants were sources of a chronic political irritation. Between the newly-formed class known as the *curiales*, a body of officers trained in the king's household, and the militant nobles who claimed the rights of hereditary counsellors, there was a fundamental difference of principle. Especially was the antagonism of the nobles directed against the 'favourites', the men most prominently identified with the system, whom they accused of acquiring wealth for themselves and of misguiding the king by their 'evil counsel'.[1] By a threatening attitude in 1308 the barons obtained the banishment of Piers Gaveston, the king's favourite minister, who was chiefly blamed for all that was done.[2] At the same time they named Hugh Despenser, Nicholas Segrave, William Berford, and William

[1] 'It is the antagonism between the court and the administration, between the *curia* and the *camera*,' says Stubbs, *Const. Hist.*, § 247. In this point I fail to follow him, except as the anger of the barons was turned particularly against the newer members of the *curia*.

[2] As a minister he is called *secretarius et camerarius regni summus* (*Ann. Paulini*, 258).

Inge as traitors, who ought to be removed from the king's council.[1] In 1310, proceeding to stronger measures, the barons declared that the king was guided by ' unworthy and evil counsel ', and recalling the methods that had been followed under Henry III, they went on to place the government in the hands of a commission. The Lords Ordainers, as the commissioners were called, were not intended to act as a permanent council,[2] but were given authority to effect ' the reform of the realm and the royal household '. And yet in the celebrated articles known as the Ordinances, which they drew up during the following year, they reserved for themselves certain conciliar functions, particularly in the article (§ 3) which required that no grants of the crown should be made without the assent of the Ordainers, or at least six of them. In accordance with their general aims the ordinances (article 4) required further that suitable men be appointed to the great offices ; and as regards the council (article 13) they said, ' forasmuch as the king has been guided and counselled by bad councillors, we do ordain that all evil councillors be put away and removed altogether . . . and other more fit persons be put in their places.' As to the evil councillors in particular, only Hugh Despenser, Piers Gaveston, and Henry Beaumont at this time were mentioned.[3] For the actual

[1] Despenser was a baron, Segrave the Marshal, while Berford and Inge were lawyers who afterwards became chief justices. One wonders why the barons did not name also Thomas Charleton, who together with the others was favoured prominently in the grants of the first year. Lanercost, 212.

[2] That the council, as ordinarily constituted, continued to act during the interim when the Ordainers were in power is shown by a memorandum of May 22, 1311, when an assignment of the dower of the countess of Lincoln was made before the king's council at Westminster, in the presence of the chancellor, the treasurer, Roger Brabazon, William Berford, John Foxle, ' and others '. *Cal. Close Rolls*, 4 Edw. II, 315. On December 18, there were writs of summons to the bishop of London, Master Robert Pickering, and six other *curiales* to be at London before the earl of Lincoln, guardian of the realm, the chancellor, the treasurer, and others. Ibid. 338, &c.

[3] Despenser was named in the preliminary articles, the others in article 22. *Statutes of the Realm*, i. 163. Henry Beaumont was the son of Lewis of Brienne, viscount of Beaumont in Maine, who had been made a baron in England. He was especially influential with Edward II, who granted him the custodies of the Isle of Man, Bardney Abbey, Roxburgh, and other castles. Many grants were made to others ' at the instance of H. de B.' *Cal. Patent Rolls*. In 1323 he became disaffected by the king's policy, and was afterwards identified with the cause of the barons.

appointment of 'good councillors', strange to say, no more positive plans were proposed. The attention of the Ordainers was directed rather to strengthening the position of parliament, which was expected to meet at least once and possibly twice a year. Beyond this, it was thought, a permanent council of barons was not a necessity. As a result of all this legislation, neither the methods nor the personnel of the existing system of administration were materially affected. After a few specific acts had been passed the Ordainers dispersed,[1] the favourites returned to court, and the council was conducted in the same manner as before. The opponents of the court continued to make complaints,[2] and they directed attacks upon individual ministers; Gaveston was killed, while Despenser, Beaumont, and the treasurer Langton were successively declared to be removed.[3] But not until 1316, in the noted parliament of Lincoln, were any definite steps taken toward the construction of a council in accordance with the wishes of the barons. It was then proposed that there should be appointed a number of prelates, earls, and barons to act as a council, without whose advice the king should do nothing serious or arduous.[4] The earl of Lancaster was asked to take the position of 'chief of the council', and upon his acceptance of this responsibility he was solemnly sworn according to an oath that was especially framed for the purpose. At the same time the bishops of Norwich, Chichester, Exeter, and Salisbury were publicly sworn to be of the king's council'.[5] But as to the other

[1] Certain grants 'by the king with the assent of the Ordainers' were made between October and December 18. After that grants in the interests of Lord Beaumont and the others reappear.

[2] In 1313, the monk of Malmesbury says, 'Revera quicquid dolose actum est in curia regis processit ex consiliariis, sed consilium eorum est inefficax et machinatio peritura.' The earl of Hereford, he also declares, remained in the royal household, but all the other earls went to their homes. The blame for the disastrous Scottish expedition in 1314 is laid particularly upon the *consiliarii et domestici*, who then advised the king. *Vita Edwardi Secundi*, 194, 196.

[3] Ibid. 208–9.

[4] 'Ordinatum erat quod dominus rex sine consilio comitum et procerum nihil grave, nihil arduum inchoaret, et comitem Lancastriae de consilio principaliter retineret' (Malmesbury, p. 224). 'Et les busoignes tochantes li e son roiaume ne seient faites ne perfumes sanz assent de li (the earl of Lancaster) e des autres prelatz, countes, e barons qi de li conseiller serront ordenetz' (*Rot. Parl.*, i. 351).

[5] Ibid. 350.

lords nothing is said of any particular group being chosen or sworn, and it is not likely that anything of the kind was done. The earl of Lancaster, after procuring a few measures in his own favour, shortly absented himself from court, while the Despensers and other courtiers returned. As Lancaster himself wrote in a letter of the next year, ' wherefore, sire, nothing has been done, but you have held them (i.e. the favourites) dearer than they were before, and others you have taken to you.'[1] In 1317 also we are told of a compact between the earl of Pembroke, Lord d'Amory, and Lord Badlesmere for holding supreme influence in the king's council.[2] Nothing came of this plan, but Lord Badlesmere was individually retained by the king 'for the benefit of his counsel', with a grant of 1,000 marks a year, while for undertaking a mission to Rome he was allowed 4,000 marks for four years.[3] But the failures of the government in 1318, the fall of Berwick Castle and the outbreak of a local civil war, moved the king to accept from his barons a still more radical plan for the reconstruction of his council. The provision of the Ordinances that every important matter should be acted upon by the barons in parliament was not sufficient, it was shown, ' since it was difficult in every case that came up in the *curia regis* to assemble all the magnates of the realm.'[4] According to a first proposal there were to be chosen a body of twelve lords to act as the king's council. But when all interests were considered this number was increased to twenty-four, including eight bishops, four earls, four barons, and instead of the earl of Lancaster himself a banneret to be named by him, besides seven officers of the court.[5] These men were to remain with the king for the next quarter of a year until the following parliament, and as they could not all

[1] Murimuth, *Contin.*, 271.

[2] *Parl. Writs*, II, part ii, 120 ; Malmesbury, 235.

[3] *Cal. Patent Rolls*, 11 Edw. II, 14. Various grants were made upon his ' information '.

[4] Malmesbury, 236.

[5] The list includes the bishops of Norwich, Ely (the chancellor), Chichester, Salisbury, Saint David's, Hereford, Worcester, Carlisle ; the earls of Pembroke, Arundel, Richmond, Hereford ; barons Hugh Courtenay, Roger Mortimer, John Segrave, John Gray ; the banneret whose name is not given ; the officers Hugh Despenser the younger, chamberlain, Bartholomew Badlesmere, steward of the household, Roger Mortimer of Chirk, William Martin, John Somery, John Giffard, John Bottetourt. *Parl. Writs*, II, part ii, 184 ; *Rot. Parl.*, i. 453.

be constantly in attendance, it was stipulated that at least two of the bishops, one earl, one baron, and the banneret should always be present. Considered as a representative body of lords the group was not badly chosen, but not even for a month does it appear to have been maintained under any pretence of unity or consistency. Much less was there an effort in any subsequent parliament to resume or continue the plan, so that the council inevitably fell back into its former grooves. Against the favourites there continued to be as many complaints as ever, while the earl of Lancaster was bitterly reproached for his negligence which was thought to amount to treason, but for the present the lords were unable to form any constructive plan of reform. So that during the rest of the reign their struggles become more and more a desultory warfare, consisting of attacks upon individual ministers and quarrels with one another. In 1321, while the Despensers father and son held supremacy, an armed league among the barons was formed, and in an ensuing parliament charges were drawn up against the favourites. In accordance with current beliefs, they were accused specifically of preventing the magnates from having proper access to the king, of removing the 'good councillors', and of causing the advancement of various 'evil councillors'.[1] The favourites were sentenced and dismissed, only to be restored by another turn of events. Again in 1323 John Stratford, a clerk of the council who had recently acquired the bishopric of Winchester, was dismissed in disgrace, but he returned to wield greater influence than before.[2] During these years it is true the barons were summoned and came to parliaments and great councils with unusual frequency, but so long as there was no settlement of the real question at issue, whether the government of England should be carried on by an aristocracy or a bureaucracy, the only tangible

[1] The appointment of Robert Baldock as keeper of the privy seal, and that of William Cusance, a foreigner and private clerk of the younger Hugh, as keeper of the wardrobe, are particularly noticed. Objection was made also to William Clyff, a clerk sworn of the council—'et dominum Willelmum de Clyff similiter eiusdem clericum de consilio regis fecerunt iurari'. Bridlington, *Gesta Edwardi* II, 67.

[2] '(Rex) episcopum gratanter admisit, restitutum de consilio suo privato iuratum, caeteris de caetero tenuit cariorem.' Blaneforde, 148.

results were a continuation of warfare, a series of political murders, among which both Lancaster and the Despensers were victims, and finally the deposition of the king himself. In the articles of accusation that were drawn up against Edward II the first point to be mentioned was that he had been controlled by 'evil counsel' and had failed to do as was required by 'the great and wise men of his realm'.

Similar attempts under Edward III.

With the accession of Edward III and the prospect of the reign of a minor, there was another opportunity for the lords to put their plans into practice. Accordingly, in the first parliament there was chosen a body of fourteen magnates, including four bishops, four earls, and six barons, who 'should remain with the king to counsel him'. The men then selected, at the head of whom was placed Henry, earl of Lancaster, were not lacking in reputation or experience,[1] but either because of their own inattention or because of the superior adroitness of Lord Mortimer and Queen Isabella, the earl and his associates were completely thwarted in their attempts to govern.[2] According to all complaints they were not permitted even to approach the king, to say nothing of reorganizing the royal household. Under the personal supremacy of Mortimer and Isabella, then the king's council continued to be mainly a body of *curiales*, of officers, judges, and clerks. Not until after the fall of Mortimer, which occurred in 1330, was there any new suggestion for the reform of the council. Probably it was in response to the wishes of parliament, during the session of 1332, that the chancellor announced that the king desired to have certain wise men of the realm near him to give counsel, naming the archbishop of York, the bishop of Norwich, Lord Percy, William Clinton, William Denham, and William

[1] They were Bishop Orlton of Hereford, then treasurer, Archbishop Melton of York, Reynolds of Canterbury, and Stratford of Winchester; the earls of Lancaster, Kent, Norfolk, and Earl Warenne; Lords Wake, Percy, Ros, and Sir Oliver Ingham. For some reason, Bishop Hotham, the chancellor, is not mentioned. Leland, *Coll.* ii. 476; Stubbs, § 256.

[2] 'In tantum isti duo regina et Rogerus (Mortimer) asciverunt sibi potestatem, quod comes Lancastriae Henricus qui deputatus et ordinatus est capitalis custos et supremus consiliarius regis in tempore coronationis . . . non potuit ei appropinquare nec quicquam consilii dare.' Knighton, i. 447, 455; *Rot. Parl.* ii. 52.

Shareshull.[1] Again in 1338, when the king went to France, his son Edward, duke of Cornwall, was made guardian of the realm, while the earl of Huntingdon, the earl of Arundel, and Ralph Neville were appointed to be of the duke's council.[2] Once more in 1341 an attempt was made in parliament to reform the king's government in accordance with the ideals that had many times already been suggested. This time as an outcome of a conflict that had arisen between the king and Archbishop Stratford, along the lines that are now familiar, demands were made that the chancellor and other great officers and the judges should be appointed in parliament, and that upon the occurrence of any ministerial vacancy the peers in parliament should be consulted, 'whom the king with his privy council should no longer thwart'.[3] Under the leadership of the archbishop the aims of the lords were the more clearly stated. 'Wherefore, Sire,' he writes in a letter to the king, 'for the salvation of your honour and your land, and that your interests may be brought to a happy issue, be willing to act with the assent of your elders and magnates, without whose counsel and aid you can neither rule your land nor maintain the war.'[4] Although the rolls of parliament make no mention of the fact, there is reason to believe that a scheme for the reconstruction of the council was also prepared. At all events we find a letter which seems to be the expression of a league or a group of lords, who bound themselves by an oath loyally to counsel the king according to their ability, to manage his business profitably for him, to take no profit for themselves, and to redress all evils that had formerly been suffered to exist.[5] But just as had happened before these plans fell to the ground, because the king immediately repudiated all his concessions. Within a brief time Archbishop Stratford was restored to favour and became known again as the king's principal councillor. During the following thirty-five years, so far as we know, no further attempt was made to reorganize the

[1] *Rot. Parl.* ii. 69.
[2] *Cal. Patent Rolls,* 12 Edw. III, 112.
[3] Murimuth, *Contin.* 119.
[4] W. de Hemingburgh (Eng. Hist. Soc.), ii. 365.
[5] This letter I have quoted at length in connexion with the councillor's oath treated in Chapter XIII, p. 351.

council on these lines. From time to time, it is true, certain lords and bishops were appointed or retained to act as councillors. In 1345 a group was selected to assist the king's son Lionel during the time that he was guardian of the realm,[1] and again the same thing was done in 1372 under the prince of Wales.[2] In 1352 the bishop of Norwich was retained as one of the council with a grant for life of the profits of a town 'for the livery of himself and his men'.[3] But besides the great prelates who commonly held the principal offices, it must be admitted that hardly any other instances of the kind can be cited before the end of the reign. In the chronicles the lords are commonly described as 'coming' to the council. This they did whenever they were especially asked or when they found it convenient to do so. Edward III made a practice of summoning small and secret councils possibly as often as two or three times a year. Some of the lords also were more attentive to these demands than others. But this is not the statement of any new principle, but only the preparation for a later series of experiments.

No permanent council of magnates as yet.

From all these incidents it is obvious that a council consisting of a permanent body of magnates was an ideal exceedingly difficult to realize. The lords appreciated the importance of the council, and willingly accepted appointments thereto, but in their own private interests they came to court and quickly went away in the same manner as before. Just like the men of lower rank, the nobles were not usually disposed to give much of their time to the king's business, unless they were induced by grants of office or rewards of money. These the king could not always afford to give upon the larger scale. So that it was the invariable experience thus far that any council made up mainly of lords and depending upon their support fell to pieces almost as soon as it was formed.

Moreover, there is reason to say, the great lords as a rule

1 These were the archbishop of Canterbury, the bishop of London, the bishop of Chichester, the bishop-elect of Durham, the earl of Lancaster, the earl of Surrey, the chancellor, the treasurer, the prior of Rochester, Simon Islip, William Trussel, and Andrew Ufford. *Cal. Patent Rolls*, 19 Edw. III, 487.

2 *Dipl. Documents Chancery*, Portf. 320.

3 *Cal. Patent Rolls*, 26 Edw. III, 241.

were reluctant to take the councillor's oath, considering it to be beneath their dignity to be bound, as were knights and clerks, by an official form. The status of a lord spiritual or a lord temporal was a far higher one, and within these ranks the theory still survived that the king was free to ask for counsel, and the lord was free to give it without further qualification. As an illustration of this feeling, in 1386 the archbishop of Canterbury was unwilling to be sworn, claiming as a general prerogative of the church of Canterbury the right to be present at all parliaments and councils, 'secret or other.'[1] Undoubtedly there was good reason for such a claim in the fourteenth century, although it was not allowed to be established. Again, in 1410 the prince of Wales was excused from taking the oath which was then imposed upon others of the council then appointed, as was explained, 'because of his highness and the excellence of his honourable person.'[2] The reluctance of the lords either to attend the council with regularity or to bind themselves by an oath so to do, was no doubt a reason for the repeated insistence of parliament that they should be sworn. It was the irregular and uncertain attendance of the lords, too, which left the work, for the greater part, in the hands of lesser men, who were of course the more ready tools of royal influence. Several times during the fourteenth century the barons revolted, and sought to reorganize the council according to their own ideals. The next reaction of this kind, as a following chapter will show, occurred in 1376, and this time it continued with perceptible effect during the entire reign of Richard II.

Reluctance of the lords to serve.

In the light of all the facts here gathered, it is evident that the sworn councillors of the Edwards formed a wide and heterogeneous body. Among them may usually be counted several score of men, including officers, prelates, barons, knights, clerks, honorary members, foreigners, and favourites. Some of these, within the period in view, were eliminated as sworn members of the council, although they continued to act as councillors for certain purposes. Others were retained purely as an honour, or from special reasons of diplomacy, or out of sheer favouritism. As a whole they

The council not a homogeneous body.

[1] *Rot. Parl.* iii. 223.

[2] Ibid. 632.

could not have formed an effective working body, and this they probably were not intended to be. Most of the councillors were chosen in fact for their individual services, and this consideration was more important than their collective capacity. But among them there is always to be found a faithful working group with strongly-marked official tendencies. The nobles still formed in the main a varying and shifting element, whose attendance at all times was desired but could not beyond reasonable limits be required. The councillor's oath indeed was not intended to form an exclusive body or to grant a personal right of attendance, but to impose an obligation of service ; for the lords it was an extra obligation which could not be exacted without their personal consent. It would be some time yet before a rule could be made or in any wise enforced that the council should be controlled only by its sworn members.

It may be thought that a useful comparison can here be made between the mediaeval council and the privy council as it exists at the present day. The council now is a large body of more than three hundred members ; it includes men of diverse classes and political opinions ; its membership is mainly conferred as an honour, while the practical work is performed by various inner groups. But the likeness, however striking, is only a superficial one. The council to-day stands out in all the clearness of modern definitions. Its membership, even though it does not necessarily impose any serious duties, is certain, since all councillors are formally sworn. The attendance of non-members would not be permitted ; the early distinction of estates also is here practically obliterated ; and all confusion which lingered between the council and the house of lords as well as between the council and other courts has been cleared away. Moreover, the title of 'Right Honourable' is an exalted one, and is not associated with the ordinary grades of government service. The modern idea of a council in its privilege, its exclusiveness, and its mutual cohesion is almost the reverse of the thought of the middle ages. There are many steps yet to be taken, therefore, before the council of the Edwards is transformed into its modern counterpart.

CHAPTER V

THE 'PRIVY' COUNCIL, THE 'GREAT' COUNCIL, AND THE 'ORDINARY' COUNCIL

Terms of current usage.

BEFORE proceeding further with this work it will be necessary to explain certain terms of current usage, such as *privatum* or *secretum consilium*, *magnum consilium*, and *consilium ordinarium*. In the varied nomenclature of the fourteenth century there were also *bonum consilium*, *sapiens consilium*, *totum consilium*, *plenum consilium*, *commune consilium*, and the list could be extended indefinitely, if the French language also were taken into account. How many councils were there ? has been asked in despair.[1] No one, to be sure, has understood that there was a 'good' council in distinction from a 'wise' council, but it is generally supposed that there was a series of councils, more or less concentric and overlapping, each with its powers marked off and assigned to it.[2] In particular it has been argued that there was more than one circle of sworn councillors. The question, however, has been a ceaseless source of difficulty for every one who has touched upon it, because no hypothesis of the kind could positively be proved. There can be no evasion of the problem here. The grounds of opinion in this regard must be carefully scrutinized before any further headway is made.

[1] Sir Matthew Hale undertook to name and define four distinct councils, (1) the *consilium privatum* or *assiduum*, (2) the *consilium ordinarium*, (3) the *magnum consilium*, (4) the *commune consilium*, embracing both houses of parliament. *Jurisdiction of the Lords' House*, chap. ii.

[2] Mr. Pike has carried this view to the utmost extreme, saying, 'it is clear from the records . . . that there were many kinds of Council known to the law'. He mentions 'the Common Council of the Realm, the Great Council which was different from the former, the Secret Council which is distinguished from the official or ordinary Council, the "Whole Council" which may or may not have been identical with the Great Council, and lastly the King's Council without any qualifying epithet.' *Constitutional History of the House of Lords* (London, 1894), p. 46.

Indefiniteness of the Latin.

In the first place it must be recognized that mediaeval Latin was a very imperfect medium of the thought of the time. It was mainly a written, rather than a spoken, language, of small vocabulary and fixed terminology. Especially in an official department like the chancery did the use of the language become formulaic and unyielding to an extreme degree. Thus the term *consilium regis* continued to have currency throughout the middle ages, in spite of all the changes of ideas pertaining to it, and even when it might mean two different institutions. In reference to the early Saxons and their efforts to express themselves in the ways of civilization, Maitland has said, 'there lies a besetting danger for us in the barbarian's use of a language which is too good for his thought.' [1] But by the thirteenth century the Saxon had ceased to be a barbarian, and then the difficulty is that he was struggling with a language too rigid for his thought. Thus *concilium* or *consilium* is the same whichever way it is spelt, and means equally 'counsel' or 'council'; likewise *consiliarius* may be translated either 'counsellor' or 'councillor'. No doubt the ideas of the abstract and the concrete were closely blended, but even when the distinction was clearly perceived it could hardly be expressed. Yet there was plainly a consciousness of the double meaning of the word when one wrote *de consilio totius consilii*, and *de consilio procerum de consilio*.[2] Moreover, the lack of the definite and indefinite articles in Latin leaves it uncertain whether *a* council or *the* council is meant. Undoubtedly such indefiniteness in the use of words was the expression of an underlying indefiniteness of thought, but here again the need of a better vehicle was felt, as the advance of the Norman-French and later of the native English in official usage most clearly shows. The French, of course, never fails to make the distinction between *un conseil* and *le conseil*, and when we can find a Latin phrase like *magnum et secretum consilium* translated into French we may see its meaning more accurately. In this wise we may sometimes determine the point whether the adjec-

[1] *Domesday and Beyond* (Cambridge, 1897), 225, 334.
[2] *Foedera* (Record Ed.), i. 365.

tives are used descriptively or with reference to distinct institutions.

The 'privy' or 'secret' council.

During the thirteenth century any reference to a 'privy' council was sedulously avoided in official documents. During the reign of Edward II, *secretum consilium* and *privatum consilium* appear upon the regular rolls. French equivalents also gain currency, such as *le prive conseil, les prives de conseil, les plus secretz, les privez et nurriz*, and the like.[1] But never during the middle ages did 'the privy council' become a term of general acceptance, as it is in modern times. It was seldom used, in fact, unless a certain distinction was necessary, and then it meant not especially a small council, nor yet a more highly organized or more select council than usual, but simply a *secret* council.[2] This was neither a body of lords exclusively, nor a body of officers and clerks, but it might be of lords, knights, officers, clerks, and others in the usual proportions, whenever they met under conditions of secrecy.[3] But during the middle ages this was not the normal aspect of the council as it is in modern times. Moreover, the term 'privy council' was not generally liked, and often conveyed a sinister and reproachful meaning. Many times it was used with reference to the 'favourites' and 'evil councillors' of Edward II, and again under Edward III when parliament declared that no grant should be made or statute repealed by the 'privy council'.[4] The name was still avoided generally in official documents.[5] The king, it is true, is known to have summoned a secret council,[6] and to have members sworn thereof,[7] but it is doubtful if he would

[1] *Rot. Parl.* ii. 163, 201, 256, 311.

[2] In 1344, it is said, 'super quibus dominus rex habuit secretum concilium cum archiepiscopo et quibusdam praelatis et comitibus valde paucis.' Murimuth, *Contin.*, 159.

[3] Again in 1345, a secret council was held for eight days, 'cui concilio interfuerunt rex, archiepiscopus Cantuariensis, Norwicensis et Dunelmensis episcopi, comes de Warewykia, de Arundellia, de Huntyngdona, magister Johannis de Offord decanus Lincolniensis (keeper of the privy seal), et alii clerici et milites de secreto concilio regis.' Ibid. 177.

[4] *Rot. Parl.* ii. 311.

[5] Instances like the following, wherein a case is heard by the treasurer *et alii de privato consilio*, are exceedingly rare. *Memoranda Roll, Exch., K. R.*, 26 Edw. III, Mich., Communia, Cant.

[6] *Cal. Close Rolls*, 12 Edw. III, 517.

[7] Philip Slane is described upon one roll as *iuratus de consilio*, and upon

ever proclaim an act or ordinance on such authority. An order of the king ' by advice of his great council ', or ' of the wise men of his council ', would have strong sanction, but it would be a poor endorsement to say ' by the advice of the privy council '. A term free from any such implication was found in *le conseil continuel* which appears for the first time prominently in 1376, and it arose from the desire which had been stated many times before of having councillors ' continually present '. Still no new form of designation found favour sufficiently to supersede the older term, *consilium regis*, which was well enough understood for all practical purposes.

The ' great ' councils.

But we are told that there were ' secret councils and others '.[1] What were the others ? There were certainly the great councils which antedated the constitutional formation of parliament, and which continued to be brought together in the old way during the fourteenth century. The distinguishing trait of a great council, as it is commonly regarded, was the general use of writs of summons, stating in the usual form the time, the place, and the general cause for which the assembly was called. A great council, then, differed from a parliament only as the latter organization was given definite form. The peers, for instance, gained a *right* to be summoned to parliaments, but no such right was acknowledged in regard to councils. That the king was free to summon ' whom he wills ' to his councils was a statement of general acceptation. Any assemblage of the estates, then, which was not of sufficient formality to be considered a parliament continued to be known as a great council. Moreover, the term *magnum consilium* was accurate enough to describe the parliament itself or at least the part corresponding to the house of lords. But it has been observed that after the twenty-seventh year of Edward III, or possibly the forty-fifth year, great councils ceased to be summoned in the old way, and that they were then somehow differently conducted.[2] They cease then to be noticed in the rolls of

another as *de secreto consilio iuratus*. *Roman Roll*, 11–14 Edw. II, m. 7 d. ; *Close Roll*, 13 Edw. II, m. 15.

[1] *Cal. Patent Rolls*, 10 Edw. II, 655.

[2] *Report on the Dignity of a Peer*, i. 324, 328, n. 67.

parliament. The change which mystified the authors of the Lords' Report was this. At about the time mentioned, during the reign of Edward III, all councils apart from parliament began to be summoned by writs of the privy seal, instead of the great seal as before.[1] Likewise the whole clerical work of the councils was more or less rapidly transferred from the chancery to the office and the clerks of the privy seal. In the reign of Richard II this work was performed in particular by the clerk of the council, and thus the great councils were drawn away from the methods of parliament and assimilated closely to the privy council. Stubbs has observed that the great councils 'may be regarded either as extra-parliamentary sessions of the house of lords or as enlarged meetings of the royal council'.[2] Of these two aspects of the case, the first was true down to a certain date during the fourteenth century, and the latter was the prevailing system afterwards. An excellent illustration of this tendency is found in a description of the great council which was held at Eltham in 1395.[3] Although it was an assemblage of a large number of lords who had been summoned for a specific occasion, it was held entirely after the manner of a privy council, and its proceedings were written in the usual style of the clerk of the council. In accordance with this tendency, the knights of the shires, who had sometimes been called to great councils in earlier days, ceased to be summoned after the reign of Henry IV.[4] During the period from Richard II to Henry VI, when the idea of a 'continual' council was most frequently asserted, there appears now and again the suggestion that the great council held a place distinct from the parliament on the one hand, and from the privy council on the other. This view was expressed in 1415 by the duke of Bedford, who declared that he had often given warning of

[1] The tendency is most easily observed in the entries of the issue rolls where payments to messengers are recorded for carrying these writs of the privy seal, e.g. *Issue Roll*, 44 Edw. III, &c. Sometimes two or three lords are especially asked to come, and again they are called in larger groups.

[2] *Const. Hist.* iii. 274.

[3] Appendix II, p. 504.

[4] In 1401 Henry IV summoned the knights in this manner (Nicolas, i. 155 ff.), and then for the last time, so far as we know, the great council included so wide a representation. Henceforth there were summoned lords, knights, and others individually.

the defenceless condition of the Scottish Marches, 'sibien en plusours et diverses parlementz come en grandes conseils et especialment pardevant le conseil assigne pour le governance du roialme.'[1] But the stronger tendency, which was manifested during the reign of Henry VI, was to assimilate the great councils still further with what is otherwise known as the privy council. During the years of general disintegration no sufficient number of lords could be induced to remain with the council for any considerable length of time. The only way then for the king to obtain a council of repute was by recourse to the traditional method of special summons. Sometimes this was done as many as four or five times a year, and on rare occasions possibly twenty-five or thirty lords obeyed the summons. Under these circumstances the great council was only an expanded session of the small council; in point of organization and functions there was indeed but one council, which appears sometimes in a larger and sometimes in a smaller form. The conditions which caused this reversion to a primitive type will be brought out more clearly in a chapter dealing with the period.

A sworn great council?

Another aspect of the problem has caused more difficulty. The view has been maintained on high authority that there was also a great council of permanent standing, the members of which were bound by an oath and formed a body not the same in constituency as the privy council. Evidence is cited in the passage concerning Lord Beaumont, which describes him as one *de magno et secreto consilio ipsius domini Regis iuratus*.[2] Should these words be translated 'sworn of the great and of the secret council', or simply 'of the great and secret council'? In the former sense there have been understood to be two councils to which his lordship belonged and two oaths by which he was sworn.[3] This view, however, is not required by strict translation, nor is it corroborated by other evidence. The meaning of the above

[1] Nicolas, ii. 136.

[2] *Abbreviatio Placitorum*, p. 342; *Parliamentary Writs*, ii. 157. There is also the curious reference to William of Wykeham as *clericus privati sigilli, et capitalis secreti consilii ac gubernator magni consilii* (*Rot. Parl.* iii. 388).

[3] This view is stated most emphatically in Pike, *House of Lords*, p. 45.

Latin quotation will easily be made clear when it is compared with a few French phrases of the same character. In 1346, for example, by a similar juxtaposition of words a member of the council is called 'un grant et prive'.[1] In 1386, when a council of twelve was named in parliament, they were appointed 'to our great and continual council'.[2] Again in 1404 the twenty-two men then appointed were announced as being 'de son grant et continuel conseil'.[3] A member of this council, Sir Arnold Savage, in one roll is said to have been appointed to the king's council, and in another is called 'one of our great council'.[4] In 1406, when another such body was chosen, it was required that all 'those of the great council' should be sworn in parliament.[5] Finally, in 1450, the duke of Suffolk is described as 'beyng oon of your grete and pryve Counseill'.[6] A little further comparison of phrases and of usages will show that the word 'great' did not necessarily indicate anything different from what we would otherwise recognize as the privy council. For example, Edward II in the usual manner writes to his regent, 'facez assembler notre grant consail, cest a savoir notre chanceller, tresorer, justices, barons de notre eschekier et autres de notre consail.'[7] In the statute, 37 Edw. III, it was enacted that those making false suggestions should be sent before the chancellor, the treasurer, and the 'grand council'.[8]

Why, then, was the adjective 'great' used at all in this manner, to our lasting confusion? Perhaps a suggestion may be found in the contemporary usage with regard to the king's council in France. Here *le conseil du Roi* was commonly known also as *le grand conseil*, and in the fourteenth century *le grand et secret conseil* was the appellation preferred.[9] One spoke also of *le grand et étroit conseil*, and *conseillers du grand et secret conseil*. In England as well as in France the council

[1] *Rot. Parl.* ii. 163.
[2] *Cal. Patent Rolls*, 10 Ric. II, 244.
[3] *Rot. Parl.* iii. 530.
[4] *Issue Roll*, 6 Hen. IV, Mich., December 2; *Close Roll*, 6 Hen. IV, m. 13.
[5] *Rot. Parl.* iii. 589.
[6] Ibid., v. 178.
[7] *Ancient Correspondence*, vol. xlv, no. 149.
[8] *Statutes of the Realm*, i. 382.
[9] Valois, *Le Conseil du Roi aux xive, xve, et xvie siècles*, p. 3 ff.; ibid., *Inventaire des arrêts*, i. pp. xxxviii, cx.

was called 'great', not because it was large, surely, but rather because of the great men and great authority associated with it, in the same sense as one spoke of '*les grauntz et autres sages de notre conseil*'.[1] Sometimes indeed it was thus designated when so few as eleven or even six lords were indicated as present.[2] There was a fondness, too, for these high-sounding adjectives, which was carried to the utmost lengths in many of the petitions elsewhere cited.[3] As Sir John Fortescue in the fifteenth century said, 'truly such a continual council may well be called *multa consilia* for often and every day it counselleth.'[4] For these reasons the councils which on several occasions were appointed in parliament during the reigns of Richard II, Henry IV, and Henry VI, were properly considered to be 'great'.[5] Except for the fact that an unusual number of great lords were named, they were in no wise different from the usual sworn councils. Likewise in the difficulties of the later years of Henry VI, when, as will be shown, the regular attendance of great lords at the king's council fell to the vanishing point, the king was compelled more often than ever before to issue special summons to the great lords to be present. Whether they were sworn members or not was immaterial. The government, indeed, would be glad of the attendance of all who were willing to come. Such an assemblage would be called a 'great council', with much stress laid upon its full attendance, at a time when every effort was put forth to bolster the failing authority of the government by words if not by deeds. It would not be worth the while to labour this point at so great length, if it had not been held by the latest writer upon the subject, that there were in the fifteenth century at least two concentric councils, the

[1] *Statutes of the Realm*, i. 303.

[2] *Cal. Patent Rolls*, 22 Edw. III, 131; Nicolas, i. 222, &c.

[3] A petition of the duke of Geldres begins, 'Reverendissimis et eximie circumspectis dominis de Magno Consilio domini mei Regis Anglie et Francie.' *Le Cotton Manuscrit*, Galba B I. (ed. Scott, 1896), p. 44; again, 'quant ces seigneurs furent tous assemblez ilz eurent très grand conseil et long.' *Chronique de Jehan le Bel* (Brussels, 1863), i. 139.

[4] *Governance of England* (ed. Plummer), chap. xiv.

[5] In 1440 John Durward was granted a letter of exemption, excusing him from holding office and from being a resident of the great council—*residens magni consilii* (*Cal. Patent Rolls*, 19 Hen. VI, 467).

members of each of which respectively were sworn.[1] The privy council, it is said, was made up of officers, civilians, clerks, and others; while the great council included also prelates, peers, and others who were specially summoned. Nothing in the language or the usages of the time warrants this artificial definition. Lords, it is true, were specially summoned, but when they were sworn there was but one oath for them to take, and this was the same for all cases. In spite of great diversities in membership and responsibilities, there was but one sworn king's council, whether it was called secret, continual, wise, or great.

The 'whole' council, &c.

As to the *totum consilium* and *plenum consilium*, the obvious meaning of the words should be sufficient without further refinement. These were expressions of the feeling that in any organic body a stronger sanction was gained by full attendance, by full deliberation and unanimity. In view of the fact that the council varied extremely in regard to its attendance, that it might legitimately fall to six or four persons, and sometimes was reduced to two or three officers, there was a strong reason for emphasizing this point whenever possible. An act which was passed *in pleno consilio*,[2] therefore, was given an added validity like one *in pleno parliamento*. *Totum consilium* does not mean necessarily a large council but an entire council so far as it was present. In one case an action was held *par tout le conseil* when twelve men were stated to be in attendance,[3] and at another time *coram toto consilio* when fifteen names are given.[4] Again, a case 'before the whole council' was adjourned because a sufficient number were not present.[5] In the reign of Edward III a case occurs in which action was taken 'in full council', 'by the whole council,' in accordance with a statute which had given powers to 'the great council'.[6]

[1] R. Steele, *Bibliography of Royal Proclamations* (Oxford, 1910), containing certain introductory chapters on the king's council. See p. lxii; also Nicolas, vii. p. xvi.

[2] *Parl. Writs*, i. 6, &c.

[3] *Parliamentary Proceedings*, file vii, no. 21.

[4] *Close Roll*, 32 Edw. I, m. 8 d.; *Calendar*, 216.

[5] *Rot. Parl.* i. 79.

[6] 'Consideratum fuit in pleno consilio per ipsum Regem et totum consilium,' etc. *Close Roll*, 39 Edw. III, m. 26–23, *Calendar*, 123.

The adjectives are only an expression of the thought of the scribe on this or that particular occasion.

The 'ordinary' council.

With regard to the *consilium ordinarium* there has likewise been some confusion of thought. The term nowhere occurs in the middle ages, and not until the reign of Henry VIII is there mention of 'the king's ordinary counsellors'. Yet the idea has been projected into the histories of the middle ages. On this point Sir Matthew Hale, whose work in the main has stood the test of time, ventured to say, 'the *consilium ordinarium* . . . was that generally mentioned in acts of parliament under the name *consilium regis* and *coram rege et consilio*.'[1] The Lord's Report on the Dignity of a Peer falls into the same anachronism.[2] The idea too has been transplanted into a current textbook which says that 'this [distinction] seems to have become clear during the minority of Henry VI'.[3] Now there are reasons for these assertions, although they are not after all well founded.

The *consilium regis* of Edward I, as has been shown, was composed mainly of officers, judges, and other professional men, who resemble the ordinary councillors of a later day. When at length, after many experiments, the council was given over to a body of lords, there was something anomalous in the position of the former class of men, who were lowered in certain respects to the position of assistants. Nevertheless, the anomaly was allowed to continue, and in spite of all inconsistencies no definition of the kind suggested was made throughout the middle ages. On the contrary, the mediaeval king's council was intended to be a comprehensive body including 'of every estate some'. The king's councillors, with great differences of rank and employment, as the facts of the last chapter tend to show, were retained largely for their individual services, some for law cases, some for

[1] *Jurisdiction of the Lords' House*, p. 5. The membership in particular is stated to include (1) all those of the privy council; (2) the great officers of state like the chancellor, the treasurer, the lord steward, &c.; (3) certain less prominent officials like the master of the wardrobe, the treasurer, and controller of the household; (4) the justices of both benches, the barons of the exchequer, the masters in chancery, &c.; (5) sometimes judges itinerant, the master of the rolls, and others.

[2] Op. cit., i. 32, 184, &c.

[3] Medley, *Constitutional History* (Oxford, 1898), p. 99.

diplomatic work, some to serve on commissions, and others for political counsel. That an organic division on these lines should be made did not seem to the statesmen of the time either necessary or desirable. There is no doubt that the difference between the higher and the lower ranks of councillors was more strongly felt from the time of Edward IV. But even in the reign of Henry VIII, when 'ordinary councillors' are for the first time specifically mentioned,[1] the distinction was not drawn so clearly as some have understood. Prior to 1540 it appears only in a few individual cases, and in these it appears to have been made in an uncertain and tentative way. Moreover the history of the later period will show that the ordinary councillors are not the same as the judges and learned men who formed the outer circle of advisers during the middle ages. They are generally lawyers retained for the express purpose of hearing cases in the star chamber and the white hall, and of expediting other legal business; but unlike the judges, they are strictly members, individually sworn of the council, although they are not given the full rank and privileges of privy councillors. The ordinary council then represents not the line of division which separates the members from the judges, but a new line of division among the members themselves. Still beyond these are the judges and other learned men, who continue to bear their *ex-officio* relations to the council the same as before. This is emphatically stated by the chancellor in 1541, who then calls 'His Majesty's Counsellors of all sorts, spiritual and temporal, with the judges and learned men of his council'.[2] A fuller explanation of these and other features of the council of Henry VIII will be made in the last chapter of this work. The point is brought forward now only to show that the *consilium ordinarium*, either as a term in current usage or as a living conception, throughout the middle ages is entirely lacking in validity.

Probably a reason which lies behind all these futile assumptions is the feeling which exists in the modern mind, that a council, and especially a privy council, must needs be an homogeneous body. It is thought also that the language

[1] Nicolas, vii, pp. xvi, 49, 51, 60. [2] Nicolas, vii, p. xix.

used to describe the institution must be consistent, and still more must there be consistency in the usages of an established organ of state. In all this it is overlooked that the mediaeval mind did not seek definitions of this kind, and was not disturbed by the ill-adjustment of theories to facts. Moreover, it is mainly not the records of the council itself but the observations of divers outsiders that have caused this confusion. The council, it must be remembered, was not a court of record like the king's bench, which was bound by series of precedents both in word and action. The main fact, which takes away all reason for subdivision, is that the *consilium regis* unqualified by any adjective was inclusive and flexible enough to answer all the purposes required of the great council, the secret council, and the ordinary council. The only vital distinction of this kind which the middle ages really demanded was that between the parliament and the council. Here were two institutions of a common origin, which came to be positively differentiated both in organization and functions. Because of its length and importance, this phase of the subject must be reserved for a separate treatment.[1]

[1] Possibly another distinction of practical value should be mentioned in the growth of 'the council in chancery' apart from 'the council in star chamber', as it comes to be called. This phase also I shall deal with in its proper place.

PLATE IV

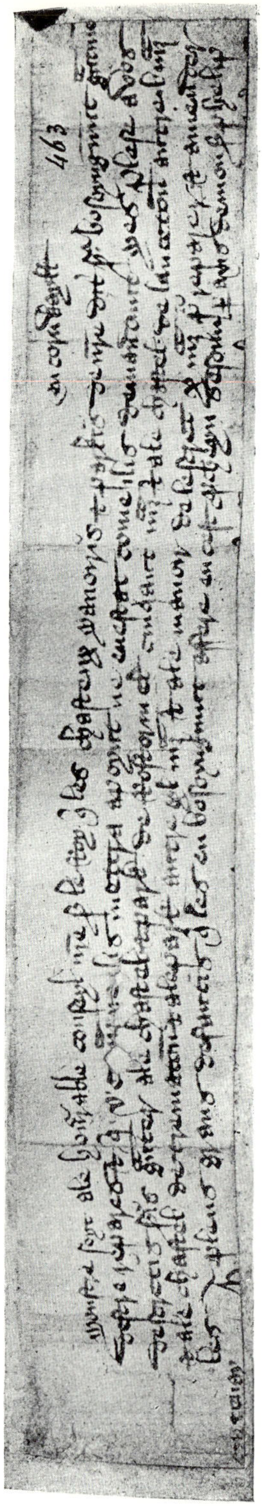

INFORMATION THAT THE KING'S CASTLES NEED REPAIR, SIGNED BY BISHOP COURTENAY, EARLY RIC. II.

CHAPTER VI

THE COUNCIL IN THE TIME OF RICHARD II

THE time of Richard II is generally regarded as one of marked transition and change in the history of the council. According to a current opinion this body then began to emerge as a separate institution. In view of the transformation that occurs, Stubbs has said, ' the privy council, from the reign of Richard II onwards, although it inherited and amplified the functions of the permanent council of Edward I, differed widely in its organization '.[1] What these changes of organization were, their connexion with the past, and their bearing upon the future, are matters requiring further explanation. Fortunately the consideration of the subject is greatly facilitated by the existence of evidence, in clearness and abundance, such as is not afforded during any previous period. This was due in part to the minority of the reigning king, when the council of necessity assumed the powers of a regency and emerged from its former obscurity. The controversies which were consequently waged in parliament over the conduct of the government brought the whole question of the organization and functions of the council into a fierce light of publicity. Powers were given to it, and powers were taken away, while definitions of all kinds were made more sharply than ever before. The rolls of parliament indeed are filled with illuminating references to the king's council, which was then prominently before the minds of all. Another reason why a study of the subject at this point becomes especially fruitful, is the fact that the records of the council itself, although they are by no means new, become considerably more plentiful. Some of these have been collected in the noted publication of ' the Proceedings and Ordinances of the Privy Council '. Even these are not all that remain. There is also a newly-found journal or register

A change of organization noticed.

[1] *Const. Hist.*, vol. ii, § 230, p. 284.

of the fifteenth and sixteenth years, besides many other notes and memoranda to which we shall have reason to refer.[1]

Attempts on the part of parliament to control the king's council certainly were no new thing. But the movements that had been made under Henry III, Edward II, and Edward III were spasmodic and ineffective in producing any permanent results. From these experiments, however, there had been learned a method of attack, which was now resumed with greater vigour and persistency. This policy was actually taken up before the close of the reign of Edward III, when the time seemed to be ripe for an examination and adjustment of the position of the council. A plan of reform was suggested by the 'Good Parliament' of 1376, and the same line of action was followed during the early years of Richard II. Again after a brief interval similar methods were taken up under Henry IV and under Henry VI with remarkable tenacity and effect. So that those years extending from the attempt of the Good Parliament in 1376 until 1437, the close of the latter king's minority, may be marked as a special period in the history of the council, a period when it was most under parliamentary pressure. The powers of parliament were exercised mainly in three ways: (1) by appointments and removals, (2) by judicial prosecutions, and (3) by regulative legislation. It will be seen that its actions taken together reveal a fairly consistent plan or conception of what the council should be. What this policy was and to what extent it was effective may now be explained.

A well-marked period, 1376–1437.

The Good Parliament, 1376.

Beginning with the events of 1376, there were abundant causes for a widespread discontent with the conduct of the aged king's government.[2] The recent military fiasco of the duke of Lancaster, a fruitless Spanish alliance, extraordinary expenditures, the domination of the household by John of Gaunt and Alice Perrers, rumours of the corruption of the king's councillors, all gave good grounds for the concerted attack which was made by lords and commons upon the entire management of the government. So definite a plan could not have been put forward without able leadership, and this for the moment was afforded by the Black Prince.

[1] Appendix II.

[2] Stubbs, *Const. Hist.* § 262.

Without mentioning most of the issues that were raised, the principal object now held in view was the reconstruction of the king's council. Although the sequence of events, as given by different authorities, is not perfectly clear, the first move towards the desired end appears to have been the punishment and removal of the most unpopular councillors. Just as had happened before, these were especially the officers and attendants of the royal household. The duke of Lancaster himself was much too powerful to be attacked, but the wrath of parliament was turned effectively upon several of his well-known supporters. Chief of these was Lord Latimer, who for the last seven years had been the king's chamberlain, and had wielded extraordinary influence in the distribution of royal grants.[1] In the noted impeachment which followed he was accused of taking bribes on many occasions; in one article particularly, it was said that at the time he was chamberlain and one of the privy council, he had procured patents and writs licensing the carriage of merchandise to other ports than Calais. He was convicted and imprisoned, and declared to be removed from all his offices and from the privy council, as some would have it, 'for all time'.[2] At the same time Richard Lyons, a merchant of London, was impeached upon charges of deceptions, extortions, and crimes committed 'when he was in attendance upon the household and council of the king', as well as when he was a collector of revenues. He was implicated with Latimer and others of the privy council in defrauding the king on one occasion of 10,000 marks, by negotiating a loan of 20,000 marks for which the king was afterwards obliged to pay 30,000 marks.[3] While these trials were being held, Lord Neville, the steward of the household, by seeking to intercede

[1] He was the fourth baron of his family, had held governorships in France, was warden of the forests beyond Trent in 1368, chamberlain of the household in 1369, and Constable of Dover Castle in 1374. Petitions to the king commonly passed through his hands, and some were addressed to him (Chap. XI, p. 284). There is also the petition of John Burdet, a monk, who makes complaint to the king and parliament that he has lost a suit because of the procurement and maintenance of Lord Latimer. *Record Trans.*, vol. 105, no. 6.

[2] *Rot. Parl.* ii. 325, 372.

[3] Ibid. 323; *Chron. Angl.* 78; Adams and Stephens, *Select Documents* (New York, 1901), no. 82.

in behalf of the accused men, drew an impeachment upon himself as well. It was charged that while he was an officer and a member of the council he had purchased of the king's creditors, presumably at a reduced price, tallies of assignment for which he afterwards received full payment at the exchequer.[1] Of the truth of these charges upon the face of the evidence, it is impossible now to judge. They can only be taken to show what was thought about the council at the time, and to bring into greater clearness the political position of a councillor. At all events in spite of the duke of Lancaster a certain group, which had hitherto been powerful, including Lord Latimer, Lord Neville, Sir Richard Stafford, Sir Richard Stury, and Lady Alice Perrers, were declared to be removed from their offices and the king's council.[2] A proposal of the commons that the officers and councillors convicted of fraud or deceit should never be restored, was answered that the king with the advice of his council would act according to each individual case.[3]

Proposals for a new council.

Proposals of a more constructive kind were made when the commons went on to demand that ' the council be strengthened with the presence of lords, prelates, and others to the number of ten or twelve, according to the will of the king '.[4] The words of this petition are very suggestive of the casual relations which the nobles had usually borne to the king's council. It was now requested that the ten or twelve lords should be appointed to ' remain continually ' ; in such wise that no great business should pass without the consent and advice of all, while matters of less account might be determined by the advice of six or four ; so that six or four of the councillors at least should always be in residence. To eliminate if possible all tendencies to corruption, it was insisted further that these men should be ' faithful, discreet, and free from bribes '. It is remarkable that the commons

[1] *Rot. Parl.* ii. 328.

[2] A narrative slightly different at certain points from that contained in the Rolls of Parliament is given in *Chronicon Angliae* (Rolls Series), p. lxvii ff. The chronicle is probably correct in placing the impeachments prior to the plan for a new council.

[3] *Rot. Parl.* ii. 322.

[4] Ibid. ; *Chron. Angl.*, p. lxxi ; another transcript of the chronicle is in *Archaeologia*, xxii. 212 ff.

did not ask for the appointment also of new officers. On this score something like a bargain was made, for the king accepted the proposals of parliament on the express condition that the chancellor, the treasurer, and the keeper of the privy seal should be free to perform the business of their offices without the presence of the council. This was a point of great weakness in the scheme, for without the co-operation of the ministers the council could hardly be an effective body. On the advice of many of the nobles, we are told that the king appointed the following nine lords as his 'continual councillors'; the archbishop of Canterbury, the bishops of London and Winchester, the earls of Arundel, March, and Stafford, lords Percy, Brian, and Beauchamp.[1] These together with the three great officers made the number twelve. Before the assembled parliament the duke of Lancaster declared what had been done, and the nine lords were accordingly sworn 'loyally to counsel and govern the king and the realm according to their powers'. For his part in the matter the duke was cordially thanked by the commons, who thought that the king's council was now sufficiently safeguarded.

Failure of the plan.

But a fatal mistake had been committed in the failure to give the duke of Lancaster an influence in the council that was at all commensurate with his actual power. The duke, as a chronicler hostile to him said, 'was not well satisfied but was sore grieved and vexed because he himself was not chosen to be of the king's council.' It is not likely, however, that the royal duke desired his own appointment so much as that of his partisans. This by his influence with the king he was immediately able to secure. No sooner had the parliament departed than he caused the removal of the lords recently appointed, 'commanding them to depart home to their houses, for the king had no more need of their counsel.' Lord Latimer and the other deposed councillors were restored, and even Alice Perrers was permitted to return to the court. Because of the complete reversal of all the plans of the Good Parliament, its acts have not been reputed

[1] The names are not given in the parliament roll, but are found in Harleian MS., no. 247, p. 143; *Archaeologia*, xxii. 239.

to have much practical value. Stubbs has said, 'it asserted some sound principles without being a starting-point of new history.' [1] But in view of the fact that in their attempts to control the council the parliaments of Richard II followed the same line of action, we venture to question whether the year 1376 may not be taken for this purpose as a starting-point.

Problem of the minority of Richard II.

With the accession of the young Richard II, in the light of the experience of two previous reigns of minority, it was certain that the council would be the ruling power in the state for the time. No special law or definition of a regency was considered to be necessary, as the government was conducted under the usual forms by authority of the king and council. The only question was whether the council should be left to the king's officers, with the more or less casual association of nobles, or whether it should be chosen and given definite responsibilities in parliament. In the first parliament which was speedily assembled, the commons rose to their opportunity, taking very much the same course of action as they had taken in the previous year. In a petition addressed to the king they asked that a sufficient number of persons *of the different estates* be ordained and named to be continual residents of the council together with the great officers.[2] They suggested the number seven, and apparently to guard against the danger of a settled oligarchy, they proposed that fresh elections should be held every year, and that none of the members now to be chosen should be re-eligible for two years. Other requirements concerning the faithfulness and incorruptibility of the councillors were repetitions of their actions in the year before. On July 17, 1377, the day after the coronation, the choice of the council, as made by the king 'on the advice of the lords of parliament', was announced. It was decided to have twelve councillors, including two bishops, two earls, two barons, two bannerets, and four knights, besides the king's ministers. For the first time the entire council was given a commission by letters patent,[3] and on July 20 the members were sworn in the king's presence. On this occasion the duke of Lancaster was

[1] *Const. Hist.* ii. 465.

[2] *Rot. Parl.* iii. 5–6.

[3] *Rot. Parl.* iii. 386; *Cal. Patent Rolls*, 1 Ric. II, 19.

The council of 1377.

more successful than he had been before in securing the appointment of several of his adherents, including Ralph Erghum his own chancellor. The list, in fact, was carefully drawn to include the partisans of the duke and his opponents in almost equal numbers.[1] Another important feature of the plan of this year was that most of the councillors, possibly all, should receive salaries for their services. During the previous reigns, it will be remembered there was no regular usage in this regard. Individual councillors had been remunerated, either by annuities, by daily wages, or by special payments, according to the king's favour. So that the present plan of a general system of salaries was a new departure, which was designed to overcome the difficulty that had always been experienced in holding a council of lords together. In the following list, which has been drawn up with the aid of the exchequer rolls,[2] it will be found that a few changes were made since the original appointments. Probably some of the men first chosen were unable to serve.

Adam Houghton, bishop of St. David's, chancellor, whose official salary was 500 *m.*
Henry Wakefield, bishop of Worcester, treasurer.
John Fordham, keeper of the privy seal.
The bishop of Carlisle with a salary of 400 *m.*
The bishop of London with a salary of 200*l.*
The earl of March, with 200*l.*
The earl of Stafford, with 200 *m.*
Lord Latimer (removed after 3 months), receiving 40*l.*
Lord Cobham (removed after 3 months), receiving 40*l.*
Richard Stafford, banneret, 200 *m.*
Roger Beauchamp, banneret (removed), 40 *m.*
Henry le Scrope, knight, 200 *m.*
Hugh Segrave, knight, at 6*s.* 8*d.* a day, for 340 days, 113*l.* 6*s.* 8*d.*[3]
John Devereux, knight, at 6*s.* 8*d.* a day.

---

[1] William Courtenay, bishop of London, was balanced by Ralph Erghum, bishop of Salisbury, and Lord Latimer by Lord Cobham. The two earls, Edmund of March and Richard of Arundel, represented the opponents of the duke, while Richard Stafford and Roger Beauchamp, bannerets, were his allies. The four knights were John Knyvet, Ralph Ferrers, John Devereux, and Hugh Segrave.

[2] *Issue Rolls*, 1 & 2 Ric. II, *passim*.

[3] Segrave's accounts in detail are found in *Accounts Exch. K. R.*, 96/14. It is stated that he received wages at the same rate as ' one other knight remaining in the council '. The other knight undoubtedly was Devereux.

The position of the justices, the barons of the exchequer and similar officials, who were no longer regarded as members of the council, was clearly set forth in a petition of the commons requesting that Magna Charta be confirmed, and that if any point be obscure it should be declared 'by those who shall be ordained to be of the continual council, with the advice of the justices and serjeants-at-law and other such men, whom they shall see fit to summon '.[1]

When the parliament met again in the following October, there was another outbreak against the duke of Lancaster, so that the removal of several of his friends from the council was required. Lord Latimer was disqualified from further service by a resolution 'that none being duly deprived out of the council in the time of Edward III be any more restored to be about the king's person '.[2] But Richard Stafford, although he fell equally under the same enactment, was permitted to remain. At the same time Lord Cobham and Roger Beauchamp ceased to serve, and it is possible that still other changes were made. The council was then sworn again in the presence of the lords. A proposal that the officers and councillors should receive their charges and have their commission declared before the commons, was not acted upon.[3]

Of the actual work of this council we have no information from any specific records. There is no doubt, however, that with the inducements of salaries and great power the members actually carried on the government according to their commission. They were considered, indeed, to have served until October 30, 1378. This is the first time in fact that a council appointed under pressure of the barons can be said to have been held together even for a year.

A second council named in November 1378.

In the parliament which met at Gloucester during the following month of November, the commons returned to the subject of the council with a request that they might know the names of such as were to be the king's great officers and councillors.[4] They were answered that the king would select as pleased him, but of the names the commons should be

[1] *Rot. Parl.* iii. 15.
[2] Ibid. 16.
[3] Ibid. 7, 14.
[4] Ibid. 35–6.

informed. But as the parliament of Gloucester ended abruptly, the names were not announced, nor were they placed upon the parliament roll. For this omission apologies were made to the commons at their next meeting. Nevertheless a council was said to have been 'chosen with the assent of the prelates and magnates at the parliament of Gloucester'. As the names of the councillors do not appear upon the rolls of parliament, they can be ascertained only from the statements of their wages in the exchequer. In the list of names which follows, it will be observed that, according to one of the resolutions of the first parliament, no member of the previous council was permitted to serve again. Under the complete change which was now brought about, the choice fell upon a body of men who were personally by no means so strong as those who were displaced. This time also the unusual experiment was tried of making all payments to the councillors by daily wages, instead of by salaries, bishops and earls receiving two marks a day, bannerets one mark, and knights half a mark. This method had the advantage of requiring from the lords strict statements of their services, and from these we judge that they were by no means lax in their attendance. The list, so far as it can now be put together,[1] is as follows:

	Rate of Wages.	*Days of Service.*	*Amounts received.*		
	m.		*l.*	*s.*	*d.*
Richard lord Scrope, chancellor.					
Thomas Brantingham, bishop of Exeter, treasurer.					
John Fordham, keeper of the privy seal.					
The bishop of Winchester	2	276	368	0	0
The bishop of Bath	2	278	370	13	4
The earl of Arundel	2	155	206	13	4
The earl of Suffolk	2	171	228	0	0
Robert Hales, Prior of the Hospital of St. John's, Jerusalem, banneret	1	238	158	13	4
Roger Beauchamp, banneret	1	277	184	13	4
Aubrey de Vere, knight	$\frac{1}{2}$	113	37	13	4
Robert Rous, knight	$\frac{1}{2}$	80	27	0	0

[1] *Issue Roll*, 3 Ric. II. There may, of course, have been others whose names are not found here.

Attack of parliament, January 1380.

This council also was successful in the bare endeavour to live out its term. Apparently it was permitted to serve a little more than a year, until the meeting of a parliament which opened in January 1380. In a speech the chancellor then said it was due that they should render an account of their stewardship. He explained that on their first meeting they had found that there were no funds in the treasury, that for the purpose of the war they had been compelled to contract loans, and even to pawn the crown jewels. They were still £22,000 in arrears and therefore asked for further supplies. These words were heard by the commons with anger, and they immediately asked that the lords of the continual council be entirely discharged, and that no such councillors be longer retained about the king. In disgust with the entire system of elective councils, they asked that only the five great officers be chosen in parliament, saying, with doubtful correctness, that at the beginning of the reign the king had no other councillors than these.[1]

Relapse of the parliamentary plan.

From this time for several years, parliament gave up the idea of securing the appointment of a council, trying instead other methods of controlling the government. Already in 1379 the commons, in their distrust of the council, had secured the appointment of a commission to examine the condition of the king's household.[2] Again such a commission was asked for in the parliament of 1380,[3] and at the same time an important petition, instead of being referred to the council, was given to a special commission for consideration.[4] In personnel these commissions closely resembled the elective councils. They differed materially from the councils in that they were appointed only for certain specific purposes. Since the duties of the commissioners were the more quickly and easily performed, the lords showed more willingness to serve in this capacity than the other. In the same year also

[1] *Rot. Parl.* iii. 71–3.

[2] Ibid. 57. This commission included several of the lords and knights appointed to the council in 1377. There were the archbishop of Canterbury, the bishops of London and Rochester, the earls of March, Warwick, and Stafford, Lord Latimer, Guy Brian or John Cobham, and Roger Beauchamp. Walsingham, *Historia Anglicana* (Rolls Series), i. 447–8; *Chron. Angl.*, 210, 278, 281.

[3] *Rot. Parl.* iii. 73.

[4] Ibid. 79.

an attack was made on Sir Ralph Ferrers, a member of the council, who was accused of sending treasonable letters revealing state secrets to the French.[1] But when the incriminating letters were examined by a judicial committee in parliament, they were found to be forgeries and Ferrers was exonerated.

After the terrors of the peasants' revolt in 1381, the commons renewed its attacks on the government, and returned to the subject of the council. 'And for God's sake,' they urged, 'let it not be forgotten that there be put about the king and of his council the best lords and knights that can be found in the kingdom.'[2] Instead of a council, however, the king granted that a committee of inquiry should be appointed to investigate abuses and to suggest remedies. The commissioners, we are told, sat several days *en prive conseil*.[3] As a further concession it was announced to the commons that the earl of Arundel and Sir Michael de la Pole 'were elected, ordained, and sworn to be about the person of the king in his household, to counsel and govern him'.[4] They were expected to counteract the influence of such men as Sir Simon Burley, the king's tutor, and Robert de Vere, who was already pointed out as a royal favourite.[5] But without the continued pressure of parliament, the tendency was for the council to fall back into its former grooves, while the lords as a rule were summoned and were present only on occasion.[6] Sir Michael de la Pole, a royalist at heart, in

[1] Ferrers had been a prominent soldier in the war, had participated in the battle of Poitiers, and had been made captain of Calais. In 1370 he was one of the admirals, and in 1376 he appears as one of the 'mainpernors' of Lord Latimer. He was therefore identified with the adherents of the court, and for this reason probably the present attack was made upon him. *Rot. Parl.* iii. 90, 93.

[2] Ibid. 100.

[3] Ibid. 101.

[4] Ibid. 104. 'And this time, king Richard made the erlle of Oxenforde and ser Michael de la Pole and othir flaterers chief of his counsel and be thaym was governed.' *Eng. Chron.* (Camden Soc.), p. 3.

[5] Burley had been a trusted servant of the Black Prince, and held many minor offices. In 1380 he was known as a 'knight of the king's chamber', and was one of a commission to treat for the king's marriage. In 1381 he was under-chamberlain of the household, and in 1383 was Constable of Dover Castle. His loyalty to Richard during the stormy events of 1386 afterwards cost him his life.

[6] There are plenty of instances when small groups of lords were invited to come to the council. On one occasion messages of this kind were sent to the archbishop of Canterbury, the bishops of Winchester, Durham, and

1383 was made the king's chancellor, and was allied with de Vere, earl of Oxford, and Simon Burley in holding a short-lived ascendancy. Certain minor men of the household also enjoyed a similar patronage. In 1384, a chronicler opposed to the court declares that the king in a certain affair consulted 'not the lords, not the peers of the realm, nor those who were strong in the kingdom, but his accustomed counsellors, namely, two clerks of his chapel'.[1] During all these years there is no lack of evidence as to the constant activity and power of the council in appointments to office and all other matters of government.[2] It was only a question as to which interests should dominate. It was generally believed that the duke of Lancaster, through his numerous adherents, still exercised an undue amount of influence, and this was the basis for most of the attacks which were made upon individual councillors. In 1385 again the commons asked to know who were to be the king's principal officers, but they were answered that the king had sufficient officers and would change them when he pleased.[3] In another petition the commons asked to be informed as to the lords who were to be ordained of the council, and in answer instead of a comprehensive list, they were given the names only of the bishops of Winchester and Exeter, and two bannerets.[4]

The impeachment of Suffolk, 1386.

The growing tension between the court party and the baronage brought matters to a crisis in the noted parliament of 1386. All the efforts which had been made in former years for controlling the king's government were now renewed and further extended. With the encouragement of the lords, especially the duke of Gloucester and the earl of

Rochester, the duke of Lancaster, the earls of Buckingham and Arundel, and others. *Issue Roll*, 5 Ric. II, Mich., &c. Again, a record of October 4, 1383, notes the presence of the archbishop of Canterbury, the bishops of London, Winchester, Worcester, Bath, Hereford, the three officers, the earl of Arundel, Lords Roos and Furnival, Masters Genant and Savage.

[1] Walsingham, ii. 113.

[2] In 1381 it was provided in parliament that no grant of land, marriage, wardship, or escheat should be made without the assent of the lords and others of the council, until the king was free of debt and war charges. *Rot. Parl.* iii. 115.

[3] Ibid. 213. Furthermore the commons asked that no grants be made from the king's revenues for a year.

[4] Ibid. 213–14. There may have been others, but the roll at this point is damaged.

Arundel, the commons began the attack by asking for the removal of the chancellor and the treasurer. This the king bluntly refused to do, making reply that at such a request he would not dismiss even a servant of his kitchen. But after it was hinted that his deposition was possible, he became more amenable to this demand. The commons then proceeded to the impeachment of the chancellor Michael de la Pole, now earl of Suffolk.[1] Among the numerous articles, making charges of every conceivable kind, as usual great stress was laid upon the misuse of the grants of the crown. In detail it was stated that while the earl was one of the privy council and sworn thereto, he had accepted or purchased great estates of the king below their real value, an act which would be a direct violation of the councillor's oath. In answer to the murmurs that he was a merchant and the son of a merchant, his brother-in-law, Sir Richard le Scrope, referred to his creditable career in war and peace, declaring that he 'had long been a privy councillor and chancellor, and that he possessed the property necessary for the support of that rank which was next to the rank of an earl'. Some of the accusations were preposterous certainly, and others were lacking in proof; but the desired end was accomplished when the lords convicted him on three counts, while as to the rest they said that since his guilt was shared by others of the council the earl should not be condemned alone.[2]

A new parliamentary council.

Having been successful in driving the ministers from office, the commons went on in the same manner as before to require the appointment of a group of lords and knights 'to be of the king's great and continual council'. The lords and knights whose names were then announced were the two archbishops, the duke of York, the duke of Gloucester, the bishops of Winchester and Exeter, the abbot of Waltham, the earl of Arundel, lord Cobham, Sir Richard le Scrope, and Sir John Devereux, who were to act in conjunction with the usual three great officers.[3] It will be seen that the influence of

[1] Ibid. 216 ff.; Knighton, cc. 2681, 2682; Stubbs, § 266.
[2] *Rot. Parl.* iii. 219.
[3] Bishop Arundel of Ely was made chancellor, and Bishop Gilbert of Hereford treasurer.

the duke of Lancaster, though no longer predominant, was by no means eliminated. These lords were to have not only the usual powers of a council, but also those of an extraordinary commission, as was immediately set forth in extended letters patent.[1] For this reason they have been called 'the commission council', although it was by no means the first time that a council had been appointed by letters patent. In this statement of their duties, the council was to examine the condition of the king's household and to amend all faults found therein, to inquire into the revenues and expenditures, to enter the courts, to compel the production of rolls and other evidences, and to hear complaints which cannot be redressed and terminated by the ordinary course of law. Lest the members of the council be changed in any way, it was declared further that no other persons should be associated with or assigned to this body; and if the lords in any way should be prevented from carrying out their duties, the validity of all grants should cease. Moreover, no person of whatever estate or condition should privily or openly give the king counsel contrary to the terms of the commission under grievous penalty. Finally the provisions of the commission were given the validity of a statute, and when the council at length was sworn to execute their powers, it seemed as though the resources of parliament were exhausted in the efforts to secure the success of the plan.

Failure of the council of 1386.

There is not lacking evidence that the members of this council made an attempt to carry out the terms of their commission.[2] Yet it is familiar history that every effort of the kind was thwarted by the king and his so-called 'false councillors'. They immediately advised the king that if he yielded to the insurrection of the lords he might expect to be king only in name, while they enjoyed the power. Of these false or evil councillors, as they were called, there were six who were given special notoriety.[3] Archbishop Neville, though he was a member of the commission, remained

[1] *Rot. Parl.* iii. 221; *Statutes of the Realm*, ii. 39–42; *Cal. Patent Rolls*, 10 Ric. II, 244.

[2] The first page of Nicolas contains the points of the commission in a series of articles which one would take for an *agenda*. *Proceedings*, i. 3.

[3] Stubbs, *Const. Hist.* ii. § 266.

at court to encourage the king in his policy of resistance. Robert de Vere, now duke of Ireland, the earl of Suffolk, and Sir Simon Burley, old favourites, returned. Nicholas Brember, an ex-mayor of London, was identified with a party in the city which supported the struggle for absolutism, while chief justice Tressilian presided over a court which declared the commission unlawful and contrary to the prerogative of the crown. Of their actions further the most that we know is contained in the appeals of treason and the charges that were afterwards on their impeachment made against them. It was then declared that by false covin they had not suffered the magnates of the realm nor the good councillors to approach the king or to speak with him; that they caused the king to remove himself to distant parts so that the lords appointed could not counsel him; and that they had wrongfully procured the decision of the justices against the validity of the commission.[1] It is also made clear that the king caused other men to be sworn as councillors. One of these was John Blake, an apprentice-at-law, against whom this charge was made on his impeachment. The fact Blake himself admitted, but claimed that the king had a right so to retain him.[2]

One more attempt by parliament, 1388.

After a series of impeachments and condemnations, which were carried through with vengeance in the 'Merciless Parliament' of 1388, the lords and commons essayed once more to provide for the selection of a continual council. On the initiative of the commons it was enacted with severe penalties that no person of whatsoever estate or condition, except those assigned and ordained in the present parliament, should interfere with the government in any way, unless it be by order of the continual council and with the assent of the king. The officers and councillors were required to swear especially that they would not suffer any act of that parliament to be annulled, reversed, or repealed.[3] Who

[1] *Rot. Parl.* iii. 232, 376.

[2] Ibid. 240. Besides those already named there were Robert Belknap, Roger Fulthorp, John Holt, William Burgh, justices of the common pleas; John Cary, chief baron of the exchequer, John Lockton, serjeant-at-law, and Thomas Usk, who were connected with the court declaring the commission unlawful.

[3] Ibid. 246, 258.

were the members of this council was not formally announced. But it is well understood that the five 'lords appellant', Gloucester, Arundel, Warwick, Derby, and Nottingham, who had been the leaders of the barons in making the charges of treason, were given a predominant place. For a brief interval, then, they controlled the grants of the crown, and for their own use they did not hesitate to require the enormous allowance of £20,000 out of the subsidy for that year.[1] By another turn of events their career was shortly interrupted, when on May 3, 1389, the king entered the council chamber and declared himself of age, saying if the chronicle be correct, 'I will call whom I will to the council.'[2] The aforesaid lords were said to have been then removed, and at the same time a new chancellor was appointed in the person of William of Wykeham.

Aspect of the council after 1389.

With the close of the period of the king's minority the history of the council is now to be followed during the mature years of Richard, with reference both to the effectiveness of the influence of parliament and the changes produced by the personal policy of the king. At first the changes certainly were not so sweeping or so abrupt as the words of the chronicler just quoted seem to imply. If the attendance at the council during the thirteenth year, 1389–90, be followed,[3] as can easily be done, it will be found that the influence of the previous régime still continues in considerable strength. The duke of Gloucester shortly returns, while as many as eight other lords who had served in previous councils, and four of the lords appellant are prominently in evidence. At one meeting in 1390 the councillors expressed their fear of parliament more than of the king, when they refused and could not be persuaded to accede to a proposed expenditure, lest in the first parliament it should be imputed to them that they had burdened the kingdom with a larger sum of money than was necessary or honest.[4] Something like the former parliamentary methods were revived in the same year, when the chancellor, the treasurer, and all the lords of the council were constrained to resign their places, in order that charges

[1] *Rot. Parl.* iii. 248.
[2] Walsingham, ii. 181.
[3] Nicolas, i, *passim.*
[4] Ibid. 12c, 17.

might be brought against them.[1] As the commons declared there was no fault to be found, they were immediately re-appointed and re-sworn in parliament, the king protesting that this action should not be taken as a precedent. At the same time a series of ordinances, 'for the governance of the council',[2] embodied in succinct form and with certain extensions many of the regulations that had been enacted before. Whether these ordinances were ever passed by parliament is not clear, but they were evidently forced upon the king by the parliamentary party. The hand of the Gloucester faction in particular is seen in the requirement that no gift or grant to the decrease of the king's profit should be made without the advice of the council and the individual consent of the dukes of Lancaster, York, and Gloucester, and the chancellor, or two of them. This article alone is sufficient to account for all the subsequent contention between the king and the barons. The control of the grants of the crown was indeed the most valued power of the government. If it fell in this wise to the council, the barons were easily supreme; and if it was taken from the king, he was virtually reduced to the position of a minor. The aim of the lords plainly was to take the government completely out of the king's hands. As was expressed further, 'the king should give full credence to the council in all things touching the government, and suffer them to govern duly, without commanding them by message or letter anything to the contrary.'[3] In matters of law or litigation, it was said, he should not in person interfere at all. Another article having a political bearing was that all members of the council should receive payments, the lords 'according to their rank and expenses', or in other words, salaries, the 'bachelors' by reasonable wages for their time.[4] Since the experiment of

Ordinances of 1390.

[1] *Rot. Parl.* iii. 258. The keeper of the privy seal, or 'clerk' as he was still commonly called, was not held to the same political responsibility as the other officers. In 1379 John Fordham was permitted to remain in office although all the other councillors were changed. On the present occasion the keeper was not required to resign, as did all his colleagues. Again, nearly the same thing was true after the revolution of 1399.

[2] Nicolas, i. 18a.

[3] The date of this enactment is uncertain, but it must have been in 1392 or shortly afterwards. Ibid. 84.

[4] Ibid. 18b.

the second year, in fact, the system of salaries and wages for attendance at the council had quite broken down. All these events of the year 1390 are characteristic of the period commonly known as that of Richard's constitutional government.

Royalist influences.

But just as had happened before, the plans of the barons were brought to naught by the opposite influence exerted by the king and his ministers in the management of the council. This royal policy in some ways shows a reversion to the usages of Edward III. For one thing, as an offset to the power of the older nobles, Richard added many new men, so that the membership of the council, which parliament had reduced to twelve or fifteen, immediately became larger. At one meeting of the thirteenth year, there were twenty-one present,[1] while during the year as many as thirty-four councillors of all ranks may be counted. Of these a larger proportion than before were officers and knights, whose usefulness was plainly enhanced. Beside the traditional officers of the household, the under-chamberlain was now given a place. On one occasion a series of ordinances was passed by the king in the presence of a council of thirteen, seven of whom were of knightly rank.[2] At another time may be noted the presence of the master of the rolls, and again that of a baron of the exchequer. Altogether, it is true, there were not so many men as belonged to the council of Edward III. But again it is found that, with less participation on the part of the nobles, the work of the council came to depend mainly upon the men of minor estate. In the matter of salaries and wages, the ordinance of 1390, requiring the equitable payment of all members, was quite ignored, while the king's policy again was to give rewards only in special cases, and with greater generosity to the men of lower rank. To some of these, reviving a practice of his predecessor, he even granted life annuities. Of the men who served most constantly in the king's council at this time, we will give a few examples.

Prominent councillors.

Among the knights who rose in the king's service the most prominent at this time was Sir Edward Dalynrigg.

[1] Nicolas, i. 17.

[2] Ibid. 6.

He had formerly been a friend of John of Gaunt, and a member of parliament for Sussex.[1] He was brought into the council in the thirteenth year, where he served steadily for the following four years, without apparently holding any other office. For his attendance he was granted a life annuity of one hundred marks, besides wages at the rate of ten shillings a day.[2] How industrious a councillor he was is shown by his accounts at the exchequer, which state that from January 8 of the fifteenth year to February 21 of the sixteenth year he served 207 days. He appears sometimes to have attended the king in his peregrinations about the country, while upon the council records no name appears more frequently than his. For his good service in continually attending the council, as a mark of favour, he received also a grant of two tuns of red Gascon wine each year.[3] Sir Richard Stury was a knight of the king's chamber who had first gained prominence under the patronage of John of Gaunt. He was known under Edward III as a councillor 'intimate with the king', was reputed to be a supporter of the Lollards, and had been called 'a liar and a sower of sedition'. He was one of the courtiers especially assailed and removed by the Good Parliament in 1376. After a period of retirement, he returned to the council of Richard II about 1390. During the following five years he was rewarded with grants of £100 a year, ten shillings a day, and two tuns of wine just as Dalynrigg was.[4] Sir Lewis Clifford was another experienced knight of the king's household, likewise a patron of the Lollards, who received an annuity of 100 marks since the thirteenth year.[5] Upon the various com-

[1] He had served in the expeditions of Edward III, in the retinue of the earl of Arundel; was one of the commissioners of inquiry appointed in 1380, was a member for Sussex in the parliament of 1386, in 1390 was one of a commission to conclude a truce with France, and in 1392 when the mayor and sheriffs of London were arrested, he was temporarily governor of the city. Nicolas, *De Controversia Scrope vs Grosvenor* (1832), ii. 370; Armitage-Smith, *John of Gaunt* (Westminster, 1904), 137.

[2] Nicolas, i. 8; *Accounts Exch. K. R.*, 96/1.

[3] *Cal. Patent Rolls*, 15 Ric. II, 37.

[4] In the sixteenth year he is recorded as attending the council at London for 159 consecutive days, and in the eighteenth year for seven months. *Issue Roll* (*Pells*), 16 Ric. II, Mich., m. 18; 18 Ric. II, Easter, m. 22; *Cal. Patent Rolls*, 15 Ric. II, 37.

[5] Nicolas, *Scrope vs Grosvenor*, ii. 427; *Issue Roll* (*Pells*), 14 Ric. II,

missions and committees no men were employed more constantly than these knights. They represent indeed a type of skilled men such as were rapidly being trained in the work of the council. Since the reign of Edward III the presence of a foreigner is rarely found, but this occurs in the case of Master Peregrino de Fano, a doctor of laws from Aquitaine, who in 1394 was summoned by the king to attend the council and was sent as an envoy to treat for peace with the king of France. For this he received a fee of forty pounds.[1]

Acts of the council, 1392–3.

Concerning the conduct of the council at this time we are given full information by the fortunate discovery of a record, which gives its proceedings day by day during the fifteenth and sixteenth years.[2] In this remarkable register it is apparent that the bureaucratic tendencies heretofore visible were even more strongly accentuated. In the carefully made record of attendance it is shown that most of the time only the officers together with one or more of the knights did duty as a council. Often three, four, or five were a sufficient number. A few of the clergy, like the bishops of Winchester, Durham, and Chester were more faithful in this regard than the lay lords. Lesser lords, like Cobham and Lovell, appear with less frequency than the bishops. But the great lords apparently, unless there was a personal interest at stake, came only on occasions of special summons. Of the issue of such writs of summons under the privy seal we are given abundant evidence.[3] It is thus made perfectly clear, as has been suggested before, how completely the great councils, as known under the Edwards, had become assimilated to the privy council of Richard II. Whether it is called a great council or a privy council, the writs, records, and methods of procedure were the same. A notable council of this kind, at which more than a score of lords and bishops were present

Mich., m. 14 ; 15 Ric. II, m. 23. He had fought in the battle of St. George in 1352, and had served in several subsequent campaigns in Aquitaine, Spain, and Scotland. In 1385 he was commanded to remain in attendance upon the king's mother, and was one of the ambassadors to France in 1390. He was known as one of the 'king's knights', and in 1398 was made a knight of the Garter.

[1] *Issue Roll* (*Pells*), 17 Ric. II, Mich., December 3.

[2] Appendix II.

[3] Messengers were sent forth with the writs and paid. *Issue Rolls, passim.*

besides the usual officers, was assembled February 12, 1392.[1] It was then decided to send a commission to treat with France for peace. At the same time either as a threat or in fear lest peace might not be obtained, it was also ordained that the usual writs to mobilize troops for war should be issued, and that ships should be assembled for transportation. In the same council, it is worthy of notice, the lords made to the king *en sa main* a solemn assurance of loyalty, agreeing to do nothing against the king, against each other, or against the people in any way contrary to law, and to compel each other to seek redress only by lawful means. For the assurance of the lords Richard on his part promised on the word of a king that he would do no harm to any lord or other of his subjects for anything which had been done before. Furthermore, with reference to the impeachments of former years, he declared it was not his intention to restore to his realm any person who had been judged in full parliament. These pacific words hardly conceal the underlying distrust that was felt on both sides, and they may be taken as a premonition of the strife yet to come.

A great council at Eltham, 1395.

Another session of the council, at which most of the great lords were present, was held on July 22, 1395. On this occasion we are fortunate in possessing not only the official statements of the clerk of the council, but an elaborate description by the chronicler Froissart as well.[2] The description is worth repeating for what it reveals on various important points. The question to be determined was concerning the government of Gascony, whether a new charter given by the duke of Lancaster as governor of the province should be valid against an earlier charter of Edward III. The charter of Edward was regarded as a more favourable statement of the liberties of the province. That the matter might be discussed, the king, we are told, summoned the principal barons and prelates to meet in the palace at Eltham. The king arrived on Tuesday, the chronicler says, and the lords by the following Thursday. First certain deputies from Gascony brought

[1] Appendix II, p. 493.

[2] Appendix II; Froissart, *Chroniques*, Book IV, chaps. lxiii–lxv. The chronicle gives the year as 1394, and this date has been followed by Armitage-Smith. But the record of the council and the patent rolls are explicit in reference to the year 1395.

their credentials and the letters patent of King Edward as well as a copy of an agreement made by the duke of Lancaster, in which he mentions the oath of the king to preserve the privileges of Gascony. Likewise two knights came in behalf of the duke of Lancaster and submitted the evidence on their side. All writings were first given to a group of clerks who were to investigate the matter and give their advice the next day. The great meeting or 'parliament', as Froissart calls it, began on Thursday morning at eight o'clock, 'in the presence of the king, his uncles, and the council.' At the command of the king the chancellor formally charged the five clerks and doctors of law, who had considered the question, that they should inform the king and the lords of the council whether the royal grant to the duke of Lancaster,[1] and therefore the duke's charter to Aquitaine, should remain in force or not. Thereupon the clerks individually said, that inasmuch as King Edward by his letters patent to the city of Bordeaux had declared the town annexed to the crown of England, with the promise that the city should not be granted to any one but the heir to the throne, and had also sworn to uphold these privileges, it was their opinion that the present king was bound to revoke the grant made to the duke of Lancaster. Then all the lords, being asked for their opinion—*examinez sur celle partie*—expressed their agreement with the opinion of the clerks. But the duke of Gloucester, who is inclined to be favourable to his brother's claim, assented only on condition that the aforesaid grant and oath of Edward III should be proved as a matter of record. He urged further that the deputies of the duke should be heard in the matter, and in this proposal he was seconded by the earl of Derby. What happened in this debate Froissart describes more fully than the record. He says that when the lords were asked what answer should be made, they seemed at first afraid to speak. The bishops wished to refer the question to two royal

[1] It should be made clear that the validity of the duke of Lancaster's charter to Aquitaine, which was the real issue, hinged upon the nature of the powers vested in him. Hence the discussion bore upon the validity of Richard's grant made to the duke in 1390. See *Foedera* (Orig. Ed.), vii. 659–63.

dukes who were present, Gloucester and York, but the dukes at first excused themselves, saying that the matter should be deliberated in common. So that for a time no opinion was expressed. The duke of Gloucester at length, being desired to speak, said that it would be a strong measure to annul a grant which had been made with the unanimous consent of the council, and he favoured upholding the position of his brother the duke of Lancaster. Some commented on this speech, while others had not the courage to say the answer was unreasonable, 'for the duke of Gloucester was much feared.' The earl of Derby, son of the duke of Lancaster, added, 'good uncle, you have spoken and justly explained the matter and I support what you have said.' After this the council began to separate and the members to murmur one to another, but they did not call in the envoys again. While the discussion was going on in small groups, Gloucester accompanied by the earl of Derby went to the dining-room, where the duke of York soon joined them. After dinner the duke of Gloucester took leave of the king, and mounting his horse rode away to London. What was done by the council in the afternoon, we are not informed, except that the deputies from Aquitaine were unable to obtain any answer to their petitions. By Sunday the whole council had gone away except the duke of York and Sir Richard Stury, who remained with the king. It was then that Froissart, who was interested in these proceedings but had not been admitted to hear them, approached his old friend, 'that ancient and valiant knight,' Sir Richard Stury, and asked him what had been done. 'Having mused awhile (Stury) said he would tell me, for it was not worth while to conceal what must shortly be made public.' Undeterred by his oath of secrecy, says Froissart, 'Stury told me everything word for word as I have written it.'

Minute work of the council.

But the everyday work of the council, as the aforesaid journal shows, was not concerned with great questions of policy, so much as with innumerable matters of detail in administration and jurisdiction. There were rewards for services to the crown, and remissions of payments at the exchequer. Likewise there were a great many minor ordinances concerning customs, exports, and other matters of commerce. An ordinance which must have had far-reaching consequences in respect of the wool trade was passed on February 13, 1392. Although a statute of 1390 had declared the staple removed from Calais to England, this ordinance permitted English merchants to pass with their wool to Calais without paying the duties in England, provided they found security for their payments later at Calais. Under these conditions the wool might be exported without coming to the towns or cities determined by parliament, while several towns were added to the list of licensed ports. The tendency of the council to alter the statutes and to make ordinances beyond what was intended by acts of parliament, had been a matter of complaint in the parliament of 1390; but the practice nevertheless was not visibly checked. A still greater cause of solicitude in the same quarter was felt concerning the judicial activities of the council. The commission of 1386 and the ordinance of 1390 already contained warnings in this regard. But the pages of the journal and other records have only to be turned to show that the extra-legal methods of the council were fully developed and that they were now extensively used in defiance of the principles of the common law. Because of their technical character these methods will be explained in a separate chapter. They are mentioned here only as one of the causes of friction between the king and parliament, which soon brought the reign to a revolutionary end.

The period of absolutism, 1397–9.

The last two years of the reign, from 1397 to 1399, are known as the period of Richard's absolutism.[1] The assertion of this policy has generally been represented as denoting an abrupt change on the part of the king, that was the result possibly of a stroke of insanity. It is thought too that his marriage with the daughter of Charles VI of France may have had an influence. But the history of the council shows that there were marked tendencies in this direction for many years before, and that these were at length brought to the surface. The policy is also explained as springing from the personal initiative of the king, but his councillors

[1] Stubbs, *Const. Hist.* ii. § 268.

were implicated to such an extent that we cannot tell who was most the originator of it. Behind the king's absolutism there was a bureaucracy of the household that the nobles had been vainly seeking to suppress. After a series of provocations both sides were now goaded to extreme measures. In fact there was every reason to believe that the barons were planning a new attempt to place the government in the hands of a commission. In a fury of alarm Richard forestalled them by striking the first blow which suddenly fell in 1397. The duke of Gloucester was arrested and secretly put to death,[1] Arundel and Warwick were tried and condemned, and Hereford and Norfolk were afterwards driven into exile.[2] Thus the king succeeded for the moment in breaking up the group of nobles, who had sometimes actually controlled and at other times had powerfully influenced the government during the past ten years. It is well known also that certain new members of the council, entering into communications with the sheriffs, to a great extent controlled the ensuing elections, so that the house of commons was made completely subservient to the wishes of the king. All the petitions then before the parliament were placed in the hands of a committee, while the bishops and barons were required to swear that they would repeal nothing that had been done. With the power of parliament thus brought to nought, the government then rested entirely with the king and council.

Councillors of the period.

The chronicles of the time generally speak of Richard's councillors as enemies of the law, and it is customary still to regard them as indulging in a public policy of a most fatuous kind. It is fair to observe, however, that the king's supporters were not a body of adventurers, much less were they *novi homines* or mere personal favourites. As a rule they were men of experience and ability, some of them younger sons of good families, who had taken positions in the royal household, and had gained advancement from one office to another. The chancellor of the time was Edmund Stafford, son of Sir Richard, who had been keeper of the

[1] That Gloucester's death was positively planned by Richard and announced before the event has been demonstrated by Professor Tait, *Owens College Essays* (Manchester, 1902), 193 ff.

[2] *Rot. Parl.* iii. 350 ff., 377 ff.; Stubbs, *Const. Hist.* § 268.

privy seal since 1389, bishop of Exeter since 1394, and in 1396 was raised to his present position. More aggressive in the assertion of the present policy was William le Scrope, also of a noted family, who had held one office after another since the later years of Edward III. He had served in the council since 1390, was under-chamberlain in 1393, and two years later chamberlain of the household. As the spokesman of the court party, although he was not himself a baron, he made the appeal of treason against Gloucester, Arundel, and Warwick, and soon as earl of Wiltshire he was granted many of the forfeited estates.[1] In 1398 he was made treasurer and served on the committee to terminate the business of parliament. In the lively events which follow, no one was more closely concerned than he. Master Richard Clifford, who was possibly a son of Sir Lewis Clifford, was a king's clerk who rose from a minor position to be keeper of the wardrobe in 1397, and later in the same year to be keeper of the privy seal. Sir Thomas Percy, a younger son of the noted Northumberland family, had been steward of the household since 1392, and is frequently mentioned in the proceedings of the council from that time. He took the king's part actively in the parliament of 1398, serving particularly on the committee to answer all petitions. In the same year he was given a higher rank and title as earl of Worcester. Another man who was especially identified with the policy of these years was Guy Mone, a king's clerk, who for his services in the government had been rewarded with various church preferments. In 1397 he was made treasurer and at the same time bishop of St. David's. The treasurership he gave up during the next year, but he continued to be a member of the council to the end of the reign. Besides an annuity of 100 marks he received as a councillor wages at twenty shillings a day for 164 days during the twenty-first year, and in the twenty-second year the same for 128 days.[2]

Among the great lords the duke of York, as a rival to his brother the late duke of Gloucester, stood by the king.

[1] *Dict. National Biog.*; Nicolas, *Scrope vs Grosvenor*, ii. 40.

[2] *Cal. Patent Rolls*, 21 Ric. II, 288; *Issue Rolls* (*Pells*), 21 Ric. II, Mich., m. 16; 22 Ric. II, Easter, m. 11.

There were also the duke of Albemarle, the duke of Exeter, the duke of Surrey, and the earl of Wiltshire, whose exalted titles were newly granted. As was usually the case, none of the magnates received salaries as councillors, although they were rewarded conspicuously in other ways.[1] The estates recently confiscated were in large measure turned over to them. As a single example, the duke of Exeter himself petitioned that he might be given the properties taken from the earl of Arundel, and these were granted him with the assent of the council.[2] Among the knights of the council were John Bussy, who was speaker of the house of commons in the first parliament of 1397, Henry Greene, William Bagot, and John Russel. Bussy, Greene, and Bagot gained a special notoriety for promoting the king's schemes in the final parliament of 1398. They were unceasingly active in the council, and were accustomed there to report the wishes of the king.[3] On one occasion it was declared that for the arrangement of certain fines none should be present in the council but the chancellor, the treasurer, the keeper of the privy seal, and these three knights.[4] They were richly rewarded in various ways. Besides annuities of £100 each, like the afore-named lords, they were granted confiscated estates and the custody of castles to an astonishing extent.[5] For such actions a day of retribution was sure

[1] The duke of York in the twenty-second year received annuities amounting to £2,000, besides various estates, and he was made steward of England during the absence of the duke of Lancaster, to whom the office belonged by inheritance. *Cal. Patent Rolls*, 22 Ric. II, 400, 404, 490, &c.

[2] One of his petitions was granted October 19, 1397, with the consent of the king and the council in the presence of the archbishop of York, the chancellor, the bishop of Durham, the earl of Worcester, John Bussy and Henry Greene, knights, besides the two chief justices. *Ancient Petitions*, no. 13406; also 13421; *Cal. Patent Rolls*, 22 Ric. II, 472, 514, &c.

[3] In the petition of the duke of Exeter, just cited, it is said, 'et sur ce messrs Johan Bussy et Henry Grene reporterent au consail qe la voluntee du Roy estoit,' &c.

[4] Nicolas, i. 76. In one instance a petition for favour was granted by the king in the presence solely of Bussy and Green. *Ancient Petitions*, no. 11253.

[5] Bussy and Green were permitted to hold all the confiscated possessions of the duke of Norfolk, and in 1399 Wiltshire, Bussy, Breen, and Bagot were given the custody of Wallingford Castle, where the young Queen Isabella was lodged, as well as the important castles of Rochester, Leeds, and Bristol. On the Bagot family see William Salt, *Staffordshire Society*, New Series, xi. 45–53; *Cal. Patent Rolls*, 22–3 Ric. II.

to come. The other knight, John Russel, had long been known as a keeper of the king's horses, and on being relieved of this office he was granted a life annuity of £50 besides other favours.[1] He was less prominent politically than the other knights, but was not the less industrious in ordinary administrative and judicial work. In labours of this kind probably the most efficient of all the councillors was Sir Richard Waldegrave. He had been a member of parliament for Suffolk, and was speaker of the house of commons in 1381. He became a member of the council, apparently in the seventeenth year, and although he kept clear of political quarrels, certainly no man served on so many judicial commissions as did he.[2] Faithful to the last, he received 100 marks each year, besides many other favours.[3] It was upon men of this stamp that the extensive judicial functions now assumed by the council mainly depended.

Among the men of lower estate it is necessary to mention also Lawrence Drew. He was an esquire, who in the seventeenth year was retained for life to be with the king besides being appointed to attend the council with an annuity of 100 marks.[4] He is found acting as a ' reporter ', or bearer of messages, being once entrusted by the council with money to distribute in the expenses of the war in Ireland, and returning with information from the king.[5] Yet he was not in the full sense a member of the council, as it was declared that he was retained for law cases only. A councillor of still lower status was Master Ralph Selby, a doctor of laws, who has already appeared as one of the clerks to whom reference was made in the council at Eltham. Although he came only to render his expert advice, he was retained as one of the council with an allowance of 50 marks a year, which was revoked at the time he was made a baron of the exchequer.[6] Taken altogether the council had never before been so clearly outlined as a staff of expert men.

[1] *Cal. Patent Rolls,* 21 Ric. II, 314, 359, &c.

[2] Ibid., *passim.*

[3] Ibid., 17 Ric. II, 415 ; *Issue Rolls,* 17–22 Ric. II, *passim.*

[4] *Cal. Patent Rolls,* 17 Ric. II, 391.

[5] *Issue Roll* (*Pells*), 18 Ric. II, Easter, m. 14 ; Nicolas, i. 57.

[6] *Cal. Patent Rolls,* 17 Ric. II, 328 ; Nicolas, i. 75 ; *Issue Roll* (*Pells*), 22 Ric. II, Easter, m. 12.

Conduct of the council, 1398–9.

Concerning the actions of the council at this fateful time, we possess but a few fragmentary records besides the inaccurate descriptions given by observers. Some things also are suggested by the impeachments that take place later. The councillors certainly carried matters with a high hand as regards arbitrary arrests and confiscations. In the absence of parliament also they seem to have treated an unprecedented number of judicial cases. In May 1399, Richard went on a campaign into Ireland, leaving the duke of York as guardian of the realm in association with the council.[1] The invasion of Henry, duke of Lancaster, which occurred in the following July, came as a complete surprise both to the king and the council. At the first intimation of the invasion the guardian and council evidently expected the attack to be made in the south and issued orders for raising forces in Kent.[2] When the progress of Henry from the north became known, we are told that the duke of York hastily called together the chancellor, the treasurer, and the knights Bussy, Bagot, Greene, and Russel, to take counsel as to what should be done.[3] Pursued by their enemies they fled to Bristol Castle, where they were captured, and Wiltshire, Greene, and Bussy without a trial were hanged upon the spot. What purports to be a dying statement of Bussy, is a confession that he had wrongfully obtained a certain manor in Lincolnshire.[4] Later the king himself and his remaining councillors were taken prisoners, and held to be dealt with at a later time. The first step in the ensuing revolution was merely a change of the king's councillors. Henry went about the country making grants, still in the name of King Richard with the consent of his council. Under these circumstances the council was said to include the archbishop of Canterbury, the duke of Lancaster, the earls of Northumberland and Westmoreland, and ' other lords and magnates '.[5]

[1] By a chronicler hostile to the court it is declared that Richard ' entrusted and let to farm ' his kingdom to the duke of York acting as protector, the earl of Wiltshire treasurer, and John Bussy, Henry Greene, John Bagot, knights. *Chronicle of Croyland* (London, 1854), p. 353.

[2] *Cal. Patent Rolls*, 23 Ric. II, 592.

[3] Walsingham, ii. 232 ; *Annales Ricardi Secundi* (Rolls Series), 243.

[4] *Dip. Doc. Chancery*, Portf. 464.

[5] *Cal. Patent Rolls*, 23 Ric. II, 589, 595, &c.

The revolution of 1399.

The revolution was finally accomplished by the deposition of Richard and the punishment of his former councillors. The articles of accusation that were drawn up against the late king reviewing his past career bore mainly upon his personal tyranny.[1] It was charged that he said 'the laws were in his own mouth'. Concerning his relations with the council it was alleged that contrary to the enactment (*quod statutum erat*) that each year officers and councillors should be chosen, the king had not permitted this to be done, but had selected for his council favourites and others who would not resist his will. There was a manifest exaggeration here, for it had never been a statutory requirement, but only an expressed intention, that such appointments should be made every year. The question of the king's right freely to select his council of course was the root of the whole controversy. On the one side there was the powerful argument of the barons that they were the king's natural councillors and should in no wise be excluded. On the other hand, if the council was to be a selected body, the king's right to make appointments could hardly be questioned. The overthrow of the commission of 1386, which was probably uppermost in the mind of parliament, was more plainly illegal, because with the king's consent the measure had been given a statutory basis.

Punishment of the councillors.

The subject of the deposed king's council was more specifically dealt with in the first parliament of Henry IV. In view of its recent judicial activities, one of the first demands of the house of commons was that all personal actions, between party and party, in which the king was not directly concerned, should henceforth be tried by common law and never before the council; and that all such actions still pending should be turned over to the courts of common law.[2] This request was allowed with an important reservation, 'except when one party was so great and rich, and the other party so poor that there could be no other means of recovery.' But the indignation of parliament was turned more especially against the 'false councillors' of the late king, who were not included in Henry's proclamation of amnesty. Several of

[1] *Rot. Parl.* iii. 417 ff.

[2] Ibid. 446.

the former councillors, it is true, were successful in making their peace with the new king. The earl of Worcester, whether traitorously or not is uncertain, in the moment of defeat went over to the victorious side. Richard Clifford had friends in parliament who offered a petition in his behalf, and he was permitted to remain in his office as keeper of the privy seal.[1] Richard Waldegrave, also, who had played no conspicuous political part, on a petition of his own to the king was granted a comprehensive pardon for all the crimes imputed to him.[2] Edmund Stafford continued to sit in the council of Henry, and in the following year was made chancellor again. As for the rest, the knights of the shire in the house of commons demanded their immediate arrest and impeachment. It happened that the only survivor of the three most conspicuous knights was William Bagot, who was now brought forth and given over to a committee of his fellow knights to be examined.[3] Bagot defended himself by seeking to implicate others, accusing the duke of Albemarle in particular of counselling the king to bring about the death of Gloucester. Lest he might incriminate others in high station, Bagot was not permitted to complete his accusations, but was led away to prison. As he had formerly been serviceable to Henry, he was afterwards released and permitted to retire to his home in Warwickshire. The house of lords continued to resound with accusations and appeals of treason, but no striking evidence was disclosed. After the dukes of Albemarle, Surrey, and Exeter were degraded to their former rank as earls, and when the earls of Kent and Salisbury in the following year were killed by a mob, the spirit of vengeance on this score at length was satisfied.

In conclusion, it is manifest that the conflicts under Richard II had certain permanent effects upon the history of the council. On the one side the efforts of parliament were put forth to secure a council of limited membership, of definite responsibility, in which men of rank were to be

[1] Ibid. 428. He was made bishop of Bath and Wells in 1401, whence he was transferred to the see of Worcester.

[2] *Ancient Petitions*, no. 12555.

[3] *Rot. Parl.* iii. 428 ff. ; *Annales Henrici Quarti*, 303–6 ; *Archaeologia*, xx. 278.

induced to serve with regularity. This policy, it is true, was only intermittently asserted, and in its specific attempts it was generally a failure. Nevertheless the many definitions that were made were not wholly ineffective, the ideal of a body selected from the higher estates was not lost to sight, nor did the council ever again revert to its earlier formlessness. On the other hand, the king was in a position to appreciate the impracticability of the plans of parliament, even if these were sustained in the best of faith. The royalist influence, then, was to create in addition to the lords a body of official and bureaucratic character. But neither was this plan wholly successful, for between the old nobility and the men known to their opponents as 'favourites' and 'evil councillors' there was an irrepressible antagonism. Yet the council was made to contain both of these elements, and thus far no state of equilibrium between them had been reached. With this problem in view, it is necessary to follow the events of the next period, to see what was done under the house of Lancaster. Still the general result thus far, both of the parliamentary and the royalist influences, was to make the council a body more narrowly circumscribed and exclusive than it had been before. The lords were accustomed to be sworn and to take up their duties as councillors with seriousness, while the relations of the justices, serjeants, and doctors of law were satisfactorily defined. The council also in its personnel and methods was made a political question, and so was drawn into the light of publicity and criticism.

CHAPTER VII

THE COUNCIL UNDER HENRY IV AND HENRY V

UNDER the house of Lancaster the council reached a period of supreme power and prominence. It continued to be the centre of political conflict, for the questions raised in the reign of Richard II were by no means settled. The great question at issue was whether the council should be maintained as a department of the royal household in the interests of the monarchy, or whether it should be like the parliament a body representative of the estates of the realm. The success at certain times of the latter principle has caused it to be said that 'the council of the Lancastrian kings is the real, though perhaps not strictly the historical germ of the cabinet ministries of modern times '.[1] It will be seen, however, that on the whole the royal bureaucratic influences were equally strong. Between these two elements there was an almost constant rivalry with quick alternations of success and failure between them.

The problem under the Lancasters.

After the deposition of Richard II, attended by the dissolution of his council and the punishment of his surviving councillors, it might be expected that no similar body would appear for a time. The question of Henry's council was not immediately taken up in parliament, nor did the king himself make it prominent in any way. In the reconstruction of the government we learn that the justices and other officers were appointed and sworn,[2] but no such publicity was given to the appointment of the king's councillors. There was a council in action nevertheless within a month of the recognition of the new king,[3] but the names of the members were not announced nor are they now easily ascertained. It is noticeable too that no important tasks at this time were

Obscurity during the first years.

[1] Stubbs, *Const. Hist.* iii. § 367.

[2] *Rot. Parl.* iii. 423 ff.

[3] Henry's reign began on September 30. The first act of the council, so far as I have noticed, is seen in the endorsement of a bill on November 11. *Council and Privy Seal* (Exch. T. R.), file 7.

entrusted to the council.[1] During the first month of the reign there was an unusual amount of business in the way of filling offices, revoking former grants, making new grants and confirmations of old ones, but these things were done almost entirely under forms of the royal authority and not with the 'consent' or 'advice' of the council.[2] Only a few cases of doubt and dispute, apparently, were left to its decision. In view of the number of rebellions that had to be met, it is strange that the king did not leave the concerns of government to a greater extent in the hands of his council. However much he may have been aided in these matters by his chamberlain and secretary, it is not to be doubted that the extraordinary labours of this time seriously impaired the king's health, so that he was obliged to be all the more dependent on his council in later years. So great an assertion of the royal prerogative certainly was not desired in parliament, where it was soon suggested on the part of the commons that all gifts or grants of the crown should be made 'by advice of the council'. But the king answered with evasion that he would 'be counselled by the sages of his council in things touching the estate of the king and the realm, saving, however, his liberty'.[3] The weakness of Henry's position in his relation to parliament was not at first made manifest.

Appointments.

There was evidently some difficulty experienced in the appointment of a council at the start. For the same reason that the king was away from London most of the time, it is true that scarcely any of the great lords, upon whom Henry especially relied, were able to give their regular attendance as councillors. Not only was there military work for them in the numerous revolts following the revolution, but they had supreme concern for the security of their own estates. For this reason they were precluded at first from holding the offices which were usually given to men of high rank. The chancellorship was first given to Archbishop Arundel,

[1] On November 9 a Provisors case, instead of being brought before the council, is ordered to be heard before the king in chancery. *Cal. Patent Rolls*, 1 Hen. IV, 82; also 173.

[2] *Cal. Patent Rolls, passim.*

[3] *Rot. Parl.* iii. 433, 479, 495.

but he held the office only to the time when the revolution was successful, and then resigned it in favour of a much less prominent man, Sir John Scarle, previously master of the rolls. Likewise John Norbury, a serviceable esquire, was made treasurer ; Sir Thomas Erpingham, an old follower of the dukes of Lancaster, became the king's chamberlain ; and Master Richard Clifford was permitted still to hold the office of the privy seal until the early period of unrest was over.[1]

Attendance of the lords.

The records of the council, such as are found in fragmentary form for a period of three or four years, are sufficient to show that on the part of the great lords an extremely varying attendance was given. The earls of Northumberland, Westmoreland, Arundel, and Worcester, besides several of the bishops, it is true, manifested an active interest in the government, but the lords generally seem to have fallen back upon their former liberty of giving the council only their casual attention. Sometimes a fairly large number was brought together by means of special summons,[2] and again there were sessions at which not a single lay lord was present.[3] There were not always as many as four members on duty.[4] Here was an initial problem, which might well have caused some anxiety, since it was not possible at that time for the council to be of great weight unless it were actively supported by the barons.

Lesser men.

In lieu of the presence of the lords a number of lesser men were retained, some with salaries, to give the council a certain degree of stability. Several of them had had experience in the government of Richard, while others were promoted for their services in the duchy of Lancaster. Besides the officers, Scarle, Norbury, Erpingham, and Clifford, already

[1] A list of the officers during the reign is given in the work of J. H. Wylie, *England under Henry IV* (London, 1884–98), iv, Appendix V.

[2] By letters of the privy seal, January 14, 1402, Henry cancelled the summons of a parliament, which was to meet on February 2, calling instead a great council for January 25. *Council and Privy Seal*, file 11.

[3] There is an instance in the third year when the following names are given upon a warrant : the bishop of Exeter chancellor, the bishop of Bath treasurer, the bishop of Bangor keeper of the privy seal, the bishops also of Lincoln and Hereford, and John Scarle, John Prophet, and John Curson. *Warrants (Chancery)*, no. 1546.

[4] In the fourth year a petition is answered by the archbishop of Canterbury, the treasurer, and the keeper of the privy seal, who alone were said to be *praesens en counsail. Ancient Petitions*, no. 13454.

mentioned, perhaps the most notable appointment was that of Master John Prophet, the former clerk of the council, now dean of Hereford. Without apparently holding any other office in the state, he was immediately retained with a salary of £100, 'so long as he should remain of the king's council'.[1] Prophet became one of the most assiduous members, as the recurrence of his name upon the records testifies, and since he was almost the only member who had been engaged in the work before, his experience must have been valuable in reviving the traditions of former years. He rose still higher in the service of the government, as in 1403 he is known as the king's secretary,[2] and in 1406 he became keeper of the privy seal. A name scarcely less prominent in the records was that of John Durward, an esquire of Essex. He had been a minor officer and one of the council of Richard, as well as a member of parliament for his shire. With the king's approval he was made speaker of the commons in Henry's first parliament, and immediately afterwards is found to have been appointed to the council with a salary of 100 marks, which in the second year was raised to £200.[3] As a man of industry and discretion, he became the special emissary or 'reporter', who was entrusted with confidential messages passing between the king and the council, as well as to absent lords.[4] Sir John Cheyne of Gloucestershire was the first to be elected speaker in the parliament of Henry IV, but he immediately resigned the post and became a member of the council with a grant of 50 marks, which was afterwards increased by £54 yearly.[5] There was, no doubt, good reason for Henry's choice of so many members of parliament. Other men who served steadily in the council of the first years of the reign are Hugh Waterton, John Curson, Thomas Coggeshale, John Frome, and John Fremington.[6]

[1] *Issue Roll* (*Pells*), 1 Hen. IV, Easter, m. 9, &c.
[2] Nicolas, ii. 78.
[3] *Issue Roll* (*Pells*), 1 Hen. IV, Easter, m. 6; 2 Hen. IV, Mich., m. 21.
[4] *Council and Privy Seal*, file 7, *passim*.
[5] *Ancient Petitions*, no. 13219; *Cal. Patent Rolls*, 7 Hen. IV, 183, 237.
[6] With dying words, says Dr. Wylie, Henry IV mentions especially the loyalty of the Erpinghams, the Watertons, and the Cheynes. Op. cit., iv. 142.

Commoners.

Still another and less familiar element in the membership of the council at this time is found in three citizens of London. These were Richard Whittington, already once mayor, John Shadworth, warden of the Mercers' Mystery, and William Brampton, who on November 1, 1400, were formally 'ordained and assigned' as councillors with a fee of 50 marks each.[1] This is not the first time indeed that an alliance between the king and certain parties in the city had been expressed in this way. Moreover there was a prevalent theory that the council should represent all the estates of the realm, and in this light the city undoubtedly had its claims. In these cases the bond seems to have been a series of loans and commercial contracts. As a mercer Whittington had already supplied the household of Henry, when earl of Derby, and by reason of his wealth he had been useful to Richard II.[2] He now furnished Henry's daughters with rich bridal outfits, and lent the king money to the extent of £6,400 at a time.[3] Probably Shadworth was concerned in the same transactions. Brampton in one instance served on a diplomatic mission.[4] Their connexion with the council, however, proves to be merely a formal one. They were hardly ever present at the meetings,[5] and their appointments are probably to be regarded as a survival of the earlier practice of retaining councillors for individual and temporary reasons.

Councillors 'with the king'.

Another observation, which is suggested by the early years of Henry IV, is that while the king was required to move on his campaigns about the country, he took some of his officers and councillors with him, while the others remained at London or Westminster. In this way a distinction was frequently made between those of the council who were 'about the king's person', and those 'remaining at London'.[6] John Prophet, we are told, was *retentus penes dominum*

[1] *Issue Roll* (*Pells*), 2 Hen. IV, Mich., m. 2.

[2] Fortunately for him a loan of 1,000 marks was now repaid. Ibid., 1 Hen. IV, Easter, m. 6.

[3] Wylie, ii. 442, 448 ; iii. 65.

[4] Ibid., ii. 71.

[5] I have found Brampton's name noted twice and Whittington's only once. Nicolas, i. 107, 114 ,122 ; *Council and Privy Seal*, file 7, November 28.

[6] Nicolas, ii. 52, 54, 103, &c. In 1406 the commons prayed the king *envoier les billes a son dit conseil* (i.e. at Westminster), *par aucuns* (*sic*) *du dit conseil demurrantz entour sa persone*. *Rot. Parl.* iii. 586.

Regem de essendo uno consiliariorum,[1] although he afterwards appears among those acting at Westminster. Arnold Savage, too, in 1404 was engaged as *unus consiliariorum qui circa personam nostram morabuntur*.[2] The tendency to distinguish these different groups of councillors, however, is for the present of no special consequence, since no permanent cleavage in the council on this line was as yet made. It is suggestive, however, of an important division that was made at a later time.

Resumption of normal activities.

After a year or more of comparative obscurity the normal activities of the council may be seen to have been revived. No doubt this process was quickened by the appointment of stronger men to the leading offices. Before the end of the year 1400 Edmund Stafford, bishop of Exeter, was again made chancellor, and in 1403 the office was given to Bishop Beaufort ; Thomas Allerthorpe became treasurer in 1401, and in 1402 the bishop of Bath, and after him in the same year the bishop of St. David's ; Thomas Langley was keeper of the privy seal in 1402, and Lord Lovell in 1403.[3] It does not appear that the council, as a body, guided the king in his policies or appointments, but it served in determining many questions of administration. There were numerous cases of conflicting grants, of rewards for services in the past and the like, which were referred by the king to the council for determination.[4] Parliament likewise, though with caution, turned over to it a number of petitions for adjudication, besides giving it authority to make certain ordinances on weights and measures, and other minor matters.[5] There were orders for the arrest of dangerous criminals, and the hearing of a case of an attack at sea, which show that the peculiar judicial powers of the council were not entirely dormant.[6] But its authority for the time was seriously impaired, as appears in the case of a prominent knight who openly refused to obey a summons.[7]

[1] *Issue Roll* (*Pells*), 1 Hen. IV, Easter, no. 351, m. 9.

[2] *Patent Roll*, 4 Hen. IV, part ii, m. 20.

[3] Wylie, vol. iv, Appendix V.

[4] *Council and Privy Seal*, file 8, *passim*.

[5] *Rot. Parl.* iii. 469, 496, 506, 593.

[6] *Cal. Patent Rolls*, 164, &c. ; *Council and Privy Seal*, file 8, December 10, 18.

[7] Sir Philip Courtenay, *Rot. Parl.* iii. 489.

Weakness of the council and plans of reform, 1404.

In the attacks which were soon made upon Henry's government, it was not the tyranny but the weakness and inefficiency of the council that was the object of complaint. In 1403 the earl of Northumberland directed a letter to the council, asking that payment be made of the arrears due to him and his son for their military services.[1] Getting no satisfaction from this demand, the Percies made their revolt in the same year, when one of their avowed objects was to reform the government, and in particular 'to establish wise councillors to the advantage of the king and the realm'.[2] A similar feeling was manifested in the fifth parliament, which met January 14, 1404. On a previous Friday a small council attended by the archbishop of Canterbury, the bishop of Rochester, Thomas Erpingham, and John Norbury had met to arrange preliminaries. Their plans seem to have been completely upset, for by a united action of the lords and commons a general attack upon the government was made. While the complaints, then presented by the commons, were directed mainly against the management of the king's household, it becomes evident that much was said also concerning the king's council, more, in fact, than the rolls of parliament have revealed. Apparently certain complaints and demands were made in the manner that was familiar in the reign of Richard II. Of these demands we know nothing in particular. But on March 1 the king announced that 'at the strong instances and special requests made at divers times in this parliament by the commons, he had ordained certain lords and others to be of his great and continual council'.[3] The list, which was read, is as follows:

The archbishop of Canterbury.
The bishops of Lincoln (chancellor), Rochester, Worcester, Bath, and Bangor.
The duke of York.
The earls of Somerset and Westmoreland.
Lord Roos (treasurer).
Thomas Langley (keeper of the privy seal).
Lords Berkeley, Willoughby, Furnival, Lovell.

[1] Nicolas, i. 203.
[2] *Annales Henrici Quarti* (Rolls Series), 361–2.
[3] *Rot. Parl.* iii. 530.

Messrs. Piers Courtenay, Hugh Waterton, John Cheyne, Arnold Savage, John Norbury, John Durward, John Curson.

It has been remarked that in naming these councillors there was no great concession on the part of the king, since no one of these men was new to the council, all of them were supporters of the monarchy, and most of them were Henry's special friends. In this view of the case the point is lost that it was not then a question of throwing the council into the hands of one party or another, but of establishing 'wise' councillors, especially lords, who by their continuous presence would give the council greater weight than it had had before. Neither was it intended to substitute a group of new councillors for old, but to have them publicly named and thus made definitely responsible. In the announcement of the names of the six bishops, nine lay lords, and the others, this parliamentary advantage was secured. Concerning this council there is nothing more to be learned from the rolls of parliament, but a letter is found which discusses at great length certain further problems connected with these appointments. This letter we learn was framed at a meeting of the council, probably of the men previously named, who came together at the house of the Black Friars one morning at seven o'clock in the same month of March.[1] It was sent to the king by the hands of John Durward, whom the king was requested to receive in the presence of his chamberlain and steward, and to entrust with a gracious answer. With regard to the officers and councillors, who by ordinance of parliament, it was said, were to serve until the next parliament, the question was raised in what manner the appointees should be charged and sworn. It seemed to the councillors expedient that the lords and others should be charged not in parliament but only in the presence of the king, like household officers. Although if it pleased the king they conceded that certain of the commons, not more than two or three,

[1] *Council and Privy Seal*, file 28. The letter is poorly written, upon coarse paper, with many mistakes, erasures, and interlineations. There is also a copy of it in better form. As I have given its contents closely paraphrased, it seems hardly necessary to present the text, which is uncertain in various points.

might be present. In the case of the great lords, it was argued to be sufficient that they be charged upon the oaths which they had formerly sworn as members of the council, but if the king desired them to be sworn again together with others of minor estate, they should make a protestation that the oath was taken not at the instance of the commons but out of reverence for the king. In regard to another question, the letter continues, considering the great number of prelates, lords, and others named to be of the council, it would be too burdensome for the king to pay them all salaries, and likewise it would be grievous for them to make long-continued residence away from home. Therefore they suggested that after their common advice concerning the government should have been given, they should make provision for absenting themselves for suitable lengths of time, in such a way that a sufficient number of each estate might always be in attendance. What the king's answer to the letter was we are not informed, but he seems to have agreed with his advisers on the point that the councillors should not be compelled to take their oaths in parliament.

None of the enactments of the ' unlearned parliament ', as it was called, were famous for their success, and the arrangements concerning the council were as unpractical as any. Most of the lords then appointed, it is true, did serve in the council during the following year, but with their wonted irregularity. In one meeting we find as many as twelve members present,[1] and again not one of the great lords or bishops was in attendance.[2] The king also was not hindered from making changes in the personnel from time to time.[3] Moreover, nothing further was said about the termination of their service at the next parliament. On the contrary, the parliament which met in 1405 was much more favourable to the government, and the commons voted their subsidies willingly ' for the great confidence which they had in the lords elected and ordained to be of the continual council '.[4]

[1] Nicolas, i. 222. [2] Ibid. 246.

[3] A list which was drawn up on November 21, 1404, shows a considerable number of changes. Nicolas, ii. 243.

[4] *Rot. Parl.* iii. 568.

The Long Parliament of 1406.

But the methods of attack followed in 1404 were remembered, and were renewed with greater vigour in the long active parliament of 1406.[1] On the military failures and expenditures, for which the government was held to be responsible, the commons spoke with displeasure and exasperation, demanding an account of all public moneys. 'Kings do not give account,' they were curtly answered. 'Then their officers must,' was the reply. On this occasion the attention of the houses plainly was focused upon the appointment of the chief officers and the council. The commons made their grants upon the express condition that the money should be expended 'by the advice of the lords and officers to be named and elected by the king in this present parliament'. Many times, declared the speaker, he had prayed the king 'for sufficient government', and the answer which he brought was, that the king assented 'to be counselled by the wisest lords of the realm'. Pressed in this manner, it is stated that the king himself framed a bill, which was read May 22, naming a council and defining its powers. The list was as follows:

Names of the councillors publicly read.

Archbishop Arundel of Canterbury.
Bishop Beaufort of Winchester.
Bishop Stafford of Exeter.
The duke of York.
The earl of Somerset.
Lords Roos, Burnell, Lovell, Willoughby.
Bishop Langley of Durham, chancellor.
Lord Furnival, treasurer.
Bishop Bubwith of London, keeper of the privy seal.
Prince Thomas, steward of England.
Lord Grey, chamberlain.
Sir Hugh Waterton, Sir John Cheyne, Sir Arnold Savage.

As was true before on a similar occasion, none of these men were new to the council, and all of them were the king's friends. It will not suffice, however, for this reason to call the action 'a mere flourish on the part of the commons'.

[1] A full account of the proceedings of this 'Long Parliament' is given in Wylie, op. cit., vol. ii, chap. lxii.

On the contrary, the concessions were regarded as real and substantial, and their effect proves to have been considerable, even though it was not all that was desired. Not the least of these concessions was the fact that the lords were now given a stronger predominance than they had held in the council of 1404. In the further discussion of the problem, the king announced that the newly appointed members should publicly declare their willingness to serve. At first the lords showed reluctance toward committing themselves so strongly, and asked to be excused ; but when the king definitely asked them, they made it plain that they were obedient only to the royal command. Lord Lovell was excused on the ground that he was interested in pleas then pending in court. When the speaker on a following day asked to be informed whether the lords would undertake the task or not, 'Decidedly,' answered the archbishop, 'if there are funds enough, but not otherwise.' Accordingly the commons suggested salaries, praying that 'the lords of the council be reasonably guerdoned for their labour'. They voted further grants of money on the condition that 'the lords of the estates chosen should undertake to be of the continual council'.[1] In their eagerness to provide for all future contingencies the commons caused an unprecedented number of ordinances on the conduct of the council to be passed. They desired that the council make an inquiry into the value of all crown properties and that it ensure these were let at the utmost profit. They required that all bills endorsed by the chamberlain and letters under the signet, as well as other warrants addressed to the chancellor, the treasurer, and the keeper of the privy seal, should either be endorsed by the council or written by its advice. This provision alone would leave the king practically nothing of his independent prerogative. 'In all matters,' it was added, 'the king should govern by the advice of his councillors and trust them.' A 'reasonable number' of the councillors should continually remain about the royal person, and they should make report to the others from time to time. The king feebly agreed to these demands, even to the extent of

[1] *Rot. Parl.* iii. 568, 573 ff.

withdrawing his hand from the government entirely—*desportez en sa roiale persone.* Before the close of the parliament the commons drew up at great length a series of thirty-one articles to be observed by the council.[1] Most of these articles were, indeed, only repetitions of former enactments, which by this time had become familiar, as for instance, that the council should not treat of matters determinable at common law, and that a councillor should not maintain pleas, or act as a judge in a dispute to which he was a party. The problem of absentees was met by a curious provision which required those who were present in the council to consult absent members, and to gain their consent to all matters passed. The absurdity of this article was pointed out by the councillors themselves, saying that some of their number might be in Wales or elsewhere at a great distance.[2] As a result the requirement was practically negatived by the addition of a modifying clause, that this should be done only in great matters when the council deemed it necessary.

Finally, before the close of the parliament in December, the question of receiving the oaths of the councillors and giving them their charges was again discussed. This was more than a mere matter of ceremony, since it was an expression of the intention to make the council actually responsible to the estates. The speaker demanded that the lords of the council be sworn in parliament before the king and all the estates to obey each of the previous enactments. To this the archbishop, speaking for himself and all his colleagues, made protestation that they would in no wise take this charge, unless it were by the king's own will and motion. Even this the king commanded them to do, so that after some further altercation most of the lords were sworn, as they said, 'at the instance of the commons and at the command of the king.'[3] Lord Roos and several others who were not present at the time were permitted to take the oath after the dissolution of parliament. It is noticeable that by December 22 the list of councillors in more than one point was changed since it was first presented in the month

[1] *Rot. Parl.* iii. 578 ff.
[2] Ibid. 587 ; Nicolas, i. 298.
[3] *Rot. Parl.* iii. 585.

of May. It was finally decided to include the controller of the royal household in addition to the five officers previously named. One other concession made by the king, different from what had been done in 1404, was the order that all the foregoing enactments should be entered upon the parliament roll. In view of all that was done, Stubbs has said, 'the parliament of 1406 seems almost to stand for an exponent of the most advanced principles of mediaeval constitutional life in England.'[1]

It remains to be seen how far the enactments and policies declared in the parliament of 1406 were afterwards carried out. Not all of the ordinances, indeed, could be enforced, but they did not fail to produce certain marked effects in the conduct of the government. That the men should be 'guerdoned for their labour' was understood to mean a liberal distribution of salaries, such as in several instances they were receiving already. The council itself took this matter up, advising that the exchequer be searched for the usages of Edward III.[2] Probably the usages of Richard II were considered too. All of the bishops were granted salaries according to the scale that was now customary. Archbishop Arundel continued to receive £200 a year,[3] while Bishop Beaufort and Bishop Bubwith were granted similar sums.[4] Of the lay lords the duke of York seems to have been the only one to be awarded a salary. He had £200 which had been assigned him in the previous year.[5] Of the others Sir Arnold Savage[6] and Hugh Waterton continued to draw £100.[7] Those who held offices, of course, found remuneration in other ways. In the face of the difficulty that the government felt in paying these amounts, it is fair to notice that Bishop Bubwith generously returned to the exchequer sums which he might have claimed.[8] It was not so with the

Great power and success of the council.

[1] *Constitutional History*, iii. 61. [2] Nicolas, i. 297.

[3] *Issue Roll* (*Pells*), 8 Hen. IV, Easter, m. 2.

[4] Ibid., 12 Hen. IV, Easter, May 11.

[5] Ibid., 10 Hen. IV, Easter, m. 7; 13 Hen. IV., Mich., February 13.

[6] Ibid., 6 Hen. IV, Mich., December 2; 7 Hen. IV, Easter, m. 14.

[7] Ibid., 7 Hen. IV, Mich., m. 8; 8 Hen. IV, Easter, July 18.

[8] He was entitled to 20*s*. a day as keeper of the privy seal, besides his salary as councillor. *Issue Roll* (*Pells*), 7 Hen. IV, Easter, May 18, June 26; Mich., October 3, November 13, &c.

archbishop of Canterbury, who in 1411 gave a receipt for the sums which he had steadily received since December 22, 1405.

As to the conduct of the government there can be no doubt that the lords of the council took up their duties with more seriousness and energy than ever before. This they were induced to do, not alone by reason of the acts of parliament and the salaries bestowed upon them, but also because of the king's sickness and need of retirement, so that the entire powers of the government were practically thrown into their hands. The best evidence of this increase of responsibility is found in the files of bills or warrants both of the great seal and the privy seal, which show that from this time few grants or orders of any kind were made that were not written or at least endorsed by order of the council.[1] Only a few letters of the signet from time to time reveal the personal interposition of the king. With the power of filling offices and disposing of royal grants placed so fully under their control, the position of the lords of the council was similar to that enjoyed during the former king's minority. Indeed, their power for the time was even greater, since they were not now limited to the making only of temporary grants. The lords, therefore, who had formerly held themselves aloof from the king's council, as the records abundantly attest, now found sufficient inducement to attend to their duties with an unwonted degree of regularity.

Failure to sustain the plan.

But the project of temporary appointments, with a view to changing the council at every succeeding parliament, broke down completely, since the same political purpose was hardly maintained in any two consecutive parliaments. In the next parliament, which met less than a year later at Gloucester in 1407, the king and council had chosen their own ground and were possessed of every tactical advantage.[2] When the commons, through their speaker, then mentioned the subsidies which had been entrusted to the lords of the council, Archbishop Arundel, now chancellor, answered them that he had already reported to the commons privately upon the matter.[3] The lords of the council, he said, had

[1] *Warrants* (*Chancery*); *Council and Privy Seal*; Nicolas, i. *passim.*
[2] Wylie, iii. 120 ff.
[3] *Rot. Parl.* iii. 609.

loyally performed their labours, even to the extent of lending their own credit for large amounts of money. They had found their task, indeed, to have been a thankless one, and to avoid further questions they begged to be excused from the obligations of the oath they had sworn in the last parliament. This prayer the king intervened graciously to grant them. The commons did not press the subject further, but made their complaints upon other matters, and no new council was appointed at this time.

Reassertion in parliament, January 27, 1410.

During the two years following there were dissensions among the lords, which caused a rift in the council and divided even the royal family itself. For some time the Arundels and the Beauforts had not been friendly, and now, in 1407, the archbishop, as soon as he was made chancellor, gave positive proof of his hostility.[1] At the same time the vigorous policy of the archbishop toward the Lollards gave offence in other quarters. Already the Prince of Wales had come into the council and gave support to his old friend Bishop Beaufort, while Prince Thomas of Lancaster adhered to the Arundels. Before the end of the year 1409 the party of the Prince of Wales had gained ground,[2] so that Arundel gave up the seals in December. The parliament which met in the following January carried the attack still further and demanded the appointment of a new council. Voicing strongly the anti-clerical spirit of the day, the house of commons took the aggressive in framing a series of articles which were presented in the interests of 'good and substantial government'.[3] The first of these articles requested the king 'to ordain and assign in the present parliament the most valiant, wise, and discreet lords of his realm to be of his council', who, together with the justices, should be publicly sworn. When on a later day the king gave his

[1] The act legitimatizing the Beauforts was revised so as to contain the important reservation *excepta dignitate regali*, which expressly denied them any claim to the throne. For this interpolation the chancellor was believed to be responsible. Stubbs, *Const. Hist.* § 314.

[2] In 1408 an act is passed, par Monsieur le Prince et par les autres seignurs du counsail; again, in 1409 the prince is deputed by the council to speak with the king concerning the appointment of a lieutenant of Ireland. The prince was made Warden of the Cinque Ports and Constable of Dover Castle also in 1409. Nicolas, i. 308, 318, 320, &c.

[3] *Rot. Parl.* iii. 623.

answer to the commons, he declared that certain lords whom he had selected had excused themselves for reasons which he considered good. It may readily be surmised that the lords who were reluctant to serve at this time were most likely the archbishop and his friends. By reason of this defection the list of names which the king now offered was an unusually brief one, consisting only of seven lords, at the head of whom was placed the Prince of Wales. Probably the prince had much to do with the selection of his colleagues, who were Bishop Beaufort of Winchester, Langley of Durham, and Bubwith of Bath and Wells, the earls of Arundel and Westmoreland, and Lord Burnell,[1] each of whom was well known and experienced in this capacity. Besides these there were Sir Thomas Beaufort, the new chancellor, Lord le Scrope, the treasurer, and the keeper of the privy seal, who were the only officers to be included in the council at this time. A week later, when it was found that the bishop of Durham and the earl of Westmoreland were needed on the Scottish Marches, the bishop of St. David's and the earl of Warwick also were appointed. It was due, no doubt, to the influence of the Prince of Wales that the council was made so strongly partisan and so exclusively aristocratic. The entire absence of knights and squires in a council appointed in parliament would seem surprising, were it not plainly evident that the advancement of men of their own estate was not strongly desired by the commons. Much importance again was attached to the project of requiring the lords to take their oaths and to receive their charges in a manner suggesting their responsibility to parliament. This the Prince of Wales and his associates refused to do unless sufficient supplies were voted to support the government, and on this condition they gave their oaths to govern in accordance with the aforesaid articles. The prince, as a noteworthy fact, was exempted from taking the oath, 'because of the highness and excellence of his honourable person.' The commons, however, finally had their way, for on the last day of their session they asked to be informed of the completed list of the coun-

[1] *Rot. Parl.* iii. 632.

cillors, who they said should now be charged and sworn without conditions.[1] We are not informed, but since the commons afterwards expressed themselves as satisfied, it may be presumed that this was done.

The council under the Prince of Wales.

The subsequent history of this council shows a more complete success of the parliamentary plan than in any previous experiment. For over a year the same councillors, with slight exceptions, served with substantial regularity and without change of membership until the next parliament. This result was chiefly due to the strong position that had been given to the Prince of Wales, who held the small group easily together and practically controlled the government, while the king was shown only the slightest deference. This fact was recognized by several petitioners who were careful to make address to 'the prince and other lords of the king's council',[2] instead of to the king, and in one case a petition was answered in parliament, *respectuatur per dominum principem et consilium.*[3] The grants of the crown also were actually at their disposal.[4] In one important matter of policy, when it was a question whether England should support the Burgundians or the Armagnacs in France, the prince and council leaned to an alliance with the duke of Burgundy, and ultimately sent an expedition to co-operate with him. To consider the necessary expenditures a wider consultation than usual was desired, and for this reason on March 19, 1411, a great council was attended by as many as thirty-two lords and knights.[5] Before the end of the year the breach in the royal family widened, until there was a serious proposal that the king should resign and allow the prince to reign. This the king indignantly refused to do, and with the aid of the Arundels roused himself once more to throw off the yoke that had been placed upon him. In the parliament which met during the following November, the influence of the royalists was strong enough to bring about the dismissal of the council, after it had been praised for its conduct of the government. With expressions of

[1] Ibid. 634. [2] Nicolas, i. 339. [3] *Rot. Parl.* iii. 643.

[4] In one instance a grant of land and a wardship were determined in the presence of the prince, the chancellor, and the treasurer. Nicolas, i. 331.

[5] Nicolas, ii. 6.

complete satisfaction the commons prayed the king to thank the Prince of Wales and all other lords and officers of the council, who had loyally fulfilled their promises. Then, kneeling before the king, the prince and his colleagues received the thanks of his majesty for their diligence and good counsel.[1] For the rest of the reign the prince withdrew from further participation in the government, receiving a reward of 1,000 marks 'for the time that he was of the council'.[2] At the same time Thomas Beaufort resigned the seals and his brother the bishop ceased any longer to give his attendance.

Last years of Henry IV, 1411–13. A few further changes mark the king's intention to resume the control of affairs and to reverse the policy of the previous régime. Archbishop Arundel, now for the fifth time, was again made chancellor, and a new treasurer was appointed in Sir John Pelham. Prince Thomas, now duke of Clarence, returned to the council, archbishop Bowet of York was retained with a salary of £200,[3] and Lord Roos with £100.[4] Other members of the former council, like the bishops of Durham and of Bath and Wells, continued to serve. Instead of an alliance with Burgundy, the cause of the Armagnacs now was favoured, and in conjunction with them an expedition was sent forth in 1412.[5] Otherwise the last year of the reign was uneventful. From failing health the hand of the king grew increasingly feeble, so that the council must needs be the effective ruling body. No efforts were made again either on the part of the king or of parliament to bring the subject into public notice.

Policy of Henry V. With the accession of Henry V there was another reversal of political conditions affecting the ministers, the council, and the policies of the government. The king immediately appointed Bishop Beaufort again to the chancellorship, the earl of Arundel to the treasurership, and recalled others of his former associates to the council. Because of

[1] *Rot. Parl.* iii. 649.

[2] *Issue Roll* (*Pells*), 13 Hen. IV, Mich., February 18.

[3] Ibid., 14 Hen. IV, Mich., March 17. [4] Ibid., October 27.

[5] In the preparations for the expedition under Prince Thomas, we note the presence of the archbishop of Canterbury, the archbishop of York, the bishop of Bath, the bishop of Durham, the treasurer, the keeper of the privy seal, and Lord Roos. Nicolas, ii. 31.

the masterful personality of Henry V one expects to find the council again in a position of marked subordination to the monarchy. But there may be a feeling of surprise when it is learned that the council of this reign represents a voluntary attempt on the part of the king to carry out the ideas that had usually been expressed in parliament, rather than the traditional policy of the monarchy. After an active career as Prince of Wales, Henry's associations and preferences were strongly aristocratic, so that now in the appointment and management of his council he is inclined to the same general policy that was asserted by him in 1410. In other words, the aim of the king was to maintain a small and select council, consisting of the great officers, prelates, and lords, who are also his personal confidants. At no time, apparently, were there more than a dozen regular councillors, while the actual number of attendants was usually much less. Strange to say there was no plan of salaries or other system of compensation, but a reliance mainly upon the loyalty of the lords and their willingness to serve. The only exception to the rule, so far as we are informed, was in favour of Bishop Beaufort, who, during his term of chancellor, continued to receive the customary £200 a year for attending the council.[1] On at least one occasion, during the year 1414, there was a general assemblage of lords and knights who advised the king to take measures in support of his claim to the crown of France.[2] But for the reasons already given, it is not surprising to find that the usual attendance of lords in the formal proceedings of the council was actually smaller than ever. This fact is to be noted even before the war required the services of the military leaders in other directions. Upon the king's departure for France in 1415 he named his brother the duke of Bedford as guardian of the realm, with the commission to 'do all things with the consent of the council'. The councillors then selected were the archbishop of Canterbury, the bishops of Winchester and Durham, the earl of Westmoreland, the prior of the Hospital, Lords Grey,

[1] *Issue Roll* (*Pells*), 3 Hen. V, Easter, m. 1.

[2] Lavis des seigneurs et chevaliers en le Consail a Westminster. Nicolas, i. 142.

Ruthin, Berkeley, Powys, and Morley.[1] But the proceedings of the following months fail to show that the council was strongly supported by these men. The duke himself was not frequently present, the lay lords were actively engaged in defending the frontier,[2] while the work of the council was actually performed in the main by the bishops and officers. A similar commission of government was named in 1417, and again in 1421,[3] but even at those times it does not appear that the amount of attention given by the lords was materially increased.

In the absence of the lords we have usually found the business of the government carried on by a more or less definable body of officers. During these years, according to the records, the chancellor, the treasurer, and the keeper of the privy seal, in spite of all rules requiring the presence of six or four members, were frequently the only ones in attendance to do duty as a council, and sometimes even two of them sufficed.[4] On other occasions there came also the chamberlain of England, the steward of the royal household, the controller of the household, the keeper of the wardrobe, and even the king's secretary ; so that often the council was practically a meeting of the king's officers with little if any other support. But the circle did not extend to a host of minor functionaries such as we have noticed before. Justices and clerks were called upon for their advice and assistance, and for the conduct of law cases, but the king was little inclined to dignify many of the lesser men as his councillors. There were a few, however, like Master Philip Morgan, a doctor of laws, whom the king calls ' our faithful councillor ', and Master John Honingham, who attended the council and served on various embassies.[5] Another man who was now beginning an important career was Sir Walter Hungerford, a knight of the king's retinue, who had gained distinction in

[1] *Cal. Patent Rolls*, 3 Hen. V, 353 ; Nicolas, ii. 157.

[2] The duke of Bedford at the time was keeper of the eastern march, and now the earl of Westmoreland, Lord Grey, and Lord Morley were also appointed to defend the Scottish marches. Nicolas, ii. 136, 157, 165.

[3] *Cal. Patent Rolls*, 5 Hen. V, 113 ; 9 Hen. V, 373.

[4] *Council and Privy Seal*, esp. file 30 ; in one instance an act is warranted *par avis et assent des chanceller et tresorer*. Ibid., file 34. Nicolas, ii. *passim*.

[5] Nicolas, ii. 155, 191, 193, 236 ; *Foedera*, ix. 168, 221.

the battle of Agincourt. Under the duke of Bedford in 1417 he was made admiral of the fleet, and in the next year steward of the king's household and a member of the council. There were also Sir John Pelham, Sir Richard Redman, Sir Thomas Erpingham, and William Alyngton, Esquire, whose names are noted in the records. Otherwise the usual group of minor attendants is indicated by the general and impersonal phrase 'and others'. But so slight was the prominence given to men of inferior rank, that Henry V was never criticized, as his predecessors had been, for retaining 'evil' or 'low-born' advisers.

Administration and judicature. As has already been intimated the council at this time was in no wise permitted to be a dominant or controlling power, and its functions were mainly confined to questions of administration and judicature. Royal proclamations and grants of the crown were usually made, not 'by the advice (or consent) of our council', but on the independent authority of the king or the regent. Seldom, indeed, were acts of this kind determined without the king's consent even when he was in France. To the council then by the king's command it was given to determine the form of the letters patent and commissions, to direct the writing of diplomatic letters, to give instructions to ambassadors, to arrange for the reinforcements of castles and other military supplies, to award payments for services, and to give security for the king's loans.[1] Moreover, since the council at this time enjoyed to an unusual degree the confidence of parliament, a considerable amount of business was committed to it from this source. According to various acts of parliament suitable persons to serve as justices of the peace were to be selected 'by advice of the chancellor and the king's council'; the council also was enabled to make ordinances concerning the currency and the exportation of money, concerning the practice of surgery, and several times to provide security for the king's loans.[2] Under these conditions the council was permitted to give a great amount of attention to the law cases and judicial

[1] Before the council in 1421 the king's crown was given into the custody of Bishop Beaufort as security for a loan of £14,000. Nicolas, ii. 288.

[2] *Rot. Parl.* iv. 35, 51, 118 130, 210, &c.

questions which called for special treatment. It was authorized by parliament to provide remedy for the grievances of sheriffs, likewise for the complaints of those serving abroad, and to summon and deal with malefactors.[1] By an active correspondence the king also was constantly committing to the council petitions for judicial action. As a result the council was never more vigorous in its pursuit of lawbreakers. At one time when there was reason to fear that two knights who were opposing each other in a suit were about to provoke a riot with their respective supporters, the council caused letters to be sent to each of the parties warning them against any breach of the king's peace.[2] At other times important suits were heard by the council, particularly in the line of the new cases in equity for which the common law provided no remedy.[3] As an example of what was done in this field, there is the following letter under the signet which was sent from France by the king to his brother the duke of Gloucester, who was then, in 1420, acting as guardian of the realm.

'Right trusty and well-beloved brother. We grete yow wel, And we sende yow closed with ynne thees owre lettrees a supplicacion putte unto us on the behalve of William Goddard and Agneis his wyf, wolnyng that knowelache hadde of the trouthe of the matere contened in the same supplicacion, ye calle unto yow oure justices, and by thaire advice ordeineth that bothe parties nemped in the forsaide supplicacion have right, soo that nouther of thaim have cause to compleine hereafter for defaute of justice ; and (God) have you in his kepyng. Geven under oure signet at oure town of Maine the xii day of Juill.'[4]

At no time previously and not for a long time afterwards, in fact, are the records so satisfactory in what they reveal of the council's procedure in this field. The only attempts made by parliament in this reign to control or limit the council were with regard to its judicature, which was steadily inclined to ignore the principles of the common law. Of these matters there will be further explanation in a chapter devoted to this particular phase of the subject.

[1] *Rot. Parl.* iv. 12, 99, 147, 307.

[2] Nicolas, ii. 272–4.

[3] A trust and uses case, Nicolas, ii. 328 ; also 303, 308 ; iv. 145.

[4] *Council and Privy Seal*, file 33, July 12, 1420.

CHAPTER VIII

THE COUNCIL UNDER HENRY VI

Recurrence of a royal minority, 1422–37.

THE premature death of Henry V and the accession of his infant son again threw upon the country the problem of the reign of a minor. In meeting these recurring crises two guiding principles seem to have been held in mind. The one was the general feudal law of wardship, that the property of an heir must for the time be managed for him and ultimately restored to his control. But this rule was not more than partially applicable, because the king was not in a position of a vassal and no one could act as his lord. The second and more prominent thought was that by the active power of the council no change of the public law was required, for the government could still be conducted in the name of the king and council. Under these conditions it is hardly correct to speak of a 'council of regency' as a special institution, for it differed from the organ of normal times only as its activities and responsibilities were increased. At the time, however, the more practical difficulty lay in the appointment of a council with sufficient legal sanction. On the demise of the crown, of course, all officers lost their commissions, and the council was *ipso facto* dissolved. In this case the emergency was met by the duke of Gloucester and a group of magnates, who acted in their capacity as lords of the realm to override all legal obstacles in causing the first parliament to be summoned.[1] They sanctioned the issue of writs in the name of the duke of Gloucester, whom they called 'lord commissioner for holding a parliament', but they insisted that the summons should be given not in his name alone, but 'with the advice of the council'.[2] Thus the interregnum was tided over.

[1] This action of the lords was declared with the words 'ordinatum erat per dominos et proceres ibidem existentes'. Nicolas, iii. 3–5.

[2] Ibid. 6; *Rot. Parl.* iv. 170.

Appointments in parliament of officers and councillors.

In this parliament, which met November 9, 1422, the chancellor, the treasurer, and the keeper of the privy seal, who held office in the previous reign, were immediately re-appointed, 'by advice of the duke commissioner and all the lords spiritual and temporal.'[1] Upon the further construction of the council there was probably much deliberation, the results of which do not appear until December 9. Upon this occasion, we may observe, not only was the council named *in* parliament, as had been done before, but it was expressly chosen *by* the lords of parliament, with several other new features in the manner of appointment. At the head of the government was placed the elder of the king's uncles, the duke of Bedford, with the title 'Protector, Defender of the Realm, and principal Councillor', while the duke of Gloucester was to bear the same title during the absence of his brother.[2] Thereupon, 'by the advice and assent of all the lords' were selected the councillors who were to assist in the government. Now the task of selecting a council at any time during the middle ages was different from that of forming a modern cabinet, in that it was considered right that no one party or estate should be given control, but that all interests in due measure should be represented. In this respect the council should be on a small scale the counterpart of parliament. This ideal was probably never more successfully carried out than was done on this occasion. The body then chosen, says Stubbs, was one 'in which every interest was represented and every honoured name appears'.[3] Each of the men appointed had done conspicuous service under Henry V, and most of them had been in his council at one time or another. The list in all numbered twenty-one, and marks a return to a larger body than the late king had been accustomed to retain. This list may be reproduced as follows:

The duke of Bedford, Protector.
The duke of Gloucester, Protector during the absence of the former.
The archbishop of Canterbury.
The bishop of Durham, chancellor.

[1] *Rot. Parl.* iv. 171. [2] Ibid. 175. [3] *Const. Hist.* iii. § 330.

William Kinwelmersh, treasurer.[1]
John Stafford, keeper of the privy seal.
The bishops of London, Winchester, Norwich, and Worcester.
The duke of Exeter.
The earls of March, Warwick, Northumberland, Westmoreland, and the Earl Marshal.
Lord Fitz Hugh, chamberlain.
Ralph Cromwell, Walter Hungerford, John Tiptoft, Walter Beauchamp, knights.[2]

Discussion of the powers of the council.

There was much discussion further on the powers, scope of authority, and remunerations to be enjoyed by the councillors. On this occasion, instead of submitting to the conditions laid down by parliament, the members of the council were in a position to dictate the terms upon which they

[1] Within a week Kinwelmersh died, and John Stafford was made treasurer, while William Alnwick became keeper of the privy seal.

[2] There is reason to notice particularly the careers of these knights. Cromwell was by inheritance the fourth baron of the name, and the owner of Tattershall Castle in Lincolnshire. Although his father had died in 1417, he was still ranked as a knight at the age of twenty-eight. Under Henry V he served most of the time in France, where he was *in curia militari*, but so far as I have noticed he attended the council in England only once. In the council of Henry VI his attendance is noted more regularly than any other man. He soon became the king's chamberlain, and held many other posts of profit. In 1433 he was made treasurer. He was a partisan of Beaufort's, and was involved in many personal quarrels.

Sir Walter Hungerford was formerly a steward in the household of John of Gaunt. In the war he gained renown in battles and tournaments. He was a member of parliament for Wiltshire, and speaker of the house of commons in 1413–14. He was once an ambassador to the Emperor Sigismund, and attended the council of Constance. His services as an officer and councillor under Henry V have already been noticed. In 1424 he was steward of the household of Henry VI, and in 1425 was summoned as a baron. He succeeded Bishop Stafford as treasurer in 1426. In the events which follow, his career is hardly less notable than that of Cromwell.

Sir John Tiptoft began service under Henry of Bolingbroke. In 1403 he is called *miles camerarii* (*sic*) *regis et aulae*. He was a member of parliament for Huntingdon and speaker during the 'long parliament' of 1406. He was successively keeper of the wardrobe, treasurer of the household, chief butler, and in 1407 treasurer of England. One of his biographers calls him an 'assistant councillor' in 1422, but there was in reality no such position. In 1427 he was steward of the household, a position from which he was removed by the duke of Gloucester in 1432. Like other members of the council at this time, he acquired the custody of numerous castles and lordships.

Sir Walter Beauchamp was a trained lawyer as well as a soldier. Inasmuch as no other professional men were recognized as responsible councillors, most of the routine work in fact devolved upon the regular officers and knights.

would serve. They accepted their responsibilities—'condescenderent emprendre tiele assistence a la governance'—only on the conditions stated in five articles which they offered for acceptance.[1] In these articles it was provided that all offices and benefices, not especially excepted, should be filled only by their advice; all farms, wards, and marriages in the gift of the crown should be at their disposal; nothing was to be done in the council without the presence of six or at least four of them; furthermore the officers of the exchequer were to tell no man what the king had in his treasury except the lords of the council. In this way the councillors sought to grasp the most important powers of the government, as well as to defend themselves from being over-reached by the protector.

In other particulars the plans of parliament were not so carefully laid as had been done on several other occasions. It does not appear that in this instance the councillors were sworn before either of the houses. Most likely they were not, for several of them certainly took the oath under other circumstances afterwards.[2] Moreover, in the first parliament nothing was said as to the length of time for which the men were to serve. Nevertheless, in the following year, 1423, the commons made 'divers and special requests to have knowledge of the persons assigned and elected to be of the council'; whereupon 'for the ease and consolation' of the commons, with the assent of the lords a list of councillors was again publicly read.[3] This list, containing twenty-three names, was slightly longer than the former one, but it presented no conspicuous changes, except the addition of two prominent esquires, Thomas Chaucer, who had several times been speaker of the house of commons, and William Alington,

[1] *Rot. Parl.* iv. 176; Nicolas, iii. 17.

[2] 'Eodem die (January 26) Walterus Hungerford chevalier apud Fratres (Predicatores) praestitit sacramentum, etc., (eodem) modo quo alii domini, assumptus ad consilium Regis et admissus fuit.' Nicolas, iii. 22, 274.

[3] *Rot. Parl.* iv. 201. They were the archbishop of Canterbury, the bishops of London, Winchester, Norwich, and Worcester; the usual three officers; the duke of Exeter; the earls of March, Warwick, the Marshal, the earls of Northumberland and Warwick; Lords Cromwell, Fitz Hugh, Bourchier, Scrope; Walter Hungerford and John Tiptoft, knights; Thomas Chaucer and William Alington.

a former member of the council of Henry V.[1] Again the councillors accepted appointment only on the condition of certain articles, which reveal more plainly than before their fear of the supremacy of the duke of Gloucester. Neither the duke nor any other member, they declared, should grant any favour either in bills of right, office, or benefice which belong to the council. It was great shame, they said, that in relations with foreign countries any one should write in the name of the council contrary to the opinion of the rest; 'let no man of the council presume to do it.' The requirement of the presence of six or four members was repeated as a safeguard. On this occasion we may be sure that the councillors were not sworn or given their charges in parliament, but the new members were afterwards sworn before the council itself.[2]

Remarkable stability of the arrangement.

In no succeeding parliament do we understand was any new council appointed or list of names publicly read. In 1426, it is true, the bishop of Durham was said to have been 'named and elected by the king's council in his parliament',[3] but this was only an individual case. It is possible, too, that a list of the council which appears in the fifth year was drawn up for this purpose.[4] But at other times, certainly, new members were chosen and sworn within the council itself.[5]

[1] Thomas Chaucer of Ewelme was a cousin of Bishop Beaufort. He had been speaker in 1407, 1410, 1411, and 1421, and was noted as a vigorous asserter of parliamentary privilege. In 1415 also he held the office of butler of England (Nicolas, ii. 159).

William Alington of Horseheath, Cambridgeshire, is found in 1399 acting as an attorney for John, duke of Exeter. He was once at least in the council of Henry V, and held the office of treasurer-general of Normandy (*Exchequer Accounts*, bundle 187, no. 14; 188, no. 7). After his appointment to the council of Henry VI, he served on various commissions, one in 1426 to raise a loan for the king, and another for the same purpose in 1428. We find his accounts for attending the council during the following ten years in *Exchequer Accounts*, bundle 96, no. 22.

[2] Nicolas, iii. 155.

[3] Namely, the parliament at Leicester. Ibid. 197.

[4] The names are almost the same as those mentioned earlier, including the dukes of Bedford, Gloucester, Exeter, and Norfolk; the two archbishops; the bishops of London, Winchester, Durham, Bath, Norwich, and Ely; the earls of Huntingdon, Warwick, Stafford, Salisbury, and Northumberland; Lords Cromwell, Scrope, Bourchier, Hungerford, and Tiptoft. *Rot. Parl.* v. 407.

[5] Of Lord Scrope, Alington, and Chaucer, it was said, 'xxv° die Ianuarii dicto anno secundo consimiliter per dictos dominos ad consilium Regis predictum electi fuerunt et iurati.' Nicolas, iii. 155.

With individual changes such as were inevitable from time to time, the council remained on the whole a remarkably stable body. In this respect the period of the minority of Henry VI differs materially from that of Richard II, for it was substantially the same body which now controlled the government throughout all these years. At no time, certainly, was one set of councillors dismissed and another group appointed. Neither were there any signs of a reversion to a circle of officials and royal favourites as in the time of Richard II. Moreover, instead of periodic attacks on the part of parliament, the relations of the two bodies had never been so harmonious. Factions and strifes of course existed, but they did not take the form of a contest between the parliament and the council, because the aristocracy which controlled the one likewise dominated the other. There was, however, a great deal of legislation passed from time to time, in the form of ' ordinances for the governance of the council '. These may be regarded as extensions and elaborations of those enacted in 1390 and in 1406. Besides the articles already mentioned there was a set of ordinances of this kind passed in 1424, which were re-enacted with additions in 1426, and again in 1430.[1] Taken together these ordinances form a veritable code of rules for the procedure of the council, to which there will be reason to refer again.[2] In 1424 also there was a complete revision or ' correction ' of the councillor's oath, in which a special clause bearing on the king's minority was inserted ; that ' ye will also with all your might and power help, strengthen, and assist unto the king's said council, during the king's tender age . . . for the universal good of the king and of his land '.[3]

Salaries. In holding the council together the question of salaries was most important. This matter was taken up by the council itself in 1424, when it was ordained that ' all councillors should receive (salaries) for their attendance according to their estate and rank '.[4] After a scrutiny of the rolls and

[1] Nicolas, iii. 148, 214 ; iv. 60.

[2] It will be more convenient to deal with these in connexion with the problems treated in Chapter XV.

[3] *Rot. Parl.* iv. 407.

[4] Nicolas, iii. 154.

a consideration of the usages under Richard II and Henry IV, a far more consistent plan was evolved than anything which had been attempted before. The protector, whether it were the duke of Bedford or the duke of Gloucester who was serving at the time, was to receive 8,000 marks a year,[1] besides a number of offices and other perquisites which were placed at the disposal of each. The scale which was decided upon for the other councillors may be stated as follows :[2]

An archbishop	200*l.*
A duke	200*l.*
The chancellor	200*l.*
Henry Beaufort	200*l.*
Other bishops, each	200*m.*
Earls	200*m.*
The treasurer	200*m.*
Barons, bannerets, and knights	100*l.*
Esquires	40*l.*

It was a rule that if a member of the council held any other office, his salary as a councillor should be proportionately reduced. Still, the chancellor and the treasurer were permitted regularly to receive salaries for attendance at the council, besides their official incomes, although the keeper of the privy seal was not given any salary beyond his official wage of twenty shillings a day.

A novel feature of the present scheme, which was intended to secure a more constant attendance on the part of members, was a provision that deductions should be made for absences. A councillor receiving £200 a year should lose one pound for every day that he was absent during the term ; one receiving 200 marks should lose one mark, and others at the the same rate. This was a complication which caused some perplexity at the exchequer, since the council's records were by no means so carefully kept that it was possible to ascertain the days of each man's service. To surmount the difficulty, in several instances the king ordered the treasurer and barons of the exchequer to accept the statements of the councillors themselves when they rendered their accounts.[3]

[1] Ibid. 26, 197. [2] Ibid. 154 ; *Accounts Exchequer, K. R.*, 96/16.

[3] Some of these individual statements of account are found in *Accounts Exchequer, K. R.*, 96/16–20.

So constant did the members report their attendance to have been, that as a matter of fact very little was saved to the treasury by the plan of deductions. There was much argument subsequently concerning the amounts to be paid the two great dukes, who were disposed to make the most of their opportunities. In 1426, during Bedford's presence in England, Gloucester was allowed 3,000 marks as 'chief councillor next to his brother'.[1] In 1429, on the abolition of the protectorship, it was agreed that Gloucester should have 2,000 marks as councillor and 4,000 marks when regent during the king's absence.[2] In 1431 he succeeded in getting the council to raise these sums to 5,000 marks and 6,000 marks respectively.[3] Even these salaries were small compared with the amounts which the dukes acquired in other ways. Thus in 1427 Gloucester was said to have been provided with 20,000 marks in assignments at a single parliament.[4] The system of salaries on so extensive a scale was plainly a burden to a government which was already financially embarrassed. The councillors could easily provide themselves with assignments, but the exchequer was far from able to pay the sums assigned. In some instances, indeed, the accounts fell twelve years or more in arrears. It was for this reason, no doubt, that in 1431 the additional sanction of an act of parliament was obtained for the payment of councillors, and the very form of the warrant to be directed to the exchequer was included in the enactment.[5] Under the continued difficulty of making these payments, a considerable relief was felt, when in 1433 several of the bishops with commendable self-denial agreed to give their services during term time for nothing.[6] Likewise it was an acceptable concession when at the instance of Bedford the two dukes agreed to reduce their salaries to £1,000 each.[7] Nevertheless, we find Gloucester afterwards receiving his old salary of 2,000 marks.[8]

But salaries were not the only inducement to the coun-

[1] Nicolas, iii. 210, 228.
[2] Ibid. iv. 12; Devon, *Issue Roll*, p. 44.
[3] Nicolas, iv. 104–6; Devon, 414, 415.
[4] Nicolas, iii. 271.
[5] *Rot. Parl.* iv. 374, 436.
[6] Ibid. 446.
[7] Nicolas, iv. 185, 218.
[8] Ibid. vi. 314.

cillors for taking a lively interest in the government. This was the time when the power and dignity of the mediaeval council may easily be said to have reached its height. Associated with the protector it now absorbed almost the whole of the royal prerogative, the only limits on this side which were recognized being the grants of the king's inheritance and annulments of his letters patent. The king, it is true, was not entirely a legal fiction, for on several occasions it was considered necessary to have him present with the council, confirming its acts *ore proprio*, even though he were sitting upon his mother's lap.[1] In 1427 a statement was made by the lords, that in spite of the king's tender age, 'never the lesse the same autoritee resteth and is at this day in his persone that shall be in him at eny tyme hereafter.' But 'the execution of the king's said authority . . . belongeth unto the lords spiritual and temporal of this land at such time as they be assembled in parliament or in great council, and else, they not being so assembled unto the lords chosen and named to be of his continual council'.[2]

Great power and responsibilities of the council.

As to the protector, there were no material powers which he was acknowledged to exercise without the participation of the council. As a matter of fact, it does not appear that any letters patent or other acts of the government were issued in his name. But it was alleged that he was inclined to do things in the name of the council without sufficiently consulting his colleagues. For this reason many of the aforementioned ordinances were enacted, as, for instance, that no act of the council should be passed without the presence of six or four besides the officers. It was partly for the same reason, no doubt, that all members of the council, whether supporters of the duke or his opponents, found it for their interests to give an amount of attention to the council hitherto unequalled. All doubt, however, as to the unusual powers which were implied in the protectorship was finally ended in 1429, when at the time of the king's coronation this title was abolished and only that of 'chief councillor' was per-

[1] See the expression, *in presentia Regis*, ibid. iii. 323, &c. In 1426 Lord Roos, it is said, was knighted by the king 'with his own hands'. Ibid. 225.

[2] Ibid. 233.

mitted to be continued.[1] In 1430 the strong position of the councillors was further entrenched by an act that no great officer or sworn member of the council should be removed, and that no one should be added to their number without the consent of the council.[2] With this degree of power in their hands, it is not surprising to find that the councillors were generally willing to serve, and to be in attendance with a degree of regularity hitherto unprecedented. In 1433, when at the close of a long and active parliament the lords of the council were asked by the commons if they intended to serve, three of the bishops (York, Ely, and Lincoln) made diverse excuses, saying that they needed better to care for their sees and their own souls. But they finally declared their willingness to attend the council, not continuously, but in term time, and this they would do without salaries. At the same time, the bishop of Durham, who had wished to retire before, was excused on account of his old age. But all the other lords spiritual and temporal agreed to be present as they had been before.[3] Among all the complaints which were made concerning the king's council during the period now in view, that of the unwillingness of members to attend was not one.[4]

Conduct of the government

In their conduct of the government the lords of the council can hardly be praised for living up to the terms of their oaths and pretensions. For the ruinous policy of keeping up the war with France they cannot well be blamed, since it was a policy inherited by them and equally supported by the nation at large. The war undoubtedly was the greatest factor in causing the deficit of the government to increase, until in 1429 it was reported by the treasurer to amount to £20,000 a year.[5] This deficit, in fact, the councillors did nothing to diminish, for in every way they exercised a liberality in the way of grants and assignments which was well over the border of extravagance. A single embassy on one occasion was made to cost 500 marks, and in another instance 1,000 marks ;[6] a messenger from Paris was paid ten pounds ;

[1] *Rot. Parl.* iv. 337. [2] Nicolas, iv. 38. [3] *Rot. Parl.* iv. 446.

[4] Not infrequently it is stated that 'all the lords' were present. Nicolas, iii. 118, 198, 199, &c. [5] Ibid. 322.

[6] Ibid. 319 ; iv. 314 ; for similar services others were paid 100 marks, or £200. Ibid. iv. 29, 71, 308.

the king's nurse was granted forty pounds a year, the salary of a councillor or a judge;[1] a royal physician the same amount, and eleven minstrels five pounds a year each.[2] The liberality of the councillors to themselves, not only in the matter of salaries, which was supported by precedents, but in countless individual grants was also a feature of this régime. The great dukes, it has been shown, virtually helped themselves to huge sums, and the lesser men followed their example. The patent rolls in fact are filled with grants to Lords Cromwell, Hungerford, Tiptoft, and others. It cannot be said, in any case, that these grants were dishonestly acquired, but it is possible to point to petitions that were endorsed by the very men who presented them.[3] The same influence which the councillors used for themselves could likewise be lent to others. With all the patronage of the government at their disposal, the members of the council were besought by office seekers and all who had favours to ask. A petition indeed had small chance of success unless it were promoted by one or another of the lords. In such cases the lords could hardly be personally disinterested, so that favouritism, bribery, 'brocage', and maintenance were evils that were generally believed to be rife in the council. Upon these subjects the legislation of the time was constantly brought to bear, as for instance the requirement that no one of the council should take any enfeoffment of land in dispute without the privity of the council; and that if he take a bribe or bond to place any one in office, he should be removed under forfeiture.[4] Against Lord Cromwell, in particular, there is found the following complaint on the part of a widow who declares that he has cheated her of her inheritance. The petition is addressed not to the council, but to the king and lords in parliament. The writing is not wholly legible, but its tenor can be discerned with sufficient clearness:

'Supplie humblement votre povre vieue et Oratrice Elizabeth . . . par force de diverses fyns levez en la courte de Seigneur Edward . . . Cromwell un des Seigneurs de votre

[1] Ibid. iii. 131.
[2] Ibid., pp. lxx, 84.
[3] *Council and Privy Seal*, file 47, especially petitions of Hungerford.
[4] *Ordinances* 1422–30, cited.

conseil, tresoverein Seigneur, par sa grant puissance favour et obeisance q'il ad en diverses parties du roialme par son grand avoir et . . . faitz ont estez a luy trop favorable prestez et obeisantz de perfourmir son plesir en sez affaires vexe et destourbe la dite suppliant de sa dite heritage . . . al entent pur avoir recovere de dite heritage envers la dite suppliant.' [1]

The interests of the councillors in the government were bound further by the sums of money which they lent from time to time. Often the projects of war and peace could not be carried out, unless the lords at the moment either lent the necessary funds or gave their names in security for the amounts. In 1425, on the occasion of a loan, the members of the council gave security to the extent of 5,000 marks,[2] and again the same thing happened at least six times during the period of the king's minority.[3] By his great loans to the government Bishop Beaufort is well known to have attained an unequalled position of power and profit. In 1436 is found a memorandum of the sums lent to the government at different times by his ' kindness '. It mentions the securities and assignments given for each of the following sums : 10,000 marks, 1,000 marks, 11,000 marks, and £20,000.[4] So long as there were valid securities to be had, there was no lack of enthusiasm for lending the king money. More than once the lords of the council were asked by parliament to take measures for the inspection of the revenues, and to adjust the payments of the king's debts,[5] but this task they did not seriously undertake.

Dissensions among the lords.

A greater cause for anxiety at the moment was found in the persistent dissensions among the lords and the growth of factions which rent the council as well as the parliament. The rivalry of the duke of Gloucester and Bishop Beaufort, with their respective adherents, is a well-known subject of political history,[6] which need be referred to here only so far

[1] *Ancient Petitions*, no. 5526.
[2] Nicolas, iii. 167 ; *Cal. Patent Rolls*, 3 Hen. VI, 271.
[3] Nicolas, iii. 199 ; iv. 16, 89, 202, 233, 316 ff. ; v. 13.
[4] *Council and Privy Seal*, file 55, February 20.
[5] *Rot. Parl.* iv. 432, 439.
[6] K. H. Vickers, *Humphrey, Duke of Gloucester* (London, 1907) ; Stubbs, *Const. Hist.* iii. §§ 334–6.

as it affected the council. Most of the legislation, in fact, which has been cited in this chapter, was inspired by the desire of one party to limit the power of the other. Along these lines the followers of Beaufort were generally successful, but the duke possessed greater resources outside the sphere of politics in the way of personal popularity and military forces. In 1425 the danger of a warlike outbreak was felt to be imminent, when, for the sake of 'peace, concord, and tranquillity', an ordinance was drafted by the council and passed in parliament, requiring each of the lords to give a pledge to the king to keep the peace, and that in case of 'quarrel or matter of debate or heaviness' affecting them, they would in no wise proceed by violence. If any of the lords or councillors should do anything in violation of this act, in lack of any other remedy, it was ordained that 'the other lords and persons shall wholly let and withstand him'.[1] Again in 1426, when it was reported that Gloucester refused to attend a parliament at Northampton in case the bishop were present, the council deputed certain members to remonstrate with the duke. It was known, they said, that his highness had long borne 'heaviness and displeasure' against the chancellor, and how to cause them to keep the peace had long been 'communed' in the council. To prevent riot, it was suggested that the two lords need not be lodged in the same town, while on behalf of the council the duke was asked to promise to keep his men from all riot and to come accompanied only by a reasonable number of retainers.[2] At the ensuing parliament held at Leicester, since known as 'the Parliament of Bats', a formal though insincere reconciliation was effected. In the same year the acceptance by the ambitious bishop of a cardinalship from Rome, 'the great mistake of his life,' as it has been called, caused an eclipse of his political influence for a time. In 1427 the presumption of the duke of Gloucester was held in check only by the intervention of the duke of Bedford.[3] In 1428 Gloucester evidently won a victory in the council, since he was given full authority to prorogue or to continue

[1] Nicolas, iii. 174 ff.; *Rot. Parl.* v. 406–7.
[2] Nicolas, iii. 181 ff.
[3] Ibid. 231 ff.

the parliament then in session.[1] The question of Beaufort and the cardinalship, whether by a violation of the statute of *praemunire* he had vacated the bishopric of Winchester, came before the council in April 1429. It was then debated whether the cardinal could perform a certain anniversary service at Windsor by virtue of a prescriptive right of the bishopric of Winchester. Without settling the main question the council then advised that he should refrain from going to Windsor.[2] Later in the year the question of the cardinal's right to sit as a councillor was determined by parliament in his favour. While it was not usual, the house of lords declared, for an Englishman who was made cardinal by the pope to be present in the king's councils, yet considering the near relationship of Henry Beaufort to the king, and in view of his valuable services, he should not only be permitted to attend as one of the councillors, but should be required to do so.[3] But the influence of Beaufort in the council was certainly weakened, for in 1431 the question of his right to the see of Winchester was again discussed there, while at the same time a larger salary was voted for the duke of Gloucester [4]

Offices seized by the duke of Gloucester.

The cardinal being called to France upon an ėmbassy in 1432, an opportunity was given to the Gloucester party of removing three of the most prominent supporters of Beaufort from office. These were Lord Hungerford the treasurer, Lord Cromwell the king's chamberlain, and Lord Tiptoft the steward of the household. Each of these men had served in the council since the first year of the reign, they had been the most conspicuous of all the councillors in the regularity of their attendance, and especially assiduous in those duties for which men of business were necessary. There was hardly an important committee that failed to be attended by each of these younger lords. For their services

[1] *Warrants* (*Chancery*), file 1545, December 8.

[2] Nicolas, iii. 323.

[3] *Rot. Parl.* iv. 338.

[4] Nicolas, iv. 100, 104. In all the contests Lord Scrope was the most consistent supporter of the duke within the council. Among the others I do not find any particular group which can be designated as the Gloucester party. Members rallied to him or fell away according to the expediency of the moment. On one occasion, in 1429, the duke was supported by Lord Scrope, but opposed by all the others present. Ibid. 8.

they had reaped abundant rewards, and had enjoyed an extraordinary amount of the government patronage. Their sudden removal at this time provoked a conflict between the parties. Cromwell made an appeal to the lords in parliament on the ground that he had been removed without warning, through no fault of his own, at the mere pleasure of the Gloucester faction, and in violation of the ordinances of 1430.[1] The lords gave Cromwell a complete exoneration in the form of an extensive declaration of innocence, and his restoration to favour is marked shortly afterwards by his appointment to the higher office of treasurer. But Hungerford and Tiptoft, though they remained in the council, were not similarly vindicated. In 1433 the tension of the factions was so great as to cause the return of the duke of Bedford from France, who came with purposes of his own to further. In the presence of parliament he accepted the title of *principal councillor* to the king, on the conditions laid down by him in the form of six articles which were accepted.[2] Certain of these articles re-affirmed the intent of previous ordinances concerning the council, while others strengthened the duke's personal position. He was to know who were to be the king's councillors; no great officer or councillor should be removed without the consent of the council, 'and my advice had'; parliament should be called only with the advice of the council, and with the certification of its intent and purpose; and in cases of vacancies in cathedrals, no letters should be written to the pope or to the chapter without the opinion of the council being certified, 'and also mine'. The efforts of the duke of Bedford to regain his supremacy in the government were not successful without a struggle. In 1434 a formal debate between the two dukes over their respective powers was held before a great council, which was terminated only by a request of the king that the proceedings should not be carried further.[3] Again when in the presence of his colleagues Bedford asked what salary he was to receive, 'the lords of the council sat still for a time, giving him no answer, but deliberating and

[1] *Rot. Parl.* iv. 392.
[2] Ibid. 423–4.
[3] Nicolas, iv. 210 ff.

advising among themselves what they might answer.'[1] When at length after further argument the duke offered his services at a stipend of £1,000, the lords thanked him and agreed. But when the duke asked that certain castles and lordships in Gascony be given him as an inheritance, he was answered with the following protest: 'the lords of the council neither dare take upon themselves to give away the king's inheritance nor to break his letters patent.' The duke of Bedford, if not less selfish, was at least a wiser man than his brother, for when his request had failed he did not press it further.[2]

Passing of the king's minority, 1437.

An assuagement of the strifes among the lords was looked for in the passing of the king's nonage and the full restoration of royal rights. Already in 1435–6 the king's personal intervention in the matter of favours may be observed, as in his own boyish hand the royal signature appears upon various bills, *R.H. nous avons graunte.*[3] The liberality of the king in granting offices caused the council no little solicitude, so that it was thought fit to advise him, 'that he geve office to such persones as the office were convenient to, not to high estat a small office, nether to lowe estat a grete office.'[4] The assertion of the complete independence of the crown was made on November 12, 1437, before the lords of the council, when the king made a formal reappointment of all his officers and councillors.[5] There was no intention of bringing in a body of new councillors. 'They that were of councils (*sic*) before are appointed to be of the council now,' declared the king, but the conditions of service in

Council reappointed

many respects now were changed. The list which was then announced, together with the salaries awarded, may be stated as follows:

The duke of Gloucester	2,000*m*.
Cardinal Beaufort	—
The archbishops of Canterbury and York	—
The bishops of Lincoln and Saint David's	—
The earl of Huntingdon	100*l*.

---

[1] Nicolas, iv. 220.
[2] Ibid. 246.
[3] *Council and Privy Seal*, file 58.
[4] Nicolas, v. 3.
[5] Ibid. 71; and vi. 312 ff.

The earl of Stafford	200*m.*
The earl of Salisbury	100*l.*
The earl of Northumberland	100*l.*
The earl of Suffolk	100*l.*
The earl of Devon	100*l.*
Lord Hungerford	100*m.*
Lord Tiptoft	100*m.*
The bishop of Bath, chancellor	200*l.*
Lord Cromwell, treasurer	100*m.*
William Lindwood, keeper of the privy seal (regular wages of the office, 20*s.* a day)	—
William Philip, chamberlain	—
John Stourton, a knight of the household	40*l.*[1]
Robert Rolleston, keeper of the wardrobe	—

In the award of salaries it will be seen that the schedule of 1424 was considerably altered. A salary now was a matter of favour which might or might not be granted, and it could be made greater or smaller. For example, in the case of Lord Cromwell a few years later, it is stated that 'the king wishing to reward (him) before other councillors of his status grants (him) 200 marks a year so long as he remains of the council '.[2] It was the rule also that, with the exception of the chancellor and the treasurer, those holding office of sufficient profit should not receive salaries as councillors. As regards the bishops, probably their self-denying offer of 1433 was remembered, so that no salaries at the time were awarded them. Nevertheless, exceptions were made, since one finds the archbishop of York for many years receiving £200, while other bishops were similarly favoured.[3] It was perhaps intended as a signal of the resumption of the royal prerogative, that the grants to the councillors were made by letters patent 'for the term of their lives '.[4] Even though one fell into 'unwieldiness or impotence ', it was said, still the king willed him to have the fee for life. In a government

[1] He is noted as attending the council only since the previous October. Likewise Rolleston began to appear in November, 1436. Possibly it is a sign of royal influence that these members of the household are recognized.

[2] *Issue Roll* (*Pells*), 22 Hen. VI, Easter, m. 5.

[3] Ibid., 19 Hen. VI, Mich., m. 3, &c. The archbishop of Canterbury a few years later received £200. Ibid., 21 Hen. VI, Easter, m. 3. The Bishop of Carlisle was given £600 for coming many times from a great distance to the council at Westminster. Ibid., Mich., m. 15.

[4] *Cal. Patent Rolls*, 17 Hen. VI, 240, 289.

which could not fairly pay its debts, there was for the recipients a manifest advantage in this form of grant, since annuities by inheritance or for life were given preference over other obligations.[1] It is evident also that the councillors preferred to convert their salaries into the more stable form of the farm of an estate.[2] In subsequent years, however, grants were not made in this form, but men were given fees 'for the time they should be of the council'.

Its changed relations.

The members of the council were each newly sworn before the king 'to counsaille him wel and trewly . . . and to kepe ye Kinges consailx secree'. In giving them their charges, the king commanded that in the matters to be moved in his said council they should put forth their whole labours and diligences for his worship and profit.[3] He gave them power 'to hear, treat, commune, appoint, conclude, and determine such matters as shall happen to be moved among them'; but matters of great weight they were not to conclude fully without his advice. Finally, to guide their actions, he caused to be read the articles which were enacted in 1406 concerning the council of Henry IV. These had been understood before to give the council the utmost degree of power, but a reservation was now made in favour of the rights of the crown, that 'charters of pardon, collations of benefices, and offices and other things that are matters of grace shall be reserved for the king'.

As thus constituted the council remained without material alteration for the following six years or more. Additions and removals of individual members, it is true, were made from time to time in the normal way. For example, Thomas Beckington, doctor of laws, the king's secretary, who was destined to have a prominent diplomatic career, appears in the council in 1439. Lord Fanhope, who had served steadily up to 1437, but for some reason was not included in the list

[1] Nicolas, iv. 339.

[2] Lord Tiptoft particularly asks that his annuity of 100*m.* be converted in this manner. His petition concludes, 'Please to youre hynesse considering ye long service . . . to graunte . . . youre manoir of Bassyngbourn and ye baillywyk of Badburgham of the honour of Richmond in the counte of Cantebrige . . . in recompens of the seid hundred marcs.' The request was granted. *Council and Privy Seal,* file 60, May 5.

[3] Nicolas, v. 72; vi. 313.

of that year, returned in 1441.[1] In 1443 Adam Moleyns, hitherto clerk of the council, assumed an important place as a member of the council, and the next year was made keeper of the privy seal.[2] The duke of Gloucester, by reason of the prosecution of his wife for witchcraft in 1441, was thrown into retirement for a while, but he returned to the council in 1443, where he was frequently present until 1446, the year before he died.[3] At the same time Cardinal Beaufort recovered most of his former influence and was able on occasion fairly to dictate the decisions of the council,[4] until he too passed away in 1447. Whatever may be thought of the quarrels of the duke and the bishop, at this point we should not fail to observe that they had fought their battles mainly in the council chamber, and by centring their interests here they had made the council for the time the principal organ in the state. Never before, indeed, and not for a long time afterwards, did any men of similar rank and influence attend so closely to its routine daily affairs.[5] On the other hand, the disaffection of the earl of Northumberland, and his withdrawal from further attendance at the council in 1443, is to be remarked as one of the ominous signs for the future.[6]

Its continued power and stability.

There is naturally some difference to be observed in the conduct of the government after the reappointment of the council in 1437. But the dictum of Stubbs, that 'it became again a mere instrument in the hands of the king and the court',[7] is extreme, and cannot be maintained without qualification. In the main there was no immediate change

[1] Nicolas, v. 173 ff.

[2] On September 22, it is said, 'iurari fecit (rex) unum de consilio,' with a salary of £100, 'quamdiu ipsum Magistrum Adam custodem sigilli Regis de eodem consilio fore contigerit.' *Issue Roll* (*Pells*), 23 Hen. VI, Easter, m. 3.

[3] I find his name on the bills of the council so late as February 1446. *Warrants* (*Chancery*), file 1546.

[4] Nicolas, v. 27, 216.

[5] The extent to which these magnates heard petitions and served upon committees and commissions is entirely unparalleled. The duke is known to have acted on a commission of oyer and terminer: e. g. *Rot. Parl.* iv. 334; *Cal. Patent Rolls*, 17 Hen. VI, 313, &c.

[6] It was proposed in the council to examine the earl in respect of a letter which was said to have been written by him instigating certain riots. Northumberland sent to the council a schedule of answers to the charges, but he did not himself appear. Nicolas, v. 273–5.

[7] *Const. Hist.* iii. § 367.

either in point of personnel or in methods of work. Most of the lords, in fact, who had been prominent before, continued to give their services now, and there was no sudden reversion to a circle of household attendants. Not only did the lords repeatedly lend the king money in sums larger than their own salaries, but they were active in securing similar loans from others.[1] The great material difference lay in the appointments to office and other grants of the crown. In normal times these were undoubtedly matters of the royal prerogative, and now it is true grants were made consistently under the forms of royal authority.[2] For example, in 1441, when certain emissaries from Guienne approached the council with a request concerning the seneschalcy of that province, they were answered 'that it was not ye Kynges consailles part to graunte any such thing for it lay but oonly to ye Kyng and to noon other persone'.[3] The lords, however, did not hesitate to express their opinion that the office should be held by an Englishman rather than a native. But the changes of which we speak seem to have been much more a matter of form than of fact, for there was no lack of pressure exerted by the councillors both collectively and individually upon the king in the distribution of favours. Unfortunately Henry's generosity and pliability made him an easy prey to the self-seeking men who surrounded him. In the records we find no end of examples of grants made 'at the instance of the earl of Desmond', or 'of my lord Somerset and Adam Moleyns'; or perchance a statement that 'the king granted John Stourton's bill'. Sometimes a bill of this kind appears with the single signature of the earl of Suffolk or some other councillor.[4] Moreover, it was plainly the intention of the council to establish its power firmly in this most important point. In the guise of a series of suggestions, not to say ordinances, regarding the 'rule and order' to be followed in the treatment of petitions, the

[1] Nicolas, v. 199, 218; vi. 28.

[2] There were many royal letters under the signet, besides instances of the sign manual. Often a bill too is endorsed with the words, 'the kyng hath granted.' *Council and Privy Seal*, file 59, and others.

[3] Nicolas, v. 161.

[4] Ibid. 256, 274, 310, &c.; *Council and Privy Seal*, file 64.

following proposals were made : first, that if any lord of the council or any other person attending the king should be concerned in furthering any bill at court, he should subscribe his name thereto ' in order that it may be known at all times by whose means and labour every bill is ' ; bills of justice should be sent to the council, which was to decide whether the matter should be given to the courts of common law for adjudication ; but in regard to petitions of grace, there was a studied arrangement according to which the persons concerned were to write upon the back of the bill just what was asked for, and then ' the king *may* send it to his council to have their advice '. In case the king did not ask the advice of his council in this manner, there was a further provision that whatever grants were made by the king's grace should be issued by order of letters under the signet, which should be directed to the keeper of the privy seal, and by him warrants under the privy seal might be directed to the chancellor. In case the keeper of the privy seal deemed the matter to be 'of great charge', he was to 'have recourse to the lords of the council, and open to them the matter, to the intent that if it be thought necessary to them the king be advertised thereof, ere it pass '.[1] The numerous endorsements that were made upon the bills passed during these years, particularly in 1443 and 1444, leave no room for doubt that the lords of the council were temporarily successful in carrying out the intent of these ordinances.[2] In other words, the council that had ruled during the king's minority did not cease to rule him now, and the same aristocratic junto, which had formerly controlled and exploited the government, still retained its actual supremacy.

Influence of Suffolk.

A very material change in the affairs of the council is connected with the rise of the earl of Suffolk.[3] He was one

[1] Nicolas, v. 316–20.

[2] For a brief period, indeed, it would be difficult to find a bill for favour that was not passed upon by the council. *Council and Privy Seal*, file 73 ; *Cal. Patent Rolls*, 22 Hen. VI.

[3] William de la Pole was the fourth earl of this conspicuous family, which was never forgotten to have been of merchant origin. So distinguished were his achievements in the war under Henry V and the duke of Bedford, that one would not suppose that the charge of treason could ever be laid against him. In 1419 he was admiral of Normandy, in 1425

of the less prominent members as early as 1431, and was known as a supporter of Cardinal Beaufort in his policy of peace with France. For this reason he had been sent on various embassies, the most noted of which was the commission sent to the congress of Arras in 1435.[1] In 1444 he was made to take a decisive political step in spite of himself.[2] In response to the growing desire for peace, it was proposed in the council that he should be sent to France once more to open negotiations, but Suffolk protested that by reason of his friendship for the duke of Orleans he should not be entrusted with the mission. But on the advice of the council his objections were overruled, and the king insisted that he should go. The results of this embassy, as every one knows, gave a new turning-point to English politics. To gain the hand of Margaret of Anjou, in a moment of weakness, the commissioners made the fatal concession of the counties of Maine and Anjou. Although the act was approved at the time by the council, it was intensely unpopular with the war party, and brought the earl of Suffolk into open hostility with the duke of Gloucester. But by his influence with the king and queen, Suffolk's ascendancy at court from this time was assured. Probably he was acceptable to the king because he was the only man at the moment who could free him from the yoke that the duke of Gloucester and others had imposed upon the royal authority. Unlike Gloucester or Beaufort, Suffolk did not frequently show himself in the council, but with excessive disregard for his

lieutenant-general of Caen and Lower Normandy, besides holding various minor governorships and commands. His military career practically ended in 1430, when he returned to England and the next year came into the council. His marriage made him a connexion of the Beauforts, while his knowledge of events in France also led him to support their policy. In 1433 he became steward of the household; in 1435 he served on the commission which attended the congress of Arras; in 1437 he was steward of the duchy of Lancaster north of the Trent, and in 1440 chief justice of North Wales and of South Wales. He fairly outrivalled his predecessors in the acquisition of offices and posts of profit. In 1441 he was one of the commissioners to inquire into the sorceries of the duchess of Gloucester. It was his project to bring about the marriage of the king with Margaret of Anjou, and by his success in carrying out the plan, he was regarded as the most influential of Henry's advisers next to Cardinal Beaufort.

[1] *Foedera*, xi. 66, 80.

[2] The date of this event is incorrectly given as 1445 in Nicolas, vi. 32–5.

enemies carried his policy with the king independently of colleagues. This he was best in a position to do after the death of the former great leaders,[1] and when he was made chamberlain in 1447.[2] In the council it is true he had supporters, most notably Adam Moleyns, now bishop of Chichester, also Lord Saye and Sele, but it does not appear that he ever controlled a clear majority there. By the lords generally he was regarded with the jealousy and suspicion that they had always felt towards a predominating minister, whom they were likely to look upon as a royal favourite. Under the circumstances the council was not entrusted with important business as much as before, it was not able to enforce its demands that bills should be sent there for approval, and so by a rapid transition it entered upon a period of feebleness and inaction. This we may safely infer not only from the paucity of records which survive for these years, but also from the unimportant matters which are contained in them.[3] No longer were questions of policy and authority debated at length by the councillors, much less were grants of favour determined by them, but subjects like extra pay for the king's secretary, the compensation of messengers, the support of isolated garrisons, and the regulation of the wool trade were left to their serious consideration. The system of salaries, too, broke down almost entirely. So that with a lack of vital interest a conspicuous abstention on the part of the lords of the council was the result. Usually there were less than the required traditional number of six or four, and not infrequently there were only three or still fewer to do duty as a council. We find instances of the presence only of the chancellor and Moleyns, or of the chancellor and the keeper of the privy seal, or even of the chancellor alone.[4] Under these conditions of disintegration,

[1] Mr. Vickers believes that the evidence points to Suffolk as the one who chiefly connived at the death of the duke of Gloucester. On the very next day, it is proved, he received some of the offices lately held by the victim. *Humphrey, Duke of Gloucester*, 297 ff.

[2] The chamberlain was the officer who regularly received all petitions addressed to the king, and would be the one to transmit them to the council in case this was done. In the same year Suffolk was made admiral of England, and in 1448, at the summit of his power, he became a duke.

[3] Nicolas, *passim*.

[4] Ibid. v. 232, 240, 267, &c.

the only way for the government to hold a consultation of lords was to fall back upon the method of special summons.[1] In 1447 it was found necessary to urge the attendance of a greater number, by an order that 'the lords of the council and such others as shall be thought good to the lord chancellor be written to be here in the beginning of next term'.[2] It was, of course, the duty of councillors to be present during the term without special summons. In the same year, Suffolk came before a great council to defend his conduct in the cession of Anjou, but the council was not permitted to express an opinion, and the king gave him letters of vindication.[3] Again an attack was made upon the government in a council held in 1449, when a series of questions were put to the duke of Somerset concerning his conduct as governor in Normandy.[4] But as had been found to be true many times before, a council specially assembled and immediately dissolved was not able to enforce any policy. The main assault, therefore, upon the ministry of Suffolk came from another direction.

Quarrels of Lord Cromwell.

Of all his fellow councillors the one who had strongest reason to resent the rise of the king's favourite minister was Lord Cromwell. He was now the oldest member in point of service, and could well remember the days when the council was all-powerful. Although he had not failed to be in constant attendance, for reasons that we can only surmise he had given up the treasurership in 1443 and had seen most of his patronage taken away. In 1449 a quarrel broke out between Cromwell and William Tailboys, an esquire of the same neighbourhood, who on his side was believed to have the powerful support of the duke of Suffolk. During the parliament which met in November, Tailboys made a bodily attack upon Cromwell as he was coming to a meeting in the

[1] For the purpose of considering a convention with the king of France, a council was especially summoned to meet, October 6, 1446, to which the following lords were invited; the cardinal archbishop of York, the bishops of Norwich, Bath, Rochester, and Lincoln; the duke of Exeter, the duke of Buckingham, Lord Cromwell, Lord Hungerford, Sir John Stourton, the marquis of Dorset (Edmund Beaufort), and the marquis of Suffolk. *Council and Privy Seal*, file 77.

[2] Ibid. vi. 60.

[3] *Rot. Parl.* v. 447; *Cal. Patent Rolls*, 25 Hen. VI, 78.

[4] Stevenson, *Letters of the English in France* (Rolls Series), ii. 718 ff.

star chamber. Cromwell appealed to the house of lords, where, without a trial, he obtained a statement vindicating himself and declaring Tailboys to be known as a murderer and a breaker of the peace, and to have committed 'the greatest, most heinous and most odious riot that hath been seen'.[1] At the same time the resignation of Lumley the treasurer, and of Moleyns the keeper of the privy seal, was also a blow to the power of Suffolk. Bishop Moleyns, who had been an eager partisan during the recent strifes, was murdered shortly afterwards. How far other lords of the council were concerned we do not know, but Cromwell's great opportunity for revenge came during the second session of the same parliament in 1450, when he took advantage of the discontent of the commons, and led them to the impeachment of Suffolk.[2] The articles containing the charges in this famous case were stated with extreme partisanship and with obvious distortions of the truth, but they nevertheless reveal much of what was thought concerning the duke and the council. Much was made of his 'untrue coloured counseilles'; he was accused of revealing to the French 'the privite, ordenaunce and provision of your (i.e. the king's) counseill'; he was alleged to have boasted that 'he had his place in the counsail hous of the Frenesh Kyng'; it was said that 'beyng next and pryvyest of your Counsaill' he had allured the king to give and to grant many of his possessions to the impoverishment of the royal domains; that 'without the knowing or assent of the lords of the council' he had brought about the convention with France. Underneath a mass of exaggerations, we can see that the portion of the accusations against Suffolk alleging that he had acted as 'sole councillor' and in disregard of the others, is supported by the facts; and this was in reality the main reason for his downfall. In the same year Jack Cade's revolt broke out with a special political bearing. Among the articles of complaint which are reported then to have been made, is the following one concerning the king's council: 'that the lords of his royal blood have been put from his daily presence, and other mean persons of lower

Impeachment of Suffolk, 1450.

Cade's rebellion

[1] *Rot. Parl.* v. 200. [2] Ibid. 177 ff.

nature exalted and made chief of his privy council.'[1] So corrupt was this body, it was declared, that no redress could be obtained 'but if bribes and gifts be messengers to the hands of the said council'. Furthermore, there were said to be grave cases of injustice, in which people were accused of treason and kept in prison without trial, on the information of persons about the court who had influence to obtain grants of the confiscated lands. The political designs of the movement are seen in further demands that the king 'remove the evil counsellors', and that he take about his person such 'true lords' as the duke of York, the duke of Exeter, the dukes of Norfolk and of Buckingham. The advocates of these and all similar proposals were likely to forget a fact which the experience of former years had abundantly proved, that even when great lords were appointed to the council it was still another matter to induce them to serve. Much less was it assured that they would be devoted to the interests of the state when they were willing to come.

Efforts to reform the council, 1450–1.

From this time all efforts whether of reform or of opposition to the government were directed toward the reconstruction of the king's council. In this movement the duke of York was the natural leader.[2] Coming home from Ireland he presented letters of protest to the king, who gave in reply the following promise: '(we) have determined in our soul to establish a sad and a substantial council, giving them more ample authority and power than ever we did before this; in the which we have appointed you to be one. (And since it is not customary to take counsel from one alone) we have determined to send for our chancellor and for other lords of

[1] This is not a contemporary account, but a narrative that has been preserved in Stowe, *General Chronicle* (ed. 1614), p. 389, and Gregory's *Chronicle* (Camden Society, 1876), pp. 195 ff.

[2] Richard, duke of York, representative of two lines of descent from Edward III, in 1436 was made lieutenant-general of France and Normandy. At his own request he was recalled in 1437, although the council wrote letters urging him to stay. In 1440 he was again appointed the king's lieutenant with a salary of £20,000 a year. He was an adherent of Gloucester and after the latter became the chief rival of Suffolk and the Beauforts. In 1447, to get him out of the way, the government made him lieutenant in Ireland, where he was allowed to hold unrestricted authority. His return to England in 1450 was a definite challenge to the existing régime.

our council . . . to commune these and other great matters.' [1] But under the duke of Somerset, who became the real successor of Suffolk as the leading minister, no such reform was made, although two of the older councillors, Lord Dudley and the abbot of Gloucester, who had been identified with the peace policy of Suffolk, were at the moment removed and for a short time imprisoned. The duke of York, however, gained support in parliament and accomplished something here in the way of legislation. The Resumption Act of 1451, which attempted to annul a large portion of the king's grants, contained a clause that grants which were passed by the advice of the chancellor, the treasurer, the keeper of the privy seal, and six lords of the council should have full validity, 'provided their names be subscribed and it be a matter of record.' [2] In the same spirit an order to the officials of the exchequer commanded them that in their judicial proceedings they should obey no warrants to surcease, 'save only such as pass by the advice of our council.' [3] Some effort, too, was made to bring adherents of the duke of York into the council, as is seen in a letter of summons to Lord Cobham. The king remonstrates with him for his failure to attend, considering it a 'great untruth and disobedience meant', and commands him to come without delay to perform such service as he ought to do.[4]

Strifes and failures, 1453.

But nothing that was done under the duke of Somerset to re-establish the council in its constitutional form was successful. By 1453 the strife of the Percies and the Nevilles in the north had broken into civil war, while the letters of summons, the commissions of inquiry, and the commissions of oyer and terminer sent out by the council were defied.[5] To Lord Egremont in particular the king writes, 'divers tymes heretofore we have yeve you in commaundement by oure letters for suche causes as moeved us to have be and appered before us and oure counsaille . . . to the which our letters and commaundement ye in no wyse obeying have differed so to appere.' The only part which the government could

[1] Stowe, p. 395; cited in Gairdner, *Paston Letters* (London, 1900–1), Introd., pp. xcvi ff.
[2] *Rot. Parl.* v. 218.
[3] Nicolas, vi. 104.
[4] Ibid. 116.
[5] Ibid. 140 ff.

play, in fact, was to take the side of the Percies against the Nevilles, commending them for their efforts to repress lawlessness.[1] In the face of many flagrant local disorders, the council proved to be never so powerless as at this time when its writs were commonly evaded or defied, and when the number of pardons granted in hundreds of cases amounted practically to a suspension of the course of justice.[2]

The duke of York and the council, November 21, 1453.

In the same year the fall of Bordeaux and also the failure of the king's health brought the problem of the government to a crisis. A great council was called for November 21, to which the duke of York was invited not in the regular way but by special letters on the part of his friends. Somerset did not join in the invitation to his rival, but he evidently could not prevent the action of the others. The duke of York understood the summons as an expression of willingness to accept his services, and he came to the council, which was attended by twenty-five prelates and lords, especially of his own supporters. The duke then made a declaration, which he was careful to have put on record, to the effect that he was the king's true liegeman and subject, and was ready to work with all diligence for the welfare of the king and his subjects. Observing the absence of various older councillors, who had been warned not to come, he continued, 'but for asmoche as it soo was that divers persones such as of longe tyme have been of (the king's) counsail have be commaunded . . . not to entende upon him but to withdrawe thaim of any counsail to be yeven unto him, the which is to his greet hurte and causeth that he can not procede with suche matiers as he hath to doo in the kinges courtes and ellus where, (the duke) desired the lordes of the counsail above said that they wolde soo assente and agree that suche as have been of his counsail afore this tyme might frely w[t]oute any impediment resort unto him and withoute any charge to be leide unto thaim yeve him counsail from tyme

[1] Nicolas, vi. 158 ff.

[2] *Cal. Patent Rolls, passim* ; also a *Pardon Roll*, 30–31 Hen. VI, described in Gairdner, *Paston Letters*, Introd., p. cxxvii. Among a host of less interesting names on the latter roll, one finds particularly the dukes of York, Norfolk, and Suffolk, Thomas Percy Lord Egremont, the earl of Devon, Lord Cromwell, Sir Henry Percy, Lord Poynings, and others.

to tyme in such matiers as he hath or shal have to doo. To the which desire that was thought unto thaim juste and resounable, and (he) fully licensed alle suche persones as he wolde calle to his counsail frely withoute any impediment to entende unto him, and commaunded this to be enacted a monge th'actes of the counsaill.' [1]

Plans in parliament, 1454.

The duke of York, now supported by a strong body of nobles, was fully victorious in the council and began the work of transforming the government. Somerset was put in prison on charges presented by the duke of Norfolk.[2] On February 13, 1454, as many as twenty-nine lords were present to advise that the duke of York be given full power to hold and dissolve a parliament.[3] The schemes proposed in this parliament, which met at Westminster, February 14, show a vivid recollection of the methods taken in former years.[4] In an opening speech the chancellor declared 'that there should be ordained a sad and wise council of the right discreet lords and others of this land, to whom all people might have recourse for the ministering of justice, equity, and righteousness, whereof they have no knowledge as yet'. On receiving a report that the king was quite helpless, the lords decided that the duke of York should be 'chief of the king's council', and then, devising, as they said, a name different from other councillors, they chose him to be 'Protector and

[1] *Cal. Patent Rolls,* 32 Hen. VI, 143. [2] *Paston Letters,* i, no. 191.

[3] This commission is mentioned but is not embodied in the parliament roll. It is found among the acts of the council, the full text of which is as follows:

'The xjij^th daye of Feverer the yere of the Regne of our souverain lorde the king Henri the VIth, XXXII^t at Westm in the greet counseel chambre it was demaunded by the chaunceller of Englande to whoom the kinges power sholde be committed for the holding of the parlement at this tyme, and it was aunswered advised and accorded by the lordes here undre subscribed that the said power sholde be committed to the Duc of Yorke and that the said chaunceller of England sholde doo make a commission in due and ample fourme to the said duc of York under the greet seal to thentent abovesaid, and to procede ende and dissolve ye said parlement and to do all thyng yt shalbe necessarie yerfore to any of ye premisses . . .

'Die mense anno et loco supradictis advisatum et concordatum fuit ut supra presentibus dominis Card. Cant., Archiepo. Ebor., Epis. London., Winton., Elien., Norwicen., Hereford., Sar., Lincoln., Dunelm., Comitibus War., Sar., Devon., Wigorn., Thes. Anglie, Oxon., Salop., Baronibus P. S. Joh., Cromwel, Greystok, Grey, Ruthyn, FitzHugh, Duddelay, Clynton, FitzWaren, Stourton, Scrop, Rotland.' *Warrants (Chancery)*, file 1546.

[4] *Rot. Parl.* v. 238 ff.

Defender of the Realm '.[1] In accepting this position the duke proposed that after the manner of previous precedents a council should be named, and that the members should ' take upon them so to be and also accept and admit the charge thereof '. To this suggestion the councillors, who were apparently already selected, themselves objected, asking that they might first be permitted to confer with one another. As a result, no council was named in public, nor was any list of councillors read before the present parliament. But on a later day every one concurred in the enactment that all offices and benefices in the gift of the king should be disposed of, ' by advice of the protector and council.' [2] The prevalent unwillingness, too, of the lords to attend either parliaments or councils was met by an ordinance that fines should be imposed upon absentees at the discretion of the council. It afterwards appears that the proposal to reorganize the council was more definitely drawn than appears upon the rolls of parliament. Mention is made of a certain act of the council of April 15, and this, taken in connexion with the assignments of the year,[3] enables us to draw up a list of the councillors as follows :

Richard, earl of Salisbury, the protector's brother-in-law, was appointed chancellor April 1, with a salary of 200*l.* for attending the council.

John Tiptoft, earl of Worcester, a friend of York's, retained his office of treasurer, with a salary as councillor of 200*m.*

Lord Dudley, treasurer of the royal household, although he had been removed in 1450, was restored to the council in 1452, and was allowed a salary of 100*m.*[4]

The bishop of Winchester	200*m.*
The bishop of Lincoln	200*m.*
The earl of Warwick	200*m.*
Lord Cromwell	200*m.*
Viscount Beaumont	200*m.*
John Say, esquire	40*l.*

It is not unlikely that the act of April 15 was still more

[1] *Rot. Parl.* v. 242. On July 18, York was made captain of Calais in place of Somerset.

[2] Ibid., 248.

[3] *Issue Roll* (*Pells*), 34 Hen. VI, Easter, m. 9 ; 36 Hen. VI, Easter, m. 2, &c.

[4] Ibid., 33 Hen. VI, Mich., m. 11.

comprehensive in its scope, as it was probably modelled on the earlier enactments of the kind.[1]

Brief revival of council forms.

For over a year, while the duke of York held supremacy, there was a manifest revival of the forms of conciliar procedure. This, it is true, arose from the necessities of the duke's political position, and was directed largely to a partisan advantage,[2] but without doubt the effect was to postpone the disintegration of the council. It was the stated policy of the protector that the council should not be composed exclusively of one party, yet such was the inevitable result. It was also his manifest intention not to maintain the council as a small exclusive body, but to gather into it as many lords as possible. When the lords in attendance were not sufficient he caused the others to be summoned. On April 16 letters were sent to as many as twenty-four lords, all Yorkists, reminding them 'for somoche we have ordened that our Counsaill shall in goodely haste be assembled . . . of the whiche ye be oon,'[3] &c. Again, on July 24, similar letters were sent forth admonishing the lords for their disobedience in not coming before.[4] This was done as many as four or five times during the year, so that it is not unusual to find as many as twenty or thirty lords in the council. At other times the number shrinks to six or seven. On these occasions, it may be excusable to repeat, there was not the slightest distinction between the great council and the privy council as regards organization or procedure. The former was simply an expanded and therefore more dignified session of the latter, but with the same methods of business and subjects of control. Instead of a clearer definition of the

[1] If the record of attendance during the following months be taken, of course the list of councillors would be greatly extended. Nicolas, vi. 174 ff.

[2] See, for instance, the long declaration that was made and put on record at the request of Lord Cromwell in February 1453. The original statement covered fifty-six sheets of paper, in which he protests his loyalty and vindicates himself against Robert Collison, who had slandered him. All these articles were said to have been read before the council, and after an 'examination' was held, Collison was sent to prison until he should give satisfaction. *Additional Manuscripts* (*British Museum*), vol. 4521, ff. 99–100. *Cal. Patent Rolls*, 31 Hen. VI, 93. The council itself recommended Thomas Bourchier who was elected archbishop of Canterbury, and designated George Neville, the chancellor's son, for the next vacant bishopric. Nicolas, vi. 168, 170.

[3] Ibid. 174.

[4] Ibid. 216.

privy council, as distinguished from the great council and so-called *consilium ordinarium*, the peculiar difficulties of these years nearly caused the abandonment of the idea of a small continual council, while in its stead was revived the earlier form of special assemblies. Resuming then a large share of its former powers, the council (or councils) took up with much vigour the problems of the government, giving attention particularly to the disorders that troubled the country. On June 13 the riotous scholars of Cambridge were summoned, and on July 8 the rioters of Bath.[1] With reference to the civil war in the north, letters of summons were sent to the duke of Exeter, Lord Egremont, Lord Roos, Richard Percy, and others, to answer for their conduct.[2] On the occasion of the summons of his son, the earl of Northumberland was invited to be present in a message to the following effect: '(we) think your presence here with us and our council should be right expedient'. But the Percies now were as unwilling to trust themselves to the arbitrament of the council as the Nevilles had been before. The duke of Somerset, however, was a prisoner and could be dealt with. On July 18 a great council was assembled to discuss his case.[3] In an address the protector justified the summary arrest of the duke on the ground that it had been done by the lords of the council, 'at that time being of great number'. As to the question of releasing him on bail, the protector urged that the advice of the judges as well as the opinion of absent lords first be obtained. It was then agreed that the charges made against him should not be heard until October 28.[4] It does not appear, however, that anything was done even on that day.

Alternations during 1455.

In 1455 the king's recovery of his senses brought a reversal in the government once more. On March 4, before a great council, at which the duke of York was present, Somerset was released and returned to power.[5] The king's council, we

[1] *Council and Privy Seal*, file 84.
[2] Nicolas, vi. 178 ff.
[3] Ibid. 206.
[4] Ibid. 218.
[5] This act of the council recites that the duke had been kept in the Tower for a year, until February 7, 1455, when he was released on bail. He was now set free and vindicated, while a copy of the act was given by the keeper of the privy seal to the chancery for an enrolment. *Cal. Patent Rolls*, 33 Hen. VI, 226.

are told, was reconstructed, although of its personnel we know nothing except that the duke of York wrote as follows concerning it: 'for asmoche as we understonde that other lords of this lande have be late sent fore, by the Kynges commaundement under his letters, to comen unto his consail privately late called at Westmynstre, where unto we have not been among the said Lordes called, we conceyve a jelosy had ayenst us.' [1] The duke of York, however, fully recovered his position by the battle of Saint Albans. In a parliament, which was opened on July 9, he accepted again the title of protector, making further proposals for the rehabilitation of the council.[2] He expressed his complete willingness to rule with the advice and assent either of the lords in parliament or of those whom it may please the king to name of his privy council. 'Whereas some have not given so diligent attendance as they should have done,' so that affairs had been 'thrown into jeopardous omission, not executed', he asked parliament to appoint a proper number 'not of favour nor affection, but such as be approved of virtuous and righteous disposition'. As to inducements to serve, the protector shows a knowledge of the past when he continues, 'and foras muchas it accordeth not with reason that any lord give attendance or bear the charge, unless the pension or annuity assigned him be duly paid according to his attendance and the continuance thereof'; he urges, therefore, the house of lords to ordain that 'sufficient, agreeable, and undelayed payment' be made to the lords to be named of the council. The protector also complained that his own annuity of 2,000 marks, awarded in the last parliament, had not been paid, and he asked for himself a 'sufficient and agreeable payment'. It was agreed that he should have a salary of 3,000 marks. As to the problem of absences he suggested that these be permitted only with the special consent of the council, and that the cause should be certified in writing. The schemes of the protector were readily accepted, and it was added that the council should have the unusual power of appointment to all offices and benefices not otherwise specified. There is evidence, finally,

The duke Protector.

[1] *Rot. Parl.* v. 281. [2] Ibid. 286 ff.

that the councillors were ordained, or at least received their charges, formally in parliament, for the king expressed his will that they work for the welfare of his person, and the lords replied that they would serve him as well as ' ever did any councillors or subjects '.[1] During the second protectorate of the duke of York there was another brief period of conciliar activity. Concerning the work done there is not much to be said, except that offices were the spoils of one party instead of the other, although at no time was there anything like a ' clean sweep ' in this respect.

Failure of the protectorate and of the council, 1456.

On the improvement of the king's mental health the termination of the protectorate was confidently predicted. It was regarded as possible, however, that the duke of York might still be retained as chief councillor, but with diminished powers. As was observed by one in touch with the court, ' the kyng, as it was tolde me by a grete man, wolde have hym chief and princepall counciller, and soo to be called hise chief counciller and lieutenant as longe as hit shulde lyke the Kyng : and his patent to be made in that form, and not soo large as it is by Parlement.'[2] But the influence now exercised by the queen was strong enough to cause his commission as protector to be withdrawn entirely on February 26, 1456. Whether the duke had still any claim to the title of chief councillor, is a question of no consequence, since he ceased to hold the leading influence. In a council held at Coventry during the following October the duke of Buckingham strongly urged the king to take York again into his favour, but though Henry was willing the queen was hostile to the proposal. After the fall of the duke then there was no other attempt to organize a council in accordance with the familiar ideals of the period. Instead of a ' great and continual council ' the king could only summon the lords on special occasions, when they came with evident

[1] *Rot. Parl.* v. 290. We are not given a list of the councillors on this occasion, nor has it been possible to determine precisely who they were, but during the month of August acts were passed in the presence of Archbishop Bourchier, chancellor, Viscount Bourchier, treasurer; the bishops of London and Winchester; the earls of Warwick, Salisbury, and Worcester; Lords Fauconberg and Stanley; the prior of Saint John's, the dean of Saint Severin, and John Say. Nicolas, vi. 257–8.

[2] *Paston Letters*, no. 275.

reluctance, while at other times their attendance fell to the vanishing point. Manifestly the real issues of the time were passing from the control of parliaments and councils into the fields of battle. For the remaining years of the reign the records fail more completely than for any previous time during the century.[1] From the few notes and hints that remain we infer that the sessions were not regularly kept up and that suitors were turned away in disappointment. One of the Paston letters, of June 7, 1456, says: 'the Lords Chaunceller, Tresorier, and th'Erle of Sar(esbury) (were) in London, and noo more Lords at the begynyng this day of the grete Counsail. Many men say that there shuld be, but thei wote not what'.[2] And again, on October 8, the same correspondent writes from London, 'for here til this day come noo counsaill . . . the Kyng and the Quene ar at Coventre. The Counsail be ganne there yesterday';[3] and on October 16, 'sum men seyn, the counseal is dissolved and that the Kyng is forth to Chester'.[4] Still the king needed the lords at times, and he would remind them of their duties with pathetic urgency. Planning to hold a great council at Westminster in November, 1457, he wrote, 'we shall have noon excused of his comyng to our said Consaill in any wise that oweth to be there.'[5] This council succeeded in excluding Bishop Pecock for his heretical leanings, but because of dissensions it broke up on November 29 to meet again January 27. Although the king himself was present on the day set, the lords came with marked tardiness, till on February 14 it was found the earl of Arundel, by reason of disaffection, was still absent.[6] He did not appear in fact until the king had sent a special letter peremptorily commanding his attendance. It was explained, 'we called oure said Counsaill in especial to sette apart suche variances as ben betwixt divers lordes of this oure reaume.'[7] In the following

[1] No notes whatever are found between January 1456 and the end of November 1457. I do not regard the loss of records at this point a mere accident, since the files of warrants show a similar gap as regards bills answered by the council.

[2] *Paston Letters*, no. 285.

[3] Ibid., no. 295.

[4] Ibid., no. 298.

[5] Nicolas, vi. 290 ff.

[6] *Paston Letters*, no. 313.

[7] Nicolas, vi. 293.

August the king summoned all the lords of the council in a letter stating their duties in the following manner :

Summons, August 26, 1458.

'Reverent fader in God ; How be it as ye know well all the lordes and other persones suche as be of oure Counsail owen in the terme tyme to yeve attendaunce to the same, yit for suche matiers as concerne specially oure honeure and worship, the welfare of this oure land and subgittes, we write unto you that be of oure Counsaill thees our lettres praying and also charging [you] that withoute any faille ye wol be atte oure paleys of Westminster the xi day of October next comyng to yeve youre sadde advys in the said matiers and othir suche as shalbe treted in oure Counsail there.'[1]

Disintegration of the council.

The number of those whom the king considered to be of his council on this occasion was no less than thirty-three, among whom are found the duke of York and about a dozen of his partisans.

During these years of disintegration the tendency of the council to resume its earlier and more primitive aspect is very manifest. Since the lords more and more failed to give their regular attendance as councillors, while many of them were reluctant to come even upon the most urgent request, we notice once more the inclination to retain in their places a number of lesser men. For example, in 1453 two knights in the king's employ, William Lucy and Thomas Tyrell, are called councillors, and as such they were employed on various commissions and in the judicial proceedings of the star chamber.[2] Again, in 1455, Master John Derby, a clerk of the chancery and a doctor of laws, is named among those in attendance.[3] Even so there was no resemblance to the active council which Richard II had brought together from among his officers and household attendants.[4] The degree of strangulation that now was reached is shown also by several of the particular measures taken.

During the last struggles to keep up the dying monarchy,

[1] Nicolas, vi. 297. [2] Ibid. 148, 153 ; *Cal. Patent Rolls,* 31 Hen. VI, 93.

[3] *Warrants* (*Chancery*), file 1546.

[4] The last bill which I have found signed by those present in the council is of the date June 7, 1459, and bears the names of the archbishop of York, the bishops of Winchester, London, Norwich, Durham, the dean of St. Severin, Lord Dudley, and Richard of York. *Council and Privy Seal,* file 88.

in 1459 a revocation of letters patent was ordered by advice of the chancellor, the justices, the serjeants-at-law, and the king's attorney.[1] Another order given in 1460 was that all persons lending the king money should have repayment out of the confiscated possessions of the duke of York and the lords adhering to him.[2] Finally, in the parliament of 1460, when the duke of York's claim to the throne was asserted, the following colloquy with the justices took place. The lords, it is said, desiring to have 'the advice and good counsel' of all the king's councillors (or counsellors) sent for the justices, the serjeants-at-law, and the king's attorney.[3] The justices then prayed to be excused as the matter 'must needs exceed their learning', saying that 'between party and party', that is political parties, they were not of the council. But they were answered in behalf of the lords, that they might not be so excused, 'for they were the king's particular councillors and therefore they had their fees and wages.' But the serjeants and the attorney insisted that 'they were the king's councillors in law, but this matter was above their authority'. This is a clearer statement of the position of the justices than any previously made.

Its powerlessness in administration and judicature.

In no wise was the failure of the Lancastrian council more complete than in its special field of judicature. While in former years the complaints of parliament were constantly directed against the excessive powers assumed in this regard, now even the voice of complaint was stopped. Suitors in fact ceased to seek redress in a court which failed them so completely, and prosecutions for violence were given up from sheer futility. Amid the overt rebellions of Yorkist lords, the council was powerless to compel either attendance or obedience. In 1457 there occurs the curious record of a case in which the duke of Norfolk after repeated disobedience to the writs of summons, was finally discharged. The passage is worth quoting in full.

[1] *Cal. Patent Rolls*, 37 Hen. VI, 485.

[2] Among the proscribed adherents of the duke of York were the earls of March, Warwick, Salisbury, and Rutland; the countess of Salisbury, Thomas and John Neville, Thomas Harington, Sir Thomas Parr, Sir John Wenlock, James Pickering, John and Edward Bourchier, Thomas Colt, Thomas Vaughan, &c. Ibid., 38 Hen. VI, 597.

[3] *Rot. Parl.* v. 376.

'XV Pasch. 35 H. VI, att Westm in the starr chamber before the councell of the kinge, John Duke of Norfolke against whom upon a statute made at Readinge there went forth severall writts as well to the sheriffes of London as to the sheriffs of Suffolke to make proclamation that the said duke should appeare before the Counsell aforesaid to answeare to the Kinge, as well for a contempte for not appearinge by virtue of another writt to him directed, as to certaine riotts and offenses specified in the said writt of proclamation, of the which processe the said duke was discharged as by the Record appeareth.' [1]

Reflections of Sir John Fortescue.

A last word on the Lancastrian privy council may be obtained from the writings of Sir John Fortescue, the eminent chief justice of the king's bench during the later years of Henry VI. He is well known for various works, political and theoretical, but the one entitled *On the Governance of England* [2] is the one most based upon practical experience, and shows real insight into the failure of the Lancastrian system. The treatise is believed to have been written after 1470, possibly with the purpose of suggesting to the government of that time certain desired reforms; but as these reforms were never carried out it is valuable mainly for its reflections of Lancastrian conditions. In his observations on the king's council, to which two chapters are devoted besides various other allusions, Fortescue spoke from abundant knowledge, for he had been constantly called to attend its sessions and had served on various commissions. Once indeed he received the formal thanks of the council for his services in these ways. His chapters upon this subject give us certain definitions and opinions which no one else has stated so clearly.

As to the composition of the council Fortescue takes the strongly aristocratic point of view. 'The kynges counsell', he begins, 'was wonned to be chosen off grete princes and off the gretteste lordes off ye lande both spirituelles and temporelles, and also off oyer men that were in grete auctorite, and offices.' [3] The suitable number of members he suggests

[1] *Additional Manuscripts* (*British Museum*), vol. 4521, f. 92. The entire problem of judicature will be treated at greater length in chap. xi.

[2] Ed. Charles Plummer (Oxford, 1885), especially chaps. xiv and xv; also Appendix A contains tract on 'Good Counseill'. The editor gives a brief historical survey of the council in his Introduction.

[3] Op. cit., chap. xiv.

is twenty-four. As to the officers he places these in a position of secondary importance.

'Yer may be off this counsell, when thai liste come yerto, or yat thai be desired be ye said counsellours, ye grete officers off ye lande, as Chaunceler, tresorer, and prive seell; off wich ye chaunceler, when he is present, mey be presydent, and have ye suppreme rule off all ye counsell. Also the Juges, the Barons off ye exchequier, ye clerk off the rolles, and suche lordes as ye forsaid counsellours woll desire to be with thaym for materes off grete difficulte, mey be off this counsell when thai be so desyred, and ellis not.'

That certain men might be of the council for the time being is the true explanation of the relations held by the judges as well as the lords whose attendance was only occasional. Strange to say, Fortescue does not advocate in his scheme any degree of parliamentary control; but he thinks that the king's power should be limited, in that councillors should be removed only for some definite offence, and then with the consent of a majority of their colleagues. He had no high opinion of the abilities of parliament, which in matters of legislation he thought was quite incapable of devising measures, unless they were first prepared by the council. 'Ye parlementes shall mowe do more gode in a moneth to ye mendynge off the lawe, then thai shall mowe do in a yere yff ye amendynge yer off be not debated and be such counsell ryped to thair handes.'[1] The members, he thought, should be sworn after a form of oath 'to be devised', as though revision were constantly necessary, 'and in especiall yat thai shall take no fee nor clothynge nor no rewarde off any man except only off ye kynge.' As to the difficulty of maintaining secrecy, he seems to be giving an historical fact when he declares, 'then couude no mater treted in the counsell be kept prive. Ffor the lordes often tymes tolde ther owne counsellours and servantes, that had suyd to hem ffor the maters, how thai had sped in ham, and who was ayen ham.' The king should give his full confidence to his regular councillors, and 'not be counseled by men of his chambre, of his housholde, nor other which can not counsele hym'. In

[1] Ibid., chap. xv.

a tract on 'Good Counseill', all the misfortunes of England are traced by him to the fact that 'our kinges have bene ruled by private counselloures, such as have offered their service and counseile and were not chosen thereto'.[1] To maintain a council of the right character, salaries, he urges, should be paid, although they 'seme a newe and a grete charge to ye kynge'. But the expense would be small compared with the great advantages to be gained, for only in this way could a sufficient body of men be held together. 'Trewly such a continuall counsell mey wel be called *multa consilia* ffor it is ofte and euere day counsellith.' Members of unequal rank should be free in their deliberations, as was formerly enjoined 'always with due reverence kept to every estat and persone'. Fortescue complains that no 'lower man . . . durste say ayen the openyon off any off the grete lordis'. He reveals the prevalence of private interests in the council, saying 'when thai come togedre, thai were so occupied with thair owne maters, and with the maters off thair kynne, seruantes, and tenantes, yat thai entendet but litle, and oyer while no thynge, to ye kynges maters'. Finally, as a matter of record, all the acts of the council should be 'putt in a boke, and that boke kept in this counsell as a registir or a ordinarye, how thai shall doo in euery thynge'. The words of this great theorist reflect unmistakably the aims of the period we have just covered. These of course had never been fully realized, and they had proved a failure in many essential respects. In spite of all weaknesses and deficiencies, however, Fortescue remained an advocate of the council more than of the king or parliament. How these ideas were to be received and altered during the Yorkist régime we shall be prepared to treat in a succeeding chapter.

[1] Op. cit., Appendix A.

CHAPTER IX

THE COUNCIL AND THE EXCHEQUER

In the previous chapters the subject of this work has been followed through certain well-marked periods, wherein the council was considered in its composition and general political bearings. There now remain certain phases of the history which can best be presented by a topical method of treatment. In particular there is the problem, already suggested in the third chapter, of the relations of the council and its kindred branches. It was intended to be made clear at the start that the king's council was never a specially created institution, and at no time during the middle ages did it lose its original character as a single controlling organ in the state. Moreover, the differentiation of the various courts did not occur at any specific time, the process in fact continued for over a century, while a reversion to the original type at any moment was easily made. During the reign of Edward I certainly there were at least three important bodies, which were as yet only partially defined and not entirely separated from one another, namely, the king's bench, the exchequer, and the parliament. The king's bench, as has been shown, was at that time not fully a court of common law, but it was rapidly being drawn away from the council into the prevailing judicial current. There is now the same question to be asked as regards the exchequer. To what extent were the council and the exchequer still identified with each other? and when does the exchequer, after the manner of the other courts, become separated from the council as a specialized body? This question has already been answered only as regards the purely fiscal operations, which were made a matter of rule and routine at a much earlier day. But the answer has yet to be given in regard to the general administrative and judicial functions, which

Problem of the council and the courts.

are known to have been exercised here in the time of Edward I and afterwards.

The exchequer a general secretariat;

It will be remembered that in the beginning the exchequer was not solely a revenue department. The machinery that was devised for one purpose was found to be efficient for other purposes as well. So that the exchequer was actually a general secretariat for all kinds of government business. Even after the chancery was made a separate department, the older organization did not cease to exercise a share of these general functions, and to retain a certain primacy among the government departments. With its staff of officers, including the treasurer and barons, the chamberlains, and clerks, maintaining as many as three contemporaneous rolls, and exercising a direct control over the sheriffs, the exchequer was for a long time undoubtedly the best equipped of all the existing courts and offices. It has been said, however, upon the weighty authority of Madox, that already during the reign of Henry III a decline of its power began to be felt,[1] and this view has been supported by the still weightier authority of Stubbs and Maitland, who have been disposed to regard the chancery from this time as the more prominent department. 'Since the fall of the great justiciar,' says Stubbs, 'the Chancellor was in dignity, as well as in power and influence, second to the king.'[2] This view of the situation can have been derived only from a partial reading of the records, for at the present day the rolls of the chancery are far more accessible than those of the exchequer. But when a wider survey is taken, it will be found that upon the relative positions of the treasurer and the chancellor, and likewise those of the exchequer and the chancery, there is at least room for argument. Upon this point it is likely that the history of the council will afford further information.

[1] *History of the Exchequer*, ii. 2.

[2] *Const. Hist.* ii. 282. At first we have said that the chancellor, or keeper of the seal, held a certain advantage by virtue of his personal attendance upon the king. But during the reign of Edward I this relationship was altered, since the privy seal became the immediate instrument of the king's will, and the chancery became like the exchequer, a department located at Westminster.

In the first place, it is evident that the exchequer did not lose its character as a court of general assemblage. The traditional principle of the earlier *curia regis* was that there should be consultation in proportion to the importance and difficulty of the questions to be determined. There would be no need, we understand, to hold such an assemblage except in a court of discretionary power. Under Edward I early usages in this regard were actively maintained in the exchequer. To a considerable extent its sessions were still the sessions of the council. Magnates, justices, and others of the council are described as 'sitting', 'assisting', or 'residing' at the exchequer.[1] This was a matter of some regularity and planned for in advance, as is shown by various writs of summons citing men on set days to come *coram consilio regis existente hic in scaccariis*.[2] Moreover, when the exchequer was moved to York, as was done in 1298, the council is found to have gathered there with no less regularity than formerly at Westminster. On one occasion a petitioner is told, *expectet usque ad reditum aliorum de consilio regis apud Eboracum*.[3]

as a court of general assemblage.

The manner of assembling the council in addition to the regular officials under these circumstances is also made clear. While it was customary for parliaments and great councils to be summoned by writs in the name of the king, the gathering of smaller councils was committed to the treasurer, or the chancellor. To the treasurer, for example, the king would send a writ of the privy seal, enclosing a petition or specifying the business to be treated, and directing that the council be called in the following words :

How assembled.

'. . . et a cele busoigne deliverer appelez a vous notre chancellier et de notre justices et des autres gentz qui sont de notre consail a Londres les queux vous verrez,' &c. [4]

[1] 'Et per Thesaurarium et Barones, fratrem W. de Hotham et H. le Despenser de consilio Regis iuratos eis assidentes concordatum est.' *Memoranda Roll, Exchequer K. R.*, 25 Edw. I, m. 54 d. ; also *L. T. R.*, 2 Edw. II, m. 60 ; *K. R.*, 4 Edw. II, m. 54, &c.

[2] *Memoranda Roll*, 34–35 Edw. I, Mich. Com., m. 19 d., 22 d., 20, &c.

[3] *Ancient Petitions*, E. 431 ; also *Memoranda Roll*, 30–31 Edw. I, Hil. Brev., m. 69.

[4] *Ancient Correspondence*, xlv, nos. 121, 131, 137, &c. ; *ante*, p. 73.

Writs of this kind, according to the business in hand, were likewise sent to the chancellor, sometimes to the treasurer and chancellor jointly, but in the time of Edward I the greater number were directed to the treasurer. In the writ just quoted, it is important to observe that the council was regarded as a special assemblage, called *ad hoc* for the purpose of considering a certain matter of business and presumably nothing else. There could hardly be a king's council without some such definite mandate. It will be noticed also that in calling together the council the treasurer was usually given a measure of discretion, since he was commanded to summon those 'whom he shall see fit', or 'who ought to be summoned', or 'others of the council if it be necessary'. It was well understood, however, that in all questions of law the exchequer should act with the counsel of the justices.[1] Sometimes there was doubt whether the presence of the council was necessary, as in one instance the clause to this effect was inserted between the lines of the letter, as though it were an after-thought.[2] Again the king assumed the presence of the council directing the writ, *a noz Tresorier et as autres de notre Conseil*.[3] The matters thus referred to the treasurer were usually questions for adjudication, and these were said to be heard *coram thesaurario et consilio*. In summoning the individual men of the council, when they were near at hand, the formality of writs was not always necessary.[4] But when there was good reason, explicit writs of summons were sent. An example of such a writ, which was issued in the name of the treasurer under the seal of the exchequer, may be quoted in part as follows:

'. . . veniatis ad scaccarium nostrum . . . cum thesaurario et baronibus et aliis de consilio nostro ibidem existentibus,

[1] In 1305 the following order is given: 'Rex . . . mandat Baronibus (scaccarii) quod inspecta carta praefatae Floriae per consilium Iustitiariorum Regis in dicto Scaccario ex hac causa evocandorum fieri faciant quod de iure fuerit faciendum, et secundum quod in causa consimili hactenus in regno Regis fuerit usitatum.' *Memoranda de Parliamento*, p. 107.

[2] *Ancient Correspondence*, xlv. 131.

[3] *Rot. Parl.* i. 208. Again a petition is answered, 'qe le Roi vult qil seit oye et qe dreit ly seit fait et sur ceo avoit iour devaunt le Tresorer et le consail le Roi a Everwyk.' *Parl. Proceedings*, file ii, no. 30.

[4] Once it was declared by the barons, 'si avons sur ce ordine remedie par le conseil *pres de nous*.' *Red Book of the Exchequer* (Rolls Series), iii. 908.

super quibusdam arduis negotiis nos specialiter tangentibus tractaturi, et ulterius facturi quod vobis ibidem iniungetur. Per ipsum thesaurarium.'[1]

We find similar writs under the great seal, but for ordinary purposes no doubt the seal of the exchequer was more convenient and more frequent.

Why assembled at the exchequer.

The reasons for calling the council to the assistance of the treasurer and barons are apparent when the extensive functions of the exchequer are considered. Sometimes, it is true, the presence of the council is noted when there could have been no strong reason for it, as once, for instance, on the occasion of an examination of assays,[2] but usually there was some act of discretionary power to be sanctioned. There are many ordinances of the time of Edward I which are described as enacted by ' the council at the exchequer ', and these were placed on record in the Memoranda Rolls.[3] Many of these enactments, it is true, were on subjects of finance like the forms of taxation, regulations of the currency and of the customs. Most of them were of minor and incidental importance, although in one instance at least a statute, namely, that ' concerning the sheriffs ', 26 Edw. I, is declared to have been made by the council assembled at the exchequer.[4] It is well known that much of the business

[1] *Memoranda Roll, K. R.*, 9 Edw. II, Brev. Pasch., m. 167 d.; Madox, ii. 31.

[2] *Cal. Patent Rolls*, 9 Edw. I, 448, &c. Sometimes it seems to make no difference whether men were told to come before the council or before the exchequer. Compare examples in *Parl. Writs*, ii. 160.

[3] Several examples are found in *Memoranda Rolls, K. R.*, 25 Edw. I, mm. 10 d., 14 d., 89. In 34 Edw. I the following enactment concerning the confiscation of the property of felons is noticed : ' Sachiez qe nos feismes la chose monstrer a tut le conseil le Roy et acorde est par eux toutz, qe de futifs pur felonie apres la felonie faite et la suite faite soit atteinte, lour chateux seint forfatz au Roi, e des autres fugitifs pur trespas home ne deit mie seisir leur chateux avaunt quil soient utlagez, et apres le utlagerie soient leur chateux forfetz.' Ibid., m. 26 d. In another instance the entry is introduced with the words : ' Memorandum quod Johan de Sandale thesaurarius liberavit hic . . . quandam ordinationem factam per Regem et consilium suum super compto Garderobe . . . et eam precepit irrotulari.' Ibid., 3 Edw. II, Trinity. Another is : ' Quedam ordinatio facta per consilium Regis hic super scrutatione monete proclamata in Londonia.' Ibid., 4 Edw. II, 59 d. Another : ' Forma ordinata per consilium Regis de vinis vendendis in Londonia.' Ibid., m. 60.

[4] There were then present the archbishop of Dublin, the bishops of Ely and London, the treasurer, the chancellor, the barons of the exchequer, and the justices of both benches, and others. *Statutes of the Realm*, i. 213.

which came before parliament was left in an incomplete stage to be concluded by the council. In 1301 the subsidy of a fifteenth was granted to the king at the parliament of Lincoln, leaving to the council the task of devising the 'form' containing all the particular directions as to how the tax was to be levied. This 'form', we are told, was 'ordained by the king's council at York', where the exchequer was. When certain of the clergy came there to urge that, as they had already given out of their spiritualities and temporalities a tenth for the Holy Land, the same temporalities should not be taxed for the fifteenth, it was deemed necessary to assemble the council to take advisement on this point. It was decided that the temporalities should be charged, and to this effect a writ of the privy seal was directed to the barons of the exchequer.[1] This is an excellent illustration of the point that has been made before, that the regular officers very quickly reached the limits of their prescribed authority.

Wide range of functions.

Still more remarkable in demonstrating the wide range of the powers of the exchequer are the many acts which do not relate to the subject of finance. It can be shown, for example, that on several occasions, in order to raise soldiers for war, the king took the course of sending a letter of the privy seal to the treasurer, and by him the warrants were sent to the chancellor to issue the necessary writs under the great seal.[2] Many times in fact the form of the letters in the chancery were determined by the council at the exchequer. It was a custom of very general bearing that the king's officers were regularly sworn here, and it is likely that the councillor's oath also was generally administered in the same way. Unfortunately the ceremony is rarely described. In 1306, it is true, certain councillors were sworn in the presence of parliament, but this action was exceptional. The form of the oath, we are told, was then brought forth by one of the clerks of the exchequer.[3] It was probably for this reason that a form of the councillor's oath was engrossed in the Red Book of the Exchequer in England, as well as in

[1] *Memoranda Roll, K. R.*, 30 Edw. I, mm. 8, 52; *Rot. Parl.*, i. 266; *Parl. Writs*, i. 104.

[2] Madox, ii. 106, 109, 110.

[3] *Rot. Parl.*, i. 219.

a similar book kept in Dublin.[1] In the case of Walter Langton, the deposed treasurer of Edward II, we find the command of the king, which was received at the exchequer: *quod sit de consilio suo et quod admittatur inter alios consiliarios . . . et statim super hoc idem episcopus evocatus assessus est inter alios de consilio regis.*[2] Of other oaths which were required to be taken by the king's officers, we are told in one instance that the form was prescribed by the council.[3]

Control of foreign relations.

The whole subject of foreign relations, with numberless special cases arising therefrom, was one which constantly received the attention of the council. It was inevitable that this should be so, not only because of the great importance of the subject, but also because such matters could not be treated in any prescribed or routine manner. That the exchequer was the principal custodian of treaties and other diplomatic documents which were deposited in the treasury has been well understood, but to what extent these affairs were controlled from this department has not been made equally clear. Among the numerous archives of the kind, especially those known as 'Diplomatic Documents, Exchequer', there are a great many passages which describe the action of the king's council in association with the barons of the exchequer, so that the only conclusion to be drawn is, that in all matters of the kind this was the normal mode of procedure. To give a few illustrations, in the fourteenth year of Edward I, the king directed the barons of the exchequer to postpone all other affairs and to consider especially the relations of the merchants of England with those of Flanders. Apparently the barons could carry the negotiations to a certain point without further assistance, but subsequently in the same year when a composition between the king of England and the count of Flanders was framed, the matter was formally announced at Westminster in the presence of a number of councillors 'then residing at the exchequer'.[4] In relations with Scotland on several

[1] *Red Book*, fol. 5, m. 15; also Madox, chap. xxii, § 4–5.

[2] *Memoranda Roll, K. R.*, 5 Edw. II, m. 41.

[3] Ibid., 4 Edw. II, m. 54.

[4] Madox, ii. 103; also *Diplomatic Documents, Exchequer Treasury of Receipt*, Box 50, no. 1366.

occasions, submissions and fealties, which were rendered by the Scots, are described as being made 'before the council in the exchequer'.[1] At length in the thirty-fifth year there appears the 'form' of a peace to be observed in England and Scotland. Having been agreed to by the king and council, this instrument was delivered by the treasurer to be enrolled in the exchequer.[2] In relations with France there were endless arguments on the question of the homage due from the king of England for the duchy of Aquitaine. One of the documents used by Edward II in this controversy contains the assertions which were made upon the question in 1306, *in presencia Thesaurarii Garderobe patris domini nostri Regis et Cancellarii et Baronum Scaccarii et ceterorum de consilio in parvo Scaccario apud Westmonasterium.*[3]

For a time the responsibility for the government of Gascony lay especially with the exchequer. Under Edward I it was enacted by parliament that returns from the exchequer of Gascony should be made directly to the exchequer in England. It seems that this was done not only in fiscal matters but likewise in all questions of government. The communications concerning Gascony were usually drafted in the form of articles consisting of propositions or petitions which were submitted to the council in England and answered one by one. In the fourth year of Edward II, the king sends to the treasurer certain notes touching Gascony, commanding that having called the justices and others of the council he cause the notes to be examined, debated, and answered in due form. The answers were to be communicated through the chancery.[4] With all of these examples taken from the reigns of Edward I and Edward II it is hard to believe that the political power of the exchequer was as yet considerably diminished. But before any change in this regard is noted, there is one other field of authority to be described.

[1] *Cal. Close Rolls*, 26 Edw. I, 202; *Memoranda Roll, K. R.*, 34 Edw. I, m. 48.

[2] Ibid., 35 Edw. I, m. 22.

[3] *Miscellanea (Chancery)*, bundle 27, no. 11. For some reason it was the treasurer or keeper of the wardrobe who is mentioned in this conference, and not the treasurer of the exchequer.

[4] *Memoranda Roll, K. R.*, 4 Edw. II, m. 58; another of the year 1328 is in *Dipl. Doc. Exch.*, box 50, no. 1369.

Extensive judicial authority

The wide scope of the judicial authority held by the exchequer has never been fully appreciated.[1] Probably because the subject is somewhat external to the development of the common law, it has not been deemed so important as that of the other courts. But the fact that the methods of the exchequer stand in contrast to those of the common law is a very good reason why they should be studied, for it was chiefly by a divergence of procedure that the various courts were separated from each other. In particular the distinction that is ultimately made between the exchequer and the council can be traced only upon this line. It will be a valuable point to determine, therefore, when the exchequer in its judicial procedure was placed under the limitations of a court of common law.

Why the exchequer was sought.

It is a well-known phenomenon that cases in great variety, including not only those concerning the king's revenue but pleas between private parties, were heard in the exchequer from the earliest times. The explanation that the court was in reality the *curia regis* sitting in the chamber of the exchequer is correct only when it is understood that there was as yet no division of the original body. But after the formation of the court of common pleas, as heretofore described, with its special forms and requirements, a difference between the methods of the one body and the other begins to appear. While the court of common pleas was accustomed to receive cases only upon an original writ or warrant, the exchequer was not bound by any of these particular forms. Continuing the older and freer procedure of the *curia regis*, it might hear the parties who came to make their complaints without any writ.[2] In the reign of Henry III, it is true that certain initiatory writs are mentioned,[3] but these were not necessarily writs of the chancery. In one case that was being

[1] Bracton speaks of the exchequer in its judicial capacity as an alternative to the king's bench, 'per barones de scaccario vel coram ipso rege,' *De Legibus*, ii. 242.

[2] *Exchequer Plea Rolls*, beginning 20 Hen. III.

[3] 'Quia constat nobis, quod per Placita mota coram vobis per brevia nostra Originalia, de debitis diversorum, et ibidem pendencia,' &c. *Mem. L. T. R.*, Mich. Com., 56 Hen. III, m. 1 d.; Madox, ii. 73. These writs are mentioned only in connexion with actions *de debitis*, and it does not appear that they were essential to every kind of plea.

reviewed it was definitely decided that a process might properly be begun upon a writ under the seal of the exchequer.[1] There were certain advantages in these methods of the court, which attracted suitors in increasing numbers. For one thing, an item of expense in the purchase of a chancery writ was thus saved. Another point of advantage was found in the superior facilities of the exchequer in collecting debts and damages. The same agencies that were employed in obtaining the king's revenues could also be used to the advantage of private parties. As a result, more than half of the cases on record were of this kind. Moreover, by the stern process of attachment of goods it is shown that a defendant could be brought to court after the king's bench had failed.[2] As a result of these tendencies in the reign of Henry III the pleas of the exchequer received so much attention that a separate roll for them was begun.[3]

Restrictions of this authority.

On the other hand, for the same reasons, the methods of the exchequer aroused a certain opposition, which called for a restriction of its powers by means of legislation.[4] In the statute of Rhuddlan, 12 Edw. I, it was enacted that pleas should be held in the exchequer only in such matters as especially concern the king or the officers of the exchequer; and in the articles on the charters, 28 Edw. I, c. 4, that common pleas should not be held in the exchequer contrary to Magna Carta. These restrictions, however, were largely evaded by the invention of legal fictions, the favourite subterfuge at this time being for the interested party to become a 'servant' of the treasurer, the chancellor of the exchequer, or some other officer. There was also the device of alleging that the king's revenue would be affected, long before the peculiar writ *quominus* was invented.[5] At the same time it is fair to notice that the officers of the exchequer made efforts to observe the limitations laid down for them.

[1] *Exchequer Plea Rolls*, 8 Edw. II, m. 58.

[2] Walter Kelk, *Memoranda Roll, K. R.*, 35 Edw. I, m. 28.

[3] The earliest roll of this kind is for the year 20–21 Hen. III; there are two for 43–45 Hen. III, and from the 51st year they continue regularly.

[4] Upon this subject a brief but valuable article was contributed by the late Professor Gross in the *Law Quarterly Review*, 1909 (pp. 138 ff.), including the texts of several cases.

[5] Ibid., case 5.

The claim that 'by the king's special grace' any plea could be terminated in the exchequer was not allowed.[1] If the aforesaid legal fictions were not duly established, it was often a valid and successful defence to say, 'this is a common plea and should not be held here', and the plaintiff would be told to seek redress elsewhere if he wished. In one instance the statement of the treasurer to this effect is worth quoting, since in so many words he declares that the exchequer is not a court of common law.

'. . . Et que Thesaurarius non vult quod ratione servicii sui aliqua in favorem suorum que communem legem tangunt hic in processu deducantur, dictum est per eundem Thesaurarium et Barones predicto Rogero (*the plaintiff*) quod adeat communem legem sive super hoc impetretur, si voluerit, eo quod istud placitum est de arreragiis redditis et tangit communem legem.'[2]

The council at the exchequer an extraordinary court.

So long as the exchequer was not a court of common law or of prescribed jurisdiction, it was the most convenient organ for dealing with a variety of cases for which the common law provided no remedy. The failure of the law to expand with the needs of the country left all these cases to be treated individually by the king's council, which for this purpose was mainly identified with the exchequer. Most of the subjects involved are familiar as belonging to the jurisdiction of the chancery at a later time. The reasons for this change will afterwards be made apparent. Without attempting a complete enumeration of these subjects, it will be sufficient to say that the numerous disputes of merchants and foreigners, as well as those concerning shipping and customs, were likely to involve persons and things outside the realm of England, and so beyond the territory of the common law. Serious crimes like riots, trespass, and contempt of the king, in which parties refused to obey the ordinary writs, often proved beyond the power of the common law to deal with. Many times, too, the actions of the common-law courts were restricted by franchises and liberties within which the ordinary

[1] Ibid., case 2.

[2] *Exchequer Plea Rolls*, 33 Edw. I, m. 15. The phrase *ratione servicii* has reference to the aforesaid subterfuge by which one entered the 'services' of a member of the exchequer, in order to be *de gremio scaccarii*.

writs could not be delivered.[1] Questions affecting the king's ecclesiastical rights, such as advowsons and conflicts with Rome, were matters of political interest not to be entrusted to the courts in their usual operations. Moreover, when under the prevailing rigidity of the law, suitors were unable to find a writ in the chancery to fit their case, there was no court that could provide a remedy except the king's council. To make this matter clear it will be necessary to give a few illustrations of the cases which were heard before the council in the exchequer. It will be evident that in all cases of this kind a consultation wider than that of the treasurer and barons was necessary.

Mercantile cases.

Among the many mercantile cases, there was one of the thirty-second year of Edward I, in which by a letter of the privy seal the king commanded the treasurer and barons to hear the grievances of certain Lombard merchants. In this letter the clause was inserted that they should summon also the chancellor and others of the council.[2] Probably some such initiatory writ was used in most of the cases which follow. Again in the thirty-fourth year several Italian merchants were brought before the treasurer, the chancellor, barons of the exchequer, justices, and others of the council, apparently on charges of engaging in the trade of the realm without a licence. Having been arraigned on the king's behalf, they were enjoined by the council not to go out of the realm or to export anything without leave. As they failed to find surety, they were committed to prison, but were afterwards released on their giving surety for one another.[3] In the thirty-fifth year the king referred to the exchequer a case which arose from the complaints of certain merchants of France, who claimed that their goods had been wrongly appraised by the customers at the port. The case was brought, we are told, before the treasurer and barons, and many others of the council who were specially called 'to hear and terminate the premises and to do justice to the

[1] Sometimes a writ would fail to be effective because the sheriff would deliver it not to the party directly but to the bailiff of the liberty. Phillimore, *Placita coram Rege*.

[2] *Ancient Correspondence*, xlv, no. 131.

[3] Madox, ii. 107.

merchants'. But the treasurer and barons and others of the council found themselves to such an extent engaged with other business, that they could not come to a final discussion of the case of the merchants. Whereupon there was appointed a committee of four men, who should examine the matter and report to the council. After a new appraisement of the goods had been made in this manner, the judgement awarding damages was given 'before the treasurer, the chancellor, the barons, and many others of the council'.[1] It is of interest to find that the procedure of the council by the aid of committees was followed at so early a date.

Cases of contempt and violence.

Of cases involving contempt of the king there is one of the same year in which it was alleged that Walter Kelk had repeatedly evaded the writs of the king's bench. The greater efficiency of the processes of the exchequer is shown by the fact that the defendant was brought to court only when the sheriff, who had failed to capture him, succeeded in attaching his goods. On being arraigned before the council he claimed that he was on military service at the time of the previous summons.[2] Again, in the sixth year of Edward II, on the testimony of an informer, a charge was made against John Bedewind that when he was sheriff of Cornwall he had declared in full county court that the king had evil counsellors and was badly advised in making a certain grant. This is an early instance of a prosecution based upon private information or delation.[3] In the twelfth year of the latter reign a good description of the case of a London riot is given. It was brought to the notice of the treasurer and barons and others of the council, we are told, particularly by the pope's nuncio, that a tumult had arisen against certain Lombards, wherein it was declared that divers murders, robberies, and other outrages had been committed, and that four or five hundred armed men had invaded the cathedral. The mayor

[1] *Memoranda Roll, K. R.*, 35 Edw I, m. 30.

[2] Ibid., m. 28.

[3] Ibid., *L. T. R.*, 6 Edw. II, Com. Hil., m. 1 d. The record of another such case is as follows: 'Philippus de Violer de Newenton exhibuit Consilio Domini Regis hic (i.e. in the exchequer) quandam Cedulam per quam ipse suggessit quod Robertus le Messager de Newenton nuper protulit inreverenter plura verba indecentia de Domino Rege, in contemptum Domini Regis, offerens se hoc velle verificare pro Domino Rege contra eundem Robertum,' &c. Ibid., 9 Edw. II, Mich. Com., m. 89 d.

and aldermen were brought before the council at the exchequer, and the mayor was asked to explain how these outrages were permitted without any punishment being inflicted. The representatives of the city were finally commanded to take action against the rioters under threat of forfeiting their liberties.[1]

Cases of ecclesiastical rights.

Cases concerning the king's ecclesiastical rights, particularly in the disputes with the pope over appointments, are to be found long before the statutes of *provisors* and of *praemunire* assigned this jurisdiction to the council. In the last year of Edward I occurs a case of this kind, in which the procedure of the council is more fully described than in any of the previous examples. The king by a letter of the privy seal refers to his council, ' residing at the exchequer,' a dispute concerning the appointment of the treasurership of the church at York, which on the other side the cardinal-bishop of Sabina claimed on behalf of the pope. The council was asked to examine the question, to ordain concerning the rights of the crown, and to frame an answer which should be sent to Rome. At the trial an attorney for the cardinal presented a petition which was read and understood. After an adjournment was taken for an examination of the rolls, precedents were found in favour of the king's right. It was finally agreed by the council that letters of the chancery should be issued in defence of the royal rights and a report was made to the king of their action.[2] Again a conflict of

[1] *Memoranda Roll*, 12 Edw. II, m. 31 d.

[2] Ibid., *K. R.*, 35 Edw. I, m. 41. The letter which was finally written containing the report to the king is worth quoting at length. ' Sire, endreit de ce qe vous nous maundastes qe oye la mustrance qe lounorable pere en dieu Pierres par la grace de dieu evesqe de Sabyne cardenal de la seinte eglise de Rome voudreit faire devant nous et les autres de votre consail pur celi qui fu tresorer en leglise Deverwik endreit de meismes la tresorre nous vous fecoms savoir qe oye la mustraunce (petition qe fu livree a votre parlement a Cardoil sur meismes la chose et la quele aremnee hors du dite parlement jusque devant votre consail a Londres et la quele petition—this clause is erased) qe on clerk de par le dit cardenal *ad faite devant nous et vos justices et les autres de votre consail a Londres* et bien et diligeanment examinee la dite busoigne nous trovoms qe la dite tresorre fu vacante en la temps lercheveschee de Everwyk fu vacante par la mort Johan le Romeyn aucun archevesque iloques et la la temporarie meismes lercheveschee fu en vostre mayn par la reson de cele vacacion, E pur ce sire qe nul ne curt a vous en tiel cas (il) semble a nous et a vos justices et as autres de vostre consail qe la collacion de la dite tresorie apendent a vous de

royal and papal rights is shown in the next reign, when one William Servat was heard before the council at the exchequer, on his complaint that he had been summoned to Rome for a debt in spite of a prohibition of the king.[1] There were advowson cases also. One recently published is described as having been heard before certain justices and officers 'assembled in the place of the exchequer usual for holding councils'.[2] To mention only one other example, the burghers of Great Yarmouth complained of an infringement of their charters by men of other towns who made forestallments by purchasing of the ships coming to that port. The case was heard at the exchequer before the treasurer, the chancellor, a justice of the king's bench, the barons of the exchequer, a justice of the common pleas, and others of the king's council. After an examination of the charter it was decided that the town was a free burgh and no one had a right to forestall its market.[3]

Consciousness of a quasi-equitable jurisdiction.

All these cases taken from the reigns of Edward I and Edward II, both in substance and in methods of treatment, point to the outlines of an equitable, in distinction from a common-law, jurisdiction. A certain consciousness of this fact was revealed at the time, when these subjects were said to be treated in accordance with 'reason', 'justice', and 'equity'. In the foregoing initiatory writs clauses like the following are freely used: *quod fuerit rationis, q'ils ordeinerent quei enserroit a faire par resoun* and *quod juris fuerit et consonum equitati*. On one occasion in a revenue case, judgement was given with the words, *ideo de equitate curiae mandatum est*.[4] The existence of an equitable juris-

dreit de vostre coroune, et qe vous la poiez et deviez doner a votre volente sicome vous avez fait, sauntz tort faire a nule *et qe votre doun est resonable por le dreit de votre coroune* par quoi sire nous avoms ordenee qe lettres souz votre grant seal soient faites a Wautier de Bedewynde votre clerk a qui vous avez donee la dite tresorre tieles come mester li sont *ou seront* pur son dreit et sa possession meintenir.' The parts in italics are later insertions. *Ancient Correspondence*, vol. l, no. 101.

[1] Ibid., 4 Edw. II, m. 57; another, 5 Edw. II, m. 55 d.

[2] 'Coram dominis Wilhelmo de Bereford, Galfrido de Scrop, Rogero Beler, et Johanne de Mitford congregatis in loco de scaccario pro consiliis habendis consueto.' Contribution of Mr. Charles Johnson, *Eng. Hist. Rev.*, xxi. 727.

[3] Ibid., 34 Edw. I, m. 43.

[4] George Price, *Treatise on the Law of the Exchequer* (London, 1830), p. 260, n. 1.

diction in the exchequer at a later day has been pointed out by many writers, but it has generally been believed that the court of the treasurer only followed the example set by the chancellor.[1] But the evidence here gathered tends to support the opposite view, that the treasurer was in the field before the chancellor, and that cases of the kind mentioned were commonly treated in the exchequer before the same thing was done in the chancery. A still greater mistake is to regard the system of equity as a development subsequent to that of the common law. It was indeed a feature of the king's court from the very beginning, and came to stand in contrast with the common law only after the latter system had acquired positive form. On the other hand it must be admitted that the early jurisdiction of this kind was by no means extensively exercised, and that there were many technical features of the system yet to be devised.

Methods of procedure.

The nature of the jurisdiction exercised by the council, whether it were in the exchequer or in the chancery, will be seen more clearly when its methods of procedure are considered. The records, it is true, are not sufficiently descriptive to reveal the practice of the court at every step, so that not much can be learned in this regard from any single case. The evidence can be obtained only from the fragments and hints which are given here and there. As was explained in a former chapter, when suitors failed to find a remedy at common law, their recourse was to address a petition, also known as a 'complaint' or 'supplication', either to the king or to the king and council. So far as these petitions required a special application of the law, they were brought in first instance, not to the king's bench, the exchequer, or the chancery, but to the greater court known as 'the council in parliament'. Here was a sufficient authority for any legal action that might be required. If a judicial process was necessary the case might then be committed to any one of the established courts. Thus an endorsement

[1] 'It was only natural that the Court of Exchequer should assume a general equitable jurisdiction like that assumed by the Lord Chancellor.' Holdsworth, *History of English Law*, i. 106. By a singular lapse of memory Dr. Poole has said, 'The Court of Exchequer did not acquire jurisdiction in equity until Tudor times.' *Exchequer in the Twelfth Century*, 184.

authorizing the treasurer to proceed with the assistance of the council reads as follows :

> ' Mittatur ista petitio thesaurario inclusa in litteris Regis, et mandetur eidem quod vocatis illis de consilio Regis Londoniae examinari faciat istam petitionem et contenta in eadem et fieri faciat conquerenti quod fuerit rationis.' [1]

The 'letters of the king' mentioned are those under the privy seal such as have been quoted before. Among the many examples of this kind, it is noticeable that not only cases affecting the king's revenue, but a large number, which we may call quasi-equitable in character, in the time of Edward I were referred to the exchequer rather than the chancery. The assemblage of the council is mentioned because ' reason ' took the place of rules of law. From first to last the case was treated as an exception ; it could not be dealt with according to precedents, nor was it expected to create a precedent for the future. The body which was brought together for consultation might be anything from a group of justices to a general assemblage of the magnates. As an illustration of the close inter-relation of the exchequer, the council, and parliament at this time, we have the record of a case in which a widow claims the custody of a manor as the heir of her late husband. A petition to the king and council was treated in the parliament of 1306, where answer was made that the lady should sue before the treasurer, who should call the justices and others of the council to render speedy justice. One stage of the proceedings, we are told, was held before the treasurer and council, but a final discussion was held before all the magnates in full parliament.[2]

Petitions to the treasurer and council.

It was a further step in the development of this procedure, when suitors instead of directing their petitions to the king, or the king and the council, made their address to the treasurer and council. In one case, for instance, the petition begins with the words, *al Tresorer et al cunsail notre Seigneur le Roi monstre Williaume le Druyn*,[3] and in another instance

[1] *Ancient Petitions*, no. 11872 ; also *Memoranda Roll, K. R.*, 35 Edw. I, m. 53 ; 5 Edw. II, m. 22.

[2] The process was not transferred from one court to another, but it was said, ' sic continuato processu usque in Parliamento ipsius Regis.' *Rot. Parl.* i. 214 ; also 167.

[3] *Ancient Petitions*, no. E. 545, 15564, &c.

a suitor is described as coming to the exchequer with a petition addressed, *au conseil notre seigneur le roi et as barons de son escheqer*.[1] In this way the parties not only expressed the wish to be heard before the treasurer, but they endeavoured to save the preliminary step of having their petitions first considered in parliament. As a survival of an earlier usage, it is also true that parties were permitted to come to the exchequer and state their complaints without the form of a written petition.[2] Another indication of the tendency to exalt the treasurer is found in a petition addressed to him beseeching him to exert his influence with the chancellor and others of the council. These petitions to the treasurer are a matter of interest, because it was in just such a way that the court of the chancellor at a later time may be seen to branch from the council and to gain an independent footing. As regards the treasurer, this departure was only a tentative one, which failed to create as yet any settled mode of procedure.

Writs of summons and arrest.

Another essential feature of the procedure now before us may be studied in the writs of summons and arrest by which defendants were brought to court. The form most frequently used was that known as 'the summons of the exchequer', which commanded the parties to come, at a fixed time and place, 'to do and receive what shall be ordered by the king and the council'. If the simple summons was not sufficient, a writ of arrest was sent to an officer, to the following effect :

> 'A. B. scire facias quod in propria persona ad scaccarium coram consilio nostro fuerit.' [3]

The *venire facias* was similar but more coercive. A still stronger form of compulsion is found in the writ of attachment by which the sheriff or other officer was commanded,

> 'quod attacheret A. B. per corpus suum ubicunque eum inveniret ita quod eum haberet hic coram consilio regis . . .

[1] *Memoranda Roll*, 30 Edw. III, Mich., December 12, dors.

[2] 'Johanna . . . venit hic coram W. Wygornensi Episcopo Thesaurario, H. comite Lincolnie, Baronibus de Scaccario et aliis de consilio, et supplicavit.' Ibid., *L. T. R.*, 3 Edw. II, Com. Mich., m. 5.

[3] *Close Roll*, 31 Edw. III, m. 4 ; Calendar, 54.

ad respondendum super illis que ei obicerentur ex parte Regis.'[1]

But, however cogent, these writs were all of common-law character, in respect of the important detail that they necessarily contained a clause giving the cause of the summons or arrest. But in the reign of Edward III certain writs known as the *quibusdam certis de causis* and the *sub poena* were devised without containing any such essential clause. These writs first appeared in the chancery, but they were afterwards used in the exchequer as well.[2] In this important point it must be granted the procedure of the exchequer followed that of the chancery.

Still another feature of the council's procedure which afterwards became very noted is found in the method of drawing evidence from defendants by means of questions. The inquisitorial examination, as the method is called, has been commonly understood to have been brought into secular practice by the chancellors from their experience in the ecclesiastical courts. Of the success of the chancellors in developing this procedure, there will be abundant evidence later on, but it must also be admitted that a rudimentary practice of the kind was known in the exchequer at a date quite as early as is found in the chancery. The chancellors in fact were not the only judges to be acquainted with the practices of the clerical tribunals, and other courts of the king were tempted to act in the same manner. It was a recognized rule of the common law that a defendant should be arraigned—that is, permitted to answer the charges before the court proceeded to judgement.[3] It was a step beyond this when the defendants were asked questions and were required to make damaging admissions. This was done in several of the cases previously cited. In one case we are told the accused person was *positus ad rationem per plures de*

Questioning the defendant.

[1] *Memoranda Roll, L. T. R.*, 2 Edw. II, m. 60.

[2] *Rot. Parl.* iii. 478 ; iv. 84. A petitioner asks the keeper of the privy seal to grant a writ of subpoena, summoning his opponent to the exchequer, because he says no ordinary writ could penetrate the liberties of the Cinq Ports. *Council and Privy Seal*, file 58, September 15, 15 Hen. VI.

[3] Pike, *Year Books* (Rolls Series), 19 Edw. III, pp. xli–xlvi ; it was ground for an appeal on error if the arraignment was not on the record. *Cal. Patent Rolls*, 1 Edw. III, 142.

consilio Regis et per eosdem Thesaurarium et Barones et requisitus, and again, *quesitus idem Walterus per consilium*. Even these acts did not overstep the bounds which were then commonly permitted to the courts, but it was another matter when in the reign of Edward III, we are told, the defendants were put under oath and diligently examined—*de precepto curie jurati et postmodum diligentius examinati*.[1] The instance may have been an exceptional one, for it happened at a time when the government was seeking to punish the officials who had stolen the money collected under the Statutes of Labourers, but it is of great interest nevertheless in showing that the chancellor's court was not the only one to follow this feature of the civil law.

A check upon this development.

It remains now to ask, and if possible to answer, the question why this equitable or quasi-equitable jurisdiction, which had at least made a good beginning in the exchequer, did not continue there to expand, and why the greater development after all took place in the chancery and in the court of star chamber. For neither the jurisdiction nor the great political powers held by the treasurer and the exchequer were permitted to enjoy an uninterrupted development. In the rising power of the chancery a rival was found, which was able to challenge and to wrest from the older body many of its most valuable functions, while in other respects the powers of the exchequer were closely limited. This happened largely as the result of a political convulsion which must now be described.

Rivalry of the chancery.

At the beginning of this chapter the question was suggested whether the treasurer or the chancellor was the first of the king's officers in the time of Edward I. Many of the passages cited show that in official documents precedence was commonly given to the treasurer. The rolls of parliament and the statutes likewise use the expression,

[1] *Memoranda Roll, L. T. R.*, 28 Edw. III, m. 28; one of the documents transcribed in Putnam, *Enforcement of the Statutes of Labourers* (New York, 1908), Appendix, p. 270. Again, in 1409–10, it was agreed, 'qe les Tresorer et Barons du dit Escheqer aient poair par auctoritee de Parlement d'examiner les Custumers en ces cas.' *Rot. Parl.* iii. 626. There was likewise a complaint against the procedure of the exchequer upon *information* without inquest. Ibid. 478. A fuller explanation of this feature will be given in chap. xi.

'the treasurer, the chancellor, and others of the council' more frequently than 'the chancellor and the treasurer'. That the chancellor was sometimes mentioned first, shows that there was at least room for doubt upon the point, and suggests that the rivalry of the clerks of the chancery and the barons of the exchequer had already begun. The undisputed primacy of the chancellor and of his department certainly was not attained without a struggle, and this opportunity came with the political strife of the reign of Edward II. The treasurer of the time was Walter Langton, bishop of Coventry and Lichfield, who held the office from the year 1295.[1] Langton was a man of great force and influence, and under him the exchequer was led to its widest assumptions of power. Opposition was aroused, and in the parliament of 1301 an attack upon the government was made with charges against the treasurer. But Langton's influence with Edward I was only strengthened, until by the end of the reign he was credited with being the king's sole confidant, while his unpopularity was increased to a corresponding degree. Immediately in the first year of Edward II the opposition, under the leadership of Archbishop Winchelsey and the chancellor,[2] was renewed with such success that the treasurer was removed from office.[3] But the struggle was more than a personal one against Langton. It was an attack upon the entire administration of the exchequer, in which the parliamentary party aligned itself with the interests of the chancery.

The contest under Edward II.

The movements of this contest are not entirely clear, but in 1311 we find the chancellor, Walter Reynolds, coming to the exchequer, where he announced that he had the king's commands to remove John Sandale, then treasurer, and to appoint Walter of Norwich for the time as *locum tenens*.[4] Langton, however, was admitted to the council, and in 1312 he was restored to the treasurership, only to be driven out

[1] T. F. T., in *Dict. Nat. Biography*.

[2] John Langton, not a relative of the treasurer.

[3] There is a petition of Little Yarmouth complaining that Walter Langton had granted a charter to Great Yarmouth contrary to their liberties. *Ancient Petitions*, no. 2667.

[4] *Memoranda Roll, K. R.*, 5 Edw. II, m. 41.

again by the Lords Ordainers. Again, in 1315, he was deposed together with Hugh Despenser. Between the parties of the chancery and of the exchequer a crisis was reached in the notable parliament of Lincoln in 1316, which has been described in a recent publication.[1] The special point of contest here was the method of appointing the sheriffs, and a signal victory for the chancery was won when it was determined that henceforth the sheriffs should be assigned 'by the *chancellor*, the treasurer, the barons of the exchequer, and the justices'.[2] As a matter of fact, henceforth the sheriffs were appointed through the chancellor's office, and their names were listed upon the rolls of that department. At the same time, it is equally significant, the Rolls of Parliament, which had hitherto been kept by the clerks of the exchequer, were now turned over to the clerks of the chancery. The more narrative style of the records of the chancery is immediately apparent.

Ascendancy of the chancery.

This reversal of the relative positions of the chancery and the exchequer was a revolution of more far-reaching consequences than anything otherwise accomplished by the Lords Ordainers. Who was the first minister of the crown, there was no longer room for doubt, for every document of the time gives precedence to the chancellor rather than the treasurer. As William of Wykeham later had reason to claim, the chancellor was 'ye secondary in England next to ye kinge'.[3] To him now were referred the important questions that were to be submitted to the council for deliberation and adjudication. The chancery in fact became the general secretariat for the council, as well as of the parliament, while its notes, indentures, and ordinances were written by the clerks of this office, and its orders were communicated by the letters and writs under the great seal. For the reign of Edward III therefore we look for the records of the council upon the close and patent rolls rather than upon the memoranda rolls. On the other hand, the separation of the council from the exchequer is shown, even when financial

[1] See the valuable article of Mr. Hughes, *Trans. Royal Hist. Society*, new series, vol. x, pp. 41–58.

[2] *Statutes of the Realm*, i. 174.

[3] *Chron. Anglic* (Rolls Series), p. lxxix.

policies were considered. In the levy of the new wool subsidies under Edward III, for instance, the arrangements were all determined by the council, not sitting in the exchequer as was done in former years, but communicating its orders through the agencies of the chancery.[1] Even the contracts which were made by the council with the coiners of money are regularly to be found upon the close rolls. Matters of diplomacy were likewise treated in the chancery, although such documents were still left in the treasury as a depository. Possibly the erection of a new building for the council, namely, the star chamber, may be regarded as another evidence of the detachment of the council from the exchequer.

Contraction of the powers of the exchequer.

At the same time the judicial functions of the exchequer were greatly contracted. This tendency, it is true, was due not entirely to political causes, for early in the reign of Edward II it appears that the procedure of the exchequer in respect of pleas was so far formalized as to be subject to review on error.[2] In the first year of Edward III the treasurer and barons were sharply reminded of their limitations, when they had summoned a man to answer before the council for certain properties held of the crown. The king declared that such writs should not be issued by the exchequer without his knowledge, and that the defendant was not bound to answer for the freehold *at common law* without the king's writ.[3] To this extent has the exchequer become a court of common law. Another striking illustration of the same general tendency is found about the same time in a certain petition addressed by a merchant of Gloucester to the treasurer and council, in the form which had just begun to be followed—*au Tresorer nostre Seigneur le Roi et a son conseil*.[4] The plaintiff alleged that men of Calais by force of arms had attacked and robbed his ship off the coast of Dover, wherefore he prayed for remedy and aid. Now cases of this kind had certainly been heard in the exchequer, as the petitioner no

[1] *Cal. Close Rolls, passim.*

[2] *Rot. Parl.* i. 274; also a good example of a case is in *Exchequer Plea Roll*, 8 Edw. II, mm. 57, 58.

[3] *Cal. Close Roll*, 1 Edw. III, 194.

[4] *Ancient Petitions*, no. 15564.

doubt had reason to believe, but the answer then given was that cases of this kind should be sued in the chancery—*sequatur in cancellaria et fiat ei sicut fit aliis in consimili casu.*

Survivals of an equitable system.

What was left to the exchequer in the way of an equitable jurisdiction was hardly more than a fragment of its original authority. There were isolated cases in which the *sub poena,* the inquisitorial examination, and 'procedure by bill' were resorted to, and these are sufficient to show that the original authority was not entirely lost.[1] But it was not until modern times that the system of equity in the exchequer was permitted to undergo any marked expansion. Most of the cases such as we have seen given to the treasurer, were now in a similar manner committed to the chancellor, who was to summon others of the council and to do what reason or justice required. How the jurisdiction of the chancery, or more properly 'the council in chancery', was extended far beyond anything achieved in the exchequer will be the subject of a later chapter.

The question of appeals on error.

In spite of a great number of changes along these lines, it is true that in one respect the treasurer and barons were successful in maintaining their former dignity and independence. As the exchequer came to be a court of fixed procedure, analogous to that of the common law, there inevitably arose the question how its cases should be reviewed on appeal of error. It was claimed on the one hand that as a court of common law its judgements should be revised in the king's bench, whose special function it was 'to amend false judgements'. Now it was the most marked sign of the inferiority of any court that its processes might be reviewed, corrected, or reversed by another tribunal, and there was cause for much strife between the courts before their rights in this regard were finally adjusted. In the struggle which now arose between the exchequer and the king's bench, it was the contention of the exchequer that its errors might be amended only in the exchequer itself.

[1] See the case, for example, of John Stourton v. the abbot of Saint Albans before the treasurer and barons of the exchequer in 1451. The procedure is by petition, response, replication, and again response, petition, &c. Joh. Whethamstede, i. 56 ff.

There were not lacking precedents to support this contention. In the second year of Edward II, for example, certain sheriffs presented a petition complaining that the treasurer and barons had wrongfully made certain distraints. It was answered that the treasurer, calling certain justices and others of the council, should hear all petitions and complaints made at the time alleging errors in the exchequer.[1] Other cases we learn were treated in this manner by the council at the exchequer.[2] When, therefore, in the reign of Edward III a demand was made that a record of the exchequer be sent for review to the king's bench, the barons stoutly refused and addressed a lengthy memorial to the crown arguing that the king's bench never had this right.[3] The precedents were not all on one side, for in the eighteenth year of the same reign it is recorded that the king's council, apparently in parliament, annulled and repealed an exchequer process on the ground that it was erroneous.[4] There is an instance, too, in the early years of Edward III, in which an exchequer case was reversed by the justices of the king's bench, who confirmed the previous judgement, whereupon an appeal was made to have it reviewed in parliament.[5] In the twenty-first year, with some political *animus* no doubt, a concerted demand was made in parliament that errors in the exchequer, like those of the common pleas, should be reversed in the king's bench, but the king's answer was, that on complaint of error the chancellor, the treasurer, and two justices should be named who should cause the case to come before them, and that they should make the review in the exchequer.[6] In the next year a renewal of the demand brought forth the same answer.[7] This statement was the basis for the famous act of 31 Edw. III, 1357, which is considered to be the foundation of the statutory court of exchequer chamber. The statute provides. Statute, 31 Edw. III.

'that in all cases where a man complains of error made in a process in the exchequer, the chancellor and the treasurer

[1] *Rot. Parl.* i. 274.

[2] *Exchequer Plea Roll*, 8 Edw. II, mm. 57–8; *Cal. Close Rolls*, 8 Edw. III, 342; Coke, *Fourth Institutes*, chap. xi.

[3] Pike, *Year Books*, 14 Edw. III, pp. xxi–xxv.

[4] *Rot. Parl.* ii. 154.

[5] *Ancient Petitions*, no. 12838.

[6] *Rot. Parl.* ii. 168.

[7] Ibid. 203.

shall cause to come before them in any council chamber near the exchequer, the record of the process out of the exchequer, taking to themselves the justices and other sage persons such as ought to be taken; and they shall also cause to be called before them the barons of the exchequer to hear their informations and the causes of their judgements and thereupon shall duly examine the business; and if any error be found they shall correct and amend the rolls and afterwards send them into the exchequer for execution.'[1]

The court of exchequer chamber.

This enactment may be explained as a recognition of the previous practices of the exchequer with important modifications. The court thus constituted was none other than the historic 'council at the exchequer', which was assembled now for a certain specific purpose. It was not yet described as a regular court, but was still a special assemblage for emergencies. Contrary to the original usages, however, the chancellor was given precedence over the treasurer in this as in every other relation. The chancellor and the treasurer together are mentioned as holding the authority of the court, while the justices and others were to come *before* them, and are represented in the light of assessors. The barons were to come only to give information and to explain their judgements. So strongly was the position of the chancellor emphasized, that in the time of Richard II there is found a petition addressed to him, beseeching him to hear and correct certain errors of the exchequer, although at the same time the writ of error is mentioned as returnable to the chancellor and the treasurer.[2] That the chancellor and the treasurer acted jointly as judges was the usual opinion.[3] The special victory which the exchequer gained by the statute lay in the fact that the judgements of the court were sent back to the exchequer for execution. That is, the special tribunal was not a separate court of record, so that the revised judgements were placed upon the exchequer rolls in the same manner as before. In any court, of course, the record is the all-essential thing. For the further execution of the judgement the usual writs and seals likewise would be used. Subsequent cases show that the provisions of the

[1] *Statutes of the Realm*, i. 351. [2] *Ancient Petitions*, no. 14922.
[3] *Rot. Parl.* iii. 563.

statute in the main were carried out, although there were exceptions. In the fortieth year an appeal of this kind was heard by the lords in parliament.[1] In the reign of Richard II opponents of the exchequer once more renewed their demands that errors in this court should be reviewed either in the king's bench or in parliament, but the answer to this and other demands of the kind was that the statute of Edward III should be maintained.[2]

Divergence of this court from the council.

As the newly-defined court continued to meet in the old council chamber near the receipt of the exchequer, it was soon known by the name of the exchequer chamber. It differed distinctly from the king's council, as otherwise operative, in that it was a court of prescribed jurisdiction, and as such was under 'the domination of the writs'. That it was conceived as a separate court is shown in the reign of Henry IV when a case was definitely committed by the council to the justices in the exchequer chamber.[3] Again, the difference between the council and a court of fixed procedure is shown in a case which upon petition in parliament was committed to the council rather than to the court of exchequer chamber, because there were technical difficulties in obtaining the usual writ of error.[4] How the jurisdiction of the latter court was still further enlarged by its use for other purposes than the one originally contemplated, how it began even to receive appeals on error from the king's bench, is a matter of interest which would repay further investigation, but as the field is now far removed from the history of the council, it cannot be treated here.

[1] *Memoranda Roll, K. R.*, 40 Edw. III, Hilary, 'de processu tangenti Williamum de Furnivall.'

[2] *Rot. Parl.* iii. 24, 563.

[3] *Year Books*, Mich., 13 Hen. IV, no. 10. This is the first time, so far as we know, that the court was designated in this manner.

[4] *Rot. Parl.* iv. 469–70.

CHAPTER X

THE COUNCIL AND THE CHANCERY

The unique development of the chancery.

THERE is nothing in the institutional history of England more remarkable than the development of the office of the chancellor. In view of the great antiquity of the office, the wide variety of its functions, and its adaptability at all times to the needs of the nation, surely no other position in the government stands in comparison with it. The chief justiciar and the treasurer, it is true, have each held supremacy for certain periods of time, but neither of these has shown the same sustained ability of making his office of practical value in every period. Recalling rapidly the achievements of the chancery, at the time of the Norman Conquest it was principally a bureau of the charters; in the thirteenth century it became also the source of the original writs and the means of approach to the law courts; in the fourteenth century it was made the principal organ of the king's council in matters both administrative and judicial; in the fifteenth century it branched off from the council as a court of equity; and after several further transformations the chancellor's prestige to-day is sustained by his position as the presiding officer of the house of lords and chief judge of a court of appeals. Referring to the complex functions of the chancery at the time of Edward I, Maitland has said 'it was a great secretarial bureau, a home office, a foreign office, and a ministry of justice'.[1] It should not be forgotten, however, that at this time the chancery was not the only secretariat of the government, for there was also the older department of the exchequer as well as the wardrobe which held the custody

[1] Pollock and Maitland, *History of English Law* (Cambridge, 1898), i. 193. Again, Maitland has written, 'The chancery is still the great secretarial department; it does nearly all the king's writing for him, whether such writing concerns foreign affairs or the government of England.' *Mem. de Parl.*, p. xxxvi.

of the privy seal. In their methods of work these departments differed widely, but there was great uncertainty and rivalry as to their respective functions. Matters of finance, it was already settled, belonged to the exchequer, and the issue of original writs to the chancery; but whether the equitable jurisdiction of the future should fall to the treasurer or the chancellor, was still an open question. It was indeed a mysterious transformation by which a purely administrative office grasped judicial functions, and ultimately became a court of great renown. Naturally the subject has not failed to receive attention, as much as anything in legal history, but there are still points of difficulty and obscurity. In particular the relations of the council and the chancery, and especially the later differentiation of the council and the chancery, are a part of the history upon which more light is now needed.

Its origin as a branch of the *curia regis.*

Much depends upon a proper conception of the origin of the chancery as a distinct department. This is not a question of date or of the diplomatic forms in its letters and charters,[1] but of the nature of its authority. From the records of the thirteenth century, it appears that the chancery was not merely an executive office, but a branch of the *curia regis* retaining a degree of discretionary power and acting in a measure as a council. In 1264, for instance, it is declared that a certain letter under the great seal was written 'without the counsel and assent of any clerk of the chancery'.[2] The inference is that such letters were usually composed with the counsel and assent of the chancellor and his clerks. Later records bear out the theory that the chancery from its very inception followed the methods of the *curia regis* as a body of consultation. In the reign of Edward I we find many references to 'the chancellor and others of the council'.[3] In 1319 we are told that the chancellor, in the presence of certain clerks and others of the *curia regis*, who formed 'the

[1] Upon the administration of this department, see F. M. Powicke, 'The Chancery during the Minority of Henry III' (*Eng. Hist. Rev.* xxiii. 220–35); also L. B. Dibben (Ibid. xxvii. 39–53).

[2] *Cal. Patent Rolls*, 48 Hen. III, 317. In 1262 also it is said that certain letters recorded in the chancery were made before the king's council. Ibid., 46 Hen. III, 226.

[3] *Cal. Close Rolls*, 30 Edw. I, 565.

council of the chancery ', as it was called, formally ordered the alteration of a record.[1] From this time the presence of magnates, justices, and others of the council, who came to the assistance of the chancellor and his clerks, will be shown to be a matter of frequent occurrence. From its very inception, therefore, the chancery, supported by the king's council, appears like the exchequer and the early king's bench, as a body of general and consultative powers. This fact is very essential to all its later developments.

As *officina brevium*.

It is well understood that the chancery was first brought into daily touch with the business of the law courts by its issue of the original writs.[2] No regular legal action in fact could be begun without an order of this kind from the chancery. The mere issue of the writs was a perfectly normal function for a secretarial bureau, but the formulation of new writs was a different matter. According to the methods of justice that were being evolved in the thirteenth century, it is manifest that the power to select and to devise the commanding writs was a very material one. For a certain period prior to Bracton there is every evidence of a phenomenal activity in this direction. Now from every analogy and attendant circumstance it must be inferred that the formulation of these instruments was made to a large extent by the officials of the chancery, who acted more or less in consultation with the justices. If this process had been permitted to go on in response to the demand for new remedies, there is no doubt that the whole subsequent history of the law and of the courts would have been very different. But the power of the chancery to issue new writs was placed under severe restrictions. According to the Provisions of Oxford, in 1258, the chancellor was made to swear that he would seal no writ except those *de cursu*, in other words, those of formal judicial character which were of accepted usage, without the commandment of the king and his council.[3] This restriction was carried further in the statute,

[1] *Parl. Writs*, ii, part ii, 200; *Foedera* (Rec. Ed.), vol. ii, part ii, p. 710; see also an order to appear before the king's council in chancery on Monday next to inform the king on certain affairs. *Cal. Close Rolls*, 19 Edw. II, 493.

[2] Maitland, *Harvard Law Quarterly*, iii. 97 ff., 167, 212.

[3] *Ann. Burton*, p. 413; *Select Charters*, p. 389.

13 Edw. I, c. 24, wherein it was stated that the clerks of the chancery on their own initiative might issue only such writs as were of established usage, *in consimili casu*, and that all questions as to form they should refer to the next parliament. Still it was said by Fleta to be the duty of the clerks of the chancery to hear and examine the petitions of complainants and to afford remedy by means of the king's writs.[1] But the aforesaid rule was generally observed, and resulted in a material curtailment of the power of the chancery in this regard. The judges indeed would even refuse to recognize a writ that was not duly sanctioned. It is not clear, however, that every new writ was considered in parliament, for in some cases it is said that they were either created or adapted 'according to the form ordained by the king and council'.[2] With this remedial power of the chancery curtailed, we look in other directions for its greatest success.

As a court of justice.

It is well known also that with characteristic versatility the chancellors at an early day became responsible for certain proceedings of a veritably judicial character. Just how such a function began has never been clearly demonstrated, but it probably arose from the fact that there were many judicial questions necessarily connected with the secretarial work of the chancery. In the first place difficulties constantly arose in the issue of the writs; it was often a question whether this or that writ should be granted, whether a certain writ was valid, or had been properly executed. Many of the earliest cases referred to the chancery in fact were of this kind. Then too there were a great many questions that could be determined only from the rolls of the chancery, wherein were registered innumerable charters, confirmations of charters, concords, quit-claims, and recognizances. Whenever questions of record arose in the king's bench or elsewhere it was customary to refer them to the chancery for determination. As we have already observed, a judicial body was readily brought together here, which in its origin was plainly conceived as an assemblage of the king's council.[3]

[1] Liber ii, c. 13 (ed. 1685), p. 77.
[2] *Ancient Petitions*, nos. 14570, 14573, &c.
[3] On one occasion the personnel is described as follows: 'en chauncelerie

Fleta speaks of it as the king's court in the chancery—*habet etiam (rex) curiam in cancellaria.*[1] Among the pleas of the chancery held in the time of Edward I, for example, are those specially designated as *Placita coram Rege et Consilio suo.*[2] A little later the action of the court is described in the following words: *De avisamento iusticiariorum et servientium ipsius domini Regis ad legem, ac aliorum peritorum de Consilio in eadem Cancellaria consideratum fuit quod litterae praedictae revocentur et adnullentur.*[3] These pleas of the chancery consisted of certain well-understood actions that were rapidly formulated. As soon as they are positively defined, of course they are distinguishable from actions before the council. They form the basis for what is known as the common-law jurisdiction or Latin side of the chancery.[4] It is not necessary to dwell upon these, because the chancery never became a strong or self-sufficient court of common law. In this respect the scope of its jurisdiction was limited, while its procedure was further restricted by the fact that it did not employ juries. On the contrary, it was soon realized that the strength of the chancery lay in the fact that it was mainly not a court of common law or as yet of fixed procedure. It was indeed the singular success of the chancellors that, while both the exchequer and the king's bench were being drawn into the current of the common law, their own court remained comparatively free from this system. For this

a Westmonster, devaunt sire Johan de Laungton adonk chaunceler en presence de sire Roger Brabazoun, Sire Rauf de Hengham, sire Gilbert de Roubury, sire Williame de Bereford, sire William Haward e autres bones gentz du conseil.' *Parl. Writs*, i. 131.

[1] Op. cit., lib. ii, c. 2.

[2] *Placita in Cancellaria*, 30 Edw. I, no. 37; in ibid., 34 Edw. I, no. 1A, there is the following passage referring to the court as being held in no fixed place: 'habeatis in eadem cancellaria nostra in quindena, &c., *ubicunque fuerit* in Anglia, ut tunc fiat prout consilio nostro fore videbitur faciendum;' also 18 Edw. III, no. 16, &c.

[3] Quoted by Pike, *Law Quarterly Review*, i. 444.

[4] 'The chancellor under his ordinary jurisdiction,' says Spence, 'held pleas of *scire facias* for the repeal of letters patent, of petitions of right, and *monstrans de droit* for obtaining possession or restitution of property from the crown, Traverses of offices, *scire facias* upon recognizances, executions upon recognizances, executions upon statutes, and pleas of all personal actions by or against any officer or minister of the court of chancery.' Spence, *Equitable Jurisdiction of the Court of Chancery* (1846–9), i. 336; D. M. Kerly, *Equitable Jurisdiction of the Court of Chancery* (Cambridge, 1890), p. 70 ff.; Maitland, *Equity* (Cambridge, 1909), p. 4 ff.

reason it was possible, in the course of time, to make the chancery the principal organ of a jurisdiction outside the realm of the common law.

As a court of extra-ordinary juris-diction.

The beginning of a jurisdiction that may be distinguished from the common law is found in a way similar to what was done in the exchequer. It has already been described how cases calling for special treatment were made the subjects of petition to the king, or the king and council. Many of these petitions were committed to the treasurer, or to the treasurer and chancellor, who were to act in association with others of the king's council. Just such messages were likewise sent to the chancellor. As early as the eleventh year of Edward I, the king refers a petition to the chancellor by a writ of the privy seal in the following words : *Mandamus vobis quod inspecta petitione ... quam vobis mittimus inclusam, et habita super ea deliberatione de iure et gratia curie nostre videritis faciendum.*[1] In a later and more expanded form a letter of this kind reads as follows :

'Edward, etc. Nous vous enveons cy dedeinz close une petition quelle nous feust baillee par Martyn de Chaundry marchant Despaigne, si vous mandoms que appellez a vous ceux de notre conseil queux vous verrez qe serroit a ce appeller, et veue et entendue la dite petition, facez ordiner faire et mander entre pur le dit Martyn solonc ce qe vous verrez, par avisement de notre dit conseil qe serra a faire par reson. Don, etc.'[2]

According to such an order, it is to be noted, the court is authorized to take counsel and to act with 'justice and grace' according to the needs of the individual case. Under these circumstances, it is understood, the chancery was not regarded as a mere branch of the king's council ; for the immediate occasion and purpose it *was* the king's council, with all of the powers thus implied.[3] The earliest of these

[1] *Warrants* (*Chancery*), 11 Edw. I, file 151, October 14 ; see also a letter of the king to his chancellor Langton, which reads : 'vos requirimus et rogamus quatenus in negociis suis (i.e. a suit of the prior of Trinity, York) que in curia habet expedire eidem sitis adiuvantes et consilium prebentes utile cum favore.' *Ancient Correspondence*, xxvi, no. 111.

[2] *Privy Seals*, year 1338, no. 10724 ; also 10883, 11379 A.

[3] Upon this point Campbell has given utterance to an entire misconception which seems still to be believed. He says, 'they (the chancellors under

cases were given to the chancellor, no doubt, because they touched upon the normal functions of his office. In most instances probably the chancery, with the assistance of the council, was not expected to do more than provide the writ that was necessary for legal action elsewhere. Yet there are cases, even as early as Edward I, when the petitioners were instructed to go to the chancellor to obtain justice—*veniant partes coram cancellario . . . et fiat eis iustitia.*[1] In the reign of Edward II, however, when the authority of the exchequer was visibly reduced, it becomes plain that cases for which the common law failed to provide a remedy were in this wise regularly committed to the chancery.

Impetus of the statutes.

The impetus that was given to the jurisdiction of the chancery at the start came from the acts of parliament as much as from the favour of the king. There was, indeed, a material connexion between the parliament and the chancery, as soon as the rolls of parliament and all of its clerical work fell into the hands of this department. From the reign of Edward II certainly a large portion of the petitions considered in parliament were endorsed with words like the following : *Soit ceste petitioun maunde en chancellerie . . . et le chaunceller appellez devant lui ceux qui sont appeller face outre droit et reson.*[2] In a number of instances it is plain that where there was a choice between one court and another, the chancery was given the preference.[3] Sometimes the order was sent by the king's writ, *per litteras Regis,* but ordinarily the endorsement upon the petition was a sufficient warrant for the court to proceed. That the chancery in these cases acted not as an independent court, but 'by authority of parliament', was carefully maintained.[4] In one

Edward I) exercised important judicial functions both in the King's Council and in their own court, where they sometimes had the assistance of others, and sometimes sat alone. No case of importance was heard in the Council when the Chancellor was absent ; and cases were referred by the Council for his consideration in Chancery, either by himself, or with the advice of specified persons whom he was to summon to assist him.' *Lives of the Chancellors* (1845), i. 185.

[1] This case arose from the violation of a writ, 'quod Adam Gordon eos eiecit de pastura contra tenorem Brevis Regis.' *Rot. Parl.* i. 60.

[2] Ibid., *passim.*

[3] *Ancient Petitions*, nos. 9975, 12841, 15564.

[4] 'Ait le chanceller poaire par autorite du parlement de faire venir devaunt lui,' &c. Ibid., nos. 9879, 11046, 11531, 11598, &c.

instance a petition was committed to the chancellor, with instructions to summon lords of parliament as well as others of the council—*Soit ceste petition mande en chauncellerie et illoeque appellez ascunes des grantz du parlement et autres du consail le Roi*, etc.[1] During the fourteenth century probably the great bulk of the judicial business treated in the chancery was created by the delegation of individual cases in this manner. By the same general authority several statutes were enacted expressly assigning subjects to the jurisdiction of the chancellor and the council.

Stat. 20 Edw. III, c. 6, in all cases of misdemeanours on the part of sheriffs, escheators, and other officers, declares 'we have charged our chancellor and treasurer to hear the complaints of all those who will complain, and to ordain speedy remedy'. The chancellor and treasurer we know never acted in such matters without the assistance of the council.

Stat. 36 Edw. III, c. 9, regarding the misdemeanours of purveyors in particular, promised, 'if any man feeling himself aggrieved will come into the chancery, and make his complaint, he shall presently there have remedy . . . without pursuing elsewhere.'

Stat. 1, 27 Edw. III, c. 1, of *Praemunire*, required that all persons suing in a foreign court, for matters cognizable in the king's court, should be made 'to appear before the king and his council, or in his chancery, or before the justices of one bench or the other to answer for their contempt'.

Stat. 2, 38 Edw. III, c. 1, extended the former with respect to persons obtaining citations or benefices from the court of Rome. They 'shall be presented to the king and his council, there to remain and stand to right, to receive what the law will give them'.

Stat. 37 Edw. III, c. 18, to guard against the damage caused by people making false suggestions or accusations to the king, required 'that they who make suggestions be sent before the chancellor, the treasurer, and grand council, and that they there find surety to pursue their suggestions'. These statutes go far to recognize, if they do not create, an

[1] Ibid., no. 10464.

independent standing of the court of chancery. This is not to say that it was dissociated from the council, for the substantial identity of council and chancery in all these matters was carefully maintained. The degree of independence is stated in the clauses that men might bring their complaints directly to the chancery, without going first to parliament. It is an over-emphasis of the statutes, however, to say that they marked in any way the beginning of a special jurisdiction, for there were cases in abundance prior to the statutes. Neither did the subjects specified comprise a large share of the jurisdiction actually wielded here. The acts also show us that at that time the attitude of parliament toward the chancery was in the main one of confidence, and that the opposition which was just beginning to be expressed against the extra-legal methods of the council was not as yet strongly felt.[1]

Efficiency of the chancery.

The extension of the power of the chancery at this time was without doubt based upon its general efficiency and popularity. This is shown by the expressions of many individual petitioners, who particularly asked to have their cases referred to the chancellor. One man beseeches the king, *Plaise . . . par voz lettres comaunder a votre chaunceller qe assembleez voz justices sergeauntz et autres sages de votre consail il face ceste busoigne oue toutes les circumstances debatre diligeanment et . . . ils ent facent ordainer si covenable remedie.*[2] Under Richard II the suggestion is made by a suitor that as the council in the usual course was not to meet before Michaelmas the chancellor be commanded to assemble it without delay.[3] That the chancellor's court might be held at any time and was not restricted to regular terms, was certainly a strong reason for its popularity and success.

The court was the council.

The court which the chancellor was instructed to assemble was the king's council, sometimes including 'the lords and

[1] This jurisdiction, so far as it was granted by acts of parliament, has been considered by some to belong to the common-law side of the chancery. But the consequent cases, as we shall show, do not warrant this classification, for the procedure was based upon petitions and in other respects followed the methods that were foreign to the common law.

[2] This is of 21 Edw. III, *Ancient Petitions*, no. 12144. Some are earlier, e.g. no. 12220 is of 17 Edw. III; also 12309, &c.

[3] *Warrants Privy Seal*, series i, section ii, file 6.

those skilled in the law', or more often those of the council 'who ought to be summoned', 'whom you see fit', or 'come fait a faire'.[1] It was left therefore largely to his discretion, or to the opportunity of the moment, how many bishops, lords, justices, serjeants-at-law, and clerks should be summoned. There seemed to be an indefinite obligation to summon an appropriate number, as was suggested in a case where an objection was raised that there was not a sufficiency of learned men present to do justice.[2] On one occasion in the trial of a great criminal case under Richard II, there was a proposal to call a number of bachelors and men-at-arms.[3] For yet an indefinite time, it is to be noted, the council was not a fixed tribunal, but an assemblage called *ad hoc*, according to convenience or the nature of the case. Sometimes there were jurists only, sometimes mainly lords, who composed the court under the chancellor. Neither was there any field of jurisdiction defined at first, but cases were referred apparently on no other ground than that of convenience and expediency.

The chancellor's presiding duties.

Processes were said to be heard 'before the chancellor and others of the council'. In various ways the function of the chancellor as a presiding officer is plainly indicated. He summons the parties;[4] assigns a day for the case;[5] addresses a question to the litigants;[6] answers an objection;[7] admits an attorney in spite of the opposition of other councillors;[8] dismisses a case on his own responsibility;[9] and announces the decision of the court.[10] For his influence in the case affecting the abbey of Meaux, a long and important litigation

1 'Appellez a vous ceux de notre Conseil queux vous verrez qe serroit a ce appeller', was the usual tenor of these instructions. *Warrants* (*Chancery*), no. 10724; *Rot. Parl.* i. 362, &c.

2 Moleyns' case, *Cal. Patent Rolls*, 20 Edw. III, 136.

3 'Soit ceste bille mande en la Chancellerie, illoeqes appellez les Justices et sergeantz le Roi, et avant suffisantz bachelors et gentz darmes et autres queux y sont appellez, et illoeqes oiez et declarez ceste matire et les circumstances et dependentes dicelle plein droyt illoeqes ent soit fait,' &c. *Ancient Petitions*, no. 5094.

4 *Cal. Patent Rolls*, 20 Edw. III, 136.

5 *Ancient Petitions*, no. 12289, 23 Edw. III.

6 *Cal. Close Rolls*, 26 Edw. III, 470.

7 The case of the Audeleys, ibid., 40 Edw. III, 238.

8 *Chron. de Melsa* (Rolls Series), iii. 135.

9 Baildon, *Select Cases in Chancery* (*Selden Society*, 1896), no. 106.

10 *Ancient Petitions*, no. 14957.

lasting from 1356 to 1367, it is confessed that he was extensively bribed.[1] The other members of the council are represented as assessors or advisors, when in the reign of Richard II the chancellor was instructed to act 'by his discretion with the advice of the council';[2] and again, he is 'to take such of the council as he shall see fit'.[3] It is important to observe, however, that throughout the fourteenth and most of the fifteenth century the chancellor was unable to act in these matters without the council, and that the rendering of decrees was thus far always on the authority not of the chancellor, but of the council—*ordinatum* or *decretum est per consilium* being still the proper form.[4]

Steps toward a more independent court.

To this point the chancery has been represented mainly as a subordinate authority, to which judicial functions were delegated by the king or the parliament. It is now possible to trace some of the steps by which the chancellor acquired a greater degree of independence, proceeding in judicial matters upon his own authority. 'It may readily be supposed,' says Dicey, 'that the pressure of other business, and a distaste for the niceties of legal discussion, made the Council glad to first refer matters of law to the Chancellor, and next to leave them entirely to his decision.'[5] A certain suggestion of this kind has already been given in the statutes. But there are earlier signs of an advance in this direction, as is seen in the petitions which suitors began to address to the chancellor instead of to the king and council. Already in the reign of Edward I, he was given prominence in an ordinance that no petition should come before the king and council except by the hands of the chancellor or other

[1] 'Contra quem diem, abbas noster Londonias accedens, muneribus quibusdam non parvis regis cancellario, tunc Wintoniensi episcopo, aliis de consilio renitentibus, promeruit ut ibidem per attornatos suos posset respondere.' *Chron. de Melsa*, iii. 135.

[2] *Rot. Parl.* iii. 14. Again, in 1382, with reference to lands taken by the escheators it was proposed, 'en cas qe aucun viegne devaunt le chanceller et monstre son droit, qe le Chanceller par sa bone discretion et avis de Conseil, si le semble qe lui busoigne d'avoir Conseil, q'il lease et baille les Terres issint en debate au tenant.' Ibid., p. 140.

[3] *Ancient Petitions*, no. 12947.

[4] A slight modification of this form of statement is found in 1397, when a decree was made 'by advice of the justices and other skilled persons of the chancery.' *Cal. Patent Rolls*, 21 Ric. II, 264, 426, 455.

[5] *Privy Council*, p. 16.

chief minister.[1] It was a well understood custom, in fact, for men to direct letters or petitions to any of the ministers upon matters within their official powers. There was nothing peculiar, therefore, in the earliest petitions to the chancellor, which asked for a writ or a change of writ, or complained that a writ was ineffective. It was probably with reference to a writ that the chancellor also was asked 'to provide a suitable remedy',[2] and sometimes in these cases he is besought to obtain the consent of the council. In the reign of Edward I, for example, Chancellor Langton was requested by the king to aid an aggrieved suitor in the following words: '(il) vous pri et requei pur lamour demoy qe au portour de ceste lettre voyles doner teu remedie com la court peut suffrir.'[3] In the year 1325 there is a petition which reads as follows: 'A Chaunceller notre Seigneur le Roi Emma la femme Roger de Plat prie grace et deliveraunce, pur Dieu, qe vous voillez regarder la Peticioun qe feust livere au commun Parlement et respondu par Comun Conseil, et a Vous livere; et vous commaundastes de suyvre bref,' etc.[4]

In a petition to the chancellor of the second or third year of Edward III the keeper of the forest of Galtres complains of a conspiracy to rob the forest, and asks, *pleise a vous sire conseiller issi qen cas notre Seigneur le Roi mette remedy*.[5] About the ninth year of the same reign a man made complaint to the chancellor that he had lost money in the king's service, whereupon he was told to come before the council to explain the matter further.[6] All of these petitions may be regarded as directed to the chancellor as an executive officer, but it can be seen that he was regarded as a means of approach to the council. This fact is still more clearly illustrated in the frequent requests which were made to

[1] The importance of this ordinance has been greatly exaggerated. The function was a purely ministerial one, and besides, the chancellor is not the only minister mentioned. See Hardy, *Introduction to the Close Rolls*, p. xxviii; also *Calendar*, 8 Edw. I, p. 108.

[2] A petition to Chancellor Hamilton in 1304 concludes with the words, 'Quare convenerabili dominationi humiliter supplicant quatinus pro prefato Williamo de aliquo congruo remedio in hac parte velitis subvenire.' *Ancient Petitions*, no. 15097.

[3] *Ancient Correspondence*, xxvi, no. 78.

[4] *Rot. Parl.* i. 437.

[5] *Ancient Petitions*, no. 15119.

[6] Ibid., no. 14774.

him for writs of summons and arrest, thus : *qe vous please granter un brief pour arrester le corps du dit Henry et lui amesner devaunt le conseil de respondre vers le conseil.*[1] To obtain the writ was to begin a council process.

Petitions to the chancellor and council.

For the same fundamental reason, namely, the prevailing belief that the chancellor was the actual head of the council, suitors began to address their petitions 'to the chancellor *and* council'. This form is analogous to that already begun in the address to the treasurer and council. In the reign of Edward II, about 1320, a petition of the subprior and convent of Dover, making claim to certain franchises, is addressed to the chancellor and treasurer in the following unusual manner : *Ceo est la enfourmeson fait a Chancelier et Tresorier et as autres grantz seigneurs du Conseil notre Seigneur le Roy.*[2] In the twelfth year of Edward III, 1338, a petition for a confirmation of charters was addressed, *Venerabili domino domini nostri Regis illustris cancellario et ipsius consilio.*[3] In the same year a petition is similarly addressed by a monk and prior of Jersey, who complains that he has suffered loss of goods as though he were an alien, whereas he declares he is a native of the island.[4] From this time scores of legal petitions to the chancellor and council appear, showing in their variety and frequent incorrectness of style a still unsettled usage. One as early as Edward I begins with the words :

'Pleise al chanceller et al conseil notre Seigneur le Roi.'[5]

Another about 1340 begins :

'A (*sic*) treshonorable pier en dieu et lour treschier Seigneur, si luy plest, sire John par la grace de dieu Erchevesque de Caunterbyrs et Chaunceler notre Seigneur le Roi et au bon conseil le dit notre Seigneur le Roi.'[6]

Other forms are :

'Al Chaunceler et as autres Seigneurs du counsail notre Seigneur le Roy.'[7]

[1] *Ancient Petitions*, nos. 14847, 15176, &c. ; *Calendars of Proceedings in Chancery*, vol. i, p. xii.

[2] *Ancient Correspondence*, xxxvi, no. 129.

[3] *Ancient Petitions*, no. 11961.

[4] Ibid., no. 13077 ; translated in 'Société Jersiaise', *Ancient Petitions* (Jersey, 1902), p. 66.

[5] *Ancient Petitions*, no. 15235.

[6] Ibid., no. 14915.

[7] Ibid., no. 10471, 28 Edw. III.

'As treshonorez Seigneurs le Chaunceller notre Seigneur le Roy et son tressage conseil en le chauncellerie.'[1]

'As treshonourables et tresreverentz seigneurs Chaunceller, Tresorer, Prive Seal, et touz autres honourables et tressages Seigneurs du conseil notre Seigneur le Roi.'[2]

'A trespuissant et tresredoute Seigneur le Roy et a son Chanceller et a tout le sage conseil.'[3]

'A honourez sires le Chanceller, Tresorer et gardein du Prive Seal.'[4]

These forms may be regarded as transitional, appearing with less frequency after the reign of Edward III, when they were superseded by the single address to the chancellor.

Petitions to the chancellor alone.

The next step then toward the independent position of the court of the chancellor is found in the petitions for remedy that were directed to him alone—*au chancellor du Roi*—instead of to the king and council. From all that has been said this was not a great step, nor does it mark any change of thought as regards the chancellor's function. The motive of suitors in resorting to all these later devices is plain enough, that in the face of the delays occasioned by bringing their petitions first to the king or to parliament they might have more direct access to the chancellor's court. It is perhaps more remarkable that the king and parliament acquiesced in this change of procedure, but such was the pressure of business in parliament that some outlet had to be found. In these cases presumably the chancellor, with the assistance of the council, could proceed without any preliminary writ or warrant. The earliest of the petitions of this class that the writer is able to identify is of the years 1343–5,[5] after which time they are numerous enough to indicate a frequent, though by no means the most usual, procedure. Under Richard II they occur in such numbers and regularity of form as to reveal an established usage and to indicate the beginning of a new stage of

[1] Ibid., nos. 15740, 14755, 15781, &c. This form is found more frequently in the time of Henry VI.

[2] Ibid., no. 14955, 10 Ric. II.

[3] Ibid., no. 983, 5 Ric. II.

[4] Ibid., no. 14882, tem. Edw. III.

[5] *Ancient Petitions*, no. 14865; file 303 contains many others. An instance purporting to be of 14 Edw. III is quoted in Spence (op. cit., i. 338), but unfortunately an error has been made in the reference, which belongs properly to the reign of Edward IV, not that of Edward III.

development in the separation of the chancellor's court from the council. Whether addressed to the council or the chancellor, these petitions are alike in their recital of grievances, including violent attacks, fraud, seizures at sea, and inability to obtain remedy in the ordinary courts. They plead for remedy in terms like the following : *pur quei le dit A. B. prie votre graciouse Seignurie que vous ordinez remedie, pour lonneur de dieu et en oevre de charite.*[1]

With the greater prominence of the chancellor the very style of the address was made more elaborate. To the simple words *au chanceller* of the earlier petitions are now added ' reverend father in God ', ' honorable ', ' gracious ', ' sage ', or ' puissant lord '. Something like a judicial title is expressed in the words *votre droiturele Seignurie.*[2] In the time of Richard II, also, in accordance with the tendency to emphasize this feature, the words of the address were commonly set apart from the body of the bill in the upper margin of the parchment. The reasons which guided suitors in thus directing their petitions to the chancellor seem perfectly clear. There was, in the first place, his influence as head of the council, a position which was shared to some extent by the treasurer and the keeper of the privy seal ; there was also his peculiar function of issuing the writs that were especially desired ; and above all there was his recognized power as an executive officer of enforcing the law. This last consideration was expressed by a plaintiff, who in 1388 asked the chancellor to proceed against his enemy, *et en oevre de charite luy chastier come vous bien puissez de votre droiturele Seignurie* ;[3] and still more positively within the years 1391–6, *depuisque vous avetz les leyes soveraignment a gouverner desouz notre Seigneur le Roy et sa pees a mayntenir et tielx riotes a contreester et des malefeassours et rebelx deinz la Roialme pur duement punire et chastier.*[4] The

[1] *Ancient Petitions*, nos. 12264, 13313, &c.

[2] Ibid., no. 15085.

[3] Ibid.

[4] Ibid., no. 15216. In the next century, probably during the chancellorship of Henry Beaufort, cir. 1413, a poor widow holding certain lands that had been purchased with her marriage money declared she wished to have no other judge. She asks, ' que si ascune homme voudrait compleindre de le ou dascune dez voz loials serviteurs a cause de lequele purroit estre en votre presence en respounse pur monstrer son droit come cele que iamais

reputation also of the chancellors for acting not only with power but with promptness, greater than was afforded in parliament or the council in any other relation, was a very material inducement to suitors. In one instance of the same reign the king was especially requested, *qe plese comander le dit Chaunceller faire droit et ley as dit suppliantz en cest present terme saunz ascun autre delay.*[1] To practical considerations such as these undoubtedly the popularity of the chancellor's court originally was due, rather than to any theory of his position as ' holding the prerogative of the king's grace ' as ' keeper of the king's conscience ', or as ' the head of justice ', which was as yet unformulated. In the history of this institution as well as others the facts came first and the theories afterwards.

A definable stage under Richard II.

The exact stage of development that was reached by the reign of Richard II is perhaps best shown by a certain well-expressed petition within the years 1389–91.[2] It was addressed to the chancellor, William of Wykeham, by certain foreign merchants complaining of a seizure at sea, and prayed him to consider the matter and ordain remedy—*que plese a votre tresnoble et tresgracieuse Seigneurie considerer ceste matiere et ent ordeigner de remedie par manere qils eyent restitucion . . . pour dieu et en oevre de charite.* In the endorsement it is stated that the hearing was before the council, by whom it was decreed—*per idem consilium consideratum fuit et decretum*—that damages should be paid to the plaintiffs. The chancellor then gave the order—*de mandato venerabili patris*[3]—that the money should be paid. Still more clearly the thought of the chancellor acting as a mediator, in behalf of the suitor in his dealings with parliament as well as with the council, is expressed in a remarkable petition of the time of Henry IV.

' Plese a treshonore et tresgraciouse Seigneur le Chaunceller Dengleterre de votre treshabundante grace et benignite, considerer la bille touchant lez grevances et extorcions

ne prendra autre seignour ne juge forsque vous mesmes sil vous plust de votre grace et ceo pur dieu et en oevre de charite.' Ibid., no. 15051.

[1] Ibid., no. 4399. [2] Ibid., no. 14957.

[3] Proceedings of this character one expects to find recorded in French rather than Latin, but no rule of this kind was as yet consistently followed.

faitz a lez poveres comunes del counte de Kent par lez officers del Chastel de Dovre, et coment lez tresreverendes et tressages Seigneurs de le tressage et tresdiscreet conseill notre tresredoute Seigneur le Roy ount plein poair par lassent de tout le parlement a finier et determiner lez ditz grevances et extorcions solonc lour bone avys et tressage discretion, et a ceo mettre votre graciouse mayn quant vous estez entre lez ditz Seigneurs au fyn qe la dit bille *par votre tresgraciouse mediation* poet estre bien et hastivement esployte pur dieu et oevre de charite, considerantz la bone voloir de le tresreverend piere en dieu larchivesqe de Canterbyrs en ceste matiere quant il vous pria vous especialment qe la dit bille poet estre esployte.'[1]

Further definitions of the court of chancery.

At the time of Richard II, when the cleavage of the council and the chancery was to a certain extent effected, it should be remarked that the petitions to the chancellor as yet formed a small class compared with the number of petitions to council and parliament. The bulk of the business of the chancery was still created in the old way by delegation either from the king or the parliament. From this time, however, such was the success of the new procedure, that the number of petitions in chancery quickly exceeds that of all the others. At this point the history of the chancellor's court begins to separate from the council, although throughout the fifteenth century it still retained the main features of its former constitution. In his judicial capacity the chancellor was still regarded as the head of the council, and was sought as the most favourable means of approach thereto. In a few instances petitions were addressed to the chancellor and the king's council, while one in particular mentions the council in the chancery with the words, *au treshonorez Seigneurs le Chaunceller notre Seigneur le Roi et son tressage conseil en le chauncellerie*.[2] The attendance of the council in the chancery was a feature of diminishing importance until it became a mere shadow of the body formerly assembled here.[3] The presence of lords and knights is rarely found,[4] but an

[1] *Council and Privy Seal*, file 11, 4 (?) Hen. IV.

[2] *Ancient Petitions*, no. 15740.

[3] In the year 1406 the court of chancery is described as 'cancellario cum co-officialibus suis et alio (*sic*) consilio regio.' *Chron. de Melsa*, iii. 300.

[4] In 1398 a record of a case in chancery contains the names of the chancellor, the treasurer, the keeper of the privy seal, the master of the rolls,

attendance of at least two of the justices was still deemed essential. A notable picture of the court as it existed in the time of Henry VI shows the chancellor, together with the master of the rolls, two judges, and four 'masters' sitting on the bench.[1] Three serjeants-at-law stand at the bar, and beyond these are various clerks and apprentices. In the reign of Edward IV a question upon this point was raised, when a decision pursuant to the statute, 31 Hen. VI, was challenged on the ground that it was not on record that any judge was with the chancellor at the time.[2] It was answered that the chancellor on this occasion did call one of the justices to him, and although there was not a record of the fact, this was said to make no difference, since it was not customary to mention the justices in the records. Under Richard III it was claimed that in cases of merchants despoiled at sea, according to the statute, 27 Edw. III, c. 13, the chancellor might proceed alone, *per se sine aliquo iusticiario*.[3] Still in 1487 one finds the chancellor giving an award and judgement in association with Sir Reginald Bray, a privy councillor, and two others, the latter presumably being justices.[4] Yet decrees on the authority of the chancellor are mentioned in the reign of Henry V,[5] and under Edward IV they were issued 'by the chancellor and the authority of the chancery'.[6] In 1463 in the absence of the chancellor the custody of the great seal was temporarily given to the master of the rolls, who was instructed in the administration of justice to call to his assistance certain clerks of the chancery, but nothing was said of the presence of the justices.

The passage reads as follows:

'... ad finem et effectum quod vos, in absentia sua (i.e. the chancellor's), sigillum illud occupare, et executionem rerum Iustitiae ac cursus Cancellariae nostrae praedictae

Sir John Bussy, Sir Henry Greene, Sir John Russel (well-known knights of Richard's council), and Robert Farington, clerk. Baildon, *Select Cases in Chancery*, no. 34.

[1] *Archaeologia*, xxxix. 358

[2] *Year Books*, 14 Edw. IV, f. 1.

[3] *Year Books*, 2 Ric. III, f. 2, no. 4.

[4] *Paston Letters*, no. 1013.

[5] 'Omnia acta et actitata ... per Dominum Cancellarium decreta conscribant.' Sanders, *Orders in Chancery*, vol. i, part i, p. 7 c.

[6] *Calendars of Proceedings in Chancery*, vol. i, pp. xcvii ff.

facere valeatis et exercere, vocatis vobis Ricardo Welton et Ricardo Fryston Clericis eiusdem Cancellariae quandocumque per vos visum fuerit expediens et necesse.'[1]

At this point we may leave the development of the court of chancery, with a summary statement of the stages through which it has passed. In general outline there was (1) the council, which was not necessarily identified with the chancery; (2) the council *in* chancery, by which the operations of the court were carried through this administrative office; (3) the chancellor *and* council, which emphasizes the position of the chancellor as chief executive officer; (4) the chancellor, who is regarded as the actual judge. This latter stage is hardly reached by the close of the middle ages, for a certain representation of the council was still considered necessary, however much it was only a formality. By these steps it is clear the chancellor came ultimately to exercise functions that did not belong to him in the beginning, and were not a natural outgrowth of his original authority. There is now to be considered one other stage of development, which belongs in point of time before the fourth, and this is (5) the chancellor *or* the council. In other words, what other mode of conciliar action was there that helped to cause the separate growth of the chancery?

A distinction between the council and the chancery.

The recognition of the chancery as a different, or at least an alternative, authority to that of the council begins to appear in the reign of Edward III. The statute of praemunire, previously quoted, declares that the parties shall be brought *devant le Roi et son conseil*, ou *en sa chancellerie, ou devant les justices*.[2] In the reign of Richard II such references can be multiplied. In the thirteenth year, 1389, the commons demand that on false suggestions parties shall not be brought by writs *quibusdam certis de causis*, or any similar writs, *devant le Chanceller* ou *le Conseill le Roy de respondre*;[3] and again in the seventeenth year they say that false suggestions are made *si bien a Conseill nostre seigneur le Roi come en la Chancellerie*, and they ask that the wrongdoers be made to appear *devant le dit Conseill* ou *en la*

[1] *Foedera* (Orig. Ed.), xi. 507.
[2] *Statutes of the Realm*, i. 329.
[3] *Rot. Parl.* iii. 267.

Chancellerie.[1] Now what is the distinction that is implied in the alternative of the council *or* the chancery? It is evident that a process of differentiation is going on, similar to that of the early law courts from the *curia regis*, but on what line does the cleavage occur? At first sight there would seem to be no material difference, whether it were the council wherein the chancellor was still the chief officer or the chancellor acting with the assistance of the council. In the words of Dicey again, 'there is little reason to suppose that in the fifteenth century persons brought before the Council and those summoned to the presence of the chancellor came before an essentially different court'.[2] In point of personnel at the time of Richard II there was no separation of two bodies of men. It is true that in the chancery men of legal proficiency especially were required, while the king's council in its political capacity under pressure of parliament was being composed of bishops, barons, and knights. Under the Lancasters also there was a logical tendency toward a division of the council into two separately working bodies, the one political and the other legal. There were times, as during the minority of Henry VI, when the council was so much absorbed in political affairs that it could scarcely give any attention to judicial business. But this has not proved to be a satisfactory explanation of the relations of the two courts, because no such line of division was consistently followed. On the whole this suggestion has very little weight compared with a certain difference of procedure, which grew up within the council and ultimately caused a cleft in its organization.

The methods of the privy seal.

It has already been made apparent that purely administrative methods may make a point of departure in the formation of organic bodies. Now the root of a new development of this kind is found in the extended use of the privy seal and in the clerical methods of this office, which differed widely from those of the chancery. The privy seal, it is well understood, was originally invented for the personal communications of the king, but before the close of the thirteenth century it ceased to be a private seal and became one of the

[1] Ibid. 323; also iv. 156. [2] *Privy Council*, p. 70.

regular instruments of the government.[1] It was used mostly for official communications, especially for the warrants directing the actions of the treasurer and the chancellor. For these purposes it was a subsidiary instrument, but for many other purposes it came to be used in preference to the great seal. This tendency was due partly to the necessity of relieving the chancery of an excessive amount of business, but partly also to the greater convenience and less formality attending the operation of the minor seal. According to the long-established customs of the chancery, letters under the great seal must be written upon parchment, in the Latin language, and were encumbered with tedious formulae; except for the writs of established usage the chancellors were not permitted to seal anything without a warrant, and for this purpose a warrant under the privy seal was preferred; the regular writs of the chancery also were registered, and a record of their issue thus was kept; special rolls also were maintained for letters close and letters patent. The more these forms were elaborated, the greater necessarily became the expense, and the fees of the chancery for any of its services were exceedingly high.[2] In much of its work, too, the chancery laboured under the aforesaid statutory restrictions, which sought to bring the department in a measure under parliamentary control.

From these limitations and inconveniences the privy seal was comparatively free. In all points its diplomatic forms were briefer and simpler. Written usually in French, in the fifteenth century sometimes in English, not necessarily upon parchment, its letters were issued without sealed warrants, and they were never registered or enrolled.[3] For these reasons the operations of the office were not easily made public, and it was never held under constitutional control. According to an early statute, therefore, it was not

[1] Eugène Déprez, *Le Sceau Privé* (Paris, 1908), is a valuable study on the diplomatic side.

[2] One of the ordinances of 1406 in regard to the officers of the chancery declared, 'qils ne preignent de nulluy excessive regard pur lour labours.' *Rot. Parl.* iii. 588.

[3] Déprez has suggested that the beginning of a register here was once undertaken, but the evidence on this point is not at all convincing.

allowed to issue any writ concerning the common law,[1] and the ordinances of 1311 declared that any letters of the privy seal seeking to delay or disturb the law of the land should be held invalid.[2] Nevertheless there were writs of the privy seal, and as these were not subject to the restrictions of the common law, they were used to penetrate districts protected by franchise, and became the natural instruments of any extraordinary procedure.[3] Moreover the advantages of expedition and secrecy caused the privy seal to be grasped in turn by more than one of the government departments as a medium of communication. It was for a time the special instrument of the wardrobe,[4] until in the reign of Edward II the clerk of the privy seal was drawn away from that department; later it became the direct and authoritative organ of the king's council, while the king for his private purposes was thrown back upon the signet.[5] This transformation in the procedure of the council came about very gradually. It first appears in the warrants to the treasurer and the chancellor, some of which are attested *per consilium* in the reign of Edward II. It is soon made evident that an act of the council was itself a warrant for a letter of the privy seal, but for a letter of the chancery, if all the formalities were observed,[6] a warrant under the privy seal was required. In the reign of Edward III an important change occurs when writs of summons to the king's council were issued under the privy seal, while those to parliaments continued to be by the great seal. The clerks who wrote the warrants and writs

[1] *Articuli super Cartas*, c. 6; *Statutes of the Realm*, i. 139.

[2] Ibid. 165.

[3] In the year 1 Edw. II a case occurs for which there proves to be no remedy at common law, since the manor in question was of ancient demesne, wherein no writ ran except 'the little writ close of the king'. *Abb. Plac.*, p. 302. Naturally the writs of this kind were disliked, and their validity questioned. In 1318 it was reported that when certain writs of the privy seal were delivered, the men threw them upon the ground and trampled upon them. *Cal. Patent Rolls*, 11 Edw. II, 176.

[4] T. F. Tout, *Eng. Hist. Rev.* (July, 1909), 496.

[5] In the reign of Henry VI it will be found that the council sometimes commanded the signet, but these instances are exceptional and did not open any new channel of action.

[6] Needless to say, the chancery did not always insist upon sealed warrants. But in regard to the more important letters patent this rule was well observed from the tenth year of Richard II. Titles to property might indeed be questioned if due formalities were not observed.

were also employed for the other secretarial work of the council, until, after a period of alternation and rivalry, the clerks of the chancery were quite displaced from this service. The first to hold the special office of clerk of the council was Master John Prophet in the reign of Richard II, one of the staff of the privy seal, as was each of his successors.[1] In the hands of these men the records of the council and therefore its procedure followed the methods of this office, which differed materially from those of the chancery. The chirography is recognizable as rounder and more cursive, the notes and memoranda were briefer, on thinner parchment or on paper, in French or English more often than in Latin; petitions and warrants were kept in files, but with no enrolments as in the chancery,[2] while the final depository of these records was the treasury of the exchequer instead of the Rolls House or the Tower.

The keeper of the privy seal.

In the course of this transformation the dignity of the keeper of the privy seal was naturally advanced. In the reign of Edward III he was supported by a staff of five clerks,[3] which was increased to nine under Henry IV.[4] Not only was he acknowledged to be one of the three great ministers in the council, but for certain purposes he was called upon to relieve the chancellor as its chief executive officer. In 1349 a proclamation was made that petitions of grace, such as were commonly acted upon by the king with the advice of the council, should first be brought either to the chancellor or to the keeper of the privy seal.[5] One such petition is answered with the words, *notre Seigneur le Roy graunta ceste supplication sur lavis de son conseil et bailla mesme la bille au Gardien de son prive seal par celle cause*;[6] another is endorsed, *a ceste bille est responduz par monsieur du prive seal qe le Roi ad confermez le grant.*[7] There was a marked

[1] Chap. XIII, § 4.

[2] Although there were no enrolments the office kept its warrants well enough to make a return upon a writ of *certiorari*.

[3] *Ordinances for the Royal Household* (Society of Antiquaries, 1790), p. 10; also Nicolas, i. 88.

[4] See a petition of the privy seal clerks for their wages, *Council and Privy Seal*, file 9, July 23.

[5] *Cal. Close Roll*, 22 Edw. III, 615.

[6] *Ancient Petitions*, no. 11119, temp. Edw. III.

[7] *Council and Privy Seal*, file 25, temp. Hen. IV.

inclination in judicial proceedings also to assemble the council under the keeper of the privy seal in the absence of the chancellor. In 1364 we read that a certain indenture was drawn up in the presence of William of Wykeham, keeper of the privy seal, and others of the council.[1] According to the ordinances of 1390, in which the hand of William of Wykeham is visible, it was provided that all business ' of great charge ' should be determined in the presence of the chancellor and certain other members, but that all bills of the people ' of less charge ' might be treated before the keeper of the privy seal together with those of the council who were present at the time.[2] This ordinance has been understood to indicate a prototype of the later court of requests.[3] But the words of the ordinance hardly warrant this assumption, for in the context bills ' of less charge ' do not necessarily mean ' poor men's causes ', but private bills of ordinary character. How closely the position of the keeper of the privy seal was analogous to that of the chancellor is well shown in the various petitions that were addressed to him for the favours which he could grant or secure. Some of these asked simply for a writ such as it was within the province of his office to issue.[4] The following example of the time of Henry IV is exactly parallel, in its content, to that found in the petitions most frequently addressed to the council or the chancellor.

' A son honourable et gracious Seigneur le Gardeyn del privee seal notre Seigneur le Roy, supplie humblement un povre homme Walter Dru de Hendon qe plese votre graciouse Seigneurie de considerer lez tortz et injuriis qe John Dru son frere ad fait au dit suppliant ; cest assavoir . . . le dit John oue force et armes ensemble oue autres disconez entrason le cloos du dit suppliant en la paroch de Hendon avandit et coupa lez arbres al value de XL s. del dit suppliant, et apres cc fagottes de bois pres x s. du dit suppliant prist et emporta, et outre ceo il fist assaut au dit suppliant et ly manassa ly occire issint q'il nest hardy aler alarge pour doute de sa mort ; dount prie remedie solonc votre tressage

[1] *Cal. Close Roll*, 38 Edw. III, 59. [2] Nicolas, i. 18 b.

[3] Palgrave, *Original Authority*, p. 79.

[4] A petition of Thomas de Skelton and his wife complains of a delay in an assize of novel disseisin and asks the keeper for a writ to the justices to proceed. This was indeed a writ of the common law. *Council and Privy Seal*, file 2, m. 4.

discretion ou outrement vous plese luy graunter license de pursuer envers le dit John par le commune ley pour dieu et en oevre de charite.' [1]

Petitions like these, however, are exceptional, and are simply indicative of the experiments that were being made to find a new channel of action. The keeper of the privy seal at this time established no permanent court of resort, nor did he in any wise displace the chancellor as the active head of the council. But his office remained the regular organ of the council, in matters both administrative and judicial, while the chancery was thereby one degree removed. In the reign of Richard II, we learn specifically of judicial processes according to the methods of the privy seal. These include not only writs of summons, but executory writs as well,[2] besides a meagre form of record. There was evidently a positive policy on the part of the government to extend these processes, as well as those of the chancery, in rivalry with the courts of common law. The aggression of the council, as it was regarded, was strenuously resisted in parliament, where objection was particularly directed against 'the writs and processes of the privy seal'.[3] The continued activity of the council, especially in its use of writs under the privy seal, has already been mentioned as one of the causes of the revolution of 1399, when the council suffered a check but not a hindrance to its further development. Under these conditions, therefore, we may speak of the council and the chancery not as two distinct bodies of authority, but as the same body in two diverging methods of operation. More correctly, one was the 'council in chancery', which continued the older forms of action,[4] and the other, to make a con-

The council (privy seal) distinguished from the council in chancery.

[1] *Council and Privy Seal*, file 27, 2 (?) Hen. IV; also file 21. It is to be noticed that not all of the petitions to the keeper avowed poverty as the ground of appeal.

[2] 'Le consail estoit acordee que le suppliant en ceste bille avera executories briefs et lettres du privee seal.' *Ancient Petitions*, no. 11010.

[3] *Rot. Parl.* iii. 21, 44, 267. In the first year of Henry IV the commons prayed that all personal actions be tried at common law, and not by writ of privy seal. Ibid. 446.

[4] Still, in the reign of Henry V and of Henry VI, according to the records, the council and the court of chancery were treated as one and the same thing. A mainprise to come before the council is fulfilled by one's coming to the chancery; mainprise was made in the chancery to come before the council; and a case in the chancery at alternate stages is a case for the council. Take, for example, the following extracts from the Close Roll

venient designation, was the 'council (privy seal)'. In the light of subsequent events we should call the latter 'the council in star chamber', but at first the star chamber was used by the council in its chancery proceedings as well as the other,[1] while the fundamental difference lay in the writs and records which had a practical bearing in all matters of administration and judicature. With the government there was the alternative between the greater secrecy and dispatch of the one procedure and the greater formality and security afforded by the other. The method of the privy seal, therefore, was adopted by the council in all its political activities and for such judicature as most affected interests of state. To the suitor, on the other hand, there was offered a measure of choice whether he would have his case determined more expeditiously and at less cost by the summary procedure of the privy seal, or at greater expense but with more security in the chancery. To some such considerations as these was it due that the council in time became the great tribunal for criminal trials, while the chancery was mainly a court for cases concerning property. These general tendencies can be shown to have reality only as they are illustrated by a great number of concrete cases. These will be taken up in the succeeding chapter, for the purpose of showing more in detail the relations and differentiations of the council and the chancery. Thus far it has been the intention only to draw in outline the structure of the court and its two forms of authority. It remains now to consider both the subject-matter and the methods of the jurisdiction to which allusion has frequently been made.

(9 Hen. V, m. 10 d). John Meverell gives security *in cancellaria* 'quod ipse personaliter comparebit coram dicto Rege et consilio suo,' &c. Later, 'ad quem diem predictus Iohannes in cancellaria comparuit iuxta formam manucaptionis predicte.'

[1] While the department of the chancery is reputed to have gained a fixed place in the time of Edward I, its legal proceedings are still reported to have been held in one spot or another *ubicunque fuerit.* It might be in the star chamber, in the chapter house of the Black Friars, or in the chancellor's residence. In 1356 we are told of the 'place' at the upper end of Westminster Hall, 'where the chancery is held.' Here there was a marble table before which the chancellor or his deputy sat, receiving suitors and affixing the seal to writs and charters. Frequently the chancellor's advisers were assembled here, but for cases requiring deliberation the court was more suitably held in a council chamber. *Cal. Close Rolls,* 30 Edw. III, 332; 32 Edw. III, 534. On the council chamber see chap. xiii, § 2.

CHAPTER XI

THE JURISDICTION OF THE COUNCIL

Ordinary *v.* extraordinary jurisdiction.

In comparison with the 'ordinary' jurisdiction, as it is called, of the common law, it is customary to speak of the 'extraordinary' jurisdiction of the king's council. This was not the original conception, since the council was a court of general and undefined authority long before the courts of special character came into existence. Naturally the distinction did not arise until the common law was recognized as the prevailing system within the king's courts, while the council was felt to represent certain rival and even antagonistic methods. In order that this phase of the history may be clear, it is necessary now to describe the jurisdiction of the council, as it was practically exercised, with especial reference to the distinctive methods of procedure that were herein developed. So far as is possible, the contrast of these methods to those of the common law will at every step be pointed out. At the same time it must be borne in mind that there was a process of differentiation within the council itself, between the branch identified with the chancery and that associated with the office of the privy seal. The points of distinction between these two branches should also be noticed as soon as they occur. Continuing the argument that was started in the last chapter, these lines of development can now be followed only in the light of the cases, particularly during the fourteenth and fifteenth centuries. There are first the cases that are found in the records of the chancery, and later those produced by the department of the privy seal.

Records of the chancery and of the privy seal.

As might reasonably be expected, the records of the chancery are by far the more complete and abundant. In the fourteenth century the most important cases were frequently enrolled with the letters close and patent, where they are now readily accessible. But from the time of

Richard II, whether because the rolls were too much encumbered, or because other means of keeping the records were more satisfactory, this usage almost disappears. The bundles of proceedings in chancery which were then thrown together are in a very faulty condition of preservation ; so that for the fifteenth century we have petitions in great quantity, but records of the processes are scarce.

Of conciliar cases distinct from the chancery there has seemed to be a still greater dearth, for hitherto scarcely any have been known prior to the time of Henry VII.[1] A considerable number may be found, however, among the piles of miscellaneous parchments and papers of the privy seal. Characteristically of the methods of this office, these were briefly written, sparing of parchment, showing no sign of arrangement or care for their preservation. Not until the time of the Tudors apparently did the practice begin of putting these proceedings together in bundles. Still for a century earlier they may be counted by the hundred, attesting the constant activity of the council in this direction. Most of them consist only of the petitions, upon which it was enough simply to endorse the judgements or orders of the council. A few fragments that remain, however, contain at one stage or another the hearings at length, and reveal the procedure of the council more clearly even than any of the contemporary records of the chancery. With this material, fragmentary as it is, from both sources a fairly complete view may be obtained of the judicial business, which at first belonged alike to the council and the chancery, and which in time came to be divided between them.

Origin of cases before the council.

Looking at the subject from the beginning, there was at first no *field* of jurisdiction which was understood to belong to the council apart from other courts. As appears in the time of Edward I, there were innumerable instances of legal difficulty for which there was then no relief at common law, and for these cases there was no remedy except by petition. To give a list of all the legal points thus raised would hardly

[1] Several cases between 1477 and 1487 are included in Mr. Leadam's work, *Select Cases in the Star Chamber*, Selden Society (London, 1903), xvi. 1–16. Others are to be presented in a forthcoming volume announced by the Society under the hand of the same distinguished editor.

be practicable, but it will be useful to mention one or two of the most frequent causes for resorting to this procedure. If one had a grievance or complaint against the king himself, by reason particularly of the excessive exactions of sheriffs or escheators, it was not possible to sue the king, but a petition would be received and turned over to the exchequer or the chancery for consideration as a matter of course. Sometimes the mere delay of the courts, for reasons perhaps inexplicable, was made the subject of grievance. The following letter of Edward I to his chancellor will show how a case on this ground was committed to the council.

'Edward, &c. Quia Isabella de Clifford et Idonia de Leybourn asserunt iustitiam sibi esse dilatam coram iusticiariis nostris de banco in placito quod est coram eis inter nos et ipsas Isabellam et Idoniam de advocatione ecclesie de Burgh subtus Staynmor, vobis mandamus quod intellecto a prefatis Iusticiariis processu inde habito coram eis et convocatis si opus fuerit venerabili patre J. Eliensi episcopo Thesaurario nostro et aliis de consilio nostro ibidem, hinc inde fieri faciatis in placito predicto plene et celeris iusticie complementum, prout vos et alii de consilio nostro secundum legem et consuetudinem regni nostri videritis faciendum.' [1]

It has already been shown that the council did not usually conduct the trials, but confined itself rather to aiding or correcting the processes of other courts. Even when the parties were summoned to appear and to explain themselves, their cases were generally committed to one or another of the ordinary courts or commissions for trial. The council might give its advice, and would sometimes communicate a very positive opinion, but it was usually preferred that the decision should be rendered by 'due process of law' in a regular court of record.[2] The few cases that the council did consent

[1] *Ancient Correspondence*, vol. xlv, no. 51.

[2] In a record of Edward III, a certain heiress was actually examined by the council and found to be an idiot, so that the alienations of her property were invalid. But in order that this might be determined by 'due process', the following word was sent to the king's bench: 'we command you cause the aforesaid Joanna to come personally before you to be diligently examined, and if it shall be evident to you, as she surely seems to us and our council, then . . . do you cause to be done what in justice and according to the law and custom of our realm should be done.' *Close Roll*, 47 Edw. III, m. 29.

to hear were received more likely because of the prominence of the individuals or of the interests concerned than because of the nature of the litigation. Only after a considerable time, when it was made evident that the courts of common law for certain purposes had failed or proved inadequate, was the council induced to receive cases of certain kinds and to become itself a court for trials. Upon this point the evidence is not that the council usurped the function suddenly or eagerly, but rather that it was persuaded to do so by the pressure of necessity and at the wishes of the people as expressed in their petitions. Let us notice for a few pages the subjects that especially called for attention.

Cases of violence.

In the first place, a problem that the government constantly had to face lay in the crimes of great violence which afflicted every century of the middle ages and sometimes spread beyond control. In an age of prevalent warfare these evils, under different conditions, were at all times essentially the same, namely, the rebellions and oppressions of powerful men and their armed bands. They invaded the property of weaker people and made seizures, often under forms of law. All legal authorities, including sheriffs, judges, and juries, were likely to be corrupted or intimidated by them. Whether it was under the feudal relations of lord and vassal, or under the subsequent practices known as livery and maintenance, there were recurring outbursts of crimes described as trespass, riots, armed attacks, unlawful assemblages, robberies, misprision, abduction, embraceries, extortions, and many others. One of the most frequent causes of violence is found in the conduct of private parties who, having secured the judgement of a court, would undertake themselves *vi et armis* to enforce it. All such forcible entries and violent dispossessions were firmly forbidden, first by ordinance, and then by statute; nevertheless, the practice of self-help, as it is called, was exceedingly difficult to eradicate.[1] Sometimes the source of the evil lay in the great power of a single individual, sometimes in the

[1] An act of the second year of Edward I reads as follows:
'Prohibendum est ex parte Regis sub periculo incarcerationis et redemptionis ad voluntatem Regis, ne quis in regno unum aliquem armis exerceat

general anarchy of entire counties. To meet such cases the government resorted to one method after another, none of which was adequate for all emergencies. In the thirteenth century the king's bench was especially deputed to receive actions of trespass, and became the great criminal court, but under the forms of common law it was unable to cope with the entire problem.[1] Another method, which was begun apparently by Henry III [2] and extended by Edward I, was found in the appointment of special commissions, particularly those of *trailbaston* and of *oyer et terminer*, who were to act with power and promptness in a given case or group of cases. In comparison with the operations of the king's bench the commissions appeared as an extraordinary procedure, and, although the necessity for them was admitted, in parliament they were immediately regarded with disfavour. The statute of Westminster, 13 Edw. I, c. 29, required that no such commissions should be granted except to regular justices, 'unless it be for a heinous trespass, where it is necessary to provide speedy remedy.' Still the commissions were widely sought and employed,[3] until in the reign of Edward II complaint was

aut vi armata terras seu possessiones alicuius usurpare presumat, set unusquisque ius suum per viam iusticie in curia eiusdem Regis consequatur.

'Simili quoque modo est prohibendum ne qui cum equis et armis per terram incedat seu discurrat, exceptis domini Regis ministris quibus ratione officii sui publici hoc propter pacis conservationem incumbit, seu hiis quos Rex ipse aut eius locum tenentes pro pacis conservatione aut aliis negotiis ipsis specialiter mutuatis ad eadem explenda negotia in manu armata duxerit assignandos, et hiis qui in evidenti necessitate pro transgressoribus insequendis arma sumpserunt ut familiam suam in armis duxerint et de hoc indubitanter constare possit.' An unfiled document.

The same idea was stated more explicitly in the well-known statute of Richard II, declaring that 'the king forbids any one to make entry upon lands or tenements except when given by law, and then never by force or with a multitude of men, but peaceably and according to law.' *Rot. Parl.* iii. 114; *Statutes of the Realm*, ii. 20.

[1] There was every effort to support the common law in this regard. Many a petitioner who complained of violence and oppression was answered *sequatur ad communem legem.*

[2] Special commissioners were sent to hold court in a given place, to deal with a specific case. *Cal. Patent Rolls*, 36 Hen. III, 155, 156, 159. In 1259 such a commission was appointed to punish a sheriff. Ibid. 41 Hen. III, 539.

[3] In 1290 a man complains of the extortions of the bishop of Exeter, and he asks to be granted either a commission of *oyer et terminer* or a hearing before the king and council. *Rot. Parl.* i. 60.

renewed in parliament that they were appointed much too freely and to the detriment of the law. An ensuing statute, 2 Edw. III, required that writs of *oyer et terminer* should be granted only for 'grievous and horrible trespass'.[1] According to a later statute, the justices of *oyer et terminer* were required to take a professional oath.[2] The more the commissions were regularized the more plainly do their limitations appear, and the less were they able to deal satisfactorily with extreme conditions. From a few scanty records of their proceedings, it appears that they employed juries and other forms of common law, while for their protection and the execution of their orders they generally depended upon the sheriffs.[3] Consequently they were often corrupted and defied in much the same way as other courts. In a flagrant instance described in 1354, a certain knight came into the hall where the commissioners were sitting, and with drawn sword threatened to kill one of the justices, whom he seized by the throat, and it was said that he would have killed other men had he not been prevented.[4] At the same time various petitioners declare that because of the power of their enemies they cannot sue at common law,[5] they dare not pursue even by *oyer et terminer*;[6] that the commissioners are hindered in the execution of their offices;[7] that officers

[1] In the fourth year of Edward III a petition for a commission was granted with the words, 'Eyt en Chauncelerie oyer et terminer pur le horribilite du trespas.' *Rot. Parl.* ii. 33. A commission was once revoked because the case was not one of 'grievous and horrible trespass'. *Cal. Close Rolls*, 41 Edw. III, 392.

[2] *Statutes of the Realm*, 20 Edw. III, i. 304.

[3] *Assize Rolls*, especially nos. 1551, 1560. One prays for a writ of trespass 'according to common law'. *Rot. Parl.* ii. 33.

[4] *Cal. Patent Rolls*, 28 Edw. III, 166.

[5] *Ancient Petitions*, no. 10626.

[6] Ibid., no. 12298, 29 Edw. III.

[7] The following petition is of a later time than the other references given in this connexion, but it illustrates the same chronic difficulty: 'To the right reverent fader in god the Bisshop of Carlile Tresorer of Engelond. Please unto youre good lordship to be informed, where that Robert Pylton and his ffelows have a commission of the King whiche hath been schowed un to divers personys that longith to gyf intendaunce to the seide commissioun and nought ys obeyed in their behalf, Whereby the king hath sustened grete harme; Wherefore like it un to youre hie dignite to directe this bill under your signet un to the Worschipful sire Maister Thomas Kent clerk of the Kinges Counseill willing hym to do make out lettres of the privy seal directed un to the seide personys . . . to appiere in theyr propre personys to for the Kinges Counseill,' &c. *Council and Privy Seal*, file 77.

are in collusion with wrongdoers;[1] that sheriffs refuse to serve writs;[2] that bailiffs will not arrest;[3] that juries are controlled and coroners are under procurement.[4] In the reign of Edward III plaintiffs in the greatest distress began to ask that they might be served not by a commission, but that they might be heard before the council instead. A petition of the parson of a church in Southampton, 5 Ric. II, made complaint to the king and lords of parliament of the oppression of the prior of Huntingdon, who, it was alleged, was seeking to enforce certain covenants that could not be enforced without simony. The prior resorted to violence, and also, it was said, obtained a commission of *oyer et terminer*, whereby he falsely obtained an award of £90 against the parson. The petitioner asked that the matter be examined by good men of the country now in parliament, and particularly that no *oyer et terminer* again be granted.[5] The system of commissions was by no means abandoned; with all its faults it remained the more frequent form of action. On the whole it was the method the least likely to suffer delay, because any requisite number of commissions might be appointed. But for the most dangerous cases in emergency the council was recognized as the more effective power. As was said in the first year of Richard II, there were actions 'against such high personages that right could not be done elsewhere'. From this time the number of cases treated either wholly or in part by the council increases beyond all estimation. In the early years of Henry VI there is mention of a special file of 'riot bills' that were turned over to the council in a single session of parliament.[6] At this time, however, there was nothing to determine whether the jurisdiction thus begun belonged properly to the council or the chancery. As a matter of fact the early petitions to the chancellor, already described, were mainly burdened with complaints of this nature. During most of the fifteenth

[1] *Ancient Petitions*, no. 15200.
[2] Ibid., no. 14969.
[3] Ibid., no. 15200.
[4] Ibid., no. 12824, 1 Ric. II.
[5] Ibid., no. 7129. In 1386 it is asked, 'qe les parties soient faitz venir devant votre conseil estre finalment terminez *non obstante* ascun commission ou autre chose faite a lencontre.' Ibid., no. 13443.
[6] *Early Chancery Proceedings*, bundle 5, no. 41.

century, indeed, it seemed to depend on the convenience of the instant whether the cases of great violence calling for summary treatment should be dealt with by the council or the chancery. At certain periods like the minority of Henry VI and the first years of Edward IV they seem to have been thrown mainly into the chancery. Any distinctions that we may try to make upon this point, therefore, are likely to be premature until we reach the statute of Henry VII concerning the star chamber.

Cases of fraud.

A group of cases that began to receive the attention of the council quite as early as the former may be classified as those arising from *fraud* of one kind or another. It is well understood that the forms of common law, by their very rigidity, were readily perverted by methods of chicanery that could be penetrated only by a court of summary powers. According to the statements of many aggrieved parties they were being harassed by processes that were begun in the courts and then continued or delayed indefinitely. Litigation, we know, was frequently held back for years, and this of course was to the advantage of the stronger party. In complications of this kind the only way to cut the knot was by means of an appeal to the king and council. Many cases relating to forged charters,[1] false claims,[2] counterfeit money,[3] 'covin and procurement,'[4] covenants extorted under duress,[5] malicious indictments,[6] and others of the kind were consistently heard by the council in chancery under Edward III. A good illustration is given in the case of a deaf and dumb girl who was being imposed upon by certain men acting as her guardians. The matter was brought to the attention of the king on private information, and the men were commanded to appear and to bring the girl before the council. On being interrogated, the men claimed to have a certain enfeoffment by which the heiress had made over her property to

[1] *Cal. Patent Rolls*, 22 Edw. III, 131; *Cal. Close Rolls*, 24 Edw. III, 225; *Close Roll*, 42 Edw. III, m. 8 d.

[2] An unfiled document, petition of Hamon Lestineur, which I can only indicate as found in 'Exchequer Box'.

[3] *Cal. Patent Rolls*, 24 Edw. III, 595.

[4] *Ancient Petitions*, nos. 11302, 12264, 12287, 14937.

[5] Ibid., nos. 11028, 15149.

[6] Ibid., no. 15571.

them. But when it was found that the girl was deaf and dumb, the council immediately determined that the enfeofment was of no validity. Upon confession of their guilt, the men were committed to the Fleet prison, whence they were liberated on the payment of fines.[1] That a jurisdiction of this kind properly belonged to the chancellor and council was declared further by the several statutes assigning to them the power to deal with misdemeanours in office and false accusations.[2] A noteworthy example of the success of the council in treating such subjects is given in the Chesterfield case, 39 Edw. III, wherein a clerk of the exchequer was accused of falsifying his accounts and defrauding the king to the extent of £1,000.[3] After an examination of the testimony by 'legal and discreet auditors', who pointedly questioned the men on both sides, it was found that the accusers had given false suggestions, as they themselves were afterwards forced to admit. It was in the cases of fraud that certain features of the peculiar procedure of the council may first be observed, for in allegations of this kind often the truth could be ascertained not by any existing rules of evidence, but only by a free examination of all the attendant circumstances. The seals of the charter in question had to be inspected by experts,[4] the records searched and compared,[5] and even the defendant questioned as to his motives. Although no division of this jurisdiction was formally made, by general acquiescence it was properly inherited by the later court of chancery, whose clerks were the acknowledged experts in these matters.

The king's person and all rights pertaining to the crown

[1] *Close Roll*, 49 Edw. III, m. 13 d.

[2] *Statutes*, 20 Edw. III, c. 6; 36 Edw. III, c. 9; 37 Edw. III, c. 18; 38 Edw. III, c. 9; 42 Edw. III, c. 3; 17 Ric. II, c. 6.

[3] *Cal. Close Rolls*, 39 Edw. III, 114–25; *Patent Roll*, 40 Edw. III, part i, m. 11.

[4] *Ancient Petitions*, no. 12168, 22 Edw. III, is an instance in which a charter, which was being used in a case pending before the king's bench, was proved a forgery before the king and council. Likewise, 26 Edw. III, a document which was being used as a certification in chancery was invalidated because the date was wrongly stated, and the man who presented it was punished as a forger. (An unfiled document.)

[5] In 1360 the council examined a certain certificate in order to determine whether it was a fraud upon the statute of mortmain. *Cal. Close Rolls*, 34 Edw. III, 8.

Cases affecting the rights of the crown.

were considered to be above the jurisdiction of the ordinary courts. When any such rights or interests appeared in the course of litigation, either the king would command the judges to surcease, or the judges themselves would refuse to proceed without a special order. Cases of sufficient importance were treated by the council. Among these inevitably are found many criminal charges of treason, conspiracy, espionage, evasion of the customs, and contempt.[1] Arraignments for contempt were incurred by defying the orders of a court or of the king, or most likely by pursuing litigation contrary to an existing judgement.[2] It was possible at any time for the king to make an order especially reserving a case, or a group of cases, to be heard before the council. When in 1358 a number of indictments were pending against certain ministers of the crown, a writ was issued to the justices saying, 'for certain causes the king wishes the indictments and presentations to be examined and tried before the council.'[3] In 1364 while certain fishers were being prosecuted in the king's bench for violations of law in buying and selling fish, the justices were commanded to postpone the actions, as 'the king considers that such excesses may be debated and terminated before him and the council at Westminster better than elsewhere'.[4] In no respect were the royal rights more carefully guarded than in the matter of ecclesiastical presentations, particularly when there were collisions between the claims of the pope and those of the king. There were not lacking cases of this kind even before they were expressly assigned to the council by the statutes of provisors and praemunire.[5] No questions certainly were

[1] *Ancient Petitions*, nos. 14915, 15119; *Cal. Patent Rolls*, 22 Edw. III, 151; *Cal. Close Rolls*, 21 Edw. III, 241; 32 Edw. III, 484, &c.

[2] These were indeed very numerous. *Cal. Close Rolls*, 17 Edw. III, 265; *Cal. Patent Rolls*, 16 Edw. III, 548; 22 Edw. III, 66, 165; 23 Edw. III, 315, 317, &c.

[3] Possibly the statute 20 Edw. III, c. 6, was held in mind. *Cal. Close Rolls*, 32 Edw. III, 540.

[4] Ibid., 38 Edw. III, 57; a similar order regarding unlicensed travellers, ibid. 90. In 1353 a clerk was appointed to be chancellor of the exchequer at Dublin, who, it was provided, should not be removed without reasonable cause; and such cause should be examined before the council in England. *Cal. Patent Rolls*, 27 Edw. III, 434.

[5] In 1343 there was a dispute concerning the benefices that had been provided by the pope for two of the cardinals, reputed nephews of his.

more intricate and perplexing than those bearing upon the respective rights of church and state. One of the most frequent subjects of complaint was with reference to persons making appeals to Rome in spite of the judgements of the king's court. On the other hand, the king is known to have been petitioned to uphold a presentation made by the pope against one made by himself.[1] There were also certain free chapels of the king which were declared to be exempt from the authority of every other court. When a question arose regarding the chapel of Bosham, the justices were notified that it was free from all 'ordinary jurisdiction'; moreover, the writ declared, 'for certain causes the king wishes that the said affair be determined by him and his council, and not by any other process.'[2] Once the matter came before the council, it was not permitted by any process of law to be considered by another court.[3]

Maritime and mercantile cases.

There was a large class of cases also that came to the attention of the council because they arose outside the territory wherein the common law was effective. Either the parties concerned were not subjects of the king, or the scene of the dispute was beyond the realm of England. A group of cases, then, hardly less numerous on the whole than those relating to violence, may be designated as maritime and international. Seizures at sea, piracies, shipping claims, questions of wreck, contraband, and evasion of customs were among the earliest to require a special manner of treatment.[4] In the reign of Edward I a few such cases were

The proctors of the cardinals were called 'coram cancellario regis et aliis iusticiariis regisque concilio.' Murimuth, *Contin.*, p. 142; also *Ancient Petitions*, nos. 14898, 15074; *Cal. Patent Rolls*, 18 Edw. III, 284; 20 Edw. III, 229; 23 Edw. III, *passim.*

[1] *Ancient Petitions*, no. 12264.

[2] *Cal. Close Rolls*, 29 Edw. III, 157; 30 Edw. III, 228; 32 Edw. III, 540; also the chapel of Hammepreston. *Ancient Petitions*, no. 15074.

[3] When the abbot of St. Augustine's, Canterbury, sought to bring actions at common law in a case of this kind, the sheriff was commanded by a writ of the king to serve no such process, 'quia non est iuri consonum aut honestum quod aliquis de hiis quae coram nobis et consilio nostro in discussione pendant, alibi inde interim placitari debeat, aut apparere.' *Close Roll*, 16 Ric. II, m. 11 d.

[4] *Cal. Patent Rolls*, 20 Edw. III, 135; 23 Edw. III, 83, 319; *Cal. Close Rolls*, 23 Edw. III, 65; 31 Edw. III, 386; 39 Edw. III, 156; *Ancient Petitions*, nos. 14930, 14955, 15124, 15155.

given to commissions of *oyer et terminer*, the commissioners to take instructions from the council if necessary. The commissions continued to be used for the purpose, but, like other methods of the common law, they were proved to be not entirely adequate. Under Edward II it was declared to be customary for cases of the kind to be referred to the chancery, where ' justice should be done according to the custom of the chancery '.[1] In the time of Edward III the chancellor and council found themselves so seriously pressed, that the beginning of a new court was made in the delegation of a part of this jurisdiction to the admirals.[2] The first steps in this direction appear in the questions that were individually committed to be heard ' before the admiral and others of the council '.[3] It was likewise customary to employ the admirals to make inquisitions and to return the information. As a result, there came to be defined a sphere of ' maritime law ', in which the authority of the admirals was clearly recognized. The following passages will be of interest because they antedate by a few years the time when the court of admiralty is believed to have been permanently established. In 1359 Guy Brian was named admiral of the fleet toward the west, and in association with ' other skilled persons of the king's council ' he was to have cognizance of accidents at sea.[4] In 1361 this policy is stated more definitely in a letter of the king which reads, ' it is thought agreeable to law and custom that felonies, trespasses, and wrongs committed at sea should be brought before the king's admirals according to maritime law, and not before the justices at common law.'[5] In the same year Robert Herle was appointed admiral of all fleets, ' with full power of hearing plaints touching the office of admiral and having cognizance in maritime cases, of doing justice and correcting excesses,

[1] *Rot. Parl.* i. 317, 435.

[2] Marsden, *Select Pleas in the Court of Admiralty*, Selden Society, vol. vi (London, 1892). To the excellent account given here of the origin of this court my own studies have produced a few additional facts and considerations.

[3] In 1352 we learn that a claim of certain merchants to a cargo of wool which had been seized by pirates near Calais was actually heard ' before the admiral and others of the council '. *Cal. Close Rolls*, 26 Edw. III, 425.

[4] *Cal. Close Rolls*, 32 Edw. III, 442.

[5] Ibid., 35 Edw. III, 265.

of chastising delinquents, of imprisoning and delivering out of prison, and of doing all other things pertaining to the office of admiral as of right and according to maritime law, and of substituting and deputing others to do as he is not able.' [1] Cases follow, showing that at this time the judgements rendered by the admiral were strongly upheld.[2] During the reign of Richard II the proceedings of the court attracted a considerable amount of attention. There is no doubt of the need of a division of the labour of the council, as is seen at the same time in the separate formation of the court of chancery. But the success of the admirals in their judicial functions was very different from that of the chancellors. For one thing, the admirals did not give to the court the prestige of their personal attention, but left the work generally to be performed by deputies. The court was never popular, it was not widely sought, nor at any time during the middle ages was it strengthened or given authority by statute. The only acts of parliament relating to the subject sought to restrict its authority to matters of the sea, and to provide a means of appeal from its judgements.[3] As a result, the admiralty fell far short of becoming a court of strong competence. Appeals on the ground of error or of violation of the statutes were authorized and made easy.[4] The council readily received such appeals, but gave them to be heard usually before commissions of *oyer et terminer*. Regarding the court of admiralty as an ancillary agency, the council constantly interfered with its operations, sending it writs to surcease and orders to bring the matter in hand before the council.[5] Naturally suitors were not strongly

[1] *Cal. Patent Rolls*, 35 Edw. III, 531.

[2] In 1365 there is an order to the justices of the king's bench to stay proceedings in certain actions relating to the right to raise weirs in the waters flowing into the port of Colchester, because the matter had been decided by Robert Herle lately admiral. The process had come before the king in chancery, where the admiral's judgement was sustained. *Cal. Close Rolls*, 39 Edw. III, 157.

[3] *Statutes*, 13 Ric. II, c. 5 ; 15 Ric. II, c. 3. See also the complaint of the commons that the admiralty was violating the statutes. *Rot. Parl.* iii. 498.

[4] The ground of appeal most readily taken was that the action was 'contrary to the law and form of the court'.

[5] There was a case, 5 Ric. II, involving the question of a wreck, which was committed to the admiral of the north for adjudication. The admiral

attracted to a tribunal wherein the proceedings and judgements were so little secure, so that even at greater expense and risk of delay they might better direct their petitions to the chancellor or the council. Throughout the fifteenth century indeed the bulk of this jurisdiction, including practically all civil disputes, remained in the hands of the council and the chancery just as before. As in other matters, for practical reasons the tendency was to bring the greater number of cases of this kind before the chancellor.[1] It was not until the time of Henry VIII, therefore, that one may look for the foundations of a vigorous and effective court of maritime jurisdiction. A closely analogous jurisdiction was that of the mercantile law, which was claimed especially by the chancery. In the reign of Edward IV a question was raised whether a foreign merchant under a safe-conduct could be required to sue according to the ordinary course of the common law. The chancellor answered that under the circumstances aliens were not bound to know the statutes of England, and that they 'ought to sue here where the matter would be determined according to the *law of nature* in the chancery '.[2]

Cases of heresy.

Occasionally the council took cognizance of the subjects of heresy, sorcery, and witchcraft. This was not a difficult departure, since the procedure of the council followed closely that of the ecclesiastical courts. In 1388, during a moment of religious zeal, Richard II appointed a commission with instructions to search for, take, and bring before the council all heretical books, and to arrest persons buying and selling the same.[3] In 1392, at the request of the bishop of Hereford,

and his court had already made a decision, when 'for making a better and more speedy execution of justice' an order was given to have the entire record and process brought before the king and council. *Close Roll*, 5 Ric. II, m. 9. Again in the tenth year of the same reign, on the petition of certain merchants, the admirals themselves were required to come before the council to answer for their conduct in seizing a ship. *Dipl. Documents, Chancery*, portf. 329. In the fourteenth year a merchant complains that he is being sued extortionately and fraudulently in the admiralty and 'water-court' of Plymouth. *Ancient Petitions*, no. 14939.

[1] There was an ordinance in 1426 that whenever any one complains to the chancellor of a seizure at sea, *he* shall have the power to arrest the delinquents. Nicolas, iii. 208.

[2] *Year Books*, 13 Edw. IV, f. 9–10. [3] *Cal. Patent Rolls*, 11 Ric. II, 430.

who confessed his inability to effect the arrest of two men in his diocese named as heretics, the king granted the bishop authority with the aid of the sheriffs to arrest the men wherever they might be found, and to bring them before the king and council.[1] Again, in 1441, at the time of the prosecution of the duchess of Gloucester for witchcraft, one Roger Bolingbroke, a clerk associated with her, was arraigned before the lords of the king's council and all the judges of the land, while the duchess was made to appear before the king and all the lords spiritual and temporal.[2] In the same year a certain 'witch of Eye', who also was implicated in the Gloucester affair, was prosecuted by the clerk of the council before a special commission.[3] These instances show that the council made excursions into the field usually held by the clerical courts, but during the middle ages its concern with cases of heresy was slight. Not before the Reformation, in fact, was any continuous or well-sustained policy in this direction undertaken.

Poverty of suitors.

A very different ground upon which suitors gained the attention of the council, and also of the chancellor, was stated in their poverty or disability. As early as Edward I, certain evicted parties say they know not how they may be relieved 'because they are poor', and they especially ask that the king by his grace may provide remedy in the chancery.[4] Petitioners commonly represented themselves as 'your poor clerk', 'your simple and poor wax-chandler', 'poor tenants', 'poor mariners', or as 'old and feeble', 'reduced to poverty and misery', while they asked for relief 'for God', 'pity', and 'work of charity'. In one instance a petition of the masters and scholars of University Hall, Oxford, was read before the lords in parliament, by whom it was agreed that 'because of their excessive poverty' the masters and scholars could not defend themselves at common law, and so the matter was sent to the council for examination.[5] Moreover, it was stated in various ordinances that

[1] *Cal. Patent Rolls*, 15 Ric. II, 40.
[2] *Chronicle of London* (ed. Nicolas, 1827), p. 128.
[3] *English Chronicle, Richard II to Henry VI* (Camden Society, 1856), p. 58.
[4] *Rot. Parl.* i. 60. [5] *Close Roll*, 12 Ric. II, m. 42; *Rot. Parl.* iii. 404.

the bill of the poorest suitor should be selected first, and that he should be given legal advice without fees.[1] There is no doubt that the assertions of poverty and loyalty were often pure fiction, and that they easily became perfunctory phrases like those of the king's majesty and the chancellor's benevolence. The richest religious houses and most prominent towns, in fact, did not blush to allege poverty. On grounds that were practically analogous, suitors appeared before the council who had no other recourse by reason of positive legal disability. A foreigner could gain access to the king's courts only by special favour, and for this he must address a petition.[2] A married woman could not take action at common law without the concurrence of her husband. In the noted case of the Audeleys, 40–41 Edw. III, a wife was enabled before the council to uphold a claim based on a pre-marital contract that her husband's family was unwilling to carry out.[3]

Cases of trusts and uses.

There is yet to be mentioned a class of cases that are of more distinctive character than any of the others. Most of the subjects hitherto described did not fall exclusively to the jurisdiction of the council. The crimes of great violence, for example, might with equal propriety be brought before the king's bench, or the house of lords, or given to commissions of *oyer et terminer*. Similarly suits were brought to the council not because of any peculiarity of the subjects of litigation, but usually on account of some incidental difficulty of procedure. In exceptional circumstances, then, the council would intervene. So far as we have shown as yet, the only subjects that were positively withheld from the courts of common law were those given to the admiralty. There is one peculiar feature, however, that appears in these cases at an early date. In suits arising from loss of goods

[1] Nicolas, iii. 150, 217.

[2] The lord of Enghien came before the council to clear himself of a charge made against him in Flanders. *Cal. Close Rolls*, 25 Edw. III, 366. A bill of the duchess of Guelders is in *Ancient Petitions*, no. 12352. In 1355 a merchant of Venice under the king's safe-conduct complains that actions had been taken against him, his goods had been attached, and for fear of his enemies he dared not sue. The parties were ordered to come before the king in chancery. *Cal. Patent Rolls*, 29 Edw. III, 225.

[3] *Cal. Close Rolls*, 40 Edw. III, 237–9 ; 41 Edw. III, 344.

it was customary for the injured party to ask not for 'damages', as at common law, but for 'recovery' and 'restitution'.[1] This was interpreted to mean not merely the damage as usually computed, but all attendant losses and expenses, even possible profits, such as only the council or the chancellor and council were empowered to decree. Other than these, the first cases to create a field of substantive law, internal to England and not administered by any other secular courts, are found in the enforcement of certain fiduciary relationships known as uses, trusts, and confidences.[2] These practices had grown up and spread widely without the recognition of the common law. So far as they were matters of oral understanding, the courts of ordinary procedure were not fitted to deal with them according to existing rules of evidence. The truth could hardly be ascertained, in fact, without the testimony of the defendants as well as the plaintiffs. At first the only resort in cases of dispute was found in the spiritual courts, so that when the chancellor consented to give ear to complaints of this kind and to enforce such obligations by the power of the state, the great utility and popularity of his court was assured. There is no reason to say that this was done any earlier than Richard II, but from this time the cases multiply rapidly during the fifteenth century. They did not belong to the chancery to the exclusion of the council, for there was a case of trust certainly before the privy council of Henry V.[3] But just as was true in other matters, the greater accessibility of the chancery and its willingness to serve, made it the court more generally sought. *Nullus recedat a curia cancellarie sine remedio*,[4] was a maxim effectively stating its policy.

Restrictions by parliament.

This extensive but ill-defined jurisdiction the council and the chancery were permitted to carry to a certain point without any serious hindrance. To a considerable extent, as we have shown, these subjects were given to the council

[1] There are innumerable examples, especially among the maritime cases of the time of Edward III and afterwards, e.g. *Ancient Petitions*, nos. 13442, 14934, 15149, &c.

[2] An excellent article by Justice Holmes is found in *Select Essays* (ed. Wigmore, Cambridge, Mass., 1908), ii. 705–36.

[3] Nicolas, ii. 328–31.

[4] *Year Books*, 5 Hen. VII, no. 8.

both by the king and the parliament. Not until the peculiar nature of this authority in contrast to the common law began to be perceived was any serious question raised with regard to it. It then came to be looked upon with jealousy and dislike by all the conservative classes in parliament, by lords and commons even more emphatically than lawyers and judges. Instead of a policy of progressive legislation, that might have precluded the need of courts of equity, the efforts of parliament were directed preferably to a defence of the common law from all encroachments. The tendency of the council to override the forms of law and to pass judgements in summary fashion was then a subject of perpetual complaint, and brought forth a number of restrictive statutes. Possibly the earliest measure of this kind is found in the statute, 5 Edw. III, c. 9, wherein it was enacted that no man be attached, nor his possessions seized, contrary to the Great Charter and the law of the land. In the twenty-fifth year of the same reign the commons demanded that no man should answer for his freehold or for matters of life and limb before the council, but the king consented to the restriction only as regards freeholds, for which one should be required to answer only by course of law.[1] This was a material limitation upon the authority of the council, and one which it was to some extent careful to observe, for it is found returning a number of cases on this ground to the common-law courts.[2] Moreover, with a feeling of restraint, the council was always reluctant to inflict penalties of life and limb, although there was no statute to this effect. The aforesaid law, which was several times re-enacted,[3] was almost the only restriction of positive character that the parliament ever succeeded in making. It was a problem of some difficulty, because with all its hostility to the extra-legal methods of the council, parliament did not fail to recognize that summary processes at times were necessary. There were incessant complaints against the special writs and processes of the privy seal, while ordinance after ordinance was enacted under the Lancastrians to the effect that matters

[1] *Rot. Parl.* ii. 228.
[2] *Ancient Petitions*, nos. 12289, 12299.
[3] *Rot. Parl.* iii. 21, 323.

'touching the common law' should be determined by the common-law courts. But there was always a saving clause, 'unless it were against such high personages that right could not be obtained elsewhere', or as otherwise expressed, 'unless there be too much might on the one side and too much unmight on the other';[1] so that the discretionary power of the council was left practically undiminished. A characteristically spasmodic action, of no enduring effect, occurred after the fall of Richard II, when all cases of this nature then pending before the council were quashed and turned over to the common law. It was not long before conciliar cases again accumulated and complaints were renewed as before.

Peculiar methods of procedure.

As has already been suggested, it was not the field of its jurisdiction so much as its methods of procedure that gave the council its special distinction. In the thirteenth century, it is understood, the comparatively free procedure of the older *curia regis* was maintained, but the council did not then devise any new forms of its own. In the fourteenth century certain distinctive methods begin to appear. It is believed that an influence in this direction came from the Roman law through the example of the existing ecclesiastical courts. The chancellors were almost invariably churchmen, and they were assisted by other bishops as well as by doctors of civil law, who were retained probably for this very purpose. No one doubts the reality of this influence, but the extent to which the chancellors borrowed their methods is still a disputed matter. Spence has argued for the Romanist theory and Justice Holmes against it, while Maitland has expressed the opinion that beyond a few maxims and general principles even the knowledge of Roman law was not great. 'In treatment,' says he, the chancellors 'stuck marvellously close to the common law, with common lawyers and common-law judges to assist them'.[2] There was no slavish imitation certainly, for while a few features in the practice of the court can be shown to have been directly borrowed, other forms were invented with great independence. Moreover, with all its freedom of procedure, it is true that throughout the

1 *Rot. Parl.* iii. 21, 446; iv. 201, 343.
2 Maitland, *Equity* (Cambridge, 1909), p. 9.

fourteenth century most of the actions before the council were treated in full consonance with the common law. Suitors were not always clear in mind whether to base their claims upon ' right and reason ' or the ' law of the realm ' ; sometimes they stated both grounds.[1] Likewise, when it came to the judgement of the court, whether it was according to one formula or the other, *adiudicatum est, ordinatum est*, or *decretum est*, probably no material difference was perceived at the time. The new departures indeed were made slowly and cautiously, and are inextricably mixed with the older practices. Even so late as the reign of Henry V traces of common law procedure have been shown to linger in a court of equity.[2] To these points of contrast attention will be called as the forms of conciliar procedure are now to be described in detail.

Petitions.

The beginning of all special procedure, it is well understood, lay in the petitions for favour and redress, that were first addressed to the king or the king and council. The elementary idea of a petition or a supplication is too universal to be assigned any particular origin, but the system that appears in England was practically an indigenous growth. What gave the system its peculiar importance here was the rigidity of the common law, which did not claim to provide a remedy for every ill, so that for all unusual cases the only resort for suitors, as they themselves often declare, lay in a personal petition. This ground of complaint is apparent in numberless instances under Edward I, but possibly the first time that the defect of the law is openly stated occurs in the reign of Edward II, when a lady finds a writ of dower not applicable to her case, and she is sent to the chancery ' because she could not be helped at common law '.[3] Often

[1] Observe, for example, the following extract from a petition of 17 Ric. II: ' Plese a votre treshaut et tresroial mageste comander votre chaunceller et ordiner par avys de votre tressage conseill qe hastive remede et redresse sibien touchant les grevances tortz extortions issint faitz a voz ditz tenauntz come pur la salvation de votre droiturel seignurie, qe droit et reson soit fait sicome la commune ley demande.' *Inquisitions Misc. Chanc.*, file 254.

[2] Pike, *Law Quarterly Review*, i. 445–53. Moreover, in the reign of Edward IV it was claimed, ' the law of the chancery is the common law of the land.' *Year Books*, 4 Edw. IV, f. viii.

[3] *Rot. Parl.* i. 340. In the time of Edward III Lucy Langton declares that on coming to London she was detained and robbed. She asks the

the petition was simply the means of obtaining an original writ, and then the action would go on through the ordinary channels. But when the petition, or 'bill', as it was also called, was made the basis of the litigation, the first step in an extraordinary procedure was taken. The 'bill', then, in distinction from the original writ, was the natural means of approach to all the courts not bound by the common law, including the council, the house of lords, the chancery, and the admiralty. The form and substance of these petitions is therefore of the utmost importance in all this history.

A petition differed from a writ in every essential respect. Written usually in French, before the end of the fourteenth century sometimes in English, its very appearance suggests a departure from the procedure of common law, every instrument of which was given in Latin. Moreover, a petition was not bound by any form of words, whereas form was the essence of a writ. If it was inaccurate or inexplicit, it was not therefore invalidated, but might be explained or amended orally; according to early practices, as has been said, complaints might be made without any form of writing, but the court preferred that the matter should be written.[1] There is no evidence that any fee was required upon the presentation of a petition, as there was on the purchase of a writ, so that it was the natural course of action for all who called themselves poor. Some of the earliest petitions in general style were not different from ordinary letters; possibly they were composed in some cases by professional letter-writers. But most of them, there is reason to believe, were written for the suitors by lower grade scribes of the king's court. Although there was never a set formula, a petition was properly composed of the following parts, as many of our illustrations show:

1. The address, whether it was intended for the king, the council, the chancellor, or some other minister.

2. The statement of grievance or complaint. This is the

chancellor to have the parties brought before him, as she has nothing in the common law to defend her. *Ancient Petitions*, no. 15011.

[1] Still in the fifteenth century parties are known to have come before the council and the chancery without any written petition, but the court would ask them to put their grievances in writing; e.g. Nicolas, ii. 286.

only part which we may be sure was essential; some of the early examples, in fact, are confined to a single sentence.

3. The prayer for remedy, usually with a pious exhortation for God', 'for God and charity', or 'for the sake of pity'.

For reasons that will be made evident there was a tendency during the fourteenth century to elaborate each of these elemental features. By reason of its simplicity and freedom from technicality, suitors might easily prefer this mode of procedure to any other; possibly they would have followed it exclusively, had they not found certain obstacles in the way. From the time of Edward I certainly there were hundreds of petitions every year, making statements of every kind of need and desire.[1] They formed always a principal part of the work of parliament and the council. In parliament special committees were appointed to receive and answer them, while the council dealt with those that were left over from parliament or were received between sessions.[2] Such was the number of petitions at all times that both parliament and the council plainly were overburdened with the work, until there was every danger that public interests would suffer. It was primarily this pressure of business that caused great numbers of petitions first to be committed to the chancery, as already described, and subsequently gave rise to the distinct class of petitions in chancery. Still the council was not sufficiently relieved, and there was ground for complaint either because too much time was given to private interests, or because personal bills were not properly

Difficulties in treating petitions.

[1] In a recent volume of the Selden Society (*Eyre of Kent*, vol. ii, p. xxi ff.) Mr. Bolland has produced a number of petitions that were addressed to the king's itinerant justices in the time of Edward I and Edward II. They were 'bills of complaint' which were used as a basis of action instead of the usual writs. Probably they were presented by very poor people who had not the means of getting a hearing in any other way. The feature is indeed an interesting one, for it is an early assertion of the equitable principle. But I cannot agree with the learned editor when he claims 'that there can be no doubt that these bills are the very beginning of the equitable jurisdiction' (p. xxviii). I should prefer to say that we have here one of the many manifestations of an equitable jurisdiction which was then exercised not only by the king's council, but by the king's court in its various branches. Have we not also at the same time petitions of the kind addressed to the treasurer and the chancellor, who were sought as a means of approach to the king and council?

[2] The procedure of parliament in this regard is explained in chapter xii.

attended to. This problem received attention in the ordinances of 1390, previously cited, wherein it was stated that business of the king and the realm should be given precedence, and that petitions of the people 'of less charge' might be considered in the presence of the keeper of the privy seal and those who might be present,[1] that is, a limited number. Later on it was provided that Wednesdays should be especially reserved for the hearing of petitions, and that these should be answered and returned to the petitioners on the following Friday. The bill of the poorest suitor was to be especially selected and considered first.[2] Still we find that with its manifold responsibilities in the reign of Henry VI, the council was unable to read all of the bills brought to it, as on one occasion at the close of a term, it ordered that the determination of all petitions remaining unheard should be committed to the lord chancellor and the chancery.[3]

Urgency of petitioners.

Under these circumstances suitors needed to make special efforts to gain the attention of parliament and the council.[4] They drew up their petitions with greater care, making it clear in the form of address whether they expected to be heard by the lords of parliament or by the council. For the same reasons they sought other avenues of approach, soliciting the mediation of various officers and even individual lords.[5] To say nothing further of the petitions to the chancellor, the treasurer, and the keeper of the privy seal, there were also those directed to the chamberlain and the steward of the household. A certain merchant of Florence, for example, in trouble over the arrest of his ship, addresses his petition to the influential Lord Latimer, the king's chamberlain, beseeching him particularly to write to the king's council:

'Sur quey plaise a votre graciouse Seignurie en œvre de droit et de charite escrire par voz lettres al conseil de notre

[1] Nicolas, i. 18a, 18b; *ante*, p. 131.

[2] Ibid. iii. 149, 214; 150, 217.

[3] Ibid. 36.

[4] In 1405 we find the curious example of a supplication made by the duke of York that an earlier petition of his be considered. *Foedera* (Orig. Ed.), viii. 387.

[5] On a date prior to 1348 Richard Spynk, we are told, approached Archbishop Stratford, who was at the time not chancellor but one of the council, praying him of his charity to obtain for the said Richard a hearing before the king. *Cal. Patent Rolls*, 38 Edw. III, 502.

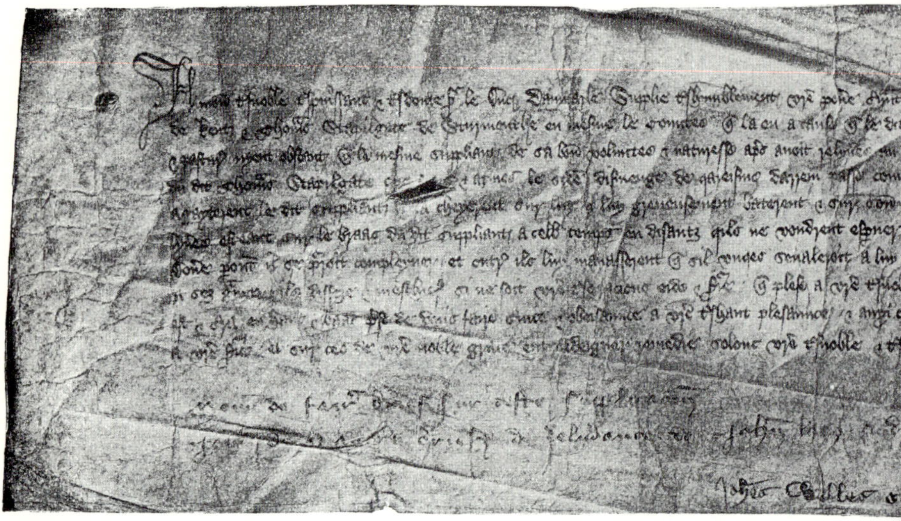

A PETITION OF GRIEVANCE ADDRES

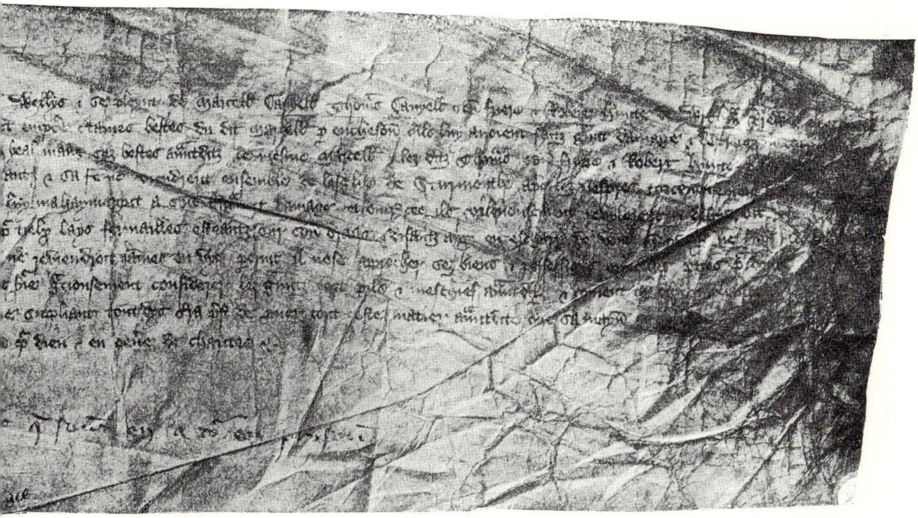

DUKE OF ALBEMARLE, LATE RIC. II.

Seigneur le Roi et a votre honorable filz le Seigneur de Nevyll ou a les ministres de la ville de Bristwich (Bristol) susdit pour la deliverance de la nief et des marchandises et biens susditz.'

Whereupon the chamberlain writes a letter addressed to the chancellor, the treasurer, and the keeper of the privy seal, rehearsing the facts and making the following recommendation:

'Sur quoy il me semble qe droit voet qe lez ditz marchantz ne perdent mye lour biens par tiel cause, et vous prie qe vous facez tiel deliverance dez ditz nief et marchandises come vous voiez par votre bone avys qe droit et reson serra sy hastifment come vous bonement porrez.' [1]

A petition to the steward of the household begins with the words, *au noble et puissantz Seigneur Monsieur Henry le Scrop et as sages conseulx notre Seigneur le Roi.*[2] A very curious petition to Richard's queen, Anne, on the part of certain of her tenants asks,

'pleise a votre souveraintee denvoier al Chanceller Dengleterre notre dit Seigneur le Roy endesirant denvoier par briefs severalment hors de la Chauncelerie sur grevous peynes pur les malefeisours suisditz pur vous a respondre de les riotz et malefeisons.' [3]

There were likewise petitions to John of Gaunt in the time of his ascendancy. One directed to the duke of Exeter under Richard II asks him 'to command the council to hear the suppliant'. About the same time a petition to the duke of Albemarle beseeches him to pray the king to charge the chancellor to bring an oppressor before the king and council.[4] There were similar petitions to the earl of March and to Henry, prince of Wales, and during the minority of Henry VI one might expect to find a considerable number addressed to the duke of Bedford and the duke of Gloucester.[5] It is needless to multiply these examples further. They are of

[1] *Ancient Petitions*, nos. 14881, 14882.

[2] *Ancient Correspondence*, vol. l, no. 146. In 1368 there was a complaint that the steward of the household was seeking to extend the bounds of his court, causing men to be brought before him 'as though it were before the king's council'. *Rot. Parl.* ii. 297.

[3] *Ancient Correspondence*, vol. xliii, no. 65.

[4] Plate, no. 5.

[5] *Council and Privy Seal*, file 4, &c., and several unfiled documents.

no consequence in themselves, except as they show the strong demands that were made upon the attention of the council and the need that was felt for new channels of action.

Sugges-tions and delations.

A large share of the complaints before the council consisted inevitably of criminal charges.[1] These were made by the 'suggestions' of private parties, either on their own initiative or at the solicitation of the government. As the proceedings were secret, the way was opened for all kinds of false and malicious accusations, until the attention of parliament was called to the evil. In 1354 the commons alleged that certain of the king's purveyors, because legal proceedings had been taken against them, had made 'false suggestions' in order to bring their opponents before the king and council.[2] As a safeguard against this danger, an act was passed and several times repeated, requiring that accusers offer security before the council, as they did in other courts, to prove their suggestions.[3] These were the *plegii de prosequendo*, as the pledges were called, which the council and the chancery, with a fair degree of consistency, required in all cases of private interest;[4] likewise, in order to secure the attention of the court, men would offer to give security. But there were also cases of state in which the council did its utmost to obtain information in the form of suggestions or depositions without any guarantees. Persons were summoned and required 'to give *information*, and to do and receive what shall be ordered by the king and council'.[5] Under Richard II the council offered a reward to all those reporting evasions of the customs,[6] and again it gave assurances that the

[1] I dissent from the view that the council's jurisdiction from the beginning was mainly criminal, and that it was distinguished in this way from the chancery. The distinctive feature of the council was its summary powers and procedure in whatever direction these were exercised.

[2] *Rot. Parl.* ii. 260. In the same year there is an instance of a person being examined before the council at the 'suggestion' of the king's serjeant-at-arms. *Cal. Close Rolls*, 28 Edw. III, 72.

[3] *Statutes*, 37 Edw. III, c. 18; 38 Edw. III, c. 9; 42 Edw. III, c. 3; 17 Ric. II, c. 6.

[4] In the chancery the names of the pledges were commonly written upon the bill, but for reasons that will appear this was rarely done in the privy seal or star chamber proceedings of the council. See also the remarks of Mr. Leadam, *Sel. Cases, Star Chamber*, ii. 21 n.

[5] *Cal. Close Rolls*, 39 Edw. III, 181.

[6] 'Quicunque ad nos et consilium nostrum volentes accedere ad nos et

informers would be heard.[1] In the fifteenth year Walter Sibille was awarded £40 for his work 'in pursuing cases before the council'.[2] Again, an arrest was ordered 'on the information of Thomas Rempston'.[3] Sometimes these depositions were made in the written form of bills; one of these suggests that a writ of summons be sent to a certain man, another names a monk who is pointed out as a spy.[4] There is also in the reign of Richard II a lengthy pamphlet of anonymous origin, making extensive and indefinite charges against Alexander Neville, the unpopular archbishop of York, suggesting among other things that he should be examined before the king and council for his extortions, maintenances, and tyrannies.[5] Under Henry IV there is found a formal deposition made by one William Stokes, who declares it to be the duty of every loyal subject to safeguard the honour and profit of the crown, and informs the council of certain illegal exportations of wool and skins.[6] Whether it was for this or some other service, the informer was not without reward.[7] In 1420 there appears a letter of a more dignified character, wherein Sir Thomas Erpingham, himself a member of the council, acquaints the chancellor of the probability of a riot in Suffolk, owing to the rivalry of two knights who were about to attend an assize supported, each of them, by a body of armed followers. The council ordered that the men be warned to attend the assize peaceably and to make no breach of the king's peace.[8] It is likely, however,

consilium nostrum informandum habebunt pro labore suo sufficiens rewardum.' *Close Roll*, 10 Ric. II, m. 15 d.

[1] Ibid., 12 Ric. II, m. 19 d.

[2] *Journal*, 15–16 Ric. II, Appendix, p. 499.

[3] *Cal. Patent Rolls*, 23 Ric. II, 597.

[4] *Ancient Petitions*, nos. 14948, 15176.

[5] 'The comunes of Ingelond wherfor blame ye the Kyng and his conseil of the unhappe and disese and myschief of this Reaume . . . Wer Kyng Alisaundre wel examynd of his extorciones and his meyntenances and his tyrranttrie of that he hath take falsly ageyne the Kynges lawes he shuld leve for ever the Kyng lx. M[l]. li.' *Archaeologia*, xvi. 82–3.

[6] British Museum, Cotton MS., Galba, B 1, nos. 23, 24; Appendix, p. 523.

[7] *Cal. Patent Rolls*, 1 & 2 Hen. IV, 322, 431. In 1423 parliament was willing that in cases of persons illegally carrying gold out of the country the informers who should bring notice of the fact to the council or the treasurer should receive half of the goods forfeited. But the king consented to allow only a fourth part. *Rot. Parl.* iv. 252; vi. 184.

[8] Nicolas, ii. 272.

that secret suggestions of this kind were usually not put in writing, but were made orally, as was said, by 'soden reporte'. But the extent to which this practice was carried can only be a matter of conjecture.

Writs. Next in order were the writs of summons and arrest to bring parties before the council. In this respect, as in others, there was at first nothing distinctive in the council's procedure. In the time of Edward I, there were used the ordinary writs both of the exchequer and the chancery, among which are recognized the *monstravit*, the *scire facias*, the *venire facias*, and the *corpus cum causa*. It was a marked departure from the older methods when, about 1346, there was devised in the chancery a certain form of writ that was peculiarly adapted for the purposes of the council.[1] Possibly the essential idea was suggested by the customary writs summoning men to take part in parliaments or councils *super quibusdam negotiis*; the business to be discussed was not necessarily stated. At all events the peculiarity of the new writs lay in their omission of any statement as to the cause of summons. The *quibusdam certis de causis* ran as follows:

> 'Rex, etc. Quibusdam certis de causis coram consilio nostro propositis, tibi praecipimus firmiter iniungentes, quod omnibus praetermissis, sis in propria persona tua coram consilio nostro in cancellaria nostra, die, etc., ad respondendum ibidem super hiis quae tunc tibi obicientur ex parte nostra, et ad faciendum ulterius et recipiendum quod curia nostra consideraverit in hac parte. Et habeas ibi hoc breve. Teste, etc.'[2]

A kindred writ appearing soon afterwards is known as the *praemunire*, which was directed to a sheriff to warn the parties to come in words to the same effect. It begins with the clause,

> 'Quibusdam certis de causis vobis mandamus, firmiter iniungentes, quod praemunire faciatis Henricum Cove, etc., quod quilibet eorum, sub poena centum librarum, in propria

[1] A satisfactory description of these writs is given in Palgrave, *Original Authority*, pp. 40–1. It will be noticed that the phrase 'for certain causes' was frequently used in other writs of the council; e.g. *ante*, pp. 271–2.

[2] *Cal. Close Rolls*, 20 Edw. III, 175; given in Palgrave, p. 132.

persona sua, sit coram consilio nostro apud Westmonasterium, etc.'[1]

By a slight change of the formula first quoted, namely, the addition at the end of a penal clause—*et hoc sub poena centum librarum nullatenus omittas*—the writ became the more famous *sub poena*. Often the penalty was fixed at £200, and sometimes as high as £1,000, although in ordinary cases the amounts were more reasonably fixed at £20 or £40. In devising the latter form, possibly the clerks were given a suggestion from the peremptory citations used in the ecclesiastical courts, as for instance: *citamus eundem peremptorie, ut . . . coram nobis legitime compareat . . . et hoc sub poena excommunicationis maioris.*[2] However the thought may have been derived, the new writs differed from any corresponding instruments of the common law in several essential points. The most radical departure lay not in the threat, or even the penal clause, for the latter seems not to have been of any practical effect,[3] but in the initial words 'for certain causes' whereby a defendant was given no warning or hint of the charges to be made against him. Moreover, no record of the writs was kept in the chancery, and so they were required to be 'returned' by the party addressed. The most serious objection of all was the fact that they were not sanctioned by parliament, and so according to the statutes they remained of an extra-legal, if not positively illegal, character. For these very reasons they were not under the limitations of the ordinary legal writs, so that they could be used to penetrate districts under franchise like Cheshire and the Welsh marches. Although they were originally devised in the chancery and issued under the great seal, the writs were immediately translated into French and issued under the privy seal, an instrument well adapted for any extra-legal processes. As writs of the privy seal, then, they

[1] Ibid. 131. I do not find that this writ was ever extensively used. Orders of this kind were more often transmitted by the older *venire facias*, which was known in French as *pour faire venir*.

[2] Wilkins, *Concilia*, ii. 87, &c.

[3] In cases of disobedience the parties were punished for contempt, a process that had a better legal basis than the new device of the penalty.

became most familiarly known.[1] Illustrations of these writs, both in Latin and in French, belonging to the time of Richard II, are given in one of our plates. Sometimes, particularly when any of the great lords was addressed, the rigid form of the writ was changed into a letter of more suavity, but of the same general purport. One such letter of the time of Henry V reads as follows :

'Chere et bien ame. Pour certaines causes nous et notre consail especialment moevantes, de lavis et assent de mesme notre counsail volons et vous mandons estroitement enchargeant qe toutes autres choses lessees et excusations cessantes, soiez en votre propre persone devant mesme notre counsail la ou il serra le darrein jour Daverill prochein venant saunz nulle defaulte pur y oyer et receivre ce qe par notre dit counsail vous serra monstree et declaree a votre venue illoeqes. Et ce sur peine de cent livres ne lessez en nulle manere. Doun souz notre prive seal a Westminster le xx iour de Aprill.' [2]

In addition to all that has been said concerning the usages of the privy seal, an advantage afforded by the latter method of issuing the writs is seen in the customary mode of delivery. While letters under the great seal were conveyed by regularly employed messengers, first to the sheriffs and by them to the parties addressed, those under the privy seal could be carried by any person hired for the purpose, and delivered directly to the persons wanted.[3]

Contention over the writs.

From their very inception these letters and writs became the most conspicuous and essential feature of the council's procedure. It was for the writs specially that suitors prayed, while against them in particular the opposition of parliament was concentrated.[4] In the contests that

[1] The *sub poena* is then designated as *le brief sur certeine peine*. Palgrave is quite misleading upon this point, as he speaks of the writs under the privy seal as though they were different from the *sub poena*. A summons by privy seal, probably one of this kind, is mentioned as early as 1354. *Rot. Parl.* ii. 260.

[2] *Warrants Privy Seal*, ser. i, sec. ii, file 28.

[3] Special messengers in the king's service known as 'pursuivants' appear in the reign of Edward IV.

[4] Under Henry IV the commons complained particularly of the *sub poena*, asking that such writ be used only in cases where it should be deemed necessary at the discretion of the chancellor or the council. *Rot. Parl.* iii. 471.

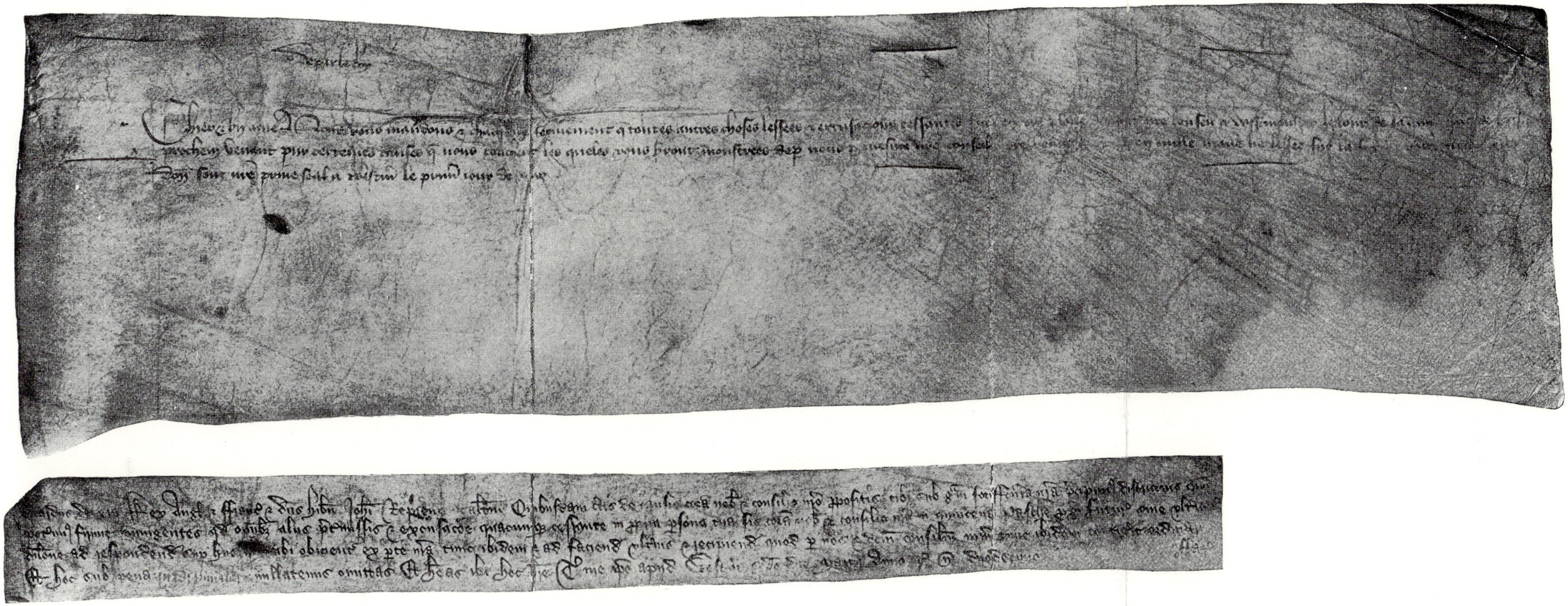

SUBPOENAS, ONE IN FRENCH AND ONE IN LATIN, TEM. RIC. II.

followed, they were stigmatized as a novelty, and incorrectly they were said never to have been known before the time of Richard II.[1] In that reign men complained that due course of law was being impeded by the king's letters under the privy seal, and consequently acts were passed with the intention of restricting their use to the most necessary cases. Where action at common law was possible, it was urged that no man should be required to appear before the council upon a *quibusdam certis de causis*, and that the clerk who made such a writ should lose his office.[2] In 1421 the commons reiterated their former complaints on the ground that the writs were not due process of law, and made the further drastic proposal that no such writs as the subpoenas be granted in future.[3] And if any such were granted, they suggested that the defendant by declaring the action to be one of common law might take exception to the jurisdiction of the court; and if the exception were not allowed he might safely go without responding or appearing. But the king refused his consent to any such nugatory measure. Nevertheless the doubtful validity of the writs was always a source of weakness, for there were persons bold enough to refuse obedience to them upon this ground. Failing in the efforts to prohibit the writs or materially to check their use, parliament sought to have them altered and made conformable to the law. It was particularly urged that the cause and matter of the suit be put into the writs and that they be enrolled and made patent without being returned.[4] With some inconsistency parliament was constantly authorizing the use of the writs in individual instances, and in these cases sometimes a statement of the cause was actually inserted. At length under the stress of Jack Cade's rebellion, parliament consented temporarily to legitimatize the writs for a period of seven years in riot cases only.[5] On this ground it was afterwards claimed that the writs used pursuant to the statute should contain the words *de riottis*,

[1] *Rot. Parl.* iv [illegible]4.

[2] Ibid. iii. 267.

[3] Ibid. iv. 156.

[4] Ibid. iv. 84.

[5] *Statutes*, 31 Hen. VI, c. 2. In spite of the limitation of the act to seven years, it is still cited and treated as in force during the reign of Edward IV. *Year Books*, 14 Edw. IV, f. 1.

and at least one party refused to obey a summons that was not so framed.[1] But such was the lawlessness of the later years of Henry VI that the evasion and defiance of the king's writs was acknowledged to be very general, and one finds the subpoenas brought back with explanations that the parties would not receive them, that the men absented themselves and could not be found.

Arrests and detentions.

In case of the failure of any of the aforesaid writs there were still more forceful means of compelling the parties to appear. In extreme cases commissions of arrest, consisting of a half dozen or more competent persons, were appointed, 'to have A. B. before the king and council to answer what shall be charged against him and to abide their order.'[2] Such commissions appear with unusual frequency during the later years of Richard II and likewise under Henry VI.[3] In 1399, the government on 'information' that divers felons and malefactors were gathered in Kent, Surrey, and Middlesex, named a commission with extraordinary powers to ascertain the names of the delinquents and 'to arrest all whom they might reasonably suspect, imprisoning them until further order'.[4] Another mode of compelling attendance and good behaviour during the meantime was by placing the parties under bonds and surety, *mainprise* it was called, to keep the peace for a certain time and to appear at a certain day. Sometimes the bondsmen or *mainpernors* were made responsible for bringing the party *corps pour corps* before the court. The bonds might be placed as high as £5,000 or £10,000. Failing to furnish bonds, men were sent to prison to await further proceedings. In the third year of Henry VI, the commons made the following complaint against such practices :

'for as mych as divers persones that here to for havyn bene arettyd ⁊ acusyd of treson felonye lollardrie ⁊ other such playntes bene commytted al day by the Kynges comaund-

[1] An unfiled series of six articles, 35 Hen. VI, 'Exchequer Box'.

[2] These are found certainly as early as 14 Edw. III. *Cal. Patent Rolls*, 88. Often the commissioners were instructed also 'to keep safely' their charges.

[3] *Cal. Patent Rolls*, 23 Ric. II, *passim*. In 1443 Sir John Neville was charged under penalty of £1,000 to bring certain misdoers before the council. Nicolas, v. 241.

[4] *Cal. Patent Rolls*, 23 Ric. II, p. 597.

ment ⁊ his counceayll some to the Tour of London ⁊ some to other Castels ⁊ holdes in the rewme, whereas they lye long tyme other while a yeer or two without eny processe or execucion,'[1] &c.

It was asked that these men be brought before judges to be tried as they deserve for the peculiar reason, as stated:

'in eschewyng of excessive costes of our Lord the Kyng done about the long kepyng of such prisoners ⁊ the grete perill fere ⁊ labour of her kepers.'

Possibly the strongest measure that could be taken against an individual was a proclamation of outlawry. This was an old practice that was followed by justices of the peace, commissioners of *oyer et terminer*, and likewise was taken up for the purposes of the council. It was nothing less than a public announcement made in one or more of the counties through the agency of the sheriff, that the party should appear or be made to appear before the council, the chancery, or wherever he was wanted, under threat of the severest penalties and perhaps with reward to the captors. In 1427 such an order was given to the sheriff of Bedfordshire and Buckinghamshire with the words, 'we direct you to make proclamation in all fairs and markets, that if any one should arrest said William (Wawe) or produce his body or head, alive or dead, before us or our council he shall have £100 reward . . . that no one should give him food, drink, or lodging under penalty.'[2] In this case we learn that the one who succeeded in capturing the outlaw was given a reward of £60.[3] Sometimes the sheriff was threatened with a penalty lest he fail to deliver the proclamation.[4] When even this means of compulsion failed, as commonly happened after 1453, there was nothing left but a state of civil war. In 1459 there is a record of the following four successive methods which were taken without complete success to bring before the court certain parties in Cornwall. (1) They were cited to appear by the usual writs of the privy seal, and likewise by

[1] *Record Transcripts*, series i, vol. 114; not given in the rolls of parliament. [2] Nicolas, iii. 256. [3] Ibid., p. 312.

[4] In 1453, owing to the general disobedience to these writs, it was enacted that the sheriffs should make the proclamations under threat of a penalty of £200 and loss of office. *Rot. Parl.* v. 266.

writs under the great seal; (2) the king commanded the sheriffs to publish a proclamation that the men should appear before the council within a month, yet one of the men did not appear; (3) inasmuch as this man still resisted, a commission of arrest was appointed; and (4) in case the commission failed, a proclamation was to be made in the counties calling him to appear under threat of forfeiture.[1]

Parties received by the council.

The parties summoned were usually allowed ten days or a fortnight in which to come before the court. It was not possible for the council always to hear them at the appointed time, for in the midst of political affairs there were no particular days or hours reserved for judicial business. So that often the parties were required to wait 'from day to day' for a convenient moment.[2] During the litigation involving the abbey of Croyland, 1390–1, the abbot is said to have come again and again without being heard. On one day when he appeared it was explained, 'that during that term, the king's council was so busied upon arduous affairs of the kingdom, that it had no time to attend to less important matters of merely incidental nature, or indeed to give any serious thought thereto.'[3] When all was ready, it is described as customary for the name of the person to be cried at the door of the council chamber.[4] Most of the cases, whether civil or criminal, could be treated very expeditiously. By the petition or other means of information the council was likely to have some knowledge of the matter in advance. By an early confession,[5] or an accord[6] that the litigants were advised

[1] *Cal. Patent Rolls*, 37 Hen. VI, 493; also 516.

[2] 'He shal from day to day awaite on ye kinges consail unto ye tyme yt be dismissed.' Nicolas, v. 277.

[3] *Chron. of Abbey of Croyland* (trans. H. T. Riley, 1854), pp. 338 ff. This chronicle is known to be spurious in part. But, since it was composed in the fourteenth century, the suggestion of procedure seems not lacking in value.

[4] One of the returned writs under Henry VI bears the following statement: 'vocatus in dictis Octavis ad Hostium camere prout moris est non comperuit.. Unfiled, 'Chancery Box.' Once in the time of Richard II it was said, A. B. 'solemniter vocatus non venit.' *Ancient Petitions*, no. 11059.

[5] In one instance a clerk accused of falsifying a record, on being 'spoken to' before the council, immediately admitted the fact. *Cal. Patent Rolls*, 22 Edw. III, 113.

[6] In a case of 22 Ric. II the parties were commanded to treat and make an end themselves if they could accord. *Ancient Petitions*, no. 12549.

to make, the trial might be ended at once. By the system of *mainprise,* if bonds were offered, the parties were most often bound over to keep the peace or to appear at another time, without any trial at all. At any stage of the proceedings, too, the case might be given for trial and decision to a commission or to some other court.[1] In times of great pressure also hearings were postponed from time to time and finally dropped from sheer inability to give them attention. But for the cases that were actually heard before the council, there were certain distinctive methods of procedure which may now be described. Naturally there was a difference between criminal cases and civil cases, although the line between them was by no means clear.

Treatment of suits.

In civil actions or suits, which the parties brought voluntarily, they were required to make submission to the court, *in alto et basso,* agreeing to abide by its decision.[2] Since no one could well be bound against his will by an extra-legal procedure,[3] this act was deemed to be essential, it being once declared that without the submission the trial could not go on.[4] In one instance a person agreed under bond of £5,000 to abide by the award of the council.[5] Having bound themselves in this manner, neither side was afterwards at liberty to take exception to the authority or procedure of the court. The hearing was opened with the reading of the bill, when an adjournment was likely to be taken to allow the defendant time to prepare his answer. This he might do with the aid of counsel. All matters of evidence so far as possible the council preferred to have in writing. Suitors were asked to be fully informed as to their contentions, and were likely

[1] There is an instance in which a complaint was examined and the first hearing held before the council; it was then delivered to a commission of *oyer et terminer*. *Cal. Patent Rolls,* 16 Hen. VI, 199.

[2] The willingness of the parties to do this was sometimes stated in the petition. For example, 'qar le dit Abbe ne Priour voillent nullement countrepleder mes humblement perfourmer ceo qe le dit counseil aiugera en le cas.' *Ancient Petitions,* no. 10449.

[3] As was said by Fleta, lib. ii, c. 13 'quia non tenetur quis sine brevi respondere nisi gratis voluerit, et cum fecerit quis, ex hoc ei non iniuriabitur, volenti enim et scienti non fit iniuria.'

[4] Audeley case, *Cal. Close Rolls,* 40 Edw. III, 238.

[5] *Close Roll,* 51 Edw. III, m. 6 d.; again both parties agreed to a bond of £2,000. Nicolas, v. 158, 174; also iii. 165.

to bring charters, letters, and other documents. Both parties were commonly sworn to tell the truth. The defendants were required to answer the points of complaint in detail, and as early as the reign of Edward III these answers began to be given in written form.[1] This was another feature manifestly borrowed from the practices of the clerical courts. In the reign of Richard II, if not before, the statements and counter-statements of the litigants appear in the form of replications and rejoinders.[2] Sometimes a defendant took the course of presenting a counter-petition. Other than the parties immediately concerned, witnesses were rarely summoned, although in some instances they do appear.[3] Juries were never directly employed. Questions of fact from outside sources were obtained by writs of inquisition directed to the sheriffs, or writs of *certiorari* sent to the justices and other authorities requiring them to search the records and return the information.

The inquisitorial examinations.

If the facts could not be ascertained by any of the simpler methods, recourse was had to the most drastic means within the power of the council, namely, the inquisitorial examination. This method was naturally most effective in criminal prosecutions, although it was not confined solely to these. It was a feature most clearly derived from the ecclesiastical courts, where it was employed especially, though not exclusively, in the prosecutions of heresy.[4] The practice was to require the parties, usually the defendants, but sometimes both plaintiffs and defendants, to answer questions under oath. A beginning of this procedure appears as early as the reign of Edward II, when we are told that

[1] See the case of the prior of Dunstable *v.* the burgesses of the town. The answers and claims of the defendants were reduced in writing to seven points. *Cal. Close Rolls*, 40 Edw. III, 302.

[2] The arguments that were at one time carried on between the king of England and the king of France appear to have been reduced to the same form. In 1311 I find mention of a *quadruplicatio* rendered by the French king in answer to the *triplicatio* of his rival. *Chanc. Misc.*, bundle 29, file 7, no 2.

[3] In 1363 testimony was obtained by the 'examination of credible persons'. *Cal. Close Rolls*, 37 Edw. III, 445.

[4] Observe, for instance, the examination of witnesses—*iurati et examinati*—in the process against the Templars in 1309. This was not a trial of heresy. Wilkins, *Concilia*, ii. 329 ff.

certain persons accused of being madmen or lepers were 'examined' before the council.[1] A few years later several men accused of plotting against Queen Isabella were each 'examined' separately before a council then in session.[2] About the first year of Edward III we learn that the parties were sworn and examined—*iurez et examinez en la chauncellerie.*[3] The oath, which was an essential part of the system, was exacted in the name of the king who alone had the right to require it. As this system develops, it was customary to draw up a series of questions, based upon the facts contained in the accusations or depositions previously made; the questions were then addressed to the defendant and his answers were noted.[4] It is likely that questions were asked orally as well. Any discrepancies or self-contradictions in the statements of the one questioned were quickly turned to his disadvantage, and were likely to cause him to break down and confess.[5] Written confessions were desired and obtained wherever possible. If more than one person was examined, each was taken separately so that inconsistencies in the testimony were all the more easily brought out.[6] Considering that in the writs of summons the defendant received no intimation of the charges against him, and that in prosecutions for felony no one was allowed the aid of counsel, it is manifest that any one subjected to this system was placed at a serious disadvantage. Nothing, in fact, was more antagonistic to the practices of the common law than to require a man thus to incriminate himself. With good reason, therefore, the examinations were assailed as 'a feature

[1] *Cal. Close Rolls*, 2 Edw. II, 132; 6 Edw. II, 559.

[2] The *Scalachronica* of Sir Thomas Gray, *Scottish Historical Review*, iv. 33.

[3] *Ancient Petitions*, nos. 10608, 10640.

[4] The system of interrogatory examinations develops rapidly during the reign of Edward III, the time when most of the special departures originated. *Cal. Close Rolls*, 34 Edw. III, 123; 39 Edw. III, 205. In the Chesterfield case the accusations were given in the form of a roll of articles to which the answers of the defendant were made *seriatim*. Ibid., 39 Edw. III, 114 ff. See also the confessions of William Stiles, *Cal. Patent Rolls*, 46 Edw. III.

[5] Appendix III, p. 519. In 1421 Jacob Berkeley, being interrogated by the chancellor, on oath confessed that he had employed armed men against the countess of Warwick. Nicolas, ii. 286.

[6] In 1415 the chaplain and the steward of the household of the late Lord Scrope, who had been convicted of treason, were examined before the council. Ibid. ii. 182.

of the civil law in subversion of the law of the land'. It was also objected that they were held in secret and 'without record or entry'. Nevertheless, in an age when the art of cross-questioning witnesses was unknown, and when the corruption of juries was very prevalent, and when every form of law was easily perverted, there was much to be said in favour of the star chamber method. In extreme cases it can be shown that the same thing was done both in the exchequer and the king's bench,[1] while on rare occasions even parliament seemed to permit it.[2] From the inquisitorial examination it is, of course, an easy step to physical torture as a means of extorting confessions. Strange to say, while torture was a not infrequent expedient of the common-law courts during the fifteenth century, the council was always very reluctant to lay hands upon life or limb. Something of the kind was done in the case of the aforesaid Roger Bolingbroke, who was first held in the Tower and then brought forth to be exhibited before the people, with his instruments hung about him, until at length he was led before the lords of the council to be examined.[3]

An early case in the Star Chamber.

An excellent example of a typical case in the star chamber, with a full account of the procedure, is found in the year 1438–9. Attached to a petition is a small roll or fold of paper that is partly torn away, containing the articles of examination with the answers of the defendants concerned in a recent riot at Bedford.[4] It is distinctly a record of the privy seal, different from any of the chancery, written in English by the clerk of the council. To explain the case, it is learned from various sources that four of the king's

[1] In 19 Edw. III a clerk accused of forging a writ was brought before the king's bench, where he was sworn and examined secretly by the justices. *Year Book*, 20 Edw. III (Rolls Series), p. l. In 1477 a man accused of sorcery was questioned before the king's bench in a very severe examination, so that he perforce confessed. *Continuation of Croyland*, p. 478. Other extra-legal practices of the same court are described by Mr. Harcourt, 'Baga de Secretis,' *Eng. Hist. Review*, xxiii. 508–29.

[2] In 1388 parliament approved of a statute declaring that all bearers of false reports affecting the great men of the realm and high officers should be punished by the council 'notwithstanding previous statutes', i.e. restricting its procedure. *Statutes of the Realm*, ii. 59. Again, in 1416, by authority of parliament, certain malefactors were to be dealt with 'by such process as the lords of the council shall determine'. *Rot. Parl.* iv. 51.

[3] *Chronicle of London*, p. 128.

[4] Appendix III, p. 529.

justices of the peace and of *oyer et terminer* were commissioned to hold sessions in Bedford, where they were badly received because certain of the lords of the locality believed that the commission had been appointed for the purpose of indicting their tenants.[1] According to a certification made by the justices, Lord Fanhope, with forty-five armed men, invaded the court in riotous manner, insulted the judges, and broke up the session. Lord Fanhope was somehow placed under fine and security, but in his own defence he addressed a petition to the king, denying the truth of the charges and asking that an examination be made. This petition was referred to the council, who proceeded to examine the justices on oath in a manner that was said to be severe. The questions consisted of nine articles on the matters of fact contained in their own allegations, as to the number of men, as to the conduct of his lordship, as to their own conduct, and the like. These were addressed in turn to each of the four defendants, and their answers taken. When, upon subsequent perusal, certain discrepancies in their assertions were found, especially in comparing their answers with the original certification, the judges, though still maintaining the truth of their charges, were forced to admit that they had been actuated by motives of anger and malice. The council, therefore, found the charges false and so must have reported to the king, who then commanded the chancellor by a letter of the privy seal to issue a patent of pardon and release for Lord Fanhope and all his followers. For a record which his lordship desired, and presumably paid for, this was enrolled after the manner of the chancery with a brief summary of the case.[2] The council would seem to have acted very leniently, if not with favour, toward the lord, as to whose conduct in breaking up the court the essential facts were not denied, but it was considered that he had not been without excuse. His lordship also, be it said, was an influential man politically, and at other times was known as a member of the council.

For obvious reasons not many cases could be heard by the

[1] A suggestion to this effect is given in Nicolas, v. 35, 39, 57

[2] *Cal. Patent Rolls*, 17 Hen. VI, 246.

council at such length. On one occasion when an examination was pending, the lords declared that under the many burdens imposed upon them they could not go on with it.[1] Fortunately the methods of the council were such that a large part of the more technical and laborious work could well be given to committees. No doubt here was a reason for the strong insistence at all times upon written evidence. The practice of appointing 'committees of examination', as they were called, can be traced to the reign of Edward III.[2] Sometimes a point of inquiry was left to the chancellor alone, or an inspection of documents to the clerks of the chancery. But more often the work was given to a limited number of lay and clerical members who were assisted by one or more of the justices. The system finds a parallel in the ecclesiastical courts where professional examiners were regularly employed.[3] Among the few existing records of the work of these committees there is a noteworthy example of the thirteenth year of Richard II, which explains itself by the following marginal notes: 'Les nouns de ceux qi feurent deputez par le conseil du Roy pur examiner [les matires] comprises deinz ceste bille et autres evidences proposeez,' &c. The names follow. Later, 'le dit conte [of Northumberland] par lui et par les deputez susditz fesoit relation au conseil du Roy qe,'[4] &c. As the latter note suggests, the committee was to make a report or 'relation' to the council of its findings. The council was likely to act and might even agree to act in accordance with the report.[5] The final relation too might be waived, when the parties to a suit were induced to submit to the arbitration of the committee. There is an instance in which the parties at first agreed to accept the decision of a committee of justices, but afterwards one of them wished

The use of committees.

[1] 'Propter varia et ardua eis per dictum dominum Regem iniuncta negocia intendere minime potuerunt.' The examination was then committed to a bishop and a lay member. Nicolas, i. 190 ff.; ii. 321, &c.

[2] The king, it is said, caused further examination to be made by some of his council. *Cal. Patent Rolls*, 22 Edw. III, 131. In 1389 an examination was held before the keeper of the privy seal, Edward Dalinrigg and Richard Stury, 'pro tunc de Regis consilio existentes per ipsum consilium ad hoc specialiter deputatos.' Nicolas, i. 14 d.

[3] On the duties of an examiner, see Wilkins, *Concilia*, ii. 689.

[4] An unfiled document in the 'Exchequer Box'; also one of 3 Hen. IV, Appendix III, pp. 517, 523.

[5] Nicolas, i. 192.

to have a decree of the council.[1] The reference of cases in this way for judicial inquiry, at one stage or another of the proceedings, was a regular feature both of the council and the chancery. To such an extent were the justices occupied in the work of examinations, that complaint was made in parliament that they were being kept from their ordinary duties of hearing pleas.[2] The committees are in no wise to be confused with the older method of delegation to commissions of *oyer et terminer*, for the latter followed in the main the procedure of the common law, while the committees assumed the peculiar powers of the council. Moreover, the commissions were empowered to render final judgements, while with the committees this prerogative was reserved to the council.

Assistance of the judges.

With these agencies of assistance, in most instances no doubt all that took place in the council was a reading or 'rehearsal' of the case, as contained in the various written forms that have been described. Sometimes the reading was performed by the chancellor and sometimes by the clerk. As was once expressed in the appointment of a committee of inquiry, upon their report nothing should remain for the council but to render judgement.[3] If there were points for deliberation these were most easily dealt with when drawn up in a succinct series of articles, which could be discussed and decided one by one. In questions of law the justices were either specially summoned or otherwise communicated with. Indeed, it was repeatedly enjoined by acts of parliament that the lords of the council should in no wise decide legal questions without the aid of the justices. On one such occasion we read of the justices being interrogated individually for their advice.[4] Consultation with the king also, as expressed in the words, 'loquendum est cum rege,' was commonly necessary before final decision was made. It will be recalled as one of the early usages of the *curia regis* that a judgement of the court did not become legally valid and compulsory until it had been confirmed or proclaimed by the king himself.[5] In the courts of common law, which

'Relation' to the king.

[1] Nicolas, ii. 333–5; also iii. 165.
[2] *Rot. Parl.* iv. 84.
[3] *Cal. Patent Rolls*, 26 Edw. I, 384.
[4] Nicolas, iii. 313.
[5] Adams, *Origin of the Constitution*, p. 64 n.

acted upon writs or commissions, naturally no such step was necessary, but in the council and the chancery, where cases were heard without any similar restrictions, there was good reason for a continuation of the original custom. The principle is best illustrated in the noted case of the Audeleys, 40 Edw. III, wherein the opinion was expressed by the council that under the circumstances it could not reach a final judgement until the king was consulted. Accordingly the entire proceedings were transmitted to the king, who then commanded by a writ of the privy seal that the council proceed to a final discussion.[1] Upon this point no controversy was ever raised, since the council was not disposed to assume responsibilities without the king's permission. Certainly he must be consulted in all questions wherein the royal rights were concerned, and this ground, according to current interpretation, was very extensive. Moreover, no change or novel application of the law could properly be made without the consent of the king. For this reason the rule was well grounded that a final reference to the king must be made in all equitable cases. It was also desirable in cases affecting property that the final orders under the great seal should be fully warranted ; this was best accomplished by the aforesaid writ of the privy seal. Still, in criminal cases, where the law was plainly understood and no deviation was contemplated, arrests were ordered and judgements executed on the sole authority of the council. These were the general rules, but we cannot insist that they were followed without variations during the fifteenth century. The final judgement or decree was one essential matter which must in some form be written in the court.[2] In cases following the method of the privy seal this was regularly inscribed by the clerk upon the back of the bill ;[3] in cases of the chancery at

[1] This example is accepted by Palgrave as 'the first equitable decree on record, grounded upon an application to the king and pronounced by virtue of his delegation to the council' (*Original Authority*, p. 67). It is true that the incident is described in the record with exceptional clearness, but it is not the earliest example that can be cited (see the Oxford case, *Close Roll*, 29 Edw. III, m. 17; the Merton case, *Plac. in Canc.*, no. 18). Moreover, the essential principle, I think, is by no means a new one.

[2] Under Edward IV, sometimes the decree was made by the king on the advice of the council.

[3] This was an early practice which disappears during the York and Tudor periods.

this time the decrees were rarely written upon the petitions. With greater formality the clerks took separate membranes upon which to draw up a longer review. The various parchments and papers were then sewn together to constitute the 'record and process'. Few, however, survive in their original condition. If a more substantial record were desired, this might be made by an 'exemplification' or abstract upon the close or patent rolls, as was done, for instance, in the case of Lord Fanhope. Except for the 'book of the council', which was not used for this purpose, there was no roll, of course, in the office of the privy seal. Such technical points as these are of importance, for it is only in this wise that the divergence of the council and the chancery at this time can be clearly seen.

Expedition *v.* delay.

The council and the chancery were in a word courts of summary procedure, acting according to a familiar maxim of the canonists, *simpliciter et de plano ac sine strepitu et figura iudicii.* As such they were appealed to by suitors against the notorious delays of the common law. 'To make an end as speedily as possible', 'to ordain hasty remedy', to give justice 'without delay', was the desire expressed in many petitions. In the main this reputation was deserved, for while the council was not always easy of access, its cases once taken up were terminated in the briefest possible time. Thus an unusually extended case, begun on November 7 and continued with several adjournments, was ended on December 18,[1] while the longest duration of a litigation which the writer has observed lasted from July 9 until April 30.[2] Still, one reads of cases postponed from day to day, partly heard or not heard at all, for the reason that the lords of the council were otherwise occupied.[3] For example, at the close of a term in 1441, it was said, 'For as moche as the said counsail is now in departing and yt ye heryng ⁊ dissecucion of the said bille ⁊ complainte wolde axe a tract of tyme wt meur advis ⁊ deberacion,'[4] the parties were commanded to appear again

[1] Case 16 Ric. II, *Warrants Privy Seal*, series i, section ii, file 3.

[2] Spynk's case, *Cal. Patent Rolls*, 38 Edw. III, 502.

[3] 'De diebus in dies continuate, quia prefati domini aliunde sic pro tunc occupati quod circa finalem decisionem prefatae litis intendere non poterant.' Nicolas, ii. 321; iii. 36; again a suit is said to be 'hanging in the council'. Ibid. v. 162.

[4] Ibid. v. 172.

during the following Hilary sessions. It is probable, too, that during the later years of Henry VI the great majority of petitions that came to the council, if we judge from the fact that they are without endorsements or other marks upon them, were simply neglected and never heard at all. The court of chancery, on the other hand, was not limited to terms, but declared itself to be 'open at all times'.[1] This was another very practical reason for the separate growth of the chancery. It is not surprising that the chancellor also found himself overburdened with work, as he declared on one occasion when he appointed a committee of examination.[2] It is remarkable, too, that the very method that was at first devised for quickening the work of the court should in time become a cause of the notorious delays in the modern chancery.

Leniency and weakness.

But the greatest weakness of the council, which had a direct bearing upon the disruption of the fifteenth century, is found in the insufficiency of its penalties and punishments. This was equally true of the council in its star chamber capacity and of the council in chancery. It held the power, in one sense, to inflict the severest penalties short of life and limb, such as the pillory, imprisonments, and fines to an indefinite extent.[3] Men were sent to the Tower, to the Fleet prison, or to the Marshalsea to be kept 'until otherwise ordered by the council'. Authority was given also to commissioners of arrest and mainpernors to keep their charges in prison. Such was the treatment of fraudulent merchants, pirates, and robbers who could not give bail and surety. But towards the lords and knights, who with their armed bands were committing the greatest offences, always a certain timidity and leniency was shown. When such men were

[1] This was in the third year of Edward IV, when other courts were closed on account of the pestilence, but the chancery *est tout temps overt*. *Year Books*, 3 Edw. IV (Tottell), f. xx.

[2] 'Cancellarius, quia occupatum circa maiora se dixit, tamen cuilibet iustitiae complementum fieri cupiens, predictam examinationem . . . comisit.' *Foedera* (Orig. Ed.), xi. 672.

[3] Edward III writes to his council, reserving to himself the fine and punishment of an offender, but requests the council to make an examination as to how much the man is willing to pay, provided it be a reasonable amount, having regard also to the excesses, extortions, and outrages he has committed. An unfiled document.

dealt with at all the favourite method was to release them upon bail and surety. It may have been a surer means of constraint, to place a man under bonds to the extent of £5,000, or £10,000, than to put him in prison, for jails certainly were easily broken, and prisoners, it is confessed, were held only 'with great peril, fear, and labour on the part of the keepers'. But bondsmen or 'mainpernors' no sooner gave security than they sought to have their obligations cancelled, and this release they were likely to obtain through channels of favour. Moreover, the necessity of finding bonds, even though one were not convicted of crime, was said to bear heavily upon poorer men, who were thus compelled to treat and accord with their enemies.[1] It would be rare, indeed, to find an instance during the long reign of Henry VI wherein any lord or great man was actually punished for a violation of the statutes regarding maintenance.[2] The lords of the council themselves were so involved in the same practices that they could hardly sit in judgement over others. On the contrary, it was the more general practice for such men to protect themselves against prosecution by obtaining pardons for every conceivable offence. In 1449, for example, there were scores of these 'blanket' pardons that were worded to cover 'all trespasses, offences, contempts, violations of the statute of liveries, murders, rapes, rebellions, riots, felonies, conspiracies, maintenances, embraceries, and treasons'.[3] After Jack Cade's rebellion the government, as an act of amnesty, promised pardons to all who should ask for them, and the number granted with the specification of every conceivable crime amounted to a veritable suspension of justice. Again, in 1459–60 there was another season of the most lavish grants of such pardons.[4] Under all these circum-

[1] *Rot. Parl.* iv. 84.

[2] Something of the kind was threatened in 1443, when Sir John Penington, a justice of the peace in Cumberland, confessed that he had participated in a riot. The chancellor would have committed him to the Fleet prison, but two of the lords gave security at 3,000 marks for his appearance in court upon another day. Nicolas, v. 270.

[3] *Cal. Patent Rolls*, *passim*.

[4] As an extreme illustration, in 1460 a pardon was granted to a certain 'gentleman' of all 'treasons, offenses, misprisions, contempts, impeachments against the statute of liveries, murders, rapes, rebellions, insurrections, felonies, conspiracies, champerties, maintenances, embraceries,

stances the council was fairly paralysed for dealing effectively with the greatest factor of disturbance, nor did the court of chancery in this respect offer any practical alternative. In last resort, it will be shown, men appealed to parliament against the weakness, favouritism, and corruption of the council. But nothing availed, so long as the government was entirely bound up in the evils that needed correction. How the people would fare under another dynasty remains to be seen. In dropping the subject at this point, we cannot fail to remark that all of the methods which ultimately made the star chamber a terrible power were well developed under the House of Lancaster, but the government did not then realize the possibilities of the extraordinary tribunal at its service nor use it to its full capacity. What was lacking was not a judicial method, but a policy of action. This did not come until after the accession of the Tudors.[1]

trespasses, negligences, extortions, ignorances, contempts, concealments, forfeitures, deceptions and consequent outlawries; all gifts, alienations, and purchases of land without license and in mortmain, and all intrusions and entries into his inheritance without due suit.' *Cal. Patent Rolls*, 38 Hen. VI, 540.

[1] Concerning the star chamber of a later time, Mr. Prothero has wisely said, 'It was thus admirably calculated to be the support of order against anarchy, or of despotism against individual and national liberty. During the Tudor period it appeared in the former light, under the Stuart in the latter.' *Encyclopaedia Britannica* (1910–11), xxv. 796. There is still the earlier phase, under the Lancastrians, when it acted in support neither of order nor despotism, but was practically the organ of an overbearing aristocracy.

CHAPTER XII

THE COUNCIL AND PARLIAMENT

THE way is now prepared for dealing with one other phase of the general subject, namely, the relations of the council and parliament, or more particularly the house of lords. As has been previously intimated, there was here the germ of two institutions springing from a single stem, so that in the minds of all historians it has been a problem how to distinguish between them.[1] In the reign of Edward I, it is true, there was a sworn council of permanent standing, but the identity of this body was immediately lost when any larger assembly was brought together. Between the small council and the large there was then no substantial difference of organization, nor any difference whatsoever in function. Little by little, as reasons occurred, distinctions were made, and a process of differentiation and separation was begun. Even so, there was a period of about a hundred years of uncertainty, transition, and occasional reversions to type. Until the close of the middle ages, indeed, there did not cease to be some confusion of language and thought as regards the king's council and the house of lords. In the treatment of this theme it will be necessary to observe the close inter-relations of the council and parliament that existed in the time of Edward I, and then to follow the steps that lead to the recognition of two forms of authority. It will be a valuable point at any time to find a function or a mode of action that was considered to belong to one body and not to the other.

The problem.

[1] In the opinion of Mr. Pike, 'It could hardly be said that the House of Lords was an offshoot of the Council, though it might, perhaps, be said that the Council was an offshoot of the House of Lords' (*House of Lords*, p. 289). I see no reason for insisting upon either of these alternatives, but should say rather that by a gradual process the one original body was divided into two.

Two words for one idea.

At the time at which we begin, even the words *consilium* and *parliamentum* were not used consistently or with settled meaning. *Consilium,* of course, was the older term, and it was still applied to any assemblage great or small. It might be construed to include all the estates gathered in parliament, as for instance in the clause, *ex assensu domini regis ac totius consilii parliamenti predicti provisum est.*[1] But the tendency was not to extend the term beyond its original meaning, so that it included the lords spiritual and temporal and the officers of the household, as many as happened to be assembled; but it was not understood to embrace the knights and commons who were an entirely new element. A *parliamentum,* on the other hand, Maitland has shown, 'is rather an act than a body of persons', a colloquy or a debate. 'It is but slowly that this word is appropriated to colloquies of a particular kind, namely, those which the king has with the estates of his realm, and still more slowly that it is transferred from the colloquy to the body of men whom the king has summoned.'[2] A conference even of a small body in 1284 was called a parliament, as in the following passage: *habito ibidem cum quisbusdam regni sui magnatibus non universali aut generali sed tanquam particulari et speciali parliamento.*[3] But the tendency of official usage was to consider it a parliament only when the estates were specially and solemnly summoned. Already in the reign of Henry III the barons were asked to come *coram nobis et consilio nostro in parliamento nostro.*[4] Again, in the reign of Edward I appears the familiar passage from Fleta:

> 'habet enim Rex curiam in concilio suo in parliamentis suis, praesentibus praelatis, comitibus, baronibus, proceribus, et aliis viris peritis' (*or* iurisperitis?).[5]

The council in parliament.

Now what was 'the council in parliament'? Regarding this significant phrase, there has been no lack of discussion

[1] *Rot. Parl.* i. 221.

[2] *Memoranda de Parliamento,* p. lxvii. It is perhaps needless to point out that the word 'exchequer' passes through the same transformations; (1) a chess board, (2) an occasion on which the *curia* used the board, and (3) the *curia* sitting for that purpose.

[3] *Chron. Wykes* (Rolls Series), p. 300.

[4] *Foedera* (Rec. Ed.), i. 449.

[5] Liber ii, cap. 2.

in various constitutional histories,[1] but the subject has yet to be treated in all its bearings. At the risk of some repetition, it must be stated that the parliaments of Edward I, before their organization was fixed, were more widely inclusive of the estates of the realm than they afterwards became. At different times the king is known to have sent writs of summons to each of the following groups: the great prelates, sometimes also the lower clergy, the earls and barons, the knights of the shire, the commons, and lastly, a varying number of judges and officers who were asked to come 'with others of the council'.[2] It is important to notice that long before the formation of the 'houses', these groups or estates were treated in a manner distinct from one another, each on its own footing. The writs, for instance, sent to one group were differently worded from those sent to another, although the forms used for the lords temporal and those for the members of the council differed only in one or two essential clauses. The names of the men also of each group were carefully set apart in the records. It is also to be noted that although there were bishops and lords sworn of the king's council, in parliament they preferred to stand not as councillors, but as lords or peers of the realm. It was, of course, a higher status to be a peer than to be a member of the council. This fact goes far to explain why the king's small council had so little distinctness in parliament, and why it was so readily merged in the larger body.

Comprehensiveness of the early parliaments.

With great comprehensiveness the parliaments of Edward I were made to include not only the several estates, but all of the existing courts of law. In the re-merging of these branches there seems to have been a survival of the conception of a single governing institution. Thus we find reference to an action *ad scaccarium in parliamento regis*,[3] although it is true that the exchequer generally held a greater degree

[1] Stubbs, *Const. Hist.* § 228. Says Mr. Pike, 'we know precisely what was meant by the expression "the King in his Council in his Parliament". . . . This kind of Parliament was not necessarily a Parliament including the Commons, but a Parliament of Lords Spiritual and Temporal with the King and his Council sitting therein.' *House of Lords*, p. 50.

[2] *Parliamentary Writs, passim.*

[3] Madox, *History of the Exchequer*, ii. 8.

of independence than other courts. More frequently do the rolls contain *placita coram rege in parliamento*, and *placita coram consilio in parliamento*,[1] in which the distinctness of the king's bench and the council as institutions is for the time being lost to sight. The chancellor, the treasurer, and the justices were instructed to bring forward in writing the cases which they could not determine outside of parliament.[2] Repeatedly the justices are found adjourning and postponing cases in order that they might have the added presence and advice of the magnates.[3] Even without any positive assistance being given by the lords, the mere occasion of a parliament lent an added dignity, not to say authority, to the proceedings of each and every one of these courts. In these instances the parliament was not regarded as a separate court, but as a strongly reinforced session of the exchequer, the king's bench, or the council. It has been said that there was here 'a council within a council'. But men did not then reason in this way. They spoke not of two councils, but always of one council, which varied greatly as it was enlarged or contracted according to the number of men or estates that were consulted.

The council continues after a parliament.

When a parliament was broken up the council and the courts resumed their normal form. Upon this point the proclamation of Edward I in 1305 is very illuminating. The archbishops, bishops, and other prelates, earls, barons, knights of the shires, citizens, burgesses, and other men of the community, who had come to the parliament by the king's command, were thanked for their coming and asked to withdraw in peace, in order that they might return promptly when summoned again; except that the bishops, earls, barons, and justices who were of the king's council should not go away without the king's special licence.[4]

[1] *Abbreviatio Placitorum*; *Rot. Parl.* i, *passim.*

[2] 'Post hec iniunctum fuit predictis Cancellario et Thesaurario et Iusticiariis de utroque Banco quod ipsi negocia coram eis in placeis; uis pendencia que extra parliamentum non possent terminari, sub compendio in scriptis facerent, et ea in parliamento referrent ita quod ibi de eisdem fieret quod deberet.' *Parl. Writs*, ii. 156; also *Statutes*, 13 Edw. I, Westm. ii, c. 24.

[3] *Rot. Parl.* i. 354; Hale, *Jurisdiction of the Lords' House*, p. 114.

[4] *Rot. Parl.* i. 159 ff.; *Parl. Writs*, i. 156 ff.

How many of the bishops and barons were included we do not know;[1] but we have definite information that a clerk, Robert Pickering, remained until he was permitted to withdraw. What was done by the council after March 21, the day of the proclamation, can in part be ascertained. On March 26 a memorandum concerning the state of the kingdom of Scotland was read and answers to the questions raised were made. On April 6 commissions were issued to justices of Trailbaston 'according to the form of an ordinance made by us and our council and delivered in our parliament'. On this and other occasions the council simply went on with the unfinished business of parliament. Matters of detail were often purposely left to the council. In a parliament of the following year, for instance, at the request of the king for an aid, the barons and knights granted a thirteenth and the commons a twentieth. The 'form' of taxation providing for the levy of these aids was afterwards devised by the king's council.[2] In none of these matters do we find a line of division beyond the convenience of the moment. Between a parliament and a small council there were different degrees of dignity, but there was as yet no difference in *kind* of authority or in methods of action.

The groups in parliament.

There is still the question just what group or groups of men were included in the recurring phrase, 'the council in parliament'. It certainly was not restricted to the sworn councillors, who lost their distinctness in the general system of estates. It failed to have any application to the knights and commons, because they were not admitted to bear a consultative part. But concerning the other groups usage was still unsettled. Sometimes we find mention of 'the prelates, earls, barons, and others of the king's council', and again we see 'the prelates, earls, barons, *and* the council', and also 'the prelates, barons, councillors, and commons'.[3]

[1] On March 31 a hearing took place in the presence of the treasurer, three bishops, two chief justices, and others. Again, on April 6, the Salisbury case was taken up by 'the whole council'.

[2] *Parl. Writs*, i. 104, 164, 395; *Memoranda Roll, Exch. K. R.*, 34 Edw. I, m. 40. Similar actions appear in other years, as seen in *Rot. Parl.* i. 266, and *Mem. Roll, Exch. K. R.*, 30 Edw. I, m. 8.

[3] *Rot. Parl.* i. 159; iii. 166; *Statutes of the Realm*, i. 71, 195, &c.

From these and many other passages it is evident that the council in parliament included in varying numbers the same groups as had always been found in the king's council. These were the magnates and the officers of the *curia regis*. As to the share of influence which properly belonged to each of these elements there was still a condition of uncertainty. For practical purposes sometimes the prelates and barons were particularly consulted, sometimes only the justices and officers, and again under other circumstances the magnates and justices were brought together. Upon the further relations of these estates to each other the future organization of parliament will largely depend. In order to reach an ultimate definition upon the point in question it will be necessary to follow for a time the actions of these groups.

The *curiales*.

The group of professional men, here referred to, were the *curiales*, including a varying number of justices, barons of the exchequer, clerks of the chancery, and other 'learned men'. As we have elsewhere shown, many of these were formally sworn of the king's council, and are especially known as the king's councillors. They were given great prominence by Edward I, who summoned as many as thirty of them at a time to his parliaments. Unlike the lords, they never gained a right to be summoned, so that it was never certain how many should come. In every parliament these men were an important factor, whose action as a separate estate is often clearly visible. Their special function naturally lay in the treatment of legal questions, whether these were in the form of judicial cases or of legislation. A few examples of the independent action of the professional council can readily be given. In the law case of Geoffrey Stanton, we read that the chief justice brought the record into parliament, and there assembled the chancellor, the treasurer, the justices of either bench, the barons of the exchequer and others of the council.[1] Again, in disposing of the lands of the Templars, it was the opinion of the greater part of

[1] It is quite inconceivable that the clerk should have neglected to mention the magnates in case any of them were present. *Rot. Parl.*, ii. 123; also *Year Books*, 13–14 Edw. III, no. 15.

the king's council, 'that is, the justices and other lay persons', that the lands should not go to the lords of the fees ; it was afterwards decided by the king, the nobles, and others assembled in parliament, that the estates should be given to the Hospitallers.[1] Perhaps the utmost distinctness of the councillors as a separate group in parliament is seen in the eighth year of Edward II, when a petition was addressed to the king and council by the archbishops, bishops, earls, and barons, that the prices of cattle, poultry, eggs, and other articles be fixed.[2] The petition we are told was exhibited before the council, surely not the body which presented it, and was endorsed in the usual way. A list of prices was afterwards drawn up and ordained by the council—*il semble au conseil.* In the ensuing orders to the sheriffs to put the schedule in force, it was stated, *ordinavimus de consilio et assensu prelatorum, comitum, baronum, et omnium aliorum de consilio nostro existentium in ultimo parliamento.*[3]

The councillors in legislation.

Probably the relation of the council to the other estates in parliament can best be observed in the function of legislation. This is not to say that legislation was then the most important work of parliament, or that it was a process essentially different from adjudication. It has been abundantly demonstrated, in fact, that the statutes of Edward I were hardly more than judicial interpretations in legislative form.[4] For this very reason it was deemed proper that the form of the statutes should be left largely to the king's professional councillors. The statutes of Edward I, in fact, contain a series of statements like the following. In 1274 certain ordinances were enacted, *par son conseil, e par le assentement des erceveskes, eveskẹs, abbes, priurs, contes, barons, et la communaute de la tere ileokes sumons.*[5] The first statute of Westminster in 1275 was declared to have been passed in words almost the same.[6]

[1] *Statutes of the Realm*, i. 195. [2] *Rot. Parl.* i. 295 ; another, 383.

[3] In 1369 we find the following note in answer to a petition, 'la response donee depar le counseil du Roi . . . ouesque les prelatz, piers, seigneurs, grantz et sages de son Roialme.' *Dipl. Documents, Exch. Treasury of Receipt*, no. 255.

[4] McIlwain, *High Court of Parliament* (New Haven, 1910), pp. 51 ff.

[5] Red Book of the Exchequer at Dublin, cited in *Lords' Report*, p. 173.

[6] *Statutes of the Realm*, i. 26.

The statute *de Bigamis* in 1276 was first read before a special group of councillors, including the treasurer, the chancellor, one dean, three archdeacons, fourteen justices and officers, besides the Italian jurist Francisco Accursi. The articles were afterwards rehearsed in parliament and confirmed.[1] The statute of Acton Burnel in 1283 was declared to have been made *par luy* (i.e. the king) *et par sun consail a sun parlement*.[2] The statute *de Escaetoribus* in 1300–1 was enacted 'by the advice of the treasurer, the chancellor, and others of the council there present'.[3] An act of Edward II is described as passing under the review of three successive councils.[4] Other acts of this time, with less clearness of statement, are declared to have been made by 'the council in parliament', or simply by the council. Language like this can only mean that the real origin of the statutes at this time was in the king's council, and especially with the justices, who acted not as draftsmen but as the authority responsible for the sanction of the acts. The added assent of the lords and of the commons was sometimes given, but their part was by no means always essential. This was the view emphatically stated in the argument of a case that arose in 1305 on the construction of the second statute of Westminster of 1285, when the chief justice cut short the argument with the remark, 'do not gloss the statute; we understand it better than you do, for we made it!'[5] If the tendency to employ the king's councillors as a distinct estate in parliament had been permitted to continue, it is possible that a third house might have been formed upon these lines.[6]

[1] *Statutes of the Realm*, i. 42.

[2] Ibid., p. 53; also p. 98.

[3] Ibid., p. 142.

[4] Ibid., p. 192, n. a.

[5] *Year Books*, 33–5 Edw. I (Roll Series), p. 82. It will be seen that the justices held practically a dual position. As judges of the common law they acted upon commissions, to the terms of which they were held very strictly. As king's councillors they were bound by no such restrictions, and they easily became legislators. When a judge in the course of a trial reserved a point for the consideration of the council, it was to consult with a body of which he was most likely a member. What the judges, then, were not able to do in one capacity they could readily do in another.

[6] In 1333 there is the curious and exceptional instance of three separate assemblages in a parliament at York. First there were twelve lords, presumably those acting at the time as the king's councillors, namely, the archbishop of York, the bishops of Ely, Winchester, Lincoln, Chester,

Conflict of the magnates and the councillors.

Thus far, whatever was done by the prelates and lords, and whatever was done by the king's council, there was no division of authority between them. So long as these estates did not represent conflicting interests there was no reason for raising any question of the kind. But a rift begins to appear as soon as the conflict between the barons and the *curiales* was imminent. Until the death of Edward I the strife was repressed with difficulty, but it came all the more surely during the reign of his successor. In the movement of the Lords Ordainers there was revealed not only an antagonism to the 'evil councillors', who were to be 'removed and put away', but there was an outspoken distrust of the king's council as it was then constituted. The effects of this crisis upon the relations of the council and the exchequer have already been pointed out. The consequences as regards the estates in parliament are equally striking. This is well shown in 1322 when it was proposed to frame a statute repealing the ordinances of 1311. The king sent a message to the council, concluding with the following words:

> 'and be it known that the king wishes that each sage of his council consider these points, that they may amend the law for the profit of the king and the people; that they submit their agreement in the form of a statute or make some other remedy if it will suffice, and that such thing should be put into form in order that he may be advised before the parliament the more readily to deliver to the people who come to parliament.' [1]

In the famous act which followed, it was declared that such matters in future 'shall be treated, accorded, and established in parliaments by our lord the king, and by the assent of the prelates, earls, and barons, and the commonalty of the realm'.[2] The importance of this declaration in its recognition of the commons as an essential part of parliament has been fully appreciated, but it is perhaps equally significant

and Norwich; the earl Warenne and the earl of Warwick; Lords Percy, Beaumont, Courtenay, and Clinton. At the same time the other prelates, earls, and barons met by themselves; and the knights and commons in another chamber. On this occasion nothing is said of the justices and officers. *Rot. Parl.* ii. 69.

1 *Parliamentary Proceedings*, file v, no. 10.

2 *Statutes of the Realm*, i. 189.

that the justices and 'others of the council' were in no wise mentioned. From this time certainly the acts of parliament show that the former prominence of the councillors was not permitted to continue. With an entirely different emphasis the statutes of Edward III were declared to be accorded by the prelates, earls, and barons, 'at the request of' or 'with the assent of the commons', while the participation of 'others of the council' was seldom recognized. In other words, this function was absorbed by the house of lords. The council, it is true, continued to prepare measures for the consideration of parliament, but this was not *making* the law. How the ordinance of the staple, in the twenty-eighth year of Edward III, was constructed and passed is described in the following manner. First, certain 'sages of the council' were assigned to draft the ordinance, and then the articles were read in full council (presumably the lords) and here accepted. They were afterwards to be read in parliament, the knights of the shires being given copies that they might put into writing any amendments they might have to offer.[1] There was some mistrust of the king's councillors even in this capacity, for on one occasion when special assistance was required in order to draft a statute, rather than leave the work to the council, parliament appointed a committee composed mainly of lords.[2] These facts may help to account for the tendency, which others have noted, toward a deterioration in the scope and quality of parliamentary legislation. 'After an extraordinary outburst of legislation under Edward I, when parliament, if we may speak of one at all, was in its primordial fragments, there ceased, with a few noteworthy exceptions in the fourteenth century, to be any important law-making until the Tudor period.'[3]

Altered status of the judges in parliament.

The altered status of the judges and officers in parliament is seen in various other ways, which enable us ultimately to define their position with accuracy. It is noticeable that in point of numbers, while Edward I would summon as many as thirty such officials at a time, Edward III rarely invited

[1] *Rot. Parl.* ii. 254. [2] Ibid. 113.

[3] A. B. White, *Making of the English Constitution* (New York and London, 1908), p. 208.

more than ten, sometimes only seven or five or less, to come to parliament.[1] Even in purely judicial matters the justices were not left to act by themselves. In the first year of Edward III, instead of *placita coram rege et concilio suo in parliamento*, as had been commonly stated before, we find *placita coram domino rege et consilio suo in presentia regis, procerum et magnatum regni in parliamento suo*,[2] and again a response to a petition is given *depar le counseil du roi . . . ouesque les prelates, piers, seigneurs de sa roialme.*[3] It has been thought by the authors of the Lords' Report that at this point is marked the beginning of a change, by which the justices ceased to be the *equals* of the lords in parliament.[4] It should rather be said that the professional men were never on an equality with the lords, but their importance and independence as a group in parliament was now visibly lowered. Possibly under Edward III some of their former independence of action still remained, but in the reign of Richard II, after the events of 1376 and other years had had their effect, it is clear that the justices are considered to be no more than advisers in the house of lords. In proof of this the action of the justices in 1398, when they delivered their opinion concerning the validity of the impeachments of 1386, has often been cited.[5] But the matter then in question was a strongly political one and does not prove the point so well as a similar action of the justices in the thirteenth year of the same reign, in the case of a purely private petition concerning the validity of a judicial commission. The endorsement is:

'Ceste peticioun lieu en parlement et la commission (i.e. of *oyer* and *terminer*) dont ceste peticion fait mencion ensemblement ove le proces ent fait, et auxint les evidences

[1] *Lords' Report, passim.*

[2] *Rot. Parl.* iii. 3.

[3] *Diplomatic Documents, Exchequer*, no. 255.

[4] The authors of the Report expressed their doubts in the sentence, 'When this jurisdiction ceased to be exercised by the Sworn Council of the King, and the part of it which remains was transferred to the Lords Spiritual and Temporal in Parliament, the Committee have been unable to determine' (*Lords' Report on the Dignity of a Peer*, i. 296). The mistake made here is in the assumption that the jurisdiction in question ever belonged specifically to the sworn council. The change was a gradual one by which the prominence of one group was diminished and the other enhanced. It was never a transference from one distinct body to another.

[5] McIlwain, op. cit., p. 39.

des suppliantz vieues et *examinez par les justices* ove bone deliberacion, et *report ent fait* en parlement par les ditz justices qe la dite commission estoit noun duement faite et encontre la ley . . . *agardez est en parlement* qe la dite comission soit outrement repelle t adnulle.' [1]

The council in parliament is the house of lords.

As the prelates and lords therefore absorbed all the independent functions of the justices and their associates, 'the council in parliament' as an expression inevitably shifted from its original meaning. Although it was used less frequently than before, it meant nothing less than the house of lords, wherein a few of the law officers of the crown remained in a subordinate capacity.[2] By this time also 'the council *out of* parliament', as it was sometimes called, had developed certain functions and methods of work that stand in contrast to those of the house of lords. In order to show the growth of an organic differentiation, these lines will now be traced.

Discernment of two bodies.

One material point of contrast is found in the legislative power that was exercised by the council either apart from or supplementary to the acts of parliament. There were, of course, enactments by the council from the earliest times, but until a rivalry of the two bodies was felt, no question as to the propriety or validity of these acts was raised. The beginning of a discrimination is seen when the justices of Edward II doubted the authority of the king and council to make an amendment to an act of parliament.[3] The strife of that reign further stimulated this feeling. At the accession of Edward III a certain charter of the late king, containing a series of mercantile ordinances, was annulled

[1] *Ancient Petitions*, no. 1043; *Rot. Parl.* iii. 298.

[2] It was therefore maintained by Prynne (*Brief Register*, i. 361) that the professional councillors were 'no essential members of the Parliaments or Great Councils'. In all arguments of this kind too much stress is laid upon the point that they did not vote or in other ways have the same rights as the lords. Under Edward I the councillors were an estate as truly as any of the others. Even in their later position as advisers their presence and services were still regarded as necessary.

[3] The statute of Gloucester, 6 Edw. I, had been made by 'les plus descrez de sun regne, ausi bien de greindres come de meindres'. A certain article had subsequently been altered by the king and council. *Lords' Report*, i. 183. In 1327 the council refused to consider an allegation of error in a case on the ground that what had been decided in parliament could be revoked only in parliament. *Foedera*, ii, part ii, p. 710.

on the ground that it had been prepared by the 'evil councillors' without the assent of the prelates and lords.[1] The statutes of Edward III contain many positive restrictions on the authority of the council. In 1348, on demand of the commons, it was agreed that no imposition, tallage, or charge by way of loan should be imposed 'by the privy council' without the assent of parliament.[2] In spite of several enactments of this kind, the power of the council to make ordinances did not fail to extend widely. Perhaps the best illustration that can be given of the effectiveness of an act of the council in comparison with an act of parliament, is found in the famous Ordinance of Labourers. This was passed at a minor council in 1349, at a time when no parliament or great council could be summoned because of the pestilence. The ordinance was put into operation, and although the Statute of Labourers containing different provisions was passed by a parliament in 1351, yet it was the ordinance and not the statute that the courts continued to enforce.[3] Parliament admitted the necessity of conciliar ordinances in many minor matters of government, not infrequently making provision in the statutes for further regulation by the council. The Statute of Provisors of 1351 was to be revised and amended if necessary.[4] In the same reign it was allowed that the chancellor and treasurer, with the advice of others of the king's council, might defer the term of the passage of wool or stop the importation of wine when there was need.[5] The power which the council was granted in certain instances, was likely to be assumed on other occasions as well. It was even claimed to be a usual right of the council to examine and amend the acts of parliament after they were written.[6] With some inconsistency parliament raised strenuous objection to the action of the council in altering the statutes. The commons brought petitions that the law be not altered with-

[1] *Rot. Parl.* ii. 9.

[2] Ibid. 201.

[3] This is the special discovery of Miss Bertha Putnam in *The Enforcement of the Statutes of Labourers* (Columbia Studies, 1908), pp. 215 ff.

[4] *Rot. Parl.* ii. 241.

[5] *Statutes of the Realm*, i. 351, 384, &c.

[6] 'Salvo domino Regi et eius consilio quod ipsi huius modi ordinationes postquam scriptae fuerint examinare et emendare valeant.' *Modus tenendi Parliamentum*, p. 21.

out a new statute; that 'with good counsel the king ordain in accordance with the statutes'; that no article of a statute be repealed by the privy council; and that neither the chancellor nor the council after parliament is ended make any ordinance against the common law.[1] But as the king answered these petitions only with evasion, no settlement of the controversy was reached.

Suspending power of the council.

To what extent in practice acts of parliament were suspended or altered it is not easy to say, because not many concrete illustrations can be given. In 1337 there was an order by the king and council temporarily suspending the publication and enforcement of a statute passed in the ninth year giving freedom of trade to merchants, because, it was said, the enforcement would be to the prejudice of the liberties of the duke of Cornwall.[2] In 1380 there is the record of an ordinance allowing herring fishers to export money contrary to the statute.[3] A more frequent form of action on the part of the king and council was in individual cases to make grants with the *non obstante* clause, that is, 'notwithstanding any statute or former grant to the contrary'. While there was no settlement during the middle ages of the question how far the suspending power might go, it was complained of bitterly. 'Of what use are statutes made in parliament?' a chronicler of the time of Richard II exclaims. 'They have no effect. The king and his privy council habitually alter and efface what has previously been established in parliament, not merely by the commonalty, but even by the nobility.'[4]

Peculiar methods of the council.

It is pertinent now to ask, why was the exercise of a legislative power on the part of the council so strongly disliked? No doubt, as has already been suggested, the house of lords and the council at times represented divergent political interests. But a reason that lay deeper than any passing conflict was suggested by the commons in 1353, when they asked that certain articles be rehearsed at the next parliament, 'since the ordinances and agreements made in councils are not matters of record, as if they had

[1] *Rot. Parl.* ii. 203, 266, 287, 311, 318. [2] *Cal. Close Rolls*, 141.
[3] *Close Roll*, 3 Ric. II, m. 24. [4] *Walsingham* (Rolls Series), ii. 48.

been made by general parliament.'[1] Now, as a matter of fact, in the time of Edward I the rolls of parliament were extensively used for records of the council, and so long as this was done there is a difficulty in distinguishing between the two bodies. But later events caused these rolls to be used more exclusively for the purposes of parliament, while the council, under political pressure, was led to seek greater secrecy of operation. This end was attained by the extensive use of the privy seal, in the manner that has been described in a former chapter. Just as the council was thereby given a development which ultimately separated it from the court of chancery, so for the first time it found a method of action that clearly distinguishes it from the houses of parliament. For while parliament, together with all great councils similarly organized, was served by the older secretariat of the chancery, the king's council became identified with the rival department of the privy seal. As to the time of this far-reaching change, it is not possible to assign any particular date, but tendencies in this direction are visible in the reign of Edward II, and by the year 1353 when the above protest was made, the fact was clearly appreciated. In the vital matter of record, then, the difference between the two bodies was as wide as that of the two seals, especially as it was not the practice of the clerks of the privy seal to make enrolments. There was abundant reason, therefore, why all acts of the council, whether legislative or judicial, should be especially suspected and disliked, for without enrolment they were not subject to scrutiny and correction.

Parliamentary and conciliar jurisdiction.

But pure legislation, it has been remarked, fills a very small space in mediaeval history. No doubt the more important work of parliament as well as of the council lay in the field of jurisdiction, and it is here that the relations of the two bodies can best be studied. It will be remembered that parliament is often mentioned as a court and judicial action as one of its principal objects, but never in the middle ages was it regarded as primarily a legislature. It is not strange to find a Frenchman at that time speaking of the parliament of England and the *parlement* of Paris as similar

[1] *Rot. Parl.* ii. 253.

institutions.[1] This jurisdiction was exercised not so much by hearing cases as in dealing with the petitions which were brought to parliament as well as to the council in vast numbers. It was by affording remedy in these individual cases, in fact, that the necessity of general legislation was mainly avoided. As to the petitions which should be considered in parliament, and those which might be treated apart by the council, there was no reason for making any distinction at first. Most of them indeed were brought to parliament, because these sessions were the more public and better known. At one of the parliaments of Edward I nearly five hundred petitions of all kinds may be counted.[2] In the face of a manifest danger that the business of the realm might be submerged by a flood of private interests, special arrangements were made for dealing with the petitions. These arrangements began in a tentative way. In the eighth year of Edward I it was ordered that petitions should be considered, in the first instance, by the officers of the departments to which they belonged, and not brought to the king and council unless they related to matters of importance.[3] There are petitions which are found to have been answered in this manner by the treasurer and by the justices. But the plan apparently did not work well, perhaps because it was often uncertain to which department the matter properly belonged. It was also ordained that no petition should come to the king and council but by the hands of the chancellor or other minister. In the twenty-third year another plan was tried, when it was proposed to appoint certain men known as 'receivers', who were to examine and separate into files the petitions, which were then to be delivered to the chancery and the other departments.[4] How the

Treatment of petitions, especially in parliament.

[1] A certain petitioner, Pierre de Saint Pol, states that he has sued for four years 'a touz les parlementz Dengleterre et de France'. *Ancient Petitions*, no. 14432.

[2] *Memoranda de Parliamento* (Rolls Series), *passim*.

[3] *Cal. Close Rolls*, 8 Edw. I, 56.

[4] 'Those (petitions) that concern the chancery shall be put on a file by themselves, and the others that concern the exchequer in another file; and those that concern the justices shall be treated in like manner. And afterwards those that shall be before the king and his council shall be kept separately on another file.' Ibid., 21 Edw. I, 289.

petitions reserved for the king and council were treated, we are not specifically informed, but from every analogy we infer that petitions involving points of law were then especially considered by the judicial members of the council, and the magnates were consulted only as there were questions of exceptional importance. Even then the work was burdensome, so that for the relief of parliament still another change was made. In 1305 certain committees known as 'hearers' of petitions were appointed; one group 'to receive and answer' all petitions from Gascony that could be answered without the king, a second group for petitions from Ireland, and a third for Scotland.[1] For petitions of England no hearers were expressly named. A time for presenting petitions too was set, and a proclamation to this effect was cried through the halls.

Receivers and hearers of petitions.

During a period of ten years nothing further is said of the appointment of these committees. Apparently the work of hearing petitions suffered considerably, for a desire expressed in the ordinances of 1311 was that 'the bills shall be finished which are delivered in parliament'.[2] For the same reason, no doubt, it was proposed that a parliament should be held at least once a year. Another provision of the Lords Ordainers, manifestly intended to thwart the king's council, was that a special committee consisting of one bishop, two earls, and two barons should be assigned in every parliament to hear and determine complaints against the king's ministers. Of this particular plan nothing further is heard, but in 1316 the former system of committees was revived and extended.[3] First, there were certain groups of 'receivers', generally clerks of the chancery, who were to do no more than receive and classify the bills. Then there were three groups of 'hearers', one 'to hear and determine' the petitions coming from England, a second group for Gascony and the Channel Islands, and a third for Wales, Ireland, and Scotland. Henceforth there were both receivers and hearers of petitions regularly appointed at the opening of every parliament, while the number of these groups was increased to five or six.

[1] *Mem. de Parl.*, pp. lvii ff.
[2] *Statutes of the Realm*, i. 165.
[3] *Rot. Parl.* i. 350.

Just as was done in matters of legislation, it was plainly the intention of parliament to supersede the council in this work. The hearers were different from the council in that they were for the most part bishops and barons, with only a few of the judges and officers to aid them. It was a mark of distinction among the lords to be named in this way. They must perform their duties too during the session of parliament, when, to a certain degree, they were subject to control. On one occasion they are described as working through Saturday, Sunday, and Monday, in order to answer and return a given instalment of petitions.[1] Cases which were deemed of sufficient importance they brought before the house of lords, although there were no rules to guide them in this regard. For the most part the answers which they gave were considered to be the answers of parliament, and required no further confirmation. Having no authority after the close of parliament, the hearers did not by any means prevent the council being incessantly occupied with petitions at other times. Indeed, there was not yet sufficient reason to distinguish between parliamentary and conciliar petitions, the chief concern still being to deal with the quantity.

For a limited period the system thus inaugurated worked well, in that petitions were generally heard, were not often delayed for an answer, and in most cases are found to have been endorsed. People were encouraged to present their claims and grievances even more freely. It was promised that any man aggrieved by the king or his officers might have remedy in this wise.[2] It was also promised that sheriffs and other persons might recover by petition in parliament, if the exchequer refused to allow their acquittances.[3] The petitions, or 'bills' as they were also called, came from the commons, from separate counties and towns, from the province of Gascony, as well as from private individuals.[4] It is to be noted that there was no discrimination between public bills and private bills, although, as a matter of

[1] *Rot. Parl.* ii. 160. [2] Ibid., 127. [3] Ibid., 284, 289.

[4] Probably the best summary description of these bills was given by Sir F. Palgrave, in the *Report of Select Committee on Public Petitions* (Parliamentary Papers, 1833, vol. xii), pp. 19–24.

legislative history, probably ninety-nine per cent of the bills were of individual or local interest. In the reign of Edward III the distinction was made between petitions of grace and petitions of right—*de chescun droit*. By far the greater number were petitions of grace, which were simply requests for favour. These were properly addressed to the king in the first place, as it was one of the rules best understood that matters of grace must be referred to the crown. In regard to bills of this kind there is no special problem, since they were either to be granted or refused. Petitions of right, on the other hand, were based upon claims of law or justice, and so required judicial or quasi-judicial action. Most of these were easily determined with the necessary mandate stating which writ or which court was to be sought. Cases involving greater legal difficulty might be referred to the lords with the words, *coram magno consilio*. Some petitions, in fact, are found to have been answered by the hearers, but the answers were afterwards amended by the lords. There was no certainty, however, that every case of this kind would be referred to the lords, and here lay a difficulty.

Difficulties in parliament.

In the reign of Edward III it was realized that by the accumulations of petitions and answers the common law might be seriously affected. On more than one occasion the commons prayed that the law of the land be not superseded or altered on the petition of any private person, and they further expressed the desire that such petitions be especially considered by the lords. Anything 'touching the law of the land', they said, could be finally discussed only in parliament. The effect was to reduce the power committed to the hearers or 'triers', as they were also called, who from the twenty-eighth year of Edward III, so nearly as one can observe, were given authority 'to hear' but not 'to determine' the petitions, and so were constrained to return all petitions of law to the house of lords.[1] The petitions in question are understood to have formed a small class in

[1] Sir Matthew Hale at this point has sought to make a distinction between the 'auditors' or hearers preceding this date and the 'triers' subsequent to it (op. cit., p. 76). The words, however, continued to be used interchangeably, while another alternative term was that of 'examiners'

point of numbers, but one requiring the most careful attention. This step gave rise to a new problem which affected the procedure of parliament very seriously, and in particular caused the rivalry of parliament and the council to appear in a new light. With the utmost effort it was manifestly impossible for the lords to deal with the stream of public and private bills which came before them. Other demands, too, were made upon their time, as when the king requested them to suspend the treatment of petitions and other private business, in order to consider 'the perils and damages of the realm'.[1] The result was that scores of petitions, both public and private, 'from the brevity of time', as was said, went unanswered and were left over from parliament to parliament. This condition became a chronic matter of grievance which was voiced by all concerned. The commons repeatedly urged that pending petitions should be heard and answered by the lords 'before the departure of parliament'.[2] Individual petitioners expressed themselves even more emphatically. One was delayed, he said, 'by the high business of the king', another had made continual suit 'in the last three parliaments'; another had pursued 'from parliament to parliament' in the time of the late king Richard II as well as under Henry IV.[3] The same grievance is mutely shown in a far greater number of petitions, which contain no endorsements or other marks to indicate that they were ever heard.

Jealousy of the council.

The lords, there is reason to assert, made manful efforts to deal with the petitions, that they might hold a jurisdiction, the importance of which was fully realized. But the task was an impossible one without special means of assistance. It might be expected that the council was the body best fitted to take up the unfinished business of parliament, but for reasons already given there was a deeply-rooted objection to any increase of the powers of the council. For the treatment of petitions in parliament, then, other agencies were

[1] *Rot. Parl.* ii. 316.

[2] Ibid. 272; again, 'les ditz Communes priont, qe les Petitions de Chescung Droit dont remedie ne peot estre suy en nul autere Court mes en Parlement, q'elles soient ore en ceste present Parlement acceptez.' Ibid. 318.

[3] *Ancient Petitions*, nos. 9994, 6056, 6057, 1074, 1099, 14432.

first tried. In 1351 a special committee was appointed to examine and answer all petitions presented by the archbishop of Canterbury in the last parliament.[1] Again, in 1371 a proposal of the commons met with acceptance, that in view of the large number of petitions, both public and private, which were then before the parliament, certain lords should be appointed to hear and conclude them. With a significant allusion to the council it was urged that ‘ right could better be done in parliament than elsewhere ’.[2] This plan was tried again, although in the seventh year of Richard II it was allowed that petitions which could be treated by the king's council, apart from parliament, should be given to the council.[3] In the eleventh year of the same reign, it was declared both by the lords and by the commons, that there were many special bills pending which, ‘ on account of the brevity of the time ’, could not be endorsed or answered before their departure, and they asked that certain lords be assigned for this work not only in the present parliament but in all future parliaments.[4] There was reluctance, however, to allow even these committees to become a regular feature. These later committees, it may be explained, did not supersede the hearers or ‘ triers ’; they differed from the triers in that instead of treating the petitions at the beginning of parliament they took only those left over at the close. It was all a useless complication of business arising from the efforts of the lords to keep the authority in their own hands. Rather than commit the work to the council, or any other single body, they resorted to an indefinite number of committees. How this procedure could be turned against them was shown by Richard II, when he caused his last parliament in 1398 virtually to resign its powers by the appointment of a committee of lords to answer all petitions at their discretion.[5] But everything that was done by these lords in the way of statutes, ordinances, and judgements, was annulled after the revolution, and it was further declared that no such commissions should be granted in the future.[6] After

[1] *Cal. Patent Rolls,* 25 Edw. III, 133.
[2] *Rot. Parl.* ii. 304.
[3] Ibid. iii. 163.
[4] Ibid. 256.
[5] Ibid. 368.
[6] Ibid. 425.

a few more experiments which were plainly ineffective in meeting the problem, parliament at last did the inevitable thing in turning over its unanswered petitions to the council.[1] Without any rule being made, this was repeatedly done under Henry VI, when, as has been previously indicated, the relations of the two bodies were most harmonious. With some caution it was stipulated that the council should act with the advice of the justices, that it should give the answers within a limited time, and that it should cause the bills to be recorded upon the rolls of parliament.[2] How the council likewise was overburdened and in turn committed its unanswered petitions to the chancery, is still another matter.[3]

Aspect of the individual petitions.

All these difficulties and strifes of parliamentary history are reflected still more acutely in the petitions themselves. Not only do suitors complain of their failure to be heard, but in order to gain attention they strive to express themselves more cogently and persuasively. They prove even to be ingenious in finding new forms of expression and procedure. Under these conditions it is plain that the average suitor was not concerned with the rivalry of parliament and the council in their spheres of authority. His interest was the immediate one, how best to obtain a hearing for his petition and a remedy for his grievance. Between several alternatives he was even ready to take chances, and would learn by experience. It will be in historical order, therefore, first to consider certain questions of procedure as they affected the individual suitor, and then to observe the division of jurisdiction which was the result.

How to address a petition.

In the first place, should the petitioner address his bill to the king, to the council, to the chancellor, or to the parliament? In earlier days the form of address made very little difference, for petitions were then readily transmitted from one authority to another, and in fact generally found an answer. Petitions might still be transferred from the parliament to the council, and from the council to the chancery, but in later days there was danger of their being delayed or ignored. The petitioner, therefore, was constrained to direct his bill to the authority most likely to consider or

[1] *Rot. Parl.* iv. 174, 285, 301, 334, 506. [2] Ibid. 334. [3] *Ante*, p. 284.

promote it. He might even draw up more than one petition making address to different authorities, so that if he failed with one, he might succeed with the other. As a result there sprang up a great variety and elaboration in the part of the petition making the address, which was more than a mere form as it involved also a question of procedure. The earlier petitions begin with the words 'au roi', 'au conseil du roy', 'au conseil du parlement', 'au conseil en cest present parlement', or others in similar style. Except for an occasional expletive, like 'good' or 'wise' in speaking of the council, they were without elaboration. In the later years of Edward III a new form appears which distinguishes more clearly the lords of parliament from the council—'a notre Seigneur le Roy et touz les Prelatz et autres grantz du parlement'.[1] This address to the lords, however, was infrequent before the reign of Richard II, when it is expressed with more unction, 'a notre tresexcellent et tresgracious seigneur le roi et autres seigneurs de son gracious parlement.'[2] In keeping with this tendency the words of the address were given greater prominence by being set apart from the body of the petition in the upper margin of the bill.

Experimental forms.

At the same time various irregular forms appear, which reveal at once the anxiety and uncertainty of petitioners as to the course they should take. Some made address to the council *and* the lords of parliament.[3] One man, in his endeavour to make sure, includes the king, the council, and the lords—'a notre tresredoute Seigneur le Roi et son tressage conseil et touz autres Prelatz et Seigneurs de cest Parlement'.[4] Some named also the commons, and thus raised a question in the relations of the two houses. One man writes, 'a notre tresexcellent et tresgracious Seigneur notre Seigneur le Roi et son tressage conseil et les tresnobles seigneurs et les communes de cest parlement';[5] another, 'a notre seigneur le Roi son tressage conseille et as chevaliers des countees pur les communies Dengleterre.'[6] It seems as though every

[1] *Ancient Petitions*, no. 6830.
[2] Ibid., no. 5323, &c.
[3] Ibid., no. 2242; also *Record Transcripts*, series i, vol. 106.
[4] *Ancient Petitions*, no. 6666.
[5] Ibid., no. 5419.
[6] Ibid., no. 6870.

possible alternative of the kind was tried, until after a period of transition certain forms of procedure became settled.

There was a marked inclination also to send petitions to the commons alone. One is strangely worded, 'as chivalers, citesynes, burgeis, et communes des contees';[1] but most were, 'as tressages communes en ceste presente parlement.' Although some precedent can be found for their participation in judicial proceedings,[2] the commons were not ambitious to claim the responsibility of answering petitions, which they passed to the lords with the words 'soit parle as Seigneurs'. Under Henry IV the tendency to treat the commons as a court, or even an integral part of the court, was checked by the resolution that the commons were to be regarded as petitioners but not as judges in parliament.[3] It became increasingly frequent, nevertheless, for suitors to address their petitions to the commons for the sake of their mediation, as a means of approach to the lords and the king. 'Please your very wise discretion to offer this bill to the king,' says one.[4] As a result it was made a regular procedure for the commons, together with their own bills, to present to the lords also a great many private bills. While other methods of action were still maintained, for petitions in parliament this was the course that was found in the long run to be most practicable.

Address to individual lords.

The same need of mediation caused petitioners to seek other avenues of approach both to the house of lords and the council. It was primarily for this reason, as has been shown, that bills were delivered 'to the chancellor and council', and 'to the chancellor'. It is of interest to find, as one of the experiments of the time, that address was likewise made to the chancellor and the lords of parliament, thus: 'a chanceller notre Seigneur le Roi et as autres Seigneurs de parlement monstre une povre veue Elyn Broustre.'[5] In view

[1] *Ancient Petitions*, no. 896; *Rot. Parl.* iii. 50.

[2] On one occasion a judgement was rendered 'coram nobis et magnatibus et communitate eiusdem regni in eodem parliamento'. *Close Roll*, 39 Edw. III, m. 27. Another action is described with the words, 'par quoi notre Seigneur le Roi, et les ditz Prelatz, Prince, et Ducs, Countes, et Barons, par acord des Chivalers des Countees, et des dites Communes . . . ajuggent les Record et Jugement susditz.' *Rot. Parl.* ii. 256.

[3] *Rot. Parl.* iii. 427.

[4] *Ancient Petitions*, no. 5034.

[5] Ibid., no. 4667.

of the close association of the chancellor with parliament, it seems not fanciful to say that, if this tendency had been carried further, the jurisdiction of the chancery might have sprung from the house of lords instead of the council. In the same light are to be regarded various petitions to individual lords and councillors. For example, in the time of the ascendancy of John of Gaunt, one suitor makes address:

'A tresreverent et treshonourable Seigneur le Roi de Chastill et Duc de Lancaster et a tressage conseil notre Seigneur le Roi;'[1]

while another begins:

'A tresnoble et puissant Seigneur le Roi de Chastille et de Leon et autres Seigneurs de parlement.'[2]

In a petition to Humphrey, Duke of Gloucester, a man asks to have his enemy brought either before the council or the parliament, in the following words:

'... Please to your high Princeshod to do the seid Baron apperyn outher before the hye Pryncehodes of my lord your brother and youres ꝛ your sage Conseile outher in pleyn parlement to answer to thesu poyntes.'[3]

Another petition to the duke of Gloucester and lords of parliament, 7 Hen. V, is committed to the council with the endorsement:

'Soit ceste petition mande au counseil du Roy et y les Seigneurs de mesme le counseil pur le temps esteantz eient poer par auctorite de ceste parlement ... examiner ꝛ terminer mesmes les maters ꝛ ordoner ꝛ mettre tiele remedie as ditz suppliantz cestes partis come semblera as ditz Seigneurs le plus covenable en le cas.'[4]

Further elaborations in the petitions.

The struggle of a century had still other effects in the form and character of petitions, as they came to be prepared with greater care. At the time of Edward I they were characteristically brief and succinct, covering generally less than a dozen lines of manuscript, stating the complaint in simplest terms, and asking vaguely for 'remedy and aid'. Except the services of a professional scribe, no legal assistance

[1] Ibid., nos. 10406, 12595, 12596, &c.
[2] Ibid., nos. 7269, 7347.
[3] Ibid., nos. 6703, 5825, 15297.
[4] Ibid., no. E. 978.

apparently was required. The early petitions show many mistakes and were especially prone to indefiniteness of statement. One petitioner, for instance, mentions 'the archbishop', and in the response is asked which archbishop is meant:[1] another, complaining that a manor has been taken from him into the king's hand, is answered with patience that he should tell who holds the manor now.[2] It was the experience of others, however, that if they were not sufficiently explicit, their petitions would very probably be ignored.[3] With the more technical forms of address and other questions of procedure it was more necessary for suitors to secure legal advice. One petitioner who failed with his bill afterwards acknowledged that its defects were due to his lack of counsel.[4] For services of this kind the king's serjeants-at-law stood ready to be employed. Under the more lawyer-like influences of Richard II's time embellishments of style were added, as in the high-sounding adjectives of the passages already quoted, 'sage', 'excellent', 'gracious', 'honourable', 'puissant', 'redoubtable'. The statement of grievance, which constitutes the body of the bill, is made with the particularity and tautology of a legal document. In cases of maintenance, for instance, the bands of armed men, the weapons, assaults, riots, intimidation, bribery, and other acts of violence are set forth with far more vividness than is found in any of the literary productions of the time. Their excess of detail has been taken to indicate the greater historical accuracy. It must be admitted, however, that in the difficulties of obtaining a hearing, plaintiffs were tempted to exaggerations, and in some cases were proved to have done this for effect.[5] The petition concluded with the prayer for 'remedy and aid'. This part also was found to be more effective if it specified the remedy desired, whether it were a writ to a court, a commission of inquiry, or of *oyer et terminer*, a *subpoena*, or a hearing before the lords or the council. The petitioner also recommended him-

[1] Roger Damory, *Record Transcripts*, series i, vol. 97.
[2] *Ancient Petitions*, no. 4732; also nos. 5786, 6622.
[3] *Rot. Parl.* ii. 41.
[4] *Ancient Petitions*, nos. 7259, 7260.
[5] For instance, the case of Lord Fanhope, *ante*, p. 299.

self by his poverty, humility, and loyalty, although this was sometimes a fiction, and urged relief 'for God', 'pity', and 'work of charity'. In petitions to the chancellor it was added, 'the suppliant shall not cease to pray for your soul.' As a practical charity, the poorest suitor was allowed legal advice without fees.[1]

Costs of litigation.

All these elaborations appearing in the later petitions were obviously obtained only at greater cost. While it was understood that procedure by bill was more expeditious and cheaper than the corresponding processes of the courts, this was true, of course, only when the petitions were successful. With the delay of their cases suitors had an added grievance of expense, which they frequently mention. What their expenses were, however, we should not know but for a single instance under the Lancastrians, when, for some reason, very likely as a basis of litigation, a memorandum was made of the 'costage and expens for to sywe to the King and the counseyll'.[2] Among the items there were three successive bills costing 'for the making', respectively, 6*s*. 8*d*., 3*s*. 4*d*., and 6*s*. 8*d*.; there were several letters of the privy seal and copies at 3*s*. 4*d*., and other sums; there was an equal number of fees to the king's secretary, probably for warrants, 'for a letter of ye privy seal'; a fee also 'to a squyer of my lord pryvy seall for to help yat yit mygth be seled'; fees to the secretary of the chamberlain and to the chancellor's registrar; 'wyne to squyers and other genthilmen at dyverse tymys'; fish for the lord chancellor, and lampreys for some one else; besides sums 'for rydyng and costage to London and for his labour ꝛ his horse'. In the face of an indefinite number of fees, it is not strange that suitors pleaded poverty and asked for charity.

Tendency to a division of jurisdiction.

Having made these explanations as to form and procedure, it is now possible to consider the subject-matter of the petitions, with reference to the division of jurisdiction. What cases, in other words, was the suitor bound to bring to parliament, and what ones might he take to the council? In the

[1] Nicolas, iii. 150; iv. 63.

[2] This is as yet an unfiled document, which for the present I can only refer to as a Bill of Costs, *Miscellanea* (*Chancery*); Appendix III, p. 533.

reign of Edward II there were declared to be cases which could not be determined outside of parliament, and again under Edward III there were petitions which could be answered only in parliament, and rights which could be sued in no other court.[1] In the seventh year of Richard II a further distinction was made between the petitions which could be treated only in parliament and those which could be treated in the king's council.[2] But which were petitions for parliament, and which for the council, there was still room to question. The clearest line of distinction is found in the jealousy frequently expressed in parliament concerning the integrity of the law of the land. From the time that the council became known for its summary writs and inquisitorial examinations, the efforts of parliament were directed to a defence of the common law against the extra-legal procedure of the council. The various resolutions and restrictive statutes that were intended to warn the council off the field of the common law, especially as regards freeholds and suits, need not be repeated. The practical difference that was felt to exist between the house of lords and the council will be seen in a number of concrete cases which will now be described.

Cases of appeal on error.

A question which had to be settled was as regards jurisdiction in error, whether final appeals on such cases should be taken to the council or to the house of lords. It is well known in legal history that the right of one court to review and reverse the judgements of another had been a matter of serious contest, which resulted in the king's bench gaining the right to hear appeals from the court of common pleas. Whether the next appeal should be to the council or the house

[1] *Rot. Parl.* i. 350; ii. 254, 318.

[2] Ibid. iii. 163. There is a current opinion that by this resolution the separation of parliament and the council was fully accomplished (see Palgrave, *Original Authority*, p. 79). The point is an important one, but it should not be exaggerated to this extent. The differentiation of the two bodies was a gradual process and this was only one step. Even in the time of Richard II it was not fully accomplished. We find cases, for instance, that were heard at different stages alternately before the house of lords and the council without change of venue, just as in the very early days. That this might be a matter of purely casual convenience is shown in a case, 10 Ric. II, which was ordered to come before the council in chancery on a certain day 'nisi parliamentum interim fuerit'. *Ancient Petitions*, no. 10590.

of lords was the question. There was a conflict of precedents arising from the fact that these two bodies of authority were not clearly distinguished. There is no doubt that in earlier days it had been given to the king's council to hear appeals on error from the court of common pleas and other minor courts.[1] In the fourth year of Edward II, for example, the king commanded that a petition alleging such an error be examined by the chancellor, the treasurer, the justices, the barons of the exchequer, the clerks of the chancery, and others of the council.[2] Whether the same could be proved with regard to the more formidable king's bench is more doubtful.[3] A number of cases of the kind are on record as being heard 'before the council', but as they are found in the roll of parliament, they do not clearly favour the authority of the council.[4] Moreover, it was strongly insisted that such cases should be heard only in parliament. In the twenty-second year of Edward III a certain committee appointed for the purpose of reviewing a case declared itself unable to proceed after parliament had ended.[5] A critical and decisive case was heard in the thirty-ninth year of the same reign, when on writ of error, the record of a case pending before the court of common pleas was ordered to be removed and taken before the council. The judgement of the former court was reversed 'by the chancellor before the council'. 'But the justices', it is said, 'paid no regard to the reversal before the council for the reason that it was not the place where judgement could be reversed.'[6] The council was regarded as not the proper place, because it was not a court of common law, and all the courts were ready to resist any such subjugation to the utmost. Parliament, on the other hand, was a court of record, which might review its own

[1] An appeal from a forest court is found in *Ancient Correspondence*, vol. xxv, no. 45; one from the marshal's court in *Ancient Petitions*, no. 2777.

[2] *Ancient Correspondence*, vol. xlv, no. 163; also 36.

[3] To a certain point, as we have shown, the council was affiliated with the king's bench. A good example of a case which was removed on appeal of error from the common bench at Dublin, and heard *coram rege et eius consilio*, is found in *Coram Rege Roll*, Mich., 17 Edw. I, m. 37.

[4] *Rot. Parl.* i. 20, 41, 132, 337.

[5] *Year Books*, 22 Edw. III, f. 3.

[6] *Year Books*, 39 Edw. III (ed. Tottill, 1585), f. 14; (ed. Redman, 1533), f. 18.

judgements on appeal of error. As Mr. Pike in dealing with this subject in another connexion has said, 'it was indeed a strange anomaly that although the aid of the King and Council might have been asked and obtained again and again before judgement was given, in the Court below, yet if error was alleged after judgement . . . the Jurisdiction in error was, in the reign of Edward III, as in later times, in the Court of King's Bench,' [1] and, it should be added, in the house of lords. But the reason for the anomaly is plain ; a judicial opinion or word of advice need not be a matter of record, but a final judgement it was thought should only be made by a court of record. There were no further efforts on the part of the council to exercise this kind of authority over the great courts of common law.[2] But there remained a certain appellate jurisdiction over the courts outside the common law. On one occasion the correction of a purely verbal error in a record of the chancery was determined before the council.[3] In 1393, on complaint of error, a record of the king's court in South Wales was ordered to be brought before the council, that the errors might be examined and justice be done according to the laws and customs of the lordship of Wales.[4] The council also received appeals with considerable frequency from the court of the constable and marshal. The ground here was not error, but the curious one of exception to the jurisdiction of a court irregularly organized.[5] The council usually gave these cases to commissions of *oyer et terminer*.

[1] *Year Books*, 12–13 Edw. III (Rolls Series), p. c.

[2] It was still possible for the council, as well as the house of lords, to receive a case and proceed to a judgement *de novo*, even though the matter had been already decided by a court of law. In the reign of Henry IV this was one of the complaints of the commons, who asked that no judgement in this wise should be annulled unless it were by regular process of error. To this demand the king gave his assent. *Rot. Parl.* iii. 510.

[3] *Cal. Close Rolls*, 45 Edw. III, 322.

[4] *Cal. Patent Rolls*, 17 Ric. II, 359.

[5] L. W. V. Harcourt, *His Grace the Steward and Trial by Peers* (London, 1907), chap. xi. According to the statute, 13 Ric. II, c. 2, 'if any one complain that a plea (pending in the court of chivalry) might be tried by common law, the plaintiff shall without difficulty have a writ of the privy seal directed to the constable and marshal to surcease in that plea, until it be discussed by the king's council whether the matter ought to be tried in that court or otherwise by common law.'

Appellate jurisdiction of the lords.

It may next be asked, how did the lords succeed in exercising the appellate jurisdiction which they thus wrested from the council? Not without difficulty, surely, for the house of lords was already overburdened with business, and it was in no way organized for hearing a large number of cases. As appeals on error were freely brought to it before the close of the fourteenth century, there was evidently need of a delegation of this function as well as of others. One petitioner under Edward III, alleging errors in a process of the common pleas which had been confirmed by the king's bench, makes the following suggestion: 'may it please the king to have the said record and process come before the hearers assigned in parliament, since elsewhere than in parliament redress cannot duly be made.'[1] There was no inclination, however, to give such authority to the hearers, and the case was ordered to be brought before parliament. Other suitors suggested that their cases might be committed to the chancellor, and as all things at this time were favourable to the chancery, this was repeatedly done. In the seventh year of Richard II a petition alleging error in the king's bench was answered in the following manner:

'. . . pur ce qe les seigneurs du parlement pur la grande occupacion qils ont entour les [busoignes] du roialme ne pourront au present pur briefte de temps . . . discusser la matire deinz ceste peticioun . . . ensement en consideracion a la poverte des suppliantz accorde estoit [par le] parlement qe les record et processe, dont ceste peticion fait mencion, et toutes les eux tochantz soient faitz venir en la chancellerie et illeqes,' etc.[2]

In these cases the lords were careful to maintain that the chancellor himself had no such jurisdiction, but in each instance acted only 'by authority of parliament'. The chancellor's court would then necessarily follow the common law. These facts may afford sufficient explanation of a circumstance which has been widely observed, that the house of lords, having once grasped this jurisdiction, let

[1] *Ancient Petitions*, no. 12273.

[2] The membrane is badly damaged so that I cannot be sure of all the words. Ibid., no. 6590.

it fall in the fifteenth century. Between Henry V and James I, indeed, hardly any cases of the kind are known.[1] There is an instance under Henry VI of a petition alleging error in the king's bench of Ireland, whereupon the case was ordered to be brought to the parliament of England,[2] but whether it ever was heard there does not appear.

Cases of violence.

Another class of cases, which concerned both the parliament and the council, is found in their criminal jurisdiction. It is well known that the crimes of great violence, such as are familiarly associated with the practices of livery and maintenance, 'riot cases' they were particularly called, were the greatest trouble of the time. There is a prevailing opinion that cases of this kind belonged peculiarly to the council. A survey, however, of the petitions from Richard II to Henry VI indicates that persons suffering from these oppressions addressed their complaints to the lords in parliament as frequently as they did to the council or the chancellor. Sometimes a complainant, in his anxiety for relief, would apparently offer more than one petition at the same time, so that if he failed before one body, he might then turn to the other.[3] Between the parliament and the council, therefore, the difference lay not in the nature of the cases, but in the way they were treated. It was for just such cases, indeed, that the council made its first departures from the common law, in the writs of summons, in swearing defendants and subjecting them to examination. These methods were not 'due process of law', but they were very effective. The house of lords, on the other hand, while it was not a court of restricted powers, was consistently allied with the common law. One cannot rely, it is true, upon consistency in a political body, but the cases prove that this was so. The petitions to the lords were answered with the old standing remedies of common law, such as writs to the courts and commissions of *oyer et terminer*, while a limited number of cases were brought to the lords themselves. Only in

[1] Maitland, *Constitutional History* (Cambridge, 1908), p. 215.

[2] Petition of the Prior of Llanthony, *Rot. Parl.* iv. 361.

[3] William Laken, it is said, came to London to prosecute his enemies both in parliament and before the council. *Calendar of Patent Rolls*, 22 Ric. II, 427.

exceptional instances does it appear that the lords in their own procedure resorted to the extra-legal practices of the council and the chancery. Several times, it is true, under the stress of a political prosecution they are known to have subjected men to the inquisitorial examination,[1] and not infrequently did they use or warrant the use of the *subpoena*.[2] In such cases the writ then would read, 'Quibusdam certis de causis coram nobis et consilio in presenti parliamento,' etc. On one occasion a writ of summons to the council in parliament was so far modified as to give complete information of the cause with the words, 'Tenorem cuiusdam peticionis coram nobis et consilio nostro in presenti parliamento nostro . . . vobis mittimus presentibus interclusum,' and ending with a penal clause, 'et hoc sub pena ducentarum librarum nullatenus omittatis.'[3] But if extraordinary remedies were required, the more usual method was for the lords to commit the case to the council, or they would warrant a *subpoena* to bring the parties before the council. This was done in countless individual instances rather than according to any general rule, for there was always a certain distrust of the special procedure of the council. Yet more and more was parliament compelled to recognize the necessity for it. It was admitted that there were cases 'against such high personages that right could not be done elsewhere', and, as again expressed, when 'there be too much might on the one side and too much unmight on the other'. In the first parliament of Henry VI it is mentioned that an entire file of 'riot bills' was turned over to the council for consideration.[4] A few years later, under stress of a widespread rebellion, we have said that the act 31 Hen. VI even sanctioned the writs of *subpoena* for cases of this kind. In this field, therefore, the council in star

[1] Certain associates of Ralph Ferrers in 1380, it is said, 'furent par celle cause faitz venir en Parlement, et illoeqes examinez diligeaument et singulerement de la matire . . . par les Justices notre Seigneur le Roy et autres sages a ceo assignez.' *Rot. Parl.* iii. 93. Something of the kind was done during the trial of the 'false councillors' in 1388. Ibid. 238.

[2] In 1402 the commons complained of the manner in which parties were made to come *sur grief peyne* before the king, or the council, or the parliament. Ibid. 510.

[3] Ibid. 259.

[4] *Early Chancery Proceedings*, bundle 5, no. 41.

chamber was entirely successful in its competition with parliament.

Appeals to the lords from the council.

There were cases also in which appeal was made to parliament, as to a higher court, on the ground of the incompetence or abuses of the council. From its summary methods the council, in fact, was peculiarly liable to abuse. According to allegations, it was open to 'false suggestions', especially as it proceeded upon secret information;[1] subpoenas were purchased, it was said, for personal revenge;[2] there were postponements and delays, for like parliament the council was harassed with a variety of work and kept its litigation in suspense;[3] excessive bonds were required, or in lack of bonds men were thrown into prison, even though they had not been convicted.[4] The procedure, too, of the council was of doubtful validity, and on this pretext it might be successfully resisted. An illustration of the latter difficulty is given in 1402, when the house of lords in a case of violence showed itself to be more effective than the council. The abbot of Newnham complained of the oppression of Sir Philip Courtenay, who with a band of sixty men had made a forcible entry upon his estate, assaulting the abbot, dispossessing him, and detaining him in prison. The plaintiff had first sued before the council, by whom a writ of *subpoena* at 1,000 marks had been sent to the aforesaid knight. But Sir Philip, who was said to be a powerful man in the maintenance of the earl of Devon, refused to obey the *subpoena*, and continued his attacks upon the abbot. The plaintiff then resorted to a petition in parliament, which was first passed by the commons and then read before the lords. Sir Philip showed no hesitation in coming before the lords, who after a hearing sentenced him to be imprisoned during the pleasure of the crown.[5] It is rare, indeed, at this time to find an instance in which a powerful man was actually punished either by the council or by the lords in parliament. By the statute, 25 Edw. III, the council was not allowed to determine questions of freehold, but as freeholds were commonly

[1] *Rot. Parl.* ii. 280, 282; iii. 323.
[2] Ibid. ii. 260.
[3] Nicolas, ii. 321; iii. 36.
[4] *Rot. Parl.* iv. 84.
[5] *Rot. Parl.* iii. 489.

involved in the cases of violence, this line was easily crossed. In one instance a man tells how he was prevented by his enemy from entering upon a tenement, which he claimed in accordance with a judgement of the court of common pleas. He then appealed to the council, which likewise gave a judgement in his favour, but his opponent would not obey the order of the council because it related to a free tenement.[1] The plaintiff then addressed a petition to the king, lords, and commons in parliament, but how well he succeeded in this course does not appear. The council was also by law restrained from receiving suits, and on this ground in the reign of Henry V the countess of Kent addressed a petition to the commons, which in turn was delivered to the lords, that on a bill of false suggestion she was being sued for debt before the council as by common law.[2] Under Henry VI a Londoner complained that he and other good men, having been falsely impeached before the council, had been arrested and put into great danger. Although the council had entirely excused and acquitted them, and had sentenced the false accuser to be put in the pillory for three days and to be sent to prison, yet for certain causes the sentence was put to respite by the council. The complainant prayed the lords to command the execution of the sentence or else to impose a different punishment as a warning to others.[3] In the fifteenth year of Henry VI the abbot of Buckfast in a contest with an enemy, who had invaded his land after the manner of the times with a band of armed men, presented a petition to the commons. His complaint is worth quoting, as it shows more clearly than anything else the clash of the council with the common law.

'. . . for whiche trespasse the same besecher hath suid accions yn the kyngis court at communie lawe ayen dyvers of the said misdoers, by cause of which accione the same mysdoers have suid divers billis to the Kyng oure sovereyn Lord and to the Lordis of his counceile comprehendyng oonely matere determynable by the communie [lawe] . . : where uppon the said besecher hath be send fore by letters under the Kyngis privy seal ⁊ writtis *sub pena* and made to

[1] *Ancient Petitions*, no. 5730.
[2] *Rot. Parl.* iv. 143.
[3] *Ancient Petitions*, no. 4397.

appere before the Kyngis counceile and thanne ajournyd froe day to day to appere before the Kyngis counceile and thanne ajourned froe day to day to appere before the same counceile and so holden ⁊ kepte here the more partie of al this ii yere and yit is here ovne dismysid or dischargid froe the said counseile, ayen the communie lawe of this land ⁊ the goode statutis yn the like case purveiid to his importable cost and ynpoverysshing of his hous,'[1] &c.

The petition was ordered to be delivered to the lords—'soit baille as Seigneurs'—but whether any relief was afforded in this case or in similar ones is nowhere apparent. It is particularly to be noticed that while the council pretended to be the defender of the poor and the weak against the strong, in plenty of instances it appears rather to be acting in the interests of the strong in oppression of the weak.

Failure of the petitions in parliament.

In the later years of Henry VI the evidence is more and more overwhelming that there were far too many petitions both in parliament and the council, and that most of them failed in their purpose. Either they were not heard at all or they were suspended at some later stage. Many of the petitions already cited, in fact, speak of years of delay, and then at last perhaps the judgement was not given or was not executed. To this end the indifference and non-attendance of the lords, as described in an earlier chapter, strongly contributed, while their own interests in the practice of livery and maintenance unfitted them for dealing with the greatest factor of disturbance. In the realm of judicature, indeed, the lords had grasped a function which they were unable to exercise. 'The trial and failure of a great constitutional experiment,' as the Lancastrian régime has been called, is a statement that is strikingly true of this feature. The fall of the Lancastrians, then, marks the close of a period of parliamentary petitions. Under the Yorkists there was a decided reaction and an almost complete cessation of litigation in parliament. Petitions there were for resumptions, release from attainders, pardons, and other favours, but as to petitions of legal right a few exceptions only emphasize the rule that there was no remedy to be obtained

[1] *Ancient Petitions*, no. 4642.

from parliament. Under these circumstances the only courts open to plaintiffs by petition were the council and the chancery. But in the revolution just mentioned the council suffered a depression which was hardly less than that of the house of lords. The chancery, then, remained for a time the only court to which petitioners were encouraged to resort, and its jurisdiction underwent a marvellous development in the numerous cases in equity. How the council, on the other hand, retained an important part of its former jurisdiction, and how this was ultimately developed in the so-called court of star chamber, it will require yet another chapter to show.

Summary.

All these details of legislative and judicial history have been given to show how the council and the house of lords, from a single origin, came to be differently organized and differently working bodies. Throughout the middle ages, however, they continued to have a common name and to exercise many functions without discrimination, while only on certain lines was a positive division of authority made. In other respects, we might have shown, a division of authority was not accomplished before modern times.[1] At the time of Edward I the only distinction was that between a large body and a small body, each of which carried on the same kind of work and was supplementary to the other. Under Edward II a political motive was introduced, which caused it to be said that a council is less than a parliament, and that for certain things it is not a sufficient authority. In the reign of Edward III it was perceived further that the king's council represented a peculiar method of work, which was useful for some purposes, but in matters of jurisdiction was antagonistic to the common law. The house of lords, on the other hand, under the more conservative influence of the magnates, threw itself into the defence of the common law and kept its procedure in sympathy with it. The full conse-

[1] Take, for example, the subject of foreign and colonial jurisdiction, which, as is well known, to-day belongs to the judicial committee of the privy council. To the end of the middle ages, petitions from Gascony and other dependent lands were treated in parliament, and still during the reign of Henry VII there were 'Receptores petitionum Vasconie et aliarum Terrarum et Patriarum exterrarum ac Insularum'. *Rot. Parl.* vi. 441, 521.

quences of this divergence were hardly appreciated until the reign of Richard II, when political interests again caused assertions and definitions to be made. With unwonted energy a series of attempts to control the council and limit its authority followed, but as the efforts of parliament were fitful and inconsistent, the vague discretionary power of the council was not greatly affected. Under the Lancastrians, if not before, the general principle was accepted that the council might properly exercise a wide jurisdiction that was external to the common law, although its bounds were difficult to determine. No final adjustment was reached when the Wars of the Roses interrupted every normal development. How the council was affected during this period will be the theme of a subsequent chapter.

CHAPTER XIII

ANTIQUITIES OF THE KING'S COUNCIL[1]

BECAUSE the council was ever a shifting and varying body, there is much in its history as an institution that is of necessity uncertain and indefinite. For this reason it is desirable to follow every tangible clue that helps to give the subject a semblance of historical reality. To this end there are to be considered several material and antiquarian features relating to the council. These are the councillor's oath in its specific form, the council chamber and other places of meeting, expenses for breakfasts and dinners, the clerk of the council, and possibly others. Necessarily some allusions to these features have already been made, but they could not heretofore be fully described.

1. THE COUNCILLOR'S OATH

The oath is the earliest mark of distinction that was possessed by the council. This is important not merely because it defined the duties of a councillor, but also because it established a certain criterion of membership. Until the oath appears we cannot be sure that there was any element of permanency or stability whatsoever in this body. This is not to say that the oath was taken by all who attended the council or who bore the title councillor. Probably never during the middle ages was any such rule strictly adhered to. It was at first, we know, imposed rather upon the official members, while the prelates and barons were sworn only in exceptional instances. In a way the growth of the council can be followed in the evolution of the form of the oath and the manner of its application. This can be done from

[1] The headline of this chapter has been suggested by the title 'Parliamentary Antiquities' found in Stubbs, *Const. Hist.*, vol. iii, chap. xx.

the early years of Henry III, when the council begins to be distinguished from other bodies in the state.

So far as we know, next to the customary oaths of homage and fealty, the earliest official oath of any kind was that required of the itinerant justices on receiving their commissions.[1] The same idea was then extended to all justices, barons of the exchequer, other officers, and councillors. The first mention of a councillor's oath is a rather indefinite allusion made in 1233, when Richard Marshall accused the king's councillors of breaking the oaths which they had sworn to furnish the king with faithful counsel.[2] Another uncertain reference to an oath of this kind is made in 1237,[3] but of its form and contents we know nothing further until 1257. In this year, it will be recalled, the council was in whole or part reconstituted, while the clergy in their own assembly drew up a statement which was intended to serve as a general official oath. This draft or 'form' has fortunately been preserved by a chronicler.[4] Since it proves to be the basis of every subsequent statement of the duties of officers and councillors, the contents will be given in full.

Oath of 1257.

(1) Primo iuraverunt quod fidele consilium praestabunt domino regi, quoties viderint profuturum.

(2) Item quod nemini revelabunt consilium domini regis cui non revelandum et unde credant damnum posse venire.

(3) Item quod nihil consentient alienari de his quae ad antiquum dominium coronae pertinent.

(4) Item quod procurabunt quod iustitia fiat omnibus tam divitibus quam pauperibus, magnis et parvis, secundum rectas consuetudines et leges regni.

(5) Item quod libere permittent de seipsis, amicis, et consanguineis, iustitiam fieri cuicumque petenti. Nec per eos impedietur iustitia fieri prece vel pretio, favore vel odio, sed bona fide procurabunt, quod magnus sicut parvus iudicetur, secundum legem et consuetudinem regni. Nec

[1] Upon the appointment of Martin Pateshull in 1218 the king writes, 'capitula autem itineris vestri et formam sacramenti quod facere debetis commisimus domino R. Dunelmensi episcopo.' *Rot. Lit. Cl.* i. 403.

[2] Matthew Paris, *Chronica Maiora*, iii. 260; mentioned in chap. ii.

[3] 'Qui super sacrosancta iuraverunt quod fidele consilium praestarent, et ipse (rex) similiter iuravit quod eorum consiliis obediret.' *Dunstable Ann.*, p. 145; Matthew Paris, *Hist.* ii. 394.

[4] *Ann. Burton*, p. 395; Matthew Paris, *Chronica Maiora* v. 638.

sustentabunt vel defendent iniuriantes in iniuriis suis, opere vel sermone.

(6) Item quod a nullo quem sciverint habere facere in curia regis, vel ballivorum suorum, aliquod donum vel servitium recipient, per se vel per alium, quocumque modo, vel quacumque arte, occasione huiusmodi.

(7) Item si alicui de consilio pro certo innotuerit, vel a fide dignis audierit, aliquem alium consiliarium munus vel donum aliquod recepisse, exceptis esculento vel poculento, hoc deferet in publicam notionem totius consilii. Et si super hoc convictus fuerit inperpetuum excludatur a consilio; et perdat terras et redditus suos, vel proventus bonorum suorum per unum annum. Et si tales proventus non habuerit, alias puniatur secundum arbitrium consiliariorum.

This oath was taken, we are told, not only by the prelates and lords then elected, but also by the barons of the exchequer, the justices, and all of the king's bailiffs except the sheriffs. The substance of the articles, it will be seen, bears equally upon official and conciliar duties; the first three impose the duties of loyalty, secrecy, and defence of the royal domains, while the latter four relate mainly to the impartiality and integrity required of a judge. They are a clear reflection of the formal unity that was still maintained between the council, the exchequer, and the *curia regis*. A separation of these functions is bound to be indicated in time.

Whether the form of oath of 1257 continued to be used under Henry III, we have no positive evidence. It was not forgotten surely, for the same formula reappears under Edward I. Writing about 1290, Fleta reproduces it clause for clause, and almost word for word; but he gives it not as a councillor's oath but as an oath for the justices, barons of the exchequer, and other ministers.[1] The last clause also he indicates as intended for the justices only. Before the end of the reign the articles are further elaborated, and in 1307 are stated as the councillor's oath in the following form:[2]

(1) Qe bien e loiaument consaillerez le Roy solunc votre sen et votre poair. Oath of 1307.

[1] Lib. i, c. 17, §§ 16–19.

[2] Found in the *Close Roll*, 35 Edw. I, m. 7 d. *Rot. Parl.* i. 218; *Statutes of the Realm*, i. 248.

(2) E qe bien e loiaument son consail celerez.[1]

(3) E qe vous ne encuserez autre de chose quil dirra au consail.

(4) E qe votre peyne eide e consail e tot votre poair dorrez e metterez as droitures le Roy et de la corone garder et maintenir sauver et repeller par la ou vous porrez, santz tort faire.

(5) E la ou vous saverez les choses de la corone et les droitz le Roy concelez, ou a tort alienez, ou soustretz qe vous le frez saver au Roy.

(6) E qe la corone acrestrez a votre poair et en loiale manere.

(7) E qe vous ne serrez en lieu ne a consail ou le Roi se decresse de chose qe a la corone appent, si ce ne seit chose qe vous conveigne faire.

(8) E qe vous ne lerrez pur nully, pur amur, ne haour, pur bon gre ne pur mauveis gre, qe vous ne facez faire a chescun, de quel estat ou condicion quil soit, droiture et reson solunc votre poair et a votre escient, e qe de nully rien ne prendrez pur tort faire ne droit delaier.

(9) E qe en jugement, ou droiture faire, la ou vous serrez assignez, vous nesparnierez nully pur hautesce, ne pur poverte, ne pur richesce, qe droit ne soit fait.

(10) E si vous eez fait alliaunce a seignurage ou a autre, par quey vous ne peussez cestes choses faire, ou tenir sauntz cele alliaunce enfreindre, qe vous le dirrez ou frez saver au Roy.

(11) E qe desormes alliance de serment ne freetz a nulli sauntz conge le Roy.

(12) (To be taken by the justices only.)

E qe rien ne prendrez de doun de nully, pur pled ne pur autre chose, quil eit a faire devant vous, si ceo ne soit manger et beiver a la journee.

It requires only a brief comparison of the two forms to show that the oath of 1307 was directly derived from that of 1257, with a few significant modifications. The clause regarding loyalty at the beginning is substantially the same in both. The clause about secrecy remains, with the addition of the third article in the later form. The single clause in the earlier against the alienation of the royal domains is in the later one expanded into four clauses guarding the rights of the crown. The clauses regarding impartial justice to rich and poor, without favour or price, and according to law, though

[1] Stubbs has incorrectly translated this 'to expedite counsel', *Const. Hist.* ii. 281.

differently expressed, are strikingly similar in substance. The tenth and eleventh clauses of Edward's oath have sprung from some other source. The last clause, that none of the council shall receive any gift except food and drink, in the latter instance follows the suggestion of Fleta in that it was imposed upon the justices only.

Another revision of the oath was made in the first year of Edward II, when an exemplification again was placed upon the close rolls.[1] The changes which then appear are matters of detail merely. They consist of the addition or insertion of certain qualifying phrases that were intended to clarify the meaning. There was reason apparently for additional safeguards. Thus, in the third clause to the words *de chose quil dirra au consail* are added *qe touche le Roi*; to the fourth clause is added *et solunc ce qil affert a son office*; and to the ninth, *a votre poair*. The greatest change is in the fifth clause, where instead of *qe vous le frez saver au Roy* there stands *qe vous le freez adrescer a votre poer ou qe vous le frez saver au Roi ou a son conseil en la manere qe a vous appent*. Oath of Edw. II.

At the same time different stages in the gradual unfolding of the councillor's oath are revealed in the forms used by the king's council in Ireland, and also in Gascony. The Irish oath appears to be a somewhat earlier statement than that of 1307.[2] Although no date is given, the spellings of the words are suggestive of the thirteenth rather than the fourteenth century, as for instance *rey* for *roy*, *sey* for *se*, *poer* for *poair*, and *solume* for *solunc*. Moreover in one point at least the oath used in Ireland lacks a qualifying phrase contained in the other. In the seventh clause the former Oath in Ireland.

[1] *Close Roll*, 1 Edw. II, m. 19 d; printed in *Parliamentary Writs*, ii, part ii, p. 3.

[2] This is found in the Red Book of the Exchequer at Dublin. The text is obscure, but with the necessary omissions it can be reproduced to the following extent:

'[Iuramentum] de consilio Regis.

'. . . loiaument conseilleit le Rey solume sun sen et sun poer; E qe sun conseal bien e leaument celerat . . . de chose qil dirat en le conseil; E qe sa leale peine eyde e conseil a tut sun poer dorrat . . . de la corune garder meintenir sauver e reapeler par la ou il porrat sant tort fere . . . les droit le rey concilleret ou . . . alieneret ou sustreret, il le frat saver il Rey . . . E qil ne serra ou le Rey sey descresse de chose qe a la Corune appent si . . . pur nully ne pur amour ne pur haur ne pur bon gre ne pur maugre qil ne . . . reson e en jugement e en droiture . . .'

statement reads *e qe il ne serra ou le Rey sey descresse,* while the English oath in ampler phrase says *e qe vous ne serrez en lieu ne a consail ou le Roi se decresse.* Finally, the Irish oath does not appear to contain more than eight clauses. So the tendency was for new phrases and clauses to be added with every successive revision. The oath found in Gascony in 1310, however, is important for what it reveals of a tendency in the opposite direction.[1] The statement, which we will reproduce, is much briefer, and shows for the first time a discrimination between conciliar and official duties. It contains indeed hardly more than the clauses relating to loyalty, secrecy, and the defence of the rights of the crown. The articles concerned with the duties of judges are signally lacking.

Oath in Gascony, 1310.

'*Forma autem iuramenti scripti manu Prioris Mansi in presencia omnium talis est.*

'Iurarunt quod requisiti bonum consilium et fidele secundum suam conscienciam dabunt bona fide, prece, precio, odio, timore, amore et affeccione subductis; quod ea que in consilio dicentur partem aliquam vel dominum Regem tangencia, nemini pandent quavis occasione vel modo nec signum ad pandendum aliquod dabunt, quod possit redundare in preiudicium alicui de consilio vel alterius cuiuscumque, quodque super iuribus domini nostri Regis que possent tangere statum suum vel honorem aut utilitatem bona fide dominos avisabunt, et in apponendo remedio dabunt consilium quodque palam se excusabunt de consulendo tantum cum agitur de negociis tangentibus personas illas quibus obligati sunt per alia sua iuramenta.'

Differentiation of the oath.

From this time the councillor's oath, as applied in England, was not further extended. In accordance with certain tendencies already observed, its derivatives were differentiated in response to the needs of individual offices and departments. Most conspicuously the justices and barons of the exchequer were drawn away from the council and accordingly a separate form of oath for them was devised. Already in the twenty-sixth year of Edward I a justice of the common pleas was sworn in his office 'according to a form provided by the king's council'.[2] Soon afterwards there appears a distinct

[1] *Diplomatic Documents, Chancery,* no. 228; *ante,* p. 69.
[2] *Memoranda Roll, K. R.,* 26 Edw. I, m. 15.

oath also of the barons of the exchequer.[1] The regular oath of the justices, as it finally appears in the 'Red Book of the Exchequer',[2] retains many of the clauses and most striking phrases of the old councillor's oath; as, for instance, *qe pur hautesce ne pur richesce ne pur amour ne pur haour ne pur estat de nuly*, etc., *qe riens ne prendrount de nuly*, except *mangier et beyvre quant a la journee.* It was not forgotten, however, that the justices continued to be councillors in a qualified sense, and an oath especially for them in the twentieth year of Edward III begins with the words: *vous iurez qe bien et loialment serverez a notre Seigneur le Roi et a son poeple en loffice de justice et qe loialment counseillerez notre dit Seigneur le Roi en ses busoignes.*[3]

A councillor's oath of 1341.

In accordance with the altered status of the justices and barons of the exchequer, the next statement of the councillor's oath in England shows a marked departure from the articles of Edward I. This is discovered in a certain letter that was written by several newly-appointed councillors, who undertook loyally to counsel the king, to care for his interests, and particularly to redress the wrongs created by evil counsellors in the past. The date is uncertain, but it seems most likely to belong to the fifteenth year of Edward III, 1341, when one of the repeated attempts of parliament was made to dictate the appointment of a council.[4] The statement is a lengthy and ill-constructed one, which was composed most likely by the lords concerned, certainly not by the king's clerks. It is valuable, however, for showing that the councillor's duties were by this time clearly distinguished from those of the officers. The letter reads as follows:

'Nous jurroms et promettoms par noz fois et noz serementz qe nous serroms loialx devers vous notre Seigneur

[1] Mentioned during the years 34–35 Edw. I. Madox, *Hist. of Exch.* ii. 57, 61, 91.

[2] Printed in the *First Report of the Public Records* (London, 1800), p. 236.

[3] *Close Roll*, 20 Edw. III, m. 12 d; the ordinance is in the *Statutes of the Realm*, i. 303.

[4] The parchment is endorsed in a modern hand, 15 Edw. III. For giving this date there was very likely a reason which was apparent at the time it was written. The document is not filed as yet, but may be found in the box of Parliamentary and Council Proceedings, Chancery.

lige et loialment vous conseilleroms selonc noz sens; cest a savoir de bien et loialment mesner et guyer les busoignes qe vous touchount, selonc ce qe nous verroms qe soit a plus graunt honeur et profit de vous et plus hastief exploit de votre emprise saunz avoir regard a nul singular profit, par quel vos dites busoignes porroient de riens estre areriz ou empeschez ; et aussi mettrons entierement et saunz fryntise notre loial poair de faire redrescer totes les choses meprises devers vous par quecunqes vos counseilliers, ministres et autres vos subgiz en quecunqe manere qe ce soit auxi bien de temps passe come pur le temps a venir, et de mettre remeide et punissement selonc la qualite de lour mesprision vers quecunqe persone qe ce touche sanz nully esparnier pur doun promesse affinite doute ou affection, et de restreindre tous ceux de quel estat ou condition qil soient les queux nous purroms savoir quont este nuysours ou destourbours de votre profit, ou de l'exploit de vos busoignes en ascun manere. Et nully qi se avera mauporte ou mespris devers vos officers ou autre queconque persone ne meyntiendroms ne lui ferroms eide faveur ou confort ne riens ne prendroms de nully pur despoit faire ne pur execucion faire de droiture, einz ferroms et pursuiroms en totes choses et quant come nous purroms ce qe nous verroms qe fort honorable et profitable pour vous et lestat de votre realme et lexploit de vos busoignes, et nulle alliance ne ferroms ouesqe nully ne ne tendroms qe purra estre prejudiciale a vous et votre estat ou a vos busoignes en ascune manere, et rien pur amiste ne pur hatie de nully ne procureroms ne pursuieroms, si noun choses qe nous quidons veritables selonc Dieu et bon conscience, si Dieu nous eide et les seinz.'

The oath under Rich. II.

During the subsequent period of parliamentary dictation much was made of the point that all members of the council should be sworn, preferably in the presence of parliament itself. In 1376 it was required that the new councillors should be specially sworn to keep the ordinances then made concerning them. Again in the first parliament of Richard II it was proposed that the councillors then appointed should be sworn to certain articles that recall the first two clauses of the old oath, as regards loyalty and secrecy.

'Soient serementz . . . bien et loialment conseiller le Roy en toutes choses qe serront moevez ou tretez devant eux solonc lours sen et poairs.

'Et qe toute chose qe y doit estre tenuz en secret sanz descovrir, ne descovriront a aucun estrange, autrement qe nel doivent faire par reson.'[1]

That there was also a clause to guard the rights of the crown, is suggested in the impeachment of Suffolk in 1386.[2] But the portions relating to the duties of the judges no longer appear. In other years, particularly in 1388, and in 1406, and in 1409, when the council was made a subject of legislation, special oaths with reference to the ordinances passed were required. Again in the third year of Henry VI the form of the oath was put 'under correction' and prescribed by authority of parliament. The great extension of all the clauses relating to bribery, favouritism, and the revelation of secrets is particularly significant. The statement is given as follows :

Under Henry VI.

'Ye shall as fer furth as your connyng and discretion suffiseth, trewely, justely and evenly counsaille and advyse the Kyng in all matiers to be comoned, treted and demened in the Kyng's Counsaille, or by You as the Kynges Counsailler, and generally in all thinges that may be to the Kynges worship, proufit and behove, and to the gode of his Reaumes, Lordeships and Subgittz, withouten parcialtie or acceptation of persons, not levyng or eschewing so to do for affection, love, mede, doubte or drede, of eny persone or persones.

'And ye shall kepe secrete the Kynges Counsaill, and alle that shall be comuned by way of Counsaille in the same, withouten that ye shall common it, publish it, or discover it by worde, wryting, or in eny wyse, to eny persone oute of the same Counsaille, or to any of the same Counsaille, yf it touch hym, or if he be partie thereto.

'And that ye shall no yift, mede nor gode, ne promisse of goode, by you nor by meen persone, receyve nor admitt, for promotion, favouryng, nor for declaryng, lettyng or hinderyng, of eny matiere or thing to be treted or do in the said Counsaille.

'Ye shall also with all your might and poair, help, strength and assiste, unto the Kynges said Counsaille, duryng the Kynges tendre age, in all that be thoght unto the same Counsaille for the universale gode of the Kynge and of his Land, and for the Pees, Rest and Tranquillitee of the same ; and withstonde any persone or persones, of what condition,

[1] *Rot. Parl.* iii. 7.

[2] Ibid. 219.

estate or degree that thei be of, that wold by way of feet or ellus, attempte or entende unto the contrarie.

'And generally ye shall observe, kepe and do, alle that a gode and trewe Counsailler oweth to doo unto his Souveraine Lorde.'[1]

With the elimination of the portion relating to the king's tender age, this form appears henceforth to have been regularly used, and for this purpose it was inscribed with other official forms in the 'Book of Oaths'.[2] Inasmuch as it is then a well-understood feature of the constitution, there is no need here to pursue the topic further.

2. The Council Chamber

Meeting-place of the council.

Hardly less important in this history are the facts that can be gathered concerning the customary place of meeting. It is true that the council was not limited to any fixed place, and never ceased to bear a certain migratory character. Moreover, there was always a varying number of councillors attending the king wherever he might be, at home or abroad, while special sessions were likely to be called at any of the royal residences. At the same time, the council was considered to be mainly located at London or Westminster, especially during the regular terms of the courts. This fact was assumed when in 1314 certain conservators of the peace in Kent were instructed to make returns from month to month to the council at Westminster.[3] In the event of the council meeting at any other place and undertaking its customary work, there was the risk and expense of conveying the rolls and other records that might be wanted. In the fourth year of Edward II we find the king's clerk, Elias Jonestone, receiving by indenture certain rolls and charters from the treasurer and chamberlains of the exchequer at Westminster, which he was to bear to the council at Osney and for the safe return of which he was responsible.[4] Various payments are recorded as made to the messengers bearing books and other materials to the council at one place or another.[5]

[1] *Rot. Parl.* v. 407.
[2] Given in *First Report on the Public Records*, p. 222.
[3] *Cal. Patent Rolls*, 7 Edw. II, 122.
[4] *Chancery Miscellaneous Roll*, 17/11.
[5] *Issue Roll* (*Pells*), 45 Edw. III, m. 15.

The ancient chamber of the exchequer.

At Westminster, the usual place of resort in the earliest days was the council chamber of the exchequer. In the thirteenth century a certain building was erected near the receipt of the exchequer, containing a small upper chamber, wherein we are told 'the king's council was commonly held '.[1] So long as the council was mainly associated with the exchequer, this served the purpose very well. There were also other meeting places in the palace, such as the 'green chamber', the Marcolf chamber, the Oule chamber, the chapel of St. Stephen, and 'the great council chamber', as well as a room in the Tower of London. Even private houses occasionally were used for conferences. In the *hospitium* of the archbishop of York near Westminster there was a king's chamber where meetings of the council sometimes were held,[2] and in the same manner was used the house of Otto Grandison.[3] Of all places outside the royal buildings, the favourite meeting ground certainly was the house of the Black Friars. Edward I and Eleanor were great benefactors of the order, and their successors continued to make gifts. In the large, richly-furnished chapel divers parliaments were held, while the chapter-house and the refectory in turn were used for the purposes of the council.[4] So well was this understood that sometimes one speaks of the 'council chamber here'.[5] Other houses in the city that were resorted to in the same manner were the house of the Carmelites in Fleet Street and the New Temple.[6]

The star chamber under Edw. III.

For the special use of the council a new building was erected in the reign of Edward III. It was placed within the grounds of the palace at Westminster, upon the river front next to the exchequer, where it is represented in many existing diagrams and pictures.[7] The work seems to have been started somewhat earlier than 1347, the commonly

[1] *Cal. Close Rolls*, 6 Edw. III, 573.

[2] *Cal. Close Rolls*, 30 Edw. I, 594.

[3] *Rot. Parl.* i. 76.

[4] As early as 1311 I find the house of the Black Friars was used in this way. Riley, *Memorials of London* (1868), p. 90.

[5] *Cal. Close Rolls*, 23 Edw. III, 84.

[6] *Foedera* (Rec. Ed.), ii, part ii, p. 1101; *Cal. Close Rolls*, 6 Edw. II, 563; 38 Edw. III, 60; *Ancient Petitions*, no. 14933, &c.

[7] Several excellent plates are hung upon the walls of the Charing Cross Public Library.

accepted date.[1] In 1343 mention is made of a 'new chamber upon the water',[2] and again in 1344, a delivery of the great seal was made 'in the new chamber at Westminster'.[3] In 1346 it is stated that a case in chancery was heard in 'the new council chamber next to the exchequer'.[4] This reference can mean nothing else than the star chamber. It is recorded that the new chamber was expressly 'ordained' for the use of the council.[5] The name 'star chamber' also appears from the very start,[6] although for many years it was more commonly known as 'the council chamber next to the receipt of the exchequer'. How its peculiar name was derived has been a matter of speculation. 'I suppose,' said Hudson, 'the name to be given according to the nature of the judges thereof,' who were likened to stars in the firmament. Blackstone is hardly more plausible in his explanation that the place was used as a depository for certain Jewish contracts or bonds, which were called *starra*. With all of its improbabilities, it is strange that this theory should still be given currency, for in point of time it was then fifty years since the Jews had been exiled from England. Moreover the form of the name, in Latin *camera stellata*, or *camera stellarum*, in French, *chambre estoillee* or *chambre des estoilles*, in English also 'starred' or 'sterne' chamber, leaves no doubt as to its etymology. One is bound, therefore, to accept the simple and obvious meaning as was suggested long ago by Stow, that the star chamber was so called because its ceiling was decorated with stars. These we know were gilded at a later time, in all likelihood according to the original design.

From time to time we are given information of articles purchased for the equipment of the star chamber and the use

[1] The work of Mr. W. P. Baildon, *The Court of Star Chamber* (London, 1894), is the most satisfactory account of the subject on the antiquarian side. To the statements which he has made, I am able to offer a few additional facts and remarks.

[2] *Cal. Close Rolls*, 17 Edw. III, 233.

[3] *Cal. Patent Rolls*, 18 Edw. III, 304.

[4] *Placita in Cancellaria*, no. 21.

[5] In the twenty-third year a conference was held 'en la nouvele chambre iouste la receyte del Escheqier ordeine pur le counseil'. *Memoranda Roll, K. R.*, 23 Edw. III, Trinity, m. 3; and *Close Roll*, 23 Edw. III, part i, m. 2 d.

[6] We have the tiler's accounts in regard to work on the building, *Exchequer Accounts, K. R.*, 470/17; the name also is in the *Close Roll*, 29 Edw. III; and *Issue Roll* (*Pells*), 50 Edw. III, Mich., m. 32.

of the council. In 1376, when, it will be recalled, certain reforms were undertaken, there was the significant expense of 64 shillings for the purchase of twelve cushions for the star chamber, 'for the use of the lords of the council who were there to consult.' [1] Under Richard II a calendar was purchased for seven shillings, expressly for the use of the lords of the council in the star chamber.[2] Rushes and mats also were provided, the same as for the receipt of the exchequer.[3] In the reign of Henry IV the furnishings became more luxurious, for in the first year by command of the council there were purchased five rich cloths and twelve cushions worked with the arms and collar of the king's livery, also some tapestry and a dozen green cloths, at a cost of £7 18*s*. 10*d*., for the advantage and accommodation, it is stated, of the lords and nobility appointed to consult in the star chamber.[4] A copy of the gospels also was kept that oaths might be sworn,[5] and there was of necessity a table.[6] The custody of the building was given to the usher of the receipt of the exchequer, who by the end of the reign of Edward III was known also as the keeper of the star chamber.[7] This office was of sufficient dignity to be granted, sometimes for life, by letters patent. It received the fair emolument of forty shillings a year, besides other 'accustomed fees and profits'.[8] It was a position given for previous good service, and was allowed to be held by deputy.

Articles for the use of the council.

Most of the proceedings of the council, there is no doubt, were held in the star chamber. 'The home of the council,' it was frequently called. Yet other accustomed places were

[1] *Issue Rolls* (*Pells*), 50 Edw. III, Mich., m. 32.

[2] *Issues of the Exchequer* (ed. Devon), p. 237.

[3] *Issue Roll* (*Pells*), 14 Ric. II, Mich., October 26; 18 Ric. II, Mich., October 18, &c.

[4] *Issues of the Exchequer*, p. 274.

[5] *Rot. Parl.*.v. 410.

[6] Richard III struck the table a blow and one of the lords in fright fell under it. Sir Thomas More, *Richard III* (Cambridge, 1883), p. 47. The table, however, either in the star chamber or elsewhere, is not mentioned as a necessary feature during the middle ages as it was in modern times. More is said of the seats and the arrangement of seats for the councillors. There was no particular reason why they should be close to the table. It seems like an anachronism therefore to speak at this time of the 'council board'.

[7] *Cal. Close Rolls*, 33 Edw. III, 564; also a reference to these offices as known in 51 Edw. III, *Materials for the History of Henry VII* (Rolls Series), i. 17.

[8] *Issue Roll* (*Pells*), 3 Ric. II, Mich., m. 12; *Cal. Patent Rolls*, 1 Hen. VI, 51.

Other houses resorted to.

by no means abandoned.[1] When royal audiences were held the council was commonly called to one or another of the king's private chambers. There was in fact a small room next to the star chamber used for this purpose. Often the councillors preferred to meet in one or another of the accustomed places in London, especially in the house of the Black Friars. On one occasion it was said to be 'for the ease of the lords within the town', that a council was held in the forenoon at the Black Friars, and for the convenience of the lords living outside the town a meeting was held at the White Friars in the afternoon of the same day.[2] In a similar manner the council continued to be assembled, more or less formally, in private houses.[3] This was done particularly by the duke of Gloucester and also by the duke of Bedford during their protectorates. On one occasion Gloucester made complaint to the king against his brother, that he 'taketh unto him your royal estate in calling your council at divers times to his own house'.[4] That no factional advantage might be gained by holding the council in irregular places without due announcement, it was declared in one of the ordinances of 1426, 'that no bill be sped but in the place ordained for the council, being assembled in the form of the council.'[5] It is a familiar incident that Richard, Duke of Gloucester, while he was protector in 1483, in order safely to make his attack on Lord Hastings, divided the council by having some of the members called to the Tower, while others more favourable to himself he kept at Westminster.[6]

3. 'Expenses' of the Council

The business of the council was not carried on without various incidental expenses, which are useful as sidelights to its history. There were of course the necessary payments to couriers as well as the fees, wages, and robes of the councillors

[1] Certain ordinances of the year 1389 are endorsed, 'Conseilx tenuz en diverses lieux lan xiij et diverses actes du Conseil.' Nicolas, i. 6.

[2] *Paston Letters*, no. 366.

[3] In 1410 the council met at the house of the bishop of Hereford in London. Nicolas, ii. 338.

[4] *Letters of the English in France* (Rolls Series), ii. 449. Yet Gloucester did the same thing. Nicolas, iii. 65.

[5] Nicolas, iii. 216.

[6] Croyland, *Continuation*, p. 566.

themselves. But the expenses most commonly indicated were for the meals and other refreshments that were sometimes served. The sittings of the council, it will be remembered, began early, often at seven or eight o'clock,[1] so that if the work was to be continued or resumed during the afternoon, it was necessary that articles of food and drink be provided. In the way of 'light' refreshments, we frequently read of wine or fruit being purchased. In 1358–9 there is an item of two shillings for wine and perry procured for the council;[2] in 1359 the king's butler was ordered to deliver to the usher of the receipt of the exchequer two pipes of wine, 'for the refreshment of the chancellor, the treasurer, and others of the king's council when they come and stay upon the direction of the king's business';[3] in 1365 there is another order to the butler for a pipe of good wine;[4] in the first year of Richard II there was a payment of the considerable sum of seventy-five shillings for wine purchased for the lords of the council, who for several days remained late in the afternoon on the secret business of the king.[5] At another time there is an item for apples bought for the council.[6] More often the exchequer roll contains only an indefinite statement of 'expenses'.

Refreshments for the council.

Sometimes we learn of substantial breakfasts or dinners being provided. Whether it was called the *iantaculum* or the *prandium*, the meal was an early one that was served apparently before nine in the morning.[7] Of these repasts there are a few very curious records in the exchequer, made upon small and detached pieces of parchment, containing itemized accounts of the various articles of food and drink, with their prices and the cost of service.[8] The cost of such

Breakfasts and dinners.

[1] The ordinances of 1390 say as early as eight or nine, but frequently the hour of seven is noted in the records. In 1406 the commons were particularly urged to begin business at eight o'clock, while the house of lords was to meet at nine. *Rot. Parl.* iii. 568.

[2] *Issues of the Exchequer* (*Devon*), p. 168.

[3] *Cal. Close Rolls*, 33 Edw. III, 564.

[4] Ibid., 39 Edw. III, 129.

[5] *Issue Roll* (*Pells*), 1 Ric. II, Pasch., July 2.

[6] 'Pro pomis vocatis Blaunderell.' Ibid., May 18.

[7] 'And lat us dine as soon as that ye may
For by my Chilindre it is pryme of day.'
Chaucer, *The Shipmannes Tale*, ll. 205–6.

[8] *Accounts, Exchequer K. R.*, bundle 96, nos. 8–13.

a meal varied between six shillings and nine pounds a day, according to the number present and the elaborateness of the menu. Several of these statements run through three or four successive days. The earliest account that we have is of the forty-first year of Edward III.[1] Because of their antiquarian interest it seems advisable to reproduce certain of these lists. The first, which is dated June 30, 1374–5, is evidently a Friday meal, as may be seen by the ample provision of fish and the absence of meat.[2]

4 pikes	17*s.*	
Salmon	6*s.*	
Plaice and merling	8*s.*	
12 crabs and lobsters	5*s.*	6*d.*
Eels	5*s.*	6*d.*
4 salt fish	4*s.*	10*d.*
Bread	5*s.*	6½*d.*
Portage of fish		2*d.*
Boat hire		16*d.*
Oatmeal		1*d.*
Vinegar		1*d.*
Butter		5*d.*
Salt		4*d.*
Beans		10*d.*
Onions		1*d.*
Mustard		2*d.*
Vinegar and ginger		4*d.*
4 pounds of almonds		14*d.*
1 pound raisins of currants		4*d.*
½ ounce saffron		6*d.*
2 ounces of powder of ginger		6*d.*
½ ounce powder of pepper		2*d.*
1 ounce powder of cinnamon		3*d.*
Sugar		2½*d.*
Fuel	2*s.*	10*d.*
46 gallons of ale	9*s.*	7*d.*
Portage of same		2*d.*
Cups		12*d.*
Cooking and labour	6*s.*	8*d.*
	79*s.*	7*d.*

[1] It is entitled 'Expense facte apud Westminster xv° die Septembris anno regni Edwardi xli° pro iantaculo dominorum cancellarii, thesaurarii, Willelmi Wykeham, et aliorum de consilio secreto domini Regis Londoniae.' *Accounts, Exchequer K. R.*, bundle 96, no. 8.

[2] Ibid. no. 11.

On other days meat and game were provided in abundance, and wine also might be served. Spices and sweets from the East in small quantities were not wanting. The chief deficiency according to our own taste naturally lay in respect of the vegetables. In order to show the variety that was possible one other list will be given.[1]

Bread of divers kinds		6*s.*	
30 gallons of ale		5*s.*	
Boat hire for divers things to Westminster			4*d.*
Beef		10*s.*	2*d.*
Veal		9*s.*	
2 dead sheep		8*s.*	
12 capons		9*s.*	6*d.*
12 geese		8*s.*	6*d.*
3 goats		6*s.*	9*d.*
10 'butores' (? bitterns)		33*s.*	4*d.*
24 pigeons		3*s.*	6*d.*
18 rabbits		4*s.*	1*d.*
1 lamb			16*d.*
15 poultry		4*s.*	
Plucking the same			6*d.*
2 codfish		3*s.*	
3 small pikes		8*s.*	
8 plaice		3*s.*	6*d.*
1 turbot		3*s.*	
Conger-eels		3*s.*	6*d.*
3 John dorys		6*s.*	
Fresh salmon		3*s.*	
200 shrimps			20*d.*
Eels			12*d.*
Divers salted [fish]			8*d.*
Divers spices		4*s.*	0½*d.*
Fuel and coal		3*s.*	10*d.*
Salt			2*d.*
Carriage and boat hire from London and the King's Residence to Westminster			18*d.*
In fattening			10*d.*
In carriage and boat hire by John the Cook			5*d.*
	£7	14*s.*	1½*d.*
Labours of five officers	1	10*s.*	0*d.*
	£9	4*s.*	1½*d.*

[1] Ibid. no. 8.

Although these repasts were avowed to be for the purpose of 'expediting the business of the king', from the amounts of money spent and the quantities of food and drink consumed, we surmise that the breakfasts of the council easily became convivial feasts. At the close of the Good Parliament in 1376, for example, a great feast was held, to which the king contributed two tuns of claret wine and eight does of venison, while other lords also gave gold and wine.[1] When on one occasion forty-six gallons of ale were provided, it is necessary to suppose that the feast was not restricted to members only. At a feast of this kind, held in the first year of Henry V, there were said to be present the chancellor, the treasurer, and others of the council, the justices, the barons of the exchequer, and 'diverse other persons who were there for the day on business touching the welfare of the king and the realm'.[2] There is no reason to suppose that the breakfasts and dinners of the council were maintained with any degree of regularity at any period during the middle ages. Under the Yorkist reigns they disappear entirely. But they were revived under the Tudors, and became a special feature of the sessions of the court of the star chamber under Henry VIII. The great feast of the week then was held on Friday.[3]

4. The Clerk of the Council

The equipment of the council as a working body was not complete until a special clerk, to be known as the clerk of the council, was assigned to it. As to the beginning of this office there has been some uncertainty and dispute. Seeing the name of Master John Prophet frequently upon the acts of the council, Sir Harris Nicolas considered him to be the first to hold the office.[4] For this inference, which was not based upon any further facts, the aforesaid author was

Dispute upon the question.

[1] *Chron. Angl.* (Rolls Series), p. lxxii.

[2] *Issue Roll* (*Pells*), 1 Hen. V, Easter, m. 2.

[3] This custom was made the topic of a contribution by Miss Cora Scofield in the *Am. Hist. Review*, v. 85–95.

[4] 'That Prophete was clerk of the council in the thirteenth year of Richard II is to be presumed from the documents which he drew up and signed.' Nicolas, i, p. xvii.

sharply criticized by the editor of the *Roll of the Proceedings of the King's Council in Ireland*.[1] So far as it was known to these and other writers, the clerk of the council was not positively mentioned at any time prior to the ordinances of 1422. He is then referred to in a manner suggesting that the office was not at that time newly created. In this state of uncertainty the question has been allowed to rest. But in the light of additional evidence, furnished mostly by the issue rolls of the exchequer, it is now possible to give a fairly clear account of the office of clerk of the council from its very beginning.

Various clerks first noticed.

From the earliest times certainly there were clerks who were considered to belong to the king's council. Under Edward I, as has been shown, several of the clerks of the chancery in the same manner as the justices were formally sworn and retained, while appropriate tasks of one kind and another were assigned to them. Sometimes we learn of a particular clerk who served the council in its secretarial work. Under Edward I, Gilbert Roubery is more than once mentioned as *clericus de consilio*,[2] and in the reigns of Edward II and Edward III, Elias Jonestone was one who drafted a number of documents for the council besides performing many other services. In the first year of Edward III, we are informed, 'Gilbert Middleton and other clerks of the council' were assigned to examine certain articles coming from Gascony and to certify the council as to the remedies to be provided.[3] Any clerk of course might be employed on the errands of the council. In 1355 there is a description of the journeys of Adam Hilton, who was allowed 6*s*. 8*d*. a day for the time that he went as king's envoy to Scotland and then returned to the king's council at London, afterwards setting out on the same affairs from London to the archbishop of Canterbury at Mansfield, and thence to Earl William of Bohun at Northampton, then staying at Rockford and coming after-

[1] J. Graves (Rolls Series), p. xxvi.

[2] *Statutes of the Realm*, i. 216; *Coram Rege Roll*, 21 Edw. I, Mich., m. 35 d.

[3] 'Videtur consilio quod clerici sufficientes sint assignandi ad negocia examinanda . . . et fieri 'fecerint' brevia regia magistro Gilberto de Middleton et aliis clericis de consilio domini Regis,' etc. *Ancient Petitions*, no. 13586.

wards to the king at Clarendon, then going northward on the same affairs, and finally returning to the council at London.[1] But to this time there was no one regularly employed for the clerical work of the council in the sense that there was already a clerk of parliament.[2] A step in this direction was taken when a certain clerk of the privy seal, John of Wendlingburg, for a period of years was steadily engaged in the service of the council. In the forty-ninth year of Edward III, it is said, he was on two occasions sent by the council to meet the king on a matter of secret business.[3] In the second year of Richard II, Wendlingburg, then senior clerk in the office of the privy seal, was allowed forty pounds 'for his costs and labours in continually attending the king's council from the time of the coronation '.[4] For eleven years of the reign the same clerk received payments for his services, especially in bearing messages to the king and other lords of the council.[5] Guy Roclif was another clerk of the privy seal especially entrusted with secret messages of the king and council from the eighth to the eleventh year of the same reign.[6] The next clerk to appear prominently in the same service was the aforesaid Master John Prophet, also one of the staff of the privy seal, whose signature is found upon various documents in the thirteenth year. Too much stress, however, must not be laid upon this fact, for it was now a common practice for clerks to sign their names in this way, and Prophet was not the only clerk who served the council. But Prophet was a man of exceptional energy, as

Clerks of the privy seal.

John Prophet.

[1] *Cal. Close Rolls*, 49 Edw. III, 120.

[2] In the forty-sixth year of Edward III the signature of John Fordham, clerk of the privy seal, appears upon certain warrants issued by the council. *Warrants* (*Chancery*), file 1538.

[3] *Issue Roll* (*Pells*), 49 Edw. III, m. 10.

[4] Ibid., 2 Ric. II, Mich., m. 6.

[5] 'Iohanni Wendlyngburgh uni clericorum de officio privati sigilli Regis misso ex ordinatione consilii Regis versus partes Dorset pro certis negotiis domino Regi ex parte dicti consilii ibidem demonstrandis, c*s*.' Ibid., 7 Ric. II, Easter, m. 18; also 8 Ric. II, Mich., m. 2; 11 Ric. II, Mich., m. 12.

[6] 'Guydoni de Roclyff uni clericorum de officio privati sigilli Regis misso ex ordinatione consilii Regis de Londonia usque Knaresburgh cum litteris Regis et dicti consilii directis Iohanni Duci Lancastriae pro certis necessariis et secretis negotiis ipsius domini Regis . . . vi*l*. xiii*s*. iv*d*.' Ibid., 8 Ric. II, m. 24; also 10 Ric. II, Mich., m. 24; 11 Rich. II, Mich., m. 20.

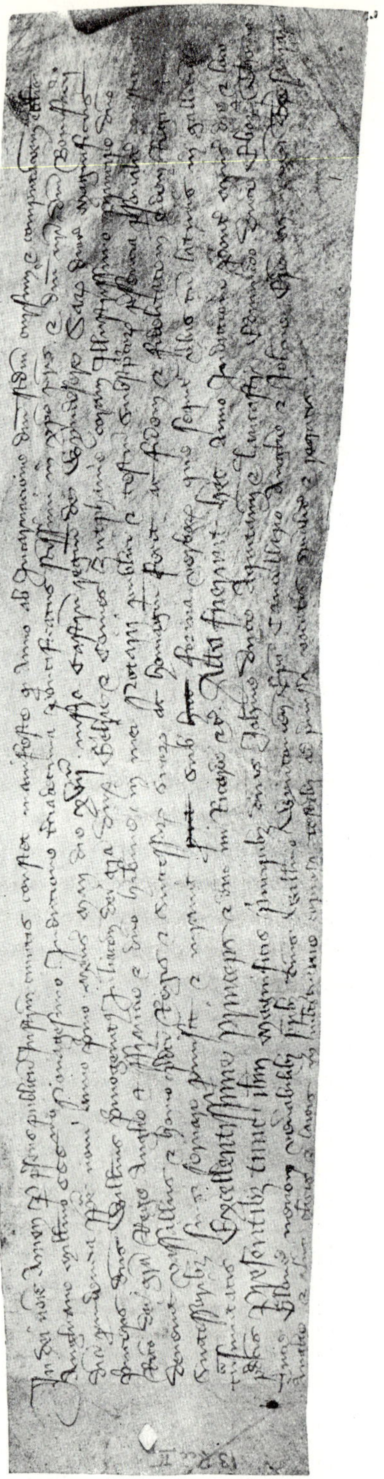

A MEMORANDUM WRITTEN BY JOHN PROPHET, 13 RIC. II.

his vigorous handwriting suggests, and as is made still more evident by the extent of his labours and the recognition which he afterwards received. In the fourteenth year, as a clerk of the privy seal, he was given 40 marks which the king commanded to be paid him 'by advice of the council' for his costs and expenses at the king's council.[1] The next year he received a similar allowance.[2] In the sixteenth year, expressly as 'clerk of the council', he was granted the sum of £40, which was said to be 'for his labours and expenses in times past, travelling to different places by command of the council, as well as remaining continuously with the council'.[3] This statement satisfactorily confirms the inference of Nicolas. The office was not then a fixed position, however, for in the following year Prophet was advanced to the position of 'secondary clerk' of the privy seal, and in the nineteenth year he was given by order of the council a special *honorarium* of £100 for his previous services.[4] To us the most valuable of his previous achievements was the compiling of the council register, which runs through the fifteenth and sixteenth years of Richard II. Prophet was also dean of Hereford and received many other preferments in the church.[5] In the first year of Henry IV he was made a member of the council with a salary of £100; in 1402 he became the king's secretary; and in 1406 he was keeper of the privy seal. Even in his higher position Prophet's handwriting and signature may be recognized among the notes of the council.

Successors of Prophet.

During the later years of Richard II, no successor to Prophet as clerk of the council was immediately found, so that there was a reversion to the earlier irregular methods. The names of James Billingford and Robert Farington, clerks of

[1] 'Iohani Prophete clerico . . . in persolutionem XL marcarum quas dominus Rex de avisamento consilii sui liberare mandavit de dono suo de regardo pro custubus et expensis per ipsum habitis circa consilium Regis.' Ibid., 14 Ric. II, Mich., m. 3.

[2] Ibid., 15 Ric. II, Mich., m. 22.

[3] 'Magistro Iohani Profete clerico consilii Regis . . . tam equitando ad diversa loca in servicio Regis de mandato consilii sui, quam morando continue circa consilium Regis predictum.' Ibid., 16 Ric. II, Mich., m. 20.

[4] Ibid., 17 Ric. II, Mich., January 30; 19 Ric. II, Mich., &c.

[5] Wylie, *Henry IV*, ii. 484.

the chancery, appear upon a number of documents. In 1398 Master William Lambroke is mentioned as 'clerk of the council',[1] but his term of service was not long or otherwise notable. In the reign of Henry IV another efficient clerk was found in Robert Fry, who had already received recognition for his twelve years of good service in the offices of the privy seal and of the signet.[2] In the second year of Henry IV we learn that upon his own request he was allowed 40 marks 'for the labours he had sustained in writing the acts of the council in times past'.[3] In the following year, as 'one of the clerks in the office of the privy seal', he received the same sum for this service.[4] In the three succeeding years his fee was £20. But in the eighth year, as 'clerk of the council', he was given a fee of 40 marks for his services in the council since the previous Christmas.[5] From this time, that is the year 1405, the position may be regarded as a permanent office, for it was held continuously by Robert Fry at the same salary of 40 marks until 1421, when he retired honourably as secondary clerk of the privy seal with a salary of £10.[6] He was succeeded by Richard Caudray, who was already associated in some way with the office; for in 1419 Caudray was one of several men sent upon an embassy to France, in which he was named as clerk of the council.[7] Not until the retirement of Fry, however, did he receive the full salary of the position.[8] In 1422, for the first time as it happened among the ordinances of the council, the office was mentioned in the requirement, 'that the clerk of the council be charged and sworn to write daily the names of all the lords that be present from time to time, to see what, how, and by whom everything passeth.'

[1] He was then appointed on a commission of inquiry. *Cal. Patent Rolls*, 21 Ric. II, 358.

[2] *Cal. Patent Rolls*, 22 Ric. II, 463. He is mentioned also as one closely associated with John Prophet. *Issue Roll* (*Pells*), 17 Ric. II, Mich., January 30.

[3] Ibid., 3 Hen. IV, Mich., m. 12.

[4] Ibid., 4 Hen. IV, Mich., m. 14; 5 Hen. IV, Mich., m. 21; 6 Hen. IV, Mich., m. 11.

[5] Ibid., 8 Hen. IV, Mich., m. 10.

[6] *Cal. Patent Rolls*, 1 Hen. VI, 22.

[7] *Foedera* (Orig. Ed.), ix. 749.

[8] 'Ricardo Caudray clerico de consilio Regis . . . in persolutionem XL marcarum . . . prout Robert Fry nuper clerico de consilio Regis solutum est.' *Issue Roll* (*Pells*), 1 Hen. VI, Easter m. 9.

Duties of the clerk.

From this time certainly the office of clerk of the council was a conspicuous post of trust and honour. The salary indicates its relative position as slightly lower than that of the clerk of parliament who received £40 a year. But the profits that were derived from the fees of suitors and other sources were probably much greater than the salary itself. From the passages already cited his duties consisted especially in conveying confidential messages, not merely delivering the letters but ‘ demonstrating and declaring ’ them. He wrote the acts of the council, and in certain years was responsible for keeping the ‘ Book of the Council ’ ; he selected the petitions to be considered, made the endorsements, and kept files of the bills. In all probability he administered the councillor's oath. He was also constantly appointed on embassies and on committees of examination. So that it is not surprising to find that much of the time the labours of the office were sufficient to require the services of two clerks, as already appears in the case of Fry and Caudray. While the clerk was not a member of the council, he might, nevertheless, add his own name to the list of councillors in attendance, as for example, *praesentibus Cancellario, Thesaurario, Domino de Beaumont, et me Adam Molyns.*[1] Several of the clerks were men of distinction and rose to higher positions in the government. One of the most remarkable careers was that of Adam Moleyns, who was clerk of the council from 1436 to 1442. He gained great influence politically, until in 1443 he was made a member of the council, and afterwards became keeper of the privy seal and bishop of Chichester.[2] During his term of office the records of the council appear mainly to have been written by Henry Benet, a minor clerk of the privy seal office, who in the sixteenth year asked to be rewarded for his services in the following petition :

(Signed) R. H.

‘ . . . Like it to the Kyng our souverain lord to considre the services and laboures that your humble servant Henri Benet oon of your Clerks in thoffice of youre prive seal hath had and souffred aboute thentendance of your counsailx

[1] Nicolas, v. 142, 145, 150, &c.

[2] *Ante*, pp. 187, 193.

this yere and an half, and yerupon to graunte unto him such reward for his said services and laboures as shal like unto youre highnesse.

(endors :—) The kyng wol that Benet with ynne written have the tyme with ynne written and for the tyme that he shal entende aboute the kynges consailx suche . . . rewards as other clercs of the Kynges consailx have hadd her afor, ⁊ yat her upon warrant be maad undre prive seal to the Tresorer ⁊ Chamberleyns to paie.' [1]

Benet served until 1443, when he was succeeded by the learned Thomas Kent, doctor of laws, who was permitted at the same time to hold the post of secondary clerk in the office of the privy seal, and likewise that of sub-constable. [2] In 1449 Kent is mentioned as a councillor,[3] and as such he was attacked in the rebellion of Jack Cade and afterwards brought to trial.[4] He did not cease to be clerk of the council, however, for in 1458 that office was granted in survivorship to him and Richard Langport, who were to receive jointly all customary fees, wages, and rewards, with a livery of linen and fur at the great wardrobe.[5] This grant was afterwards renewed by Edward IV.[6] But Kent shortly left the clerkship to Langport, while he continued to be recognized as secondary in the office of the privy seal and a king's councillor.[7] Under the conditions of Edward IV's reign the clerkship of the council sank into comparative obscurity. In 1478 William Lacy is mentioned as holding the office,[8] and during the revival of business under Richard III a second man was appointed especially to care for the bills of poor suitors.[9] Under the quickened conditions of the Tudors the office with all its perquisites was said to be worth as much as £20,000 a year.

[1] *Council and Privy Seal*, file 59, 16 Hen. VI, February 26.

[2] *Foedera*, xi. 75 ; *Cal. Patent Rolls*, 22 Hen. VI, 235, 277 ; 23 Hen. VI, 348.

[3] *Foedera*, xi. 241.

[4] He is then called 'clericus communis consilii domini Regis'. *Coram Rege Roll*, 30 Hen. VI, rex, m. 8.

[5] *Cal. Patent Rolls*, 36 Hen. VI, 425.

[6] Ibid., 1 Edw. IV, 126.

[7] Ibid., 6 Edw. IV, 520.

[8] *Issue Roll*, 18 Edw. IV, Easter, m. 3.

[9] *Cal. Patent Rolls*, 1 Ric. III, 413.

5. The 'Head' of the Council

From time to time mention is made of a 'chief councillor' or a 'head' of the council, in words such as *principalis consiliarius, de consilio regis capitalis, gubernator consilii*, and the like. From references of this kind the view was propounded by Coke[1] and accepted by Stubbs and others,[2] that there was actually an office of president of the council, which at first during the middle ages was held occasionally, and later was made a fixed position. Now the facts upon which this theory is based are indeed very meagre. In the reign of Henry III, for instance, various men were pointed out as 'principal councillor', 'special and familiar councillor', or 'moderator of the royal counsels'; William, bishop-elect of Valence, is mentioned as *consiliarius regis principalis*.[3] In 1316, under compulsion of parliament, the king asked the earl of Lancaster, *quod esset de consilio domini regis capitalis*; the earl was also called *principalis consiliarius*, and entered upon his special position by taking an oath.[4] Again in the reign of Edward III, Archbishop Stratford is mentioned as *consiliarius principalis*,[5] and in 1377 William of Wykeham is curiously styled, *capitalis secreti consilii ac gubernator magni consilii*.[6] Nothing is said of any such title again until the time of the minority of Henry VI, when the duke of Bedford was made protector and defender of the realm and 'chief councillor', while the duke of Gloucester was to hold the same position during the absence of his brother.[7] The title *consiliarius principalis* was permitted to continue even after the protectorate was ended. The same titles of 'protector' and 'chief councillor' were conferred by authority of parliament upon the duke of York in 1454 and again in 1455.[8] But one spoke also of leading councillors without any

Mention of chief councillors.

[1] 'There is and of ancient times hath been a President of the Councell.' *Fourth Institute*, chap. ii.

[2] Nicolas, i, p. iv.

[3] To these passages I have called attention in chapter ii.

[4] *Rot. Parl.* i. 351. In 1324 Roger Belers is described as 'miles et iustitiarius domini regis et consiliarius capitalis.' *Ann. Paulini*, 310.

[5] *W. de Dene Historia Roffensis* (Henry Wharton, London, 1691), i. 375. The same thing is said of Bishop Burghersh of Lincoln. Murimuth, *Contin.* 120.

[6] *Rot. Parl.* iii. 388; *Chron. Angl.* lxxvi.

[7] *Rot. Parl.* iv. 174.

[8] Ibid., v. 242, 288; *Cal. Patent Rolls*, 32 Hen. VI, 159; 34 Hen. VI, 301.

such formality. In 1455 we read of an action that was taken *per nobiles et principales consiliarios Regis*.[1] In 1461 a much less exalted man, Sir John Fortescue, at the time of his exile is mentioned as 'chief councillor'.[2] Altogether there is very little warrant for the opinion that anything like an office or a definite post was contemplated in any of these instances. The danger of magnifying descriptive phrases has many times been pointed out, but still the tendency persists. In every case the title, if we may call it such, was a purely personal one, which cannot be found to imply any particular official functions.

The actual presiding officer.

Yet, says Fortescue, there must be 'a head or a chief to rule the council, . . . chosen by the king, having his office at the king's pleasure, who may then be called *capitalis consiliarius*'. This head, he indicates, was to be the chancellor, who, 'when he is present, may be president, and have the supreme rule of all the council.'[3] In the absence of the chancellor there was the treasurer, or, as more frequently happened, the keeper of the privy seal. The practical functions of the chancellor or his substitute in presiding over the council stand out very clearly. He summoned the members; he read the letters of the king, and propounded the questions for discussion; he asked the members for their opinions and declared the votes. These presiding functions the chancellor did not fail to exercise even when the duke of Gloucester bearing the title of chief councillor was present.[4] There was no confusion, in fact, between the functions of a presiding officer and those of the chief councillor. Moreover, the post of chief councillor, as it was known during the middle ages, was not in any way a prototype of the office of president of the council, as it is seen at a later stage. Such a position is first mentioned in a connexion apart from the council in England, namely in the council of the Prince of Wales, which was appointed by

[1] Archbishop Winchelsey was said to be one of the king's principal councillors. *Cal. Close Rolls*, 33 Edw. I, 312. In 1314 we read of a session *cum primatibus consilii regis*. *Ann. London*. 232.

[2] Ed. Plummer, p. 57 *n*.

[3] Op. cit., chap. xiv.

[4] Likewise in the council at Eltham in 1395 the chancellor directed the procedure in the presence of the royal dukes.

Edward IV in 1473 to administer the principality.[1] At that time Bishop Alcock was appointed teacher of the prince and president of his council. Thence the idea seems to have been transferred to the king's council in England, when a new division of that body was made during the reign of Henry VII, and there was need of an additional executive officer to take the place of the keeper of the privy seal. Of this special development more will be said in connexion with the other events of that time, when it will be made clear that the president was never a chief councillor, as was Thomas earl of Lancaster, or Humphrey duke of Gloucester, but taking rank below the chancellor and the treasurer, he was rated as third among the active ministers of the crown.

[1] *Patent Rolls,* 13 Edw. IV, part i, m. 3; Skeel, *Council of the Welsh Marches,* pp. 283, 366.

CHAPTER XIV

RECORDS OF THE COUNCIL

An important question.

IN every treatment of the subject, the obscurity that hangs over the early history of the king's council has been attributed to the apparent lack of records. Not until the time of Richard II have any such materials been supposed to exist. Although there is much concerning the council during the fourteenth century that may be gathered from various collateral sources, the prevailing opinion is that without direct evidence our knowledge cannot be clear and definite. In reference to this problem Sir Harris Nicolas has said, 'Its history can only be traced in its proceedings, and until these proceedings are collected and printed, he is persuaded that anything which could be written would be unworthy of attention, because it must be formed of speculations founded upon most imperfect premises.' [1] The high value of the proceedings published by this eminent authority, every one surely will admit, but his opinion that no trustworthy information is to be gained from other sources may well be questioned. It has been thought, too, that before the beginning of its records the council cannot be considered to be a distinct and mature body. In emphasis of this point Professor Dicey says, 'The conjecture is therefore natural that the council's acts were first accurately recorded when its existence as a separate institution was for the first time recognized.' [2] This time was understood to be the reign of Richard II, when various new departures and organic changes are known to have occurred. A great deal therefore hinges upon the question when such records were actually first made.

The famous collection of Sir H. Nicolas, entitled *Proceed-*

[1] *Proceedings of the Privy Council*, vol. i, p. vi.
[2] *Privy Council*, p. 25.

ings and Ordinances of the Privy Council, published in 1834–7, was taken from the manuscripts then accessible in the British Museum, mainly those of the Cottonian Library. Now Sir Robert Cotton, we know, was an antiquarian of the seventeenth century, who was engaged in investigating various questions concerning the rights of kings and parliaments. He had free access to the public records, vast stores of which he ‘ cunningly scraped together ’ and appropriated. That so many public documents should be in the hands of a private individual was believed to be a positive danger to the state. Incurring the enmity of the government, Cotton was brought before the star chamber in 1629–30, when his library was confiscated and taken ultimately into the custody of the king's officers.[1] Prima facie there is no reason to suppose that Cotton secured all the records of the council for any particular period, or even that the earliest ones fell into his possession. The first entry in the aforesaid volumes of Nicolas is in the form of *agenda*, as we should say, consisting of a series of articles drawn up from the terms of the commission of 1386; the next entry contains ‘ divers acts ’ of the year 1389, and other fragmentary notes follow. There is nothing to show why the tenth or the thirteenth year of the reign was made a point of beginning in this matter. Nicolas himself afterwards discovered two isolated instances of minutes of the council, belonging to the years 1337 and 1341 respectively, which he presented in his *History of the Royal Navy*.[2] It would be strange indeed were these the only instances during a period of fifty years in which minutes of the kind were written. Now a search among the archives of the Public Record Office, where the acts of the council properly belong, reveals that there is an abundance of such material, not only of earlier date than any one has stated, but also of later times, which has not been utilized. The Cottonian Library and the editorial work of Nicolas, valuable as these are conceded to be, are not by any means exhaustive

The work of Sir Harris Nicolas.

[1] *Dictionary of National Biography*; also various works of Sir Robert Cotton.

[2] (London, 1847), ii. 188–92. The learned author, however, did not state where the manuscripts were found. In making search for these I was rewarded by finding many others of the same kind.

collections. The manuscripts of the council in fact are found for every stage of its history, even before its organization was finally determined. Because of their obvious importance an account of these records must now be given.

No records in the stricter sense.

By way of preliminary explanation, it should be said that the council was never a 'court of record' in the same sense as the king's bench or the exchequer. It was under no obligations to record its actions, and did so only so far as the utility of the moment required.[1] In the notes of the council therefore we can expect to find only the utmost brevity and often bareness of statement. It would be too much also to anticipate any revelations in the way of far-reaching legislative acts. General legislation was everywhere rare during the middle ages, and no great activity of this kind is to be found even upon the rolls of parliament. Important acts too were not hidden away, but were quickly placed upon the rolls of the exchequer or the chancery, often upon both. We should be disappointed also if we were to look for an account of the deliberations, the debates, the expressions of individual opinion and motive, such as must have taken place. These are seldom given even in the more public sessions of parliament. Besides, according to the feelings of the age, men disliked to be individualized in this way. From all that has been said one may expect the proceedings of the council, so far as they were written at all, to consist of innumerable acts of minor character, mainly private bills relating to grants of office, rewards, favours, safe conducts, charters and the renewal of charters, military supplies, loans, assignments of customs, contracts with coiners and judicial decisions. Not the importance of the individual acts, but the infinite number of acts which were constantly passed in the name of the council is the marvel. The aforesaid records, therefore, are valuable mainly not for what they contain in subject matter, but for what they reveal of the procedure of the council, showing how the work was done.

The earliest and simplest form of record made by the

[1] That acts of the council were not matters of record was repeatedly urged in parliament as a reason for restricting its powers (e.g. statute, 42 Edw. III, c. 3). Coke's well-known definition of a record was that which could be appealed on error.

council was in connexion with the petitions, concerning which much has been said already.[1] Whether these were requests for favour or for legal redress, the council was constantly occupied with both kinds. The responses were regularly written upon the backs of the same strips of parchment in words as few as possible. Between a conciliar petition and a parliamentary petition there was no perceptible difference at first, but a distinction begins to appear as soon as the two forms of authority are seen to diverge. Then it is often made plain whether the response was *per consilium regis* or *per consilium in parliamento*. In the hands of the clerks of the privy seal employed by Edward III and Richard II the endorsements of the council were made in the peculiar style of their office. Different from those treated in parliament, the endorsements and marginal notes made in the council were usually given at this time with the dates and the names of the members present.[2] Now the great bulk of the business of the council at all times consisted in the reading, passing, and endorsement of these individual bills. They are to be counted by the hundred, possibly by the thousand, every year ; sometimes a score or more were dealt with in a day. How so much business was ever transacted would remain a mystery, if it were not apparent that of all possible methods of procedure this was the one calculated to cost the least expenditure of time and attention. The request or proposition was already prepared in a definite form ; it had only to be passed with the necessary instructions ; often it was only to be granted or not granted. Moreover, as a practical matter the treatment of private bills, ' of less charge ', was generally left to a very few individuals, particularly the officers, knights, and clerks who were retained for this very purpose. Matters of greater moment

The endorsements of petitions.

[1] Most of these have been collected in the files known as *Ancient Petitions*, wherein more than 16,000 are arranged in alphabetical order. Similar petitions, however, are found in various other files, particularly in those denoted as *Council and Privy Seal*, and *Parliamentary and Council Proceedings*.

[2] Possibly the greatest number of individual acts are to be found in the files of the collection to which I have often referred, *Exchequer K. R., Council and Privy Seal*. These were formerly classified as *Warrants Privy Seal*.

were then reserved for the consideration of the 'full council'. However brief and threadbare, the endorsement of a bill, it must be understood, was treated as a record of validity equal to any other form of writing. A fact in a suit was once established with the words, *come piert par votre bille ent endorsez et de record devant le conseil.*[1]

Convenience of the petitionary form.

So well adapted to the requirements of the council was the method of petition and answer, that it was followed in all kinds of business, public as well as private. The most frequent form by which matters for the consideration of the council were stated consisted of a series of articles, each article being a distinct petition or proposition. Some of the longer petitions of this kind contained a dozen or twenty separate articles. A characteristic title upon one document of this kind in the time of Edward III reads, *fait a remembrer des choses a monstrer au conseil nostre seigneur le Roi*;[2] another is *fait a parler oue le consail nostre Seigneur le Roi qi fait a faire par reson et pur profit de defautz ensuvantz.*[3] Such a document amounted to a list of *agenda*, which could be considered point by point. Upon the wide margins on the sides of the parchment and between the paragraphs could be written the responses or decisions of the council to each point. In case the articles were accepted in their entirety the endorsement was a simple matter; in one instance the answer was, *ceux articles sont lues devant le Roi et le conseil et sont acordez en touz pointz.*[4] Single articles were sometimes accepted with a *fiat*, or *fait sil plest au Roi.* Corrections also and substitutions of words and clauses were likely to be made, so that a bill which has passed the council may be filled with erasures and interlineations. It will be noticed that this method of procedure required the very minimum of clerical work. In most instances the services

[1] *Warrants Privy Seal,* series i, section ii, file 9. An exceptional circumstance is mentioned in 1415, when a memorandum of endorsements was made—'Remembrance des endorsementz des petitions'. Nicolas, ii. 149.

[2] *Parliamentary and Council Proceedings,* file vii, no. 19. This collection has been compiled only in recent years. It contains much material relating to parliament as well as to the council. To a certain point, of course, proceedings of the council cannot be separated as a class from those of parliament.

[3] Ibid., file vi, no. 12, 2 Edw. III. The appearance of these petitions and answers is shown in Plate no. 2.

[4] Ibid., vii. 24.

of a professional scribe were not in any way needed, the brief marginal notes being written apparently by some one of the regular officers or bishops.[1] The same lack of formality in the proceedings of the council is often noticeable after the reign of Richard II as well as before, although a professional clerk was then regularly employed.

Gascon articles of 1311.

It will illustrate a whole class of documents to describe one or two of the most striking examples. In 1311 there came a series of articles from Gascony, which had possibly been drawn up by the council there, as others surely were.[2] The articles are set off from each other and punctuated with the words, *item intimandum est*, or *item consilium est*, and are written in a provincial Latin strange to England. Most likely the matter was considered at a small council summoned to meet at York, February 27, 1312, expressly to confer on affairs of Aquitaine.[3] The items in detail specify that the mayor and *iurati* of Bordeaux are increasing the taxes, that many officers commit excesses while the country is distracted by war, that commissioners with plenary powers should be appointed, that the castles of Bordeaux need repair, that in the law cases pending before the court of the king of France subjects of the king of England should be treated fairly, and for evidence in these cases diligent search should be made in the king's treasury. The responses of the council are written in a small cramped hand between the several paragraphs. Many of the questions were referred to the seneschal of Gascony, who was to act with the advice of the king's council in the province. Some of the answers are made with the additional confirmation, *placet regi*, while in other instances it was required, *informetur rex*. We learn that the appointment of a commission to go to Paris was afterwards carried out.[4]

A long document of the year 1320 shows that the same procedure was followed in the king's provincial council of

[1] Sometimes one speaks as though the writing were *by* the council without any intermediary, as for instance, *le conseil ad cy escrit son avis* and *cestes notes furent faites par le conseil*. Ibid., vii. 13.

[2] *Diplomatic Documents, Chancery*, portf. 114. This is another file into which many of the council records have naturally fallen.

[3] *Parl. Writs*, ii. 71.

[4] *Cal. Close Rolls*, 6 Edw. II, 488.

Gascony.[1] The articles in this case consist of certain petitions from Agen and other towns asking for franchises and reforms in the Agenais. These questions were first submitted to the seneschal and council of Gascony, by whom certain amendments were made. They were then sent to England, where they were submitted to the council and answered point by point in the usual manner. All the articles were accepted but one, concerning which there was to be further deliberation.[2]

Articles of John Darcy, 2 Edw. III.

There were many documents of the same kind relating to the government of Ireland. In the second year of Edward III it is stated that John Darcy laid before the council a series of petitions in sixteen articles, setting forth the conditions upon which he was willing to go to Ireland as chief justice.[3] He asks that certain men whom he names be placed in office as his associates; that the chief justice have powers of supervision over other officers; that he have the power to pardon for felony; that no grants in Ireland be made without consulting the justice and others of the council there; that it be granted by statute that all Irishmen wishing to live under English laws be permitted to do so without having to buy charters for the privilege. The answers of the council are inserted between the lines and in the margins in a handwriting clearly different from the rest of the manuscript. Most of the propositions were accepted with slight modifications. Some of the names suggested were crossed out and others substituted. As to the granting of pardons, it was answered that the power should not be exercised without consulting the king. As to the Irish freely enjoying English law, the justice was told to get the opinion of the next Irish parliament. Other items were accepted with a simple *fiat*. Apparently the assent of the king also was obtained, for the decisions thus reached were afterwards carried out on the authority of the king and council.[4] In

[1] *Chancery Miscellaneous Rolls*, bundle 5, no. 16.

[2] A final note declares ‘ Postmodum exhibitis dictis articulis et diligenter examinatis visum est consilio quod poterunt confirmari salvo iure Regis excepto xx^{mo} de quo deliberaretur ’.

[3] *Parliamentary Proceedings*, vi. 10; Appendix I, p. 473.

[4] *Cal. Patent Rolls*, 2 Edw. III, 316; *Cal. Close Rolls*, 312.

a similar series of petitions which were received from the prelates and barons of Ireland in the sixteenth year of Edward III, the following explanatory note occurs.[1] 'The king ordained that these should be diligently examined by the council and answers should be written after each petition, and then the king commanded that the answers with the articles should have full force with the penalties contained therein.' In this form the articles were afterwards sent back to Ireland to be observed.

Separate responses.

But the answers to petitions were not always of the brevity found in the examples just described. Sometimes they were rendered at such length that separate parchments were required. Of the year 1334 there is a voluminous petition sent by the seneschal and council of Gascony to the king and council in England, consisting of twenty-nine articles concerning the aggressions of the king of France.[2] A brief inscription upon one of the pages describes how the answers were returned in another roll. It says, *As touz les pointz qe touchent les articles desuzditz est respondu en le point entre en un roule sur lordenance faite par le conseil sur les ditz articles et articles suauntz.* Unfortunately in this case, as in most others when the same method was followed, petitions and answers have become separated and cannot be brought together again.[3]

Copies or transcripts.

Sometimes also for purposes of administration copies were made of the original documents passed by the council. Such transcripts are readily distinguished by the fact that petitions and responses are all in the same handwriting, while the work of copying was done by a professional scribe. In these cases of course the entire manuscript is made by the council or under its direction. A good example of a public document of this kind is one dated March 24, 1318, which embodies a report from the bishop of Worcester, one of the king's proctors for cases pending in the parliament of

[1] *Cal. Close Rolls*, 16 Edw. III, 508 ff.

[2] *Chancery Miscellaneous Rolls*, bundle 5, no. 22.

[3] There is a noteworthy set of responses sent to Gascony about the year 1314, bearing the endorsement, *avisamenta consilii Regis super quibus petitur tangens Regi.* It is more frequent to find petitions without the answers.

Paris.[1] In a number of articles in the usual form, an account is given of certain judicial processes that were being drawn into the French court, involving ministers and other subjects of the king of England in Aquitaine. Some of the recommendations of the bishop were that an effort should be made to have a joint commission appointed by the king of England and by the king of France to deal with the cases in dispute ; that penalties imposed on the appellants should not be exacted provided they would withdraw their appeals ; that in regard to certain cases request for delay should be made in the hope of a permanent peace.

Bills framed by the council.

Bills, we are told, were 'either endorsed or *made* by the advice of the council'.[2] For reasons already given the method of petition and answer was the most characteristic mode of procedure, but it was not by any means the only form of writing produced by the council. It was a different, though not necessarily a more advanced method, when the things agreed upon were set down in the shape of minutes or resolutions, without reference to any petition or other suggestion. Such minutes contain an infinite variety of recommendations, ordinances, or drafts of ordinances. They were written always upon single and detached membranes, usually in a series of articles that could be considered separately, with a preference for the French language over the more formal Latin. The statements are commonly introduced by phrases like *ordinatum est, fait a remembrer qe, accorde fust par le conseil,* or *avis est de conseil.* In some cases the appearance of the writing suggests that the articles were put down at different times, as the decisions were reached, and sometimes space is left for more. It would be possible to give illustrations of such ordinances at great length.[3] Many of them are of the reign of Edward I, before the organization of the council was fairly differentiated

[1] An explanatory note is as follows: 'Dominus T. dei gratia Wigorniensis episcopus liberavit Elie de Jonestone (*king's clerk*) infrascriptos articulos portandos dicto domino Regi, cancellario et thesaurario suis et ceteris de consilio ad quos pertinet super hiis consulere et remedia adhibere.' *Diplomatic Documents, Chancery,* no. 250.

[2] *Rot. Parl.* iii. 572.

[3] Good examples are given in Plates nos. 1 and 3.

from that of parliament. We have reason to think, however, that in those days most legislative acts, even the statutes, were passed by small councils.[1] In 1299 there is a very clear record of an act, stated as *ordinatum per Regem et consilium suum*, awarding sums of money to various Gascons who had lost their lands in the king's service.[2] The document contains the names of six councillors who were responsible for the measure. Of the same general form is an ordinance of the twenty-fourth year called *de statu religiosorum de potestate regis Franciae*, which relates to alien priories, forbidding them to exist within thirteen miles of the sea or other navigable waters.[3] In the first and second years of Edward II there are certain notable acts relating to the government of Scotland, directing appointments to office, salaries, military equipment, and various other matters.[4]

All kinds of documents inspected and passed.

But the attention of the council was not confined to any particular class of documents. Every kind of instrument in fact known to the state came under its purview, and it was a special function of the council to determine the form of words to be used in these numberless drafts of letters and writs that were submitted and passed upon.[5] Sometimes they are accompanied by side-notes like the following: *accordez est qe brief soit fait . . . solonc la contenue de ceste copie deinz escrite*, or *solonc leffect et purport de ceste copie*, or *qe commissions soient faites . . . ouesqe les additions en la cedule a icestes annexes*.[6] Generally the drafts were written only in rough outline, giving merely 'the effect and purport', and leaving much to be filled out by the clerks. As once was stated in such a matter under Henry VI, 'the king wills that the aforesaid articles be extended in ample and large form as it shall be thought necessary and behoveful.'[7] On another occasion of the same reign letters of the chancery in two alternative fashions of writing were submitted, those

[1] Discussed in chapter xii.

[2] *Chancery Miscellaneous Rolls*, bundle 5, no. 5.

[3] *Parliamentary Proceedings*, ii. 22.

[4] *Diplomatic Documents, Chancery*, nos. 217, 809.

[5] 'Decretum est per consilium quod breve predictum in casu isto et in casibus consimilibus est necessarium et rationabile.' *Rot. Parl.* i. 74; also 297; *Parl. Writs*, i. 384.

[6] Taken from unfiled documents found in a box.

[7] Nicolas, vi. 61.

written 'with the styles' and those 'without styles', and the council decided that the latter should be used.[1] Likewise indentures containing the agreements made by the government with coiners of money, military leaders, and foreign princes passed under the same inspection. In one instance the statement is made that 'this indenture was first made under the form here enrolled, word for word; and afterwards with the assent of the council all the words underlined were cancelled, and the indenture was newly made under the same date, the cancelled words being omitted'.[2] As an example of an indenture used in foreign relations, we have one of the twelfth year of Edward II, when certain ambassadors of the count of Flanders came to a parliament at York and treated with the council there upon the damages sustained by the people of Flanders as well as by the people of England because of certain depredations at sea. The content of the agreement is explained by the following note: *fait a remembrer qe come avant ces houres trete fut entre le conseil le Roi Dengleterre et certeins messengers le Conte de Flandres . . . les quex messages vindrent au dit Roi a son parlement a Everwik . . . et reherse entre le conseil le dit Roi et les ditz messages*, etc.[3] In the same manner letters of diplomatic correspondence were read before the council, and there the answers were dictated.[4]

Endorsements and notes by the king.

Of utmost interest are the records which reveal in any way the relations of the king and the council. What was done by the king apart from the council, or by the council independently of the king, it is not possible always to discern. In general there was no guiding rule, except that the rights of the crown were not to be touched without the king's assent. From a reading of the documents one gains a strong impression that the council was very little inclined to assume responsibilities without at least the formal assent of the king.

[1] Nicolas, vi. 193.

[2] *Cal. Close Rolls*, 25 Edw. III, 379; another is in *Cal. Patent Rolls*, 2 Ric. II, 340; also Appendix I.

[3] *Diplomatic Documents, Chancery*, portf. 143.

[4] For example a communication from the doge of Venice was answered by the council article by article. *Ancient Petitions*, no. 14759; see also Cotton. MS. (ed. Scott), p. 136.

Between the two there passed a great deal of correspondence, at times with daily frequency.[1] Letters of the king to the council appear in the reign of Henry III, while letters from the council to the king are found under Edward II. Messages of the king ask for the immediate consideration of a petition or some other form of proposition which he sends; letters of the council submit matters for the approval of the king and in questions of doubt ask for special instructions. In legal proceedings, we have noticed, there were certain stages when such reference had to be made. In many of the notes already described it is evident that the council awaits the approval of the king. Sometimes the petitions, or certain articles of the petitions, are answered conditionally, *s'il plest au Roy*; a second endorsement perhaps gives the king's assent, *il plest au Roy*. On one occasion the council answered favourably an entire series of articles, except one to which the response was *soit parle au Roi de ce point.*[2] Another set of ordinances is first passed in a conditional way with the words, *il semble au conseil sil plest au Roy*; and afterwards the responses of the king were given in side-notes.[3] In the seventeenth year of Edward III certain articles were given to a messenger to be delivered to the king with the statement, *Ces sont les articles bailles a William de Edington pur monstrer a nostre Seigneur le Roi depar son conseil.*[4] Still another method is shown in the tenth year of Edward II, when in the composition of certain letters under the great seal a question arose in regard to a single clause. In order that the king might decide the point, two sets of letters were issued, the one containing the clause in question and the other omitting it, and these were sent by the council at Westminster to the king then residing at Windsor. Here the letters of the latter form were chosen and sent on to Ireland, while the others were given back to the chancery.[5]

[1] *Ancient Correspondence*, in 58 volumes.

[2] *Parliamentary Proceedings*, viii. 27; also *Diplomatic Documents, Chancery*, portf. 114.

[3] *Chancery Miscellaneous Rolls*, bundle 1, no. 20.

[4] *Parliamentary Proceedings*, vii. 15; also articles, 18 Edw. III, Appendix I.

[5] *Cal. Close Rolls*, 10 Edw. II, 405.

Curious articles of 1339.

One of the most interesting of all the records in hand is a transcription of certain messages that passed between England and Flanders in the year 1339. It is entitled, 'Articles reported to the chancellor, the treasurer, and others of the king's council in England . . . from the king across the sea and the responses to the same articles.'[1] The messages from the king, who was then engaged in war, express his disappointment that he has not received from home enough of the revenues and supplies, while the answers give the explanations of the council, with more or less evasion, that they have fully done their duty. The questions bore particularly upon the extraordinary subsidy of 1338, when the king had been granted the pre-emption of 20,000 sacks of wool at a fixed price. This was a new kind of levy, and the management of it had devolved entirely upon the council. The whole scheme proved to be very disappointing. Regarding the 20,000 sacks of wool, the king in his message complained that of the assignments already made not one half had come to him; the council answered that as to this and other things they were sending messengers to explain, and asked the king to consider the facts stated in a schedule shortly to be sent. He asked further for an explanation why certain parties to whom assignments of wool had been made not only failed to receive them, but found that their assignments had been recalled and changed. The council replied that some of the assignments in question had actually been delivered and that none had been recalled or changed except by the king's command. Most of all the king complained of the corrupt and faulty methods of the levy, by which inferior wool of light weight and unmarketable had been sent to him; the council, however, claimed that every effort had been made in their writs and commissions to provide against these very evils. Certain petty financial devices that were further suggested by the king, such as the withdrawal of various assignments and the recall of ministers' fees, were pointed out by the council to be entirely impracticable. Seldom do we find a document in fact which reveals so much of the interplay of motives and feelings.

[1] *Parliamentary Proceedings*, vii. 7; Appendix I.

PLATE VIII

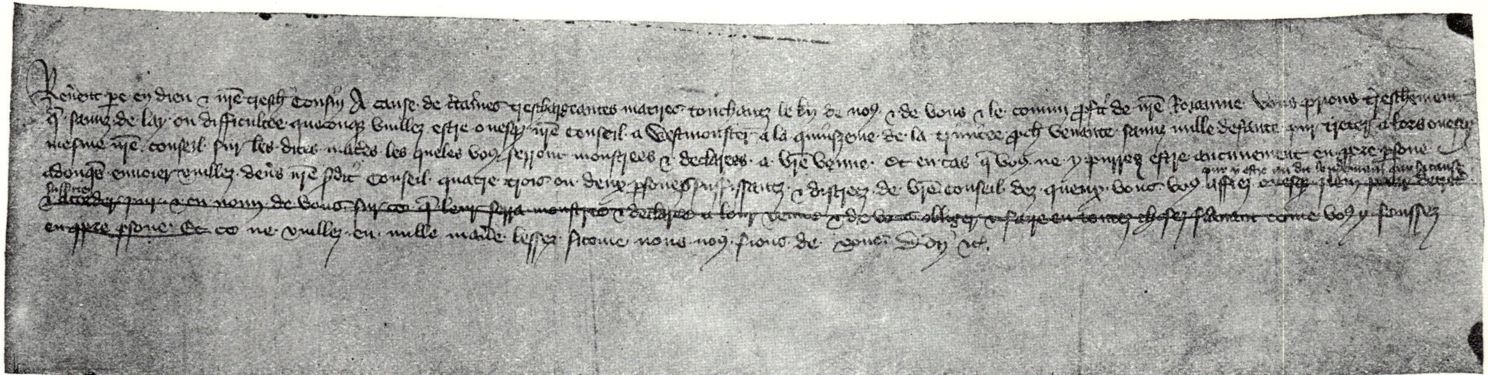

WARRANT FOR A LETTER OF SUMMONS DIRECTED TO A BISHOP, 22 RIC. II.

PLATE IX

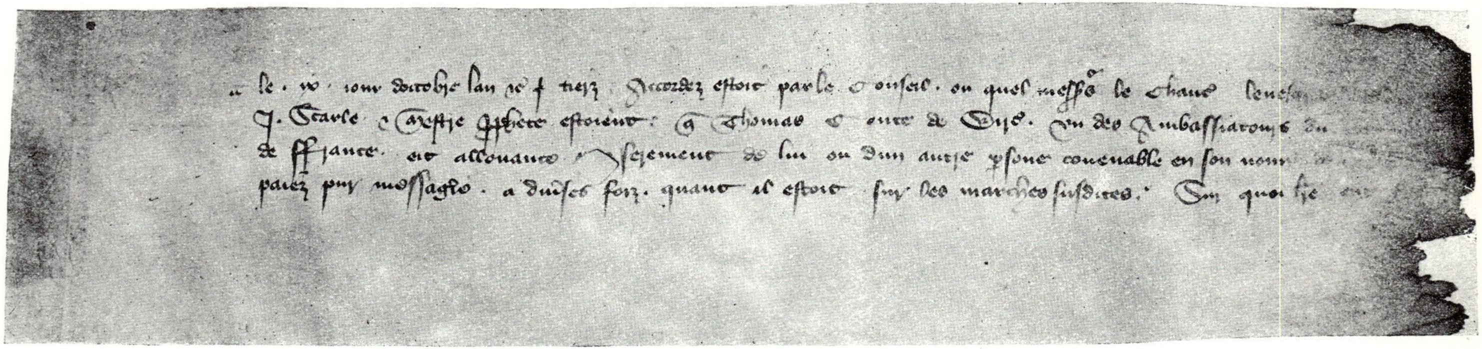

A SMALL BILL, PASSED OCTOBER 9, 3 HEN. IV.

Purpose of the council's notes.

The question naturally arises, for what purpose were these various responses, notes, and memoranda written? The intention certainly was not to make a record in the usual sense of leaving the actions subject to review and of creating precedents for the future. The aim was one of immediate practical utility. In whatever form they were made, the acts of the council were governmental orders which were to be carried into effect by one or another of the agencies at command. Sometimes the articles and responses without any change were given to the officers or authorities for their guidance. In 1351 the king wrote to the mayor and sheriff of London enclosing certain articles ordained by him and his council, ordering them to cause those articles to be proclaimed and observed, and to arrest all those found doing anything to the contrary.[1] A similar use was made of the articles relating to Ireland which have been cited from the sixteenth year of Edward III. But in the greater number of cases the acts of the council were taken as warrants for official letters either under the great seal or under the privy seal. Now and then one finds a suggestion upon the bills to the following effect: *memorandum quod concordatum et ordinatum fuit per consilium domini Regis quod diverse carte et littere patentes fiant sub magno sigillo*,[2] or *accordez estoit et assentuz que garant du prive seal soient faites solonc les trois copies cy annexees*.[3] From the reign of Edward II on, one may observe, the acts of the council were more and more taken as warrants for the privy seal, while the letters under the great seal in turn were warranted by writs of the privy seal.[4] The extreme formalities were never fully insisted upon, but from the reign of Richard II one often finds the following steps taken in the

1 *Cal. Close Rolls*, 25 Edw. III, 391; also *Rot. Parl.* iii. 386.

2 *Warrants* (*Chancery*), file 1538, 46 Edw. III; another note is, 'Les seigneurs du counsail par lour assent et bon avys ont grantez les commissions par les maneres qe desouz est escrit.'

3 *Council and Privy Seal*, file 11, October 3, 3 Hen. IV, and many others. In certain proceedings of the year 1417 a sign was made in the margin to indicate the articles intended as warrants for the privy seal. 'Concordatum est quod super articulis inscriptis tali signo O+O signatis fiant littere sub privato sigillo.' Nicolas, ii. 239.

4 In one instance, 18 Edw. III, we find the note, 'ceste bille fut livere en chauncellerie depar le Roi et le conseil, et sur ceo fut bref fait,' &c. *Warrants* (*Chancery*), file 1538.

system of warrants: (1) an act of the council, or a letter under the king's signet, (2) a letter under the privy seal, (3) a letter under the great seal. Consequently the bulk of the records of the council are found among the miscellaneous parchments of the office of the privy seal. This department, we know, kept the warrants on file for a time [1] and afterwards gave them to the Treasury of Receipt for further preservation. At various times we are told in particular how letters and rolls were delivered into the treasury, where they were put in a bag of canvas, marked with a sign, and placed in a chest.[2] The lack of care and responsibility that was shown in keeping the records beyond the years of their immediate utility easily accounts for the losses that have been suffered. Those which remain have been found in a state of great disorder.

Use of official rolls.

From all that has been said, it is manifest that enrolments were never a necessary or characteristic part of the council's procedure. Yet there were often reasons for making an act strictly a matter of record. In fact, anything in the way of general legislation was sure to be treated in this manner. Although no particular roll was reserved for the purpose, it was a simple matter to order an engrossment in any of the rolls of the chancery or the exchequer. Even the rolls of parliament did not cease to be used at the convenience of the council for placing its law cases and other proceedings on record. Sometimes one finds a statement to the following effect, *Memorandum quod Iohan de Sandale thesaurarius liberavit hic septimo die Augusti hoc anno quandam ordinationem factam per Regem et consilium suum super compto garderobe . . . et eam precepit inrotulari in hec verba*,[3] *etc.*, or *cestes notes deinz escrites furent faites par le conseil le Roi et mandees a la chauncellerie pour engrosser.*[4] Again a manu-

[1] We read of 'a certayn acte of oure Counsail among othre remembrances of ye same our Counsail remayning in y'office of our prive seal'; also 'sicut in quadam copia de manibus dominorum de consilio subscripta, et in filacibus in officio privati sigilli remanentibus plenius continetur'. Nicolas, iv. 268; vi. 206, 208. The king is known to have addressed a writ of *certiorari* to the clerk of the council, requiring a return from the records. Appendix III, p. 531.

[2] *Antient Kalendars and Inventories of the Exchequer* (ed. Palgrave), vol. i, pp. lxxiv, 201, 210, &c.

[3] *Memoranda Roll, Exchequer K. R.*, 3 Edw. II, Trinity term.

[4] *Parliamentary Proceedings*, vii. 13.

script is handed to the clerk of the rolls 'to be entered in the rolls of the chancery for a record and testimony'.[1] The close rolls and the patent rolls in fact are filled with engrossments or 'exemplifications' of indentures, legal processes, and other matters of the kind. Sometimes the enrolment was 'craved' by private parties who were willing to pay for having their rights thus safeguarded. In the same manner the printed calendars of the close rolls and patent rolls contain in great abundance letters under the great seal warranted 'by record returned from the council', 'by record and petition returned from the council', 'by conciliar petition',[2] or simply 'by the council'. With so much material concerning the council lying on every hand, therefore, it is hardly correct to say that 'its history can only be traced in its proceedings'. Properly understood, this class of records, even though it does not consist of proceedings at first hand, is quite as trustworthy and instructive as the other.

Advances under Ric. II.

Most of the illustrations thus far cited in the present chapter have been taken from the period before the reign of Richard II. This was in order to show that nothing like a beginning of the records was made at that particular time. One is now prepared to consider what changes or advances were made in this line of development during the later period. No radical change certainly is noticeable in the accustomed forms of procedure. As the pages of Nicolas clearly show, the favourite methods still continued to be the answers to petitions, the marginal notes upon letters and other documents, and the ordinances or memoranda in the form of serial articles. But certain improvements came naturally with the advanced conditions of this time. For one thing the employment of a special clerk led to a noticeable regularity in the style of the notes. Not that all the notes even now were written by the clerk. Under Richard II there is the curious example of a message sent from the council to the king; half of it was written by a professional clerk,

[1] *Cal. Close Rolls*, 32 Edw. III, 534.

[2] The phrase *per petitionem consilii* is generally translated in the calendars 'by petition of council'. The translation which I have given seems to me to convey the real meaning.

while the latter part is in the crabbed hand of an amateur.[1] The most marked improvement to be noticed at this time was the practice of placing in the notes the date and names of the councillors present. As for the date the clerks seem to have followed the usages of the office of the privy seal, where it was customary to give this in every letter. In regard to the names of the councillors, this was a change from the more obscure or secretive usages of Edward III. It was particularly the intention of parliament that the councillors, individually as well as collectively, should be responsible for their actions. The plan in this respect was also upheld by the king, so that the clerk was regularly required to enter the names of the members present in every endorsement or other form of memoranda. For example, he writes :

le second jour Doctober lan etc. tierz, praesens en consail messeurs le Chanceller, levesqe de Hereford, le Tresorer, Gardein du prive seel, John Scarle, et mestre Johan Prophete, accordez estoit, etc.

Nicolas is certainly mistaken in saying that at any time under Richard II or Henry IV the names were written by the members themselves as signatures.[2] They were inscribed by the clerk in the same hand as the rest of his record. In the ordinances of 1422 it was expressly asserted that the clerk should be charged and sworn to write daily the names of the lords present, ‘ to see what, how, and by whom everything passeth.’ [3] As to signatures, these came in more slowly. Under Richard II, it is true, a lord would write his name upon a bill for which he was sponsor, and from this grew the practice of having all the lords place their signatures upon the bills which they passed. The earliest instance that the writer has happened to find of autograph signatures by the councillors as a body occurs in the second year of Henry VI.[4] In the ordinances of 1424 it was required that in passing their bills ‘ the names of thassenteurs be writen of their own hand ’.[5] The ordinances of 1426 were said to

[1] Letter of the lords of the council in 1399 to Richard II in Ireland. Cotton. MSS. Titus B xi (British Museum), p. 7 *b*.

[2] *Proceedings*, vol. ii, p. xxvi.

[3] Ibid., iii. 18.

[4] Cotton. MSS. Vespasian C xiv, 246.

[5] Nicolas, iii. 150, 216.

have been subscribed 'by the lords of the council with their own hands'.[1] So far as we have the original manuscripts to show, this practice seems to have been consistently followed during the remainder of the reign of Henry VI. There was good reason for insisting upon this formality, since titles were likely to be disputed if every legal requirement was not complied with. In the ordinances of 1430 an additional requirement was made that not only the decisions of the majority, but also the opinions of dissent should be placed in the minutes.[2] This rule was plainly disliked, and after being followed on a few occasions was readily dropped. The royal signature upon bills of the council begins to be seen under Richard II, expressed by the letters R.R. Henry VI's sign manual, H.R., is of frequent occurrence, and under Edward IV, E.R., for certain purposes, appears with practical regularity.

A journal, 1392–3.

Another step in the evolution of the records was taken when from the separate and individual notes a journal or register was compiled. This was a departure not to be expected of the council or of the office of the privy seal, but the need of a compilation for purposes of reference was sufficient to cause an attempt in this direction to be made. The earliest that has been known hitherto of any such register is of the date 1421.[3] But a search among the files of the privy seal has just brought to light a journal of this kind for the fifteenth and sixteenth years of Richard II, 1392–3.[4] The work is in a perfect state of preservation, and from the contents it proves to be the most valuable of all the surviving remnants concerning the mediaeval council. It consists of ten good-sized membranes, closely written upon both sides of the page, and stoutly sewn together at the top after the fashion of the Memoranda Rolls. It is the work solely of the clerk John Prophet, whose vigorous handwriting is easily identified; sometimes he calls attention to himself among those present, 'and I John Prophet.' It is quite likely that the work was undertaken on his sole initiative, for it was not continued under his immediate successors. The intention was not to copy all of the separate notes that were then

[1] Ibid. 221. Illustrations of signatures are given in Plate no. 10.
[2] Ibid., iv. 62. [3] Ibid., ii. p. xxvii. [4] Appendix II, p. 489.

readily at hand, but to abridge them and summarize the proceedings as they occurred from day to day. Especial care was taken to give the names of those present at every sitting. Many points of interest are clearly brought out. Beginning with January 20, 1392, an exceedingly active term was kept, lasting until March 7 ; as many as thirty-four sittings are noted, sometimes two in a day, one in the morning and the other 'after eating' ; during the first week six sessions were held ; and at a later time business was carried on for fourteen days without a break. The usual number in attendance varies from six to twelve ; sometimes it sinks to three or four ; the officers and knights, sometimes assisted by the justices, prove to be the more faithful in this regard, while the lords, as a rule, came at irregular intervals. The smaller council of four or six readily expanded into a great council, as happened between February 12 and 16, when as many as twenty-five to twenty-nine lords and members were present. The business of the council was taken up in the usual piece-meal manner, with frequent commitments and adjournments. According to the journal a half-dozen topics were easily treated in a day, to say nothing of petitions concerning which nothing is said. In the first pages it is noted that the mayor and aldermen of London came and were listened to in a question concerning their franchises ; securities were given for the appearance of William Brian in eight days ; word from the king was received that his confessor should be rewarded ; a report was heard concerning a violation of the statute of provisors ; the earl of Devon was to be summoned, apparently for a breach of the peace ; cases of wreck and deodand were dealt with, and so on. In the great meeting of February 12, the weighty question of peace or war with France was taken up, without any positive determination being reached. Along with administrative and political questions judicial processes were frequently interspersed, showing at one stage or another the peculiar features of the council's procedure.[1] There seemed to be no division of time with reference to the kind of work.

[1] The Franceys case, for example, of which a full description is given elsewhere. Appendix, pp. 502, 517.

During the remainder of the sixteenth year the journal of John Prophet was not sustained with anything like the same fullness of material. Possibly less was actually done, so that the items were of necessity fewer and less consequential. But there is every evidence of carelessness, as one must infer from the hasty handwriting and the failure to fill several blank spaces ; moreover, when the membranes were finally sewn together, the last two pieces were placed in inverse order. So that at this point, there is every reason to believe, the work was given up. There was no lack of material, however, during the following years, as various important fragments suggest. Witness for instance the account of the great council held at Eltham in 1395.

The Book of the Council, 1421–35.

So far as is known, no other attempt to compile a register was made until 1421. The work which then appears was a roll known as the 'Book of the Council'.[1] Unfortunately it has not survived intact, since it has been cut to pieces and the pages pasted into a volume, probably by some one who thought it could be more easily handled in this form. We are not sure therefore that the entire roll has been preserved. Like the earlier journal, it consisted of transcripts and abridgements of as many of the original minutes as were deemed of sufficient importance. Certainly it did not contain all of the notes of the council, and it took slight notice of judicial actions. Compared with the splendid rolls of the chancery and the exchequer, it was by no means a well-written or evenly-sustained work. How many years it was kept we do not know. Nothing is seen of it again after 1435, but whether it was then discontinued or simply lost is merely a matter of conjecture. Mention is made of it in 1455, at the time of the supremacy of the duke of York, when it was declared that the oath of allegiance to Henry should be enacted in the roll of parliament and also 'written and incorporated in the Book of the Council there to remain among other acts and ordinances'.[2] But from this passage shall one infer that the book had been continued during the intervening years, or that there was only an intention then of renewing it ? Nicolas believes that the work was continued

[1] Nicolas, ii. 286.

[2] *Rot. Parl.* v. 283.

and in existence in 1455. But in view of the disintegration which the council suffered during the previous decade, the writer is inclined to the opinion that the book was not continued long after 1435, and for similar reasons he still more strongly believes that the effort to revive it in 1455, like other projects of the same year, was equally a failure. Still the book was not forgotten. Among the reforms suggested by Sir John Fortescue was the observation that all rules of the council should be ' put in a book, and that book kept in this council as a register or ordinary, how they shall do in every thing '.[1] Nothing is seen of any such book again, however, until the reign of Henry VIII. Whether the compilation which then appears is to be regarded as a continuation of the earlier register or a renewal of it on similar lines, is a question for future discussion. But in any case, no matter for what period of years the roll was kept, one should remember that it was never an essential part of the council's procedure. Strange to say, nothing was ever said of it in the many regulations laid down by parliament between 1376 and 1437. The passage of the year 1455 just quoted is the first reference of the kind that occurs. It was compiled solely as a matter of convenience to the clerk and others for purposes of reference. It has proved of great value too in every historical study, since in no other way could so many of the acts ever be brought together again. Nevertheless, with or without the register, the daily proceedings of the council were carried on in the same manner as before, just as we have described.

New view of the subject.

The results of this investigation place the entire problem of the council's records in a new light. The traditional view regarding their first appearance in the reign of Richard II has arisen out of a mere accident of collection, which in itself has no historical basis. Certain advances at that time, it is true, were made in the style of the notes and in an effort to preserve them, but these were by no means the first steps. It is also a mistake to regard the existence of such records as a sign of institutional maturity. Conciliar notes, memoranda, ordinances, and responses in fact have

[1] Op. cit., chap. xv.

existed from the earliest times, even during the most elementary stages of organization. To a considerable extent they reflect the conditions when this body was not fairly differentiated from the exchequer, the parliament, and the chancery. Moreover, the full extent of these archives can be realized only by a survey of the Public Record Office, where they properly belong. Those lying in the British Museum are the remains only of private collections that have strayed or been stolen from the custody of the government. This is said not entirely to the discredit of the private collectors, who often showed more interest in the preservation of public documents than did the government itself. Sometimes too they did us the service of causing transcripts to be made of materials which would otherwise have been lost entirely. In view of all the facts that have been given, it may be wondered why the existence of these records should not have been generally known before. In defence of Nicolas and all other writers of his day, it should be remembered that the Public Record Office was not then freely open to scholars, and it was due to their arguments that these archives have since been made accessible to every one.[1] Moreover, the calendars of the close rolls and patent rolls, that have frequently been cited here, are a very recent publication. Finally, we may explain, the records of the council are not easily found to-day, because among the existing lists and compilations they are nowhere classified as such. On historic grounds, indeed, there is no reason why they should be so classified. In accordance with their original purpose they are more often arranged according to their subject-matter and purpose, so that they are to be found in a half-dozen or more of the available lists, such as the Diplomatic Documents, Ancient Petitions, Warrants of the Chancery, Warrants of the Privy Seal, and others. Unfortunately, there has been a tendency in the course of time to scatter the documents even more widely. Taken out of their original setting, with responses torn from the petitions, and even one half parted from the other, it is not possible to identify or even to understand many of the stray manuscripts. Often

[1] Read the argument of the aforesaid writer, op. cit., i, pp. lxviii ff.

the single parchment is of no use whatever because a companion to it cannot be found.

Briefly to summarize what has gone before, the council records, as they are now found, exist in at least four forms that are characteristic of its procedure.

1. There were the numerous responses and marginal notes that were made upon the petitions, letters, and any other documents that were considered. The answers were made with the utmost brevity and without explanations. It was no doubt the most convenient mode of action and the one preferred wherever practicable.

2. Not altogether distinct from the former were the separate memoranda or minutes made by the council. These were usually brief, and often give the impression of hasty action. In whichever form the notes were made, most of them were intended to serve as drafts or warrants for executive orders. When their immediate purpose was fulfilled, there was no special care taken for their preservation.

3. Whenever it was desired, in special instances, entries were made in any of the rolls of the exchequer or the chancery. For this reason a special roll of the council was never a necessity. Altogether there were probably no acts of far-reaching importance that failed to find their way to one or another of the regular rolls.

4. For certain years a roll or book of selected matter was kept. Because the work has proved very convenient and illuminating in our study of the subject, there has been a tendency to exaggerate its importance. The council was not a court of record, and the roll was never a vital part of its existence. The journal under Richard II does not appear to have been more than a personal experiment. Even the later work was carried on without official sanction, and is not known to have been kept up for more than fifteen years. To say that it was maintained throughout the vicissitudes of the fifteenth century, the writer believes to be an ill-grounded assumption.

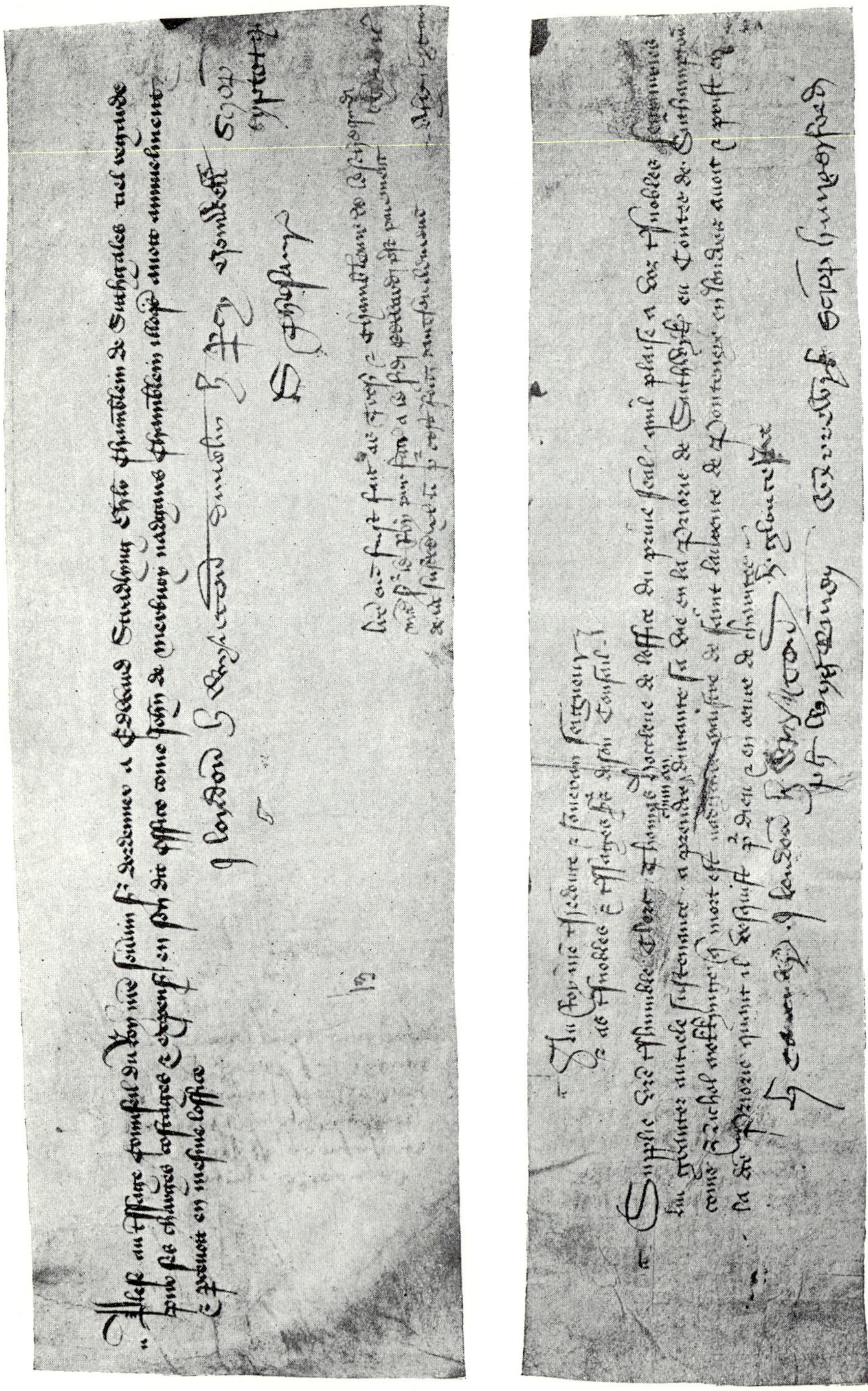

... Hen. VI, with the Signatures

CHAPTER XV

THE COUNCILLORS IN RELATION TO THE KING AND TO ONE ANOTHER

As in any other organic body the history of the council brought forth an indefinite number of usages regarding its procedure and the conduct of its members. So far as possible these features have been described or alluded to in previous chapters, but there are others which have not heretofore been mentioned for want of opportunity. Because of the meagreness of the records these matters do not generally appear upon the surface, and are only to be learned from the chance references that are given here and there. A few points of suggestion can be gathered from the numerous ordinances concerning the council, especially those that were made within the period 1376–1437. These enactments, it must be acknowledged, tell us not so much the rules that were actually observed, as the aims that were held in view. Particularly in their prohibitions and restrictive clauses do they disclose the tendencies which it was desired to counteract. As in other matters of legislation by force of repetition and by the elaboration of certain articles they reveal the points of stress and emphasis. In general they are to be accepted as a reflection of the thoughts that were current regarding the duties and demeanour of the king's councillors.

Relations of king and council usually not defined.

In the first place something can be said concerning the relations of the king and the council. Generally speaking, 'the king and his council' were regarded as a single body of authority, so far bound together by ties of personal obligation and confidence, that there was no reason to discriminate between them. How far the king trusted the council, and to what extent the council controlled or affected the action of the king was mainly a personal equation. Without any change of constitutional form this was a matter which varied in fact from one extreme to the other. Undoubtedly the council did many things on its own responsibility, which in modern times would require the sanction of the crown. On the other hand, the monarchs of the middle ages desired to have the advice and sanction of their council far more sincerely than did the later kings of autocratic ambitions. It was only under the stress of unusual circumstances then that the respective rights of the king and the council were in any wise brought into question. One of the requirements made in 1376 was that everything done by the council should be submitted to the king;[1] and again one of the ordinances under Richard II laid down the rule that the king should give credence to his council in all matters affecting the government.[2] But enactments of this kind did little to counteract historic usages. Under the Lancastrians, we have said, the general tendency was for the council to dictate to the crown and to control the powers of the government to such an extent that for the time it fairly overshadowed both the monarchy and the parliament. Again there was a sharp reaction from this condition of things.[3] So that on the whole the powers of the council in its sphere were never so well determined as were those of the house of lords in its customary lines of action.

The king usually absent.

Not to leave this phase of the subject entirely indefinite, we can point with greater confidence to the modes of intercourse, which fell into regular lines and are easily described. Now it was a well-known custom of the king to travel about the country in an almost ceaseless itinerary, so that it was necessary for the council either to move with the king or to remain in a fixed place. Just as was true of certain other branches of the *curia regis*, there was a visible tendency for the council or a part of it to follow the royal train—*ubicunque fuerit*. Usually the king on his journeys took with him

[1] *Rot. Parl.* ii. 322.

[2] Nicolas, i. 84.

[3] The surest gauge of the activities of the council, so far as I have found, lies in the files of warrants, both those of the privy seal and the great seal. It can then be seen to what extent the council assumed or was entrusted with the actual direction of the government. Did it, or did it not participate in the grants of the crown? This was always the most critical question.

a number of officers and councillors, if not the chancellor, at least the keeper of the privy seal and the chamberlain, while the assemblage of a council as well as a parliament might be called to any part of the kingdom. Many times when the subject was brought to notice, as was done in 1316 and again in 1327, it was the plan of parliament that a certain number of lords should remain with the king to counsel him, while similar statements were made concerning the council 'which the king may have about him'.[1] At other times, as described in 1342 and 1347, it is possible to discern a group of councillors in attendance upon the king in France communicating with the council in England.[2] During the reign of Henry IV we have observed that a fairly clear distinction was made between the councillors who were 'about the royal person' and those who remained at London or Westminster. But a permanent division on this line was not yet effected, although it was destined to come at a later date. After all, because the business of the council was largely administrative and judicial, and because it was bound in intimate relations with the courts at Westminster, the stronger tendency throughout the middle ages was for it to be located here.[3] At all events it was this branch and not the other that assumed organic form. Accordingly, from the time of Edward I, the deliberations of the council were usually not attended by the king himself. This custom no doubt was strengthened during the several periods of a royal minority, when the council was of necessity the ruling power, as well as on the numerous occasions when in the absence of the king the government was left in the hands of a guardian.

Correspondence.

Under these conditions it was necessary that certain regular channels of communication should be established. There was a constant stream of correspondence by means of letters under the privy seal and the signet, of which many illustrations have already been given. In this connexion a certain letter of Edward II, written at Clifton December 21, 1316,

[1] *Rot. Parl.* i. 351; ii. 132. [2] Avesbury, pp. 340, 395, 439.

[3] In 1314 certain conservators of the peace were appointed to deal with the outrages occurring in Kent. They were instructed to make reports from month to month to the council at Westminster. *Cal. Patent Rolls*, 7 Edw. II, 122.

very soon after the attempt was made to provide councillors for him, is worth quoting. In this communication the king confesses to the council at London that he has not sufficient counsel near him to decide the question in hand.

'. . . Entenduz les lettres de creance qe vous nous envoastes par notre cher clerc Wauter de Kemestys . . . et ce qil nous ad dit et les articles qil (nous ad done) depar vous par sa creance, et vous mercioms tant cherement come nous pooms de ce qe vous avez noz besoignes tant acuer, et nos . . . avez ordeinez touchant notre messagerie a notre seint pere le pape, et quant de purchacer esloignance du terme de notre voiage a la terre seint, (nous) feisoms qe nous navoms pas conseil pres de nous a ore pur si haute chose ordener, mais voloms et vous mandoms qentre vous en eiez avisement (en tiel) manere coment nous puissoms cele chose plus honorablement priere . . .' [1]

As this letter suggests, there was a constant interchange of every kind of document, including bills, articles, ordinances and decrees, which the council sent to the king for approval, or, vice versa, which the king submitted to the consideration of the council. Bills of this kind were likely to receive in turn two endorsements, the one *per regem*, the other *per consilium*.

Messengers and 'reporters'.

The bearer of these letters and documents was usually one of the minor officials of the household; often it was a clerk or serjeant-at-arms, who was said to be employed 'on the king's secret business'.[2] He was frequently entrusted further with messages which he was to deliver by word of mouth. In the thirty-first year of Edward I, for example, certain articles were brought from the king to the council by John Drokensford, and it was explained 'many other things had John to say which are not contained in the articles'. After a great deal of experience of this kind under Edward III, it was perceived that the function of bearing messages between the king and the council was an important

[1] The parchment is considerably damaged. *Ancient Correspondence*, xlv, no. 192; a letter of Edward III, no. 229.

[2] The issue rolls are filled with items like this: 'Iohanni Stonseley nuntio misso versus Wyndesore cum una littera sigillorum certorum dominorum de consilio directa domino Regi.' 1 Ric. II, Mich., March 29; also *Issue Roll* (ed. Devon), 44 Edw. III, *passim*.

one that should not be a matter of casual employment. One of the reforms insisted upon during the parliamentary period was that there should be certain accredited bearers of information, or ' reporters ', as they were called. In 1376 it was proposed that everything done by the council should be reported to the king in order that his advice or assent might be given, and that such report should be made by the councillors then appointed, or by two of them, ' and by no one else.'[1] Again under Richard II it was at one time insisted that the chamberlain, the steward of the household, and the keeper of the privy seal should be the only reporters between the king and the council, and that no other reporters for any reason should be trusted.[2] The king nevertheless employed clerks, esquires, and serjeants, just as before.[3] Under Henry IV it was emphatically declared by the council itself to be expedient that a suitable person should be found to report to the king and to certify the council of the will of the king ; and this ordinance was said to be desired not only for the advantage of the king, but also for the sake of each person in the council who wished to acquit himself loyally of his oath.[4] Such a man was found in John Durward, esquire, who acted constantly in this capacity so long as he was connected with the council. In a letter previously quoted, which the council placed in his hands to deliver to the king, it was asked :

' plese a votre roiale majestee luy escoutier benignement et luy doner ferme foy et creance en celle partie et nous ent faire assavoir par luy votre graciouse voloir et entention.'[5]

Another esquire employed in this manner was John Norbury, who became conspicuous after Durward's retirement. On one occasion a schedule was entrusted to him for delivery in the following words :

' Sur quoy ceste cedule feut baillee a lavantdit Johan Norbury pur monstrer au Roy pur ent savoir sa voluntee,

[1] *Rot. Parl.* ii. 322. [2] Nicolas, i. 85.

[3] In the eighteenth year Lawrence Drew, a baron of the exchequer, was sent by the council with money for the king in Ireland, whence he returned with a message for the council. Ibid., 57 ; *Issue Roll* (*Pells*), 18 Ric. II, Easter, m. 14.

[4] Nicolas, i. 110. [5] *Council and Privy Seal,* file 28, March, 1404.

le quel Johan reporta au dit counsail que la forme desusdite bien plest au Roy.' [1]

After Henry IV the effort to have acknowledged reporters between the king and council was not continued. In all the ordinances and arrangements that were made under Henry VI, this part of the earlier parliamentary programme seems to have been forgotten. It was not in fact a necessity, for with the increase in the dignity of the clerk of the council, especially during the careers of Adam Moleyns and Thomas Kent, this service was allowed to fall into his hands. It was made the special duty of the clerk to travel to and fro upon these errands, while the work of keeping the records was left more or less to an assistant.

A royal audience.

A still more formal mode of intercourse was adopted when the king invited or permitted the council to come before him in a meeting known as a royal audience. Such an occasion is specially denoted in the records with the words, *in presentia regis*. This occurred most frequently in connexion with certain ceremonies, as for instance when the great seal was given up or entrusted to a new keeper. It was then desired to have as many noble witnesses as possible. But the ordinary deliberations of the council could not be held in the royal presence with sufficient freedom, so that these were usually held in a chamber apart from the king, and then their conclusions were laid before him in definite form. This method of action is well illustrated in an episode which took place in 1389, when the relations of the king and the council were considerably strained. The king, it is said, summoned the council to his private chamber and commanded them to deliberate during his absence and to report to him their opinions relative to certain indentures that were about to be made.[2] The lords of the council, we are told, having

[1] An unfiled document, 3 Hen. IV, June 5. There is also a message delivered to John Cheyne with the words, 'et tant de ce come dautres matires . . . quelles declarez avons a notre chier et loial chevalier Johan Cheyne, lui vuilliez donner ferme foie et credence en nous certiffiant de temps en temps les nouvelles esteantz devers vous et plus souvent que navez fait puis notre departir de vous.' *Council and Privy Seal*, file 18, February 6.

[2] Nicolas, i. 12*b*. The question was over the expenditures to be made on Berwick castle and the East March towards Scotland.

withdrawn to deliberate by themselves, came again before the king to render their advice. In behalf of them all the chancellor reported to his majesty that the measure he had proposed did not seem to them expedient. The king tried to dissuade them, but the chancellor said that they did not dare to do otherwise, and that in this stand they were unanimous. Whereupon the king ‘ with an angry look ’ departed for Kennington. On the following day the lords continued their deliberations in the star chamber, and although they feared the displeasure of the king, they agreed not to recede from their former decision. Then making a journey themselves to Kennington, where after some delay they were admitted to the royal presence, they repeated through the mouth of the chancellor what they had said before. The king then offered a modification of his original proposition, and to this plan some of the council agreed, while others did not continue their objections ; and so the matter was settled. The incident is interesting not only for its bearing on the later years of Richard II, but also because such consultations were not usually matters of record. Undoubtedly there were occasions, most conspicuously in 1386, when the councillors experienced more or less difficulty in gaining the attention of the king. This caused the suggestion to be made in certain articles drawn up for the improvement of the government, that the king should give a suitable amount of time for audiences with his council, whenever it wished to communicate with him.[1] In 1406 it was proposed that the king give up two days each week for hearing the petitions of his subjects in the presence of the councillors attending him, and that the councillors, having examined the petitions, and presumably having given their advice, should then depart.[2] In 1443 we learn that Henry VI gave audience to his council at Eltham in his secret chamber ‘before meeting time’ and again the same day ‘after meeting ’.[3] Again when the reform of the government was undertaken by the duke of York in 1454, a decree of the council was framed ‘ concerning the councillors and their access to the king ’.[4]

[1] Nicolas, i. 84. [2] *Rot. Parl.* iii. 587. [3] Nicolas, v. 253–4.

[4] *Cal. Patent Rolls*, 32 Hen. VI, 296. Nothing is said in the act, however, concerning the meetings with the king.

The duties of a councillor

As to the councillors themselves, the character of the men desired, their duties and privileges, a great deal was said from time to time. Neither the exchequer nor any other body, in fact, was so hedged about with special legislation. All this served to give the council greater prominence and distinctness, so that at length one speaks of the 'estate' of councillor.[1] With doubtful correctness in 1386 this was claimed to be a rank next to an earl in dignity.[2] Without repeating the terms of the councillor's oath and the numerous corollary ordinances that were passed from time to time, it is desirable now to learn as much as possible concerning the actual responsibilities and personal conduct of the members.

to render counsel—difficulties in the way of free expression.

The first and foremost requirement according to the oath and every other statement of the kind was the duty to render 'faithful counsel'. That 'advice is cheap' is a poor saying, for in the midst of conflicting interests sincere advice is usually the most difficult of all things to obtain. Moreover, the average man of the middle ages, unless he had a personal interest at stake, particularly disliked to commit himself to any line of action. In this regard he had reason to fear also that if he gained repute for giving 'evil counsel', he might be removed in disgrace or even suffer a criminal conviction. There was every inclination therefore to avoid individual responsibility of this kind whenever it was possible. As an illustration of this attitude there is the extreme instance of Lord Beaumont in 1323, who resolutely refused to give counsel; and, while this was the duty of any vassal, his conduct was considered to be the more contumacious because he had been sworn of the king's council. More often there was no such defiance, but simply an evasion of the duty or a reluctance to express oneself. During the consideration of the Gascon Charter in 1395 we are told that at first there was silence in the meeting, the lords were afraid to speak, and then they wished to leave the answer to the two royal

[1] 'By reason of his estate as archbishop and also as one of the king's principal councillors.' *Cal. Close Rolls,* 33 Edw. I, 312. 'Par entier avys de toutz Seigneurs d'estate de Conseil.' *Rot. Parl.* iii. 578.

[2] Ibid. 217. This was said in defence of the earl of Suffolk on his impeachment, but surely a knight of the council did not rank higher than a baron.

dukes. Much more likely under the circumstances were the lesser men to repress their opinions entirely. Most of the difficulty that has been felt to exist in the relations of the lords and their less prominent associates, whether in the council or the parliament, would immediately be dispelled if the correct point of view were taken. Indeed, if no other rules existed, the prevailing etiquette of the age would be sufficient to determine their conduct towards one another. And yet the ideal was firmly upheld that every man in the council should have freedom to say 'what he thinketh', and that to every bill 'each man should singularly give his advice'.[1] To fix their responsibility more closely it was required further during the period of parliamentary control that the names of the members present should be recorded, that the councillors should give their own signatures to the bills, and even that dissenting opinions should be written.[2] All these rules were to be observed, it was remarked, with 'due reverence kept to every estate and person'.[3] To what extent, then, we ask, was freedom of discussion actually maintained?

Manner of discussion.

In the meetings of the council probably there was more discussion than the records generally reveal. And yet the impression is given that free and positive expressions of opinion were not easily obtained. Properly conducted, a discussion consisted in each one stating his opinion upon the bill or other form of proposition. If this was not volunteered, the chancellor would ask each member in turn for a statement. This was given sometimes reluctantly or ambiguously.[4] The councillors also were likely to change their opinions after the predominant sentiment had been shown, for no one apparently liked to be left in a minority. There was no use, they felt, in pressing an individual objection. A lord

[1] Nicolas, iii. 215, 216; iv. 60.

[2] Ibid. iii. 150; instances of diverse opinions are found in i. 144; v. 76, 223, 274.

[3] As a question of precedence, in 1443 the duke of Somerset, by virtue of his blood-relationship to the king, was given a place and seat in all parliaments and councils above the duke of Norfolk. Nicolas, v. 255.

[4] In rendering their opinions I do not find that the councillors followed any rule of precedence, whether they should begin with the highest or the lowest rank.

is known to have subscribed his name to a bill, although he expressed himself as *nolens volo*.[1] Another rule, which was in keeping with the theory of equal rights among the councillors, was that questions should be decided by the *maior pars* or numerical majority.[2] To the article, once enacted, that all things should pass with the assent of six or four, it was added that their assent should be sufficient only in case they formed 'the more part of the members then present'. An officer like the chancellor or the treasurer must surely be consulted in all matters lying especially within his knowledge, but if he would not give his assent, 'nevertheless the thing shall pass if agreed to by the majority'.[3] In order that the opinions of the minority as well as the majority might be known, in 1424 the clerk was required to make a record of the names of both parties, those who gave their assent, and those who expressed dissent to any bill.[4] Evidently the rule was distasteful, and it was not commonly followed. Always there was the stronger feeling that differences of opinion were to be avoided or reconciled if possible. In 1430 a requirement was made that when differences of opinion arose the matter should be delayed until the next day and then the majority should decide.[5] For this reason we have known questions to have been postponed until a larger assembly could be consulted.[6] In all mediaeval bodies, indeed, there was a strong belief in the practicability of unanimous consent, and any act was deemed to have added force if it could be stated as receiving unanimous approval. To this end it was desired that men should suppress their individual opinions and even to give their formal assent to measures which they did not themselves favour. In the midst of all these conditions, which were unfavourable to freedom of

[1] Lord Tiptoft in 1428. Nicolas, iii. 312.

[2] In giving their votes one would infer that certain brief words of *assent* or *dissent* were uttered. The records frequently mention the names of the lords *assentientibus* and those *dissentientibus*.

[3] *Rot. Parl.* v. 433.

[4] Nicolas, iii. 150; instances, ibid. i. 144; v. 76, 223, &c.

[5] Nicolas, iv. 62.

[6] In 1292, when the justices and others of the council were at variance upon a question of procedure, although there was plainly a majority upon one side, the question was deferred until a full parliament could be consulted. *Rot. Parl.* i. 79.

expression on the part of individual members, we find it easy to believe in the general truth of Sir John Fortescue's observation, that no 'lower man durst say anything against the opinion of the great lords '.[1]

The pledge to secrecy was one of the first articles of the oath, although it was not of the same importance as some of the others. There were always secrets, 'secret business of the king ', and 'secret councils ', although this was not the aspect generally emphasized. According to the earliest statements councillors were bound to observe this rule only as their word might injure the king. When charges were made against any of the king's officers, as in the case of Ralph Ferrers in 1381, the earl of Suffolk in 1386, and the duke of Suffolk in 1450, among the accusations most readily made was that he had revealed the plans of the government to the enemy. Not much of the true tendencies can be learned, of course, from these prejudiced incidents. But there are many other instances which suggest that men held their obligations on this score rather lightly. In 1395, we have seen, Sir Richard Stury, thinking no harm would be done, had no compunction in telling Froissart 'everything word for word ' concerning the council at Eltham. The tendency was felt to be a very mischievous one, for without accusing any one in particular, complaint was constantly made that secrets could not be kept. The usual temptation, it appears, lay not so much in the direction of treasonable correspondence, as in the information and encouragement given to suitors who were thereby enabled to gain an advantage over their opponents. It was once suggested that the leak occurred through the attendance of various irresponsible persons who were not members.[2] Fortescue, who was in a position to know, says that the lords used to give information to their own retainers and servants, so that as a result 'no matter treated in the council could be kept privy '.

Requirement of secrecy

That the councillors should be honest and free from bribery was one of the earliest requirements that was re-enacted with the utmost emphasis. The endless variety and particularity of the ordinances upon this point suggest

Requirement of honesty.

[1] Op. cit., chap. xiv.

[2] Nicolas, iii. 215.

that the tendencies to corruption were very prevalent and difficult to counteract. The particular forms of bribery which men were then most likely to follow are pointed out in various acts of legislation with words of sufficient plainness. In the oath of 1257 it was provided that no one of the council should receive any gift from persons having business in the king's court, under penalty of exclusion and forfeiture of property. Presents of meat and drink were necessarily excepted. With good reason no doubt these restrictions were carefully elaborated in every succeeding statement of the oath. After the impeachment of the dishonest councillors in 1376, it was asserted to be the special aim of parliament to secure men who would be faithful and discreet, and 'void of taking bribes'. Any one found taking a bribe was to render to the party from whom it was received double and the king six times the amount.[1] In the first year of Richard II it was ordained that no one of the council should receive any gift of escheat, wardship, marriage, rent, or other thing, except by consent of all the council or the greater part of them; and that he should not take anything from any one, except what was to eat and drink of small value, for any business that should be brought before them.[2] In 1430 this law was better stated in the following terms: 'that no one of the said lords of the king's council shall receive or suffer to be received for his profit or advantage any gift, bond or promise in order to favour or further any matter pending in the council, either for promotion or furthering any person to office or benefice that may be disposed of by the council or by any of the king's officers'.[3] During the later years of Henry VI the corruption of the councillors by bribes was one of the reproaches most easily made and readily believed. It was one of the issues raised by Jack Cade's rebellion, and also by the movement to place the duke of York in control of the government.

Bribery.

Clear cases of bribery were probably as difficult to prove in those days as they are now, even though every surrounding condition suggests it. Moreover, the law as usual left certain obvious loopholes. The permission to receive food and

[1] *Rot. Parl.* ii. 322. [2] Ibid. iii. 6. [3] Nicolas, iv. 65.

drink, for instance, was very reasonable in primitive days, but it opened the way for rich presents of fish and wine as a kind of bribery that could safely be made. We know too that in all litigation, fees, if not bribes, were of necessity handed to the chancellor and other officials, just as was done in every other court. In the case of the abbey of Meaux, previously cited, it is acknowledged as a matter of course that the chancellor was extensively bribed.[1] In 1475 Philip de Comines describes how the king of France scattered pensions and other rewards, to the extent of thousands of crowns, among the councillors and servants of Edward IV.[2] Lord Hastings refused to give a receipt for the money, regarding it, as he said, a free-will offering on the one side, with no obligation on the other.

Interests in litigation.

Probably the cruder forms of bribery were less prevalent than certain indirect and subtle means of profit, which amounted to the same thing. According to all reports the most frequent opportunities for private advantage lay in the litigation which pressed at all times upon the attention of the court. It lay in the power of any councillor to help or hinder the course of a suit, and his interest was certainly quickened if he shared in the results. There was a temptation even to speculate in the market of lawsuits. This was suggested in 1285 when it was forbidden that the chancellor, the justices, or any of the king's council should purchase titles to lands in suit.[3] A similar statement is made by Fleta that no officer or member of the council or other person in the king's service was allowed to receive benefices or gifts of any kind so that he gained an interest and became a participant in any contention pending before the king.[4] Furthermore, the statute, 1 Edw. III, declared that no councillor or other minister or member of the household should maintain pleas or quarrels in the king's court. When a few years later it was discovered that this act had neglected to prescribe any penalty, a severe one was immediately provided.[5] The maintenance of quarrels, or ' brocage ', as it was called, was

[1] *Chron. de Melsa,* iii. 135; also Appendix III, p. 534.
[2] *Mémoires* (ed. Mandrot, Paris, 1901), book iv, chap. viii.
[3] *Statutes of the Realm,* i. 95.
[4] *Commentarius,* lib. ii, c. 36.
[5] *Statutes of the Realm,* i. 256; *Rot. Parl.* ii. 10, 166; iii. 6.

regarded as a very prevalent evil at a time when the complexities of legal procedure offered every chance for chicanery. Some of the king's officers and councillors were suspected of employing special agents known as 'brocagers' to promote litigation.[1] Brocage was one of the charges made against Suffolk and several other lords in 1386,[2] and again on the fall of Richard II it was insinuated that actions had been brought to the council in this manner.[3] It was on this ground in 1406 that Lord Lovell very reasonably was excused from serving in the council, since he claimed to be interested in certain pleas and so could not honestly serve.[4] Yet the conduct of councillors continued to cause suspicions upon this point. The ordinances of Henry VI declared that no lord should acquire any land in debate without the permission of the council, and that if any matter treated in the council should concern any individual member, he should withdraw while it was under discussion.[5] During the most flourishing days of the council's power it would not be difficult to prove that men were present and helped to pass bills which were drawn in their own favour. The system of mutual favours known as 'log-rolling' is by no means a modern device.

Temptations of the councillors.

For transactions of this kind the councillors were given countless opportunities in the petitions for favour and redress, which it was their duty constantly to treat. That the business of the king and the realm should have precedence over every other concern was a rule repeatedly enacted and well understood. Nevertheless, the traffic of private business was likely to be the more lucrative, and there is reason to believe it was sometimes given the more consideration. In the midst of the difficulties and delays commonly obstructing the course of justice suitors were disposed to seek every possible means of influence and favour. We have said that for this reason primarily they addressed petitions to the chancellor and other lords individually. They found still other ways of gaining the attention and interest of one lord

[1] *Rot. Parl.* ii. 10, 12; iii. 16; *Statutes of the Realm*, i. 357.
[2] *Rot. Parl.* iii. 230, 231, 237.
[3] Ibid. 445.
[4] Ibid. 573.
[5] Nicolas, iii. 214; iv. 60.

or another, who would then promote the bills of his clients before the king, the house of lords, or the council, as the case might be. Sometimes it is declared in the endorsements that the bills were presented 'ex parte Comitis Lancastriae', 'ex parte Comitis Marchie', 'per ducem Bedford', and the like. Once it is said, *levesque de Bathe pursua ceste bille.*[1] How essential it was to have a powerful supporter at court is shown in the prolonged litigation that began in 1390 concerning the abbey of Croyland. First a complaint against the abbey was made in parliament by the earl of Kent, whose assertions were then and there denied by the duke of Lancaster. Thereupon the abbot presented to the king a bill citing the injuries committed by the earl of Kent. This bill, it is said, the king entrusted to the duke of Lancaster with instructions to have it read before the learned men of the council. As the chronicle of the abbey happily reports, 'the lord duke readily undertook the performance of this command, and efficiently fulfilled it all.'[2] Without his support, indeed, it is not likely that the abbot's petition would ever have been read at all. There was subsequently much well-intentioned legislation to check the pernicious effects of these tendencies. One rule was that business brought forward first should be treated first, so that there might be the less chance for favour. In spite of a clear perception of the danger, there is no doubt that the government of Henry VI was materially weakened by the prevailing inclination to yield everything to the individual interests of the lords and their adherents. Over this state of things Fortescue made lamentation in the following passage:

'when they (the members of the council) came together, they were so occupied with their own matters and the matters of their kin, servants, and tenants, that they attended but little, sometimes not at all, to the king's matters.'[3]

Sworn alliances.

Still another form of private interest is suggested in the article of the oath which forbids any one of the council to

[1] *Ancient Petitions*, no. 11437. Another, 'ista billa concessa fuit per Regem ad instantiam Comitis Suffolk.' Ibid., no. 11301.

[2] *Chron. Abbey of Croyland* (London, 1854), pp. 338 ff. The accuracy of the chronicle would be open to doubt, if it were not supported by the petition itself. *Ancient Petitions*, no. 5054.

[3] Op. cit.

make a sworn alliance without the king's permission. To what extent the king's permission was given we have no knowledge whatever. But we can see that the council was strongly affected by the general practice of the lords in making alliances with each other and also in keeping up great retinues. It would not have been possible for the king to maintain a body of councillors entirely free from these ties. In 1316, for example, it was stipulated that one of the council should be a banneret of the earl of Lancaster. In 1377 Ralph Erghum, bishop of Salisbury, a member of the first council under Richard II, was at the time chancellor of the duke of Lancaster. Likewise Sir Thomas Percy, at the time that he was steward of the royal household and an attendant of the council, was a member of the duke's retinue. The list of John of Gaunt's household contains a score of men who were at one time or another similarly employed in the king's service.[1] The tendency of the lords to maintain councils of their own, upon the pattern of the king's council, is suggested in the ordinance of 1426, that 'no man be of the king's council but such as be barely of his council', and again in 1437, that 'none of the council take a fee of any person except the king'.[2] Whether Lord Scrope, for instance, was bound in any such manner to Humphrey, duke of Gloucester, we are not informed, but his conduct at all times in support of the duke hardly leaves room for doubt that he was. As regards the grosser forms of maintenance, resulting in violence and coercion, there was undoubtedly a reason for the ordinance made in 1430, that 'no lord of the council nor any of his servants shall maintain riots or seek to influence judges and juries'.[3]

Privileges. But the status of councillor was known not merely by its restrictions, else there would have been none willing to serve. There were also honours and privileges that were amply recognized. To a certain extent these privileges were the same as those pertaining to the house of lords and also the

[1] Armitage-Smith, *John of Gaunt*, Appendix III, pp. 440–6. There were Sir Michael de la Pole (afterwards earl of Suffolk), Sir Richard le Scrope, Sir Thomas Erpingham, Sir Thomas Percy, William Bagot, and many others.

[2] Nicolas, iii. 219; vi. 315.

[3] Ibid. iv. 64; a similar article in 1443–4, ibid. v. 320.

royal household. Some, however, have a distinctive value in pertaining solely to the council. It was one of the regular perquisites of a councillor, like other officers and clerks, to receive a robe every year out of the king's wardrobe. Some preferred to take the money value instead, which was four marks for each garment in the time of Edward III.[1] For this reason the Statute of Liveries made an exception in favour of the king's councillors, together with justices, clerks of the chancery, barons of the exchequer, and other officers.[2] It does not appear, however, that there was a distinctive councillor's robe, such as we find was adopted in France. A certain immunity from arrest also was acknowledged by Edward I in favour of the members of his council and household. On one occasion the king refused to permit one of his council to be distrained in time of parliament.[3] Again when there was a question whether a certain man should enjoy an exemption from being summoned or attached in the king's palace, it was decided that he should not, because he was neither of the council nor household nor domicile of the king.[4] Against false accusations the councillors and other ministers were especially protected by the statute, 38 Edw. III.[5] When the danger of violent assaults became very imminent, it was enacted in 1433 that if any one makes an assault on any peer or member of parliament, or on any person coming to the council, he should be punished to the extent of attaint and the payment of damages.[6] For this reason, therefore, the assault of Tailboys upon Lord Cromwell was regarded an especially heinous one.

Proxies.

A personal privilege enjoyed by the lords to a certain extent was that of sending proxies to act in their stead. This was an early custom that was carried forward by them both in parliament and the council. In respect of the house of lords the privilege was properly granted by the king's

[1] Robert Shireburn was to have the arrears due to him as one of the king's council at 40*s.* a year and the price of a robe every year. *Cal. Close Rolls*, 8 Edw. III, 266.

[2] *Rot. Parl.* iii. 478.

[3] 'Non videtur onestum quod Rex concedat quod illi de consilio suo distringantur tempore parliamenti.' Ibid. i. 61.

[4] Ibid. 97.

[5] *Statutes of the Realm*, i. 384.

[6] *Rot. Parl.* iv. 453.

special permission,[1] but as regards the council the lords sometimes of their own accord sent proxies to present excuses and to act for them. This was done in 1322 when the bishop of Carlisle made reply to a summons, excusing himself because of the distance, the expense, and his feebleness, wherefore he sent several men as his attorneys to treat with the council.[2] In 1353 there is a letter of the abbot of Bardney naming four proctors to attend a council in his behalf and to explain the cause of his absence.[3] In the writs of summons the lords were occasionally invited to send four, three, or two trusted men, in case they could not come in person. To illustrate how a lord of the council was summoned, with special reference to his privilege of sending proxies, there is the following letter under the privy seal written in the twenty-second year of Richard II :

'Reverent pere en dieu et notre treschere cousin. A cause de certaines treschargeantes matires touchantz le bien de nous et de vous et le comun profit de notre Roiaume, vous prions trescherement qe saunz delay ou difficultee queconque vuillez estre ovesqe notre consail a Westminster a la quinzeme de la trinitee prochaine venante saunz defaute pur treter alors ouesqe mesme notre conseil sur les dites materes lesqueles vous serront monstrees et declarees a votre venue. Et en cas qe vous ne y purrez estre aucunement en propre persone, adonque envoier vuillez devers notre susdit conseil quatre trois ou deux persones suffissantz et discretz de votre conseil des queux vous vous affiez pur y estre au du lendemain par la cause susdite. Et ce ne vuillez en nulle manere lesser sicome nous nous prions de vous. Don, etc.'[4]

Occasionally in the records of the council we observe the presence of 'Lord Lovell *or* his son', 'the deputy of the treasurer', and 'the attorney of the duke of Bedford'. But for various reasons the practice did not have great vogue here.[5] It was apparently discountenanced in the more

[1] Pike, *House of Lords*, p. 243.

[2] *Parl. Writs*, vol. ii, part ii, p. 264.

[3] An unfiled document.

[4] *Warrants, Privy Seal*, series i, section ii, file 3; other examples, Nicolas, i. 76, 242.

[5] In 1461 Walter, bishop of Norwich, a king's councillor, in consideration of his age and long service, was exempted from all personal appearance in any council or parliament, provided that he appear by his proctor. *Cal. Patent Rolls*, 39 Hen. VI, 642.

numerous letters of summons requiring the members to be present 'in person'. Moreover, if the lords did not wish to come, they were not to be deterred from staying away altogether. The signatures which were regularly made upon the documents of Henry VI's time do not show the presence of deputies to any material extent. Moreover, the privilege was never allowed to councillors of lower rank.

Letters of councillors.

Another substitution for attendance is found in the letters sometimes sent to lords or received from them during their absence. In this feature the house of lords and the council differed materially. Although it is true that Edward I once obtained the consent of various barons individually by means of a circular letter,[1] the precedent seems not to have been followed thereafter in connexion with parliament. But within the council there was a lingering feeling that an absent member might properly express an opinion in this way. During the hearing of the case of the Audeleys, 40–41 Edw. III, a letter was received from the earl of Arundel stating that though his presence was required he was unable to come, that he wished the council to proceed notwithstanding his absence, and that he would assent to whatever should be ordained.[2] In 1400 John Durward was sent by the council to the archbishop of Canterbury to obtain his opinion on a question touching the liberties of the city of Cork.

> 'Sur quoi le second iour de September prochain ensuant, lavantdit Johan Doreward vient devant le dit Conseil reportant endroit de la dite matire de Cork, quil sembloit a mon dit Seigneur de Canterbirs pur le mieulz de confermer les libertees et fraunchises.' [3]

Upon the appointment of the council in 1406 the singular and impracticable scheme was proposed that before any particular measure should pass the members present should communicate with those who were absent.[4] The utter impossibility of enforcing any such rule was clearly pointed out. But there was a trace of the feeling among absent

[1] J. H. Round, 'The Barons' Letter to the Pope, 1301,' *The Ancestor*, vi. 189.

[2] *Cal. Close Rolls*, 40 Edw. III, 238.

[3] *Council and Privy Seal*, file 7, August 31.

[4] *Rot. Parl.* iii. 587.

councillors that when they had interests at stake they might give their opinion, if not their vote, in this manner. In 1437 Cardinal Beaufort from the other side of the channel sent a message to the keeper of the privy seal, with a ring as a token, that he wished a certain bill to pass.[1] In 1454 the duke of York, probably with the purpose of gaining time, urged that the advice of the absent lords be obtained as to what should be done concerning the duke of Somerset.[2] Still the prevailing rule was that bills should be passed by the majority of those 'who shall be present'.

The 'term' of attendance.

It has been abundantly shown that throughout the mediaeval period the great difficulty lay in inducing men of suitable rank to remain with any degree of constancy in the king's council. To this end the greater number of measures were obviously directed. The length of time that members should serve, and the number that should at any moment be present was a matter of perpetual concern. By degrees it was recognized that the regular time for the meetings of the council should be in conjunction with the sessions of the courts—'while our courts do sit'—and particularly the court of common pleas. Something of the kind seems to have been understood in the time of Edward I,[3] and under Richard II the 'conciliar term' is expressly mentioned.[4] There were, of course, four terms every year during the fourteenth century, although we cannot assume that there were sessions of the council at every one. Under Henry VI it was clearly stated to be the duty of councillors to be present during the term, when it was intended that all business as far as possible should be transacted, while only

[1] Nicolas, v. 27.

[2] 'And moreover it is right fitting and necessarie . . . that th'advice of mo lords than be here at this tyme were hadd.' Ibid. vi. 207.

[3] 'Et vos ipsi sitis ad prefatum terminum parati et instructi nobis et consilio nostro super premissis et eorum singulis consilium una cum avisamento vestro impensuri.' *Rot. Parl.* i. 34; also *Cal. Close Rolls*, 28 Edw. I, 358.

[4] 'In denariis . . . pro custubus et expensis factis apud Westmonasterium infra privatum palatium Regis, pro episcopis Wintonie et Exonie, dominis Cancellario, Thesaurario, Custode privati sigilli et aliis de consilio Regis ibidem attendentibus tribus diebus integris per vices termino instanti super consilio ibidem capiendo,' &c. *Issue Roll* (*Pells*), 8 Ric. II, Easter, m. 7; also Nicolas, iii. 154.

questions of emergency should be treated during the intervals. As one of the ordinances declares,

'out of term time nothing be sped in the council but such thing as for the good of the king and of his land asketh necessary . . . and may not be abiden unto the term time.'[1]

But the difficulty of getting any sufficient number of lords to attend at any stated time grew greater. During the later years of Henry VI they came only in response to the most urgent, and sometimes peremptory, letters of summons.

A *quorum.*

In the face of these difficulties there was the very practical question, how many members of the council should be present at any time for the transaction of business, or as we should say, what constituted a quorum? As it was a matter of considerable importance, there were many efforts to make a definite rule, although an agreement upon the point was by no means easy. In 1316 the number five was suggested, and in 1327 it was proposed that at least four lords should always be in attendance. In 1376 the plan was that no great business should be passed without the assent of all, and that business of less importance might be passed by six or four or less as the case required.[2] In the first year of Richard II a similar requirement was made, with the added clause that four at least should be in continual residence.[3] But in 1390 it was admitted that business of 'less charge' might be determined by those who were present together with the officers.[4] After several other tentative statements a fairly practicable rule appears in the reign of Henry VI, to the effect that 'in all great matters that shall pass the council, all shall be present or else the majority', and that in other matters nothing shall be done except in the presence of six, or at least four, besides the great officers.[5] By force of repetition this number was accepted as the traditional quorum of the council. And yet it inevitably happened that the body in attendance not infrequently fell below this mark, even to the point of two or three officers with no other

[1] Nicolas, iii. 216; iv. 62.
[2] *Rot. Parl.* ii. 322.
[3] Ibid. iii. 6, 386.
[4] Nicolas, i. 18b.
[5] Ibid. iii. 18, 150, 215; iv. 61.

support. But there was danger that acts insufficiently attested might afterwards be invalidated. The Resumption Act of 1451 undertook to annul a large number of the king's grants, but made an exception of all grants that had been passed by the advice of the chancellor, the treasurer, the keeper of the privy seal, and six other lords of the council.[1] All persons desiring grants of the crown, therefore, would naturally seek this safeguard.

Attendance of non-members.

The status of councillor was always obscured by the fact that the line was not clearly drawn between members and non-members. The king took the utmost liberty of inviting men to his councils, whether they were sworn thereof or not.[2] The lords on their part gravely assumed that they were welcome in coming, even if they were not individually invited. Likewise the council itself was accustomed to ask for the assistance of any of the professional men when there was need. There even appears at times an indefinite number of minor functionaries, commonly indicated as *et ceteri*, who were permitted to attend for no particular reason, unless it was their own curiosity. Especially on ceremonial occasions it was thought to lend dignity if an extraordinary number of lords and others were present. This was made clear in 1379, when certain new officers, we are told, were sworn in the room adjacent to the star chamber, before the magnates of the council, ' in the presence of many lords and knights and others who were especially called to attend as witnesses '.[3] In the second year of Henry V parliament referred a matter to the king and council, authorizing them to call such lords, clerks, and other persons as should be deemed necessary.[4] At another time, on the eve of the opening of parliament the council chamber is found to be thronged with peers.[5] The frequent presence of unlicensed attendants was disconcerting to the stricter ideas of conciliar responsibility. In 1426 it was said that in this way much

[1] *Rot. Parl.* v. 218.

[2] In 1447 it was the king's will that the lords of the council, and such others as the chancellor might think best, should be invited to come to the council at the beginning of the next term. Nicolas, vi. 60.

[3] *Close Roll*, 2 Ric. II, m. 1 d.

[4] *Rot. Parl.* iv. 30.

[5] Nicolas, vi. 39.

of the business which should be secret was published and discovered, so that there had been cause for suspicion among the councillors themselves, and indignation against outsiders. So that an ordinance was passed that 'henceforward no person of whatever rank or condition be suffered to abide in the council, but those that are sworn of the council, unless they be specially called by authority of the council'.[1] In this, as in other questions of the kind, time-honoured traditions were not easily broken. Moreover, the idea of a council, considered as a strictly defined and exclusive body, was very slow in being accepted. The plan was asserted again and again, but not for any considerable period during the middle ages was it consistently adhered to. The presence and participation of non-members, both lords and lesser men, we know was of constant occurrence throughout the fifteenth century,[2] and so ingrained was the practice that it lasted even into the age of the Tudors. To what extent, however, these men were actually invited, it is impossible now to say. But the fact that their presence at a later time was regarded as of questionable propriety, leads us to believe that the most primitive and careless usages in this regard were tolerated.

Unpractical ideas.

It is not from cynicism or a feeling of the superiority of a later age that these observations have been made. The purpose is rather to reveal the mediaeval council in its reality as an expression of the ideals of an age that was often hazy and unpractical in its thought. Such plans inevitably failed, but the incessant struggle to realize them against the overwhelming odds of human nature and material interests forms a history that is not lacking in pathos. The great weakness after all lay in the lack of any single controlling authority, whether this is looked for in the monarchy or within the council itself. For this reason there was during

[1] Ibid., iii. 215.

[2] The earl of Suffolk, for example, was sworn a member in 1431, but he had been present on at least two previous occasions. Nicolas, iv. 101, 104, 108. In 1441 the names of four irregular attendants, including the earls of Warwick and Dorset, the king's secretary, and Adam Moleyns, are given separately. Ibid. v. 173. Because of the persistence of this practice it is usually impossible to draw up a list of the sworn councillors for any particular time.

the fifteenth century a period of excessive individualism, then a season of weakness and disruption, and finally a decade or more of almost total obscurity. At length with the accession of the Tudors the strong hand of a new monarchy, by an assertion of power and purpose, was able to restore the council to its normal position once more. This part of the narrative has been reserved for the final chapter which immediately follows.

CHAPTER XVI

THE COUNCIL FROM EDWARD IV TO HENRY VIII

Apparent loss of records, 1460–1540.

FROM the end of the reign of Henry VI until nearly the close of the reign of Henry VIII there has been left a wide gap in the history of the council. The great work of Sir Harris Nicolas, to which reference has repeatedly been made, stops at the year 1460 in its sixth volume, and in its seventh begins again with new material at the date 1540. This fact is due to the almost total loss or failure of records within the period. The disappearance of these records has been greatly deplored by writers who have felt that much of the valuable history of the time for this reason has been withheld. As Nicolas has said, 'when the important events in the reigns of Edward the Fourth, Edward the Fifth, Richard the Third, and Henry the Seventh are remembered, the loss of the council records cannot be too much regretted. Of the constitution of the council under those monarchs nothing appears to be known.'[1] And yet there is a current belief that the period prior to 1485 'was the time of the council's greatest power', when it became 'the great executive power of the nation'.

At the start it is necessary to question and examine the grounds for each of the foregoing premises. Has there been a material loss of records once existent? and was the council during the period in view an active executive power? There is also an alternative possibility, which no one seems to have considered, that the failure of the records may be due to an interruption of the activities of the council itself. Before accepting any theory let us now consider the actual evidence upon these points.

[1] Op. cit., vii. iii.

Was there a loss of records ?

As to the records, there is no doubt that in the way of judicial proceedings, such as were produced by the court of star chamber and the court of requests, a great deal remains. But the passage just quoted has reference to notes that were systematically taken, especially of administrative and political affairs, such as were found in abundance during the preceding period. Now a loss of records of the kind kept by the council is in itself quite possible, and at times just such losses are known to have occurred. We are told of certain rolls that were deposited in the exchequer under Henry VI, but no one can find these rolls to-day.[1] Again in 1455 mention is made in parliament of the 'Book of the Council',[2] and yet we have no remains of such a book after 1435. Later Tudor writers also, like Sir Julius Caesar, show a familiarity with documents which are otherwise unknown to us. Furthermore, it must be acknowledged that in 1540 the records of the council suddenly reappear, not in a feeble tentative way as though making a beginning, but in full measure and complete form as though they had long continued. Finally, the enormous power that the council certainly wielded at that date gives support to the view that this body had not been inoperative during the period of its eclipse.

or a period of reduced activity ?

On the opposite side there are serious considerations which give colour to the view that there was for a time a failure in the operations of the council itself, and that the records fail therefore from lack of material. For the purpose of the argument, let it be supposed that for the period of the Lancastrians the Book of the Council and all other first-hand records were totally wanting. Would the historian then be in ignorance of what the council was, and of the nature of its work ? On the contrary, from numerous collateral sources the outlines would be perceived almost as clearly as they are at present, for the rolls of parliament and the patent rolls are filled with illuminating references. Moreover, from the files of warrants for the privy seal alone, if necessary, an extensive register of the acts of the council could be reconstructed. Even the chronicles of the time, which are not usually concerned with the forms of

[1] Mentioned in chapter xiv, p. 386. [2] *Rot. Parl.* v. 283.

government, would not leave one in ignorance upon the subject.

Let a similar course of investigation be followed regarding the council of Edward IV, and what is the result? Direct records, it is true, are almost entirely lacking. A few fragments exist mainly in the form of warrants with the endorsements *per consilium* for letters under the privy seal and likewise under the great seal. Of these administrative orders the quantity during the Yorkist period stands in contrast to that of the Lancastrians in the ratio of less than one to twenty.[1] During the first year of Edward IV's reign not one in a hundred of these warrants was passed by the authority of the council. In point of quality also the contents of these files will be found to be of an equally diminished value. Altogether there is less evidence of conciliar activity during the years in view than is found for any considerable period since the reign of Edward I. But still the lack of records may be due merely to an accident, so that too much stress must not be laid upon this point. It is no mere accident, however, that all collateral sources, such as the rolls of parliament, the statute rolls, the patent rolls, the issue rolls of the exchequer, the year-books and other familiar collections, are almost equally silent. The same sources are filled with references to the court of chancery, which was obviously growing and making itself felt in every direction. But everything tends to strengthen the impression that for a number of years immediately following the revolution of 1460–1 the activities and responsibilities of the council, while not entirely suspended, were reduced to a minimum.

The evidence of facts is supported strongly by the argument of motive. Under the Lancastrians the council had been, like the parliament, an instrument of the nobility, and it had been identified with all of the failures and weakness of that régime. To a considerable extent it had been used to exploit

[1] In the collection to which we have often referred, denoted *Council and Privy Seal*, files 1 to 89 are from Richard II to Henry VI; while only four files, 90–93, are found for the Yorkist period. The same disproportion of matter will be found in the *Warrants* (*Chancery*). I lay no great stress upon any one of the points alone, but the cumulative effect of every line of evidence is very strong.

the power of the crown to the profit of individual lords. Already in the later years of Henry VI the disintegration of the council was as complete as that of the parliament. In his policy of restoring the rights of the crown, it was plainly not the intention of Edward IV to maintain a council along the old lines. In this regard he departed markedly from the policy pursued by his father during the interval between 1453 and 1455. A council in form there was, as there also existed a parliament, but the one body was changed in character as much as the other. How the council of Edward IV and of Richard III was constructed and how it was employed there are some facts to show.

Appointments in the council—lords;

In the inauguration and settlement of the new government, the grants of land, the distribution of offices, the creation of peerages, the attainders and reversals of attainders were most conspicuous features.[1] But the formation of a council was mysteriously left in the background. Probably no list or large number of appointments was made at any one time, but men were retained or employed as they were needed. Archbishop Bourchier, who had welcomed the invasion of Edward and aided the revolution, we afterwards learn, was 'ordained' as one of the council on March 5, 1461, the first day after the king's accession, and for his attendance was given a salary of £200.[2] John Tiptoft, earl of Worcester and constable, was 'ordained and appointed' on November 1 with a salary of 200 marks.[3] But very few lords, in fact, are found in the king's council except those who held office. Among these there remained a few of the servants of Henry VI, but a larger number were new creations and promotions made by Edward. Bishop Neville, the chancellor of Henry VI, was reappointed, and likewise Lord Bourchier, now Lord Essex, the treasurer, and Robert Botill, prior of St. John's, the keeper of the privy seal. There were also William Neville, earl of Kent and admiral of England, Richard Woodville, Lord Rivers, whose daughter became

[1] Stubbs, *Const. Hist.*, § 356.
[2] 'Rex . . . ordinavit et constituit de essendo de consilio suo,' etc. *Issue Roll* (*Pells*), 2 Edw. IV, Mich., m. 2; 3 Edw. IV, Easter, m. 1.
[3] Ibid., 3 Edw. IV, Easter, m. 8.

queen, and William Hastings, soon Lord Hastings, the king's chamberlain.[1] Sir John Wenlock, who had formerly served in the council of Henry VI, was now made Lord Wenlock and the king's butler. The chancellor and the treasurer continued to receive their salaries of £200 and 200 marks respectively,[2] but otherwise salaries for attendance at the council were given only in exceptional instances. It is equally conspicuous that neither the king nor other great lords attended the council with any degree of frequency.[3] The earl of Warwick, for instance, whose influence at the time was greatest, is found in personal attendance upon the king rather than in the council at Westminster.

knights and squires;

As has been observed many times before, in the absence of a fixed body of lords, a considerable number of knights and squires were a feature of Edward IV's council. Most of these men likewise were office-holders, especially in the king's household. To give examples, there was Sir John Say, another member of Henry VI's council,[4] who was speaker of the house of commons in 1463; Sir John Fog, treasurer of the king's household;[5] Sir John Scott, controller of the household; Sir Thomas Vaughan, treasurer of the chamber; Sir Thomas Montgomery, John Denham esquire,[6] Richard Whitehill, William Nottingham, and others whose status it would be difficult to determine. A few of these received the traditional salary of their rank, £40 a year, but the system now was rather to reward men for their services by special grants.

doctors and clerks.

Still more marked is the tendency, already visible in the later years of Henry VI's reign, to extend the title 'councillor' to more than a score of doctors of law, clerks, and other

[1] In the seventh year he was given £200 for his office and attendance at the council, and the next year he was assigned £100 'for his costs in attending the king's person and the council'. *Issue Roll* (*Pells*), 7 Edw. IV, Mich., m. 4; 8 Edw. IV, Mich., m. 7.

[2] *Issue Rolls, passim.*

[3] On March 7, 1463, letters patent were granted in the presence of the archbishop of Canterbury, the bishop of Exeter, chancellor; the bishops of Lincoln, London, Ely, Norwich, and Salisbury; the earl of Warwick, the prior of St. John's; Lords Grey of Ruthyn, Wenlock, Dacre, Montague, Rivers; Sir John Langstrother, Sir John Scott, 'and others'. It is unusual during these years to find so many lords in attendance. *Council and Privy Seal*, file 89.

[4] *Issue Roll* (*Pells*), 4 Edw. IV, Easter, m. 1.

[5] Ibid., m. 2.

[6] Ibid., 2 Edw. IV, Mich., m. 2.

minor men of the court. Among these, most prominent was Master Peter Taster, a doctor of laws and dean of St. Severin's, who served on various embassies;[1] there was also William Hatfield, the king's secretary, an officer who from this time is generally found in the council; John Morton, master of the rolls; John Russell, secondary clerk in the office of the privy seal; Richard Martin, a clerk in the chancery and archdeacon of London; Thomas Colt, clerk of the hanaper;[2] Thomas Kent, doctor of laws, formerly clerk of the council;[3] Henry Sharp, John Lilleford, John Coke, three other doctors of law; John Gunthorp, clerk of parliament,[4] and Doctor Radclif, dean of St. Paul's. The list of attendants as given in the records usually ends with the indefinite phrase 'and others'.

Reversion to an official body

This catalogue of names, which might be still further extended, has seemed to be worth giving for the sake of showing the strong contrast between the council of this time and that of the previous régime. The reversion to a body of officials is more marked in fact than it was under Richard II, while the retainers given to men of many sorts and conditions recall the days of Edward III. The absence of the great lords from the council led in time to protests such as had been uttered on similar occasions many times before. In the insurrection of the lords in 1469 the duke of Clarence, the archbishop of York, and the earl of Warwick reminded the king of what had happened to Edward II, Richard II, and Henry VI in the following article:

'First, where the said Kynges estraingid the gret lordis of thayre blood from thaire secrete Councelle, And not avised by them: And takyng abowte them other not of thaire blood, and enclynyng only to theire counselle, rule and advise, the wheche persones take not respect ne consideracion to the wele of the said princes, ne to the comonwele of this lond, but only to theire singuler lucour and enrichyng of themself and theire bloode, as welle in theire greet possessions as in goodis; by the wheche the seid princes were so

[1] *Issue Rolls* (*Pells*), 2 Edw. IV, Mich., m. 2. St. Severin's was a church in Bordeaux, the deanship of which was still maintained as a title in England.

[2] Assigned £40 a year, ibid., 7 Edw. IV, Mich., m. 5.

[3] Sent on an embassy at 20*s*. a day. Ibid., 2 Edw. IV Mich., m. 2.

[4] *Rot. Parl.* v. 516.

enpoverysshed that they hadde not sufficient of lyvelode ne of goodis, whereby they myght kepe and mayntene theire honorable estate and ordinarie charges withynne this realme.'[1]

It is believed that the observations and criticisms of Sir John Fortescue,[2] who has repeatedly been quoted, were intended to suggest the reform of the council of Edward IV in accordance with previous experience. All the misfortunes of England he traced to the influence of the irregular and irresponsible councillors, such as had been the effective rulers in the past. But, it is needless to say, no effort under the house of York to form again a small exclusive council of lords along the old lines was successful.

No division of the council as yet.

The usages of Edward IV have proved very disconcerting to all those who have sought to define the council of this time. On the one hand there were certain nobles of undoubted political influence, and at the other extreme were scores of lesser men who were called 'king's councillors'.[3] The opinion has been suggested, on excellent authority, that these men of inferior rank were not strictly members of the privy council, but stood to it in the relation of assessors.[4] The suggestion is not well warranted, however, as it is really based on the old fallacy that the king's council must needs be a definite and homogeneous body, and that beyond this there might be a greater council of different composition. But even at this late day no such view of the matter was yet conceived. The king's council, whether it was called 'privy' or 'great', still remained a diversified body with all the anomalies of the past. It was designed to include not lords only, but men of every estate and kind of service. The lesser

[1] *Chronicle of the First Thirteen Years of Edward IV* (ed. Warkworth), Camden Society, 1839, p. 47.

[2] Upon his submission to Edward IV after the battle of Tewkesbury, the venerable jurist, we are told, was finally admitted to the council.

[3] The modern adaptation of this term, of course, is 'king's counsel', a title which is given still more widely to practising barristers, and is far removed from its original association with the council.

[4] A writer of the sixteenth century is quoted as saying, 'in former tymes . . . you shall find the names of many Bishopps doctors and others which were not of the King's Privy Councell noated to bee present at the sitting of that place (i.e. the star chamber), but it is like that they were at the least sworne to bee Counsellors.' Harg. MSS., vol. 216, p. 326; cited in Leadam, *Select Cases in Star Chamber*, p. xxxix.

men were members thereof as truly as the great men, even more positively because the oath was more strictly exacted of them. Moreover, the term 'councillor', we find, was used interchangeably with 'one of the council', and it was applied alike to lords and clerks. However widely it was used, the fact is clear also that this title was applied with discrimination, for in a list of names care was taken to indicate which ones were properly called king's councillors.[1] When the business transacted by the council is considered, it will be more evident why the attendance and services of official and professional members were required. Sometimes, in fact, a sitting of the council was held, in which only one, two, or three of the lords were present besides half a dozen or more doctors and clerks.[2]

Participation in the government.

The actual conduct of the government presents in every respect a strong contrast to the methods of the Lancastrians. Instead of a ruling or guiding council, there was at every step an emphasis of the royal authority. Grants of the crown, particularly, were made in the name of the king, and seldom was there any consent or concurrence on the part of the council. A survey of the patent rolls will show that scarcely one out of a hundred among the letters under the great seal was attested *per consilium.* In cases where the council was consulted, it appears to have been with reference to the technical forms rather than the policy involved. Likewise among the statutes of the realm none of the new acts appear either to have been framed by the council or to have been entrusted to it for execution. This fact is more than usually noticeable in the statute of liveries of the eighth year,[3] wherein summary powers of enforcement were conferred upon the king's bench, the common pleas, and other courts, but nothing was said about the king's council, although an earlier statute upon the same subject had declared that offenders should be punished, 'as shall be advised by us and our council'.[4]

Still the king needed the council, and frequently the royal acts are stated in the form, *rex de avisamento sui*

[1] See the lists for instance given in *Foedera* (Orig. Ed.), xi, *passim.*

[2] It is to be noticed that there was no reluctance to placing the names of these men upon the records, but in later times the 'ordinary councillors' were not so recognized.

[3] *Statutes of the Realm,* ii. 426.

[4] Ibid., 13 Ric. II, 75.

consilii voluit et mandavit.[1] With a sanction of this kind on one occasion he granted a pardon of an attainder which had been passed by parliament.[2] In granting letters under the great seal it was frequent for the king, either viva voce or by his signet, to command the chancellor 'in the presence of the council'. A noteworthy instance, revealing the relations of king and council, is given in 1469.[3] Before an assemblage of the council at London, the chancellor came with two letters of the king, one under the signet and the other under the sign manual. The first conveyed a message from Middleham in Yorkshire, declaring that it seemed expedient to the king, the earl of Warwick, and others of the *council there* to change the time and place of a parliament about to be held. In the second letter the king and his councillors at Sheriff Hutton charged the lord chancellor in all possible haste to issue letters under the great seal countermanding and superseding the said parliament. It is to be noticed that the distinction of the councillors attending the king and the council residing at London or Westminster was never before so clearly made. In this instance the former appear as the king's real advisers, while the latter was hardly more than an administrative board, composed mainly of officials and doctors of law. The tendency to divide the council in this manner will be more apparent in the future. For the present, however, the council at Westminster remains the only body of organic character. Even in this subordinate sphere it would be a mistake to suppose that the council had little to do. While its corporate action was indeed greatly reduced, individual councillors were never more active in the king's service. The clerks were employed incessantly in carrying messages to and fro, while the greater men were sent on diplomatic missions. It was for services of this kind especially that they were well rewarded. Certain important ambassadorial commissions which went to Brittany, to Burgundy, and to France were

[1] *Warrants (Chancery)*, files 1547, 1548.

[2] *Cal. Patent Rolls*, 4 Edw. IV, 321.

[3] On this day (September 7) there were present Bishop Stillington, chancellor, the bishop of Carlisle, the prior of St. John's, now treasurer; Lords Mountjoy and Ferrers; Doctors Winterbourne, Boniface (?), Radclif, and Alcock; Sir John Howard, and (William) Nottingham. *Warrants (Chancery)*, file 1547.

composed entirely of the king's councillors.[1] It is probable too that in these matters the deliberative functions of the council were of more weight than the bare statements of the documents generally reveal. In 1467, at all events, when certain councillors had been sent as ambassadors to the court of Burgundy, their letters were received and acted upon by the king in the following manner :

'Veues les dites lettres de nous dites ambassadeurs transcriptes, et sur icels et tout leur continue eu meur advis et deliberacion de Counseill, nos, de nostre certain sciens, plain puissance, et auctorite roiall . . . confermons et approvons.'[2]

Judicial activities reduced.

As has been remarked before, organic transformations are most easily followed in the field of judicature. In the later years of Henry VI there had been almost a complete breakdown of such functions on the part of the council. For a period which lasted through the first eight years of Edward IV, the practice of hearing cases was almost abandoned. Although both before and after the revolution the country was harried with the depredations of rebels and rioters, instead of being brought to the council, these cases were generally given for trial to special assizes, or else they were brought to the court of chancery. Up to the year 1468, in fact, it is very marked that the commissions of arrest in the majority of instances were to bring the offenders before the chancellor.[3] Not only was this tendency true in respect of criminal jurisdiction, but of all kinds of litigation. Suitors generally ceased to address their complaints to the parliament or the council, where they were not likely to be heard, but made address either to the king or to the chancellor. The number and variety of the petitions found in the chancery surpasses all powers of description or analysis. It seemed, in fact, as though the entire jurisdiction of the council, including cases of violence and maintenance as well

[1] *Foedera*, xi. 542 ff.

[2] Ibid., xi. 599.

[3] *Cal. Patent Rolls, passim.* Among the petitions in chancery of 1463 is one of John Fettiplate of Wolvele, who complained that his house had been attacked by forty men, who shot through its very walls, 'to the great distress of him self, his wife and children'. *Chancery Proceedings*, bundle 27, no. 428.

as the equitable cases concerning property, would be deflected into the court of chancery. But for reasons previously given, the chancery was better equipped for dealing with cases of property, and it did not succeed equally well with criminal cases. For the great evils of the times there was undoubtedly need of a still more vigorous authority.

On the other hand, the jurisdiction of the council had by no means been abandoned, nor was it entirely suspended. There are a few cases of the early years of Edward IV to be found, which may be taken as exceptions to the general observations just made. For example, there is the record of a case in 1462,[1] in which it appears that the tenants of the bishop of Winchester made complaint in parliament concerning the rents and services which were exacted of them. Although there is no mention of any such cases or petitions in the rolls of parliament, it is said that the matter was carefully examined and that the parties were heard. By reason of the great proofs on the side of the bishop, and the lack of good argument on the other side, it was advised that the tenants should pay their rents and continue their services as they had done before. But when it was learned that the tenants refused to follow this decision, they were asked to send men in their behalf to come before the council, and the bishop was asked to send attorneys as well, that the matter at variance might be heard and understood. But when the tenants suddenly departed and left the matter in default, it was ordered in the star chamber[2] that a proclamation be made by the sheriff of Hampshire, to the effect that the tenants should be notified and charged to pay their rent and return to their services. This decree was 'signed with ye kynges owen hande beyng present', *R. E.* In 1463 there is an account of a case in which Richard Heron, a merchant, complained that he had been unduly restrained by the king's officers at Calais in the sale of his wool. The matter had been brought before the council in 1460 under Henry VI, but it still

[1] *Warrants* (*Chancery*), file 1547, March 18.

[2] Those present in the council on this day (March 18) were the bishop of Exeter, chancellor, the earl of Essex, treasurer, the prior of St. John's, keeper of the privy seal, the dean of St. Severin's, and Thomas Colt. None of the justices or serjeants-at law are mentioned as taking any part.

remained unfinished. Upon a renewal of the complaint, the king declared the competence and readiness of the council to deal with it in the following words: *nos et domini consiliarii magni consilii . . . iudices competentes sumus et omni tempore erimus prompti et parati . . . iusticie facere complementum.*[1]

The point of utmost weakness.

Inasmuch as outbreaks of violence were the great evil of the day, it will be of interest to see how this problem was dealt with. In 1463, on the report of a riot in Lancashire, the king by a letter of the privy seal summoned the parties to come, not before the council expressly, but 'before *him*' in eight days, at the same time ordering the justices of the assizes to cease holding their sessions, lest a riot ensue if the court were kept.[2] From time to time there were commissions of arrest to bring parties before the council, but whether they were actually tried there it is impossible to ascertain. There is a case reported in 1467 which reveals the weakness and inefficiency of the council to an extent that is wellnigh incredible.[3] In a bill addressed to the king, Lord Strange complained that Roger Kinaston, second husband of his mother, had retained possession of certain estates in which his mother had only a life-interest. The dispute had at various times been put to arbitration, but each time Roger had refused to abide by the award. In spite of a board of arbitration appointed by the king, he had taken forcible possession of the lands. The suppliant had complained sundry times to the king, who then directed letters under the signet to the offender requiring him to appear before the council. This command he refused to obey. Upon advice of the council, the king then directed letters under the privy seal that he should appear before the council under threat of great penalty. But Roger, it was alleged, had beaten the king's messenger nearly to death. The king then sent a writ of proclamation to the sheriff, commanding that he should appear, and although the proclamation was made in towns, fairs and markets, Roger was still defiant. The next recourse was a commission of arrest under the great seal.

[1] *Council and Privy Seal*, file 90, March 5; *Cal. Patent Rolls*, 3 Edw. IV, 275.

[2] *Council and Privy Seal*, file 90, March 6.

[3] The record of this case is given in full by Palgrave, *Original Authority*, pp. 135–42.

But as the petitioner said the commission did not act decisively, he asked that a letter of the privy seal be sent commanding the commission to execute their order, and that further writs of proclamation be sent to the officers of other counties. It is not conceivable that all these orders could have been disobeyed with impunity, unless there was an extraordinary amount of fraud on the part of the king's officers in collusion with the offender. Even in this extreme case it is noticeable that the council by no means takes the initiative, but appears as one of several alternative authorities to which the king refers.

Signs of revival.

In 1468 there begins to be evidence of a turn of the tide in favour of a revival of the authority of the council. In the great criminal cases it is found that the commissions of arrest are then almost exclusively to bring the offenders before the council.[1] In 1469 a letter was sent to Sir John Paston, ordering him to cease making assemblages against the duke of Norfolk and stating that he had already been summoned before the council but had not complied. It continues:

'We therefore eftsones write unto yow, willing and straitly charging yow to cease of the said ryotts and assemblies; and that incontinent upon the sight of these our letters that ye dispose yow personally to appear afore the said Lords of our Councell at our Pallis, there to answere to such thinges as in that behalfe by them shall be laid and objected against yow, not failinge hereof, all excuses laid aparte, as ye will avoide our displeasure.'[2]

The records of several cases that are found upon the rolls show that the normal functions of the council were being slowly resumed.[3] Still as regards the rioters its administration was anything but vigorous or efficient. Among all the cases of this kind within the period in view, it has not been possible to find an instance of a great offender actually punished. In dealing with these men the methods of the council seem to have been as lax as ever they were under the Lancastrians. Moreover, there is testimony that the lords of

[1] *Cal. Patent Rolls, passim.*

[2] It is to be noted that letters of this kind were now often issued under the signet. *Paston Letters*, no. 599.

[3] *Cal. Patent Rolls*, 8 Edw. IV, 131; 18 Edw. IV, 145; 20 Edw. IV, 218.

the council themselves were too much involved in illegal practices to discountenance the same in others. One who was a king's attorney under Edward IV afterwards declared that he had seen all the lords sworn to guard the statutes of liveries and maintenance which they had themselves made, and that then within an hour's time in the star chamber they were making retainers contrary to their sureties and oaths.[1] Instead of effective punishments, then, all that we find in cases of this kind are incomprehensible delays, pardons of outlawry in scarcely diminished quantity, and attempts at reconciliation. Apparently the council preferred to deal with these cases as little as possible.

Technical changes.

Another important point, which appears during the years of comparative inactivity, is found in certain changes of procedure, which show that older traditions to a certain extent were broken. For one thing, as was quite consistent with the general tendencies of this government, the prominence of the king even in law cases was much greater than before. In most of the instances which we are able to cite, plaintiffs would address their petitions to the king, who might then refer the matter to the council. For example, in 1477 a man addressed his petition 'to the king our sovereign lord', asking him to command the parties to appear before his highness and the lords of the council.[2] Again, in the twenty-first year, on a complaint of violent entry and forcible dispossession, the king took the matter in hand, writing to the justice of the peace in Oxford in the following manner:

'And for asmoche as it is doon us to understand by a lamentable complaint made *unto us* by Alice Pothe . . . ye amove the said William Idle and all other occupiours there by occasion of the said entree from the said manour and alle that apparteignets to the same, charging theim to appere afore us and our counsaill at our paleys of Westminster in the xv^m^ of Saint Michell next comyng, to answer to the premisses.' [3]

This was different from the method of leaving it to the council to issue the orders. The use of the signet also for

[1] *Year Books*, 1 Hen. VII, Mich., no. 3.

[2] I. S. Leadam, *Select Cases in the Star Chamber* (Selden Society, vol. xvi), p. 2.

[3] *Council and Privy Seal*, file 93, July 31, 1481.

the purpose of summoning the parties, as occurs in several of the cases cited, was not customary before. On one occasion, after the process had been held and a report made, the king gave judgement and decreed.[1] It was more regular, however, for the king to instruct the court to make the decree. Likewise, a greater prominence was given the chancellor, when petitions were addressed to him as a means of approach to the council. Probably there was much confusion in the minds of suitors whether it was the council or the chancellor's court which they were seeking. Here is an example:

'*To the Right Reverent fader in Godd, the Bisshop of Lincoln Chaunceller of Ingland.* Mekely besecheth your good and gracious lordship your pore Oratour Thomas Shaw husbandman that where he hath late ben betyn and put in fere of his lief bi Thomas Arundell squyer and by his servauntes so that he darst not abide in his countree for fere of theym but cam to London to shewe and make his compleynt to your lordship and to other lordes of the kynges counceill, &c.'[2]

Another petitioner, who complains in the usual manner of the violence and extortion he has suffered, badly mixes two forms of action when he beseeches the chancellor,

'please . . . to graunt severelx writtes of *sub pena* in due forme to bee directed unto the said (parties) . . . by the same tappaer before our soverain lord the king and his Counsell at a certeyn day to bee lymyted upon a reasounable peyn yere to be examined of & in the premysses . . . to doo & receyve in the same as right & conscience require. And this for the love of God and in wey of charite and ye said suppliant shall tenderly prey to our lord for you.'

As an illustration of the tendency to deflect cases of this kind into the chancery, this petition is endorsed, *coram domino rege in cancellaria sua in Octavis Sancti Hillarii proximis futuris*.[3]

Quickened activity at the end of the reign.

By the end of the reign certainly cases heard by the council in star chamber are more clearly in evidence. In 1481 a hearing was given to a dispute between Richard Whele

[1] *Cal. Patent Rolls*, 20 Edw. IV, 218.

[2] *Early Chancery Proceedings*, bundle 66, no. 209.

[3] There is need of further investigation of these cases in chancery. Cannot the Selden Society give us another volume in this field?

and John Fortescue,[1] 'which matter long hath hanged in the King's council undecided'. The complaint was that Fortescue had represented his opponent as a Scotchman, while Richard offered to prove himself an Englishman. On November 21 the lords of the council examined the writings and proofs, and after hearing each of the parties, they determined that Richard was an Englishman and Fortescue should be put to silence.[2] Probably a communication with the king was considered to be necessary before a final decree was made. This was rendered on May 2, 1482, in the following words:

'In the sterer chambre at Westminster the secund day of Maye the xxij yere of the Reigne of our souveraigne lord the King Edward the iiijth, Present my lordes Tharchebishop of York Chaunceller of England, the Bisshoppes of Lincoln Prive Seal, Worcester, Norwich, Durham and Landaff; Therle Ryvers, the lordes Dudley, Ferirs, Beauchamp; Sirs Thomas Borough, William Parre, Thomas Vaghan and Thomas Greye knightis. In full and privie Counsaill was openly radde the judement and decree made by my lordis of our said souveraignes lordes counsail afore that tyme for the partie of Richard Whele otherwise called Richard Pierson, decreed, made, yeven and declared contrarie and ayenst John Fortescue squier in manere and forme and under the theime that followeth.'

It is noticeable that at neither of the two sittings of the council, although the business in hand was strictly judicial, was the presence of any of the justices mentioned.

Continuance of these tendencies under Ric. III.

Under Richard III the same tendencies within the council may be stated with greater emphasis. Even to a less extent than his brother was Richard able to command the regular services of a body of nobles in his government. But the deficiency of lords was made up by the appointment of a goodly number of professional men, some of whom were retained with annuities for life.[3] We cannot say that the

[1] He is not to be confused with the chief justice who is believed to have died in 1476 (*D. N. B.*). The record is found in *Council and Privy Seal*, file 93, June 26, 22 Edw. IV.

[2] On this day the examination was held before the chancellor, the keeper of the privy seal, the bishops of Worcester and Durham; Masters Gunthorp and Cook, the pope's collector, Lord Howard, Sir Thomas Vaughan, Sir Richard Harcourt, Thomas Thwaites, and others.

[3] Such grants I have noticed were made to the following men as coun-

council was allowed any initiative or discretionary power in the control of the government, but it was fully awake to its responsibilities in the judicial field. Evidence is now afforded that suitors in considerable numbers were positively seeking the remedies afforded by the council. In the first year of the reign we are informed that two clerks were appointed; the second one, John Harington, expressly 'for his good service before the lords and others of the council, especially in the custody, registration, and expedition of bills, requests, and supplications of poor persons'.[1] The custody and registration of the bills unfortunately were not so well managed as to leave many for the instruction of posterity. As one of the successors of this clerk a hundred years later explained, 'and the tyme alsoe when he served was in division between the two Houses of Lancaster and Yorke. By which means the Actes of the Counsell were not so exactly kept and conserved as they are now.'[2] Those cases which survive,[3] however, do not indicate that any vigorous policy was yet undertaken with regard to the evils of livery and maintenance.

Vigorous policy of Henry VII.

Under Henry VII one reaches more familiar ground. Although our knowledge is still restricted by a lack of original records, there is ample evidence of a policy not merely of rehabilitating the council, but of employing it with greater vigour than ever. On September 17, 1485, the new king entered London, and by September 30 a clerk was appointed and a council was already at work.[4] In this council are found five peers, of whom four were recent creations, two bishops, namely Morton the chancellor and Courtenay the keeper of the privy seal, besides nine lords and knights. The number of councillors increased rapidly, so that in the succeeding years one may count from twenty to

cillors: Lord Dudley, Lord Lovell, Lord Scrope of Bolton, Sir Thomas Montgomery, Edmund Chaderton, John Gunthorpe, Thomas Barowe, John Kendall. *Cal. Patent Rolls*, 1 & 2 Ric. III.

[1] Ibid., 1 Ric. III, 413.

[2] Quoted in Leadam, *Select Cases in the Court of Requests* (Selden Society, vol. xii), p. lxxxiv.

[3] There is a case of the second year, in which a Spanish merchant brings a bill against an Englishman for being despoiled at sea. *Year Book*, 2 Ric. III, no. 4.

[4] *Materials for the History of Henry VII* (Rolls Series), i. 154, 339 ff.

forty as present at different sittings. The proportion of lords and commoners may be indicated roughly in the following way :

	Number Present.	*Peers.*	*Knights and Commoners.*
1486, June 14	24	10	10
„ July 10	33	13	16
„ „ 11	25	11	11
„ „ 16	22	9	10
1494, November 10	39	13	13
1501	41	13	19 [1]

The number of men of inferior rank who attended the council was undoubtedly much greater than can be stated, since their names are not always given, but are referred to vaguely as *et ceteri*. Among them, however, we may observe several knights of the king's household,[2] royal chaplains, and clerks. A point was made too of having the lords sworn and admitted with due formality. Yet the practice continued of permitting some to be present who were not sworn members. On one occasion, in the fourteenth year, there is a record of eight lords being introduced and sworn, although three of them had been in attendance before.[3] Henry VII is reputed to have been very successful in raising a class of nobles who were serviceable to him, but the problem of maintaining a sufficient number of lords in the council, we shall see, was not yet fully solved.

Henry VII found it worth while to give the council an unusual amount of personal attention. As Bacon says, 'to his council he did refer much, and sat oft in person ; knowing it to be the way to assist his power and inform his judgment.'[4] During the first few years, in fact, his presence is indicated in nearly half of the records that are given us.[5] The council

[1] Compiled from the *Liber Intracionum*, found in Add. MSS. (British Museum), vol. 4521, fol. 104 ff. ; also Harleian MSS., vol. 297, fol. 1 ff. This work is largely reproduced by Cora L. Scofield, *Study of the Court of Star Chamber* (Chicago, 1900), pp. 6–8.

[2] Sir Reginald Bray, it was said, 'had the greatest freedom of any councillor with the king,' and for his services he was made rich by the grants of various forfeited estates. Sir Richard Empson and Edmund Dudley became especially notorious for their connexion with the levy of benevolences.

[3] Add. MSS., fol. 113.

[4] *Hist ry of Henry VII* (Cambridge, 1876), p. 217.

[5] *Liber Intracionum*, cited.

was even averse to continuing its sessions without him. On May 1, 1489, the term was ended with the following statement: 'Continued be all and singular appearances (i.e. suits) . . . until the beginninge of the next Terme, because the Kinges Majestie is gooing into the North with his armie.'[1] Whether it was the intention of the councillors to leave Westminster in order to attend the king, we are not at this time informed, but a tendency in this direction will soon be made apparent.

The 'Book of Entries'.

The council took up its work manifestly with great energy, during the term holding meetings as often as four times a week. The beginning of a new register called the 'Book of Entries' was made.[2] The original book is lost, but fortunately parts of it were copied, so that there exists a number of transcripts in incomplete and fragmentary form. These records have generally been used to show the development of the court of star chamber. Four-fifths of their contents, it is true, consist of prosecutions and suits such as commonly belonged to that tribunal. These were plainly the main consideration of the council. But judicial business was by no means separated from general administration, as the records abundantly show. On July 10, 1486, for example, there was a proposal to send a diplomatic commission to Calais to treat with the emperor concerning the trade relations of England and the Netherlands. Later in the year the council considered a bull from the pope and also a proposal of peace with Scotland. In the sixth year ambassadors from France appeared at the council, but they refused to express themselves there until they had been brought to the king's presence. In the twentieth year commissioners were appointed to provide for the reformation of idle people and vagabonds as well as 'the enormity of apparel, and the excess of meat and drink, and costly fare'. The swearing of members of the council and certain military indentures are likewise noted. Before the time, then, of any separate history of the court of star chamber, it seems that the records in question are to be regarded as those of the council

[1] Add. MSS., fol. 108.
[2] Already cited as *Liber Intracionum*.

sitting at Westminster or in London. That they are concerned mainly with judicial business, reveals as yet not a separation of these functions, but an emphasis and concentration of the duties of the council in this field.

Aim at riot cases.

There is no longer room for doubt that the policy of the government was to put an end to the disorders which afflicted the country. During the first term of his courts Henry called a conference of all his justices to consider matters with reference to the coming parliament, 'and there were moved many good statutes, most profitable to the realm, *if they could be executed*.'[1] With reference to the statutes of Edward IV relating to robberies, felonies, riots, routs, forcible entries, signs and liveries, maintenance and embraceries, the chief justice impressively said, 'the law will never be executed until all the lords temporal and spiritual are persuaded, for the love and dread which they have of God or of the king or both, effectually to execute them, and until the king on his part and the lords on their part shall make each other do this, and if they will not they shall be chastised and punished.' Such chastisement and punishment was not slow in coming, for the records just mentioned are filled with cases of riot, rebellion, treason, and the like, which were taken up boldly from the beginning of the reign. Men of knightly rank were systematically prosecuted and fined, while the lords were given to understand that positive measure would be taken also against them. On July 10, 1486, the following ordinance was passed, on the subject of riots made by the servants of lords :

'It is concluded and agreed that everie Lord and gent(leman), if anie of his servants make a riott or other excesse, the maister of the same trespassour shall have in comaundment to bringe forth the same servant, and if he so doe not abide such direction and punition as by the Kinge and his Counsell shall be thought convenient, and ouer that if the same ryott or excesse another arise, by cause or occasion of anie quarrell or displeasure conveninge the maister of him that soe exceedeth, doe readely, the same maister shall answear for the

[1] *Year Books*, 1 Hen. VII, Mich., no. 3.

same excesse (in) such wise, as shall be thought to the Kinge and his said Counsell expedient.' [1]

The foregoing ordinance was one of the preliminary steps to the great statute of 1487, afterwards known as the statute *pro camera stellata*.[2] The provisions of this act have been so well presented in other works, that they need not be repeated here. But in the light of what has gone before there are a few explanations to be made, which have not yet been fully stated. Like many another enactment of the middle ages, the statute propounded nothing new, but was designed to make a statement of policy, as well as certain definitions of the council's jurisdiction, which otherwise might be doubtful. The considerations which led to the framing of the act may be set forth in the following manner.

The statute 3 Hen. VII.

1. It was a manifest gain to have the authority of the council to this extent sanctioned by parliament. As the chief justice had said, the law could not be executed without the support of the lords spiritual and temporal, and by the passage of the act their assent was formally given. When it is remembered that the procedure of the council was of questionable legal validity, and had often been defied on this ground, the value of the assent of the lords begins to appear. A measured recognition of the council's jurisdiction, it is true, had been given before, but generally this had been done only in specific cases or for a limited period of time. It was a practical reversal too of all former conditions that parliament, which had usually felt bound to oppose and limit the authority of the council, should now give it a large measure of support.

2. The great evils of the day arising from the practices of livery and maintenance were fully recognized. 'Riots, unlawful assemblages, murders, robberies, perjuries, and unsureties of all men living' were declared to have been on the increase until 'the policy and good rule of this realm

[1] Add. MSS., 4521, fol. 106; also Lansdowne MSS., no. 83, art. 72; cited by Miss Scofield, op. cit., p. xiii.

[2] Statute, 3 Hen. VII; reproduced in Leadam, *Select Cases in Star Chamber* (Selden Society, xvi), p. i.

is almost subdued'. The present act was framed expressly for 'giving the court of star chamber authority to punish divers misdemeanours'. The excessive leniency of the government in the past and the failure of the courts, it was announced, was now to undergo a substantial 'reformation of the premises'. Never was a policy more vigorously stated, or a clearer warning given to criminals.

3. The number of cases, including both suits and prosecutions, which now pressed upon the time and attention of the council, called for a separation of such business from other interests touching the king more closely. This was not the first time that an effort was made to set apart sessions of the council for judicial purposes, but nothing of the kind had been sufficiently effective before. Moreover, it had often been found in the past that private interests tended to encroach upon the king's business. Now the very opposite was true. As one party interested in litigation complained in 1494, 'ther hath be so gret counsell for the Kynges maters, that my Lord Chawnsler kept not the Ster Chawmber thys viii days, but one day at London.'[1]

4. The uncertainty of the respective jurisdictions of the chancellor and the council in this field also called for a definition. Although the two courts had tended to separate during the last hundred years, there was still much confusion as to what cases properly belonged to one and the other. For a time the chancery had tended to absorb the entire jurisdiction of the council, and then there was a reaction in favour of the council. Many of the cases before the council, which have been cited in this chapter, might with equal propriety have gone to the chancery, and even in the reign of Henry VII cases of violence had been sent alternately to one court and the other.[2] It was now stated with all possible clearness that the criminal cases specified belonged peculiarly to the council, while by implication the bulk of the cases in equity was left to the chancery. The definition was by no means a complete one, but the line of division for the first time was clearly drawn.

[1] *Paston Letters*, no. 1058.

[2] *Materials for the History of Henry VII*, i. 109, 270, 286, 358, &c.

5. From previous experience as regards the attendance of the council, the need of a court of suitable number, of a fair degree of stability and regularity, instead of an ever varying, shifting body, was also appreciated. To this end it was stated that the chancellor, the treasurer, and the keeper of the privy seal, or two of them, should summon a bishop and a temporal lord, together with two of the justices, preferably the chief justices. In this wise the court would be composed mainly of its professional members, as had always been considered desirable in law cases. And yet this rule had not always been observed, for law cases are known to have been heard without the assistance of a single judge. The number six recalls the traditional quorum of the council. The provisions of the statute in this regard would have been very difficult to follow strictly, and probably there was no expectation that it would be carried out to the letter, but that its general intent should be observed. Certainly the sessions of the council immediately before and afterwards show that there might be a larger number or there might be a smaller number to form the court, while sometimes, instead of two or three great officers as required, only the chancellor or the keeper of the privy seal was present.[1]

6. Cases were to be brought to the court 'uppon bill or informacion put to the seid Chaunceller'. This clause reveals the break that had occurred in the older procedure, since formerly the bill or petition was most likely addressed to the council. But now the chancellor was uppermost in every one's mind, and the statute did not suggest any other form of address. Nevertheless, traditional forms were being revived, and one finds immediately that in most cases the petitions intended for this court were not addressed to the chancellor, but to the king, to the king and council, or to the lords of the council.[2]

7. Finally, it was acknowledged that in the great class of offences previously mentioned, the operations of the common law had been ineffective. 'Nothing or little may be found by enquiry', that is, by jury, the statute said. It

[1] *Liber Intracionum*; also Leadam, *Select Cases in Star Chamber, passim.*
[2] Leadam, op. cit.

had often been admitted as a matter of course that there were cases beyond the reach of the common law, but now the principle was carried to the extent of a sanction and legitimation of certain summary forms of conciliar action. These were understood especially to be the peculiar writs of summons, and the inquisitional examinations. Convictions and punishments by these processes were to have the same validity, it was declared, as ' if they (the parties) were therof convicted after the due order of the law '.

The subsequent court of star chamber.

The subsequent history of the court of star chamber has been so well treated by others that the subject may appropriately be dropped at this point. It is fully understood that the court proceeded not upon the terms of the statute, so much as the historic foundations of the council. Old usages were revived, some of which were beyond the scope of the act, while others were even contrary to its provisions. In all the operations of the court there was practically nothing new but its vigour and purpose. It was then shown how quickly the violence of the country could be subdued, and how the same powerful engine could be used not only in defence of the monarchy, but against liberty of speech and for a variety of purposes not thought of before.[1] It is only necessary to add, that while other branches of the modern council were soon formed, it is particularly the court of star chamber which is to be regarded as the institutional continuation of the original mediaeval council.

The court of requests.

Another branch of the council, which likewise has its roots in the past, came to be known as the Court of Requests. The reason for this differentiation was, in a word, pressure of business, which soon went beyond the power of the council in star chamber to handle. ' After a few yeeres King Henry the Seventh seeing his Court pestered with sutours and sometymes out of due season,' assigned certain members of his council, we are told, to the task of ' the xpedition of poore mennys causes depending in the sterred Chambre.'[2]

[1] Besides the works already cited there is also that of Miss G. Bradford, *Proceedings in the Court of Star Chamber in the reigns of Henry VII and Henry VIII* (Somerset Record Society, 1911).

[2] Leadam, *Court of Requests*, p. xi.

To treat the cases of poor suitors had always been one of the special duties of the council, and for these special arrangements had often been suggested. Lately under Richard III a particular classification of such bills had been made. The separate history of the court is considered to have begun in 1493, although its sessions were still regarded as those of the council and its decisions as made by the king and his council. Its actual beginning is difficult to state, because it did not start with any act or ordinance. It was practically a standing committee of the council, composed especially of professional members, who met under the presidency of the keeper of the privy seal. The selection of this officer to preside in the absence of the chancellor has been noticeable before, particularly in the ordinances of 1390.

The court differed from the star chamber in that it had no fixed terms, but was intended to be open to suitors throughout the year. At first it was held not in a fixed place, but moved with the king about the country. It was indeed the council attending the king *ubicunque fuerit,* while the sessions of the star chamber were fixed at Westminster. Obviously it was not easy to form a court on these lines. Among the 'Actes, Orders, and Decrees made by the King and his Counsell . . . remaining in the Court of Requests', as afterwards collected, we find a very careful provision to meet the never-ending difficulty of the attendance of members.[1] According to this ordinance of 1494, the bishops of Bath, Exeter, and Rochester were to attend continually during the year after Easter; the prior of St. John's was to be present from a fortnight after Easter until August; Lord Daubeney during August, September, and October; Lord Broke the same time as the prior of St. John's; Robert Rude from February to July, and certain other four knights, the master of the rolls, and three doctors of law for the entire year. Like many previous enactments of the kind, the ordinance in effect fell very far short of its intention. There were seldom, in fact, so many members present at any time, while frequently the number sank to

[1] Sir Julius Caesar, *Auncient State, Authoritie, and Proceedings of the Court of Requests* (1597), p. 1.

three and even less. After all, the work of the court was mainly sustained by the doctors of law, commonly known as the 'masters of requests', who were sworn and admitted to the council expressly for this purpose.[1] For the better convenience of all concerned, in the next reign this body was no longer required to follow the king, but was permanently seated in White Hall at Westminster.

In large part the business carried on in the court of requests did not differ materially from that of the star chamber. Most of the cases, it is true, were the suits of persons who presented themselves as 'poor' or 'humble'. By a writ issued on the authority of the chancellor they were entitled to justice free of charge, although to a considerable extent their poverty must have been a pure legal fiction. Among the litigants, we find, were Richard Close and other merchants of London; Lady Darrell, who sued Lord Delaware for ten pounds; and the mayor of Cambridge, who was in a dispute with the scholars of the university.[2]

A new branch of the council.

Besides the court of requests, there was a further marked development of that branch of the council, which is distinguished from the other by its attendance upon the king. It will be remembered that it had always been customary for the king on his journeys to have a number of councillors with him, and at certain times, particularly under Richard II, Henry IV, and Edward IV, fairly distinct groups were visible. But thus far the council following the king had never been more than a temporary arrangement, while the council at Westminster had always been the regular organ. Already in the reign of Henry VII we have said that councillors attending the royal person were retained for the purpose of hearing poor men's causes, and soon other functions were added. A certain recognition of this body as an alternative to the council at Westminster was made in the Statute of

[1] For example, it is said, 'Thomas Hoton decretorum Doctor iuratus admittitur in consiliarium regis, et promittit se servaturum tenorem iuramenti sibi in hac parte delati, quatenus discretio et scientia sua in ea parte eum permittent.' Caesar, op. cit., p. 6. That the duties of the doctors lay especially, if not exclusively, in the court of requests, some of the following references will make evident.

[2] Ibid., pp. 2, 7, 19, &c.

Retainers in 1503,[1] which provides that informers may present themselves either (1) before the chancellor or the keeper of the privy seal in the star chamber; (2) before the king's bench; or (3) before the king and his council attending his person, provided in this case that there be present at least three of the council, two of them being lords spiritual or temporal. Simultaneously with this differentiation and probably for this very reason, there appears a new officer known as the president of the council. We have said that there was nothing to suggest such a position during the middle ages prior to its establishment in connexion with the council of the Welsh Marches in 1473. The suggestion was then followed when the new branch of the council was formed in England. There the president is first mentioned in 1497, when he is seen taking the place of the keeper of the privy seal in the proceedings of the court of requests.[2] The new office, we may remark, was different from that of the chancellor, the treasurer, or the keeper of the privy seal, in that it was not the head of an existing department, but was created solely for the purposes of the council. It does not appear to have been steadily occupied prior to 1529, when an act of parliament gave the president an official rank in the star chamber below the chancellor and treasurer, and above the keeper of the privy seal.[3] With which branch of the council it was intended to place the president, is not made clear at first; but from the time of this act he is generally found in the sessions of the star chamber, where he was directed to exercise 'the same authority as belonged to the chancellor'.[4] The chancellor then more frequently acted with the other group of councillors, whom we have described as following the king.

Difficulties in establishing this branch.

But for an interval of twenty years the council with the king does not appear to have been a well settled arrangement. It is mentioned sometimes, and then again it disappears. In

[1] Statutes, 19 Hen. VII, c. 14.

[2] 'Coram Presidente Consilii domini Regis.' Caesar, p. 14.

[3] Statutes, 21 Hen. VIII, c. 20.

[4] This was stated in 1530 upon the appointment of the duke of Suffolk to the office. Gairdner, *Letters and Papers of the Reign of Henry VIII*, vol. iv, no. 6199.

the act of 1503, just cited, a doubt was expressed whether there might be as many as three councillors in attendance. But such was the pressure of business at Westminster that the need of a new division of labour was every year clearly manifest. At length in 1526 the problem was taken up by Henry VIII in the enactment of certain ordinances, which were devised, it is said, for the 'Establishment of a Councell'.[1] In order to show the difficulties which were encountered in the plan, the articles in part will be quoted.

'And to the intent, that as well matters of justice and complaints, touching the greaves of the King's subjects, and disorder of his realme and otherwise, which shall fortune to be made, brought, and presented unto his Highnesse, by his said subjects in his demurre or passing from place to place within the same; as also other greate occurences concerning his owne particular affaires, may be the better ordered, and with his Grace more debated, digested, and resolved, from time to time, as the case shall require; it is ordered and appointed by his Highnesse, that a good number of honourable, virtuous, sadd, wise, experte, and discreet persons of his councell, shall give their attendance upon his most royall person, whose names hereafter follow.'

There were twenty names, including Cardinal Wolsey the chancellor, the duke of Norfolk treasurer, and the bishop of London keeper of the privy seal. Strange to say, the president of the council is not mentioned, as though the office was not at the moment filled. There were also the duke of Suffolk marshal, the marquises of Dorset and of Exeter, the earl of Shrewsbury steward of the household, the lord chamberlain, the bishops of Bath and Lincoln, Lord Sandys, Sir William Fitz William treasurer of the household, Sir Henry Guilford comptroller of the household, the secretary of state, Sir Thomas More chancellor of the duchy, the dean of the king's chapel, Sir Henry Wyatt treasurer of the king's chamber, the vice-chamberlain, the captain of the guard, 'and for ordering of poore mens complaints and causes Doctor Wolman'.

In the council thus appointed we may feel some surprise

[1] *Ordinances of the Household* (Society of Antiquaries, 1790), pp. 159–60; also *Letters and Papers*, vol. iv, part i, p. 864.

in noting the strong predominance of bishops and nobles, two-thirds of whom were office-holders. The purpose of the new arrangement was stated primarily to be the hearing of complaints made by the king's subjects, while one man was engaged expressly to sit in poor men's cases. At this time, we see, the court of requests was not yet clearly separated from the council. There was also a desire expressed that the king's affairs should be better attended to than had been done in the past, and particularly that his majesty should often be consulted. The problem of the attendance of members, however, was still a troublesome one, and the ordinances go on to deal with it at great length. Some of the lords and officers, it was acknowledged, must needs be absent at times, especially during the terms of the courts. But 'to the intent the King's highnesse shall not be at any season unfurnished of an honourable presence of councellors about his grace, with whome his Highnesse may conferre upon the premises, at his pleasure; it is ordered that the persons hereafter mentioned shall give their continuall attendance in the causes of his said councell, unto what place soever his Highnesse shall resort'. These were the lord chamberlain, the bishop of Bath, the comptroller of the household, the secretary, the chancellor of the duchy, the dean of the chapel, the vice-chamberlain, the captain of the guard, and Doctor Wolman. And lest some of the last-named councillors perchance should be absent for reasonable cause, it was provided particularly that the bishop of Bath, the secretary, Sir Thomas More, and the dean, or at least two of them should always be present, unless they had the king's permission to do otherwise. The councillors so appointed were instructed further to apply themselves diligently, meeting at ten o'clock in the morning at the latest, and again at two in the afternoon, either in the king's dining-room or some other place appointed; 'there to be in readinesse, not onely in case the King's pleasure shall be to commune or conferre with them upon any cause or matter, but also for hearing and direction of poore men's complaints on matters of justice.' Clearly there was no intention, even at this late day, of making a separation of conciliar and judicial functions.

The two branches in relation to each other.

Henceforth the monarchy was generally successful in maintaining two co-ordinate boards working simultaneously. The one following the king was commonly known as the 'council at court',[1] while the other continued to be called 'the king's council in the star chamber'. The term 'privy council' did not belong exclusively to either branch, but for reasons that will be made evident it came to be attached especially to the former.[2] The two bodies were still very similar in their functions, and they were by no means distinct in their organization. Individual members moved from one to the other, sometimes they were reunited in a single body, and at other times they were in close correspondence. But the relative prominence of the two groups of councillors was now the reverse of what it had been before. According to the plan laid down in the aforesaid ordinances, the king preferred to hold conferences and to communicate with those who were near him, so that instead of the council at Westminster it was now the council at court which became the greater political power. For this reason its meetings were the more fully attended by the great ministers and nobles, who held the rank of privy councillors. It was not conceived to be a body superior to the other, except as it acquired an advantage by closer contact with the king, and so could speak upon many points with more positive authority. Sometimes indeed the council in the star chamber is represented as a body of restricted powers, 'established here to take cognisance in matters other than those of state'. In dealing with a proposal of the French ambassador, in 1540, the members here were disposed to say that 'they were assembled upon a special commission and would not meddle in such matters'.[3] In all political and diplomatic questions 'the council here' would solicit and receive instructions from 'the council there', whenever an expression of the king's pleasure was desired.

[1] Its favourite places of meeting naturally were Hampton Court, Windsor, Greenwich, and Westminster. It did not necessarily follow the king so closely as to be in every place where he resided.

[2] The term 'king's council' still predominated, although the newer name was very common. It was a 'privy council', I understand, whenever 'privy councillors' in distinction from judges and 'ordinary councillors' were assembled.

[3] *Letters and Papers*, xvi, no. 141.

The clerk and the Book of the Council.

The arrangements for the new branch of the council were not complete until, in 1540, it was provided that 'there should be a Clerk attendant upon the said Council, to write, enter, and register all such decrees, determinations, letters, and other such things as he should be appointed to enter in a Book, to remain always as a Ledger, as well for the discharge of the said Counsellors touching such things as they should pass from time to time, as also for a memorial unto them of their own proceedings'.[1] According to this statement the records were not to be left to the discretion of the clerk, as seems to have been done formerly, but were to be kept under the supervision of the council itself. To the responsible position thus created, William Paget, lately secretary to the queen, was appointed by the king and sworn in the presence of the council. Usually, in fact, there were two clerks of the privy council, besides the clerk of the star chamber, so that in this respect the work of the two bodies was clearly separated. Then begins anew the Book of the Council, the very name and form of which shows that the traditions of Henry VI had not been forgotten. By the aid of this work the proceedings of the council may be followed henceforth without interruption. Referring again to the question that was raised at the beginning of this chapter, it is now possible to say that the present book was not a continuation of the earlier work, since it pertained not to the old, but the newly formed branch of the historic council, namely, that attending the king's person.[2] The point is a material addition to the argument that between the reigns of Henry VI and Henry VIII something had happened which is not accounted for by the loss of records. There had been a subsidence in the power and usefulness of the council to a degree that its connexion with

[1] Nicolas, vii. 1. This is the first entry in the book, which now begins anew. There was nothing new certainly in the appointment of a clerk. In 1527 there was specifically a clerk of the star chamber, and in 1535 again two clerks of the council. *Letters and Papers*, viii, no. 858. The novel feature at this time was the proposal to enter the records.

[2] This fact is in evidence throughout the pages of Nicolas, vii. With frequent migrations the privy council was held at Windsor, Reading, Notley, Buckingham, Grafton, Dunstable, Windsor, &c. In time, it is true, this body also tended to gravitate toward Westminster, but its organic character was not changed thereby.

the past was nearly lost. In the revival that subsequently occurred, besides many alterations of an incidental character, there was a profound change in the character of the institution itself. As a result of the reorganization that has just been described, the modern privy council which now emerges is to be regarded not as a direct continuation of the mediaeval council, but as the special development of a branch which during the middle ages had never advanced beyond a rudimentary stage. The direct descendant of the parent stem was more nearly the body at Westminster, the name of which is for ever associated with its home, the star chamber. But as its functions tended more and more to be specialized in the judicial sphere, this body also was changed materially in character. When the court of star chamber then was abolished during the seventeenth century, we may say that the ancient king's council continued to exist only in its offshoots.

The rank of 'ordinary councillor'.

Another definition for which the time was ripe lay in the recognition of a distinction between the 'ordinary councillor' and the 'privy councillor'. The anomalous usages of the past, when men of the utmost diversity of rank were sworn according to the same formula and retained for various kinds of service, are matters to which we have repeatedly referred. And yet no classification could reasonably have been made, because the membership of the council had been subject to extreme variations. But now, for the first time in many years, the monarchy was served by a strong body of nobles, who were capable of filling the highest offices and of acting regularly as the king's advisers. At the same time there were men of lower rank, who were needed for their knowledge of law and abilities in administration. To this outer circle of advisers, therefore, who were regularly appointed to and sworn of the council, but were not given the full rank of privy councillors, a certain status was now given. The distinction first appears during the early years of Henry VIII. 'I have been sworn of (the king's) council above twenty years, and of his privy council above fourteen years,' declared Sir Robert Wingfield in 1535.[1] The case of Dr. Wolman in 1526 we have already mentioned. Again, it is learned that

[1] *Letters and Papers*, vii, no. 225.

Dr. Heath, bishop of Rochester, was sworn of the council and joined in office with Dr. Thirlby 'to hear causes determinable in the White Hall' [1] To retain a councillor expressly for law cases was no new thing surely, but the lines of duty and privilege were now laid down more clearly. Even still the position of an ordinary councillor was a matter of common understanding rather than of stated rule. In the case of Dr. William Peter, for example, we are informed that he was sworn of the king's council, no doubt according to the oath that was taken by all, and then a little later he is mentioned as 'one of the king's ordinary council'.[2] There was also a survival of the feeling that men might be sworn of the council to insure their faithfulness in any important service. In 1534 we read that Thomas Cromwell proposed 'to appoint the most assured and substantial gentlemen in every shire to be sworn of the king's council, with orders to apprehend all who speak or preach in favour of the pope's authority'.[3] But from the actual instances given, we do not infer that the number of ordinary councillors at this time was large; apparently they formed only a minority of the entire council. Their duties were important, but of a technical kind such as had always devolved upon men of this type. They received petitions, conducted examinations, and assisted at trials. As the sessions of the star chamber and the court of requests were especially given to proceedings of this kind, much of the routine business could safely be left in their hands. To this effect a statement was made in 1540, when the vice-chamberlains and other servants of the king and queen were admonished that they should not molest the king himself with suits, but should put their complaints in writing and deliver them to the ordinary council 'which was appointed for such purposes'.[4] Furthermore, they served on committees and made reports, but their names were never placed with the others upon the minutes, and presumably they did not have the right to vote. As is noticed in the cases of Sir Robert Wingfield, William Paget, and several others, the promotion of any of these men to the

[1] Nicolas, vii. 49.
[2] Ibid. 51, 60.
[3] *Letters and Papers*, vii, no. 420.
[4] Ibid., xvi, no. 127.

higher rank of a privy councillor was very easily made. Besides the ordinary councillors, there still remained the judges and serjeants-at-law, who were not specially appointed to the council, but continued to bear an *ex officio* relation to it. How well historic usages in all these matters survived, we may see in the announcement made by Henry VIII in 1541. 'His Highness had determined that to-morrow my Lord Chancellor, assembling his Majesty's Counsellors of all sorts, Spiritual and Temporal, with the Judges and learned men of his Council, should declare unto them the abominable demeanour of the Queen.' [1]

Rewards and payments.

It may next be asked how the Tudors were successful in maintaining a strong body of councillors, who were capable of filling the different ranks and branches which were now operative. With remarkable facility indeed they overrode the difficulties which had always before been felt as a hindrance. As to the long-standing problem of obtaining the regular attendance of bishops and lords, the new monarchy positively created an aristocracy of service. While the number of new peerages was by no means extraordinary, they were sufficient at all times to fill the higher offices and to furnish the main body of councillors. Only in a few instances, so far as we have ascertained, were salaries paid, and these were to men of ordinary rank.[2] But out of the vast supply of confiscated estates, especially those which came from the church, there were grants of land to an incalculable extent. The prodigality of Henry VIII in rewarding his favourites is a matter of general notoriety. In 1538 there is a particular memorandum, wherein the names of fourteen councillors, all of them laymen, are mentioned as worthy of the king's 'most benign remembrance'.[3] The great

[1] *Letters and Papers*, vii, no. 1331; Nicolas, vii, p. xix.

[2] Sir Robert Wingfield had an annuity as a king's councillor of 100 marks, and Robert Southwell was admitted to the council with a salary of £100, the same as was paid to the king's secretaries. *Letters and Papers*, iii, no. 417; xv, no. 436.

[3] These were Lord Audley the chancellor, the dukes of Norfolk and Suffolk, Thomas Cromwell the keeper of the privy seal, the marquis of Exeter, the earls of Shrewsbury, Oxford, and Sussex, Viscount Beauchamp, Lord Sandys the chamberlain, the earl of Southampton admiral, the controller, Sir William Kingston, and Sir John Russell. Ibid., xiii, part i, no. 1.

wealth accumulated by Cardinal Wolsey, Thomas Cromwell, the dukes of Norfolk and Suffolk, and likewise the advancement of Secretary Paget could not fail to be an incentive to every one in the king's service. Equally marked was the tendency, especially after the inauguration of the new ecclesiastical policy, to give clergymen less prominence and to place the main reliance upon laymen. In 1538 we find the extraordinary suggestion 'to withdraw the king's council *more secret* together, and to avoid spiritual men therehence for diverse reasons '.[1] Among the other inducements which attracted councillors of all ranks, we should not fail to mention the entertainments which were constantly provided. Elaborate dinners, both on 'meat days' and 'fish days', were a regular feature of the sessions of the star chamber;[2] the members were constantly invited to the houses of Wolsey and Cromwell, while those who followed the king enjoyed the unrivalled hospitality of the royal household. For all these reasons the lords are found to be willing and eager to attend the council, as well as to perform countless other services, to an extent that had never been known before.

A demand for the reform of the council.

At one time during the reign of Henry VIII a serious attack was made upon the council, which recalls the methods of the previous century, but the outcome now was very different. Incited by the attacks upon the church, for which the privy council was known to be largely responsible, the people of the northern shires made their noted pilgrimage and protest in 1536. Among their articles of complaint was the statement that 'the king takes of his council and has about him persons of low birth and small reputation, who have procured these things for their own advantage, whom we suspect to be Lord Cromwell and Sir Richard Riche, chancellor of the Augmentations '.[3] In Lincolnshire

[1] Ibid., xiii, part ii, no. 974.

[2] In 1535 we find a petition of John Lawrence, who avers to the lords of the council that he has been their cook for twenty-three years at wages of only 2*s*. 4*d*. a day. He claims to deserve an annuity. *Letters and Papers*, ix, no. 1119. Other items concerning these dinners are scattered through the same collection. In one term there were five dinners, eleven in another, and sixty-eight during a period of three years. Ibid., xiv, no. 1048. On one occasion the lords thanked the king for his gift of venison.

[3] Ibid., xi, no. 705.

the remonstrants asked the king to 'take noblemen into his council and remove Cromwell, the chancellor of Augmentations, and such heretical bishops as those of Lincoln, Canterbury, St. David's, and others'. Some of the insurgents went so far as to bind themselves by an oath 'to expulse all villain blood from the privy council'.[1] These aspersions upon the character of his advisers seemed to strike the king in a sore spot, for he took pains to repel the charge in the following explicit reply. 'As to the beginning of our reign, when ye say so many noblemen were counsellors; who were then counsellors I well remember, and yet of the temporality, I note but two worth calling noble; the one, Treasurer of England (Thomas Howard, then earl of Surrey, now duke of Norfolk); the other, High Steward of our House (the earl of Shrewsbury). Others, as the lords Marny and Darcy, scant well-born gentlemen, and yet of no great lands till they were promoted by us. The rest were lawyers and priests, save two bishops, Canterbury and Winchester. Why then are you not better content with us now who have so many nobles indeed, both of birth and condition? For of the temporality we have in our Privy Council the dukes of Norfolk and Suffolk, the marquis of Exeter, the lord Steward when he may come, the earls of Oxford and Sussex, lord Sandys our chamberlain, the lord Admiral, treasurer of our house, Sir William Poulet, comptroller of our house; and of the spirituality, the bishops of Hereford, Chichester, and Winchester. How came you to think there were more noblemen in our Privy Council then than now? But it does not belong to any of our subjects to appoint us our Council.'[2] In similar vein a letter of the same year to the emperor said, 'answer has been given to the ambassadors that the king will not change anything that has been settled by parliament, and therefore do nothing they ask, much less reform his Privy Council to please them, as it is a thing in which they had no right to meddle.'[3]

The king's confidence in his council.

But the success of the Tudors did not rest solely upon devices of organization. Having done these things they

[1] *Letters and Papers*, xi, nos. 828, 852. [2] Ibid., no. 957.
[3] Ibid., no. 1143.

trusted the council and gave it power, as the Yorkist kings had never been willing to do. In this regard we see a resumption of the policy of the Lancastrians, with certain important modifications. While the king either determined or was consulted in all questions of policy, in all matters of administration the council was expected freely to exercise its discretion and ingenuity. It was upon the council, in fact, rather than upon individual ministers, that the government of this time principally rested. How far its authority might extend in matters of legislation, was argued by Cromwell in a letter referring to the conveyance of coin out of the realm, 'that the king, with the advice of his council, even if there were no statute, might, to withstand so great a danger, make proclamation which should be as effective as any statute.' [1] Even the reception of foreign ambassadors, it was preferred, should be held before the council, and the king's communications to them were commonly given in the same manner.[2] At the same time, it is hardly necessary to add, there were trials of state in unprecedented number. As a result, the sessions of the council in both of its branches were long and arduous as never before. 'They give attendance constantly,' the lords protested in 1520, 'and order causes according to the laws.' [3] During the most strenuous years of the Reformation, in the midst of difficulties at home and abroad, the council is known to have been held continuously for six months, and at a juncture to have sat through the night.[4] The same events led to a degree of caution and secrecy such as had hardly been necessary before. Letters in cipher were now received and sent, and there were conferences behind closed doors from which even the clerk was excluded.[5] But in spite of every effort there was still the difficulty of delayed and unfinished business. Instead of the

[1] Ibid., viii, no. 1042.

[2] It is from the letters of the Spanish and the French ambassadors that the best descriptions of the proceedings are given.

[3] Ibid., iii, no. 896.

[4] Ibid., xvi, nos. 763, 1328, 1332.

[5] In the hearing of Lord Dacre's case, in 1541, all the lords, seventeen in number, met in the star chamber to hold a secret conference. But they spoke so loud, says Paget, that he was able to hear everything through two closed doors. Probably the keyholes were large, and the clerk had placed himself in a favourable position. Ibid., no. 932.

king's interests, however, it was now those of private persons which suffered. 'It is an evil time for suitors,' said one, 'as the king and his council have so many matters in hand daily'; again, 'suitors must abide their good hour, I live in hope.' [1] Under the circumstances inevitably it became a matter of favour for litigants to gain a hearing. As Bishop Lee once wrote to Cromwell, 'there is a case pending before your lordship and the council in star chamber concerning a special friend of mine . . . At the instance of (said) Piers and his son I beg your favour.' [2] On the other hand, the council, whether in the star chamber or elsewhere, was never so freely open to informers and deponents of charges, which were often of the most trivial kind. The enemies and critics of the government were pursued remorselessly, while against the men involved in the northern rebellion there were prosecutions lasting for years. In regard to a group of these unfortunate victims, it was said, 'hitherto the council has used them gently, but when it comes to a straiter examination, if they have known more of this rebellion than they pretend, their dull wits will not hide it.' [3] Persons are known to have been subjected to the inquisitorial process two and three, and even seven times over. One critic was dealt with because he had said, 'there was never more need to pray for the king's council than now'; [4] another was punished for observing that 'the king has wise men in his council, but *sapientia huius mundi stultitia est apud Deum*'.[5] In nearly every direction, it is possible to show that the traditional powers of the council were not only revived in their fullness, but also extended and intensified. But there was one important function that had been taken away from the council, which it was not now permitted to recover. This was in respect of the grants of the crown. Formerly these had been made 'by advice and consent of the council', and sometimes they had been brought under its complete control. Many a battle had been fought over this single issue, which had sometimes been brought into the foreground

[1] *Letters and Papers*, x, nos. 760, 789, &c.
[2] Ibid., xv, no. 128.
[3] Ibid., xi, no. 888.
[4] Ibid., xiii, part i, no. 604.
[5] Ibid., no. 981.

and sometimes was left in the background, but after the victory of the house of York the tendency was entirely in favour of the royal authority. The successors of the Yorkists were wise in making no change in this regard. The council might make necessary expenditures and determine payments for service, but the grants of favour were jealously withheld from its control. This fact alone denotes a wide difference between the council of the Tudors and that of the weaker Lancastrians. So long as the grants were safely held, the monarchy was not in danger of falling again under a conciliar domination.

Conclusion of the mediaeval problems.

At this point, it seems to the writer, a suitable stage has at length been reached for bringing the present work to a conclusion. Thus far it has been necessary to come in order to show the connexion of the mediaeval council with its modern derivatives. By this time, we may safely say, the chief problems which affected the institution during the middle ages were practically settled, although the results were far from perfect. In the matter of membership there was at last a limited body, inclusive of several different ranks, which served in this capacity both as a duty and an honour. It was the organ neither of an official bureaucracy nor of a territorial aristocracy, but combined both elements in reasonable proportions. There was still a trace of the old feeling that any of the great lords might attend the council without being sworn thereof, but it was not allowed to remain unchallenged.[1] As to the necessary division of business, especially the separation of the king's business from the trials and suits of private parties, this was in a measure accomplished by the formation of several special tribunals. Still the privy council, even the body attending the king, did not cease to be occupied with cases of treason, breach of the peace, malfeasance in office, and arbitraments just as before. But the danger of its subservience to private interests was safely past. As to several other branches, such

[1] In the reign of Elizabeth the rule was stated anew that no man should sit in the court of star chamber unless he were sworn of the council, and it was made the duty of the clerk to remind any one 'that he ought not to remain there unless he were sworn.' Harg. MSS., vol. 216, p. 202; cited by Miss Scofield, p. 13.

as the Council of the Welsh Marches,[1] the Council of the North,[2] and the Court of Augmentations, inasmuch as these are an outgrowth of modern conditions they have not been treated here. Moreover, no single work could possibly follow the manifold activities of the modern conciliar system, which has now been extended to two or three local branches. Upon several of these phases excellent treatises have already been written,[3] and others, we have reason to believe, are soon to follow. In view of all these considerations, it is the opinion of the author that the history of the king's council, regarded as a single institution, properly comes to a close with the year 1540.

[1] There is the valuable work of Miss Caroline Skeel, *The Council of the Welsh Marches* (Cambridge, 1904).

[2] The organization of the northern council was very quickly accomplished. In 1536 mention is made of the members of the council ' who should remain in these parts after the king's departure '. Within a year it was planned to establish ' a council there ' as in the Marches of Wales. The duke of Norfolk became president and the councillors there were treated as a distinct body. *Letters and Papers*, xi, no. 1410 ; xii, part i, nos. 651, &c.

[3] Besides those already cited there are the works of Lord Eustace Percy, *The Privy Council under the Tudors* (Oxford, 1907) ; and Dr. Karl Hornemann, *Das Privy Council von England zur Zeit der Königin Elisabeth* (Hanover, 1912).

CONCLUSION

AMONG all the institutions of the central government the history of the king's council holds a peculiar place. From the very beginning it was a body vaguely outlined, uncertain in composition, undefined in function, and unrestricted in scope of authority. In time its outlines appear with greater clearness, but instead of definition, always lack of definition was its distinctive trait. In the midst of a prevailing tendency for the organs of the state to become specialized, the council never lost its elemental freedom of action. In the formation of the courts of common law it was the trend toward specialization, both in respect of their fields of jurisdiction and their methods of procedure, that caused the divisions of the original *curia regis* and their separation in kind from the king's council. Even the house of lords, although it was never a body of limited authority, became closely defined in its composition and structure, while its acts were regularly a matter of record. Because of its inherent conservatism the house of lords also was closely allied with the courts of common law and certain vested interests, so that in character it stands usually in sharp contrast to the king's council. From time to time, it is true, attempts were made in parliament to limit the powers of the council, to say that it could not do this or that; while to a lesser extent certain functions were permitted or positively assigned to it. But these acts, whether they are considered singly or collectively, were never comprehensive in their scope, nor was the conduct of the council seriously affected by them. It is also true that inevitably the council fell into certain customary lines of action, until it created a jurisdiction and procedure distinctively its own. But a customary jurisdiction is not the same as a prescribed jurisdiction, nor was the council ever so far entangled by its own rules of action as was the modern court of chancery.

Because of the unsettled character of the council there was a ceaseless conflict over what it should be, particularly as to which of two dominant interests it should actually represent. As an instrument of the monarchy it easily became a circle of office-holders and retainers of the court, many of whom were experts in the services required, while generally they were bound by ties of loyalty to the interests of the crown. Carried to its logical extremity, as was attempted by Richard II during the later years of his reign, the king's council would have become little more than an adjunct of the royal household. This tendency, however, was always strongly affected by the attendance, usually on summons or invitation, of an unfixed number of prelates and nobles, who sustained the older idea that the king should be counselled preferably by his tenants-in-chief. That the magnates did not form the most stable element within the council was due, one is persuaded, not so much to the wish of the king to displace them, as to their own attitude of independence and reluctance to serve. In opposition to the policy of the monarchy, which tended perforce in the direction of an official council, there was the desire repeatedly expressed in parliament that the council, more truly in accordance with feudal traditions, should be composed of a select number of bishops and barons. Instead of being controlled by the king's officers, who were reinforced occasionally by the magnates, it was thought that the council should be predominantly under the influence of the magnates, who should be assisted by the officers. Again and again were the plans of parliament asserted and supported by every possible legislative device. But the same difficulty, the reluctance of the lords to serve with any degree of constancy, invariably appears, and causes more or less speedily a reversion to the former type. So that never during the middle ages was the parliamentary plan of a council successful for more than a brief period of time. No doubt it was best sustained during the minority of Henry VI and a few years more (for the period approximately from 1422 to 1447), when the lords completely controlled the state, and after exploiting it in their own interests abandoned it to its fate. In the rivalry and alternate success of these two principles of organization, varying from one period to another, sometimes changing even from year to year, the material of this history to a great extent has been found. The problem was not fairly settled until after the accession of the Tudors, when by an orderly arrangement both of the elements that had hitherto struggled for supremacy were included within the council. At least three concentric groups of councillors were then defined; first there was the king's privy council, wherein the traditional claims of the nobles were fully recognized; then there was the ordinary council, which was served by a less influential body of professional men; while beyond these there were the justices and 'others of the council', the remnant of the mediaeval *curia*, who were still called occasionally to render legal advice.

Another question, which was closely bound with the former, was whether the council should follow the king as his body of advisers, or should remain in a fixed place as a board of administration and judicature. Naturally there was no thought of dividing the functions of government on these lines, so that in spite of practical difficulties the council endeavoured to maintain its powers in both directions. Inevitably there was a sacrifice of one set of duties or the other. Usually, it is true, there were councillors in attendance upon the king wherever he might be, but at no time during the middle ages was this group sufficiently stable or dignified to form a regular council. Under the circumstances the king was likely to take counsel with and to be influenced in his policies by his personal attendants, often the minor officers of his household, frequently favourites, who were not recognized as members of the council. Repeatedly there was an outcry against this tendency, and a desire was expressed in parliament that the king should be advised only by his licensed councillors, while at times the stipulation was made that a certain number of lords should remain with the king continually. The formally organized council, on the other hand, in accordance with the tendency of the courts of law and most of the administrative offices, was drawn toward a fixed place, preferably the house assigned to it at Westminster, where it met during regular terms unless otherwise specially summoned. Relations with the king were kept up generally by the formal method of correspondence, advice on questions of state was constantly asked and given, and during the times of a regency the council was in every respect the actual governing power. But throughout the middle ages a strong impression is given that the attention of the council in its regular sessions was principally devoted to the more routine tasks of administration and judicature. Sometimes there was complaint that private business in the way of petitions and law cases tended to supersede the interests of the crown. Always the council was overburdened with work of this kind, to the extent that in spite of the creation of new courts and other agencies of assistance its business was constantly falling into arrear. A long step toward the solution of this question was taken by the Tudor kings, who after a series of experiments firmly established the branch of the council 'following the court' as the principal advisory board, while the council remaining at Westminster was the more free and better fitted to deal with the bulk of administrative and judicial business.

To review one other question that affected the council through all its history, there was the difficulty of offering sufficient rewards to secure the services of men of rank. In the case of active officers no special payments as a rule were required, although the chancellor and the treasurer were accustomed each to receive a salary for attendance at the council. But it was never desired that the council should consist solely or mainly of office-holders. For any extraordinary service special grants were likely to be made, but these were necessarily limited to exceptional cases. Annuities for life also were irregular and savoured of favouritism. There was then the alternative of salaries, generally in the form of assignments of the king's revenue, payable annually so long as one should remain in the council, which were offered for the first time upon a consistent plan in the reign of Richard II. The project itself was reasonable enough, but it was admitted to be a heavy burden upon the available resources of the crown. Like many other special devices, the plan was in fact not continued for any great length of time. There was always a temptation to convert the annuity into a permanent grant, and then there was likely to be less responsibility in regard to attendance. Even the salaries alone, there is reason to believe, were not effective in securing the constant interest of the lords without the addition of other perquisites whether legitimate or illegitimate. Indeed, it appears that a council of lords was hardly ever well maintained unless the members controlled also the grants of the crown as a matter of patronage. Again and again there was a struggle over this issue, and at certain times to the detriment of the state the lords were successful in gaining their ends. This was the point of contention, as this study has revealed, between Richard II and his great barons, and again it was the leading motive in the rivalry of Henry Beaufort and Humphrey duke of Gloucester. Ultimately the independence of the crown was upheld in respect of the power which was essential to its life. As a result of the civil war the strength of the older nobility was broken, and a body of lords bound by various ties of interest was reared in the service of the monarchy. It is needless to add that the resources of the crown were now sufficient to give ample rewards for every kind of service.

In respect of the work accomplished, the council was always a power most vital to the history of England. Free from the usual trend of constitutionality, of the common law and formalism, it was also industrious, persistent, and watchful. It was useful less in the way of conspicuous dramatic action than it was in the constant control and supervision of minor interests. It acted in matters for which parliament had neither the time nor the patience ; it was ready to meet emergencies that arose between the sessions of parliament ; it completed, fulfilled, and sometimes even altered the acts of parliament. In relation to the courts of common law the council was a constant recourse in solving points of difficulty ; it gave advice and issued orders that were necessary to assist the ordinary legal processes. Above all, in cases of the utmost difficulty and danger the council was the one court capable of meeting the emergency, and during one period of its history, one may fairly claim, was instrumental in saving the kingdom from utter destruction.

APPENDIX I

ACTS AND ARTICLES OF THE COUNCIL FROM EDWARD I TO EDWARD III

Ordinance by King and Council for the Redress of Grievances.[1] 26 *Edward I.*

April 4, 1298.[2]

— Come le Roy avant son passage vers Flandres eust volente et desir de fere redrescier e amender les grevances faites a son pueple en nun de lui, e suz ce envoiast ses lettres par tous les contees Dengleterre por ceste chose mettre en effect ; Ordene est par lui e son conseil qe en chescun contee seient assignes qatre, ce est asavoir deus chevaliers des queus le un serra mis par lui et lautre serra pris du conte, un clerk et un homme de religion qui seient bons e leaus e bien avises por enquerire de tous maneres de grevances, come des choses prises hors de Seinte Eglise, des prises de laynes, peaus, quirs,[3] blez, bestes, charz, peyssons, et de totes autres maneres des choses parmi le reaulme des clers e des lais puis la gerre comencir entre le Roy de Fraunce e lui, fust ce por garde de la mer ou en autre manere. E enqueriront meismes ceaus par queus et as queus e de queu e de combien e de la value e coment e en queu manere ices prises e grevances furent faites au pueple. E ceus assignes eient plein pouer de enquerir oir e terminer ausi bien par office come a suite de partie. E qant la matere de ces choses serra ateinte, le quel que ce seit, par garant ou sans garant, ce qe serra pris sans garant seit retorne atant qe le damage ont receu, si le tortz fesantz eient de quei e outre ce puni por le trespas. E si il neient de quei ceaus as queus les garantz e les commissions sont venus come vyscontes, clerks assignes, baillifs e autres tiels maneres de ministres respoignent por lor sourmis qui averont fait telz prises. E qe de ce qe serra trove pris par garant le Roy soit certifie a ce en fera tant qe il sentendront a paie par reson.[4]

[1] *Parl. Proceedings,* file ii, no. 26.

[2] Probably arranged at a small council summoned to meet at Westminster, March 30, 1298. *Parl. Writs,* i. 65.

[3] skins.

[4] The entire substance of this enactment is contained in the letters patent which were issued ' according to the form of the ordinance made thereof by king and council ', and were dated at Westminster, April 4. *Cal. Patent Rolls,* 26 Edw. I, 338.

July 26, 1303.

Memorandum of a Letter of the Privy Seal from the King in Scotland communicating with his Council at York.[1] 31 *Edward I.*

— Fait a remembrer qe come Johan de Drockenesford Gardeyn de la Garderobe nostre Seigneur le Roi eust lettre de creaunce de par le Roi de son prive seal a maistre Williame de Grenefeud [2] Chaunceler le Roi et sire Phelippe de Wylughby [3] Chaunceler del Escheker leutenaunt le Tresorer, solonc la tenour qe porra estre veu par meisme les lettres. Le dit Johan diseit sa creaunce susdite au ditz maistre Williame et Philippe Chauncelers en la presence des chefs justices de ambedeus [4] les Baunks le Roi et dautres du counseil qi y furent en les paroles qe sensuent.

— Cest asavoir qe le Roi comanda et sa volunte feust qe pur ce qe il fu en sa guerre Descoce ou il ly covendroit demorer ly et totes les bones gentz de son Roialme qi oue ly sont venuz celes parties taunt qe bon issue en auenyst a honour et profit de ly et son Roialme, qe eux feissent assembler touz ceux de son conseil qi a Everwyk [5] furent et qe eux parlassent, pensassent, et counseillassent par totes les bones voies qe il peussent en bone manere coment il peust estre servi en la dite guerre en deniers et vivres, qar en autre chose ne demoreit al aide de dieu a ce qil entendit qe la busoigne ne venyst a bone fyn. Et dit aussint le Roi qe il ne poait failler qe sa busoigne ne se poeist [6] bien si ne remeynsist es Chauncelers avant ditz, moy et les autres qi sunt demorez derere ly de son conseil et par defaute de lur peniblete et de lour ordenement.

— De rechef [7] le dit John quant a ce qe les bones gentz del Eschekier voleient savoir la volente le Roi, si le Roi vosist qe ses villes et ses burgs fussent taillez, ce qe unqes mais [8] ne furent en son temps, dit qe le Roi voleit qe en tallage des viles et totes les autres voies et maneres qils peussent bonement entre eux touz penser porveyer et ordeneir meissent peine pur hater et aver deners pur ly servir en sa dite guerre, et a ce faire et pursure feussent assignez touz les meilors du conseil et ascuns autres et touz ceux qe hom quidast [9] qi meuz [10] ussent ses busoignes a quer [11].

De rechef . . .[12]

— Ces articles furent les plus grantz de la creaunce le dit Johan, mais molt dautres avoit il a dire qe ne sont pas issi contenuz, come denquere coment les purvoiances le Roi furent faites et hastez devers li et coment ses ministres se sount portez en les dites purvoiances faire et haster et dautres diverses busoignes.

[1] *Parl. Proceedings*, iii. 9.
[2] Canon of York, dean of Chichester, afterwards archbishop of York.
[3] Dean of Lincoln.
[4] 'ambodeux' = both (*Kelham's Norman Dict.*).
[5] The exchequer was at that time located at York.
[6] 'se poeyt' = should take effect (*K. N. D.*).
[7] Trans. *Moreover.*
[8] never.
[9] Trans. *thought.*
[10] better.
[11] 'quer' = to seek (*K. N. D.*).
[12] As the manuscript is much mutilated a section here is omitted.

[*Endors.*] Istam indenturam recepit Philippus de Willughby tenens locum Thesaurarii de domino Iohanne de Drokenesford· custode garderobe domini Regis Anglie illustris die Veneris proxima post festum sancti Iacobi Apostli anno regni Regis Edwardi tricesimo primo.

Articles sent from Gascony, with the Recommendations of the Council.[1] 5 *Edward II.* 1311.

— Item est intimandum domino nostro Regi qualiter maior et iurati Burdegale et multi alii subditi domini nostri Regis conantur iura domini nostri Regis et in preiudicium rei publice indebiter et temerarie usurpare nova vegtigualia de novo instituendo et multociens antiqua augmentando et aliis modis pluribus et diversis.

Senescallus Vasconie dominus de Lebreto et Constabularius Burdegale ac magister B. Peleti prior Mansi de avisamento consilii Vasconie tractent cum maiore et Iuratis Burdegale super hiis que in eadem civitate inter Regem et ipsos de civitate in calumpnia existunt et inspectis formis tractatuum alias inde habitorum procurent aliquam certam formam ad maius commodum et honorem Regis concordari de qua forma certificent Regi, ut inde ulterius suam dicat voluntatem et super his fiant littere competentes. placet Regi.

— Item quod mittat in Vasconiam pro reformacione patrie et puniendis excessibus officialium, ballivorum, et subditorum personas autentiquas que super hoc plenariam habeant potestatem et has celeriter exequcioni mandare procurent, cum totus ducatus fere consistat in armis et guerra specialiter propter appellantes qui propter exercitum compesci non possunt quinymo ad invadendum et mutuo occidendum ballivos et officiales vestros prosiliunt, ut iam a paucis diebus citra contigit in personis xij officialium, ballivorum, et servientum qui a sex mensibus citra occisi fuerunt, sed propter delinquencium appellaciones et eorum exempciones exequcio iustitie totaliter impeditur, quibus personis detur potestas confirmandi ministros bonos et amovendi alios, et quod possint parragia, permutaciones, et empciones et alios contractus facere cum consilio consilii ad voluntatem domini nostri Regis.

Quo ad excessus officialium mandetur senescallo et constabulario quod ipsi associatis sibi aliis de consilio[2] quos duxerint associandos inquirant de gesturis dictorum officialium et ministrorum, et illos quos malos et minus idoneos invenerint amoveant et alios idoneos substituant et de transgressionibus et excessibus per ipsos factis tam pro Rege quam pro conquerentibus faciant iustitie complementum.

[1] *Diplomatic Documents, Chancery Misc.*, bundle 29, file 7, no. 13. The Gascon articles are in a Latin foreign to England. The answers of the council are written in a cramped hand with many abbreviations.

[2] i. e. the council of Gascony.

Quo ad parragia et permutaciones ac empciones faciendas detur predictis senescallo et constabulario quod ipsi ea faciant de avisamento consilii Vasconie, prout ad commodum Regis melius viderint faciendum. placet Regi.

— Item est consilium quod mandetur constabulario Burdegale et alicui vel aliquibus de consilio quod ipsi provideant castra, domos, fortalicia, et alia bona domini nostri Regis que reparacione indigent, ita quod reparent et faciant reparari et quod constabularius expensas ad hoc necessarias faciat ministrari.

Scribatur constabulario quod premissa faciat fieri per avisamentum senescalli vel aliorum de consilio Vasconie quos etc., et quod fiant per visum et testimonium proborum et legalium hominum ad hec deputandorum seu nominandorum.

placet Regi.

[*Several articles here are omitted.*]

— Item est intimandum domino nostro Regi quod faciat perquiri in thesauria sua acta et instrumenta per que nos possumus deffendere contra vicecomitem Pontiaci qui petit terram de Bornio et costam maris et Libornam et mercatum Burdegale.

— Item est intimandum eidem domino nostro Regi quod faciat perquiri in thesauria sua instrumenta et firmitates per que apparet quod comes Petragoriensis avoavit se tenere a domino progenitore suo castra de Veruh de Rossilha et de Sancto Maximo cum quibus non possumus deffendere.

Ad quinque articulos superius expressos [1] mandetur thesaurario vel eius locum tenenti et camarario quod scrutari faciant omnia scripta instrumenta et alia munimenta que ad defensionem Regis et iuris sui in proximo parliamento Paris expedire poterunt, et copiam ipsorum ac etiam ipsa originalia, si copia non sufficiat, pro defensione huiusmodi magistro Guillelmo de Case [2], quem Rex mittit pro ipso ad dictum parliamentum, et alicui alteri fideli Regis faciant liberari. Et si forte idem magister Guillelmus pro scrutinio huiusmodi faciendo non poterit Londoniis commorari, tunc duobus fidelibus Regis de quibus Rex confidere possit liberent deferenda ad dictum parliamentum et in thesauria Regis postmodum per eosdem reportanda. placet Regi, dum tamen secure tradantur.

— Item expedit et videtur consilio quod domini Norwicensis episcopus, comes Richmond, Guillelmus Ingue, et Guido Ferre [3] et dominus Iohannes de Hastings ac alii consiliarii domini nostri Regis ad certam diem Londoniis debeant convenire tractaturi ibidem

[1] Of the said five articles, two are given here as sufficient for illustration.

[2] William Case, professor of civil law, was king's proctor for the processes pending in the *parlement* of Paris.

[3] In the previous year the bishop of Norwich, the earl of Richmond, Guy Ferre, and William Inge were king's proctors for affairs in Gascony, being repeatedly sent there and to the *parlement* of Paris. They represented the king in the processes here mentioned, which were held at Périgueux. *Cal. Patent Rolls,* 4 Edw. II, 338; *Cal. Close Rolls*, 4 Edw. II, 289, 298; ibid., 6 Edw. II, 488, 496; *Rôles Gascons*, i. 38–9.

super processibus hoc anno habitis Petragoriis [1] coram commissariis domini Regis Francie et super quibusdam sibi circa dictos processus declarandis per dominum Guillelmum de Casis legis professorem, et provisuri de remediis oportunis, dum tamen ipsum Guillelmum diu remanere periculosum est, quia circa revocaccionem dicte commissionis domini Regis Francie, super qua nunc litiguatur Petragoriis, oportet cum diligentia et celeritate provideri.[2]

Memoranda containing Advice of the Council concerning the Government of Gascony.[3] 7 *Edward II.* 1313–14.

— Pour les damages qe notre Seigneur le Roy et Ducs et ses sugetz unt par mauveys baillifs ministres et officiaux en la Duchee, sicome piert par querele de plusours, sy [4] sont les remedies escrites et ordinetz.

— A de primes il est avys au consail solomc ceo qe est ordene par le dit notre Seigneur le Roy, qe touz les ministres et officiaux sentz le seneschal de Gascoyne soient de tout ostez de lour baillies et offices et autres covenables mys en lour lieu, et qe de y donkes par le dit seneschal de Gascoyne ou autre qe le Roy vodra a ceo assigner soint enquis de lour faitz et toutes plaintes de eux oies et droyture fait au Roy et as playntifs et qe soit fait par suffisante commission, et qe apres ceo ceux qui serront trovez covenables soient remis en lour baillies ou en autres en la fourme soutz dite et les autres de tout ostez.

— Item qe nul official ne ministre coment qe il soit covenable ne teigne fors qe un office en la dite Duchee, si issint ne soit qe le ministre soit si covenable et les offices et baillies si veysines [5] et petites qe ceo soit au profit le Roy qe un par avisement de dit seneschal et consail tienge deux offices et ne mie plus [6].

— Item qe chescun qe eit office en baillie en celes parties demerge personalment en sa baillie.

— Item si ascun qe eit baillie office ou beni fait en celes parties purchace lettres le Roy pur avoir autre baillie office ou bienfait en mesmes les parties rien neyt ne enporte par celes lettres si eles ne facent especiale mencion de la baillie ou office et du beni fait qil avoit du Roy avant.

[1] The Perigord cases are elsewhere thus referred to:
'De summonitione diversarum personarum pro tractatu habendo apud Westmonasterium super negotiis tangentibus processus habitos apud Petragorium.' *Rôles Gascons*, 5 Edw. II, 40. 'De tractando super complemento pacum inter Angliae et Francie Reges et negotiis processus nuper apud Petragorium habitos tangentibus.' Ibid., 6 Edw. II, 43.

[2] A council to consider affairs of Aquitaine was summoned to be at Westminster, January 13 (*Gascon Rolls*, 5 Edw. II, m. 7); and then another to meet at York, February 27. *Cal. Close Rolls*, 5 Edw. II, 449.

[3] *Diplomatic Documents, Chancery Misc.*, bundle 25, file 2, no. 10.

[4] 'sy, ci' = here.

[5] Trans. *neighbouring.*

[6] Trans. *and no more.*

— Item qe nul ne tiegne office de scribaine en la Duchee sil ne soit litreez et covenable pur faire loffice et quil demerge personalment en loffice, et qe le Roi soit respondu de ce qe [1] lui appent.

— Item qe ceux qe unt baillies ou offices du conestable [2] par assense ne le baillent pas a autres a plus haut assense.

— Item pur ceo qe grant pleinte est venue qe le paigis de Gascoyne est trop greve par trop grant nombre de serianz au damage du Roy et du paigis, soit mande au seneschal qe par avisement du consail en celes parties face cele nombre amesurer [3] issint qe le Roy et le paigis poient estre covenablement servitz.

— Et est la summe par estimacion de quoy le Roy prent damage par defaute de cestes ordenances xiij^{m}. cxxi *li.* v *s.* de bourdeaux; qe valent a lesterling vi deners bordeaux acompte pur lesterling, ij^{m} ciiij^{xx} vi *li.* xvij *s.* vi *d.*

— [*Endors.*] Et soit maunde au seneschal de Gascoigne qil certefie notre Seigneur le Roi des nouns de ceus qi teignent offices ou baillies en la Duschee a terme de lour vies et queles offices et baillies et coment il sen unt portez et envoit aussint a notre Seigneur le Roi transescritz de lour commissions. Et aussint seit fait de ceus qi teignent fermes et combien eles valent par an a la verroie value et combien les fermers rendent pur yceles.

> [*In a different hand.*] Le Roi voet escrire al Papa empriant qil voille assentir e doner conge al Evesque de Ceyntes qil puisse granter au Roi la iurisdiction qil ad en Ceyntes en eschaunge pur autres choses adoner al dit Evesque e a ses successors, es cele part ad le Roi iurisdiction melle ouec la iurisdiccion le dit Evesque.

1316.

Ordinances of the Council, with Responses of the King. [4] 9 *Edward II.*

Mons. J. filz Thomas.

— Quant a Mons. Johan le filz Thomas, accorde est par *le Conseil sil plest* [5] au Roi qil eyt c li. de terre en Hirlande a li ⁊ ses heirs males issanz de son corps oue le noun de counte; cest assavoir le chastel ouec la ville de *Kyldare* oue les terres et rentes apurtenantz a meismes le chastel ville, saue *Al Roi* le franchises reale qe feurent a mons. William de Vescy.

> [*Different ink.*] *il plest au Roi* qil les eit a li e ses heirs males issantz de son corps sauve al Roi loffice de visconte e les choses qe a office de visconte appendent par le service de deus fedz de chivaler. [6]

Mons. Arnal de Power.

— Item accorde est qe Mons. Arnale de Power eit pur son bon service du doun le Roi en les parties Dirlande le Chastiel Wareny et Ostrard a la value de c marchees de terre a li ⁊ ses heirs males issanz de lour corps.

[1] Altered from 'du profit'.
[2] Altered from 'seneschal'.
[3] Trans. *lessen.*
[4] *Parl. Proceedings*, file iv, no. 19.
[5] The words in italics are insertions.
[6] *Cal. Close Rolls*, 9 Edw. II, 288.

[*Different ink.*] Il plest al Roi qil eit en la forme avant dite par le service de deus fedz de chivaler.

— Item acorde est qe Mons. Moritz de Rocheford eyt le chastiel de Makkynegan pour li ⁊ Mons. Thomas son filz a terme de lour dieus vies oue les terres ⁊ rentes qi appartignent. Mons. Moritz de Rocheford.

[*Different ink.*] il plest au Roi qil eient fesant le service de un fed de chivaler.[1]

— Item acorde est q Mons. Johan le Power de Donoyll eyt des precheines issues des gardes ⁊ mariages qe serront en la mayn le Roi en Irlaunde du doun le Roy tanqe a la somme de v^c mars en alloaunce de ses pertes qil ad eu en le service le Roy. Mons. J. le Power de Donoyll.

il plest au Roi.[2]

— Item acorde est qe Mons. Richard de Clare eyt perdoun de m^l marcs *de ses dettes propres* les queles couront sur li des dettes son piere et de ses auncestres en les parties Dyrlaunde et Dengleterre et de tout le remenant qil devera au Roy soit le Roi acertez combien il li doit et soit endementres[3] mys en respit sur son bon port et le bon service qil ferra au Roi en temps avenir. Ric. de Clare.

il plest au Roi.

— Item accorde est qe Mons. Moritz le filz Thomas eyt pardoun de m^l mars pur li et ses auncestres de ses propres dettes et le remenant soit mys en sœffrance sur son bon port.[4] Moritz le filz Thomas.

il plest au Roi.

— Item accorde est que Mons. Nicole de Verdoun . . .[5]

Preamble of Articles brought by Elias Jonestone from the Bishop of Worcester reporting the state of the processes in the Court of the King of France.[6] 11 *Edward II.*

March 26, 1318.

Memorandum quod die dominica in crastino Annunciacionis Beate Marie Virginis anno regni Regis Edwardi filii Regis Edwardi undecimo venerabilis in Christo pater dominus T. dei gratia Wigornensis Episcopus[7] liberavit Elie de Joneston[8] Londonie infrascriptos articulos portandos dicto domino Regi, Cancellario et Thesaurario suis et ceteris de consilio suo ad quos pertinet super hiis consulere et remedia adhibere loco certificacionis super negociis dicto domino Episcopo commissis per breve de magno sigillo presentibus annexum. Et quia idem dominus Episcopus dictos articulos plenius declarare non potuit tam propter temporis brevitatem sibi in dicto brevi limitati quam propter negocia pro quibus versus Leycestriam a

[1] *Cal. Close Rolls*, 333; *Cal. Patent Rolls*, 459.

[2] *Cal. Close Rolls*, 333.

[3] meanwhile.

[4] *Cal. Patent Rolls*, 9 Edw. II, 459.

[5] The writing is not finished.

[6] *Diplomatic Documents, Chancery Misc.*, bundle 27, file 8, no. 37.

[7] Thomas Cobham, formerly one of the council called to consider Gascon affairs (*Cal. Close Rolls*, 5 Edw. II, 449), now proctor for the cases pending in the *parlement* of Paris.

[8] Elias Jonestone was a king's clerk who at various times had much to do with foreign negotiations.

Londonia in crastino erit recessurus et alias causas evidentes per dictum Eliam exprimendas iniunxit predicto Elie quod ipse predictos articulos et ceteros omnes huiusmodi certificacionem contingentes sufficienter declararet sub formis sibi ore tenus expositis et aliis quibus melius viderit faciendum et causas excusacionis per dictum Episcopum et ceteros de consilio dicti domini nostri tam de Vasconia quam Anglia super hiis nuper consultos quo ad finale remedium pro dicto domino nostro inde ordinandum sepius allegatas intimaret pro remediis alias petitis inde habendis.[1]

York, Oct. 15, 1322.

Agenda sent by the King to be considered by the Council.[2] 16 *Edward II.*

— Fait a remembrer des choses souzescrites.

— A de primes de lestatut sur le repeal des Ordenances.[3]

— Item de mettre les bons pointz en estatut.

— Item de remedier contre faus retours des baillifs des franchises.

— Item de ordener coment les chateus des felons et futifs, au et wast, deodandes, wrec de mer, et autres tiels profitz, qe ne se lievent forsque en eyre, peussent estre levez de an en an al eops le Roi, sicome autres seignurages les lievent a lour eops qe tiels profitz parnent[4] par chartre ou dantiquite.

— Item de mettre tutes balaunces enfyn auxi bien pur vendre come pur acheter, car hom dit qe toutes les balaunces du Roialme sont fauses fors celes qe sont deseures, a grant damage des grantz et a commun people.

— Item de redrescer tutes les mesures de blee, vin, et de cervoise partut le Roialme et de mettre conservatours sur ceo en chescun countee ou autre garde. . . .[5]

— Et fait asavoir qe le Roi voet qe chescun sage de son conseil sen pense de ces pointz . . . qe peussent amender la ley pur le profist du Roi et du people et [qant] eux soit accordez . . . qe serra accorde soit mis en fourme de statut ou mestier est de statut, ou de faire autre remedie la ou autre remedie suffira, et qe tiele chose issi mise en fourme soit monstre al Roi issint qil sen peusse aviser avant le parlement pur plustost deliverer le people qe veignent au parlement.[6]

[1] The articles follow at considerable length.

[2] *Parl. Proceedings*, v. 10.

[3] The repeal of the New Ordinances was accomplished by statute. *Statutes of the Realm*, i. 189. The other matters suggested, if carried out at all, were by 'other measures'.

[4] 'parner' = to take (*K. N. D.*).

[5] Several articles here are omitted.

[6] The articles being different in ink and appearance were apparently written at diverse times, and at the end space is left for more.

Order in Council for the issue of Letters to suppress the Feud between the Geroldines and the Poers in Ireland.[1] 2 *Edward III.* June 24, 1328.

— Pur ce qe le Roi et son conseil ont entenduz qe ascunes dissensions sont comencees en la terre Dirlaund entre les linages de Gerodyns et de Poers dont grantz perils purront avenir si hastif remedie ne soit mis, soit mande a les grantz dune part et dautre par lettres du grant seal qe sur forfaiture de quantqe ils purront forfaire sursessent[2] et facent les leurs surseer de faire mal ou damage par chivauches ou en autre manere et qe le Roi entend de mander justice covenable et ordiner dautres ministres qi ferront droit et reson a touz.

Les nouns des grantz as queux homme escrivera, Jacobus le Botiller, Johanes de Bermyngeham comes de Loveth, Mauritius filius Thome, Johanes filius Roberti le Poer, Walterus filius Willelmi de Burgo, Arnaldus Poer.[3]

Petitions to the Council made by John Darcy as to terms on which he is to go to Ireland as Justiciary, with answers inserted.[4] 2 *Edward III.* August, 1328.

Les Peticiouns Johan Darci sil devie aler en Irland.

— Soit Nichol Fastolf chief justice a tenir les plez suauntz la chief justic,[5] et Roger de Preston secundar.

— Item du commun Baunk soit sire Piers de Ledymeton ou sire Roberd de Thorp chief justice, Johan de Grauntsete secundar, et
Johan de Beuer
William de Saresfeld ou William Scot le tiercs.[6]

sire Elis de Stapleton sire Robert de Bluntesdon et
— Item en le Escheker sire Johan Travers ou sire Nichol de
sire Simon de Balderston
Akketon chief baron, et sire Henry de Thrapston secundar.[7]

— Item qe William de Boseworth soit guardeyn des brefs et roules en la place la chief justice.[8]

[*Inserted.*] Soit par la tesmoigne Nichol Fastolf.[9]

— Item dic le counseil notre Seigneur le Roy le quel la justice Dirlaund doit receivre a la pees les gentz Dirlaund, qe oue banere desplie ount fait diverses felounies come arsouns homicides et roberies, ou les doit mener par reddour de ley ou par guerre ou en quel autre manere treter.

[1] *Parl. Proceedings*, vi. 9. [2] Trans. *they surcease.*

[3] The ensuing letters under the great seal are found in *Cal. Close Rolls*, 2 Edw. III, 397 ; *Foedera* (Rec. Ed.), ii. 744. [4] *Parl. Proceedings*, vi. 10.

[5] Appointment of Nicholas Fastolf as chief justice for holding pleas following the justiciary of Ireland, by king and council. *Cal. Patent Rolls*, 2 Edw. III, 316.

[6] The erasures and substitutions made by a different pen are the corrections offered by the council.

[7] Appointment of Henry Thrapston, king's clerk, as second baron of the exchequer in Dublin. *Cal. Patent Rolls*, 2 Edw. III, 316.

[8] *Cal. Patent Rolls*, 2 Edw. III, 316.

[9] The insertions are closely written in the margins as answers of the council.

[*Inserted.*] Deffens en tieu cas ne pas fait en temps notre Seigneur le Roy qore est et pur ce overe la justice par bon conseil ce qe fait a faire profit du Roy et sauvacion de la pees etc., issint qe la justice face serment devant respons.

queratur rotulus. — Item qil ait poer a faire perdouns de felounies et trespas et de ceo comaunder la chartre notre Seigneur le Roy.

Fiat. — Item qil puisse surveer la Tresorie notre Seigneur le Roy deux foiz ou trois foiz pur aan et plus, si mester soit.

[*Inserted.*] Ensemblement od le chaunceller.[1]

— Item qe le Tresorer ait encomaundement de liverer touz maneres deners qe sount en la Tresorie illoeqes quel hure qe la dite Justice luy face de ceo guarnisement pur restreyndre les rebeals et ceux que voillent de guerre coure sur le people.

— Item qe notre Seigneur le Roi ne graunte chartre de pardoun de felounie fait en Irlaund a nul eyns, qil soit enfourme par sa justice Dirlaund de la manere du fait.

[*Inserted.*] Il semble qe le Roi soit enforme par sa justice.

— Item qil ne graunte terre ne tenement office ne baillie en la dite terre saunz estre sur ceo primes counseille de sa dite Justice et les autres de soun counsail illoeqes.

[*Inserted.*] Il semble qil est pur le Roy.

— Item qe la dite Justice puisse doner conge a faire eleccioun des Evesqes et Abbes quy possessiouns sount dedeyns le tax de xx li. et lours fealtez receivre et lours temporalitez a eux liverer parnaunt fait auxi bien des Evesqes et Abbes come des elisours qe notre Seigneur le Roy le fait a cele foiz de sa grace en reguard de charite pur esparnier lours travaux et coustages et qil ne tourne a notre Seigneur le Roy ne as ses heirs en prejudice.

[*Inserted.*] En nulle manere.

— Item qe le Roy maunde covenables chivalers hors Dengletere a guarder les chasteux de Raundoun, Roscoman, et Bourat, qar par guardeyns de la terre Dirlaund ne serount iammes les terres le Roy aprouwer.[2]

[*Inserted.*] Face la Justice gard tancque le Roi eit autre ordeinez.

Fiat. — Item qe notre Seigneur le Roy et soun counseil se assentent qe touz les Irreys Dirlaund eyent la ley Englesche sils voillent par statut a faire de ceo par commun assent en soun parlement en Irlaund, saunz ceo qils eyent mester de purchacer chartres sur ceo.

[*Inserted.*] Soit mande a la Justice qe au prochain parlement safforce assaie la volunte des grauntz sils voillent assenter a cel estatuit et certifie le Roy.[3]

Fiat. — Item qe la Justice eit poer a lesser les terres le Roy qe gisent en marches de guerre en fee a terme de vie ou de aunz solom ceo qil

[1] Order to the treasurer and chamberlains of the exchequer at Dublin to admit the justiciary and chancellor of Ireland to survey the king's treasury twice a year, by king and council. *Cal. Close Rolls*, 2 Edw. III, 312.

[2] The custody of Roscommon castle was given to John de Athy. *Cal. Patent Rolls*, 2 Edw. III, 339.

[3] An order to this effect was issued. *Cal. Close Rolls*, 2 Edw. III, 312.

verra a faire par le counseil notre seigneur le Roy illoeqes pur aforcement des marches encountre les Irroys.

[*Inserted.*] Soit mande a les Justice, Chanceller, et Tresorer etc., qe des terres gastees gisantes en marche perillouse il puissent lesser a ferme a terme des aunz issint qe le terme ne passe mie xx aunz.

— Item qil puisse doner conge as prelatz et gentz de seynt Esglise a porchacer terres en morte meyn qe sount en marches wastes et deshabitez nient countre estaunt lestatut de morte meyn,[1] par issint qils les asseent et inhabitent a lour poer en aforcement de lours marches. Fiat.

[*Inserted.*] Eit le poier pur trois aunz a doner conge as prelatz des eglises cathedrals qe sont assises en pleine terres de pees par res[onable] fyn sauf le fee le Roy.[2]

— Item qe touz les estatuz Dengleterre soient escrites et maundez illoeqes de soutz le seal notre Seigneur le Roy a tenir illoeqes auxi avaunt come en Engleterre. FIAT. Fiat.

— Item soit ordine ceo qe la dite Justice avera pur ses despenses outre soun fee, qar il ne purra mye de soun fee viure en lestat qe la terre est ore, et qil ait bref destre paie toute voirs de soun fee avaunt la mayn pur un quarter del an taunt come il serra justice et qe livere luy soit mille liveres a despendre pur restreyndre ceux qore sount levez de guerre par la venwe du Tresorer et autres du counseil illoeqes, qar il ny ad riens illoeqes en Tresorie a ceo qil ad entendu.

[*Inserted.*] Item ordene notre Seigneur le Roy.

— Item plese a notre Seigneur le Roy avoir reguard a ceo, qe le dit Johan poeit avoir euw del counte de Oluester ii li. de terre a terme de sa vie, robes et seles pur ses quintes chivalers, restor des chivaux, et totes maneres des sustenaunces pur xx hommes darmes, quele chose il lessa a demorer pres del corps notre seigneur a prendre de luy c liveres de terre a terme de sa vie de quoy il nest servy mes de lx liveres de terre, de quoy, si luy plest, voille a luy faire reward sil doit aler en Irlaund.

[*Inserted.*] Il semble au conseil qe ce qe faut de son covenant, qe le Roy le face perfournir.[3]

Orders in Council concerning Appointments to be made in Ireland.[4] *7 Edward III.* Oct. 2, 1333.

— Il semble au conseil sil plese au Roi qe Mons. Robert de Scardeburgh soit devers Mons. Johan Darcy chef justice de sa place et Roger de Preston soun compaignoun.

— Item Robert de Nicole chef clerk en mesme la place.

— Item en le commun bank Roger de Baukwelle chief, Johan de

[1] A *non-obstante* clause.

[2] The ensuing order is in *Cal. Patent Rolls,* 2 Edw. III, 315.

[3] John Darcy 'le neveu' was appointed to the office of justiciary of Ireland, with the right to keep the country with nineteen other men-at-arms with a yearly fee of £500, by king and council. *Cal. Patent Rolls,* 2 Edw. III, 316.

[4] *Parl. Proceedings,* file vi, no. 26.

Bray secoundair, Richard de Hattecoumbe tierz, sire Johan de Assheby chief clerk en comun bank en lu Watier de Kynefare, sire Thomas de Brailes chaunceller de escheqier, Robert de Helpeston cirograffer, sire Robert Power chief baron de escheqier, sire Thomas de Glaston secoundair, sire Williem de Emeldon clerk des Roules de la chauncellerie.[1]

April or May, 1339.

Articles sent by the King from abroad to his Council regarding his revenues, with the answers made by the Council.[2] 13 *Edward III.*

Les articles reportez as Chanceller, Tresorer et autres du Conseil notre Seigneur le Roi en Engleterre par maistre Robert de Askeby et Sire Renaud de Donyngton [3] depar notre Seigneur le Roi des parties dela et les responses a mesmes les articles.

— Primerement ils deivent dire coment le Roi puis sa primere venue devers les parties de decea unqes riens navoit des issues de son Roiaume en eide ou sustenance de lui ne de ses gentz de qoi il se merveille grauntement et touz ceux qi sont entour lui.

Le Respons. — Notre Seigneur le Roi en est pleinement respondu par Mons. Johan de Moylns [4] et les autres messages. (et entre ce pleise al conseil notre Seigneur le Roi aver consideracion a les choses contenues en une cedule cosue a cestes.) [5]

— Item ils poont dire coment il et ceux qi sont entour lui se merveillent plus de ce qe de xx^{m} saaks qe furent grauntez en son parlement avant sa venue, ne ne sont venuz a lui ne as autres as queux assignementz des dites laynes furent faitz noun pas la moitee au partir du dit conte.[6]

Le respons.—Notre Seigneur le Roi en est respondu par les ditz messages. (et aussint le transescrit de mesme le response est baille as ditz mestres Robert et Renaud.)

— Item ils poont dire coment les marcheantz de Barde, Peruch, Maistre Poul, William de la Pole et William Dunenord [7] dient bien qe la liveree des laynes qe [le Roi ait] premis, ne les est pas faite mais lour assignementz a la foitz repelez et la foitz chaungez ensi qe par celle defaute le Roi est deservi et eux ne poont tenir lours iours a paiementz faire qils avoient premis en espoir deide des dites leynes, parqoi ils sont en point de perdre creance.

[1] The ensuing letters patent contain each of these appointments, except the last, in which case Edmund Grimesby is substituted for William Emeldon. *Cal. Patent Rolls*, 7 Edw. III, 470.

[2] *Parl. Proceedings*, file vii, no. 7.

[3] Clerks.

[4] John Moleyns, a knight much in the king's service, one of the council. *Cal. Patent Rolls*, 374.

[5] The parts in parentheses are in a changed hand, being evidently added at a different time.

[6] = account.

[7] The Bardi, the Prussian Company, Master Paul Montefiore, William de la Pole, and William Dunort were receivers of wool, to whom for their advances of money the king made the assignments. *Cal. Close Rolls, passim.*

Le respons. — Qant a mons. William de Dunenordi il est pleinement servi de ses assignementz, et des assignementz des autres nomez en le dit article les primers assignementz furent faitz par lour assentz ou de lour attornez et puis riens nest repelez ne chaungez. (sil ne soit par expres comandement notre Seigneur le Roi.)

— Item ils poont dire qe les ditz marchantz de Barde et de Peruch ne sont pas assignez a la moite de ce qe le Roi ad mandez qils fussent assignez, par qoi ils noont poair deider au Roy come ils dussent si covenant les fust tenu a ce qils dient.

Le respons. — Quant as assignementz des laynes les marcheantz de Barde et de Peruch sont assignez a iiij^{m} DCCCLXIX saks et dim., xii pieres et dim. de leyne (de les cink m^{l} assignez a eux par mandement le Roi,) et as [autres paymentz] des deners ils sont assignez si avant, come les issues de la terre poont suffire, et semble au conseil qils ne deivent plus avant estre assignez tantqe . . . par aconte.

— Item [*omitted.*]

— Item ils poont dire coment les laines qe sont venues au Roi et as marchantz et autres as queux ils furent assignez furent si febles de si petite value et de si petit [pois qe ?] sarplers [1] des autres leines contrevaleient trois ou quatre sarplers de celes leines et tut par fausete des coillours [2] et defaute de surveue diceles, car il est notoirement [qe] viles lokes [3] et autres leynes nient marchandables sont mis dedeinz les sarplers merchez pur le Roi plus qe bones laines.

Le respons. — Pervours, surveiours, et receivours des laynes le Roi par tut Engleterre, eluz et nomez en parlement et le conseil de Northampton par les grantz et autres du conseil illoeqes, avaient [recevez] comissions de prendre, surveier, et recevire les dites laines et en chescune commission fust esprese mencion faite qe nule layne ne fust prise ne receue al oeps le Roi [sil ne] fust covenable et du meillour du pois sur peine de gref forfeiture ; et le conseil le Roi fust chescun iour certefiez de grant grevance faite au poeple par election [des laynes ?] faite par les ministres mais unqes nul qi fust assigne de surveier les leines et les haster au port ne certefia le conseil qe defaute y avoit, et fust [ordeine qe] les commissions de faire mercher chescun sak de la layne le Roi de certaine merche des armes le Roi, et de queu pois et sort la layne fust siqe le . . . [4] aver aperceu pardela en queux la defaute fust si nule y estoit.

— Item . . .

— Item ils deivent exciter qe les assignementz et estallementz soient hastiement repelez et qe la dette le Roi des uns et des autres et leide pur sa feille marier soient hastiement [levez] solonc les mandementz le Roi, et qe le Tresorer se enfourme hastiuement de tut leide qe se puet faire et meite mons. Robert de Sadyngton son lieutenant [5] et viege devers le Roi hastiement pur sentir entierment sa volunte et hastiuement revenir.

[1] sacks (?). ' Sarpillere ' = canvas to pack wares in (Cotgrave).
[2] ' coillours ' = collectors (*K. N. D.*).
[3] Old rags. ' Loque ' = a rag (Cotgrave). [4] Illegible.
[5] *Cal. Patent Rolls*, 13 Edw. III, 387.

Le respons. — Endroit del eide pur la feille le Roi marier les ditz messages portent au Roi lavis de son conseil pardecea, et le conseil sen soeffre de faire execucion tanqe le Roi [man]dra sa volunte. Et quant al repel des assignementz ordeine est en une overte [1] manere qe nul paiement ne se doit faire des assignementz forsqe a les per[sonnes assignez ?] tanqe notre Seigneur le Roi eit autre foitz sur ce mande sa volunte. . . .[2] Et quant a repel de fees des ministres [3] ils ent furent serviz iusques a la seint . . . avant la venue des ditz messages et dient apertement qe si lour fee soit retret ils se retrerront de lour service, porce qils ne sont de poair de le faire . . . propre a ce qils dient.

Endroit des estallementz, pleise a notre Seigneur le Roi et a son conseil savoir qe il nest de nulle dette si bien paie come de ses dettes attermine en cas qe len face execucion pur lentier les viscontes ne responderont mye de la moite de la somme attermine, sicome ceux du conseil notre Seigneur le Roi pardela le scient.

Estre ce au conseil de Northampton [4] par plusurs grauntz feust respondu quant le repel destallementz lur fust moustre, qe du temps dont memoire ne court estal[lementz] furent grauntez et suffertz as grauntz et autres pur sauvete de lur contenance et ce feust lusage du roialme, queux choses sanz assent des grauntz et ce en parlement ne r[ien] ne ne devoient estre changees et ce qils disoient purqoi ils ne voudreient al dit repel assentir ne le suffrir tantcome en eux feust. Et auxint les graundes . . . touchent les grauntz de la terre contre queux les viscontes nosent faire execucion.

July 26, 1339.[5]

Answers of the Council to various points suggested by the King, especially as to the Shipment of Wool.[6] 13 *Edward III.*

— Au primer point soit respondu qe la pes est bien garde, dieu mercie, et qe par celle cause nest pas mestir qe la chauncellerie soit movante par le pais. Item ouesqe ce soit dit qe si le chaunceller et la place et les autres du conseil feussent severez les busoignes le Roi serroient desespleitees, desicome tut le conseil ne suffit mie de esplette ses busoignes.[7]

— Item au second point cest a savoir de larray des niefs, soit le Roi certifie de larrai qe en est fait.

[1] A correction has been made to this word; whether from 'ouerte' to 'couerte', or vice versa, it is hard to say.

[2] Several items here are omitted.

[3] The order to repeal the fees of ministers is given in *Cal. Close Rolls*, 12 Edw. III, 467.

[4] This paragraph is a note of the great council held at Northampton, July 25, which was apparently written later than the rest.

[5] No doubt at the great council then held at Northampton.

[6] *Parl. Proceedings*, file vii, no. 9. In this case the answers are given on a separate membrane from the agenda.

[7] The king had sometimes taken the chancellor and the great seal abroad with him, e.g. *Cal. Close Rolls*, 14 Edw. I, 395.

— Item quant a lisle de Wight et de la ville de Suthampton, soit le Roi certifie de ce qen est ordine.[1]

— Item au point cest a savoir de espier la covyne[2] des gentz Descoce le conseil le ferra. Et quant a la trewe le conseil ad parle od[3] les grantz auxi bien du North come devers le Suth, et ils ne assentent en nulle manere qe la dite trewe soit debrusee depar eux, mes qelle soit tenue.

— Item soient certeines gentz assignees *autres qui ne ont mie este assignez avant ces heures*[4] daler en chescun port dengleterre et de surveer les laines le Roi tronees es ditz portz et de les faire eskiper et envoier outre salvement au Roi sanz nul delai. Et si ils troevent visconte ou autre quel qil soit desobeissant ou necgligent etc., qils les facent prendre etc., et qils certifient le conseil *de ce qils en averont fait et trovez*[4] du nombre des saaks de leyne qils averont tronez et envoiez etc.

— Item soient mesmes ceux assignez de garnir[5] les attorney William de la Pole, les marchantz de la compaignie des Bardes et de Peruch, mestre Poul de Mountflour et William de Dunord[6] qe les laynes notre Seigneur le Roi a eux assignees et les quelles ils ont receu ils facent envoier outre au Roi entre cy et my Martz[7] ou le jour a plus tard signifiantz a eux qe si ils ne le facent le Roi reprendra les dites laynes en sa mayn et en ferra son profit.

— Item soient assignez certeines gentz daler en chescun conte de surveer les laines notre Seigneur le Roi qe sont en mains des coillours et qe uncore sont a coiller es ditz contez et de les faire lever et venir as havenes sanz delai et envoier outre au Roi et qils certifient le conseil de ce qils en averont trovez et fait. Et si ils troevent visconte ou autre ministre desobeissant ou necgligent etc., qils facent prendre lur corps etc.

— Item soient touz les avantditz assignez chargez et jurez devant le conseil de bien et loialment perfournir les choses susdites.

— Item soit sire John de Charneles assignez de aler de Wappentake en Wapentake et de ville en ville es contez de Leycestre et de Warrwik denquerrer et soi enformer par totes les voies qil porra quelles laynes *ou argent en noun des laines* et vitailles sont paiez et levez al oeps notre Seigneur le Roi es ditz contez et de y faire autres choses des quelles il est charge.

— Item soient aporcionez m^{l} hommes darmes vi^{m} hobelours vi^{m} archers en touz les contez dengleterre hors pris les gentz darmes et autres queux les graauntz mesneront.

[1] Orders for the defence of the Isle of Wight and of Southampton are given by keeper and council. *Cal. Close Rolls*, 13 Edw. III, 55, 71, 260; *Cal. Patent Rolls*, 12 Edw. III, 143, 149, 180, 181.

[2] Secret place of meeting.

[3] 'od' = with (*K. N. D.*).

[4] Inserted.

[5] To warn.

[6] Assignments to each of these parties are found in *Cal. Close Rolls*, 467, 507, 588, 594, 595, 599, 601, &c.

[7] The middle of March.

1342–3. *Recommendations of the Council for the better Government of Ireland.*[1] 16 *Edward III.*

— Fait a remembrer de parler au Roi des pointz souzescritz toucheantz la terre Dirland.

— Primiere amener illoeqes gentz de bien puissantz et sages pur enquere sur trespas et duretez faites illoqes par les ministres le Roi et autres, et le Roi en avera un grant profit. Et certeines respons sont faites as messages Dirland sur pointz contenuz en un roule sil plese au Roi,[2] mes sur les pointz qe sensuent nest nule respons done, mes le conseil ad cy escrit son avis.

Il semble au conseil que ceo seroit grantment pur le Roi de tenir les citeez et grandes villes Dirlande en sa mayn santz granter les fermes as autres et qe ceux as queux les fermes sont assignez reteynent tant a lescheqer le Roi de Dyvelyn.

— Item quant al office de custumer de toute Irelande qest grante a mons. Thomas de Saundeby[3] a terme de sa vie et qi prent iiij^{xx} livres[4] par an du Roi pur le dit office, il semble au conseil, sil plest au Roi, qe purceo qil y ad sept portz en la dite terre qe ceo est au profist le Roi, qen chescun port soient deux custumers, un contre-roullour, un tronour et un coket, come est use en Engleterre, et qe nul homme eit loffice en fee.[5]

— Item fait a parler au Roi du chastel et du contee de Kilkenny en Irelaunde pur faire eschange od le counte de Gloucestre la dame de Clare et mons. Johan de Houthum qi tienent le chastel et contee avantditz.

— Item purceo qe leschetour Dirlande[6] prent XL li. par an pur son fee et fait peu de profit, il semble au consail qe ceo est pur le profit le Roi, qe chescun viscont soit eschetour en sa baillie come est ordine en Engleterre.[7]

— Item qe ceux qi sont ministres le Roi ne demoerent devers autres seigneurs du pais, ne ne preignent de eux robes, fees, empensions, ne office, e qe sur ceo soient jurez.[8]

— Item il semble au conseil qe quant le Tresorer Dirlande deit venir en Engleterre pur rendre son aconte, soit lacompte primes examinez par la justice et chaunceller Dirlande et les chalenges mises qils purront trover es parcelles du dit aconte. Et ensi soit laconte envoie en Engleterre souz lour sealx, et souz le seal del escheqer Dirlande

[1] *Parl. Proceedings*, file vii, no. 13.

[2] This roll contained a series of petitions sent from Ireland which were received and answered by the council. They are found engrossed upon the Close Roll (16 Edw. II, 508–16). Some of the articles in the present series are taken from the former.

[3] *Cal. Patent Rolls*, 14 Edw. III, 83 ; 16 Edw. III, 510.

[4] Altered from ' marcs '.

[5] This is ordained in the responses upon the Close Roll. *Calendar*, 516.

[6] Roger Darcy, escheator of Ireland. *Cal. Patent Rolls*.

Cal. Close Roll, 514.

[8] Councillor's oath.

ouesqes lour chalenges. Et qe la justice, chaunceller, et autres du conseil chescun an facent survewe du tresor le Roi.[1]

— Item il semble au conseil qil est au Justice de faire somondre le service le Roi quele hure qil veit, qe mestier soit de chivaucher de guerre en terre qest de guerre et fust au temps qe ceux qi deivent cel service furent feffez. Et sil voet chivaucher de guerre sur les terres qe sont purprises par les enemys puis cel temps, il nest pas a somondre service mes qe chescun homme a la somons du Justice est tenuz de chivaucher de guerre ad la Justice pur oustier les enemis hors des tieles terres sanz gages prendre ou autre riens du Roi chescun homme en eide dautre.[2]

— Item qe nul ministre neit qe un office et un fee.[3]

Proposals of the Council answered and amended by the King.[4] 18 *Edward III.* 1345.

— Fait a remembrer a mounstrer a notre Seigneur le Roi et son consail qe nul Furment, pur cherete qest avenuz, soit carie hors del Roialme Dengleterre sinoun as certains places sur forfaiture.

Il plest au Roi que nules blez soient caries hors du Roialme sil ne soit devers Caleys ou Flaundres ou par ceaux qi ount ore congie de nos mesmes de les carier devers Gascoigne, et sur ceo soient maundementz parmy le Roialme.[5]

— Item qe assignement soit fait a les gentz de la citee de Loundres de iiij^{m} DCCCXVI *li.* xiij*s.* 4*d.* les queux sont aderere de v^{m} *li.* et de ij^{m} marcs naigaires a notre Seigneur le Roi aprestes.

Il plest au Roi qe le Tresorer veie toutes les parcelles qe sont paiez par sire Williem de Cusance[6] et autres, et qil face certifier le Roi de ceo qe remeynt de cler apaier et de ceo le Roi lour ferra assignement aplus en haste qil purra bonement.

— Item qe la quinzisme de la dite citee qest avener qe amounte m^{l} et c marcs qest unqore apaier soit assigne enpartie du paiement de la somme avantdite a les gentz avantditz.

Cele some est ordeinee pur la guerre parquei le Roi ne la purra deporter a ceste foithe.[7]

— Item de D iij saks et iij quartrouns x pieres x libres et iij quartrouns de leyne sur la dite citee assis, qe partie de ceo sil plest a notre Seigneur le Roi soit abregge ou prorogacioun de partie du paiement de ceo soit fait.

Toutes les leynes grauntes au Roi sont assignes as marchauntz pour chevaunce faire en eide de la guerre parquei le Roi ne veot ne ne peut susprendre le covenaunt.

[1] *Cal. Close Roll*, 510. [2] Ibid. 515. [3] Ibid. 511.

[4] *Warrants* (*Chancery*), file 1538. The writing comes from the office of the privy seal.

[5] The ordinances are in a slightly different hand from the agenda.

[6] William Cusance was king's clerk and treasurer of the exchequer.

[7] At this time.

— Item qe les ij neefs assignes de la dite citee pur la guerre, dount delun Wygayn est mestre et Thomas Clerk delautre, soient paies par endenture par les coillours de la dite citee de ij*s*. del sak de leyne, vi*d*. del li. et xviij *d*. del tonel de vyn com avant ces hures unt este, issint qils puissent sur la guerre continuelment lenvoyer e le remenaunt qe sera coille qe isoit dilivere as admiralx.

Il plest au Roi qe solomc lordinaunce autre foithe faite toutes gentz soient paiez parmy les mains des admiralx.

— Item de fauses controvours des noveles et de lour fautours dount murmur sovent est entre le people qils soient pris et arestuz solomc lestatut de Westminster.

Il plest au Roi qe lestatut soit tenu et qe briefs ent soient faites solomc lestatut.[1]

— Item qe la monee dor eit son cours ou qe la chaunge soit resounable issint toutefoithe qe notre Seigneur le Roi eit de la dite chaunge cest qe a lui appartient.[2]

Il plest au Roi qe les chanceller et tresorer ordeinent ce qe ent put estre fait pur profit de lui et de la commune et qe remedie soit fait sur ceux qi font leschange contre lordinance.

— Item qe ij^{m} marcs assignes en partie du paiement de les susdites v^{n} *li*. nient paies soient leves et paies come appartient.

Il plest au Roi qe ceaux qi nont mie paiez soient destreintz a paier lour porcioun de la dite somme et les coillours qi ont les deners coilles de la dite somme soient constreintz a paier a ceux a les queux ils duissent paier come appartient.

Sept. 10, 1345.

Warrant for proclamation to be made concerning exchange of money.[3]

Il plest au Roi que la crie soit renouellee qe nul homme ne soit si hardy de refuser paiement dor pur le pris qest ordene et par la ou deuant ces heures feust defendu qe nulle eschange dor ne se ferroit mes seulement a la place de leschange qest ordene le Roi voet qe toutes gentz puissent faire franchement tiele eschange selonc le pris qest ordene tantqe au temps qe la place de leschange soit ouerte et en cas qe aucun homme de quel estat quil soit refuse le dit paiement dor ou preigne plus pur leschange dor qe le pris qest ordene cest assauer pur le florin de demy mark trois mailles [4] dauantage et pur les autres florins selonc lafferant [5], le Roi voet qe les corps de ceux qi le ferront soient pris et demoerrent en prisone a sa volonte. La monoie soit forfaite au Roi.

ceste bille fut liuere en Chauncellerie le x. iour de Septembre

[1] The statute of the eighteenth year. *Statutes of the Realm*, i. 299.

[2] Concerning a new coinage, see *Statutes of the Realm*, i. 299–301; *Cal. Close Rolls*, 18 Edw. III, 261.

[3] It will be noticed that this is distinctly a document of the privy seal, as described in chap. xiv. *Warrants* (*Chancery*), file 1538.

[4] 'mail, maylle' = a halfpenny (*K. N. D.*).

[5] 'solonc son afferaunt' = according to his proportion (*K.N.D.*).

lan present de par le Roi et le conseil et sur ceo fut bref fait de crier la dite monoie.

[*Endors*][1] Stury[2]
Ely[3] Bartholomu del Chastel de Doure[4]
la criee William armenter
la Fluue Thomas Cook Conest[able]
Oxenford'

lettres Bret'
Scire facias
Walsoken statut' March'.

Message from the Bishop of Durham, the Earl of Angus, Sir Henry Percy and others to the Council.[5] July 17, 1346.

Assentuz fust Lundy le xvij. iour de Ioyl a Noef Chastiell' sur Tyne par acord pris parentre Leuesque de Duresme[6], Le Counte Danegos,[7] Le seignur de Percy,[8] monsire Rauf de Neuill', le sire de Segraue et altres qi y furont que le portur de cestes serroit maunde a Loundres a Lerceuesque de Canterbire,[9] les Chaunceller,[10] Tresorer,[11] monsire Geffrey le Scrop et altres du conseill le Roi coment lour couenantes que furont faites ad eaux a Noef Chastiell sur Tyne et a Euerewyk[12] lour sont enfreintes. Cest assauer coment les seignurs demurrantz sur la Marche sont despaiez de les deniers qils dussent auer solonc le purport des endentures entre eaux faites. Et auxint[13] de monstrer au dit conseill que sire Iohan Dellerker ne se melle mye de la recette de deniers que sont assignez pur la garde de la Marche. Mais que sire Robert de Spynay que fust ordenez et assignez par Leuesque de Duresme monsire Geffrey le Scrop' et altres du conseill nostre seignur le Roi pur la dite rescette se melle de la ditte rescette en le noun des ditz Seignurs et a lour oeps et en cas que nul altre se melle de meisme la rescette que le dit sire Robert que adonques les ditz seignurs soient deschargez de lour demoere. Item que le dit sire Robert eit garraunt de faire paiementz et assignementz as ditz Seignurs et as altres; cest assauer a chescun solonc sa retenaunce fait et affaire par le maundement et la tesmoignance de Leuesque de Duresme le sire de Percy et monsire Rauf de Neuill' les trois ou

[1] This endorsement seems to be a note by the chancellor, not concerning the warrant itself.
[2] William Stury, appointed to treat in Flanders concerning coinage, September 8, 1345.
[3] Thomas de Insula or de Lisle, bishop of Ely, consecrated July 1345. The temporalities were restored to him September 10, 1345.
[4] Bartholomew Burghersh, constable of Dover Castle.
[5] *Parl. Proceedings*, file vii, no. 18. The substance of this document is printed in Joseph Bain's *Calendar of Scotch Documents*, iii. 266.
[6] Thomas Hatfield, the king's secretary, bishop of Durham, 1345–81.
[7] Gilbert Umfraville.
[8] Sir Henry Percy.
[9] John Stratford, archbishop of Canterbury, 1333–48.
[10] John Ufford, then dean of Lincoln.
[11] William Edington, bishop of Winchester.
[12] York.
[13] 'auxint' = also

deux de eaux et que lour dit maundement ouesque les acquitances de eaux de queux la dite paie se ferra soit allowance au dit sire Robert sur son accompte faite. Item soit maunde garraunt a Leuesque de Duresme a Leuesque de Cardoyll [1] et a Labbe nostre dame Deuerwyk Coillours [2] du Byvennale [3] en les Eueschees Deuerwyk et de Cardoyll et en le Countee Deuerwyk qils facent les paiementz et assignementz de la moite du dit Byennale que est assignez as dit seigneurs pur la garde de la dite Marche par maundement et tesmoignance des ditz seigneurs et nemye altrement. Et les ditz seignurs se aquitont que en cas que nul assignement ou paiement se face par garraunt de la Court a nul altre que a les ditz seignurs et as eaux que demoerent sur la Marche en eide dycell de les ditz deniers que sont assignez pur la dite Marche auxi bien del ixme come du dit Byennale que adonques ils soiont deschargez de lour demoere et sur ce voillent les endentures parentre le Roi et eaux en faites. Et soit amonstrer au Chaunceller et ceaux du conseill le Roi que les seignurs de Moutbray et de Segraue monsire Thomas de Rokeby monsire William de Falton et monsire Johan Destriuelyn [4] et ceaux de la garnison de Berewyk ount dit courtement a les ditz seignurs que en cas qils neyont paiement de deners hastiement en mayn solonc ce que lour couenantz de lour retenance voillont ils ne poont ne ne voillont plus longement demurrer. Et le dit seignur de Segraue ad dit a les ditz seignurs que sa endenture de sa retenance volet que sil ne soit mie serui de paiement deinz les trois sismaignes apres sa venue a Noef Chastiell que adonques il serra descharge de sa [demoere] sanz empeschement de nul homme et ad respoundu briuement qil ne voelt demurrer plus longement sil ne soit serui de deners.

[? 1346-7.] *Indenture containing articles on the state of Ireland furnished to the Council by Nicholas Snyterby.*[5]

Fait a remembrer des choses a monstrer au conseil nostre dit Seignur le Roi en Engleterre sur lestat de sa terre Dirland.

Primerement coment la pursuyte qest fait deuers le Count de Dessemond nest paas vnqore escheui [6] et mesqe [7] ses terres soient seises en la meyn nostre seignur le Roi si [8] ne y ad il nul profist sourdant [9] vnqore mes charge de la garde qar eles sont nettement destrutz et les tenantz les ount gerpy [10] ne les osent seer [11] tantqe fyne soit fait de luy.

Item voil le conseil estre auise qe coment qe la suyt soit fait deuers nostre seignur le Roi pur le Count de Dessemond par queil suyt la

[1] John Kirkby, bishop of Carlisle, 1332–53.
[2] 'Coillours' = collectors (*K. N. D.*).
[3] *sic* (= biennale).
[4] Striuelyn = Stirling.
[5] *Parl. Proceedings*, file vii, no. 19; a very similar document is no. 22. Nicholas Snyterby was appointed a baron of the exchequer of Dublin, October 28, 1346.
[6] performed.
[7] although.
[8] yet.
[9] arising.
[10] shunned.
[11] to reap.

protection luy est graunte [1] a sauuement venir en Engleterre qils voillent estre auisez sur le processe qest fait deuers luy auant qils voisent a fynal issu de la busoigne [2] pur lestat nostre seignur le Roi et la pees de sa terre Dirland sauuer et meyntener.

Item qe en caas que nostre seignur le Roi luy face grace de ses terres qe ses dettes queux il deit a nostre dit seignur le Roi auxibien ceux qe sont cleres come des acompts queux il deit vnqore a rendre par remembrances de recorde trouez en Lescheqer de Dyuelyn [3] soient especialment reseruez au Roi et qe les terres demurent chargez neynt contreesteantz [4] la seisyn nostre dit seignur le Roi et la liuere a luy sur ce fait.

Item qe la seignurie de Dungaruan et de Deces [5] ne luy soient liuerez en nul manere tauntqe le Roi soit acerte [6] de son droit queil il ad en meisme la seignurie mes qe le dit Count vnqes neust forfait qar en celles terres ne auoit il vnqes estat forsqe [7] par mauueys sugestion et en desceit de la Court a ce qe le conseil par de cea entent.

Item coment les demeigne terres nostre seignur le Roi fermes des Cytes les offices de la custume et Lescheteri [8] sont issint [9] donez et chargez qil ne y demort gairs de certeyn issu de la terre dount les Ministres et les autres charges pussent estre paiez.

Item coment les franchises et chiefserianties qe sont grantez par Chartres honysont [10] toute la terre et par eux est le profist le Roi grandement areri [11] et qil pleise au conseil qe les franchises qe sont ore en sa meyn par iuste cause de forfeture soient fermement retenuz saunz nul liuere faire cest assauoir la franchise de Kildare qe fust en la meyn le Count de Kildare la franchise de Kery et les seriantises des Countes de Cork et Waterford qe furent en la meyn le Count de Dessemond qar tant come les franchises et les chiefseriantises sont abatuz si est le Roi seignur del son et autrement nemye.

Item qe nostre seignur le Roi et son conseil voillent estre auisez qe en caas qe nul suyt soit fait deuers eux par Maier Bailliefs et la Comunalte de nulles des Cytes de la terre Dirland pur enlarger lour franchises ou amenuser [12] lour fermes qils ne le facent en nul manere qar eles sont si larges qe les leys sont souentfoitz le meyns bien gardes par cause qe la Justice et autres Ministres ne pount franchement vser lour iurisdiction ne faire lour offices entre eux.

[*Endors.*] Indentura super diuersis articulis versus consilium Regis per N. de Snyterby.

[1] See *Patent Roll*, 20 Edw. III, part ii, m. 29. Letters of protection for Maurice Fitzthomas, earl of Desmond, to come to England, June 28, 1346.

[2] 'busoignes' = business (*K. N. D.*).

[3] Dublin.

[4] notwithstanding.

[5] Decies, co. Waterford.

[6] certified.

[7] except.

[8] 'escheterie' = office of escheator (*K. N. D.*).

[9] 'issint' = thus.

[10] 'honnir' = to disgrace (Cotgrave).

[11] 'arrerie' = perverted, delayed, frustrated (*K. N. D.*).

[12] 'amenuser' = to diminish (*K. N. D.*).

April 30, 1350.

Ordinances of the Council regarding the Collection of Wool Customs.[1] *24 Edward III.*

In the margin the following note is inserted : Ceux articles sont lues devant le Roi et le conseil et sont acordez en touz pointz.

— Purce que le Roi est deceu de sa custume par faux poys et nule punissement nad este sur ce fait touz ces houres, si est parle de remedie ent faire sil soit avys a notre seigneur le Roi et au son conseil en la manere que sensuyt.

— Primerement que le tronour sil eit trove qil eit fait fauxine en le pois de leynes et de ce soit atteint sur le fait eit iuggement de vie et de membre.

— Item que le marchant qui avera rien done au tronour pur tieu fauxine faire et de ce peusse (en ascune manere)[2] estre atteint sur le fait ou par testmoignance du tronour[3] encourge forfaiture de ces leynes issint poises.

— Item que nul sarpler ne conteigne plus que un sak et demys.[4]

— Item que chescun sak soit poise ovelement[5] par le troner saunz avantage doner.

— Item pur ce que la custume de leynes est ore encrue plus qele ne soleit estre devant ces houres, que grante soit fait as marchantz outre le droit pois de la trone de quatre clowes au sak tancque a la seint Michel.

— Item que mande soit as touz les custumers destre a Londres devant le conseil a certein iour od lour cokettes et auxint soit mande as tronours destre a mesme le iour od lour trones doier la volente le Roi.

— Item que mande soit a les bones villes ou la custume est prise de eslire en chescune ville deux des millours de chescune ville destre custumers come ad este fait devant ces hours.

Endors.] Les articles deinz escriptz furent lues devant le Roi et son conseil a Westminster le vendredi prochein devant lascension, cest assavoir le darein iour de Averill lan du regne notre Seigneur le Roi xxiiij, et furent acordez en touz pointz.

Petition undated. Answered July 18, 1369.

Petition of envoys on behalf of masters, merchants, and mariners of Castile and Biscay. Answer of Council.[6]

[1.] Ce monstrent Piere Lopes Iohan Martin et Iohan Gonsales Messagers des Mestres Marchants et Mariners de Castille et de Viscaye[7] qe come ils eyent monstre vne letre de Messagerie et la copie de les trieues et ils prierent qe vous volsissez[8] tenir et garder ce qest contenuz en les dites trieues et demanderent les niefs de retourner ouesqes les Marchandies arrestuz a Sandwycz et de comander por garder les trieues por les temps qest auenir sibien come por le temps

[1] *Parl. Proceedings*, file vii, no. 24. [2] Inserted. [3] *Sic.*
[4] Cf. *Cal. Patent Rolls*, 16 Edw. III, 388. [5] equally.
[6] *Diplomatic Documents, Exchequer T. R.*, 255.
[7] Biscaye. [8] voulussiez.

passe selonc ce qils auoient en charge de lour message et leur fu respoundu qe le Roi ne les siens ne desbruserent les trieues mes par cause de deux niefs qe furent pris a Seuille ouesqes marchantz et marchandies de Bristuit[1] et des autres qe sont de lobbeissance Dengleterre par bone veritee selonc ce qest contenu en la chartre des trieues fu fait larrest de vj niefs a Sandwycz de les biens Despaigne. Et les diz messagers respoundirent qe ce fu fait countre la volentee et sachance des ditz marchantz Despaigne. Et leur fu respoundu qe le Roi vouldra maunder ses messages en Flandres as mestres marchanz et mariners Despaigne illeoqes certefiant qe les ditz niefs Despaigne demorassent en arrest a Sandwycz tanqe accord se feist parentre les messages Dengleterre et les ditz marchantz Despaigne des amendes touchantz les marchantz Dengleterre.

Item supplient les ditz messages Despaigne qe puis qe plesant soit au Roi et son bon Counsail qe bon amour unite et accord y soit continue enuers les ditz marchantz Despaigne durant les trieues qe maunde soit et crie par toutz les portz et hauenes es costeres Dengleterre qe nul Engleys face moleste greuance ne destourbance as ditz mestres marchantz et mariners durant le temps des trieues alant ne venant einz qils puissent marchander sanz estre empeschez par malice ou tort faire leur busoignes par mier et par terre come ils ont fait deuant ces heures en temps de trieues.

[2.] Cest la response donee depar le counseil du Roi de France et Dengleterre a Iohan Gonsales de la Caleza, Iohan Martines de Lougha et Pierres Lopes de Leghesenal messages enuoies en Engleterre depar la communiaulte des marchauntz maistres des niefs et marines du realme de Castelle et de la Countee de Viscaye.

Verite est qe bones trieues estoient nadgairs acordees et prises entre le Roi de France et Dengleterre et le Roi de Castelle et de la countee de Viscaye et les subgiz dune partie et dautre tant par terre come par meer durables par lespace de vynt auns par manere et forme comprise en les dites trieues, les queles le dit Roi de France et Dengleterre ad toutdys depuis bien et loialment fait garder pur sa partie et les gardera en apres en cas qe bone amende et satisfaccion lui soit fait et a ses subgiz des homicides roberies perdes et damages des niefs biens et marchandises qil eut suffert de leur[2] partie dedeins les ditz trieues par les gentz du Roialme de Castelle et Countee de Viscaye, qar en la dite trieue il ont par diuerse foitz robbe en lour portz et ailleurs sur sa meer aucunes[3] les gentz de la citee de Loundres et de la ville de Bristuyt et autres pluseurs et pris touz lours biens niefs et marchandises tuez les gentz et emprisonez et se sont vnqores en prison et malement tretez a Sybille[4] cinque persones marchantz de la dite ville de Bristuyt, les quielx damages perdes et vylenies le Roi ad bonement toutdys suffert en ferme esperance dauoir ev redresse et amendement por le quele ses ditz subgiz ont par diuerses foitz longement pursuy par deuers le Roi don Pierro et les gentz de la dite countee de Viscaye a lours tresgrantz traualx perils et coustages. Et

[1] Bristol.
[2] Altered from 'sa'.
[3] 'aucunes' interlined.
[4] Seville.

combien qe le dit Roi don Perro ait souent par ses letres et messages promis au dit Roi du [*sic*] France et Dengleterre qe ses subgiz deussent faire amende et satisfaccion des perdes et damages dessusditz neantmeins rien de ce na este fait tanque en cea einz pluis duretees domages et vilenies encontre le Roi et ses subgiz ont estez ia de nouel faitz et attemptez a Sibille et ailleurs par les gentz de Castelle en preiudice des ditz trieues et contre la fourme dycelles dont le dit Roi de France et Dengleterre voiant et considerant qil ne pourra par nulle voie failler a ses ditz subgiz de justice a leur grieue complainte criantz et pursuantz continuelment deuers li et ore tard en son pleine parlement requerrantz justice et amendement des robberies homicides restitution des persones par tiele manere emprisonez et des damages greuances et perdes deuantditz en sur toutes les dites choses ouesque les prelatz piers seignurs grantz et sages de son Roialme pleine deliberacion et auisement semble a eulx qe la dite amende et satisfaccion doura preceder auant ce que larrest fait en son realme sur aucuns des niefs biens et marchandies Despaigne se deura par aucune voie relesser. Mais a quiele heure que la dite satisfaccion et amende soit faite en maniere deue et si come a faire serra de raison le Roi des lours tantost oustera la main du dit arrest et ferra lealment garder et tenir meismes les trieues en toutz pointz si auant come il appartient a sa partie. Et ferra semblablement le dit Roi de France et Dengleterre por li et ses subgiz souffisant redresce et amendement a celi ou a ceulx de Castelle et de la dite Countee de Viscaye si aucune chose soit trouee mesprise ou attemptee de sa partie en preiudice ou en countre la forme des trieues auantditz. Si sont les dessusnomez messagerz assez pleinement enformez par escript des aucunes greuances homicides robberies vilenies perdes et damages sustenuz et encourruz de la partie Dengleterre encontre meismes les trieues par ceulx de Castielle et de Viscaye dont lon monstrera lealment et de bone foi et sicome a faire serra et le Roi de France et Dengleterre serra toutdis prest et apparillez de faire droit et equite tant a lune partie come a laultre sil en soit sur ce requis. Donne a la Cite de Loundres le xviij. iour de Iuyllet lan de grace Mille .ccc. soixante neof.

[*Endorsed in a modern hand*] xviij Iulij 1369 Anno 44 E. 3. Querimonia Mercatorum de Viscay facta de navibus suis arrestatis apud Sandwic durantibus treugis.

Responsio

Amendas faciant Mercatoribus London' Bristoll' et aliis pro consimilibus arestis et pro murdris hominum suorum et dimittentur.

APPENDIX II

A Journal of the Clerk of the Council during the Fifteenth and Sixteenth Years of Richard II.[1]

(Endors.) Acta Consilii, Anno xv^{mo}. [Jan. 20, 1392.]

Le xxme iour de Ianuar lan etc. xvme feurent present le Chanceller,[2] le Tresorer,[3] leuesqe de Duresme, leuesqe de Cestre, le Seneschall,[4] E. Dalingrugg.

Et lors feurent presentz le maier viscontz et aldermans et recorder de Londres et y feust rehercez coment ceux de Londres ne volent obeier au comandement du Chanceller sanz ce qe le maier enuoie celuy qi doit venir deuant le Chanceller. Et a ce feust responduz par les maier et les autres susditz qils ount franchise qe nul de la Citee doit estre arrestuz sanz assent du maier ou de ses ministres mes qant le Roi ou le Chanceller ou le Conseil enuoie pur aucun persone de la Citee par garnissement dun sergeant ou dautre il soloit venir a luy et ne doit en ce disobeir en celle partie.[5] Londres.

Item lors le maier de Londres William Venour Iohan Haddeley et Simon de Blakeborn ont empris pur William Brian chiualer de ly avoir deuant le Conseil de iour en iour par viij iours prochein ensuantz chescun corps pur corps et sur peine de mille liures. Brian.

Item illeoqes le Tresorer reporta depar le Roy qil voet qe leuesqe de Seint[6] Assaph son confessour eit du regard tout lestor des biens et chateux de la priorie de Clatford aliene et aussi qil eit pardon de xx *li.* qe coergent en demande sur mesme leuesqe en lescheqer de Cestre en recompensacion de ce qe mesme leuesqe doit prendre du Roy a cause de soun office de confessour de temps passe encea.[7] Confessour.

Le xxij. iour de Ianuer lan etc. xv. feurent presentz le Chanceller, le Euesqe de Wincestre, leuesqe de Duresme, le Tresorer, Dalingrugg, Stury.

Et lors estoit rehercez par Dalingrugg qe le Chanceller qe darrein estoit et les Seignurs du Conseil feurent en cause qe lestatut fet contre les prouisours feust fet et a lour procurement maintenuz et qe mestre William Menuse disoit ce deuant les messages du pape. Et a ce disoit le dit William qil en presence del Abbe message du pape disoit Menuse.

[1] The roll is found in *Council and Privy Seal*, file 3; *ante*, p. 389.
[2] Thomas Arundel, archbishop of York, chancellor, 1391–6.
[3] John Waltham, bishop of Salisbury, treasurer, 1391–5.
[4] Sir John Devereux, steward of the household, 1384–93.
[5] Such writs were directed to the mayor. For example, *Cal. Patent Rolls*, 15 Ric. II, 456.
[6] This word is repeated. In many points the work shows signs of haste and even of carelessness.
[7] See *Cal. Patent Rolls*, 15 Ric. II, 18.

qe vn Stoket[1] clerc de leuesqe de Wyncestre qest auriculier a luy purroit grandement eider la promocion de la matere touchant le pape. Et plus en effect il ne voloit confesser. Et outre ce il confessa deuant Seyuyle qe le Euesqe de Saresbury estoit tenu le plus suspect persone en Engleterre de la fesure de le dit estat. Et Seyuile sergeant deuant le Conseil disoit y ce mesme. Et purtant le dit William soy humblast au Chanceller et a leuesqe de Saresbury empriant qils luy voloient pardoner. Et sur ce il iura a les Seintz qil ne desclandra en temps auenir aucun Seignur du Royaume en la Courte de Rome par lettres ne autrement.[2]

Cestre. Item lors estoit le Conseil assentuz qe ceux de Cestreshire qi sont dettours au Roy en troys mille marcz a cause de lour chartre confermez sur lour franchises aueront du grace delay de lour paiement cestassauoir de paier a la feste de Seint Gregoire a Londres mille marcs et a la feste de Seint George mille marcs et a la feste de Seint Iohan Baptistre mille marcs.[3]

Le xxiij. iour de Ianuer lan etc. xv. feurent presentz le Chanceller, le Tresorer, leuesqe de Wyncestre, leuesqe de Duresme, leuesqe de Cestre, le Seneschall, le Souz Chamberlain,[4] E. Dalingrugg et Stury, et les Iustices et sergentz du Roy.

Deuonshire. Et lors estoit accordez qe lettres deuient estre faitz au Conte de Deuen de luy faire venir deuant le Conseil pur respondre sur certeines materes qe luy serront exposez. Et ce en soun ligeance et sur peine de qantqe il purra forfaire enuers le Roy et qil amesne auec luy Robert Yo soun seruant sur mesme la peine a ieody prochein apres la Chandelure. Et qe vn autre brief soit fet a monsire William Greneville visconte de Deuonshire de venir a mesme le iour sur mesme la peine.[5]

Le xxiiij. iour du dit mois feurent presentz lerceuesqe de Deuelyn, leuesqe de Wyncestre, leuesqe de Cestre, E. Dalingrugg, et Richard Stury, le Seneschall, le Souz chamberlain.

Deodande. Et lors estoient presentz les maier et viscontes de Londres et feust touchez depar Richard Hamme et Thomas Tyle[6] contre les ditz viscontz dun vessell apellez Lyhzter[7] qe feust forfait au Roy qe feust donez a les ditz Richard et Thomas come dieudande tanqe a la value de xx marcs. Et feust vn brief directe as viscontz pur paier les xx marcs par la ou le vessell ne vault la moyte. Et purtant il convient qe le vessell a eux soit donez ou autrement lexecucion de mesme le brief ne purroit estre fet sanz que preiudice de mesmes les viscontes qi sont chargez par mesme le brief de respondre du surplus quel chose serroit aussi encontre le Roy par cause qe en tiel cas le Roy ne purroit doner tiels forfaitures come deudandes. Sur quel

[1] This word is interlined and is not quite clear ; it may be 'Sto*f*et'.
[2] Such a pardon is found in *Cal. Patent Rolls,* 18 Ric. II, 446.
[3] See *Cal. Patent Rolls,* 15 Ric. II, 77–8.
[4] Sir Thomas Percy. The increasing importance of the sub-chamberlain at this time is very noticeable.
[5] *Cal. Patent Rolls,* 15 Ric. II, 24, 82.
[6] King's esquires and servants. *Cal. Patent Rolls,* 16 Ric. II, 162.
[7] Or 'Lyghter'. *Cal. Patent Rolls,* 15 Ric. II, part i, 508 ; part ii, 36.

chose les ditz viscontes ont en charge de monstrer le dit brief venderdy prochein au fin qe le Conseil ent purra ordeiner ce qe lour semblera melx le quiel brief est baille au Conseil du Roy le dit venderdy.

Le xxv. iour de Ianuer lan susdit feurent presentz le Chanceller, leuesqe de Duresme, le Seneschall, monsire Iohan Cobeham, E. Dalingrug.

Et lors estoit Iohan Arundell iure de dire la veritee disoit qil oyst qe vn Sire William Brun chiualer feust armez en les costes de Cornewaill qant William Wolley officer du Roy feust batuz par cause qil fist soun deuoir touchant larest des biens duz au Roy par cause de wrek. Wrek.

Le xxvj. iour de dit moys feurent presentz lerceuesqe de Dyuelyn, leuesqe de Wyncestre, leuesqe de Cestre, Dalingrugg et Stury, leuesqe de Duresme, le Seneschall, le Sire de Cobeham.

Et lors le dit Iohan Arundell porta au Conseil et lessa en escrit certeins articles touchant la matere du wrek susdit si auant come il sciet dire par vertue de son serement fet paramont. Wrek.

Item le Conseil commanda a monsire Iohan Peytew[1] souz Mareschal de deliuerer certeines persones par lui emprisonez contre le mande des commissioners du Conestable. Et qil eit vn iour de respondre sur le contempt fet au Roy. Souz Mareschal.

Item le dit xxvj. iour de Ianuer feust rehercez par le Seneschall coment le Roy estoit en volentee de doner a ses seruantz de deodaunde susdit xx marcs. Et purtant qe tielx deodandes deiuent estre donez dalmoigne et noun pas pur aucun seruice il semble au Chanceller qil est expedient qe le Roy de soun tresor doigne *cs.* as ses seruantz susditz par manere come le vessell estoit prise. Et qe le Roi doigne as poures aillours le deodaunde come lordenance de tielx deodandes demande. Et qe ce soit fet sil plese au Tresorer qant il vendra. Et qant a ce qe feut dit pur la partie de ceux de Londres par Shidworth qe tielx deodandes come eschetes deiuent a eux appartenir par cause qe le cas feust chieu deinz lewe de Tamys deinz lour franchise. Et a ce feust responduz par le Chanceller qe ceux de Londres naueront nulle forfaiture si noun pur trespas et purtant nulle instance feust fete en celle demande. Deodande.

Item qant as viures de bles a envoier a Burdeux il semble au Chanceller qe come plusours toneulx de frument sount envoiez a celles parties del an darrein passe et de cest an come apert de record en la Chancellerie qe lon serroit bien auisez combien soit a deliuerer a eux pendant de la chiertee des blees. Et il semble qil est expedient descrire a ceux de Bordeux lour certifiant combien des frumentz ad estez envoiez a eux et sils ont receuez a tant qil purroit suffire sanz auoir plus. Et qe le Conestable de Burdeux certifiez le Conseil combien soit venuz illeoqes. Et en cas qe ce ne purra suffire le Roy voet qils seient refresshez du frument. Sur ceste manere serra touche au Tresorer et alors serra response donez. Burdeux.

Le xxvij. iour du dit moys feurent presentz lerceuesqe de Dyuelin, leuesqe de Wyncestre, leuesqe de Duresme, le Tresorer, Dalyngrugg et Stury, leuesqe de Cestre, le Chanceller.

[1] Or *Peyto*.

Bochiers. Et lors touchant la Bocherie de Londres feust response donez par le Conseil qil plest bien a mesme le Conseil qe les Bochers soient aisez de lesser les issues des bestes ou ils soloient parentre cy et le prochein Conseil qe serra lundy a viij iours apres la Chandelure. Et qe le maier et viscontes soient le meene temps auisez de doner lour bone auys au Roy et a soun Conseil alors coment bonne ordenance purra estre fet pur les Bochers selonc leffect de lestatut ent fet le quele estatut demande qe ordenance se face deuant les Cendres prochein venant.

Deodande. Item touchant le deodaunde par cause qe len dit qe le vessell vault plus qe *cs.* le Conseil voet qe lundy prochein soit le vessel veue et alors le Conseil savisera q sur ce soit affaire.

Deuereux. Item lors estoit accordez qe monsire I. Louell I. Deuereux Seneschal et autres soient deschargez de la ferme de certeines terres et tenementz qe feurent au Conte de Penbrok et ce par cause qe le Conseil estoit certeinement enformez qils ne se ont mellez de mesme la ferme einz qe les ministres du Roy soient chargez de respondre pur les issues de mesmes les terres et tenementz.

Brian. Item monsire William Brian feust meinpris par les ditz persones tanqe a le prochein Conseil qe serra lundy a viij iours apres la Chandelure.

Le xxix. iour de Ianuer lan etc. xv. feurent presentz le Chanceller, le Tresorer, leuesqe de Duresme, leuesqe de Cestre, le Seneschall, Clifford, Dalingrugg, Stury, le Conte Darundell, le Sire de Cobeham.

Le darrein iour du dit moys feurent presentz le Chanceller, [1] leuesqe de Duresme, lerceuesqe de Dyuelyn, leuesqe de Wyncestre, leuesqe de Cestre, E. Dalingrugg.

Arundell. Et lors estoit present le Conte Darundell a cause du seel de ceux de Pruse et le busoigne feust continuez au fin qe le Conte de Arundell admiral puisse prouer qe le seel pris estoit des biens des ennemys.

[February 3, 1392.] Le iij. iour de Feuerer lan susdit feurent presentz le Chanceller, leuesqe de Duresme, leuesqe de Wyncestre, le Conte Darundell, E. Dalingrugg, R. Stury.

Le viij. iour de Feuerer lan susdit feurent presentz le Chanceller, le Tresorer, leuesqe de Wyncestre, leuesqe de Cestre, Dalingrugg, Stury, leuesqe de Duresme, le Sire de Roos, monsire William Beuchamp, et les Iustices et sergeantz du Roy.

Forfaiture des draps mottlees. Et lors estoit assentuz qe Lowys de Port Lumbard soit deschargez de xviij draps motlees mys a vent en Londres sanz le seal de laulner a ce qest dit par cause qil ad offert de paier synk marcs al eops du Roi pur eschuir le trial.

Le x. iour de Feuerer lan etc. xv. feurent presentz leuesqe de Duresme, leuesqe de Cestre, E. Dalingrugg. Et touz les Iustices.

Gloucestre. Et lors estoit la lettre touchant le duc de Gloucestre sur leschange de la priorie de Okkeborn pur la priorie de Takkeley commys a les Iustices pur ent estre auisez pur le Roy et pur certifier le Conseil.

Hampton.[2] Item lors estoit parlez de les biens et marchandises venantz au port de Hampton des queux aucuns feurent illeoqes deschargez et

[1] A space is left here. [2] Southampton.

custumez et des queux aucuns feurent cariez par la mere a Londres et custumez au dit port et combien qe le marchant eit monstrez a Londres soun coket de mesmes les biens custumez nientmoins celle coket ne purra estre allouez a Londres sanz ce qe ce soit declarez par le Conseil qe soit affaire.

Mestre Richard Mey lors estoit deuant le Conseil et les Iustices et respondist sur ce qil doit auoir fet et attemptez contre lestatut et iura destre deuant le Conseil de temps en temps selonc ce qil serreit garniz dattendre lour auys et ordenance en celle partie. Et soun frere iura y ce mesmes et emprist pur les auoir ensi deuant le Conseil. Mey.

Le xij. iour de Feuerer lan etc. xv. En presence du Roi esteantz illeoqes lerceuesqe deuerwyk, lerceuesqe de Dyuelin, le duc de Guyene,[1] le duc deuerwyk, leuesqe de Duresme, leuesqe de Wyncestre, leuesqe de Cestre, le Tresorer, leuesqe de Hereford, leuesqe de Cicestre, le Conte de Derby, le Conte de Rutland, le Conte de la March, le Conte de Huntyngdon, le Conte Mareschall, le Conte de Deuonshire, le Seneschall, le Souz Chamberlain, le Sire de Roos, le Sire de Burnell, le Sire de Louell, le Sire de Cobeham, monsire Edward Dalingrugg, monsire A. de Veer, monsire R. Stury.

Estoit accordez qe le dit duc de Guyene, leuesqe de Duresme, le Conte de Huntyndon, le Sire de Cobeham, monsire Thomas Percy, et mestre Richard Romhale deiuent aler pur traiter auec les Franceays. Et qils serront a la meer sur lour passage le iour de Cendres au fin qils puissent assembler auec le Roy Franceays lundy prochein deuant la dymy quaresme.[2] France.

Le xiij. iour du dit moys. En presence du Roy esteantz illeoqes les Seignurs desus escritz, lerceuesqe de Canterbirs, le duc de Gloucestre, monsire William Beauchamp, monsire William Brian, monsire Iohan Stanley, monsire Nichol Sharesfeld, monsire Baudewyn Bereford, monsire William Elmham, monsire Lowys Clifford, monsire Iohan Godard, le Sire de Harington, monsire Iohan Kentwode.

Estoit accordez qe Commissions soient fetz as sergeantz du Roy sur enquere de touz les Niefs et vesseulx qe purront estre assembles pur la guerre et qe les Owners soient chargez de faire lour Niefs et vesseulx prestz et apparaillez et qils soient mys a flote issint qils soient prestz dassembler as lieux a assigner qant ils serront garniz. Et le Roy est en propoos de aler as parties de dela apres ces presentes trieus finiz en cas de guerre. Et purtant le Roy et son Conseil sont assentuz qe briefs serront directes as viscontes pur faire proclamer qe touz les liges du Roy soient arraiez darmure et darcherie selonc lour estatz si qe ils soient prestz daler auec le Roy en ses guerres qant ils serront garniz en cas de guerre. Et qe certeines suffissantes persones soient esluz par le Conseil du Roy estre Commissioners en chescun contee pur enquerre de la nombre de gentz darmes et darchiers qe purront estre arraiez pur la guerre et pur dordeiner qe mesmes les gentz soient prestz arraiez et monstrez pur aler auec le Roy qant Ordenance pur la guerre.

[1] This was one of the titles of John of Gaunt.
[2] *Foedera* (Orig. Ed.), vii. 738.

ils serront garniz. Et qe mesmes les Commissioners certifient le Roy et soun Conseil de le nombre des gentz qe purront estre trouez pur la guerre.[1]

Chiualers faire.

Item qe proclamacion soit fet qe ceux qe ont terres rentes et tenementz a la value de xl*li*. par an soient fetz Chiualers entre cy et la Trinitee selonc lestatut ent fet.

Langeley.

Item qe le Roi auera soun bargain en le parc de Langeley en Contee de Kent a leops de Caleys sinoun qe le Roi achate le parc oue les membres.

Touchant lestaple.

Item le dit xiij. iour estoit accordez qe les marchandz Engleys qe voulent passer auec lour leins tout droit a Caleys puissent passer sanz paier en Engleterre les deuoirs de Caleys parensi qils trouent seuretee par lour obligacion et serement demesne qils paieront a Caleys mesmes les deuoirs et qils paieront a le voillon du Roi ce qe est ordeinez destre paiez selonc lestatut fet en le darrein parlement.[2]

Item combien qe les ditz marchantz soloient paier pur mesmes les deuoirs cestassauoir pur chescun saak dys et neof deniers nientmoins estoit accordez par assent et instance de certeins marchantz qe serra paiez tant soulement pur le saak viij*d*. et autre pur lafferant des leyns selonc le poys du surplus soient les ditz leyns amesnez a Caleys ou a aucun autre lieu hors du Roiaume.

Item lors estoit accordez qe les leyns puissent estre amesnez a les portz du Roiaume forspris le port de Londres sanz venir a les villes ou citees selonc ce qestoit ordonnez en le darrein parlement. Et ce pur le profit du Roy consideree le grand passage des leyns qe se ferroit par celle cause. Et qe les maires de lestaples soient deputez sur les portz.

Item qe les marchantz puissent faire passer lour leyns hors du Roiaume pensi qils soient obligez et iurez mesmes de faire porter a le Boillon ce qest ordeinez come desus ou autrement qils paieront as Custumes en partie du paiement de les custume et subside dor au tiel value qe le Roy responde resonablement pur ce qe luy est duz selonc lestatut.

Item qe les leyns puissent estre amesnez sibien as portz de Gypeswick, Lenne, et Melcombe, come as autres portz du Roiaume non obstant aucune ordenance fet a contraire.

Le xv[me] iour de Feuerer. En presence du Roy, esteants illeoqes lerceuesque de Canterbirs, lerceuesqe Deuerwyk, lerceuesqe de Dyuelyn, les troys ducs, leuesqe de Duresme, leuesqe de Londres, leuesqe de Wyncestre, leuesqe de Seint Dauid, leuesqe de Cestre, leuesqe de Saresbirs, leuesqe de Hereford, leuesqe de Cicestre, le Conte de Derby, le Conte de Rutland, le Conte de Arundell, le Conte de Huntyndon, le Conte Mareschall, le Conte de Deuenshire, le Seneschall, le Souz Chamberlain, le Sire de Roos, le Sire de Harington, le Sire de Cobeham, monsire Aubrey de Veer, monsire E. Dalingrugg, monsire Richard Stury, monsire Iohan Fallesley.

Asseurance fet au Roy.

Et lors feurent touz les seignurs desusescritz asseurez au Roy par

[1] These commissions of array were appointed on March 1. *Cal. Patent Rolls*, 88–95.

[2] The staple was removed from Calais to England by the Statute, 14 Ric. II. The council adds the following details.

manere qe sensuist. Les troys vncles du Roi, les prelatz, et autres seignurs desusescritz ont promys en bone foy et sont asseurez au Roy en sa meyn qils serront desore en auant loialx subgitz a luy, et ne ferront riens par fort main en priue ne en apert par eux ne par nul de siens qe serra encontre le Roy ne aucun seignur encontre seignur ne contre le people par oppression sinoun par la ley. Et si par auenture aucun seignur ou autre de qeconqe estat face au contraire, qe toutz les seignurs serront auec le Roy en afforcement de luy pur compeller le desobeisant de obeir au Roy et a ses leys. Et si par cas aucun seignur se sente greuez par aucuny,[1] il ne prendra redresse par force encontre la ley einz il pursuira la comune ley ou il se compleindra au Roy pur ent auoir redresse et remede, issint qe les leys du Roialme puissent estre meenes parentre le Roy et ses liges de qeconqe estat. Et dautre part le Roy en plein confort de ses seignurs et dautres ses liges de sa propre volentee et de bon cuer pur norir bone et entiere dilection en son Roiaume ad promys en parole du Roy qil ne ferra null mal ne damage a nul seignur ne a nul autre de ses liges pur nul chose qad este fet auant ces heures dont il auoit cause destre moeuez encontre eux ou aucun de eux. Et qil nest pas sa entencion de restituer aucune persone de ceux qi sont forsiuggez en plein parlement a son Roiaume ne a aucun lieu appurtenant a sa corone. Et ceste asseurance feust fet a Westm' le dit xv. iour de Feuerer lan M[l]CCC et iiij[xx] xij[me], Indiction xv[me], lan du pape Boneface ix[me] tierce. Esteantz illeoqes mestre Edmonsde de Stafford Gardein du priue seal et mestre Richard Romhale doctor es leys et plusours autres et moy I. Prophete.

Item lors estoit accordez qe les custumers soient deschargez par le serement de eux et des contreroullours des biens custumez deuant ces heures qe feurent rechargez en petitz vesselx et amesnez par la meer as autres portes de Roiaume combien qils ne feurent cokkettez par especiale declaracion de mesmes les biens. Et aussi estoit ordeinez qe les custumers desore en auant ne soient deschargez sur lour acconte en cas semblable sinoun qe tielx biens ensi custumez et rechargez soient cokkettez et declarez en les cokkettez et aussi la Nief en quel ils serront portez as autres portz. Custumers.

Item le xiiij. iour de Feuerer.[2] En presence du Roy feurent presentz lerceuesqe de Canterbirs, lerceuesqe deuerwyk, le duc de Guyene, le duc de Gloucestre, leuesqe de Duresme, leuesqe de Wyncestre, leuesqe de Cestre, leuesque de Saresbirs, leuesqe de Hereford, le Conte Darundell, le Conte de Deuenshire, le Sire de Cobeham, le Seneschall, le Sire de Grey, E. Dalingrugg, R. Stury, E. Depuis lerceuesqe de Dyuelin, le Conte Mareschall, le Souz Chamberlain, leuesqe de Cicestre, monsire A. de Veer, le Sire de Roos, monsire William Elmham.

Et lors estoit accordez qe ceux qont terres et tenementz a la value de xl *li*. par an soient fetz chiualers selonc lestatut.[3] Chiualers.

[1] auenny (?). [2] The record of February 14 follows that of February 15.

[3] Distraint of knighthood, imposed upon men with an income of £20 or £40, was a measure that the government frequently resorted to, but I do not know of any statute to this effect. Stubbs, *Const. Hist.*, § 239.

Lestatut. Item lors estoit accordez sur les articles touchantz la modificacion et soeffrance sur lestatut de prouisours.[1] Et qant a les prouisions qe len purra accorder qe le pape doigne la tierce foiz par voie dexpectation ou par mort de ceux qe deiuent en la Courte de Rome parensi qe le patron puisse doner les deux primers foiz. [Et][2] si ce ne purra estre acceptez par le message du pape [3] en purra accorder qe le pape dorra la seconde fois parensi s [3] veulle soeffrer les patrons doner le primer foiz p [3] checun vsera son temps quelqe benefice q [3] voudra soit il grand ou petit.

Le xvj. [iour de Feuerer] lan etc. xv. En presence du Roy feurent presentz lerceuesqe de Canterbirs, lerceuesqe Deuerwyk, lerceuesqe de Dyuelin, le duc de Gyene, leuesqe de Duresme, leuesqe de Londres, leuesqe de Wyncestre, leuesqe de [Ce]stre, leuesqe de Saresbirs, leuesqe de Hereford, leuesqe de Cicestre, le [Con]te darundell, le Conte Mareschall, le Conte de Deuenshire, le Seneschall, le Sire de Cobeham, le Sire de Grey, le Souz Chamberlain, le Sire Louell, monsire E. Dalingrugg.

Tretee de pees. Et lors estoit parlez de linstruction donez a monsire de Guyene et as autres envoiez pur le tretee de pees. Et le duc de Gloucestre estoit assentuz qe les marches de Caleys deyuent estre tenuz de la Corone de France par bone moderacion come les autres seignurs feurent accordez pardeuant en cas qe len ne purra meulx faire.

Item le xvij. et le xviij. iours de Feuerer estoit la matere touchant lestatut attainez parentre le Conseil et Damyan.[4]

Le xix. iour de mesme le moys et le xx. iour aussi feust parlez de lestatut parentre le Conseil et le dit Damyan. Et feurent illeoqes le Chanceller, le Tresorer, leuesqe de Wyncestre, leuesqe de Duresme, leuesqe de Seint Dauid, leuesqe de Cestre, leuesqe de Hereford, E. Dalingrugg, et R. Stury.

Touchant lestatut. Et lors feurent les iiij articles principalx sur les modificacions fetz sur lestatut declarez au dit Damyan par le Chanceller par assent du Conseil. Et feust protestez par le Conseil qen cas qe le dit Damyan ne veulle accorder sur mesmes les modificacions qe le Roy et son Conseil serront a lour large et si franks come ils feurent auant la declaracion de mesmes les quatre articles. Et lors feust monstrez la Bulle du pape Innocent au dit message touchant les franks elections, et aussi la copie dune autre bulle de mesme le pape touchant le grant du pape qe les esperituels patrons puissent disposer de lour benefices. Et mesme le message ent demanda la copie pur estre meulx auisez.

Item mesme le iour apres manger a les Frerers feurent presentz le Chanceller, le Tresorer, leuesqe de Wyncestre, leuesqe de Duresme, le Seneschall, le Sire Louell, le Sire de Cobeham, E. Dalingrugg, et R. Stury.

Regraterie. Et lors estoit accordez qe garrant soit fet as maire et viscontes de Londres pur faire proclaimer qe nul alien achate et engrosse les

[1] *Statutes of the Realm*, 13 Ric. II, 2, pp. 68–74.
[2] The manuscript is torn here. [3] The manuscript is torn here.
[4] No doubt the statute of *praemunire*, 16 Ric. II. James Dardani, as the name usually appears, was the papal nuntio and collector in England.

biens et marchandises du Roiaume pur les vendre arrier par voie de retaille as liges du Roiaume par cause qils ont mys pleusours marchandises cestassauoir spicerie a plus haut pris qe ne feust deuant et bien pres a la double.

Item lors firent les messages daragoun lour message.[1] Aragoun.

Item le xx. iour de Feuerer feurent presentz lerceuesqe deuerwyk, leuesqe de Wyncestre, leuesqe de Saresbirs, leuesqe de Duresme, leuesqe de Cestre, leuesqe de Hereford, le Souz Chamberlain, Dalingrugg et Stury.

Et lors estoit accordez qe le visconte deuerwyk eit pardon de xl*li.* de ce qe coergent en demande sur luy en soun acconte. Viscont deuerwyk.

Item xxj. iour du dit moys feurent presentz le Chanceller, le Tresorer, leuesqe de Wyncestre, leuesqe de Cestre, leuesqe de Hereford, le Souz Chamberlain, Louell, E. Dalingrugg.

Et lors estoit accordez qe le visconte de Surr' eit pardon de xl*li.* a cause de perde en soun office. Viscont de Surr' et de Sussex.

Item lors feurent les articles touchantes les ordenances faitz par le Roy et soun grand Conseil accordez et amendez.[2]

Item feust accordez qe brief soit fet as Baillifs de Iernemuth qils facent endenture parentre eux et les Escoces de lour biens qe sont prises en le dit port et de la value diceulx et qe les biens soient bien gardez tanqe ils eient autre mandement du Roy et qils certifient le Conseil de les biens et de la value et qils lessent a large le Nief de Gaunker en quel mesmes les biens sont par cause qils sont noz amys. Escoce et Iernemuth.

Le xxij. iour de dit moys feurent presentz le Chanceller, leuesqe de Londres, leuesqe de Wyncestre, leuesqe de Duresme, leuesqe de Saresbirs, leuesqe de Cestre, leuesqe de Hereford, Louell, Stury, Dalingrugg, lerceuesqe de Dyuelin.

Et lors estoit accordez touchant Dauid Holgreue, cestasauoir qil eit xl*li.* pur les custages qil ad fet en une ferme quelle il ad lesse pur le profit du Roy.[3] Item qil ne soit enpeschez pur nul gast illeoqes. Item qe [4] Holgreue.

Item touchant leuesqe de Cestre et le piere de monsire E. Stafford, cestassauoir qe le dit Euesqe soit deschargez de cxxxiij*li.* vj*s.* viij*d.* qe coergent en demand sur luy en lescheqer. Cestre et Stafford.

Item le xxiij. iour de Feuerer lan etc. xvme feurent presentz leuesqe de Wyncestre, leuesqe de Cestre, R. Stury, le Chanceller, le Tresorer.

Item lors estoit response donez a la supplicacion touchant les molyns pres de Rothelane.[5] Molins.

Item le Conseil estoit assentuz qe le Priour et Couent de Bridelinton eient certeine franchise pur vn fin de C. marcs et pur xiij*s.* iiij*d.* apaier en lescheqer du Roy annuelement. Bridelinton.

[1] A safe conduct for the ambassadors of the king of Aragon. *Foedera* (Orig. Ed.), vii. 710.

[2] It is uncertain what ordinances are here referred to, but from all the circumstances they may have been the acts contained in Nicolas, i. 84–6.

[3] *Cal. Patent Rolls*, 38.

[4] The entry ends thus.

[5] Many items like this, by their lack of particular data, show that the record was not intended to be of a severely official character.

Le xxiiij. iour de Feuerer lan susdit feurent presentz le duc de Guyene, le Chanceller, le Tresorer, lerceuesqe de Dyueline, leuesqe de Wyncestre, leuesqe de Cestre, le Conte de Derby, le Souz Chamberlain, monsire E. Dalingrugg, et monsire R. Stury, monsire Lowys Clifford.

Irland. Et lors estoit rehercez a monsire de Guyene touchant le rescours de la terre dirland. Et sur ce le dit Duc dona son auys. Et disoit qe luy semble resonable et expedient qe aucun de la retenue de monsire de Gloucestre [1] auec vn petit poair soit envoiez a la terre dirland si en hast qe faire se purra ensemblement auec les officers de mesme le duc pur ordeiner pur la venue de luy et pur sauuer la terre a lour poair. Et qe celle envoie des gentz pur aler auant la venue de mesme le duc soit sibien as custages du dit duc come de Roy selonc ce qe purra estre accordez parentre mesme le duc et le Conseil du Roy. Et sur ce doit estre fet vne lettre de credence par sire I. Welingborn au fin qe mesme le duc veulle venir en sa persone pur auoir parlance auec le Conseil du Roy ou qe luy plese enuoier sa volentee et entent en celle matere par aucun de siens.

Retayl. Et estoit illeoqes accordez qe proclamacion doit estre fet par les maer et viscontes de Londres qe nul alien soit hardiz de achatier les marchandises en grosse pur mettre a vent par voie de retayl sur peine denprisonement et de faire fin et raunceon a la volentee du Roy.

Collinges. Item qe reprisail soit grantez a Nicol Collynges sur soun demand parensi qe garrant soit fet par brief du Roy pur surveer qe les biens qe serront pris de ceux de Plesavnce soient mys en sauue garde par endenture affaire parentre luy et ceux qi aueront la garde au fin qe le Roy puisse estre gardez sanz damage.[2]

Foix Item qe lettres soient fetz au Conte de Foix luy certifiant coment le tretee purparlez parentre luy et les comissairs du Roy nest pas si acceptable come vn autre qe serra exposez a luy par le viscont Dort et monsire William Lescrop et par mestre Raymond Gwilliam. Et qe autres lettres soient faitz a eux lour certifiant de la tretee qest reformez et qils facent affermer mesme le tretee.[3]

Viscontesse. Et aussi qe autres lettres soient fetz a la viscontesse de Castelleone qe le Roy ad parlez au duc de Guyene et il a sa venue ferra ce qe reson demande.

Ermynak. Item qe autres lettres soient faitz a monsire William Lescrop luy certifiant de le dit tretee parentre le Roy et le Conte de Foix. Et qe le William en mesme la manere puisse fere alliance parentre le Roy et le Conte dermynak ou meulz sil purra et qil sur ce certifie le Roy.[4]

Pruce. Item qe le iuggement donez encontre le Priourr de lospital et monsire Thomas Percy nadgairs Admiralx et les Capitains et lour soudeours pur la partie de Pruce soit mys en execucion au fin qe le Roi puisse estre repaiez de les M[l] *li.* queux il ad fet paier de son tresor a la dite partie de Pruce forspris la partie qe le Roy auoit pur

[1] *Foedera* (Orig. Ed.), vii. 718; *Cal. Patent Rolls*, 15 Ric. II, 86.
[2] *Cal. Patent Rolls*, 38.
[3] *Foedera* (Orig. Ed.), vii. 712.
[4] Ibid.

sa purpartie. Et en especial qe le Tresorer et Barons de lescheqer soient certifiez desouz le priue seal de les noms de ceux qe feurent en la dite viage des queux les noms fuerent mys en escrit et par les ditz Admiralx baillez au Conseil du Roy en descharge de mesmes les Admiralx au fin qe chescun de eux soit constreint de paier au Roy ce qil auoit receuz des biens des Pruciens auantditz.[1] L. Clifford. Pur le Roy.

Le xxv. iour de Feuerer a les Freres Precheours feurent presentz le Chanceller, le Tresorer, E. Dalingrugg, et Richard Stury.

Et lors estoit accordez qe Wauter Sibille eit du regard xl *li.* pur ses custages et traualx queux il ad eue et sustenuz entour les busoignes du Roy et sibien en Pruce come en Engleterre en pursuant enuers le Conseil du Roy pur lexploit des causes pendantz al pursuit des Pruciens.[2] Et aussi pur les custages et traualx queux il auera et sustiendra en pursuant deuant le Conseil mesmes les causes parentre cy et la Pentecost prochein avenir de la quele somme le dit Wauter serra paiez ou assignez meintenant de la moyte. Et de lautre moyte il serra paiez ou assignez apres la Pentecost susdit. Sibille.

Le iour des Cendres le xxviij. iour de Feuerer lan etc. xvme a les Freres feurent presentz le Chanceller, le Tresorer, leuesqe de Cestre, monsire E. Dalingrugg, R. Stury, lerceuesqe de Dyuelin.

Lors estoit accordez touchant lappropriacion grantez au Conte dArundell pur vn fin de cynk centz marcs. Arundell.

Item lors estoit accordez touchant la confirmacion des chartres des priour et couent de Bridelinton pur vn fin de c. marcs. Et qils eient nouelle franchise paiant au Roy annuelement xiij*s.* iiij*d.* Bridelinton.

Item lors estoit accordez qe monsire William Elmham soit deschargez de les apprestz par luy receuz a cause de la iourne qil fit en alant en Guyene du comandement du Roy et qil eit outre de regard pur mesme le viage cent liures.[3] Elmham.

Le primer iour de Marcz lan etc. xv. feurent presentz le Chanceller, le Tresorer, leuesqe de Cestre, E. Dalingrugg, et R. Stury. [March 1. 1392.]

Et lors estoit accordez qe Iohan Haddeley deit mettre a vent le deodande susdit a meulx qil sauera et qil eit garrant sur ce et de paier a les persones as queux le Roy dona mesme le deodande les deux parties et la tierce partie a celuy qi perdist le deodande.[4] Deodande.

Item lors estoit response donez as messages daragon [5] par manere come le duc de Guyene dona a eux reponse deuant le Roy a Eltham. Et si estoit accordez qe lettres deuient estre faites du priue seal au Roy darragon fesantes mencion de la requisicion fet par les ditz messages et de signifier a luy les damages des liges du Roy dengleterre fetz par ceux darragon luy requerant dent faire restitucion quele Aragon.

[1] On disputes with Prussia see *Cal. Patent Rolls*, 13–14 Ric. II, pp. 196, 372, 374.

[2] Sibell was one of the ambassadors to Prussia in 1388. *Foedera* (Orig. Ed.), vii. 581.

[3] Elmham was one of the commissioners appointed in 1391 to procure the adherence of the count of Armagnac and the lord of Lebret. *Foedera* (Orig. Ed.), vii. 693.

[4] A resumption of the business treated on January 23.

[5] Ambassadors of the king of Aragon. *Foedera* (Orig. Ed.), vii. 710.

restitucion fet le Roy dengleterre serra prest de faire droit et reson sur la request fet par les messages darragon.

North-umbr'. Item lors estoit response donez as peticions du Conte de Northumbr'.[1]

Lundy le iiij. iour de Marcz lan susdit a Retherhithe feurent presentz le Chanceller, le Tresorer, Stury, et le Gardein du priue seal.

Escoce. Et lors estoit accordez qe la Commission affaire a ceux qe irront en Escoce pur y estre mes Paske a le tretee soit fet a mesmes les persones entre queux soit le Clerc mestre Alein Newerk. Et en cas qil ne soit returnez en Engleterre[2] qe leuesqe de Cestre passe sanz autre clerc. Et combien qe monsire Richard Lescrop ne purra estre a mesme le iournez qe les autres nomez puissent proceder et deux de eux.

Elkyne. Item touchant Elkyne qe report soit fet au Roy pur ent sauoir sa volentee sil soit affaire qe elle eit vne certeine somme a vn foiz pur eschure le annuitee.[3]

Burnell. Item lors estoit accordez qe le Sire de Burnell eit vj*d.* le iour par voie de regard pur la garde de la Chastel de Bruggenorth et nemy par voie de gages come il ad demandez.

Le Meskurdi le vime iour de Marcz lan etc. xv. feurent presentz le Chanceller, le Tresorer, leuesqe de Cestre.

Irland. Et lors monsire Thomas Mortymer declara au Conseil du Roy la credence a luy donez par le duc de Gloucestre par le quele il desire dauoir sys centz marcs de regard pur ordeiner pur la saluacion de la terre de Irland deuant le temps a luy assignez par ses endentures parensi qil puisse auoir son paiement de x mille marcs au temps assignez et qil ne soit tenuz a nulle certeine nombre de gentz a trouer mes a sa discrecion. Et en cas qe la terre soit empeirez le moiene temps qil soit deschargez enuers le Roy. Et a ce le Conseil dona response qe sur ce le Roy serra certifiez et a plustost qe le Conseil soit certifiez de la volentee du Roy ils ent ferront assauoir au duc de Gloucestre susdit.

Euerwyk. Item lors estoit accordez qe le duc deuerwyke eit c. marcs annuelement en lescheqer en noun de ce qil auoit des tenementz de Iohan Northampton.[4]

Marschall. Item lors estoit accordez qe [5] Marchal eit [6]

Item le vij. iour de Marcz lan susdit feurent presentz le Chanceller, le Tresorer, leuesqe de Cestre.

Laundes. Lors le Tresorer reporta au Gardein de priue seal qe le Roy voet qe Piers Arnaud de Bearne Seneschal de Landes eit de doun de Roy cent marcs et vn hanap susorrez couenable pur son estat.

Edward Sergeant. Item les estoit accordez qe Edward Dee, Sergeant, eit vj*d.* le iour tanqe autrement soit purveut pur son estat a auoir et prendre les ditz vj*d.* le iour en lescheqer.[7]

[1] This may refer to a series of petitions on the part of the earl of Northumberland, in which he asks for reinforcements to guard the northern marches. *Ancient Petitions*, no. 11454.

[2] He was on a commission sent to France. *Foedera* (Orig. Ed.), vii. 709.

[3] Grant for life of £10 a year to Joan Elkyn of Aquitaine. *Cal. Patent Rolls*, 15 Ric. II, 42.

[4] The grant is found in *Cal. Patent Rolls*, 41.

[5] A space is left in the manuscript.

[6] The entry ends thus.

[7] This grant is in *Cal. Patent Rolls*, 37.

Item lors estoit accordez qe sire Thomas Stanley[1] eit xl. marcs pur la serche des munimentz en la Toure. Stanley.

Item qe Iohan Frankes clerc eit c*s*. par cause de certein approwement fet au Roy. Frankes.

Le xxvj. iour dauerill lan etc. xv. feurent presentz le Chanceller, le Tresorer, leuesqe de Duresme, le Seneschall, Dalingrugg, Stury. [April 26.]

Et lors estoit demandez sil serroit expedient qe Damyan passe hors du Roiaume pur faire relacion au pape sur soun message ou qe Emanuell soun fitz passe en soun noun par mesme la cause. Et feust responduz par le dit Conseil qil semble a eux qe meulx est qe Damyan remeigne deinz le Roiaume et qe le dit Emanuel eit le iournez. Et depuis a la feste de Wyndesor le Roy et les seignurs de soun Conseil feurent assentuz qe Damyan remeindra. Damyan.

Le darrein iour dauerill lan etc. xvme feurent presentz le Chanceller, le Tresorer, leuesqe de Cestre, le Seneschall, Dalingrugg.

Le primer iour de May lan etc. xv. feurent presentz le Tresorer, lerceuesqe de Dyuelin, leuesqe de Duresme, le Souz Chamberlain, E. Dalingrugg et R. Stury et leuesqe de Cestre. [May 1.]

Et lors estoit accordez qe ceux qi ent apportez en lour Niefs seel a la terre descoce sanz Congie du Roy puissent faire aisez fins auec le Tresorer pur lour trespas. Seel apportez a Escoce.

Le ij. iour de May lan xvme feurent presentz le Chanceller, le Tresorer, leuesqe de Duresme, leuesqe de Cestre, le Souz Chamberlain, Dalingrugg, Stury, Lowys Clifford.

Lors estoit accordez qe le viscont de Deuenshire eit pardon de xl *li*. Deuenshire.

Item estoit lors accordez qe Robert Carboneld viscont de Northfolk et Suffolk eit pardon de l *li*. xvij*s*. vj*d*. Northfolk.

Le iiij. iour de May feurent presentz le Chanceller, le Tresorer, leuesqe de Wyncestre, Dalingrugg.

Et lors estoit accordez qe les abbe et couent de Seint Austyn de Canterbirs soient deschargez de laport qe la maison paie en chescun voidance dycelle pur l. marcs annuelement a paier au Roy.[2] Augstyn Canterbirs.

Item qe labbe et couent de Wyggem(ore) puissent amortiser xx *li*. de terres qe ne sont tenuz en chief du Roy pur vn fin affaire en la Chancellerie.[3] Wyggem(ore).

Le vj. iour de May lan etc. xv. feurent presentz le Chanceller, le Tresorer, leuesqe de Londres, le Conte de Saresbirs, Dalingrugg.

Le vij. iour de May lan etc. xv. feurent presentz leuesqe de Wyncestre, leuesqe de Duresme, le Conte de Saresbirs, monsire R. Lescrop, Dalingrugg, Stury.

Lors estoit accordez qe vn brief soit fet a Thomas Midlinton de Southhampton qil soit deuant le Conseil le ieody prochein avenir a viij iours pur respondre sur certeins materes qe luy serront declarez de part le Roy sur peine de xl *li*. Southhampton Hanse

Item le dit vij. iour estoit accordez qe vn commission soit fet as Abbe de Seint Austyn et le priour de Canterbirs pur enquere de les Gelre.

[1] A clerk of the chancery. [2] *Cal. Patent Rolls*, 55. [3] Ibid. 60.

biens de ceux de la terre de Gelre[1] qe sont venuz en la Roiaume par wrek au fin qe les biens puissent estre sauuement gardez tanqe ce soit discussez a qy les biens deiuent estre de droit.[2]

Le viij. iour de May lan etc. xv. feurent presentz leuesqe de Wyncestre, le Conte de Saresbirs, Dalingrugg, Stury.

Newenton Southgales. Lors feust accordez qe ceux de Neweton en Southgales eit franchise destre iuggez par lour comburgeays par manere come ceux de Cardygan ont du grant du Roy. Et lors feust rehercez qe le temps qe ceux de Cardigan auoient lour grant en mesme la manere estoit grantez a ceux de Newenton par le Conseil qe lors estoit present.[3]

Le xiiij. iour de May lan etc. xvme feurent presentz le Tresorer, Dalingrugg et Stury.

Cairmerthin. Lors le Tresorer et les autres estoient accordez qe le Chamberlain de Southgales eit xx*li*. pur reparailler le Chastell de Kairmerthin par survew et contreroulement du prior de Cairmerthin.

Elmham. Item lors estoit accordez qe R. Elmham alant au Roy de Portug' auec les lettres de la prorogacion des treues eit de regard x*li*.

Wygg'. Item qe R. Wygg' soit receiuour de la seignurie de Hauerford tantcome plerra au Roy rendant soun accompt deuant les auditours du Roy en celles parties.[4]

Penros. Item qe commission soit fet a Iohan Penros destre Iustice de Southgales. Et vn autre commission a luy destre Iustice de la seignurie de Hauerford.[5] Et purtant il auera xl*li* et il auera regard a soun retour en cas qil se porte bien.[6]

Le Counseil retournez. [Dec. 11, 1392.] Le xj^me^ iour de Decembre lan etc. xvj. feurent presentz le Chanceller, le Tresorer, le Souz Chamberlain, monsire Lowys Clifford.

Et lors estoit le Priour de Seint Barth' de Loundres et se compleina de son vicaire de Seint Sepulcre de ce qil deust auoir empledez le dit Priour en la Court de Rome en causes ciuiles touchant la cognicion et iurisdiction temporele.

Franceys. Et illeoques feurent presentz Iohan Sibille et William Hide executours de dame Agnes Franceys et confessoient que vn obligacion feust fet come ils disoient pardeuant et que deux centz liures feurent duz par dame Agnes Franceys et ils quident que ce foiz feust due a R. Belknap. Et ils disoient que si Batesford veulle faire acquitance a mesmes les executours ils auec lour compaignons paierent la dite summe. Et desirent que lour coexecutours soient appellez de venir deuant le Conseil et pur estre respondentz ouesques eux de la dite somme. Et sur ce les ditz Iohan et William lun pur lautre estoient mainparnours en pein de M^l^*li*. de estre deuant le Conseil de iour en iour.[7]

[1] Gueldres.

[2] After this entry by a strange confusion there follow the proceedings of December 18.

[3] *Cal. Patent Rolls*, 63.

[4] Maurice Gwyn, however, is mentioned as receiver and steward of Haverford. *Cal. Patent Rolls*, 24, 56.

[5] Ibid.

[6] There was evidently a break in the sessions at this point. The two entries which follow are found at the end of the roll, but I have given them their proper chronological place.

[7] The original manuscript of the Franceys case, describing the procedure more in detail, will be reproduced in Appendix III, p. 517.

Le xviij. iour de Decembre lan etc. xvj. feurent presentz le Chanceller, le Tresorer, le Conte de Hunt', le Souz Chamberlain, monsire Lowys Clifford, leuesque de Seint Dauid, Dalingrugg.[1]

Le Tresorer estoit assentuz que Nikel Reyner aueroit xl marcs de regard pur son trauail en alant vers le duc Aubert de Bayuere en message du Roy. Nikel.

Item lors cstoit William Hide examinez de les biens que feurent al Prouincial des Freres Carmes.

Le lundy prochein deuant la Nowel le xxiij. iour de Decembre feurent presentz le Chanceller, le Tresorer, le Souz Chamberlain.

Et lors estoit assentuz que Iohan Candelesby eit [2] a terme de vie ou tanque il soit auance a benefice de Seinte eglise de la value de xl*li*.[3] Candelby.

Item lors estoit assentuz que garrant soit fet au Tresorer pur faire suffissant et resonable regard as chamberlains de Souzwales et de Cestre et de Northgales et a les Espies selonc la discrecion du Tresorer et de la date de la feste de Seint Michel darrein passez a Wodestok. Regard des chamberlains.

Item lors estoit assentuz que Iohan Aspilon eit dys liures a terme de vie ou tanque il soit auance a xl liures quel Wauter Tirell auoit par lettres patentes etc. Aspilon.

Le Samady prochein apres la Tyffain lan etc. xvj[me] feurent presentz le [4] le Tresorer, le Souz Chamberlain. [Jan. 11, 1393.]

Lors sire Iohan Cadyn de Goldhangre, Roger atte Bregge, Symon Perkyn de mesme le lieu par cause qils vendoient a Byryk Huissome certeins leins a le port de Maldon [5] sanz custume paier sount aiuggez a prison et chescun de eux ad fet fin de xl*s*. et le dit Byryk ad forfet les leins arrestuz et son neif. Nientmains a la reuerence de Duc Alberht de Holand le Roy ad pardone la forfaiture del nief. Et sur ce soit fet lettre as custumers en port de Maldon [5] pur respit de les leins forfaites et de deliuerer le nief a la reuerence du dit duc. Forfaiture des leins. Mallyng.

Le xvij. iour de Ianuer lan etc. xvj. feurent presentz le Chanceller, le Tresorer, le Seneschall, monsire Richard Stury, monsire Iohan Cobeham, et autres du Conseil du Conte de Glouc' qi feurent illeoques du comandement de mesme le Conte pur sauoir lauys du Conseil du Roy si le dit duc soit tenuz de acconter pur les deniers qil ad despenduz a cause de la viage Dirland la quele viage feust detourbez et contremandez par auys de Roy et de son Conseil. Et depuis vient monsire Thomas Percy. Gloucestr'.

Et lors estoit rehercez que le Roy estoit assentuz que le duc de Lanc' pur ses despenses a cause de le tretee du pees eit le iour de regard xx*li*. Et si par cas il eit tresgrand charge de ses despenses illeoques par aucune resonable cause que le Tresorer de Caleys lui face paiement de ce que lui busoignera pur le temps. Lanc'.

Item lors estoit assentuz et le dit duc de Glouc' estoit assentuz Glouc'.

[1] The last two membranes of the roll were put together in inverse order. I have arranged the items chronologically. [2] A space is left here.

[3] Grant to John Candlesby, clerk, of 100*s*. a year until promoted to a benefice worth £40. *Cal. Patent Rolls*, 209, 481. [4] A space is left here.

[5] Written over ' Mallyng ', but not altered in the margin.

dacconter sur les despenses susditz. Et demanda dauoir lettres du priue seal dacconte.

Item lors estoit assentuz que mesme le duc eit pur ses despenses a cause de la dite trettee x marcs le iour de regard. Et en cas quil supporte plus de charge par cause resonable qil eit plus de regard par auys du Conseil.

[Feb. 21, 1393.] Lendemein de Cendres lan etc. xvj. a Westm' feurent presentz le Chanceller, le Tresorer, leuesque de Duresme, leuesque de Seint Dauid, monsire E. Dalingrugg.

Percy. Et lors estoit accordez touchant monsire Henri Percy qil eit xx*li*. pur la reparacion de Chastelle de Cairlell par surveue du visconte de Cumberlande et aussi qil eit xj*li*. par mesme la cause par ses mains de la ferme de la gilde.

Mewe. Et aussi feust accordez que Thomas Mewe qi auera lannuite de c*s*. aprendre en lescheqer pur terme de sa vie en recompense de loffice de la baillie du hundrede de Ayhorw' en contee de Kent eit la patente affaire sanz fee paier pur le grand seal.[1]

Blount. Item lors estoit accordez que Wauter Blount eit pardon de xx*li*. de la somme de cc. marcs duz au Roy pur la garde et mariage du fitz et heir de monsire William Moton.[2]

The Great Council at Eltham, 19 *Richard II.*[3]

[July 22, 1395.] Le xxij. iour de Iuyl lan etc. xixme a Eltham en la presence du Roy feurent presenz lerceuesque de Canterbirs, le Chanceller, le Duc Deuerwik, leuesque de Londres, leuesque de Wyncestre, leuesque de Sar', leuesque de Chichestre, leuesque Dexcestre, leuesque de Waterford, le Conte de Derby, le Conte Darrundell, le Conte Doxenford, le Conte de Warr', le Sire de Cobeham, le [Sire de Despen] [4]ser, le Priour de lospital, le Seneschall, Stury, Waldegraue, Dru.

Et lors venerent les messages de la citee de Burdeux et presenterent au Roy lettres de credence desouz le seal de Burdeux et aussi certeines articles desouz mesme le seal concernantz la dite credence et aussi vne lettre patente desouz le dit seal contenante le tenour de les lettres patentes du Roy Edward touchant la duchee de Guyene. Et depuis ils presenterent vne copie contenante tout le fait parentre le Duc de Guyene et la citee de Burdeux fesant mencion du serement du Roy faite a la conseruacion de lour priuileges. Queles feurent baillies a les clercs deinz escritz pur lour ent auiser tanque lendemain et pur doner depuis sur ce lour bone auys.

Et lendemain illeoques deuant le Roy et les seignurs susditz ceux du Conseil de monseignur de Lancastre purposerent certeines matires

[1] *Cal. Patent Rolls*, 226.

[2] At this point the journal ends. The last membrane is endorsed, *Acta anno XV^{mo}*, and *Acta Consilii. Anno XVI^{mo}.*

[3] *Council and Privy Seal*, file 4. Froissart (*Chronicles*, chap. lxiv) gives a narrative of the event, which he assigns to the year 1394. The date in the record, however, is unmistakably 1395. A comparison of the two accounts has been made in chapter vi, p. 135.

[4] Faded and almost illegible.

pur iustisier la donacion du Roy et mistrent en auant en escrit lour euidences. Et depuis le Chanceller du commandement du Roy chargea mestre Iohan Barnet, mestre Michel Sergeaux, mestre Thomas Stowe, mestre Rauf Selby, mestre Richard Bownale doctours es loys sur lour lygeance qils doiuent au Roy de enformer le Roy et les seignurs de son Conseil esteantz illeoques si la donacion du Roy faite a monseignur de Guyene touchant la Duchee puisse restier en sa force sauuante lestat et honur du Roy et le droit de sa Corone, les queux clercs et chescun par soy disoient que attenduz que le Roy Edward par ses lettres patentes granta tiele priuilege as maire et iures de la citee de Burdeux qils serroient annexez et encorporez a la Corone Dengleterre et a la chambre du Roy et de ses heirs Roys Dengleterre et que mesme la citee ne serroit alienee a loeps main ou proprietee dautri sinon a leysne heir du Roy et aussi attenduz que le Roy qor est iura par son procursur de conseruer mesme le priuilege, le Roy est tenu de reuoker la dite donacion faite a monseignur de Lancastre et de tenir et conseruer le priuilege susdit et son serement noun obstant aucunes aligaciones sur ceo faites par ceux du Conseil de monseignur de Lancastre. Et puis apres touz les ditz seignurs examinez sur celle partie chescun par soy saccorderent a les clercs susditz en effect. Et monseignur de Gloucestre saccorda a ycelle sur tiele condicion que lon purra trouer que tiel priuilege et serement soient grantez et faitz come auant est dit et ce soit trouez de record adioustez qil serroit expedient que ceux du conseil de mon dit seignur de Lancastre soient oiez de purpose plus en iustificacion de lour entent. Et monseignur de Derby saccorda a ce que mesme le duc disoit forspris qil ne desirra que ceux du dit Conseil de son piere serroient oiez de nouel.

Et le Roy disoit finalement que son

ent enuoiez si bien a ceux de Burdeux come al seignur de G[1]

Petitions of Burgesses of Calais; with replies.[2]

A nostre seignur le Roy et son sage conseil supplient les Burgeys de la ville de Caleys qe come ils ont les assises et gouernance de tout maner vitaile vendu en mesme la ville a retaile ouesqes les amendes de ycel qe vous plese granter garant as Maire et Aldermans de mesme la ville de puniser si bien les soudeours[3] trespasantz deuers la dit assise et leuer deux les amendes come ils font dautres vitailers en la dicte ville. Without date [Ric. II].

Response. La iurisdiction des Soudeours appartient au capitain et il a promys deuant le conseil qe il les iustifiera duement et selonc reson.

Item supplient les auauntditz Burgeys qe come ascuns ont purchasez lour mesons par nouelles chartres et ont abatez ascuns de les gaites[4] qe les ditz mesons deuoient depuis le conquest a greuouse

[1] The manuscript is torn away here.
[2] *Ancient Petitions*, no. 10582; Plate, no. 2. [3] soldiers. [4] watches.

charge de la dicte ville pur ce qe autres mesons sont chargez des ditz gaytes non duement qe vous plese ordeyner qe les ditz mesons issuit [1] purchasez soient chargez de lour aunciens gaytes en descharge de les auters mesons.

Response. Soit lancien Registre veu et sil poet estre troue qe ascun tiel gayte soit abatuz soit celi qi tient la meson a qi appartient de trouer tiel gayte compellez de lamendre.

Item supplient les ditz Burgeys qe la ou deuaunt qe feust ordeigne qe null estranger soit enherite en la dicte ville vostre aiel [2] qe dieux assoile granta as certeins estrangers certeins tenementz en mesme la ville en fee les queux estrangers les ont mariez as autres estrangers qe vous plese declarer si les issues de tieux estrangers serront enheritez ou nemy.[3]

Response. Soit veu lancien ordenance et desore enauant [4] soit celle ordenance tenuz.

Item supplient les auauntditz Burgéys qe vous plese granter et ordeyner qe toutz les enherites deinz la dicte ville eiant lour continuel demure en mesme la ville soient sermentez Burgeys et qe null a[utre] Burgeys tiegne herbergage [5] pur peril qe poet auener en cas estrangers herbergent estrangers.

Response. Il pleist au conseil.

Item supplient les ditz Burgeys qe vous plese granter a eux qils purrent deuiser lour biens et chateux moebles a lour femmes et les femmes a lour barons come ils peont faire as autres estrangers.

Response. Attendent de ceste article tanque au prochein parlement.

Item supplient les Burgeys auauntditz qe come lerceuesqe [6] de Canterbris qe dieux assoile adonqes Chanceller graunter par patent du Roy a vn sieur Iohan Dawe [7] la maisondieu dedeinz la dicte ville qest de fundacion dancien temps et meyntenu par lalmoigne des ditz Burgeys pur susteyner malades pouers pelryns et autres febles illoeqes qi nont sur qoi viure forsqe [8] sur lalmoigne et ore le dit Iohan ad pris tout le profit de mesme la maisondieu et est ale de illoeqes quele part nulle ne sciet et lesse la dicte maisondieu en male gouernance descouerte et despoile a grand damage dycel et descomfort as ditz pouers qi deuoient auer lour eisement illoeqes qe vous plese granter la dicte maisondieu as maynes des ditz Burgeys come el ad este tout temps deuaunt le dit Iohan nient contreesteant [9] la dicte patent non resonable issint [10] qe les ditz pouers purrent estre sustenuz illoeqes sicome ils ont este deuaunt ces heures et prier pur nostre seigneur le Roy et touz ses auncestres.

Response. Soit le dit sieur Iohan compellez de resider et

[1] 'issuit' = in such manner (*K. N. D.*).

[2] [Edward III ?]

[3] 'nemy' = not (*K. N. D.*).

[4] 'desore en avant' = from henceforth (*K. N. D.*).

[5] lodging.

[6] 'ercevesque' = archbishop (*K.N.D.*).

[7] This grant has not been found. The Patent Roll of 1408 contains revocations of protection granted to John Dawe, staying in Picardy with the governor of Calais, because he tarries at Colchester. The 'Maison Dieu' was granted in 1471 to William Marshall.

[8] except.

[9] notwithstanding.

[10] 'issint' = thus, so (*K. N. D.*).

sustenir les charges du dit hospital duement sur peine de priuacion dicelle.

Item supplient les ditz Burgeys ou qe nostre seigneur le Roy lour ad grante destre quitz de touz maners custumes et tolne de tout maner vitaile achate en Engleterre et amesne a la dicte ville qe vous plese granter as ditz Burgeys qils purrent en mesme la maner estre quitz de toutz maners custumes et tolne de tout maner vitaile achete en Flandres, Holand, Seland, Brabant et de toutz autres partz de par dela.

Estoise [1] leur chartre quant a cest darrein [2] article en sa force et soient les suppliantz contentz de cella.

APPENDIX III

RECORDS OF CASES AND OTHER LEGAL PROCEEDINGS, FROM RICHARD II TO HENRY VI

Memorandum of a confession of fraud and forgery made by John Martyn in Chancery.[3] June 13, 1383.

Fait a remembrer qe le xiij. iour de Iuyn lan du regne le Roi qore est sisme en la Chancellerie nostre dit seignur le Roi en presence del Chanceller, le chief Iustice du Roi, monsieur Richard Abburbury, Meistres del Chancellerie et plusours autres du Conseil du Roi vient vn Iohan Martyn de petit Thrillowe et confessa iurez sur seintz Ewangeliste a dire la veritee par ses seermentz coment il fist vn chartre de feoffement de fee simple de par Henry Neweland par estimacion entour vn xvme deuant sa moriance a monsieur William Clopton' de la manoir de Neweland en le Countee de Essex' a auoir a lui et ses heirs a touz iours et auxi le dit Iohan Martyn fist amesme le temps vn lettre dattourne depar le dit sieur William en le noun de Iohan Palmer pur receiuer seisin en le noun du dit sieur William Clopton' et le dit sieur William Clopton' bailla mesme le iour en le Court vne chartre et vn lettre de attourne de la mater auant dite disant qe le dit Iohan Martyn les fist par ses mayns et le dit Iohan regardant les dites chartre et lettre les ad outrement refusez et deniez disant qe vnqes ne les vist deuant cest iour.

Review of a case before the Council relating to seizure of a ship belonging to Castilian merchants.[4] Dec. 15, 1386.

Memorandum quod Iacobus Gonalous et Iohannes Amyl mercatores Arregonie de capcione et asportacione bonorum et mercandisarum suorum per subditos domini Ricardi Regis Anglie factis

[1] 'estoier' = to stand to, abide (*K. N. D.*).

[2] 'darrain' = last (*K. N. D.*).

[3] 'Exchequer Box' (unfiled). Writ annexed, and another memorandum concerning the manor of Newland.

[4] *Chancery Dipl. Doc.* (old number, P. 329).

grauiter conquerentes quandam peticionem suam consilio dicti domini Regis porrexerunt in hec verba. Al tresnoble conseil du trespuissant et tresexcellent seignur le Roy Dengleterre et de France : Supplient treshumblement Iames de Gonalous et Iohan Amyl marchantz Darragon qe come vne nief de Castille appelle Seint Alphines de quele est patrone Martin Piers de Rice la quele fuist charge partie a Barcelone et partie a Valence en la dite Roialme Darragon de lour biens [et marchandises et qe] fust pris par monsire Philip Darcy et monsire Thomas Treuet Admirals Dengleterre deuant Caleys et amesnez a Sandewic et la sont les ditz biens deschargez et departiz a graund damage [desditz marchantz]; Pleise a vostre tresnoble et tresgraciouse seignurie considerer qe le Roi Daragon lour seignur et les ditz merchantz sont amys et bien voillantz au Roi et a son roialme et ordiner qe lour ditz biens soient deliueres as ditz merchantz pur dieu et en oeuere de charite. Et postmodum prefati Admiralli ad mandatum eiusdem consilii super premissis responsuri coram dicto consilio comparentes dixerunt tam pro ipsis quam pro domino Rege quod tempore quo dicti Admiralli super mare in servicio domini Regis fuerunt viderunt quinque naves volantes super costeram Flandrie diuersis mercandisis carcatas quarum nauium tres naues fuerunt de Ispannia vnde due de Sancto Andrea et vna de Vermeawe et alie due naves de Lescluse extiterunt, qui quidem admiralli miserunt vnam bargeam et duas balingeras ad naues predictas certificando illis quod ibi fuerunt Admiralli Anglie et precipiendo illis de parte domini Regis per ipsos admirallos quod depositis velis suis venirent ad ipsos admirallos cum cartis suis ad ostendendum quorum naues bona et mercandise predicta fuerunt prout ius maritimum exigit et prout temporibus omnium admirallorum seu aliorum ligeorum dicti domini Regis ante hec tempora vsitatum fuit et consuetum. Ad quod gentes navium predictarum respondebant grossis verbis despectuose dicentes quod cum Rege Anglie vel admirallis suis nichil se intromittere habuerunt sed semper rectum cursum suum tenebant versus Lescluse quodque omnes gentes navium predictarum de guerra armate et arraiate fuerunt prompte ad preliandum et dicte naues sue vndique fortiter arraiate et signa prelii ibidem plene ostendebant predictos admirallos et totum posse suum despiciendo et gunnas suas dictis bargee et balingere fortiter eiciendo. Ita quod dicte bargea et balingere sine posse . . . [propius accedere] non audentes factum et responsum mercatorum predictorum dictis admirallis referebant, quo audito dicti admiralli versus naues predictas ad ipsas insultandas et capiendas accedebant que se tanquam inimicas domino Regi [quam tempore pacis] ostenderunt et sic per viam guerre predicti admiralli naues predictas ceperunt et eas vsque portum Sandwici duxerunt et ibidem naues ille discarcate et bona et mercandise in eisdem ad mandatum domini Regis partita fuerunt secundum legem et consuetudinem maris antiquitus vsitatas et vlterius allegarunt quod omnes gentes in nauibus predictis tempore capcionis earundem existentes fuerunt de Ispannia, Flandria et Picardia et quod dicta bona et mercandise fuerunt inimicorum domini Regis supradicti, per quod dicti admiralli per ius legis maritime hactenus consuete et vsitate intendunt quod naues predicte et gentes bona et mercandise in eisdem existencia fuerunt et sunt recte et legitime capta per viam guerre. Et vlterius dicunt quod dicta nauis de Vermeawe que fuit vna dictarum quinque nauium sic contra dictos Admirallos rebellancium fuit et est illa et eadem nauis de Castella vocata Seint Alphinos in peticione dictorum Mercatorum Arragonie contenta petendo tam pro domino Rege quam pro se ipsis quod predicti Mercatores Arragonie restitucionem dicte nauis de Vermeawe seu de bonis que in ipsa capta fuerunt non [habeant pro causis supradictis]. Et super hoc prefati Mercatores Arragonie coram eodem consilio contra premissas responsiones allegarunt quo ad bona et mercandisas que in dicta naui capta fuerunt quod bona et mercandise illa sunt bona propria ipsorum Mercatorum Arragonie [et quod] nauis illa cum bonis et mercandisis predictis apud Barcelone et Valence in Arragonia ad vsum et commodum dictorum Mercatorum Arragonie onerata et carcata fuit et hoc per literas Magnatum et diuersas cartas de fretto mercium ac aliud testimonium sufficiens offerebant se probare. Et quo ad nauem predictam similiter allegarunt quod cum certum sit et a notorio constat quod inter dictum dominum Regem Anglie et illustrem Regem Arragonie subditos et bona eorundem pax treuga et securitas efficax existit et licet hoc presuppositum sit certum quod nauis illa sit Castellanorum tamen quod exquo ad vsum mercandi Merces Cathalanorum qui sunt amici domini Regis Anglie destinatur non inferens dampnum Anglicis nec ad vsum dampnificandi disponitur est Cathalanorum qui amici Anglie reputantur et non Castellanorum et ad Cathalanorum commodum ordinatur. Item quod merces Cathalanorum que ducuntur et portantur in naui Castellanorum per Cathalanos conducta siue nauleata non inferunt dampnum Anglicis nec ad Castellanorum commodum deportantur. Item quod nauis conducta siue nauleata [1] per Cathalanos et Cathalanorum mercibus onerata ipsorum Cathalanorum nauleancium fuit ad tempus et accio de iure competit nauleanti contra quemcunque occupatorem et iniuriam inferentem et nauleator pro possessore presumitur et non debet dampnificari nec spoliari possessor qui est in pace et treuga nec impediri iure belli petendo quod nauis et bona et mercandise predicta prefatis mercatoribus restituantur. Super quo quinto decimo die Decembris anno regni regis Ricardi secundi decimo coram dicto consilio dicti domini Regis apud Westmonasterium in presencia admirallorum predictorum ibidem personaliter cum eorum consilio comparencium. Quia per diuersas literas dicti domini Regis Arragonie ac ciuitatis de Barcelone dicto domino Regi sepius directas et per literas Episcopi Burdegalensis predicto consilio domini Regis et aliis dominis similiter inde directas testatum fuit et eciam per cartas de fretto mercandisarum predictarum ostensum quod nauis predicta frettata fuit per mercatores Arragonie et quod frettata et carcata fuit cum bonis et mercandisis dictorum Mercatorum parte apud Barcelone et parte apud

[1] 'Nauleiare' = navem locare naulo convento. (Du Cange.)

Valence et quod bona et mercandise que fuerunt in naui predicta mere constabant ipsis Mercatoribus de Arragonia. Et preterea asserunt quod Mercatores et patroni subscripti nauium et caricarum que per predictos admirallos supra mare nuper capte fuerunt hoc recordari volunt et testari videlicet Iohannes Copelade, Daniel de Caluessage, Poynetus Olyare et Antonius de Burgo de plesancia, Antonius de Portugalia, Domyngus Cotus de Cateloign, Aaron de Mar[ino], Gabriel Arduuenti, Bartholomeus de Pendola, Gabriel Caluo, Franciscus Burro, Galatus Calvo, Reginaldus Gulle de Ianua et Sanso Piero de Lucebone. Et presertim quia prefati admiralli quibus premisse testificaciones ostense et opposite fuerunt non dedixerunt quin predicti Mercatores conquerentes sunt Mercatores de regno Arragonie et dicta bona et mercandise in naui predicta capta fuerunt propria bona ipsorum Mercatorum Arragonie et apud Barcelone et Valence carcata prout ijdem Mercatores superius allegarunt consideratum fuit et decretum per consilium predictum quod omnia et singula bona et mercandise predicta que in dicta naui vocata Seint Alphinos per predictos admirallos capta fuerunt eisdem Mercatoribus Arragonie in quorumcunque manibus inuenta fuerint si extent seu verus valor de illis que non extant integre restituantur et quod nauis predicta quia fuit de parte aduersa remaneat forisfacta et quod pro fretto bonorum et mercandisarum predictorum satisfiat. Salua domino Regi parte sua nauis et fretti predictorum.

Feb. 3, 1389.

Process before the Council concerning erroneous writ addressed to William of Wykeham, touching certain jewels.[1]

Pro Episcopo Wyntoniensi.[2] Memorandum quod xx^mo die Ianuarii anno regni Regis Ricardi secundi octauo [3] quoddam breue domini Regis factum fuit et magno sigillo suo sigillatum ac in rotulis Cancellarie eiusdem Regis irrotulatum in hec verba. Ricardus dei gratia Rex Anglie et Francie et dominus Hibernie Venerabili in Christo patri W. eadem gratia episcopo Wyntoniensi salutem. Cum certa diuersa iocalia magnum valorem attingencia in manus vestras per Aliciam que fuit vxor Willelmi de Wyndesore chiualer post iudicium contra ipsam in parliamento nostro anno regni nostri primo redditum pro certa summa pecunie per ipsam a vobis recepta posita et inuadiata fuissent et in custodia vestra adhuc existant vt pro certo didicimus. Nos certis de causis rationabilibus nos et consilium nostrum specialiter mouentibus vobis iniungendo mandamus firmiter et districte quod omnia iocalia predicta in manibus vestris propriis retineatis et saluo et secure custodiatis ita quod nullo modo extra custodiam vestram deliberentur quousque aliud a nobis inde habueritis specialiter in mandatis. Teste me ipso apud Westmona-

[1] *Close Roll*, 12 Ric. II, m. 19 d.
[2] William of Wykeham, bishop of Winchester, 1367–1404.
[3] January 20, 1384/1385.

sterium xx. die Ianuarii anno regni nostri octauo. per ipsum Regem.

Ac postmodum mense Nouembris anno regni predicti Regis duodecimo [1] idem Episcopus pro eo quod relatum fuit sibi per attornatum suum in scaccario domini Regis et alios de tenore huiusmodi breuis missi in extractis Cancellarie ad scaccarium Regis maxime admirabatur de breui predicto exquo idem Episcopus de tali breui nunquam antea audiuit vel sciuit nec aliqua huiusmodi iocalia ad manus suas vmquam deuenerunt. Et venit super hoc coram consilio domini Regis et asseruit et fideliter affirmauit quod nunquam constabat sibi de breui predicto ante relacionem predictam nec quod dictum breue vmquam sibi fuit liberatum nec quod aliqua iocalia per dictam Aliciam posita seu inuadiata in manu ipsius Episcopi Wyntoniensis post predictum iudicium contra prefatam Aliciam redditum nec ante aliqualiter extiterunt.

Subsequenterque eodem mense venerabilis pater Iohannes Episcopus Herefordensis [2] Thesaurarius domini Regis apud Nouum Templum London' in aula magistri eiusdem loci breue predictum clausum et sigillatum magno sigillo domini Regis Anglie cum cera alba more consueto Cancellarie ipsius domini Regis integrum et clausum in huiusmodi cera manu sua propria venerabili patri Thome Archiepiscopo Eboracensi [3] Anglie primati Cancellario Regis liberauit. Qui quidem Cancellarius breue predictum sic sigillatum integrum et clausum in cera vt premittitur recepit et breue illud in presencia predicti episcopi Wyntoniensis, venerabilium patrum Walteri episcopi Dunelmensis [4], predicti Thesaurarii ac Iohannis episcopi Sarum [5] custodis priuati sigilli Regis, Ricardi Lescrop' Baneretti, Walteri de Clopton' capitalis iusticiarii Regis, Roberti Cherlton' capitalis iusticiarii domini Regis de communi banco, Thome Pynchebek capitalis baronis de scaccario dicti domini Regis ac ceterorum baronum scaccarii predicti, Willelmi Thirnyng iusticiarii de communi banco et aliorum de consilio eiusdem Regis ibidem existencium fregit et aperuit atque legit. Et satis constabat eis quod fuit idem breue cuius tenor irrotulatus fuit in rotulis Cancellarie et missus in extractis eiusdem Cancellarie in Scaccarium ipsius domini Regis. Et insuper predicti domini cancellarius, thesaurarius, custos priuati sigilli et alij de consilio domini Regis postea eodem mense Nouembris, presentibus iusticiariis domini Regis de vtroque banco ac baronibus ipsius Regis de Scaccario, dictam Aliciam super materia in dicto breui contenta pro parte domini Regis apud Westmonasterium in camera iuxta Scaccarium ipsius domini Regis examinarunt que in eorum presencia personaliter constituta et iurata dixit per sacramentum suum quod nulla iocalia post predictum iudicium contra ipsam redditum nec ante dicto Episcopo Wyntoniensi per ipsam Aliciam liberata seu inuadiata fuerunt nec quod aliqua huiusmodi iocalia ad manus ipsius

[1] November, 1388.

[2] John Gilbert, bishop of Hereford, 1375–89, appointed treasurer of the exchequer, 1387.

[3] Thomas Arundel, archbishop of York, 1388–96.

[4] Walter Skirlaw, bishop of Durham, 1388–1406.

[5] John Waltham, bishop of Salisbury, 1388–95.

Episcopi Wyntoniensis deuenerunt. Et Robertus de Faryngton' clericus Cancellarie predicte cuius nomen impositum fuit et scriptum super breui predicto Interrogatus per dictum consilium si haberet aliquam noticiam de causa prosecucionis dicti breuis dixit quod non sciuit nec cognouit nec vmquam relatum sibi fuit de causa impetracionis seu prosecucionis breuis supradicti. Super quo prefatus Episcopus Wyntoniensis prosequebatur penes dictum dominum Regem per peticionem suam eidem domino Regi porrectam in hec verba.

A nostre tresredoute sieur le Roy monstre son humble Chapellein William Euesque de Wyncestre que vn brief est troue enroulle en vostre Chauncellarie du date de xxme iour de Ianuier lan de vostre regne oeptisme et entre les originalx de mesme lan est maunde en lescheqer de quelle brief la copie est annexe a ceste bille et quelle brief vnqes ne feust liure au dit Euesque et coment que la matire contenu en le dit brief ne soit verray le dit Euesque purroit de leger par celle cause estre endamage en temps auener tout soit il que mesme le brief issist[1] et fuist enroulle sanz fundement ou cause resonable. Par quei supplie le dit Euesque que plese a vostre haute seigneurie commaunder a vostre Chaunceller de souruoier[2] le dit enroullement et outre ceo par sa discrecion ordener et faire que si droit loy et reson le voillent que le dit Euesque ses heirs ou executours ne soient endamagez ne empechez par la cause susdite en temps auener mes qils y soient ent quitez as tous iours.

Que quidem peticio eidem Regi exposita ex certa ipsius Regis sciencia concessa fuit per predictum dominum Regem et indorsata in hec verba. Le Roy ad graunte ceste bille en toutz pointz et commaunde a Chaunceller de le parfournir[3] en manere et forme come ele est demaunde. Que quidem peticio simul cum copia breuis de qua in eadem peticione fit mencio remanent in filaciis Cancellarie. Super quo predictus Episcopus Wyntoniensis prosequebatur penes predictum Cancellarium petens remedium super peticionem predictam sibi fieri in hac parte. Et super hoc prefatus Cancellarius in crastino Purificacionis beate Marie dicto anno xij^{o}[4] euocatis coram eo in Cancellaria dicti domini Regis apud Westmonasterium iusticiariis de vtroque banco et seruientibus dicti domini Regis ad placita ac aliis iuris peritis et materia predicta coram eis ibidem cum magna et matura deliberacione declarata et examinata videbatur curie predicte quod breue predictum erronice et minus prouide et absque fundamento seu iusta causa et rationabili emanauit et irrotulatum fuit et quod nullus processus super eodem breui pro domino Rege de iure fieri posset aut deberet quouismodo quodque remedium competens inde in eadem curia Cancellarie vnde dictum breue sic erronice emanauit ordinari deberet per quod de assensu et auisamento consilij domini Regis iusticiariorum et seruientum eiusdem domini Regis ad placita et aliorum predictorum ibidem existencium, proclamacio solempniter et publice facta fuit in Cancellaria predicta quod si quis vellet venire et informare dictum consilium aut curiam ipsius domini Regis et aliquid dicere seu ostendere eisdem consilio et curie quare

[1] issued.
[2] to survey.
[3] to perform.
[4] February 3, 1389.

prefatus Episcopus Wyntoniensis ad respondendum domino Regi de predictis iocalibus seu ad computandum de eisdem exonerari non deberet veniret et audiretur. Et quia proclamacione huiusmodi publice et solempniter facta nullus venit ad informandum consilium et curiam predictam seu ad aliquid dicendum pro predicto domino Rege contra predictum episcopum Wyntoniensem in hac parte ac premissis omnibus et singulis debite consideratis et attentis consideratum fuit de assensu et auisamento predictis quod predictum breue in Cancellaria predicta restituatur et ibidem vna cum predicto irrotulamento eiusdem breuis cancelletur et dampnetur. Et quod prefatus episcopus Wyntoniensis heredes et executores sui occasione aliquorum huiusmodi iocalium seu ex causis predictis decetero nullatenus impetantur molestentur occasionentur in aliquo seu grauentur. Set inde erga dictum dominum Regem et heredes suos omnino exonerati sint et quieti imperpetuum. Et quod idem episcopus Wyntoniensis habeat breuia quot et qualia sibi fuerint in hac parte necessaria directa thesaurario et baronibus Regis de Scaccario de cancellando et dampnando in rotulis Scaccarii predicti extractas et tenorem eiusdem breuis et de supersedendo omnino execucioni breuis predicti et exonerando totaliter dictum episcopum Wyntoniensem heredes et executores suos de iocalibus predictis et de impeticione et compoto eorundem erga dictum dominum Regem et heredes suos imperpetuum.

Suit before the Council of John Cheyne versus William Brian. 13 *Richard II.*[1]

July 24, 1389.

Le Samedy la veillee de Seynt Iakes qest le xxiiij^{te} iour du Moys de Iuyl lan du regne le Roy Richard secounde puis le conquest xiij^{me} monsiur William Briene[2] proposa deuant le conseil du Roy suisdit a Westmoustier les matires queux ensuient.

Quant a ceo qe monsieur Iohan Cheyne dit par la contenwe de sa secounde bille, En primes qe apres qil auoit baille a monsieur William de Briene le brief du Roy a luy directe pur faire deliuerer a dit monsieur Iohan le Chastel de Mark le dit monsieur William fuist commaunde de soi hastiuer euers Mark pur ent faire la deliuerance a dit monsieur Iohan et sil ne le deliuereroit il dust [le] garder a ses propres costages. A ceo le dit monsieur William dit qil soi hastiua par si graunt diligence euers le Chastel susdit qil fuist apres sa venwe illeosqes demorrant gardaunt le dit Chastel per xvij iours ou plus deuaunt le iour qe le dit monsieur Iohan venoit a le dit Chastel de Mark prest dewement pur accepter le garde de ycelle en sa persone dewment requirant la liuere de ycelle. Et dit qe le dit monsieur Iohan se retenoit en la ville de Caleys apres sa venwe illeosqes par le temps susdit sanz venir en sa persone a le dit Chastel de Mark prest pur le garde de ycel dewement accepter tanqe le iij^{e} iour de Ianuer adonqes suaunt. Et procura le dit monsieur Iohan plusures duressis estre faitz

[1] 'Exchequer Box' (unfiled).
[2] Afterwards called 'de Briene' and 'Brian'.

a le dit monsieur William en li destourbaunt de faire les seruices nostre seignur le Roy et ses autres afferes dont il estoit ocupiez par charge des Tresorier [1] et Controllour [2] illeoqes pur la deliuerance le dit Chastel de Mark hastier, des queux duressis please a sieurs du conseil le Roy oier la compleint de dit monsieur William et ent de luy fere droit et reson.

Quant a ceo qe le dit monsieur Iohan dit qe le dit monsieur William apres certeins parlaunces entre eux purposes en la eglise de seint Nicholas a Caleys le dit monsieur William assigna certein iour de retourner de Mark a Caleys et de mettre certein iour pur deliuerer le Chastel de Mark le dit monsieur William quant a le iour de son retourner dit comment qil ne venoit mye [3] pur graundes ocupacionnez qil auoit a fere des seruices le Roy mesme le iour il enuoia son Clerk al Tresorier de Caleys pur luy fere excuser a le dit monsieur Iohan de sa dicte nonvenwe et ne quide [4] point le dit monsieur William qe par telle nonvenwe il ad fet au Roy ascun desobeisance et quant a le mettre ou assignement fere de certein iour pur le dit Chastel deliuerer le dit monsieur William dit qil ne le emprist vnqes sur luy qar il ne le purroit fere puy qe ly couenoit de dewete obeier les iours et termes a ly limitez par le Roy et lez Tresorier et Countrollour illeosqes a sa deliuerance fere, les queux Tresorier et Countrollour ly assignerent certeins iours et termes de leiser pur ses affeirs dewment acomplier as quelles iours et termes limitez il fuist toutditz [5] prest de fere son deuoir comment qil fuist a la foitz destourbe par les diuerses duressis a ly fetz come par sa compleinte pluis au plein y perra.

Quant a ceo qe le dit monsieur Iohan dit de bouche ou par escript en sa dicte bille qe le dit monsieur William ne voleit fere deliuerance de le dit Chastel de Mark, le dit monsieur William dit qil fuist toutditz prest pur deliuerer le dit Chastel a le dit monsieur Iohan Cheyne a toutz les foitz et a mesme le temps qe le dit monsieur Iohan fust prest dewment pur accepter la liuere de ycel la ou la liuere se dust fere de droit. Et outre dit qe le dit monsieur Iohan Cheyne ne venoit vnqes en sa persone a le dit Chastel de Mark prest dewement pur accepter la charge de ycelle tanqe mesme celle iour qe la liuere a ly fust fet et ceo le dit monsieur William prouera suffisauntement come Chiualer doit fere.

Quant as autres materes contenuz en la bille le dit monsieur Iohan Cheyne touchauntz autres persones qe ly le dit monsieur William dit a quelle heure qe les autres persones ly volount ascunement surmettre chose qe soit en blame ou deshonour de luy il serra toutditz prest de respoundre suffisauntement en saluacion de son estat si dieux plest.

Et pur final conclusion de ceste matere plese a lez honorez et sagez seignurs du conseil nostre sieur le Roy de considerer qe la liuere de dit Chastel de Mark ne se poet fere aillours qe a le lieu ou il est assis pur ce qil nest point remuable a volente. Et qe le dit monsieur Iohan Cheyne fust toutditz a large de son corps pur aler et venir a Mark

[1] Simon de Burgh, then treasurer of Calais.

[2] William Beauchamp, then captain, keeper, or comptroller of Calais.

[3] 'mie' = not (*K. N. D.*).

[4] think (*K. N. D.*).

[5] 'toutditz' = always (*K. N. D.*).

et aillours ou ly plust. Et qe pur la nonvenwe de dit monsieur Iohan et en sa defaute couenoit le dit monsieur William de garder le dit Chastel tanqe a la venwe de dit monsieur Iohan. Et qe par le primer maundement du Roy au primer iour qe le dit monsieur Iohan venoit illeoqes dewement prest pur accepter le dit Chastel le dit monsieur William li deliuera le dit Chastel mesme celle iour. Et cestez materes considerez oue [1] les autres materes queux le dit monsieur William ad proposez et declarrez par escript dont il reserue par protestacion toutditz a ly les auauntages de reson dewez. Sur ce le dit monsieur William serra toutditz prest de faire ce qe les treshonorez seignurs susditz luy auiseront de reson purueu toutdis qe es euidences queux il ad vnqore a moustrier en proue de ses allegeances susditz entant come ils serront vaillablez soient toutditz effectuelment acceptez quant ils serront producteez.

Et pur greindre declaracion de sa matere le dit monsieur William dit outre qe les materes substanciels pur ly proposez en sa defence et en sa compleinte sont verroiement pur ly proposez et telez en feit come il ad allegge et ce le dit monsieur William est et serra toutditz prest de meintenir par son corps come Chiualer doit fere suffisauntement si le dit monsieur Iohan voet en mesme la manere meintenir le contrare par son corps.

A les treshonurez et sages seignurs du conseil nostre sieur le Roy se compleint William de Briene de ce qe monsieur Iohan Cheyne quant il fust retenuz oue nostre dit sieur le Roy pur estre gardein du Chastel de Mark et tenuz par force de ses endentures et lettres patentes du Roy pur auoir accepte la charge et garde du dit Chastel al fest de seint Michel lan du regne nostre dit Sieur le Roy oeptisme le dit monsieur Iohan ne y venoit mye illeoqes a celle iour einz [2] soi retenoit aillours tanqe al tierce iour de Ianuier adonqes proschein suiant issint qe pur la nonvenwe de dit monsieur Iohan et en sa defaute couenoit a dit monsieur William oue sa retenue destre chargez par tout le temps suisditz gardantz le dit Chastel et agaitauntz [3] la venwe de dit monsieur Iohan a ses grauntz costagez et disese dont le dit monsieur William requert satisfaction.

La compleinte.

[Mich., 1384.]

Item par la ou le dit monsieur William adonqes Capitain de Mark fust oue le Tresorier et Countrollour de Caleys en la dicte ville de Caleys mesqerdy le xxj. iour de Decembre lan suisdit a vn vewe de son acompte a fere et illeosqes par lordinance de ditz Tresorier et Countrollour fust commande et garny [4] mesme celluy iour qil dust faire sa monstre le vendirdi adonqes proschein suant et issint a demurer engardant le dit Chastel tanqe a le secounde iour de Ianuer adonqes proschein suiant afin qe en le dit temps il dust auoir leiser de faire les acomptz rescectz et paiementz et autres aferes queux fuirent necessarez destre faitz auant son departir et sur ceo qil serroit prest a deliuerer le dit Chastel le secounde iour de Ianuer suisdit. Et le dit monsieur William voillant obeisauntement tenir et accomplier les ordinances suisditz as termes queux lui furount limiteez soi ordeigna

[Jan. 2, 1385.]

[1] 'oue' = avec.
[2] 'einz' = but (*K. N. D.*).
[3] 'agaitauntz' = awaiting.
[4] 'garny' = informed (*K. N. D.*).

mesme celle iour deuers soir pur Chiuacher [1] deuers Mark et donqes par procurement de le dit monsieur Iohan les portes de Caleys fuirount encountre le dit monsieur William closez et son passage ly fuist issint a cel temps par tout la noet deneiez sanz cause resonable en destourbance de dit monsieur William a son graunt damage et desaise et peril de la sauuegarde de le dit Chastel.

Item le venderdy adonqes proschein par la ou le dit monsieur William fust prest dauoir fait sa monstre honestement en pesible manere come a la season des trewez qe estoient adonqes de reson appartenoit le dit monsieur Iohan Cheyne par son procurement fist venir pardeuaunt le dit Chastel de Mark vne grant route des gentz darmes et archers en grant affray de dit monsieur William et destourbance de sa monstre ycelle iour sanz cause resonable a grant damage et desaise de dit monsieur William et ses soudeours et grant peril de safgarde de le dit Chastel come par declaracion de bouche le dit monsieur William ferra pluis aplein monstrer.

Item par la ou le dit monsieur William fuist oue le Controllour Capitain de Chastel de Caleys le primer iour de Ianuer et par tout la noet et il se tailla lendemein bien matin de chiuaucher a le Chastel de Mark pur ent fere la liuere mesme celle iour a dit monsieur Iohan Cheyne selonc le ordinance suisdicte mesme celle temps diuerses enbuscementz de gentz darmes et archers et balasters furont mys en diuerses lieus pur destourber le dit monsieur William de son passage deuers Mark et mesme celle iour ne venoit mye le dit monsieur Iohan a le dit Chastel de Mark pur ascune liuere accepter einz par son procurement fist le dit monsieur William estre detenuz en la dicte ville de Caleys et par maliciouses accusementz estre blamez deuers le Capitain de Caleys sanz resonable cause de son desert en grant desaise et damage de le dit monsieur William et peril de safgarde du dit Chastel.

Item par la ou le dit monsieur Iohan Cheyne en la presence de le honorable sieur monsieur William Beauchamp Capitain de Caleys, de le Tresorier et Countrollour et des autres bones gentz fuit pleinement acordez de accepter la garde de le dit Chastel de Mark le tierce iour de Ianuer susdit, sur quoi le dit monsieur William fist armer et appariler toutz ses gentz et ses vitailles asporter de le Chastel en le matine et fust tout prest pur la deliuerance faire, sur ceo le dit monsieur Iohan envoia deux ses esquiers a dit monsieur William pur faire mettre le liuere de dit Chastel en delay tanqe le ieosdy proschein adonqes suant pur son pluis grant eise a ceo qe ses messages disoient, sur quoi le dit monsieur William voillant le ese de dit monsieur Iohan fist ses propres gentz desarmer et ses vitailles qe furount dehors reporter oue grant labour et sur ceo mesme celle iour vient le dit
[*dorse.*] monsieur Iohan nonobstant son message suisdit amenant le Tresorier de Caleys oue luy sanz Countrollour et demandast liuere de dit Chastel en si grant haste qil ne amenoit pas oue luy adonques la moite de sa retenue et issint ne fist il mye adonqes prest selonc sa dewete de accepter la dicte garde nientmeins adonqes la liuere a luy

[1] 'chivaucher' = to ride (*K. N. D.*).

fust fet obeisauntement. Et sur cestes materes supplie le dit monsieur William qil ne soit en riens blame de ceo qe le dit monsieur Iohan Cheyne soi ad mespris deuers nostre sieur le Roy par sa lachesse ou autrement en les materes susditz. Einz soit le dit monsieur William restorez par le dit monsieur Iohan et satisfiez de les grantz damages et depenses qil ad sustenuz par cause de les duressis susditz et de la Iniuste vexacion par le dit monsieur Iohan a ly depuis fetz.

[*Endorsed.*] Touchant Monsieur Iohan Cheyne et Monsieur William Brian.

Les nouns de ceux qi feurent deputez par le Conseil du Roy pur examiner [la matere] comprise deinz ceste bille et autres euidences purposeez par Monsieur Iohan Cheyne contre Monsieur William Brian.

Le Conte de Northumbre
Le Priour de lospital
Monsieur William Neuyll
Monsieur Richard Aderbury
Monsieur Edward Dalingrugge
Monsieur Richard Stury.

Le viij. iour de Marcz lan etc. viij. le dit Conte par lui et par les deputez susditz fesoit relacion au Conseil du Roy qe le dit Monsieur William estoit trouez en defaut touchant la matere susdite. **[March 8, 1385.]**

The Franceys Case, an examination of dishonest executors.[1]

Le vii. iour de Nouembre lan etc. xvj. a les Frerers Precheours de Loundres esteantz illeoques monsire Thomas Percy Souz Chamberlain, le Gardein du priue seal, monsire Lowys Clifford, monsire Iohan de Mountagu et Iohan Slegh Butiller du Roy, lexaminacion deinz escrit feust fet par le dit monsire Thomas pur le profit du Roy sur ce que monsire Robert Belknap vn des Iustices du Roy bailla et deliuera a dame Agneys Franceys cc*li*. de monoie. Et que sur ceo la dite Agneis estoit obligee par ses lettres de paier mesme la somme a William Batesford et a William Topclif. Quele chose deust auoir estre concelez en deceit et damage du Roy a ce qest dit. **Nov. 7, 1392.**

En primes monsire Adam Franceys Chiualer fitz de la dite Katerine charge de dire la veritee sur la dite matere sur laligeance quil doit au Roy et sa foialtee qil doit a Dieu et a son lige seignur disoit et confessa illeoques que la dite dame Agneys par vn poy du temps deuant son moriant desira et pria a son dit fitz qil vorroit estre son chief executour et il ne voloit a ce assentir auant qil feust enformez par sa dite miere qele auoit assez de biens pur perfournir son testament cestassauoir M[1] M[1] cccc*li*. et plus come Iohan Sibille qi auoit conissance et disposicion de toutz ses biens purroit bien monstrer et declarer. Et depuis que le dit Adam Franceys auoit pris le charge destre vn de ses executours il auient que apres la mort de sa dite miere feust dit parentre le dit Iohan Sibille et les autres executours

[1] *Council and Privy Seal*, file 4. The record is made upon a long single membrane and contains a remarkably complete description of the procedure. The matter is briefly stated in the clerk's journal, Appendix II, p. 502.

de la dite Agneis quele auoit receu du dit Robert Belknap cc*li*. come auant est dit et que tiele obligacion feut fet. Sur quele chose le dit Iohan Sibille disoit qil serroit expedient de tenir le chose bien secree si que il ne serroit conuz et par especial au dit monsire Iohan Mountagu pur dont de damagiez qils porroient encourrer enuers le Roy. Et apres vient le dit William Batesford et demanda la dite somme de mesme les executours par vertue de la obligacion susdite. Sur quel demande par auys et comun assent de mesmes les executours response lui feust donez et deux voies offertz. Cestassauoir que en cas que le dit William vorroit trouer seuretee de garder les ditz executours sanz damage enuers touz autres persones il aueroit le paiement de mesme la somme bien prest en mein quele offre feut rehercez par le dit Iohan Sibille. Ou autrement que le dit William deust pursuir vn brief de det encontre les ditz executours et ils serroient prestz de rendre et de soffrer recouerir dicelle par vertue de la dite obligacion. Queles deux offres a lui ensi fetz le dit William ne accepta nul de eux einz delors en auant ne pursua par icelle ne nulle paiement lui en est fet.

Et le dit Adam disoit que apres ce qant il estoit en purport daler a Ierlm' pur dont destre enpeschez par le Roy en celle partie pur aucun concelement il sen ala a le Prior de Cristchurch de Loundres qi estoit confessour a la dite dame et certifia mesme le confessour la dite matere pur faire sauoir a aucune persone du Conseil du Roy mesme la matere. Et depuis le dit Adam descouera au dit monsire Iohan Mountagu ice mesme pur le profit du Roy et en descharge de lalme de sa dite miere tenant en sa conscience que la dite somme nestoit due a les auantditz William et William par vertue de la dite obligacion mes au dit Robert Belknap et vncore il tient ice mesme a ce qil disoit.

Item le dit Iohan Sibille iurez a les seintz de dire pleine veritee sur les dites materes disoit qil est vn des executours et en la vie de la dite dame il estoit son seruant et clerc et remembrancer de ses affaires et biens et il ne sauoit vnques en la vie de la dite Agneys qele auoit receue du dit Robert la dite somme. Mes apres sa mort il apperceust que vne tiele obligacion feut fet come auant est dit. Et il disoit que le dit William Batesford demanda de lui et de ses coexecutours la dite somme par vertue de sa dite obligacion quele nestoit monstrez illeoques ne delors null pursuit fet pur auoir paiement de la dite somme quele nest vncore paiez. Et il disoit qil suppose bien que la dite somme nest due a ceux par vertue de mesme lobligacion einz au dit Robert.

Item [1] White iurez et examinez come desus disoit qil est vn des executours nomez en le testament mes il ne fesoit riens sinon come seruant a les autres executours. Et il ne sciet riens dire en celle partie forsoulement qil oyst que le dit Adam disoit parentre lui et ses coexecutours que la dite somme feut due au dit Robert et nemy a les autres come desus et coment mesme celui Adam rehercea tout le chose come dit est touchant la liueree de la dite somme et la dite obligacion. Plus il ne sciet dire.

[1] A space is left here.

Item, mesme le iour apres manger de lassent du dit monsire Thomas et du dit Gardein du priue seal monsire Lowys susdit et monsire Iohan Mountagu aloient a la maison de William Hide par cause qil estoit malades en partie a ce qestoit dit. Et il feust iure et examine come les autres sur toutes les materes deinz escrites. Et il confessa bien qil estoit vn des seruantz de la dite dame et depuis vn de ses executours mes il nestoit priuee a ce quelle fesoit en son viuant touchant tieles materes ou bosoignes mes Iohan Sibille auoit conissance de ses busoignes come remembrancer de ycelles. Et le dit William Hide ne voloit confesser nul tiel deliuerance du monoie avoir este fet de sa science ne qil vist la dite obligacion mes au pein il voloit confesser clerement aucun chose sur celle matere einz que le dit William Batesford demanda la monoie et il ne monstra nulle obligacion et qil ne pursua delors pur ycelle. Et il dit aussi au pein que qant la somme feust ensi demande par le dit William Batesford feust demande de lui par les executours qil garderoit mesmes les executours sanz damage en cas que le paiement lui serroit fet. Et il disoit qil suppose meux que la dite somme feust due au dit Robert que a les ditz William et William par cause que delors nulle pursuit estoit fet pur le peiement dicelle. Plus il ne voloit dire en effect pur nulle examinacion que estoit fet par les ditz Lowys et I. Mountagu.

Et apres a Westm' le xj. iour de Decembre lan etc. xvj. esteantz illeoques le Chanceller, le Tresorer, le Gardein de priue seal, monsire Thomas Percy Souz Chamberlain, monsire Lowys Clifford la matere desusescrit feut rehercez a Iohan Sibille et a William Hide executours auantditz. Et par cause que vne lettre de priue seal feust enuoiez a William Batesford lui chargeant qil certifieroit le Conseil si la dite somme a lui estoit due et aussi de la dite obligacion li quiel par ses lettres certifia que Iohan Slegh Butiller du Roy sauoit bien assez declarer tout ce qil sauoit en la matere. Si feust le dit Iohan Slegh examinez sur ce et il dit que le dit William Batesford confessa a mesme celui Iohan que la dite somme nestoit due a lui. Et le Tresorer disoit que il examina William Topclif qant il vesquist si la dite dame Agneis estoit dettour a lui de la dite somme et il confessa que noun. Et depuis les ditz Iohan Sibille et William Hide feurent examinez par vertue de lour serement de la dite obligacion et ils confessoient bien que tiele obligacion feust fet come ils disoient pardeuant et que deux centz liures feurent duz par dame Agnes Frances par vertue de mesme lobligacion. Et ils supposent bien que mesme la somme feust duz a Robert Belknap. Et purce qils disoient qils ne sauent ou est la dite obligacion en cas que le dit William Batesford veulle faire acquitance a mesmes les executours ils paieroient au Roy la dite somme parensi que lours coexecutours soient constreintz de respondre ouesqes eux de mesme la somme. Et sur ce les ditz Iohan Sibille et William Hide estoient mainparnours lun pur lautre sur peine de M[1] *li.* de estre deuant le Conseil de iour en iour.

Et depuis le xviij. iour de Decembre feurent presentz deuant le Conseil les ditz Iohan Sibille et William Hide et confessoient de paier la dite somme de cc*li.* au Roy parensi qils eient acquitance du dit William Batesford. Et que tiel acquitance doit estre fet a eux

I. Slegh et monsire E. Dalingrugg ont promys. Et sur ce ils demandent estallement de mesme le paiement. Et outre ce feust aiugge par le Conseil que pur le dit concelement les ditz I. et William soient commys a prison et que le double et le fin soient mys en suspense pur sauoir la volontee du Roy. Et le Conseil est assentuz quils soient en bail hors de prisone le moyen temps en la garde du dit Iohan Slegh le quiel ad enpris al Conseil en peine aiugge et corps pur corps de faire venir deuant le Conseil les ditz I. et William qant le Conseil mandera pur eux. Et depuis le Conseil estoit assentuz quils ferroient vn fin de centz liures desterling' et qils en aueroient paiement des cc*li.* desusescrites.[1]

Certain merchants of Cornwall make a confession of their illegal exportations of tin.[2]

Iohannes Daubron de Lostwythiel
Iohannes Meger de Truru
Rogerus Coygne de Lostwithiel
Willelmus Budde de Graiwen.

Jan. 11, 1393. Le Samady apres la Tiffaine lan etc. xvj^me^ les persones susdites feurent iurez de dire la veritee et ils confessoient qils ont amesnez as parties de Flaundres apres la fest de Seint Iohan le Baptistre darrein passez sanz venir a lestaple de Caleys sys centz pieces et iij pieces desteym en vn nief apellez Seinte Marie de Falemouth dont les owners Iohan Meger, Dauid Page, Iohan Archer et William Rose, et le dit Dauid est mestre de la nief. Pur quel chose adiuggez est que le dit nief et lesteyme sont forfaites au Roy et sont mys en la garde de Slegh Butiler qi ad empris pur eux et pur[3]

Without date; circa 1398. *Petition of John Harpetyn to the King's Council against the prior of Lewes and John Broker; with action of the Council.*[4]

A tressage Counseil nostre seignur le Roy supplie humblement Iohan Harpetyng valet feutrer[5] nostre dit seignur le Roy qe come nostre dit seignur le Roy nadgairs grauntast[6] a dit suppliant pur terme de sa vie vn annuel rente de douze souldz issauntz dun Mees[7] en Pydyngho done al Priorie de Lewes par Iohan Herbard de Rotyngdon' et auxi terres et tenementz al value de xxviij *s.* par an in Ballesden donez al mesme le Priorie par vn William Darnell' et Alice sa femme del paroche de Southenon les qeux rent terres et

[1] March 4, 1393, there is a pardon for the fine of £100 incurred by William Hyde and John Sibell, whereof they had been convicted by the council. *Cal. Patent Rolls*, 258.

[2] *Council and Privy Seal*, file 4, no. 1.

[3] The entry ends thus. On May 9 we learn of the merchants of Cornwall upon a fine of £200 being pardoned of the forfeiture they had incurred for having made certain illegal exportations of tin. *Cal. Patent Rolls*, 263.

[4] *Ancient Petitions*, no. 10600.

[5] Yeoman-feuterer, or dog-keeper.

[6] See *Patent Roll*, 21 Ric. II, part 3, m. 21.

[7] meadow.

tenementz pur ceo qe furent donez al mort meyn saunz licence nostre dit seignur le Roy furent forfaitz a nostre dit seignur le Roy come a nostre dit seignur le Roy fuist fait a entendre. Sour qe nostre dit seignur le Roy mandast ces lettres tresgraciouses directe si bien al Priour de mesme le Priorie come a vn Iohan Broker de Radmyll' qe luy prendist title de mesmes ceux rent terres et tenementz Al oeps[1] de dit priour pur y estre deuaunt son counseill al quynsime de Pask darrein passe pur respoundre de certeins matiers qeux illeoqes serroient declarez depar nostre dit seignur le Roy et qils deyuent porter ouesqe eux toutz les munimentz et euidences par qeux eux pretenderont dauer title as ditz rent terres et tenementz. A quele quinsyme les ditz Priour et Iohan Broker viendrent et le title nostre dit seignur le Roy come desus est dit a eux fuist declaree. A quele ills ne respondrent riens et fuist demande de eux adonqes illeoqes sils sauoient rien dire pur quoy lettres patentz ne duissent estre faitz a dit Iohan Harpetyng solonc le grant Auauntdit et ills ne sauoient rien dire. Pur qoy lettres patents furent faitz a dit Iohan Harpetyng et vn brief fuist direct al Eschetour de Sussex' de mettre le dit Iohan Harpetyng en possession par force dez lettres patentz auauntditz le quele Eschetour luy mist eynz en possession. Sour quoy viendrent les ditz Priour et Iohan Broker oue fort mayn et le dit Iohan Harpetyng ousteront et les bleez cressantz sour mesmes les terres et tenementz scieront[2] et emporteront en contempt nostre dit seignur le Roy et a graunt damage de le dit suppliant, qe plese a voz tressages discrecions de graunter briefs directs as ditz priour et Iohan Broker destre deuant vous a certein iour pur respoundre a nostre dit seignur le Roy del dit contempt et auxi destre chargez qe desore en auaunt ne facent nulle tiel entree sour le possession le Roy et de faire restitucion dez issuetz ent prys puis la liuere fait a dit suppliant, pur dieux et en oeuere de charitee.

Et sur ce mande fut par brief de nostre seignur le Roy au dit Priour sur peyne de deux Centz marcz et au dit Iohan Broker sour peyne de deux Centz marcz destre cy deuant le Conseil a les oytaues de seint hiller proschein venant pur respondre a ceo qe lour serroit surmys touchant la matire comprise en la dite Supplicacion. Au quel iour le dit Priour en propre persone comparust deuant le dit conseil et le dit Iohan Brokere ne vient pas pur empeschement de maladie et partant qe par bone et due examinacion eue du dit priour estoit lors trouez qe le dit Priour ousta lauauntdit Iohan Harpetyng hors dez ditz rente terres et tenementz sanz due proces de la ley et encountre le iuggement nadgairs done cy deuant le dit Conseil enuers les ditz priour et Iohan Broker et les bleez sour la dite terre cresceantz atort prist et emporta. Apres ceo qe mesme cely Iohan Harpetyng ent fust mys duement einz en possession par vertue des lettres patentes nostre dit seignur le Roy a luy ent faitz en contempt de mesme nostre seignur le Roy, Consideretz estoit et agardez[3] qe le dit Priour pur le dit contempt face fyn a la voluntee du Roy et qe lauauntdit Johan

[1] 'oeps' = use (*K. N. D.*). [2] 'scier' = to mow (*K. N. D.*).
[3] 'agardetz' = awarded (*K. N. D.*).

Harpetyng soit restituit sibien a la possession dez rente terres et tenementz susditz come as blees et autres choses ent pris et remuez et qe le dit Priour respoigne au Roy du surplus quel le dit Iohan Harpetyng estoit tenuz de paier au Roy par force dez ditz lettres patentes pur le temps qe mesme le Priour occupia les ditz rente terres et tenementz sanz due proces come auant est dit. Et en outre ceo estoit dit au dit Priour qe sil pretende dauoir ascun droit ou title as ditz rente terres et tenementz susditz qadonqes il pursue au Roy dauoir congie de pursuer son dit droit et title par la commune ley si luy semble a faire.

Par le Conseil presens Messieurs les
Chaunceller
Tresorer
leuesqe de seint dauid
le Gardein du Priue seal
William Thirnyng chief Iustice du comune banc
Iohan Hille vn des Iustices de le banc du Roy
et Monsieur Johan Russell.

Suit of John Gunwardby and others versus Payne Tiptoft and others, concerning manors in the county of Cambridge.[1]

August 24, 1402. Fait a remembrer que le xxiiij. iour Daugst lan du regne le Roy Henri quart puis le conquest tierce accorde estoit par les seignurs du conseil nostre dit seignur le Roy que briefs seuerales de[souz] le graunde seal serroient directz a Payn Tiptoft[2] Chiualer, Iohan Tiptoft son fitz Chiualer, Iohan de Brunne,[2] Symond de Brunne et Robert de Brunne fitz du dit Iohan de Brunne que chescun de eux sur peyne de cynk centz marz serroit deuant le dit conseil a le quinzein de Seint Michell adonques proschein ensuant pur responder a la matier compris en vn bille pendant deuant mesme le conseil a le suyt de Iohan de Gunwurdby, Adam de Egleston' Chapellein et Iohan de Lund' Chapellein nadgairs enfeoffes en les Manoirs de Rampton Cotenham et Westwyk en le Countee de Cantebr' al oeps de Monsieur Richard Lescrope les qeux briefs feurent liuerez a Thomas Sayville Sergeant darmes pur liuerer as ditz Monsieur Payn, Iohan Tiptoft, Iohan de Brunne, Symond et Robert. A quelle quinzein les ditz nadgairs enfeoffes et Monsieur Richard comparauntz en lour propre persones deuant le dit conseil et le dit Thomas Sayville venoit et testmoignay par soun serement as ditz seignurs du conseil quil auoit deliuere les ditz briefs as ditz Monsieur Payn, Iohan de Brunne et Symond a Cantebr' en le veille del exaltacion de la seint croys[3] et quil [se troua] les ditz Iohan Typtot et Robert et a mesme le quinzein Iohan de Brunne aparoit en propre persone et nulles de les autres. Et alors Iohan Durward vn des seignurs de mesme le conseil rehersa illeoques coment le dit Iohan de Brunne auoit a luy moeue[4] que sil voilloit treter en la dit matier

[1] *Council and Privy Seal*, file 11, m. 45.
[2] A commissioner of the peace, co. Cambridge, 1399–1401.
[3] September 13, 1402.
[4] 'moeves' = moved (*K.N.D*).

il eut deust faire par la grace de dieu tresbone [seruice ?]. Et sur ceo par auys des ditz seignurs et par assent des ditz enfeoffes et de Monsieur Richard le dit Iohan Durward feust ordeigne et prie par les ditz seignurs du conseil pur faire sa diligence pur treter et fyn faire de la matier auantdit. Pur quelle trete par cause que Iohan de Wynde sore qi est partie a ycelle ne feust present iour feust done outre as ditz parties tancque les oeptaues de Seint Martyn adonques proschein ensuant. Et sur ceo les ditz nadgairs enfeoffes faisoient le dit Monsieur Richard, William Mounceux et Iohan de Harwod lour attournes ioyntement et seueralement pur pursuer la dit bille deuaunt les ditz seignurs du conseil come illeoques appiert de recorde, as qeux oeptaues le dit Monsieur Richard en sa propre persone, William Mounceux et Iohan de Harwod come attournes pur les ditz nadgairs enfeoffes deuaunt mesme le Conseille appareroun t et le dit Iohan de Brunne en sa propre persone a mesme le iour apparust. Et par cause que le dit Iohan Durward auoit trete en la dit matier et supposa de faire bone fyn come il mesmes testmoignay illeoqes la dit cause feust contynue par assent des ditz parties tancque a la quinzein de Seint Hiller adonqes proschein ensuant pur ent treter come deuaunt. Et sur ceo le dit Iohan de Brunne ad enpris deuaunt mesme les seignurs du conseil que estrepement [1] wast destruccion delapidacion vent ou remouement de biens chateux ne blees sur les ditz Manoirs esteauntz ne serra nullement fait durant le trete auauntdit. Et le dit Iohan de Brunne ad enpris auxi qil ferra les ditz Payn, Iohan Tiptoft et Symond estre garnez pur estre deuaunt le dit conseil au dit quinzein pur responder a la matier en la dit bille compris chescun de eux sur peyn en les ditz briefs compris si accorde [pur se] tailler [2] en mesme la matier.

Item [3] que les briefs nadgairs adressez a Iohan Brunne, Iohan Wyndesore et autres a la suite de monsieur Richard Lescrop pur estre deuant le Counsail a ceste quinzeine de seint Michiel lexecucion des queux estoit mys en suspenses a cause que les persones as queux les ditz briefs feurent directz feurent en le seruice du Roi es parties de Gales soient renouelles et que mesmes les persones eient iour destre cy deuant le Counseil lendemain des almes [4] prochein sur la peyne contenue en les primers briefs.

Deposition and petition of William Stokes to the Council concerning offences against mercantile laws.[5]

Tresnobles tresreuerens et treshonores Seignurs. Je me recommande humblement a vostre treshaulte et treshonore Reuerence de tout mon petit seruice. Tresreuerens seignurs il est veritet que cascun vray subget et loyal liege de mon tres excellent et tresredoubte seignur le Roy est tenus par droite liegance et obeissance a poingarder sauuer [Henry IV.] May 25.

[1] 'estrepement' = action d'arracher, dégât, ravage (Bonnard and Salmon).
[2] 'se tailler' = to pronounce.
[3] Same file, m. 50. Dated October 18, 4 Hen. IV (1402).
[4] Morrow of All Souls = November 3, 1402.
[5] Cotton MSS., Galba, B. 1 (British Museum).

estre diligent a le honour prosperitet et profit de mon dit excellent seignur et son Royalme a tout son peoir. Et pur moy tresreuerens Seignurs en che [1] quiter Vous plese sauoir que plusieurs mesusancez et fourfaitz sont perpetuees de certaines laines peaulx lanus [2] et autres merchandises amenees hors le Royalme de cha le mer par certains subges lieges de mondit redoubte seignur et aultres en contraire sa honour leur liegiance et sa prosperitet sans paier les coustumes et droitures du Royalme que moy de ma petite persone desplese de coer. Et des quelles fourfaitours Jay en effect troeuet primirement Robert papeingay et martin Walsham mouliniers [3] de norwych qui auoent portet en la nef de Williame pegge de grymmesby certaines laines et peaulx lanus lesquelles a ma poursieute estoient arrestes de par le duc de Hollande. En tant poursieuant que par laide de Seignurs et bonnes gens mes amis par de cha aucuns plaintours subges del dit duc descie-nomme [4] qui se plandoient de grandet damage a eux fait des subges de mon dit excellent seignur dicelles biens fourfaits puissent estre contenteez et nous marchans estans par de cha communement estre pluis asseures. Le quel dieu merchi est mis en bon exploit et bonne fin auoec icelles biens fourfaits Ancoire que enoultre chelles sont demoret en arrest iiij^{c} sarpell[ieres] [5] de laines et iiij^{c} peaulx lanus En commun ws [6] et profit de mondit excellent seignur le Roy et le dit duc. Enoultre ceste mesusance ay entendu que sont aultres fourfaiteuers en tel cas, Assauoir Williame van buske de yerremuth Iehan meyer nommet Iehan croft de saint fide qui continuelment ammenient laines hors le Royalme sans paier le droit et coustume. Item Iehan broun nommet Iehan aindelar demorant entour Guynes en la marche de Caleys de le mesme mesusance. Item Thomas Wessy de Iork et aultres comme on dist. Item vn varlet de Henry stepynk de lyndesey qui ammena hors le Royalme xij^{mil} de peaux lanus. Et enoultre ces fourfaits depuis noel venus hors le Royalme plusieurs aultres nefs chergies de peaux lanus de Lynne iusque a xl^{mil} de Hombre de yerremuth et daultres places du Royalme sans paier leur droit et coustume par qui cest ou par les coustumiers ou par les clers ou par les sercheurs, Je ne say. Et tresreuerens Seignurs pour doresenauant telles mesusances et dishonours de mondit excellent seignur le Roy et son Royalme resister comme moy et cascun vray liege sumes tenus a nostre peoir Si ay tant poursieuit enuers le dit duc de Hollande au quel a la Reuerence et fauour de mon dit excellent seignur la mesuance desplest de bon coer. Et pour ce obuijer le dit duc ait de son commun conseil ordeinet et fermet que de ores en auant ou en quelcunque poit ville et distroit par tout son paijs viengnent telles mesfaitours hors le Royalme ammenans aucunes laines peaulx lanus ou aultres marchandises sans paier le droit et coustume du Royalme que tous icelles biens seront perdues et fourfaits En tel manire que mon dit excellent seignur le Roy aura lune moitiet et le dit duc laultre moitiet. Sur quelle ordinance le dit duc et son conseil moy volent donner puissance et lettres de commission

[1] 'ce.' [2] wool-fells. [3] millers.
[4] aforesaid. [5] sacks. [6] 'ws,' 'wes,' 'ues' = use.

pour che cherchier par tout son paijs. Au quel tresreuerentz Seignurs Je ne suy pas digne ne soffisant asses et ausi ne oseroye entreprendre tel charge sans la bonne deliberacion de vous volente et plaisir et par especialment sans auoir lettres patentes Royales de certain commandement de mondit excellent seignur moy sur ce fait. Pour quoy tres nobles seignurs Je vous supplie humblement que vous plese sur ce auoir vostre pourueue deliberacion. Et a moy ou a chelui qui vous plera commander vostre bon plesir sur ceste matere tellement poingardant que en che puisse estre fait toute diligence en saluation honour et prosperitet de mondit excellent seignur le Roy et son Royalme et le plesir del dit duc enuers quel en ceste cas et tous aultres trouueres tout bien toute grace et toute amistet dont nous nous communement remerchions de bon coer. Et par la grace de dieu vostre commandement sera perfournit de tout plain peoir comme Raison Requirt. Et vous plese escrire a le dit duc lettres de Remerchiance sur la dite matere certifiant a luy le commandement et plesir de mondit excellent seignur le Roy sur ceste matere et a nous enuoier la copie dicelle par de cha si vous plest. Et tresreuerens Seignurs pour vous pluis ad plain Informer des maistres des nefs du Royalme et estraunguiers qui ammenent les dictes laines peaulx lanus et aultres marchandises hors le Royalme sans faire leur deuoir vous enuoye leurs noms escripts en la bille chi enclose[1]. Mes Reuerens et honores seignurs voillies moy toudis commander comme vostre humble et petit seruitour. Li Sires tout puissant vous voille sauuer et garder corps et aume. Escript a Middelbourgh le xxv^{e} Jour de may.

To the priuye Councell.[2]

Vostre humble et petit seruitour

Williame Stokes.[3]

[*Addressed*] As tresnobles Reuerens et honores les chaunselier Tresorier et gardain du priuet seal Seignurs du Conseil de mon tresexcellent et tresredoubte Seignur monseignur le Roy dengleterre mes tresreuerens et treshonores Seignurs.

[*Endorsed*] Litera cuiusdam . . .
in partibus Hol . . .

Case before the Council in Star Chamber concerning alteration of a record.[4]

Memorandum quod vicesimo die Iunij Anno regni Regis Henrici Sexti post conquestum vndecimo quidam Robertus Danvers personaliter optulit se [coram consilio domini] Regis in Camera stellata in palacio Westmonasterii et ibidem pubblice exposuit et declarauit quod circiter duos annos iam elapsos ipse primo retentus fuit ad essendum de Consilio cuiusdam Thome Seintcleer et feoffatorum June 20, 1433.

[1] No bill is now with the document.

[2] These four words an interpolation in a later hand.

[3] The signature in the same clerkly hand as the rest of the document. Stokes is mentioned as a farrier to whom the king granted the custody of several manors. 1399-1401. *Patent Roll*, 1 Hen. IV, part i, m. 12; 2 Hen. IV, part ii, m. 31.

[4] *Council and Privy Seal*, file 54.

suorum in hijs que ad legem pertinent de et super iure et titulo Maneriorum de Barton Sancti Iohannis et Staunton Sancti Iohannis in Comitatu Oxonie. Et pro eo quod quedam Inquisicio[1] coram Radulfo Seintowayn nuper Escaetore domini Edwardi nuper Regis Anglie tercij a conquestu in Comitatu Surreie anno regni s[ui vice]simo septimo post mortem Rogeri de Sancto Iohanne capta et in Cancellaria sua retornata probabilis et manifesta iuris et tituli predictorum euidencia existit. Et predictus Robertus vt vnus de consilio predicti Thome et feoffatorum predictorum sequebatur ad Cancellariam predicti domini Regis nunc pro tenore eiusdem Inquisicionis inter alia sub magno sigillo domini Regis secundum formam iuris exemplificando. Ac postmodum predictus dominus Rex nunc tenorem predictum per literas suas patentes quarum datum est apud Westmonasterium terciodecimo die Iulij anno regni suo nono inter alia duxit exemplificari. In quibus quidem Inquisicione et exemplificacione adtunc inter alia continebatur ista clausula: 'Et quod Petrus de Sancto Iohanne est consanguineus et heres predicti Rogeri propinquior et etatis xl annorum et amplius,' que quidem clausula in omnibus de litteratura clara et vniformi adtunc extitit et non viciosa neque in aliquo rasa aut suspecta vt idem Robertus etiam consilio predicto publice exposuit et declarauit; dicebat insuper idem Robertus quod predictus numerus xl in predicta clausula contentus quamdiu non rasus nec viciosus vt predictum est extitit in magnam euidenciam eneruacionis et adnullacionis pretensi Iuris et tituli quorundam Iohannis Lydeyard et Clemencie vxoris eius de et in Maneriis predictis manifeste redundauit. In qua quidem clausula predictus numerus xl diu citra confeccionem eiusdem exemplificacionis de nouo rasus et iterum cum nouo incausto renouatus extitit et rescriptus prout in dicta inquisicione satis aperte eminet et apparet. De quibus quidem rasura renouacione et rescripcione predictus Robertus in diuersis regni partibus per nonnullos obloquentes multipliciter extitit deffamatus in ipsius Roberti scandalum et predicti Thome et feoffatorum suorum predictorum iuris et tituli de et in Maneriis predictis preiudicium non modicum et grauamen. Super quibus predictus Robertus predictam exemplificacionem coram dicto consilio publice demonstrans humiliter supplicauit tam pro domino Rege quam pro restitucione fame sue predicte quod Thomas Smyth Clericus qui habet custodiam dicte Inquisicionis necnon ceterorum recordorum Cancellarie domini Regis apud Turrim Londonii existencium sub Iohanne Frank Clerico Custode Rotulorum Cancellarie eiusdem domini Regis et Robertus Poleyn seruiens eiusdem Thome Smyth sint vocati ad dictum consilium ad recognoscendum quid nouerint vel dicere sciuerint de rasura predicta. Qui quidem Thomas et Robertus die et loco predictis coram dicto consilio comparentes et predictam Inquisicionem vt predictum est rasam secum portantes visisque eis insimul predictis Inquisicione et exemplificacione fide qua domino Regi tenebantur matura deliberacione dixerunt et recognouerunt quod predictus Robertus Poleyn scripsit eandem

[1] *Inquisitio post mortem,* 27 Edw. III, no. 27. The very clumsy forgery is still visible.

exemplificacionem et postea dicti Thomas Smyth et Robertus Poleyn simul examinauerunt predictas Inquisicionem et exemplificacionem in qua quidem examinacione adtunc in loco dicte rasure reperierunt solomodo istas literas x et l simul et antiquiter scriptas pro isto numero quadraginta non rasas suspectas nec in aliquo viciosas prout in dicta exemplificacione scribitur ac testatur. Verumptamen pro eo quod hec rasura falso et nisi tarde vt apparet extitit perpetrata dicunt quod quidam Willelmus Broket mediacione cuiusdam Gerardi de la Hay circiter festum Sancte Katerine Virginis vltimo preteritum[1] venit ad predictam Turrim vna cum predicto Roberto Poleyn et cum venisset illuc in domo vbi dicta Inquisicio remanebat vt predictus Robertus Poleyn asseruit predictus Willelmus pecijt visum antedicte inquisicionis quam videns requisiuit eum diuersa alia recorda scrutare dummodo ipse Willelmus dicte Inquisicionis copiam scriberet. Ipseque Robertus sciens ipsum Willelmum esse Clericum Scaccarii domini Regis et prout moris est iuratum eidem domino Regi permisit ipsum Willelmum solum scribentem copiam Inquisicionis antedicte dummodo ipse Robertus circa predictum aliud Scrutinium aliunde extitit occupatus per quod ipse Robertus bene recolit quod ipse numquam aliquem habere largum suum dictam nephandam rasuram fecisse permisit nisi solomodo predictum Willelmum. Et ideo pecijt quod dictus Willelmus sit vocatus in dictum consilium de et super premissis examinari etc. Et super hoc predictus Robertus Danvers pro maiori declaracione ac vera et plena notificacione innocencie sue de rasura predicta protulit diuersas copias literarum nomine predicti Iohannis Lydeyard factarum predictam rasuram concernencium et post eandem rasuram diuulgatam predicto Willelmo directarum. Protulit eciam dictus Robertus literas rescripcionum eiusdem Willelmi propria manu sua scriptas et sigillo suo signatas predicto Iohanni Lydeyard directas credente ipso Willelmo easdem literas ad possessionem predicti Iohannis Lydeyard tantum et non ad possessionem alterius deuenisse eandem rasuram tangentes. In quibus quidem literarum copijs nomine ipsius Iohannis vt predictum est factarum et eidem Willelmo in forma predicta directarum inter alia iste clausule sequentes continentur. Videlicet in prima copia: 'Right Welbeloved frende I comaund me to you. And Wull ye Witen that hit is gretely noysed in oure contrey by Danvers that the Clerke of the Tour seyn that ye rased the record of Piers Seintion'. Wherfore I praye you send me Wurd by letter Whether any of the Clerkes of the Tour in any Wyse myght aspie you in rasyng of the seyd Record And Whether ye have tolde your counsell to any of your Felowes that is aqueynted With Davers' etc. Et quoad istam literam et clausulas predictus Robertus eciam protulit quandam literam predicti Willelmi responsoriam propria manu sua scriptam predicto Iohanni directam. In qua quidem litera iste clausule sequentes inter alia continentur: 'Reuerent and Wurshipfull Sir, I recommaund me vnto you desiryng your good Welfare praying you to recommaund me vnto my maistres your Wife Doyng you to Wite that I vndirstand your letter Wele.

[1] November 25, 1432.

And as touchyng the Clerke of the Tour *Credo quod non vidit* &c. And as touchyng the counsell *Nemini loquebar nisi quod scitis'* etc. Deinde idem Robertus protulit quandam aliam copiam cuiusdam alterius litere nomine predicti Iohannis facte et eidem Willelmo directe predictam rasuram tangentis. In qua quidem copia inter alia iste clausule continentur: 'I preie you send me redy Wurd Whether the Clerk in any Wyse might aspie you While the rasure Was in hond, And Wher aboute the Clerk Was ocupied in the mene tyme, And also send me redy Wurd whether the olde letter be clene away as ye suppose or no' etc. Et quoad hoc idem Robertus insuper protulit quandam aliam literam ipsius Willelmi responsoriam eciam propria manu sua scriptam et eidem Iohanni directam. In qua iste clausule sequentes inter alia continentur: 'As touchyng the Clerk he was busy aboute other thynges therwhile; For I do you to Wite that hit Was in a large hous. And the olde letter is clene away as I suppose' etc. Deinde idem Robertus protulit quandam aliam copiam cuiusdam alterius litere nomine predicti Iohannis facte eidem Willelmo directe predictam rasuram eciam concernentis. In qua ista clausula inter alia continetur: 'And also I preie you hertily sendeth [*sic*] me redy Wurd Whether the olde letter in the record by fore etc. Were evyn xl as the newe is nowe and nothing more ne lasse or ellys more as xliiij or a nother somme. For yet I coude neuer vndirstond that clerly for men speke much that ther shuld be a gret space seyn after the noumbre' etc. Et quoad istam literam et clausulam predictus Robertus Danvers protulit quandam aliam literam dicti Willelmi responsoriam propria manu sua vt predictum est scriptam et predicto Iohanni directam. In qua iste clausule sequentes inter alia continentur: 'And as touchyng the olde letter in the record I sawe it nether more ne lesse then xl noumbre. And ther to sayd my Maisters Martyn Cottesmore and Paston' that it Was by fore etc. the nombre of xxiiij^or^. And therfore as touchyng that neyther avaunt nor arere as to me in that case' etc. Et super hoc predictus Robertus Danvers pecijt quod predictus Willelmus vocetur singulis predictis copijs litteris et euidencijs versus eum superius allegatis coram dicto Consilio responsurus. Qui quidem Willelmus ibidem personaliter adtunc comparens auditisque visis et intellectis sibi predictis copijs litteris et euidencijs affirmauit et cognouit quod tot et tales littere et clausule nomine predicti Iohannis Lydeyard facte ad manus suas vt premittitur deuenerunt et quod ipse credens eas per predictum Iohannem factas fore et missas fecit predictas litteras et clausulas responsorias et eas propria manu sua scripsit prout superius declaratur. Cognouit insuper quod ipse solus circiter festum Sancte Katerine virginis vltimo preteritum transiuit cum predicto Roberto Poleyn' ad Turrim predictam et quod nullus eo tempore fuit in domo vbi recorda predicta fuerunt nisi ipsi duo tantum prout idem Robertus prius exposuit et quod ipse Willelmus solus adtunc vngue digiti sui predictum numerum xl in dicta inquisicione tempore aduentus sui contentum rasit et eundem numerum vt in hoc maxime videretur suspectum cum nouo incausto renouauit et blottauit. Et requisitum fuit ibidem ab eo qui numerus in predicta inquisicione primo in predicto loco raso tempore sui aduentus illuc extitit. Dixit quod iste numerus xl tantum et non maior numerus neque minor. Requisitum itaque fuit ab eo ad cuius instanciam venit apud Turrim predictam pro rasura huiusmodi facienda. Dixit quod ad instanciam predicti Johannis Lydeyard. Et super hoc dominus Thesaurarius Anglie qui circa examinacionem eiusdem Willelmi de rasura predicta diuersimode extitit laboratus ibidem aperte promisit quod idem Willelmus pro premissis transgressionibus amodo in domini Regis Scaccario minime resideret. Deinde dominus Cancellarius Anglie de assensu consilij predicti laudans labores predicti Roberti Danvers in adquisicione predictarum litterarum pro declaracione sua rasure antedicte eundem Robertum nullo modo reum set innocentem rasure huiusmodi et immunem ibidem publice declarauit. Et vlterius quod idem Willelmus non amodo scriberet neque resideret in aliqua Curia domini Regis vbi recorda occuparentur aut exstiterint. Et super hoc predictus Robertus pecijt omnia predicta pro eius declaracione irrotulari etc. Et ei conceditur etc.

H. gloucestre.[1] T. Duresme.[2] J. Bathon. Canc.[3] H. Cantuar.[4] W. Lincoln.[5] R. Londonien.[6] P. Elien.[7] H. Stafford.[8] H. Norhumbyrlond.[9]

[*Endorsed.*] x^o^ die Iulij Anno xj^mo^ apud Westmonasterium lectus et concordatus fuit presens actus et pro declaracione innocencie quantum ad Rasuram de qua infra fit mencio infrascripti Roberti Danvers concordatum et concessum fuit quod fiat Warantum sub priuato sigillo Cancellario Anglie directum includendo in eodem tenorem actus predicti mandando eidem quod tenorem eundem in rotulis Cancellarie inter Recorda eiusdem inscribi et irrotulari [10] faciat ibidem pro Recordo excusacionis predicti Roberti ab omni crimine rasure predicte remansuro de Recordo presentibus dominis se intra subscribentibus et alijs.

The Record of an Inquisitorial Examination, 17 *Henry VI*.[11]

Hi sunt articuli examinationum iiij^{or} partium sequentium infrascriptarum videlicet Thomae Wauton militis etc.[12] Et responsiones ad eosdem articulos.

The x^{e} day of Feverer the xvii^{e} year of the Kyng at Westm[inster] Feb. 10, 1439.

[1] Humphrey Plantagenet, created duke of Gloucester, 1414, *ob.* 1446.
[2] Thomas Langley, bishop of Durham, 1406–37.
[3] John Stafford, bishop of Bath and Wells, 1425–43; made chancellor of England in March 1433.
[4] Henry Chicheley, archbishop of Canterbury, 1414–43.
[5] William Grey, bishop of Lincoln, 1431–6.
[6] Robert Fitzhugh, bishop of London, 1431–6.
[7] Philip Morgan, bishop of Ely, 1426–35.
[8] Humphrey, earl of Stafford, *ob.* 1459.
[9] Henry Percy, created earl of Northumberland, 1414, *ob.* 1455.
[10] Enrolled on Close Roll, 11 Hen. VI, m. 4 d.
[11] As yet this is an unfiled document found in the 'Exchequer Box'. It relates to the case of Lord Fanhope previously described, *ante*, p. 298.
[12] These were the four justices of the peace who had made allegations against Lord Fanhope, who in turn offered a petition against them.

in ye sterre Chambre beyng yarine present ye high and migti prince Duc of Gloucestre, the bisshops of Bath Chaunceller and of Seint David, yerles of Sar[isbury] and Northumbr[land], the lord Crumwell Tresorer of Englande, William Lyndewode Keper of the kyngs prive seal, and Robert Rolleston Warderober, ye kings counsaillours examined ye persones whoos names here on follow upon ye Ryot yat was doo at Bedford ye xij^e day of Januer ye yere above seid.

And first was called before . . . Wauton and sworn . . .

[Half of the page is torn away.]

Walton is sworn and examined on a number of articles.

He answered as to ye nombre of persones with a sexti, And as to yeire array with yikke dowblett and sword and Rokelers, and yus arraid some of yeime come in to ye halle and a too of within ye barre.

It was asked yif ye seid lord Faunhop at oyer sessions afore yat tyme was wont to come in like array he answered ye.

[Half page torn.]

He was asked yif he and his felows such tyme as ye lord Faunhop come to yeime dede him eny reverence or What countenance yei made ; he seid yat his iij^e felows stode up and he sitting stille a baled his hede.

[Page torn.]

. . . and forthwith Wauton saith yat he seid to ye lord Fanhop it is ye enveulyest session yat I have ever sey in Bedford, and yif it be not oyerwise reuled I wol complaine unto ye kyngs counseill ; to ye which ye lord Faunhop shulde have seid complayne as you wolt, I deffye yi manassyng and alt ym evel will. Wawton seide he answered sette litil of yi defiance, and with yis yere rumor and noyse in ye holle and soo yei rose up both ye lord Faunhop, Wawton, Enderby and alt ye remenant and ye lord Faunhop stode upon ye Chekker borde ye which borde stode a fore ye bench.

[Page torn.]

. . . such tyme as he stode upon ye borde labored to the cessing of ye rumor and debate or ellis yat he stured and moved ye pepill to Rumor and answered yat he labored to cesse ye noyse and ye rumor yat was in ye halle ; he was asked wheder he labored effectuelly or all faintly and under colour of his labored suffird harme to be doo, he answered y^t to his understandyng he labored to ye keping of pees and to stynte ye noyse and Rumor yat was in ye halle and all soo diligently as ever he sawe man.

[Page torn.]

Enderby is examined on the same articles.

. . . of makyng of ye certificat ye which was put unto ye Kyng his felows and he wer in difference and discorde not for yan he sette his seal yereto.

As to ye ij^e to ye iij^de to ye iiij^e to ye v^e ye vi^e and vii^e articles he accordyd in his deposition and answere with Thomas Wawton.

As to ye viij^e article he seid yei stode up all such tyme as ye lord Faunhop come to yeime.

. . . x^e he accorded in substance with . . .

[Page torn.]

Another of the

In ye yridde ye iiij^e ye v^e and ye sexte articles he accorded in his deposition with Wawton and Enderby.

As to ye vii[e] article he accorded with Enderby and not with Wawton. justices is examined.

As to ye viij[e] article he accordeth also.

As to ye ix[e] article he accordeth with Wawton . . .

[Page torn.]

In ye seconde article he accorded also with his felows save he varied in noumbre, seying yet ye lord Faunhope cam to Bedford with xl or l persones. And another.

[Page torn.]

He was asked how ye Rumor began and he yerein accorded with ye seyeng of Wawton, and soo he dede in all his depositions savying in ye xi[e] article he varied fro all seyeng yat ye lord Faunhop such tyme as he stode upon he Chekker borde he made countenaunce toward Enderby as he wolde have smote him but he seith he smote him not.

Writ of 'certiorari' from the King to Thomas Kent, clerk of the Council, with reply showing disobedience of persons when summoned before the Council 'de riotis'.[1]

Ex Bundello brevium Regis de anno xxxv[to] Henrici Sexti. May 25, 1457.

Henricus dei gratia Rex Anglie et Francie et dominus Hibernie dilecto et fideli suo Thome Kent Clerico Consilij nostri salutem. Volentes certis de Causis certiorari super tenorem cuiusdam actus in quindena pasche vltimo preterita apud Westmonasterium in Camera stellata Coram Consilio nostro de et super allegacione ostensione et declaracione ex parte Iohannis Ducis Norffolcie factis de quibusdam articulis in actu predicto contentis Tibi precipimus quod tenorem actus predicti nobis in Cancellariam nostram sub Sigillo tuo distincte et aperte sine dilacione mittas et hoc breve. Teste me ipso apud Westmonasterium xxv[to] die Maij anno regni nostri xxxv[to]. Kirkbie.

Respontio huius brevis talis est quod
actum de quo fit mentio in eodem brevi
transmitto cum eodem brevi.
per Thomam Kent Clericum
Consilij domini Regis.

Quindena pasche anno xxxv[to] Regis Henrici Sexti apud Westmonasterium in Camera stellata coram Consilio domini Regis fuit allegatum ostensum et declaratum ex parte Iohannis Ducis Norffolcie quod vbi virtute cuiusdam acti [*sic*] parliamenti apud Reding inchoati[2] emanauerunt breuia separalia tam vicecomiti London quam vicecomiti Suffolcie ad faciendum proclamaciones quod dictus Dux comparere deberet coram Consilio predicto ad respondendum Regi tam de contemptu ex eo quod non comparuit virtute cuiusdam alterius breuis sibi directo quam certis Riotis et offensis specificatis et suppositis prout in eisdem brevibus de proclamacionibus continetur.

[1] This is not an original record, but a transcript of a later date. Exchequer Box (unfiled). Act 35 Hen. VI.

[2] The Statute, 31 Hen. VI.

Et fuit allegatum pro parte dicti Ducis quod breve primum supradictum super quo dicta brevia de proclamacionibus fundata fuerunt minus insufficiens fuit et invalidum in lege pro eo quod minime emanauit secundum formam dicti statuti quia nulla facta fuit mencio in eodem de Riotis et aliis contentis in eodem Statuto et per consequens prefata brevia de proclamacionibus fiendis fundata super dicto breve nullius valoris haberentur. Et ideo ex parte eiusdem Ducis petitum et postulatum fuit quod brevia predicta in forma supradicta exeuntia cassarentur et adnullarentur. Super quibus domini de Consilio examinatis predictis et habitis deliberacione et communicacione cum Iusticiariis Regis videntes quod superius allegata erant vera declarauerunt ipsa brevia in forma predicta habita et processum inde sequutum cassa ac nulla et quod pro nullis haberentur et quod predictus Dux inde penitus exonaretur et minime obligatum fuisse et esse ad comparendum virtute proclamacionum factarum per eadem brevia.

In Octabis sancti Iohannis Baptiste anno xxxv^to^ Regis Henrici Sexti Thomas Curwen miles vicecomes Comitatus Cumbrie cui preceptum fuit per breve Regis quod deliberare deberet certa brevia separalia super Statutum de Riotis Gulielmo Martindale militi Georgio Mar' et aliis de essendo coram Rege et Consilio suo etc. Certificauit in certa scedula annexa brevi sibi directo in forma vt sequitur virtute brevis domini Regis huic scedule consuti: 'ego Thomas Curwen Chiualer vicecomes Cumbrie deliberari feci Geo' Mark vnum breve domini Regis de Subpena super Statutum de Riotis apud Newton in Comitatu predicto' etc.

Subscribitur Thomas Kent:

Vicesimo quinto die Iunij Anno xxxv^to^ Regis Henrici Sexti apud Westmonasterium Willelmus Grimesby armiger prestito prius Iuramento certificauit Regio Consilio quod Ricardus Micoo valectus Corone domini nostri Regis habuit duo priuata Sigilla regia viz. vnum ad deliberandum Thome Veysey de Castle Bitham in Comitatu Lincolnie et aliud Willelmo Salfourth de eadem per que precipiebatur eisdem ad comparendum coram Rege et Consilio suo in Crastino sancti Iohannis videlicet dicto xxv^to^ die Iunij ad respondendum certis Riotis per eosdem Thomam et Willelmum Salfourth perpetratis vt surmittebatur. Qui quidem Thomas et Willelmus Sallfourth se absentarunt et retraxerunt et vterque eorum se absentauit et retraxit ad finem quod non reciperent dicta priuata Sigilla nec dicto die comparuerunt etc.

Subscribitur Thomas Kent.

Vicesimo octauo die Iunij anno xxxv^to^ dicti Regis Iohannes Yuse nuncius domine Regine Anglie iuratus certificauit Consilio regio quod habuit diversa privata Sigilla regia separalia deliberanda Ricardo Smyth et alijs etc. ad comperendum [*sic*] etc. ad respondendum certis Riotis etc. qui quidem Ricardus et ceteri et quilibet eorum absentauit et retraxit se ad finem quod non reciperent dicta priuata Sigilla nec comparuerunt dictis octabis Trinitatis.

Subscribitur Thomas Kent.

Nono die Februarii anno xxxv^{to} Henrici Sexti apud Westmonasterium Iohannes Brewster vnus Clericorum in officio priuati Sigilli domini nostri Regis prestito prius iuramento certificauit regio Consilio quod ipse habuit quoddam privatum Sigillum directum Willelmo Grindell per quod precipiebatur eidem quod compareret coram Rege et Consilio suo dicto nono die videlicet in Octabis purificationis beate Marie Virginis ad respondendum diversis Riotis et mesprisionibus per eundem perpetratis vt surmittebatur qui quidem Willelmus noluit illud privatum Sigillum supradictum recipere nec eodem die comparuit etc.

Subscribitur Thomas Kent.

Tricesimo die Iunij anno xxxv^{to} Regis Henrici Sexti apud Westmonasterium Iohannes Gravesson de Comitatu Lancastrie prestito prius Iuramento certificauit regio Consilio quod ipse habuit diversa privata Sigilla regia separalia deliberanda Thome Clapam de Bemesley, Iacobo Osbaldeston, Iacobo Ratcliff de Bradley, Iohanni Puddesey, Willelmo Clapam, Roberto Clapam et Thome Clapam filijs eiusdem Willelmi Clapam, Thome Clapam et Alexandro Clapam filijs Ricardi Clapam de Comitatu Eboraci per que precipiebatur cuilibet eorum ad comparendum coram Rege et Consilio suo in Crastino sancti Iohannis Baptiste vltimo preterito ad respondendum diversis Riottis per eosdem Commissis vt surmittebatur. Et dictus Iohannes Grauesson dicit per sacramentum suum predictum quod dicti Thomas, Iacobus, Iacobus, Iohannes Pudesey, Willelmus, Robertus, Thomas, Thomas et Alexander et quilibet eorum receperunt dicta privata Sigilla. Qui quidem Thomas, Iacobus, Iacobus, Iohannes, Willelmus, Robertus, Thomas, Thomas et Alexander non comparuerunt nec aliquis eorum comparuit ad dictum Crastinum sancti Johannis.

Subscribitur Thomas Kent.

A Bill of Costs, tem. Henry VI.[1]

Expens ex parte Richard Snellyng.

Costage and expens for to sywe to the kyng and the counseyll.

Furst for the furst bylle that we put to our soveraygne lord for the makyng	vi*s*. 8*d*.
Item for another bylle	iij*s*. iiij*d*.
Item for the thyrd bylle	vj*s*. viij*d*.
Item for the prevy seall	iij*s*. iiij*d*.
Item to the kyngis secretere	vj*s*. viij*d*.
Item in wyne gyeve to squyers and others	xij*d*.
Item for costage & expense to London & homeward of Richard Snellyng and his horse	x*s*. viij*d*.
Item to the secretere of my lord of Somersete for a letter	vj*s*. viij*d*.
Item to a squyer of my lord	iij*s*. iiij*d*.
Item for a costage thether	xij*d*.

[1] *Chanc. Misc.*, unfiled. The material is a fragment; later examples may be found in Leadam, *Select Cases in Star Chamber*, ii, 196; and in *Letters and Papers of Henry VIII, passim*.

Item for costage and expense for to hand our letteres to my lord Chaunceler iiij*s*. iij*d*.
Item to ye kyngis secretere for the endytyng of our letter to ye kyng vj*s*. viij*d*.
Item for the same letter iij nyw maket and y wryte x*s*.
Item for the privy seall and the wrytyng ther last & ye copyes makyng xx*s*.
Item to my lord chaunceleris rechester for his labour vj*s*. viij*d*.
Item in wyne to squyerse and other genthilmen at dyverse tymys ij*s*. viij*d*.
Item for my costage and expens rydyng to London and home and y beyng xv*s*. vij*d*.
Summa v*li*. xv*s*. ij*d*.
ex parte Ricardi Snellyng.
Item expens ex parte predicti Ricardi in Brittann xliij*s*. vj*d*.
Item expens ex parte predicti Ricardi pro lamprayes xvj*s*.
summa total ex parte predicti Ricardi viij*li*. xiiij*s*. viij*d*.
Item expens ex parte Nycolas Joh' in Brytann eodem vice xxv*s*.
Expens ex parte Robert Gold de Abbotsbury.
Item for the privy seal x*s*.
Item for a letter to the secretere of Bretaigne iij*s*. iiij*d*
Item for fysh to my lord chaunceler at Hoke iij*s*. iiij*d*.
Item for rydyng and costage to London and for his labour & his horse xxviij*s*.
Summa xliiij*s*. viij*d*.
ex parte Robt Gold.
Summa total omnium expensarum xij*l*. iiij*s*. iiij*d*.
Item predictus Ricardus recepit de Williamo Oliver xxxiij*s*. iiij*d*.
Item predictus Ricardus recepit de Roberto Goold xx*s*.
Item predictus Ricardus recepit de Williamo Eustas xiij*s*. iiij*d*.
Item predictus Ricardus recepit de Hourac Eustas vj*s*. viij*d*.

[to W. Oliver:]
Item in costage for the third requeste furst ye kyngis secretere for a letter to ye prive seall vj*s*. viij*d*.
Item to a gentyllman of my lord chaunceler iij*s*. iiij*d*.
Item for the makyng endytyng and wrytyng of the third request xx*s*.
Item to a squyer of my lord pryvy seall for to help y[t] yit mygth be seled vj*s*. viij*d*.
Item for a copy of the second requeste iij*s*. iiij*d*.
Item to ij men to gede me in my way xx*d*.
Item for my costage xij dayes x*s*.
Item for my costage Robert Golde & William Eustas ryder ward every man ij*s*. vj*d*.

Item for Robert Golde and William Eustas is costage homeward every of hem xv*d*.
summa ij*s*. vj*d*.

Of the summe y[t] y have payed for ye thirde requeste y have resceyved of Robert and William forseyd xx*s*.
Sum of my part for the thirde requeste xxxiij*s*. vj*d*.
Sum of Robert and Will xxvj*s*. vj*d*. Sum total iij*li*. ij*d*.

APPENDIX IV

DESCRIPTION OF SOURCES AND AUTHORITIES

The sources of information that have been drawn upon for the history of the king's council are extremely varied and extensive. They include necessarily most of the general collections of England for the middle ages. So persistent were the activities of the council in every direction that some allusion or point of description may be found in the most unexpected places. It would be manifestly useless to make an enumeration of all the references that have been given in this volume, but a brief account will be offered of the sources and authorities, both those in manuscript and those in printed form, which have proved most valuable.

Chronicles and other literary sources are not likely to be of much service in a history of this kind. The monastic writers were little concerned with the institutions of government and were usually lacking in legal understanding. Still the chronicles are not to be ignored, for they are constantly making allusions and reflecting impressions, which are often inaccurate but are not for this reason untruthful. Especially when the council became a subject of political contention, the monk was frequently an eager partisan, and his coloured description of the events is a more faithful reflection of the feelings of the time than the bare official records. Sometimes also, especially during the early period, a well-informed chronicler has given material that is not mentioned in other sources, or he has composed a flowing narrative which is an aid to the interpretation of the records. Here and there in the history of a religious house there occurs the account of a law case, revealing the peculiar difficulties of a suitor and various steps of procedure. To mention the most indispensable works of this character, for the time of Henry II the best references have been found in Benedict of Peterborough, *Gesta Regis* (2 vols. Rolls Ser. 1867); Roger of Hoveden, *Chronica* (4 vols. Rolls Ser. 1868–71); Gervase of Canterbury (2 vols. Rolls Ser. 1879–80); and the collection known as *Materials for the History of Thomas Becket* (7 vols. Ibid. 1875–85). For the events of Henry III there are Roger of Wendover, *Flores Historiarum* (Eng. Hist. Soc. 1842; and Rolls Ser. 1886–9); Richard of Morins, *Annales de Dunstaplia* (Rolls Ser. 1886); Walter of Coventry, *Historical Collections* (2 vols. Ibid. 1872–3); *Annals of Burton-upon-Trent* (Ibid. 1864), and Thomas Wykes, *Chronicon* (Ibid. 1869). But nothing of the period equals the voluminous works of Matthew Paris, England's greatest mediaeval historian, biased and inaccurate as he often is, particularly the *Chronica Majora* (7 vols. Rolls Ser. 1872–83), and the *Historia Minor* (3 vols. Ibid. 1866–9). From this time, partly because of the expansion of official records, the chronicles are less serviceable. There are to be noticed the *Chronicles of the Reigns of Edward I and Edward II*, including *Annales Londonienses*, *Annales Paulini*, and the *Gesta of Bridlington* (2 vols. Rolls Ser. 1882–3) ; Adam Murimuth, *Continuatio Chronicorum* (Ibid. 1889) ; John of Trokelowe, *Annales*, and Henry of Blaneford, *Chronica et Annales* (Ibid. 1866) ; William Rishanger, *Chronica et Annales* (Ibid. 1865) ; Robert of Avesbury, *De Gestis Edwardi Tertii* (Ibid. 1889) ; Henry Knighton, *Chronicon*, with *Continuation* (2 vols. Ibid. 1889–95) ; Walter of Hemingburgh, *Chronicon* (2 vols. Eng. Hist. Soc., 1848–9) ; and *Chronicon Angliae* (Rolls Ser. 1874 ; another edition in *Archaeologia*, vol. xxii, pp. 204–84). For the time of Richard II and the Lancastrians there are passages in Thomas Walsingham, *Historia Anglicana* (2 vols. Rolls Ser. 1863–4) ; *Annales Ricardi Secundi et Henrici Quarti* (Ibid. 1866) ; Thomas of Burton, *Chronica de Melsa* (3 vols. Ibid. 1866–8) ; *Chronicle of the Abbey of Croyland* (ed. H. T. Riley, 1854) ; John Whethamstede, *Registrum* (Rolls Ser. 1872) ; *Chronicle of Richard II, Henry IV, and Henry VI* (Camden Soc. 1856) ; and Froissart, *Chronicles* (a scholarly edition by the Société des Anciens Textes Français, 3 vols. Paris, 1895–9 ; a serviceable translation by Thomas Johnes, 5 vols. 1803–10).

A considerable amount of information has been obtained from various collections of letters, both private and official. Most important is the great series in the Public Record Office known as *Ancient Correspondence* or *Royal and Historical Letters* in 58 volumes, consisting mainly of letters and petitions that were preserved in the chancery. This is a veritable mine of official correspondence, which would be of greater service were it fully calendared. From this and other sources various smaller collections have been edited and published. For example there are *Royal and other Letters of the Reign of Henry III* (2 vols. Rolls Ser. 1862–6) ; *Letters of Robert Grosseteste* (Ibid. 1861) ; *Original Letters illustrative of English History* (ed. Henry Ellis, London, 1824) ; *Royal and Historical Letters during the Reign of Henry IV* (Rolls Ser. 1860) ; *Letters of the English in France during the Reign of Henry VI* (Ibid. 1861–4) ; *Official Correspondence of Thomas Beckington* (2 vols. Ibid. 1872) ; *Letters and Papers of Richard III and Henry VII* (2 vols. Ibid. 1861–3) ; the *Paston Letters*, 1422–1509 (ed. James Gairdner, 4 vols. 1900–1). A volume from the *Cottonian MSS.* (British Museum, Galba B, I), containing a number of letters and diplomatic documents, has been edited by Edward Scott (Académie Royale des Sciences, Bruxelles, 1896).

At every step the supreme value of the great rolls of the chancery and the exchequer has been manifest. Fortunately these are now available to a great extent in printed form. First the *Patent Rolls*, beginning with the Reign of John, continue in a practically unbroken series through the whole of the age that has been covered. The earliest of these letters of state are published in the *Rotuli Litterarum Patentium*, 1201–16 (Record Commission, 1835). In the *Calendars of State Papers*, the great series now being published under the Master of the Rolls, the *Patent Rolls of Henry III*, containing the full Latin text, have been completed to the year 1366. In the same series the *Calendars of Patent Rolls*, giving the contents of the Rolls in the form of an abridged translation, are now complete from 1272 to 1367, and from 1377 to 1485. The parallel series of the *Close Rolls* have also been extensively published. Of these there are the *Rotuli Litterarum Clausarum*, 1204–27 (2 vols. Rec. Com. 1833–44); the *Calendars of Close Rolls* of Henry III in full text have now reached the year 1242; and the same series in abridgement continues from the year 1272 to 1374. Of the Gascon Rolls a portion has been edited by F. Michel, *Rôles Gascons* (*Documents inédits sur l'Histoire de France*, 1885), and continued by Charles Bémont, *Supplément* to the same (1896), and *Rôles Gascons*, vol. ii, 1273–90. The *Roman Rolls* and the *French Rolls* constitute a less regular series of letters under the great seal which have been used only in the original manuscripts. The *Rotuli Parliamentorum* (6 vols. Rec. Com. 1767–77), another systematic record of the chancery, contains proceedings of the council as well as of parliament. The *Memoranda de Parliamento* (ed. Maitland, Rolls Ser. 1893) is a special record of the parliament of 1305. The *Statutes of the Realm* (11 vols. Rec. Com. 1810–28) is a standard collection of laws and charters. *Parliamentary Writs and Writs of Military Service* (2 vols. Rec. Com. 1827–34) contain extensive excerpts from the chancery rolls for the reigns of Edward I and Edward II. A work best mentioned in this connexion is the *Report of the Lords' Committees touching the Dignity of a Peer* (5 vols. 1820–9; another edition in Parliamentary Papers, House of Commons, 1826). Of this noted report the first volume gives a history of legislative assemblies, both parliaments and councils, while the second and third volumes contain extracts from the sources.

Among the archives of the exchequer the *Memoranda Rolls*, beginning with the reign of Henry III, have been the most important for the purpose of this work. Of these rolls there are two sets, the one having been kept by the king's remembrancer and designated as *K. R.*, the other by the lord treasurer's remembrancer and marked *L. T. R.* These records contain materials of the utmost variety in the way of writs, law cases, and ordinances. Because of their great size they are exceedingly difficult to use, and yet very few extracts from them are to be found in print. Some are given in *Transactions of the Royal Historical Society*, new series, vol. iii, pp. 281–91; the roll of 3 Hen. III is in Cooper, *Proceedings of the Royal Commissioners* (1833); and numerous passages are quoted in Madox, *History of the Exchequer*. The *Issue Rolls*, especially the series known as *Pells*, were a record of payments made in the form of assignments of the king's revenue. They have been found especially valuable for the history of the council, because the remuneration of members and other persons in the service of the council was commonly made in this manner. Extracts have been published in F. Devon, *Issue Roll of Thomas Brantingham*, 44 Edw. III (Rec. Com. 1835); and *Issues of the Exchequer* (Ibid. 1837). Certain miscellaneous items relating to dinners and other expenditures are found in the bundles of *Accounts*

Exchequer K. R., and in Palgrave, *Antient Kalendars and Inventories of the Exchequer* (Rec. Com. 1836).

Other published collections of diverse character include the *Foedera* (ed. Thomas Rymer, 'Original' edition, 17 vols. 1704–17; and 'record' edition, 4 vols. Rec. Com. 1816–69), a standard compilation of treaties and diplomatic documents. D. Wilkins, *Concilia Magnae Britanniae et Hiberniae* (4 vols. 1737), affords material concerning the procedure of ecclesiastical courts and councils. A few notes have been derived from *Ordinances and Regulations of the Royal Household* (Soc. Antiq. 1790). Mention should be made also of *Documents illustrative of the Thirteenth and Fourteenth Centuries* (ed. Cole, Rec. Com. 1844); *First Report on the Public Records* (1800); and with reference to the final chapter the *Letters and Papers of the Reign of Henry VIII* (ed. Gairdner, 21 vols. in series of State Papers). Smaller source books of general character are Stubbs, *Select Charters* (Oxford, 1890), and Adams and Stephens, *Select Documents* (London, 1901).

From the nature of the subject legal records and works of law have been drawn upon to a great extent. The rolls of the common law courts, including the early *Rotuli Curiae Regis*, the *Placita coram Rege*, and the *Placita de Banco*, are far too bulky to be used systematically in their original form, so that under present conditions one must depend mainly upon printed collections so far as these exist. M. M. Bigelow, *Placita Anglo-Normannica* (London, 1879), consists of extracts from the chronicles of the eleventh and twelfth centuries. The *Placitorum Abbreviatio*, Rich. I—Edw. II (Rec. Com. 1811), in spite of many imperfections, owing to the lack of other works of similar scope, is still very serviceable. The proceedings of the king's bench for a single typical year is given in Phillimore, *Placita coram Rege*, 25 Edw. I (British Record Society, 1898). Because of the care with which they have been edited the selections of cases published by the Selden Society are of special importance. The series begins with F. W. Maitland, *Select Pleas of the Crown*, 1200–25; and a parallel volume is W. P. Baildon, *Select Civil Pleas* (vol. iii). *Bracton's Note Book* (ed. Maitland, Cambridge, 1887) is of unequalled value for the same purpose. The *Exchequer Plea Rolls* are far less bulky than those of the *Curia Regis*, and it is to be hoped that selections from these will some day be published. W. C. Bolland has edited the *Eyre of Kent*, 6–7 *Edw. II* (Selden Society, 1912). Of proceedings in the court of chancery there are the *Placita in Cancellaria* from the reign of Edward I, and the bundles of *Chancery Proceedings* (Index in the Public Record Office), beginning in the reign of Edward III. Publications from the latter are made in *Calendar of Proceedings in Chancery* (2 vols. Rec. Com. 1827–30); Baildon, *Select Cases in Chancery* (Selden Society, vol. x); and C. T. Martin, *Some Chancery Proceedings of the Fifteenth Century* (*Archaeologia*, vol. 59, pp. 1–24). Sanders, *Orders in Chancery* (London, 1845), has various materials of the same kind. Extracts from the proceedings of other extraordinary courts are given in R. G. Marsden, *Select Pleas in the Court of Admiralty* (Selden Society, vol. vi); I. S. Leadam,

Select Cases in Star Chamber (2 vols. Ibid. vols. xvi and xxv); G. Bradford, *Proceedings in the Court of Star Chamber in the Reigns of Henry VII and Henry VIII* (Somerset Record Society); Leadam, *Select Cases in the Court of Requests* (Selden Society, vol. xii); and Sir Julius Caesar, *Ancient State, Authoritie and Proceedings of the Court of Requests* (1597).

For revealing the peculiar functions of the council no line of records has proved more valuable than the *Ancient Petitions* of which about 17,000 are on file in the Public Record Office. These manuscripts are very difficult to deal with because at one time in the history of the Record Office a reorganization of the files was made, whereby the petitions were arranged in alphabetical order irrespective of their dates and former connexions. The dates which are essential to their utility in following the development of the courts can now be ascertained only by dint of search in every case for a corroborative document. There is a *Report of Select Committee on Public Petitions* (Parl. Papers, 1833, vol. xii), containing particularly the observations of Sir Francis Palgrave (pp. 19–24). Under the direction of Sir F. Palgrave several volumes of transcripts were compiled, which are now the only means of observing the order followed in the earlier files. With the exception of the petitions that are given in the rolls of parliament and in various chancery proceedings, not many of them are to be found in printed collections. For this reason the volume of the Société Jersiaise, *Ancient Petitions of the Chancery and the Exchequer* (Jersey, 1902), and the William Salt Archaeological Society of Staffordshire (new series, vols. vi and vii), are worthy of attention.

From the time of Edward I certain unofficial reports of trials appear in the form of the *Year Books*. Less bulky than the rolls, they are valuable for descriptions of points of procedure, especially as they cover a wide range of cases and are not confined to the courts of common law. Several of the books of Edward I have been published in the Rolls Series (ed. Horwood, 5 vols. 1866–79); those of Edward II have been undertaken by the Selden Society (Year Book Series, vols. 17, 19, 20, 22); and those of Edward III, from the first to the twentieth year, have been edited for the Rolls Series by L. O. Pike. For all other years we are obliged to depend upon the less satisfactory editions of the seventeenth century, particularly those of Tottel.

Recognizing also the contributions of legal writers, there is first the pre-eminent work of Henry de Bracton or Bratton, *De Legibus et Consuetudinibus Angliae* (6 vols. Rolls Ser. 1878–83). A good edition of *Britton on the Laws of England* has been furnished by F. M. Nichols (2 vols. Oxford, 1865). But of *Fleta seu Commentarius Juris Anglicani*, there is as yet nothing better than Selden's edition of 1685. The suggestive work of Sir John Fortescue, *The Governance of England*, has been ably edited by Charles Plummer (Oxford, 1885).

Among the collections bearing especially upon the history of the council, the most prominent is the work of Sir N. H. Nicolas, *Proceedings and Ordinances of the Privy Council*, 1386–1542 (7 vols. Rec. Com. 1834–7), which is based entirely upon the manuscripts of the British Museum. To a much greater extent conciliar documents are found in the files of the Public Record Office, particularly those known as *Parliamentary and Other Proceedings*, which are chancery records running from Edward I to James I. Likewise the series known as *Chancery Warrants*, of which the files are numbered in the hundreds from Henry III to Richard III, contain writs sealed and unsealed, many of them by authority of the council, directing the issue of letters under the great seal. There are also ninety-three files designated *Council and Privy Seal* (Exchequer K. R.), running from Edward III to Richard III, which are warrants for the use of the privy seal that was largely employed by the council. *Diplomatic Documents* (Exchequer Treasury of Receipt), calendared in *Deputy Keeper's Report*, vols. xlv and xlviii; and to a lesser extent *Diplomatic Documents* (Chancery) contain materials explained in chapter xiv. Closely related to the council in England are the records of several minor and subsidiary councils such as are contained in James Graves, *Roll of the King's Council in Ireland*, 16 Rich. II (Rolls Series, 1877); *Archives municipales de Bordeaux* (Bordeaux, 1867, &c.), with materials on the council of Gascony; Sydney Armitage-Smith, *John of Gaunt's Register* (2 vols. Camden Soc. 1912); and Caroline Skeel, *Council in the Marches of Wales* (Cambridge, 1904).

Although no extended history of the council has heretofore been undertaken, there are many works which have dealt with the subject in part or have touched upon it in connexion with other institutions. Best known is the brief popular sketch by A. V. Dicey, *The Privy Council* (Arnold Essay, 1860; republished in 1887). Sir F. Palgrave, *Original Authority of the King's Council* (Rec. Com. 1834), is also a brief treatment bearing entirely upon the judicial side. Sir M. Hale, *Jurisdiction of the Lords' House* (London, 1796), is a work of great erudition giving much upon the council as well as the house of lords. W. P. Baildon, *Court of Star Chamber* (London, 1894), and Cora L. Scofield, *Study of the Court of Star Chamber* (Chicago, 1900), are also concerned with a particular aspect. Several editorial introductions to the collections already mentioned, such as Hardy, *Introduction to the Close Rolls* (separately published, Rec. Com. 1833); Maitland, *Memoranda de Parliamento*; Baildon, *Cases in Chancery*; Leadam, *Cases in Star Chamber*; and Plummer, *Sir John Fortescue*, are not to be overlooked. Robert Steele in a *Bibliography of Royal Proclamations*, 1485–1714 (2 vols. Oxford, 1910), as a part of his introduction has several chapters on the council; chapters iv and v deal with the king's council in England; chapter x with the king's council in Ireland; and chapter xi the council in Scotland. Unfortunately the editor has not always availed himself of the latest information. Charles Bémont, in his *Simon de Montfort* (Paris, 1884), devotes a part of chapter iv to the council of that time; L. O. Pike, *Constitutional History of the House of Lords* (London, 1894); L. W. V. Harcourt, *His Grace the Steward and Trial of Peers* (London, 1907); and J. H. Round, *Peerage and Pedigree* (London, 1910), have each given some attention to the council. The facts in Stubbs, *Constitutional History* (many editions), are substantially accurate, but are interpreted with too great rigidity. Pollock and Maitland, *History of English Law* (Cambridge, 1898), and W. S. Holdsworth, *History of English Law* (London, 1903), offer such information as falls naturally within the scope of these works. The essay of Eugène Déprez, *Le Sceau Privé* (Paris, 1908), has been useful in calling attention to a class of records especially related to the council. Hubert Hall has edited a *Formula Book of English Historical Documents* (Cambridge, 1908). Of general histories J. H. Wylie, *Henry IV* (4 vols. London, 1884–98); *The Political History of England*, vol. iii, by T. F. Tout, and vol. iv by C. Oman have been of service. Several biographies such as S. Armitage-Smith, *John of Gaunt* (Westminster, 1904), K. H. Vickers, *Humphrey Duke of Gloucester* (London, 1907), and various articles in the *Dictionary of National Biography* have likewise been utilized.

A parallel study of the council in France and other countries of Europe is afforded by Félix Aubert, *Histoire du Parlement de Paris, 1250–1515* (2 vols. Paris, 1894); Edgard Boutaric, *Saint Louis et Alphonse de Poitiers*; Ibid., *Actes du Parlement de Paris*; Ibid., *La France sous Philippe le Bel* (Paris, 1861); C. V. Langlois, *Le Règne de Philippe III* (Paris, 1887); L. Delisle, *Recueil des Jugements de l'Échiquier de Normandie*; N. Valois, *Le Conseil du Roi et le Grand Conseil, Charles VIII* (École des Chartes, 1839); Ibid., *Le Conseil du Roi aux xive, xve et xvie siècles* (Paris, 1888); Ibid., *Inventaire des arrêts du Conseil d'État* (Tome I contains *Étude historique sur le Conseil du Roi*); P. Alexandre, *Histoire du Conseil privé dans les anciens Pays-Bas* (l'Académie Royale des Sciences de Belgique, 1895); A. Gaillard, *Le Conseil de Brabant* (3 vols. Brussels, 1898); and E. Lameere, *Le Grand Conseil des Ducs de Bourgogne* (Brussels, 1900).

INDEX